THE MAYA AND THEIR NEIGHBORS

ESSAYS ON MIDDLE AMERICAN ANTHROPOLOGY AND ARCHAEOLOGY

Edited by Clarence L. Hay, Ralph L. Linton,
Samuel K. Lothrop,
Harry L. Shapiro and George C. Vaillant

DOVER PUBLICATIONS, INC.
NEW YORK

To

ALFRED MARSTON TOZZER

His students and colleagues dedicate this
volume, in recognition of his services
to Middle American Research and in
appreciation of their debt to him as
teacher, counsellor, and friendly critic.

Published in Canada by General Publishing Com-
pany, Ltd., 30 Lesmill Road, Don Mills, Toronto,
Ontario.
Published in the United Kingdom by Constable
and Company, Ltd., 10 Orange Street, London
WC2H 7EG.

This Dover edition, first published in 1977, is an
unabridged republication of the work first published by D. Appleton-Century Company, Inc.,
New York, in 1940.

International Standard Book Number:
0-486-23510-6
Library of Congress Catalog Card Number:
77-72861

Manufactured in the United States of America
Dover Publications, Inc.
180 Varick Street
New York, N.Y. 10014

PREFACE

The civilizations created by the Maya and their neighbors have for four centuries excited the imagination of the romantic, attracted the curiosity of the intellectually alert, and challenged the intelligence of the scholar. A truly vast literature has resulted, but pitifully few books provide critical guidance toward understanding the basic nature of the subject or toward following the general direction of the research. A vast gap yawns between the technical literature and more general books which should satisfy the intellectual curiosity of interested readers and students in other fields.

Those of us who are teachers and museum men have had the repeated experience of being forced to assign elaborate bibliographies for background reading on Indian Civilization in Middle America. Yet the inevitable lag between discovery and publication renders much of the available material out of date. Even among the universities, only one offered formal instruction in the Middle American field, Professor Tozzer's Anthropology 9 and 10, at Harvard. Therefore we decided that a collection of essays, prepared by technical scholars, might serve a very practical purpose in offering a summary of current opinion on the field of Middle American archaeology.

When we began to canvass the field, we found that most of the authors had been students of Professor Tozzer and that such a volume as we projected would be largely the result of his stimulating instruction. We had not only an enthusiastic response to requests for essays but also most generous contributions, from both the authors and friends of the project, toward the cost of preparing and reproducing illustrations. Our only regret is that unavoidable causes like illness and pressure of official duties prevented some contributors from enriching our volume.

It is therefore obvious why we have dedicated our volume to Professor Tozzer. His characteristic modesty has made him deplore the possibility that an anniversary volume be prepared in his honor. His students have always respected his feeling in this regard. However, since most of us have studied under Professor Tozzer and all of us have been stimulated and influenced by him, we trust that this volume, since it cannot be in his honor, will be to his honor as the teacher, counsellor, and friend of us all.

CLARENCE L. HAY   SAMUEL K. LOTHROP

RALPH L. LINTON   HARRY L. SHAPIRO

GEORGE C. VAILLANT

CONTENTS

PART I

THE BACKGROUND OF THE MAYA

CHAPTER   PAGE

I. W. W. HOWELLS, UNIVERSITY OF WISCONSIN
The Origins of American Indian Race Types
An analysis of the basic factors underlying
the racial affiliations of the American Indian   3

II. OLIVER G. RICKETSON, JR., CARNEGIE INSTITUTION OF WASHINGTON
An Outline of Basic Physical Factors Affecting Middle America
A study of the ocean currents, the geological
age and formation, and the types of climate
in Middle America 10

III. RALPH LINTON, COLUMBIA UNIVERSITY
Crops, Soils, and Culture in America
An hypothesis for the development of the
food supplies essential to the maintenance of
the American civilizations 32

IV. CLYDE KLUCKHOHN, HARVARD UNIVERSITY
The Conceptual Structure in Middle American Studies
A criticism of the intellectual basis on which
Middle American archaeologists conduct
their research 41

V. J. ALDEN MASON, UNIVERSITY MUSEUM, UNIVERSITY OF PENNSYLVANIA
The Native Languages of Middle America
A synthesis of results of linguistic research
in Middle America 52

CHAPTER   PAGE

VI. FREDERICK JOHNSON, DEPARTMENT OF ARCHAEOLOGY,
     PHILLIPS ACADEMY, ANDOVER
         *The Linguistic Map of Mexico and Central
         America*
             Analysis of the different linguistic maps
             made for the Middle Area and demonstra-
             tion of the map presented in these pages .   . 88

PART II

THE MAYA

VII. A. V. KIDDER, CARNEGIE INSTITUTION OF WASHINGTON
          *Archaeological Problems of the Highland
          Maya*
              A study showing how the development of
              Maya civilization is related to the problems
              of Middle American culture in general .   . 117

VIII. J. ERIC S. THOMPSON, CARNEGIE INSTITUTION OF
       WASHINGTON
           Archaeological Problems of the Lowland Maya
               An analysis of the latest research in the high-
               est centers of Maya civilization, evaluating
               the positive knowledge and the gaps in in-
               formation on that field 126

IX. SYLVANUS GRISWOLD MORLEY, CARNEGIE INSTITUTION
     OF WASHINGTON
         Maya Epigraphy
             A resumé of the history of the decipherment
             of the Maya inscriptions, which was a feat
             of scholarship almost on a par with the for-
             mulation of the original graphic system .   . 139

X. E. WYLLYS ANDREWS, HARVARD UNIVERSITY
        Chronology and Astronomy in the Maya Area
            A critical estimate of the basis of the chief
            theories for the correlation of the Mayan
            and Christian chronologies 150

CHAPTER   PAGE

XI.   HERBERT J. SPINDEN, BROOKLYN MUSEUM
Diffusion of Maya Astronomy
An interpretation of the manner in which a ritualistic use of astronomical data by the Maya was introduced in the calendric system of a Mexican tribe 162

XII.   H. E. D. POLLOCK, CARNEGIE INSTITUTION OF WASHINGTON
Sources and Methods in the Study of Maya Architecture
A history of the study of Maya architecture, which, in essence, summarizes the development of archaeological research in the Maya area 179

XIII.   A. LEDYARD SMITH, CARNEGIE INSTITUTION OF WASHINGTON
The Corbeled Arch in the New World
A summary of how a supposedly characteristic Mayan architectural feature is, in fact, not found continuously in the Maya region, and how this trait crops up in two distant regions in North and South America 202

XIV.   KARL RUPPERT, CARNEGIE INSTITUTION OF WASHINGTON
A Special Assemblage of Maya Structures
An analysis of a special plan, found in certain Maya ceremonial centers, which is sometimes thought to have an astronomical significance 222

XV.   ROBERT WAUCHOPE, UNIVERSITY OF GEORGIA
Domestic Architecture of the Maya
A study indicative of the value of examining the unspectacular remains of the common people, in order to establish a social continuity between the past and the present . . . 232

CHAPTER PAGE
XVI. ROBERT E. SMITH, CARNEGIE INSTITUTION OF WASH-
INGTON
Ceramics of the Peten
A technical study of pottery shapes and
composition which have an important bear-
ing on the historical analysis of Maya sites 242

XVII. MARY BUTLER, UNIVERSITY MUSEUM, UNIVERSITY OF
PENNSYLVANIA
*A Pottery Sequence from the Alta Verapaz,
Guatemala*
An analysis of the further use of pottery to
establish chronological levels and points of
tribal culture contact 250

XVIII. JOHN M. LONGYEAR III, CARNEGIE INSTITUTION OF
WASHINGTON
*The Ethnological Significance of Copan Pot-
tery*
An essay, giving a further example of the
value of ceramics in this reconstruction of
the history of the most important Maya site
on the eastern frontier 268

XIX. EARNEST A. HOOTON, PEABODY MUSEUM, HARVARD
UNIVERSITY
*Skeletons from the Cenote of Sacrifice at
Chichen Itzá*
A study in the neglected field of Middle
American physical anthropology, which ex-
plodes a myth concerning the victims of
human sacrifice in the Sacred Cenote at
Chichen Itzá 272

XX. OLIVER LA FARGE
Maya Ethnology: The Sequence of Cultures
An examination of how the modern Maya
were transformed from the manner of life
of their ancient predecessors, illustrating the
outward change in material and social culture affecting a people in the course of centuries 281

PART III

THE NORTHERN NEIGHBORS OF THE MAYA

CHAPTER   PAGE
XXI. GEORGE C. VAILLANT, AMERICAN MUSEUM OF NATU-
      RAL HISTORY
          Patterns in Middle American Archaeology
          An hypothesis to explain the basic difference
          between the Middle American cultures and
          those of North and South America .   .   . 295

XXII. EDUARDO NOGUERA, INSTITUTO NACIONAL DE ARQUE-
       OLOGIA E HISTORIA, SECRETARÍA DE EDUCACION PUBLICA,
       MEXICO
           Excavations at Tehuacan
           The results of excavations which indicate the
           contemporaneity of the advanced civiliza-
           tions of the Toltec and Zapotec 306

XXIII. GORDON F. EKHOLM, AMERICAN MUSEUM OF NATURAL
        HISTORY
            *The Archaeology of Northern and Western
            Mexico*
            A summary of the archaeology of the north-
            ern frontier of Middle American civilization
            and of the relationship between Mexico and
            the southwestern United States 320

XXIV. FRANK H. H. ROBERTS, JR., BUREAU OF AMERICAN
       ETHNOLOGY, SMITHSONIAN INSTITUTION
           *Pre-Pottery Horizon of the Anasazi and Mex-
           ico*
           A summary of the archaeology of the hunt-
           ing and early farming horizons in the south-
           western United States, a stage of culture
           not yet isolated by archaeological research
           in Middle America 331

CHAPTER PAGE

XXV. J. O. BREW, HARVARD UNIVERSITY
Mexican Influence upon the Indian Cultures of the Southwestern United States in the Sixteenth and Seventeenth Centuries
A digest of cultural diffusions in a time and at a place where contemporary observations were recorded 341

XXVI. PHILIP PHILLIPS, PEABODY MUSEUM, HARVARD UNIVERSITY
Middle American Influences on the Archaeology of the Southeastern United States
An evaluation of the amount of influence exerted by Middle American civilizations on the cultures of the southeastern United States, and the time factors involved . . . 349

XXVII. CARL E. GUTHE, MUSEUM OF ANTHROPOLOGY, UNIVERSITY OF MICHIGAN
Sequence of Culture in the Eastern United States
A summary of the development of culture in the eastern United States which may recapitulate social and economic factors governing, at a much earlier date, the development of Middle American civilization 368

PART IV

THE SOUTHERN NEIGHBORS OF THE MAYA

XXVIII. WM. DUNCAN STRONG, COLUMBIA UNIVERSITY
Anthropological Problems in Central America
A critical estimate of the problems of Central American anthropology and the efforts toward their solution, which indicates the southern limits of Maya civilization . . . 377

XXIX. DORIS STONE, TULANE UNIVERSITY
The Ulua Valley and Lake Yojoa
An identification of tribal with linguistic groups, and an attempt to distinguish the archaeological remains of Honduras in terms of the native peoples 386

CHAPTER   PAGE

XXX. FRANCIS B. RICHARDSON, CARNEGIE INSTITUTION OF WASHINGTON

Non-Maya Monumental Sculpture of Central America

A classification of the cultural situation in Central America, through classifying the types of sculpture which are unrelated to styles current among the ancient Maya . . 395

XXXI. SAMUEL K. LOTHROP, PEABODY MUSEUM, HARVARD UNIVERSITY

South America as Seen from Middle America

An evaluation of the amount and relative effect of cultural diffusion from Middle America discernible in the cultures of South America 417

XXXII. PHILIP AINSWORTH MEANS

The Philosophic Interrelationship between Middle American and Andean Religions

An essay discussing the intellectual and emotional differentiation between the religions of Middle America and those of the Andes 430

XXXIII. ALFRED KIDDER II, PEABODY MUSEUM, HARVARD UNIVERSITY

South American Penetrations in Middle America

A summary of the various cultural traits found in Middle America, the origin of which may be ascribed to South American peoples 441

XXXIV. A. L. KROEBER, UNIVERSITY OF CALIFORNIA

Conclusions: The Present Status of Americanistic Problems

A critical synthesis of the essays contributed to this volume in their relationship to American Anthropology as a whole . . 460

BIBLIOGRAPHY 491

INDEX 595

PLATES

(Grouped at p. 312.)

PLATE

I. Earliest Date Now Known in Yucatan

II. Hieroglyphic Stairway, Copan, Honduras

III. Vaulted Structures in South America

IV. Foreign Pottery Types from Kaminaljuyú, Guatemala

V. Cylindrical Vase, Uaxactun, Guatemala

VI. Effigy Vessels and Censers, Alta Verapaz

VII. Incised Black and Smoked Wares, Alta Verapaz

VIII. Polychrome Design, Periods I and II, Alta Verapaz

IX. Effigy Vessels and Censers, Periods III and IV, Alta Verapaz

X. Pottery Figurines and Stamps, Periods I–IV, Alta Verapaz

XI. Jewelry, Period IV, Alta Verapaz

XII. Black Vase, Incised and Painted, and Vase, Teotihuacan Style, Thin Orange Ware, Tehuacan

XIII. Pottery Fragments from Tehuacan

XIV. Polychrome Bowls, Guasave, Sinaloa, Mexico

XV. Pottery Vessels, Guasave, Sinaloa, Mexico

XVI. Pottery and Alabaster, Guasave, Sinaloa, Mexico

XVII. Polychrome Vase, Ulua Valley, Honduras

XVIII. Sculptures from the Pacific Slope of Guatemala

XIX. Sculptures from Salvador and the Pacific Slope of Guatemala

XX. Polychrome Vase with "Peruvian" Design, Cuicatlan, Oaxaca, Mexico

ILLUSTRATIONS

FIGURE   PAGE

1. Map of the Antillean-Caribbean Region 15

2. Map of Ocean Currents 21

3. Diagram of the Regions Enclosed by Isotherms of 80° in January and July, and of the Principal Wind Belts of the Atlantic 22

4. Map of Currents of the Caribbean Mediterranean . . . 25

5. Diagram of Significant Isobars and Isotherms in the Caribbean and Adjacent Regions During February and July . 30

6. Venus God Associated with Significant Dates as Depicted in Codex Vienna 167

7. Significant Dates as Depicted in the Selden Roll and Codex Vienna 169

8. Significant Dates as Depicted in the Lienzo of Yolotepec and the Codex Nuttall 173

9. Significant Dates in the Codex Vienna 175

10. Significant Date in the Lienzo of Chicomostoc 177

11. Map of the Maya Area 204

12. Examples of Maya Arches 209

13. Vaulted Constructions in South and North America . . . 219

14. Map of Group E, Uaxactun 223

15. Map of Specialized Assemblages in Maya Area 225

16. Map of Naachtun Specialized Assemblage 226

17. Map of Cahal Pichik 229

18. Map of La Muñeca 231

19. Plans and Elevations of Maya Houses and Their Substructures 235

20. Modern Maya Houses 237

21. Vessels, Period I, Chamá 252

FIGURE PAGE

22. Vessels, Period II, Chamá 255

23. Incense Burner and Jar, Chamá 256

24. Vessels, Periods III and IV, Chamá 263

25. Vessels from Tombs 1 and 2, Tehuacan 307

26. Incised Gray Ware Vase, Tomb 1, Tehuacan . . . 309

27. Pottery Fragments from Tehuacan 313

28. Oaxacan Carved Jade, Found at Awatovi, Arizona. . . 347

29. Stone Implements Suggestive of Middle American Influence 352

30. Shell Gorgets with Figures Suggestive of Middle American Influence 355

31. Copper Plates Suggestive of Middle American Influence . 357

32. Designs from Jars Suggestive of Middle American Influence 361

33. Stone Jaguar Heads from Western Salvador 400

34. Stone Jaguar Heads from Western Salvador 401

35. Sculptures from Guatemala, Honduras, and Costa Rica . . 405

36. Sculptures from Southwestern Honduras and the Guatemala Highlands 407

37. Crude Human Figure, Copan, Honduras 409

38. Sculptures from Chontales, Nicaragua 411

39. Sculptures from Chontales, Nicaragua, and Costa Rica . . 413

40. Polychrome Vase, Nasca 453

Linguistic Map of Mexico and Central America
. . . . *inside back cover*

TABLES

Table		Page
I.	Proposed Grouping of Middle American Languages	78
II.	Compass Bearings of Special Assemblages of Maya Buildings	227
III.	Sequence of Cultures at Chamá	251
IV.	Shape and Ware Frequencies in Period I, Chamá	252
V.	Shape and Ware Frequencies in Period II, Chamá	259
VI.	Shape and Ware Frequencies in Periods III and IV, Chamá	264
VII.	Cranial Measurements on Chichen Itzá Skulls	278
VIII.	Percentages of Wares at Tehuacan	315
IX.	Totals and Percentages of Wares of Tehuacan	317
X.	Mexican and Maya Pottery Sequences Compared	484
XI.	New World Ceramic Sequences Compared	488

PART I

THE BACKGROUND OF THE MAYA

1

THE ORIGINS OF AMERICAN INDIAN RACE TYPES

W. W. Howells *

RACIAL anthropology is the tardy sister among the studies of the American Indian. As a source of historical information it is still asking from other fields more than it gives in return and, so far from having provided an explicit account of the whole Indian racial group and its varieties, it has not even furnished an adequate description of the types of any particular area.[1] To ponder, therefore, anything so nebulous as the Indians' racial origins may seem little short of futile. We may, nevertheless, review certain of the probabilities as they are defined by such men as Boas, Wissler, Hrdlička, Dixon and Hooton, whose considered if sometimes discordant opinions are qualified by their extensive experience with the actual material.

First, however, we may take notice of certain matters relating to time and culture upon which there is substantial agreement. No one seriously doubts that the Indians came from Asia, where they were mainly allied with the Mongoloid stock; and that they crossed into America by way of Bering Strait, spreading from this point throughout the New World. There is more question as to when they began to come, how long they continued to come and when they stopped coming. Migration seems to have ceased many centuries before Columbus, the only recent movements which can be guessed at being intracontinental, and cultural considerations in both hemispheres make it probable that the separation, excepting possibly of the boreal peoples, has been very long indeed. On the other hand, the period of intermittent immigration must have been of considerable duration, while almost all authorities, in various fields, agree on a limit of ten or twelve thousand years (with a conceivable maximum of twenty

* Harvard, B.S. as of 1930; A.M., 1931; Ph.D., 1934; assistant in Anthropology, 1930–1931; now Assistant Professor of Anthropology, Wisconsin; Research Associate, American Museum of Natural History.

[1] This has been most nearly done for the Eskimo and for the Southwest. It is unfortunate, of course, that several large regions can never be properly represented.

thousand) for the time since it began.[2] The presence of glacial or interglacial man has not been established and, although passage to Alaska would have been easy during the last glaciation, escape from Alaska would have been impossible until the recession of the ice, which would not have left the western coastal route passable until perhaps ten thousand years ago.[3] Nelson [4] finds no traces of a culture which is thoroughly Paleolithic in type, the earliest being a partially developed Neolithic. At any rate, it is apparent that the Indians began first to arrive in quantities in immediately post-glacial times, and by several thousand years ago had already reached, or to be more precise, been forced into Patagonia.[5]

Ethnological evidence as to the immigrants is equivocal. Like archaeology, ethnology postulates a minimum cultural equipment which is not extremely primitive, but this is obscured by the vast preponderance of Indian culture which has developed in the New World. Wissler,[6] however, does not feel that this development calls for a vast period of time. As to language, Boas [7] considers that the tremendous linguistic diversity of America was formerly world-wide, being characteristic of a simple cultural plane which could not produce overpowering movements of peoples; thus the proselyting language families typical of the Old World are only suggested in America. In other words, if wide-spread linguistic stocks are not a primitive phenomenon but are a secondary development which is the function of an advanced culture and a heavy population, then the multiplicity of languages in the New World is a simple condition which does not betoken a long period of differentiation, but only reflects a linguistic diversity among the immigrants. Dixon [8] held the special view that the smaller American language stocks, found as they are in marginal or refuge areas, represented the earliest immigrants and the larger, more extended families, the later ones.

Altogether, the bulk of the cultural evidence, while far from precise, indicates that there were finite limits to the period of immigration

---

[2] See The American Aborigines. Their Origin and Antiquity. Edited by Diamond Jenness, 1933.

[3] W. A. Johnston, Quaternary Geology of North America, 1933.

[4] N. C. Nelson, The Antiquity of Man, 1933.

[5] J. Bird, Antiquity and Migrations, 1938.

[6] C. Wissler, Ethnological Diversity, 1933. See also, Wissler, The American Indian, 1922.

[7] F. Boas, Relationships between North-West America and North-East Asia, 1933. See also, The History of the American Race, 1912.

[8] R. B. Dixon, The Racial History Of Man, 1923.

to America which can be roughly estimated and which in terms of geology and racial evolution were not of important size. It is also the consensus of opinion that the pioneers came over in small lots which were by no means uniform in culture or language.

Plainly, the most significant aspect of the physical anthropology of the Indian is the diversity in type which he exhibits. Understanding of this is necessarily the key to the problem. As Hooton [9] has made it clear, the Indians are homogeneous in a number of characteristics, but differ very widely in certain others. The former are the more superficial and conspicuous. The eyes and the hair are dark, and the latter is straight or slightly wavy. The skin is somewhat variable, but its tribal distribution has no visible significance. The face is always broad and relatively heavy. On the other hand, in stature and less obvious features such as the shape of the head and nose and the length of the face, there is a very great variety; probably more, taken all together, than may be found in the White racial stock. This extends to general facial and bodily configuration, so that pronounced contrasts in group appearance and type may be cited.

This diversity must be explained primarily either as the result of differentiation out of a single type in the New World or as the perpetuation of existing varieties among the original groups of immigrants. A certain degree of specialization must be allowed for, since this tendency toward differentiation is a constant biological phenomenon, and whether the immigrants were homogeneous or not, it is to be expected that after they had settled down a sort of racial expanding universe would be instituted, corresponding on a smaller scale to that which appeared in the original Homo sapiens stock. Certain groups, of whom the Maya might be one, are probably due partly to such a factor. The apparent slowness of human evolution, however, makes it unlikely that this process can have proceeded far in demarcating various Indian types, as entities, and still more unlikely that it could have been responsible for the variations in a single feature, such as the nose, within any reasonable allowance of time. Analogies with the development of Indian culture are not proper, for culture is capable of an acceleration not to be found in physical evolution.

Besides this negative argument, there are positive reasons for sup-

[9] E. A. Hooton, Racial Types in America, 1933. This paper is the best discussion of the racial nature of the Indians, and the writer acknowledges a necessarily large debt to it. See also Hooton, The Indians of Pecos Pueblo, 1930; Up from the Ape, 1931.

posing that the primary divergences had appeared on the other side of Bering Strait. Not only is the spread in racial type apparently too great to have occurred in ten thousand years, but the lines of division correspond in some degree to those among the Asiatic Mongoloids. In special features, moreover, such as the blood groups and the cephalic index, there is evidence of imported variations. The Indians were once thought to be quite homogeneous in blood type but it now appears that they are not. Some tribes are almost entirely group O while others are largely group A, a difference which almost certainly goes back to Asia, and which may prove to have some chronological significance.[10] As to the cephalic index, there is excellent evidence that the first groups of immigrants were long-headed and that the brachycephals only appeared in later waves. It is true that in large areas of the Old World brachycephaly has evidently been tending to supplant and dominate over dolichocephaly, especially in mixed peoples, acting thus as if it were a recent, ultra-human mutation of some sort. But it is doubtful if this phenomenon can be invoked to derive the round-headed Indians from a once purely long-headed stock in America, for the few examples of such a possible change are dubious.[11] In the Southwest, for example, it is apparent that brachycephalic factors are due to invasion. It is presumable, therefore, that a watcher at Bering Strait would have seen in the immigrant current practically all the extremes in head form which have been found in this continent.

If this first explanation be accepted, that the Indian's diversity in type goes back to Asia, then a further explanation is to be sought as to its ultimate origins. To return for the moment to the cephalic index, Dixon [12] believed the dolichocephals to be the earliest type because of their marginal distribution, corresponding to the smaller, more multifarious language stocks. Hooton [13] agrees with him, having found that his long-headed "morphological types" at Pecos were commonest in the earlier strata, and all of the most recent discoveries of ancient crania [14] point in the same direction; even though some of the finds are questionable as to age, the moral certainty as to the

---

[10] Neglecting for the moment the presence of blood group B, whose distribution is insufficiently known for intelligent discussion.

[11] Dixon, Racial History, 1923.

[12] *Ibid.*

[13] Hooton, Racial Types, 1933.

[14] Bird, Antiquity and Migrations, 1938; Aynesworth, Biographic Studies, 1936; G. Woodbury, Notes on Some Skeletal Remains of Texas, 1937.

priority of dolichocephaly is such that it would be sensational should Folsom Man turn out to be a brachycephal.

Now, Hooton and Dixon both would see non-Mongoloid strains in these early dolichocephalic types, of an Australoid, Negroid and perhaps Mediterranean or Dravidian nature, supposing that these together with some Mongoloid elements immigrated as a mixture, or common solution, and were glossed over, or "Mongolized," by further mixture with later immigrants of a more strictly Mongoloid character. Hrdlička [15] has combatted this theory from every aspect, being unwilling to recognize non-"Indian" elements, imported either direct or in solution, early or late, to or by any part of the population, and he suggests another view: that many of the varieties of Indians have their counterparts entirely within the Mongoloid family in the Old World.

Hypothetically, then, the Indians are either a varying composite of several strains, or they are samples drawn off through Bering Strait from an amorphous *Rassenkreis* in Asia, constituted much as we find the Indians to be and possibly having certain proto-White relationships, but having its center of gravity well within the Mongoloid family proper. There may not seem to be a great difference between these two ideas, but there is. In the first case the Indians would represent a commingling of contrasted types (Australoid, Mediterranean, Mongoloid?) already more clearly differentiated than the Indians themselves; while in the second explanation they would be derived from one great unspecialized (but not particularly primitive) type in which the more specialized Mongoloid forms and, it may be suggested, the White forms, were merely incipient.

Although it is not a new idea, too little heed has been given to the bearing of the Asiatic Mongoloids upon the Indians. The Mongoloid family contains a wide variety of types, both specialized and unspecialized, and it is perhaps a mistake to look upon the most specialized (Chinese, Mongols) as the most typical. If the latter are removed from consideration there is something of a correspondence between the unspecialized remainder and the Indians generally. Knowledge of Asiatic peoples is too poor to say how full this correspondence may be, and it is probably indiscreet to suggest specific parallels. Nevertheless there are strong superficial resemblances between the

---

[15] A. Hrdlička, The Origin and Antiquity of the American Indian, 1923; The People of the Main American Cultures, 1926; Melanesians and Australians and the Peopling of America, 1935; The Minnesota "Man," 1937.

Eskimo (the most "Mongoloid" Indians) and the northeastern Siberians, between the Athabascans or the Plains Indians and some of the peoples of central Siberia or Tibet, and between many forest tribes of South America and certain Indonesian groups in Borneo and the Philippines. If actual measurements are brought to witness these comparisons might be untenable, but the Mongoloid peoples (always excepting the Chinese and certain others) exhibit the same vagueness of type and variation in form (cf. the cephalic index) as do the Indians and share with them the same unspecialized and somewhat primitive configuration.

Now it is possible to ascribe these unspecialized and diverse limbs of the Mongoloid family to a mixture of differing strains, as Dixon does, and as Hooton does for the Indians, but it is a question whether it is necessary. It is true that, in spreading through Asia, the Mongoloids might be expected to have absorbed other strains, in contrast to the Indians who were moving into free territory. Both groups, however, represent just such a congeries of types as might have been produced during the gradual evolution of the Mongoloid family as a whole. There are of course mixed Mongoloid groups, but this does not signify that any type which is less "Mongoloid" than the Chinese is necessarily of mixed origin.

On this basis it does not appear that the Indians have a very large non-Mongoloid residue, since their non-Mongoloid features are mostly their unspecialized ones. There is a residue, however, and it appears to point, not to the Australoids [16] or the Negroes, but toward the White group. It exhibits itself, in various tribes, in a high bridge and well developed tip of the nose, in a rarity of the epicanthic fold, and probably also a ruggedness or great length of the face. Furthermore, these features combine with a general "European" appearance in a few Indian types, or at least very commonly in individuals of certain groups, and there is at least a suggestion that these groups may be the more marginal and thus perhaps the earliest ones. This description is especially true of the Indians of the eastern United States. Little remains to tell the tale, but Hooton [17] believes that the older portraits of eastern Indians, showing this European type very generally, are not merely the conventionalizations of indifferent

[16] This is flying in the face of the Punin skull, but the occasional appearance of an "Australoid" or primitive-looking individual is of uncertain significance, and I have found one or two "Australoid" skulls on Christian Irish skeletons.

[17] Hooton, Racial Types, 1933.

artists but are accurate, and photographs from more recent times seem to bear him out.

It is a matter of pure speculation whether these European characteristics bespeak a "White" admixture to some groups of Indians before these emigrated from Asia or whether they express a parental form akin to but less specialized than either the Whites or the Mongoloids we know today. Boas [18] believes that the fundamental racial distinction in man is that between the black-skinned peoples and all others, the Whites and Mongoloids being more recently related, and it may be suggested that the two stocks approach each other most nearly through these European-looking Indians and the heavy-faced types of the Upper Paleolithic in Europe. It must be confessed, however, that much of the foregoing calls for assumptions as to the processes of racial evolution, and as yet these are matters of hypothesis and not of fact. It remains to be seen whether an acceptable classification of American Indian types will disclose more direct affinities with those of Asia and more precise indications as to the history of the peopling of America.

[18] F. Boas, The Mind of Primitive Man, 1938.

II

AN OUTLINE OF BASIC PHYSICAL FACTORS AFFECTING MIDDLE AMERICA

*Oliver G. Ricketson, Jr.**

ALTHOUGH the masonry buildings of the Maya were standing amid the jungles of Central America when Cordoba coasted Yucatan in 1517 and when Cortés made his epic march from Tenochtitlan to the Province of Honduras in 1524–1525, their existence was not generally known to the world until more than three centuries later. Their modern rediscovery may well be dated from the now classical writings of John Lloyd Stephens, whose "Travels in Yucatan" were published in 1843.

For the next half century the archaelogical explorations stimulated by the books of Stephens were carried out by less than a score of men leaving behind them records of their investigations; the scientific merit of any one of these records, naturally, reflects the effort and the acumen of the individual producing it.

Although investigation in the modern sense might well be dated from the work of such an outstanding individual as Alfred P. Maudsley (1881–1894), the past fifty years is better characterized as an epoch in which large institutions of learning have participated. Few individuals command the means for the long-sustained effort which the magnitude of the work demands.

The first institution in the field (1892) was the Peabody Museum of American Archaeology and Ethnology of Harvard University. This movement was initiated primarily by Mr. Charles P. Bowditch, the impetus thus originated being subsequently continued at Harvard by courses of instruction in the fields of Maya research under the direction of Dr. Alfred Marston Tozzer, Chairman of the Division of Anthropology from 1919 to 1937. The list of contributors to this volume bears witness to his success as a teacher in that field. No less

* Harvard, A.B., 1916; Ph.D., 1934; now Archaeologist, Carnegie Institution of Washington.

than eight institutions [1] have followed in the path blazed by the Peabody Museum, and many scientists from many institutions have cooperated in extending our knowledge in fields allied to the archaeological.

It is the purpose of this paper to summarize the basic physical factors which make Central America what it is. These factors explain Central America's geology, its violent vulcanism, its geography, the division of its seasons and point to the origins of its fauna and flora. These elemental facts will be dealt with here only in their broadest outlines.

Although political and historical considerations permit us to define Central America as that portion of the mainland American continent lying between Mexico and Colombia, this definition does not command the assent of geologists because it fails to include the whole region to its natural frontiers. In respect of climate, natural products and aboriginal settlement it is more accurate to speak of the region as Middle America and to define it roughly as lying between the southern terminus of the Rocky Mountain System in Mexico and the northern terminus of the Andean Mountain System in South America. The geological unity of this region has been shrouded by an overwhelming volcanic development which until recently has been falsely believed to be continuous with the great cordilleras of the continents lying to the north and south. The traditional continuity of these cordilleras has been broken by investigations showing that the Rocky Mountain System terminates in the belt of great volcanoes along the southern margin of the Central Plateau of Mexico—the "Great Scarp" of Oaxaca. The northernmost Andes similarly terminate before reaching Panama, from which they are separated by the valley of the Atrato River. Not only are the axes of these two cordilleras out of line, but their respective termini are 1200 miles apart. Central America, certain coastal ranges along the north margin of South America, the islands of the West Indies, and several submarine ridges connecting the latter to one another and to the Central American mainland, all belong to the Antillean Mountain System. This system is characterized by crustal folds of late geologic date trending east-west, in opposition to the north-south trends of the Andean and Rocky

[1] Archaeological Institute of America, British Museum, American Museum of Natural History, Field Museum, Carnegie Institution of Washington, University of Pennsylvania, Tulane University, Museum of the American Indian, Heye Foundation.

Mountain Systems. Overwhelming volcanic additions of still later date have concealed the Antillean crustal folds. These volcanic regions occur in two great arcs: 1, the Pacific border of Central America, extending into southern Mexico; 2, the eastern, Atlantic border of the Caribbean Sea following the line of the Lesser Antilles. The unity of this system has been overlooked also because the eastern half of the Antillean System has often subsided below sea-level, and because the volcanoes forming the most striking relief along the Pacific coast of Middle America are so arranged as to suggest continuity with the mountain systems on the north and the south. Geological studies show, however, that both the fundamental structures and the surface forms are those of a system distinct from the Cordilleran. The lowlands of Yucatan, of the Gulf Coastal Plain in both Mexico and the United States, of the peninsula of Florida, including eastward as far as the Bahaman Bank, are the emergent part of a much larger mass still submerged as the "shelf" around the "deeps" of the Gulf of Mexico. All this Middle American region is advantageously surrounded by water and, at least on the Atlantic slopes, is luxuriantly productive, though it would be as barren and desert as the Sahara were the seas replaced by land. Middle America has also been greatly altered in early Pleistocene time by an unparalleled vulcanism—Lake Nicaragua, once a bay of the Pacific, was cut off by volcanic deposits and its level so raised by the barrier thus formed that its drainage turned eastward to the Caribbean Sea across the former inter-oceanic watershed.

THE ANTILLEAN-CARIBBEAN REGION

The vast area around the perimeter of the Gulf of Mexico and the Caribbean mediterranean divides itself naturally into portions of two continents, namely: the folded and fragmented southern portion of North America and, beyond the Caribbean Sea, the equally folded and fragmented area of northern South America. These continents are now separated by a mediterranean sea with suboceanic depths, the Caribbean, and probably have been so separated since the beginning of the Palaeozoic era.

The lands framing the Caribbean mediterranean on the north and south are joined together on the west by Middle America, whose geologic history shows three main regions:

(1) The Antillean geanticlinorium or protaxis (see Fig. 1) extending in a great arc through the length of the peninsula of Lower

California southeasterly to Oaxaca, the Sierra Madre del Sur mountain ranges, across the Isthmus of Tehuantepec to the highlands of
Chiapas and Guatemala. These great crustal folds are laid down in
arcs convex to the south, and form a geologic unit, Nuclear Central
America. Sweeping eastward, these same folds form Antillia, where
a sequence of tectonic movements ending with subsidence give us
the present insular forms of which Cuba is by far the largest. To the
east, the anticlinorium drops steeply 27,972 feet below sea-level into
Brownson Deep north of Porto Rico, and to depths of over 15,000
feet into the Caribbean Sea. Its extreme eastern terminus is Anegada
Passage with a greatest depth of 7120 feet. The known topography
of the Atlantic bottom beyond Anegada Passage does not support
the theory that the anticlinorium extended farther eastward. That
portion of the Antillean geanticlinorium which sweeps east through
Guatemala–British Honduras north of the Motagua River, proceeding
to the eastern end of Cuba by way of Misteriosa Bank and the three
Cayman Islands is called the Antillean geosyncline (C–D, Fig. 1).

(2) In Oaxaca another ancient protaxis strikes northwest-southeast
from the Pacific; it soon changes its strike to east-west in an arc
convex to the south and so continues through Honduras and apparently across the Nicaraguan, Rosalind and San Pedro Banks (beneath the Caribbean waters) into Jamaica and southern Hispaniola
(Haiti–San Domingo). This old protaxis, called the Antillean geanticline (B–E, Fig. 1), then subsides; it is older than the Carboniferous
and may be as old as the Rocky Mountain System. The geologic
boundary of these two areas on the south lies north of Lake Nicaragua (9, Fig. 1) and the geologic proof that Nuclear Central America
with its Antillean protaxis has always been separate from South
America is afforded by the presence of east-west crustal folds with
suboceanic depths in the Caribbean mediterranean. Such folds are
not characteristic of ocean floors, nor do they occur in the Gulf
of Mexico—a flooded subsidence "plate" whose low-lying coastal
plains and peninsulas (Yucatan and Florida) are emergent parts of
an equally large but submerged "shelf" surrounding the mid-gulf
Sigsbee Deep (12,400 feet).

(3) The region next on the south Schuchert calls the "Isthmian
Link." This narrow land, sigmoid in form (at the surface only) lies
on a broad (200 mile) basement of volcanic rock veneered with
marine Cenozoic strata. Its geology does not concern us here other
than as a young land-bridge over which must have crossed the Neo-

tropical (i. e. South American) terrestrial animal forms which are today so characteristic a feature of the Middle American and Antillean fauna.[2] Geology and biogeography do not give evidence that North and South America were united by the Panama land-bridge before Upper Cretaceous time.

The orogeny of that portion of the Antillean-Caribbean region which we have briefly outlined above has been overlaid by a subsequent Pleistocene major vulcanism. The Pleistocene–Recent volcanoes developed on the west termini of the east-west structural folds from Tehuantepec to Costa Rica (Fig. 1). Lower volcanoes follow the line of the Cordillera de Talamanca southeast into Panama. At the same time the southern part of Mexico, as well as the southern terminus of the Rocky Mountain System (the "Great Scarp" of Oaxaca [5, Fig. 1]), was studded with volcanoes. It is also probable that the Caribbee volcanic arc, which follows the line of the Lesser Antilles, developed at about this time on an older submarine tectonic ridge. The geologically younger, true Caribbee islands constitute a unique volcanic province; the convexity of this arc faces the Atlantic Ocean, and the islands are festooned across the entrance to the Caribbean Sea like the piers of a bridge. As we mentioned, it is this overlying volcanic development on the mainland of Central America, which concealed the true nature of the structures beneath

---

[2] The avifauna is, on the contrary, decidedly Nearctic or northern, "almost all the characteristic Neotropical families are entirely lacking."

FIG. 1. THE ANTILLEAN-CARIBBEAN REGION

1. Sierra Madre Occidental.
2. Sierra Madre Oriental.
3. Lower California.
4. Mesa Central of Mexico.
5. The Great Scarp of Mexico, terminus of the Rocky Mountain System.
6. Balsas Portal.
7. Sierra Madre del Sur.
8. Tehuantepec Portal.
9. Northern boundary of "Isthmian Link."
10. Bolivar geosyncline, terminus of Andean Mountain System.

A. Isthmus of Tehuantepec.
C. Nuclear Central America.
C–D. Antillean geosyncline ⎫ anticlinorium.
B–E. Antillean geanticline ⎭

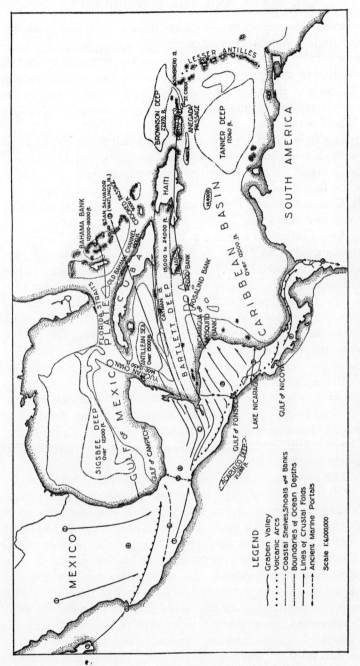

FIG. 1. THE ANTILLEAN-CARIBBEAN REGION (For description, see facing page.)

and led to the false supposition of the continuity of the Rocky Mountain and Andean Mountain systems.

Before turning from this brief outline of the Antillean system to a description of the three Middle American marine basins, mention must be made of the great portals which have at one period or another connected the Atlantic and Pacific oceans during past geologic time. These portals are:

(1) The Balsas Portal (6, Fig. 1), extending from the Gulf to the Pacific across Mexico between the Great Scarp of Oaxaca and the Sierra Madre del Sur. It derives its name from the present valley of the Rio Balsas, and was intermittently open from Late Triassic into Middle Cretaceous time. The evidence, however, tends to show that there was continuous land from North America into South America during Late Cretaceous and it was then that four or five orders of mammals spread from North to South America. Evidence of later migrations is completely lacking until Pliocene time, since when there has been wave after wave of migration across Central America.

(2) The Tehuantepec Portal (8, Fig. 1), open during Pliocene and probably during Late Miocene, connected the Gulf of Mexico with the Pacific through the present Isthmus of Tehuantepec. Though this permitted the spread of marine forms from the Gulf to the Pacific, it prevented the spread of terrestrial forms from North to South America. With the closure of this portal in Late Pliocene time, migrations of terrestrial animals from north to south was possible, but by then the Antillean bridges from Nuclear Central America to Antillia had submerged. These unstable land conditions cause the animal life of the Greater Antilles—lands of continental rocks—to resemble that of oceanic islands.

(3) The Isthmian Portals; under this generic title I have grouped many different portals piercing the so-called "Isthmian Link" (southern Nicaragua–Costa Rica–Panama) including one South American portal—that of the Bolivar geosyncline, following roughly the present course of the Atrato River (10, Fig. 1). The aperture of these portals is of significance not only as preventing the northward migration of terrestrial Neotropical animals, but of vast climatic implication as well. For with an open portal the westward drift of the warm waters of the North Equatorial Current would flow into the Pacific. With the portal closed, these waters are deflected north, so that with the breakdown of Antillia into its present insular form, these warm waters flow northward through the Yucatan Channel and the Straits

of Florida to form a true ocean "river"—the Gulf Stream, "the grandest and most mighty terrestrial phenomenon."

THE CARIBBEAN MEDITERRANEAN

Although geographers have recognized but two marine areas between North and South America—the Gulf of Mexico and the Caribbean Sea—geologists now recognize three, since the Caribbean Sea is in reality a compound of two basins. The older of these two, the Caribbean proper, is bounded on the east by the Caribbee Islands, on the south by South America, on the west by Central America, and on the north, not by Cuba, but by the Antillean geanticline—i. e. Porto Rico, Haiti, Jamaica, and the Pedro-Rosalind-Nicaraguan Banks. This sea covers 575,000 square miles; it is three miles deep over a large part of its area, and measures 1500 miles from northwest to southeast. It extends from 10° to 18° north latitude. Prior to Cretaceous time it was an abyssal seaway, long and narrow, connecting the Atlantic and Pacific; in Upper Cretaceous a submarine ridge studded with volcanoes was upthrust to form the "Isthmian Link" underlying present Panama-Costa Rica-southern Nicaragua. In Middle and Late Cenozoic arose the volcanic Caribbee arc of the Lesser Antilles which bounds the Caribbean proper on the east. The bottom is not the slightly undulating plain of the oceans but is creased by southeast trending folds—submarine continuations of the Antillean Mountain System. Suboceanic depths are also reached—the maximum depth being 17,064 feet.

The second basin of the Caribbean mediterranean is the Antillean Sea. It is bounded on the south by the Antillean geanticline (see above), on the east by Jamaica and the Cayman Islands, on the north by Cuba and on the west by Yucatan-British Honduras. Its area is 175,000 square miles. Upthrusts and subsidences marked its progress during the earlier geologic ages, but its present depths and insularity are the result of a marked subsidence accompanied by block-faulting during Late Miocene-Early Pliocene. It is the breakdown of Antillia during Pliocene time which opened the Yucatan Channel (between Cuba and Yucatan) and permitted the northward flow of currents which unite to form the Gulf Stream. The bottom of the Antillean Sea shows division into two areas, the South Cuban Sea lying north of the Cayman Ridge and the Bartlett Deep lying south of it. The latter is a drop-faulted trough running northeast, as though a continuation of the Motagua Valley in Guatemala. It extends more than 1000 miles to Haiti and maintains a depth in excess of 15,000 feet (maximum depth, 24,000 feet). North of Porto Rico the depth falls to 27,970 feet in the Brownson Deep of the Atlantic Ocean.

The remaining undescribed basin is that of the young Gulf of Mexico. It covers 615,000 square miles and comprises shoaler peripheral waters surrounding the Sigsbee Deep. This deeper portion of the Gulf basin maintains a constant depth between 12,000 and 12,425 feet over a triangular central area, the apex pointing towards Florida and the base towards Mexico. But if we reduce our soundings to 10,800 feet we find, though the same general triangular form remains, that the Sigsbee basin now has two deep-water troughs, one of which heads southeast and then east toward the Straits of Florida while the other heads northwest to the mouth of the Mississippi River. During early geologic ages, the Gulf of Mexico "plate" was sporadically submerged by shallow seas; since Middle Cretaceous time, however the bottom has sunk at least 20,000 feet, accompanied by subcrustal movements building up the geanticlines of Mexico and Central America-Antillia. This movement is not yet completed.

Yucatan is a very young Cenozoic remnant of the foreland of Central America. It extends northward beneath the sea as Campeche Bank. West of Yucatan it is 150 miles from the shore to the edge of the coastal shelf, but in another ten miles the sea bottom drops to 7200 feet; on the east, however, the coast line and the submarine contours are straight and closely adjacent, indicating a major fault belt dropping to a maximum of 12,000 feet in the Yucatan Channel. Yucatan is therefore a modified horst, tilted to the west, a part of the old Central American foreland; while it was rising in the east, the Antillean Sea sank at least 6000 feet. Since the entire sea margin of the Gulf coastal region in the United States and most of Mexico is related to one and the same phenomenon—i. e. the subsidence of the Gulf of Mexico "plate"—all these regions comprise one unit. This geologic structure explains why the Gulf of Mexico is bordered by plains instead of the mountainous coasts peripheral to the Caribbean.

THE OCEAN CURRENTS

Before we outline those ocean currents which by their proximity influence the conditions of life in Central America, it is necessary to understand certain broad principles giving rise to the currents in the first place (Fig. 2). Since we are primarily interested in Middle America, we note at once that it lies in the northern hemisphere and wholly within the tropics. We therefore must remember these facts:

(1) Ocean currents flow with the prevailing winds, except the Gulf Stream, and the Japan Current. These are true "ocean rivers," both warm, both arising off the eastern coasts of the great continental land masses, the former from North America, the latter from northern Asia. These streams both flow perpendicular to the cold northwest winds of winter without being deflected.

(2) The ocean currents of the northern hemisphere in both the Atlantic and Pacific oceans flow clockwise, while in the southern hemisphere they flow counterclockwise.

(3) The Equatorial Current flows from east to west in both oceans. It extends through 20° of latitude to the north and south of the equator, embracing a third of the earth's surface; the North Equatorial Current comprises more than one half the ocean surface in the northern hemisphere.

(4) The "return currents"—i. e. those flowing down towards the equator and then westerly in the northern hemisphere, up to it and then westerly in the southern hemisphere—are *cooling* currents (see Fig. 2). The North Equatorial and the South Equatorial Currents and their "deflected" currents (deflected by striking continental land-masses) are heating currents. It therefore follows that within the tropics the continental coasts facing the east are hotter than continental coasts facing the west.

(5) The Horse Latitudes are regions of weak winds extending from latitudes 25° to 40°. They are tropical high pressure belts. Near their northern margins, especially in winter, the prevailing winds blow from the southwest. This fact, plus the prevailing westerlies in the North Atlantic, can accelerate the drift of the Gulf Stream, though it is the constant pressure of the North Equatorial Current flowing westward which forces the overheated waters to the northeast, eventually to form the Gulf Stream. These warm waters flow on the ocean surface, forcibly submerging colder Arctic waters to lower levels. The Gulf Stream materially warms the climate of western Europe, while the "return currents" materially cool northwest Africa. The same phenomena are true on the Pacific coast as witnessed by their effects in California and Chile-Peru (Humboldt Current). These last-mentioned coasts are also cooled because the warmed surface water is blown seaward by the trades and cold, bot-

tom water rises by suction. The west coast of Central America-Mexico is hotter than the coasts of California to the north or Peru to the south, not only because the heat equator passes through the latitude of Yucatan, but also because the cooling Japan and Humboldt Currents are warmed and deflected westward before reaching there. These coasts are also heated by the action of the Counter Equatorial Current. (The latter flows from west to east between the main westerly drifts of the North and South Equatorial Currents.)

(6) The waters of the northern hemisphere are warmer than those of the southern owing to the narrowing of the continents towards the south. In other words, the Antarctic seas are not confined by great land-masses as is the Arctic Ocean; consequently Antarctica supplies a greater volume of cold water with which to chill the Equatorial currents. This fact, in conjunction with the greater land-masses in the northern tropics [3] is the chief explanation why the heat

[3] Given equal amounts of insolation on equal areas of land and water, the resulting increase of temperature on land is almost twice (10:6) that on water.

FIG. 2. OCEAN CURRENTS

Note that currents in northern hemisphere flow clockwise; in southern hemisphere, counter-clockwise.

North and South Atlantic

1. Gulf Stream (warm).
2. West Wind Drift (warm).
3. Sargasso Sea.
4. Antilles Current (warm).
5. Yucatan and Florida Streams (warm).
6. North Equatorial Current (warm).
7. Equatorial Counter current—Guinea Current (warm).
8. Canaries Current—a "return" current (cool).
9. South Equatorial Current (warm).
10. Benguela Current (cool).
11. "Return" current (cool).

North and South Pacific

12. Peru Current (cold).
13. "Return" current (cool).
14. South Equatorial Current (warm).
15. Equatorial Counter current (warm).
16. California Current (cool).
17. Kuro Siwo or Japan Stream (warm).
18. "Return" current (cool).

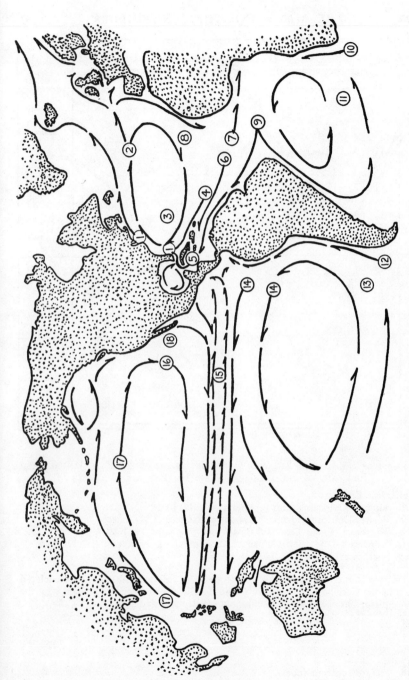

Fig. 2. Ocean Currents (For description, see facing page.)

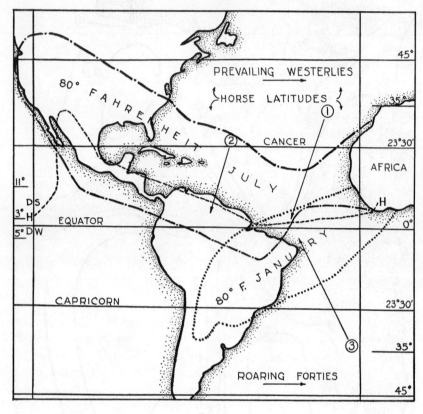

FIG. 3

DIAGRAM OF THE REGIONS ENCLOSED BY THE ISOTHERMS OF 80° F. IN JANUARY AND
JULY, AND OF THE PRINCIPAL WIND BELTS OF THE ATLANTIC

   H. Heat Equator.
  DS. Summer Doldrums (July), about 3°–11° N. Lat.
DW. Winter Doldrums (January), about 5° S. Lat. to 3° N. Lat.
    1. Northeast Trade Belt (July), 30°–35° to 5°–10° N. Lat.
    2. Northeast Trade Belt (January), about 26° to 3° N. Lat.
    3. Southeast Trades.

These two isothermic islands shift north or south following the sun. The enclosed
basin of the Caribbean and the great land-mass of North America explain why the
heat equator lies north of the geographic equator in this region.

equator does not coincide with the geographical equator, but follows as shown by the line H, Figure 3.[4]

(7) Warm water flowing to cold latitudes causes rain, because air saturated with water-vapor at high temperatures precipitates its moisture content on cooling. Hence warm currents usually bring wet climates. In Central America the prevailing trades are "drying" winds when they blow over low-lying, super-heated lands (northern Yucatan) but rain-bringers when they strike the windward slopes of bold coasts (Mosquito Coast). In the latter case the cooling effect is not one of latitude, but of increased altitude.

CARIBBEAN CURRENTS AND THE GULF STREAM

Palaeogeography indicates that in older Cenozoic time the Caribbean basin and the Gulf of Mexico were separated by an Antillia greater in extent than at present. It was as yet unsubmerged to form the present islands and was still connected with the Central American mainland. No Gulf Stream was possible under these conditions.

But with the closing of the last interoceanic portal by which the present Atlantic and Pacific waters were connected, and with the establishment of deep water connections between the Caribbean, the Gulf of Mexico and the Florida Straits by the Pliocene submergence of Antillia, the flow of the waters forming the Gulf Stream became a fact. We know this from the distribution of Pliocene marine fauna from the Caribbean into the Gulf of Mexico (Fig. 4).

The waters for 12° of latitude north and south of the equator are greatly heated by the sun; in the Caribbean region their temperatures vary from a low of 76° F. in February to a high of 84° F. in August. Within these zones there is annually a double period of insolation. The insolation is double because the sun passes directly overhead once in crossing this zone on its apparent course north to the summer solstice and again on its apparent course south to the winter solstice. At the equator there are two maxima of insolation (at the equinoxes, when the sun is vertical at noon) and two minima (at the solstices, when the sun is farthest off the equator). On the equator the values do not vary much through the year because the sun is never far from the zenith, and day and night are always equal. As

[4] Coleman, 1926, p. 270 et. seq., summarizes the theories which involve changes in the inclination of the earth's axis, eccentricity of the earth's orbit, and sun-spot activity, with special emphasis on glaciation.

latitude from the equator increases, the angle of insolation becomes more oblique and the intensity decreases, but at the same time the length of the day increases during the summer and the length of the night during the winter. The double period of insolation for the equator, however, prevails as far as about the twelfth parallel (north or south); near Latitude 15° the two maxima have united in one period of insolation, and the same is true of the minima. On the 21st of June, although the equator has a day twelve hours long, the sun does not reach the zenith and the amount of insolation is therefore less than that at the equinox. On the northern tropic—the Tropic of Cancer—the sun is vertical at noon and the day is more than twelve hours long. Hence the amount of insolation received at this latitude is greater than that received on the equator at the equinox. This annual migration of the sun is thus fully described here not only because it accounts for the heating of tropical waters, but because it must be thoroughly grasped in order to understand the march of tropical wet and dry seasons, which will be described in the section on climate. This zone of greater insolation heats the waters of the Equatorial Currents drifting to the west under the prevailing northeast and southeast trades. The North Equatorial Current drifting into the Caribbean mediterranean is the power reservoir, so to speak, whose force, on striking the continental land-mass, is deflected north and eventually northeasterly to form the affluents which unite as the Gulf Stream. (See Figs. 2, 3.)

This northerly deflection gives rise to two main currents—the Antillean passing to the east of Cuba and the Yucatan Stream flowing through the deep Yucatan Channel between Cuba and Yucatan. Instead of flowing widely into the Gulf of Mexico as has been generally believed, it is deflected northeast to submarine south Florida and thence into the narrowing and shallowing channel of the Straits of Florida and the still narrower channel between Florida and the Bahama Bank. Emerging as the Florida Stream, it is soon joined on the east by the Greater Antilles Current and the two flow conjointly as the Gulf Stream towards Cape Hatteras, where they are

FIG. 4. THE CURRENTS OF THE CARIBBEAN MEDITERRANEAN

The wind roses show the prevailing winds, the length of the arrow the percentage of time blowing from the direction indicated. Current flow in nautical miles (subject to fluctuations caused by winds). Note counter currents. (Taken from charts, United States Hydrographic Office.)

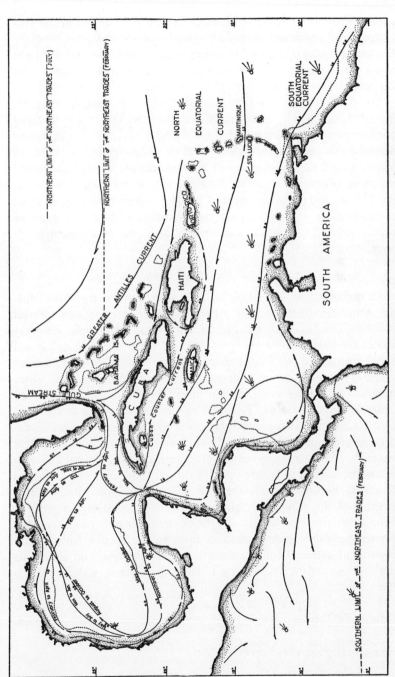

Fig. 4. The Currents of the Caribbean Mediterranean (For description, see facing page.)

again deflected northeasterly. It then flows at right angles to the prevailing, cold northwest winds of winter across the Atlantic causing Europe to enjoy the mildest winter climate and the highest mean temperature which are found anywhere in the world in corresponding latitudes.

The Gulf Stream was first noted by Ponce de Leon in 1513, although Columbus by the time of his third voyage (1498) realized how strongly the currents of the Caribbean set to the northwest.[5] Schuchert states: "The highest level of these waters, at most 30 inches above the mean level of the sea, occurs to the north and northeast of the Bahamas and is caused by the merging pressures of the Florida and Antillean streams." [6] The immense volume of these ocean currents is indicated by the estimated forty cubic miles of water which the Antillean Current conveys past Porto Rico every hour.

THE PACIFIC SLOPE

As compared with the complicated orography of the three Middle American basins on the Atlantic side of Mexico and Central America, that found on the Pacific side is relatively simple. Its overwhelming feature is the string of volcanic formations overlying and concealing the earlier folds beneath; this series of Pleistocene-Recent volcanoes extends from Tehuantepec through Nicaragua to Costa Rica and continues along the Cordillera de Talamanca of southern Costa Rica into Panama. This development is transverse to the east-west folds of late Pliocene-Pleistocene which formed the great Caribbean mediterranean, briefly outlined above. The Pacific coast differs from the Atlantic in its extremely narrow coastal plain and few indentations. The only large gulf is that of California and while the Gulfs of Fonseca, Nicoya, Dulce and Guarachiné form harbors worthy of the name, only the two first-mentioned are of modern commercial importance. It should be remembered, however, that present Lake Nicaragua was once open to the Pacific, having been closed and converted into a fresh water lake by volcanic action; its drainage now flows across the former interoceanic watershed into the Caribbean.

The Pacific slope of Mexico, like the whole of Mexico as far as the Isthmus of Tehuantepec, belongs geologically with North America;

---

[5] Churchill, 1732 (3rd edition), Vol. II, p. 558.
[6] Schuchert, 1935, p. 74.

but from the Isthmus on it belongs geologically with Nuclear Central America. The North American structural features terminate beneath the volcanic axis following from Cape Corrientes to Jalapa, Vera Cruz (5, Fig. 1); very probably the next geologic province to the south, the Sierra Madre del Sur (7, Fig. 1) belongs to Central America, being, possibly, a link between the latter and North America. Be the geology as it may, few specimens of Nearctic fauna are found south of the Mexican Plateau, the southern boundary of which follows the line of volcanoes just described.

No great ocean currents off the Pacific coast of Central America flow as dramatically as they do off the Atlantic; nevertheless, we find here the greatest stretch between mountain plateau and sea-bottom, closely adjacent. Ninety miles off the Guatemala coast lies the Acapulco Deep with a maximum depth of 21,288 feet below sea-level, while about 50 miles inland from the coast, highland plateaus rise to 11,000 feet—a difference in level of over 32,000 feet.

CLIMATE

We have shown how the mountainous framework of Middle America is a geologic unit forming the western border of the Antillean-Caribbean region, and have stressed its geological independence of the north-south trending cordilleras of North and South America. We have also described the ocean currents of the Atlantic and Pacific, here closely adjacent because of the narrowness of the land separating them; these currents, coupled with prevailing winds, have a marked influence upon the climate of Middle America, the basic features of which we will now describe.

First, we must understand clearly that the climate of Middle America is extremely complex, owing to its geographical location and to its greatly varying topography. This causes four factors to function in a very small area so that abrupt changes occur in the closest juxtaposition. According to the *dominant control*, we have solar, continental, marine, and mountain climates: latitude is the dominant control in the first, the influence of land or water in the second and third, while the effect of altitude is the essential in the fourth. The inter-action of these four factors give Middle America a physical climate as abruptly varied as any in the world. We must define these four climatic controls further.

(1) Solar climate: the solar climate is controlled by the amount

of insolation (solar radiation) which any place receives by reason of its latitude. As explained under that section dealing with the Gulf Stream, there are two maxima and two minima of insolation on the Equator, and for 12° north and south of it, the former at the equinoxes, the latter at the solstices. About Latitude 15° these two unite —i. e. they may not be distinguished because there is no appreciable time lapse between them; as the region we are chiefly concerned with lies six degrees north and south of Latitude 15°, it occupies the zone where the Equatorial type of rainfall impinges upon the tropical type. Certain regions are also subject to the trade belt type. We must also remember in connection with insolation that when equal quantities of sun heat are received on equal areas of land and of water, the resulting increase of temperature is almost twice (10 to 6) as great on the land as on the water, even when no considerable share of the heat received in the case of the water is expended in evaporation. This discrepancy in the heating of land and sea causes the phenomenon of land and sea breezes—i. e. offshore and onshore winds—often a pronounced day and night occurrence.

(2) Continental climate: this classification is usually divided into "continental" and "marine," the former being further subdivided into "desert" and "littoral," while "mountain climate" is grouped by itself, because altitude is so dominant a control. Continental climate is severe, with greater seasonal contrasts than over the oceans, less cloudiness, and greater temperature ranges, both diurnal and annual. Both the amount and frequency of rainfall decrease inland, though conditions may be affected by local topography and winds. Seasonal changes of pressure over continents cause systems of inflowing or outflowing winds; when well-developed, they become true monsoons. "Northers" in the Caribbean, though irregular storms, are seasonal and monsoonal in origin.

(2a) Littoral climate is transitional between continental and marine; the prevailing wind is the dominant control—when onshore, a marine type; offshore, continental type.

(2b) Desert climate is an extreme of continental climate.

(3) Marine climate: whereas land warms and cools quickly, oceans do not; their seasonal changes are slight and retarded; they are characterized by higher humidity, greater cloudiness, heavier rainfall, all due to abundant evaporation of the surface water.

(4) Mountain climate: mountains contrasted with lowlands show the following characteristics: a decrease in atmospheric pressure,

temperature, and absolute humidity; an increase in insolation and radiation and (generally) in precipitation. Within the tropics, on mountains with abundant rainfall, there is a definite altitude at which the air is almost constantly saturated. Throughout the trade wind belt, precipitation occurs upon the windward slope and its intensity is proportional to the elevation of the land. (The decrease in temperature is 0.5° Centigrade for every 100 m. increase of altitude.) As a corollary, leeward slopes are relatively arid, wherever specific local conditions are not so emphasized as to become the dominant control.

The Annual March of Tropical Seasons

In the tropics the year is divided into two seasons—the wet and the dry. These seasons are of two types—the Equatorial type, and the Tropical (Fig. 5). In the former, the area of greatest insolation swings back and forth across the equator according to the zenithal position of the sun (Fig. 3), the rains following where the verticality of the sun super-heats the earth and atmosphere directly beneath. On the equator itself there are two rainy seasons (when the sun is vertical, i. e. the equinoxes) and two dry seasons (when the sun is farthest from the zenith, i. e. the solstices). These conditions prevail along the equator and for 10 to 12 degrees north or south of it—that is, as long as there is a sufficient time-lapse between the zenithal position of the sun for the two seasons to be distinguishable. But at Latitude 15° the interval vanishes and the double system of Equatorial rainfall merges into a single system; this effects a Tropical type of rainfall, with one dry and one rainy season. It is found where the Equatorial type in its migration north or south with the sun encroaches upon the trade wind belts. The weather of these two types is strongly contrasted. The *single* dry season of the tropical type lasts longer than *either* dry season of the Equatorial type. It may reach eight months in typical cases, so that lowland areas become parched and dry and vegetation withers. The biotic conditions of each type differ markedly; the rhythm of the life of agricultural man also varies according to the type of rainfall, the *time* of the onset of the rains being of greater relative consequence than the *amount* of precipitation.

On either side of the belt of Equatorial rains lie the trade wind belts. At sea-level they are characterized by fair weather, steady winds averaging 10–15 miles per hour, infrequent light rains and very regular, slight ranges of temperature. The climate of ocean areas in these belts is the simplest and most equable in the world. The rainfall of these belts (roughly from 30 degrees to 10 degrees of latitude on the polar margins of the Equatorial rain-belts) is greatest in the winter when the trades are most active.[7] The greatest contrast in the trade wind belts are the leeward slopes of high islands (or the Pacific coast of southern Mexico). In cases where the trades blow throughout the year against high coasts, as on portions of the Atlantic coast of Central America, there is no true dry season.

The trades blow from tropical high pressure belts on either side of the low pressure belt which follows the thermal equator. This belt of calms—the Doldrums—shifts north and south after the sun. It is a low pressure belt because the super-heated air is constantly expanding and rising. The trades would blow straight down from the north (or up from the south) were it not for the spin of the earth from west to east; this spin imparts to them their diagonal direction—northeast in the northern hemisphere, southeast in the southern. Their margins shift after the sun—i. e., following the Doldrums—and at certain seasons they may be interrupted by the migrating Equatorial rains, by land and sea breezes, or violent cyclonic storms (hurricanes). In the Caribbean region they are frequently interrupted during the winter by "northers"—a wind of monsoon type originated by the collection of a great reservoir of cold air over the North American continent.

The inter-action of these fundamental conditions upon the abrupt topography of Middle America, peppered as it is with a phenomenal vulcanism, gives this narrowly constricted region an ecology as variable and contrasted as any in the world.

[7] The trades are most active in the winter, especially through the Caribbean region, because the cold polar air over North America is in sharpest contrast with the hot airs of the tropics (see Figs. 3, 5, 80° isotherm for January).

FIG. 5. SIGNIFICANT ISOBARS, AND ISOTHERMS FOR THE CARIBBEAN AND ADJACENT REGIONS DURING FEBRUARY AND JULY

The equatorial low pressure belts follow the isobars for 29.90, shifting north or south following the sun. The trade winds blow into this shifting belt of calms—the doldrums—from the shifting tropical high pressure areas. (See 30.10 for July and 30.20 for February.) The Northeast Trades blow steadiest in the winter. (January to June; Tropical type of rainfall.) Equatorial type of rainfall impinges on Tropical type along the isobars for 29.90. Trade type of rainfall, usually north of Latitude 15°, has maximum in winter, when Northeast Trades are most active.
1. Northeast Trades, July.
2. Northeast Trades, February.

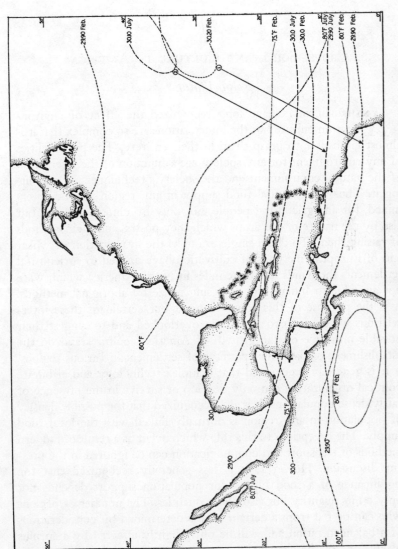

F<small>IG</small>. 5. (For description, see facing page.)

III

CROPS, SOILS, AND CULTURE IN AMERICA

Ralph Linton *

ANTHROPOLOGISTS have long recognized the effect of environment on culture but the interrelations are so complex that it is almost impossible to grasp them in their entirety. The potentialities of any environment for any society are a function of the interaction of the natural environment and the society's techniques for exploiting it. Thus the potential food supply in any region will be determined, for an agricultural people, not only by climate and soil but also by the nature of the crops which they possess and their methods of raising them. To cite a single example, the introduction of wheat and of European methods of cultivation have opened to agricultural settlements thousands of square miles in North America which were not available to Indian groups raising maize by aboriginal methods. It is the purpose of this paper to point out certain of these interrelations which seem to have been overlooked and to suggest their possible influence on the growth of American cultures and on the establishment of particular patterns of settlement in various regions.

It is generally recognized that complex technology and elaborate political organization can only develop or survive in the presence of fairly dense populations. It is also recognized that the possible density of population in any region is normally linked with the local food supply. The exceptions to this rule which occur as a result of modern methods of transport and communication can be ignored in the present discussion. However, it is less generally recognized that the significance of a food supply for population support depends not only on its quantity but also on its qualities. The number of persons who can be fed from a certain area is determined by considerations of a balanced ration and will be only slightly affected by a surplus of any one of the elements necessary for such a ration.

* Swarthmore, A.B., 1915; Pennsylvania, A.M., 1916; Harvard, Ph.D., 1925; now Professor of Anthropology, Columbia.

What constitutes a balanced ration is, in itself, an exceedingly complex problem. In spite of the rapid progress of research along this line we are still very much in the dark as to the minimum amount of vitamins and minerals necessary to insure health and it is quite possible that certain as yet unsuspected substances may enter into the picture. The writer is not an expert on nutrition and the present discussion will, therefore, be confined to one of the simplest aspects of the problem, that of a protein and starch balance. There seems to be abundant evidence that although our species can adapt itself to a starchless diet, it cannot survive on one which lacks a certain minimum of proteins and fats. Thus there are human groups who live exclusively on meat and/or fish or on a combination of meat and dairy products but there are no human groups who live on starch foods without the addition of proteins. This means that an agriculture which confines itself to the raising of starch crops cannot form the exclusive basis of a people's food economy.

If we turn to the Old World we find that throughout most of Eurasia and Africa a balanced ration was provided by a combination of starch crops and dairy products. It was the latter, rather than the simple domestication of animals which, in combination with agriculture, made possible large and settled populations. Milking the herd provided many times the proteins and fats which might have been obtained by killing from the herd. In further Asia, where the dairying pattern never penetrated, the need for protein was met in some regions by a local protein crop, the soya bean, and in others by the rearing of pigs and chickens, supplemented by fishing and local small game. Where the people were within reach of the sea sufficient proteins and fats could be obtained by fishing alone. This was the situation which obtained in most of Oceania, where the local crops were almost exclusively starch crops. In Polynesia, where there was no native game, a tribe which was cut off from the sea, was in desperate straits even when it had abundant land for agriculture. In Melanesia, where there is some game in the larger islands, we find that interior populations are usually much sparser than the quantity of land available for agriculture would seem to justify and that there is frequently a trade in fish between the coastal and interior tribes.

In America there were comparatively few domestic animals and those present made only a slight contribution to the aboriginal food supply. Dogs and turkeys were eaten in some places but were luxuries rather than staples, while the South American llama and related species were never milked and were too valuable for wool and transport to be killed except on ceremonial occasions. Proteins and fats had to be obtained by hunting and fishing, by gathering wild plants or by raising special crops. Actually, all the higher American cultures were based on a combination of starch and protein crops just as all the civilizations of the Old World were based on a combination of starch crops and domestic animals.

In his exceedingly stimulating article on American Agricultural Origins [1] Dr. Carl Sauer has stressed the large number of starch crops raised by the American Indians. He concludes on the basis of several sorts of evidence that most of these crops were domesticated independently and in different regions and suggests the probability of the independent invention of agriculture at several points in South and Middle America. He further concludes that these original centers of agriculture were all located in valleys or plateaus of moderate altitude, i. e. in inland regions.[2] This point is of considerable importance to the present discussion, for it means that the earliest American farmers were cut off from sea fishing, one of the surest and most abundant sources of proteins and fats.

In contrast with the multiplicity of American starch crops the number of protein crops was decidedly limited. There were only two of any importance, the peanut and the bean, the latter in numerous varieties. Recent investigations of Russian botanists, summarized by Dr. Sauer,[3] indicate that the peanut was originally a native of Brazil, the bean of Middle America. Whether the domestication of these two plants was contemporaneous with the domestication of starch crops in the same localities cannot be determined at present. However, maize appears in our own Southwest in much older cultural horizons than does the bean and if the two crops appeared in Middle America at the same time it is hard to see why one should have been diffused northward without the other. It seems probable, therefore, that maize culture was established in Middle America before bean culture.

An inland people who had no domestic food animals and who raised only starch crops would have great difficulty in developing or maintaining a dense population. They would have to depend upon hunting and wild foods such as nuts or legumes for their proteins

[1] Sauer, American Agricultural Origins, 1936.
[2] Op. cit., pp. 283–284.
[3] Op. cit., pp. 289–290.

and fats. This would set a fairly low upper limit to the size of population and especially of localized aggregates. To hunt and gather wild foods successfully the people would have to live in small and widely spaced communities. In time such farmers-food gatherers might develop considerable skill in cultivation but a mere increase in the quantity of starch foods raised would not solve their problem. There would be a definite ceiling, set by the supply of wild proteins, beyond which their population could not increase without encountering dietary deficiencies. This, in turn, would set a limit to the level of culture which they could maintain. Large aggregates can afford to support specialists while small aggregates cannot.

Let us assume for the sake of argument that agriculture was invented, and various starch crops domesticated, independently in several places in the New World. If so, there must have been many communities scattered over the two continents who had the habit of crop raising but who were subject to the limitations on population growth imposed by protein deficiency. The domestication of a local protein yielding plant, or the introduction of such a plant through diffusion, would remove this limitation. A new and much higher ceiling for population would be set, depending mainly upon the amount of arable land available, and until this ceiling was reached there would be boom times. The size of local aggregates could be greatly increased and the stage set for rapid cultural advance. If the protein crop was a diffused one, this change might occur with great speed. To a people already familiar with agriculture the acceptance of a new crop is an easy matter as we know from the rapidity with which American food plants spread through the Old World after the discovery of America.

It is interesting to check this hypothesis against the known development of culture in the Southwest. Here we have indisputable evidence of a comparatively brief period of very rapid cultural advance with a strong suggestion that this was correlated with a great increase in population. The period of advance seems to have been preceded by a much longer period, lower limits still unknown, during which the development of culture was slow while it was followed by another long period of comparative culture stabilization. It also seems that the period of rapid advance cannot be accounted for on the basis of sudden contact with and borrowing from some other culture. The Anasazi line of culture development runs uninterruptedly from the Basket Makers to the builders of the great pueblos and unbroken evolutionary series can be traced for most of the elements present. We must conclude that Basket Maker culture received a sudden stimulus of some sort. We know that, although the Basket Makers raised corn and squashes from early times, the bean does not appear in the Southwest until shortly before the period of culture flowering. It seems probable, therefore, that the introduction of this protein crop, with the consequent raising of the population ceiling, was responsible for the sudden release of cultural energy.

There are suggestions for such a period of rapid change and advance in the Southeast also, although the evidence there is much less conclusive and an exact chronology is lacking. The finding of seeds of domesticated and improved rag weed and amaranth in Bluff Dwellers sites and the fact that these crops seem to have been allowed to lapse by the period of first European contact may indicate an independent development of agriculture in this region. Such evidence as we have for the introduction of corn and beans into the Southeast seems to indicate that, if they were not introduced together, the time interval separating the two introductions was short. The sudden advance of Southeastern culture may, therefore, have been due to the introduction of a maize-bean complex into a region where agricultural techniques were already known but where the crops were inadequate. Such an introduction would provide a balanced ration at a single stroke and make possible a rapid population increase.

Even in Middle America there seems to be evidence of a period of rapid cultural advance. Although the Maya civilization did not rise out of darkness as abruptly as once supposed, its sudden flowering in the Old Empire certainly suggests some stimulating factor. May this not have been the addition of beans to a pre-existing agricultural complex? The apparent priority of maize over bean culture in Middle America has already been noted.

Other things being equal, one might expect the period of rapid population advance and cultural flowering to continue in any region until all available new land had been brought under cultivation. After this the population would decline with the diminishing food supply until it stabilized at a level which could be maintained by re-utilization of land. This level would be determined by a combination of the nature of the local soils and of the techniques for exploiting them provided by the particular culture. The latter would, of course, include not only methods of tillage and fertilization or crop rotation but also facilities for land clearance. The importance of weed growth to land re-utilization has been brought out by recent researches of the Carnegie Foundation in Yucatan.[4]

American agriculture, outside two or three centers of high civilization, was comparatively crude. There was only sporadic use of fertilizers or crop rotation, the main method for restoring used soils being simple fallowing. Soils naturally varied with the locality, but there were certain climatic factors which were of importance to both soil exhaustion and rejuvenation. Where rains are light, the substances necessary to crop growth remain in the upper levels of the soil where they are readily available. The fertility of most desert lands when water can be brought to them is proverbial. In tropical regions of heavy rainfall, on the other hand, the warm rains leach out the mineral content of the surface soil and carry it down beyond the reach of ordinary crop roots. In moist temperate regions the conditions are intermediate, depending on quantity and season of precipitation. Thus a soil of given mineral content will grow crops longest under semi-arid conditions, for a shorter time under moist temperate ones and for a still shorter time in a tropical rain belt.

Closely connected with these differences in moisture and temperature is the factor of weed growth. This is of the utmost importance to agriculturalists who lack metal tools. In semi-arid regions weed growth is slow and comparatively scanty, making the annual reconditioning of cleared fields easy. In moist temperate ones the growth is more rapid and abundant, but it reaches its climax in regions of tropical rainfall where the growth is so rapid and dense that almost as much labor is required to reclear a field used even the previous year as to clear long standing jungle.

These factors of soil fertility and weed growth united to impose different patterns of soil utilization in different climatic areas. While the Southwestern tribes could grow corn on the same lands generation after generation, the Indians of the Eastern Woodlands had to change their cultivation every three or four years due to a combination of soil exhaustion and weed seed accumulation. In the wet tropics the same factors, in increased intensity, made it difficult to crop a field more than two years in succession and desirable to clear new fields every year. Recuperation of the land through fallowing followed a similar order. Desert soils recuperated very slowly and areas which had been depleted by long cultivation had to be aban-

4 Emerson, Milpa System, 1935.

doned for many years. In temperate regions the recuperation was more rapid, due to the heavier plant growth while in jungle areas fifteen to twenty years were required for complete recovery.

Both the total population of an area and the possible size of residential aggregates are intimately related to these factors of soil exhaustion, weed growth and soil recuperation. With Indian techniques of agriculture the long term stabilization point for the population of any area was determined by the possibilities of turnover in fallow and cultivated land. A tribe might actually have bred up to the limits of its assured long term agricultural food supply while much of its territory appeared to be unused. The possible size of the village groups within the tribe was set by the amount of food which could be raised on land exploitable from the village. The extent of this zone of exploitation was roughly determined by the distance to which a man could travel, work in the fields and return on the same day. When it was necessary to guard the fields against raiders, the zone was correspondingly narrowed.

Given the rich soils of semi-arid regions, the scanty weed growth and crops suited to local conditions, large settlements could be established and remain on the same site for several generations. Under such circumstances the population would become so thoroughly rooted that, when soil exhaustion did make itself felt, the people would tend to cling to their settlement until the last possible moment. Perhaps the long dwindling of population which is evident for some of the Southwestern ruined pueblos may have been due to progressive soil exhaustion as well as to the drought period. With the slowness of soil recuperation, fields that had once been exhausted could not be re-utilized for so long a time that the same group would rarely return to them at all.

In tropical rain forests, on the other hand, the soil exhaustion and weed growth were so rapid that villages as large as those of the Southwest would have had to move every two or three years. Actually, the pattern in the American rain forest areas seems to have been that of much smaller local aggregates, but even so a village rarely remained in the same place for as much as a generation. The tribes here had the habit of movement and seem to have drifted long distances with ease. In moist temperate regions, such as the Eastern United States, village movement was also necessary as long as the zone of exploitation was limited by the common residence of the community's members. However, the villagers could remain in one place for a generation or more and moved with corresponding reluctance. Moreover, the rather rapid recuperation of the land under fallowing made it possible for a village to move about within a fairly restricted area, returning to the same territory time after time. This seems to have been the condition which existed among the protohistoric Iroquois and some of the northern agricultural Siouan tribes such as the Winnebago. However, it was most characteristic of the tribes living on the northern margins of the eastern agricultural area, regions in which fortified villages were useful for defense against the neighboring hunting groups. It is interesting to note that whenever this threat was removed, as in the time of Iroquois League dominance, the village populations tended to spread out and the community to remain in the same place for longer intervals.

This fact may provide a clue to the origin of the type of community organization found in the Southeast and in many parts of Middle America. In both these regions we find a development of confederacies or other large political groupings which made large areas comparatively safe from attack. Soils were rich enough here to permit villages to remain in one place long enough to take root. When the soil in the immediate neighborhood of the village began to be exhausted, safety from attack made it possible for the village to expand its zone of exploitation by having its members live at the more distant farms during the agricultural season. In due course of time it might come to be surrounded by isolated families or even hamlets whose inhabitants felt themselves members of the central community although they did not regularly reside there. Since the soil recuperated readily under fallowing, such an extended community might become very large without exceeding the assured year by year food supply. The community would be as firmly rooted in one place as a Southwestern pueblo, but would have quite different characteristics. In particular, the central town from which the scattered population had been derived would tend to become a community center, a place to which the whole group resorted for exchange of goods, councils and ceremonies. This is the pattern which obtains for certain Guatemalan Indian towns today and which probably obtained for most of the Middle American cities of pre-European times. The great temples and squares for assembly found in these cities seem to be quite out of proportion to the apparent size of their constant populations but were adapted to the function of the cities as community centers. Very similar arrangements in town planning are found in our own Southeast where we know that a similar scattering of families on isolated farms existed. These resemblances between the Southeast and Middle America are probably due to a northward diffusion of the pattern, but their acceptance in the Southeast was justified by the similarity of community organization.

In the Southwest this type of community organization never developed. This may have been due in part to the lack of political organizations larger than single villages, with the consequent danger of attack on isolated families. However, soil may also have played a part. With the slowly exhausted, slowly rejuvenated soils of this region there was less stimulus to expanding a village's zone of exploitation while the area required for a really permanent settlement with alternate cultivation and fallowing would have been enormous. The Southwestern village was a highly localized, closely knit community which needed no focal point. Perhaps the failure of the Middle American community center type of town planning to diffuse into the Southwest is due to the fact that the needs to which it was a response did not exist here.

All cultural processes involve a multiplicity of causal factors which, in combination, produce a multiplicity of results. The writer would be the first to admit that the hypotheses which have just been advanced to account for certain observed phenomena of American cultures are much too simple. However, food is the most basic of human needs and the crops and soils from which the American Indians derived it deserve more attention than they have received to date.

IV

THE CONCEPTUAL STRUCTURE IN MIDDLE
AMERICAN STUDIES

Clyde Kluckhohn *

FOR ONE who has published but a single very trivial contribution in Middle American research [1] to attempt a critical review of the theoretical bases of work in this field may well seem a gratuitous impertinence. Perhaps, however, the significance of the forest as a whole can be envisioned a little more easily if the student is not preoccupied with a particular set of trees. An intensive interest in a given set of facts is often (as Dr. Kidder has suggested) productive of a certain intellectual myopia. We can hope, therefore, that the fact that the writer has only a non-specialist's familiarity with the data is in part compensated for by the detachment which tends to be associated with lack of a research stake. Full and detailed factual knowledge would, of course, be a prerequisite to any useful commentary on the interpretation of specific assemblages of evidence, the status of concrete problems, or present frontiers of information. But (particularly since Professor Tozzer [2] and Dr. Mason [3] have recently given us admirable surveys of just this sort) this is exactly what I do not propose to do. I wish, rather, to turn to a general survey of the conceptual bases to investigations which have been carried out in this field.

Any discussion which could be given in a few pages will necessarily be somewhat schematic and generalized and will inevitably rest more upon impressions than upon exhaustive examination of the evidence and satisfactory, documented induction. First, however, I must be careful to state and discuss briefly two postulates upon which my analysis will rest: 1. archaeologists and ethnologists wish

* Wisconsin, A.B., 1928; Oxford, B.A., 1932; Harvard, Ph.D., 1936; Instructor in Anthropology, Harvard, 1935-1937; Assistant Professor, 1937–.
[1] Kluckhohn, Note, 1935.
[2] Tozzer, Maya Research, 1934; and Tozzer, Review, 1937b.
[3] Mason, Observations on Middle American Archaeology, 1938.

to be "scholarly" at least in the sense of working systematically (with provision for verification by other workers) toward the end of enriching our intellectual grasp of human experience; 2. in scholarly procedure there is a rational or conceptual element as well as a factual or evidential element. The first postulate implies that Maya archaeologists, for example, should not be interested merely in any set of facts as such—no facts are, from this point of view, their own justification simply because they satisfy our intellectual curiosity on a given point. Gathering, analyzing, and synthesizing all the data on, let us say, the calendar system of the Aztecs is justified only if all this industry can be viewed as contributing, however indirectly, toward our understanding of human behavior or human history. Clearly, it cannot be demanded that the precise relevance of each research undertaking to some broad induction should be known and stated in advance. But unless data are gathered and presented in such a way that they can be so conceptualized by other workers they are intellectually useless. Hence the broad outlines of a conceptual scheme should be present in the consciousness of the investigator and clearly stated. It is not sufficient that there should be a sense of problem in so far as clearing up obscurities of fact are concerned. The second postulate is very closely related to the first. As my colleague, Professor Talcott Parsons, has long insisted: "The content of science cannot be wholly fact. For if it were there would be no 'crucial experiments.' . . . The facts do not speak for themselves; they have to be cross-examined." The thesis that the conceptual aspect of anthropological procedure needs at least as careful examination as the verificational aspect (Whitehead's "observational order") I have elaborated elsewhere.[4]

Let us now turn directly to Middle American studies. To begin with, I should like to record an overwhelming impression that many students in this field are but slightly reformed antiquarians. To one who is a layman in these highly specialized realms there seems a great deal of obsessive wallowing in detail of and for itself. No one can feel more urgently than the writer the imperative obligation of anthropologists to set their descriptions in such a rich context of detail that they can properly be used for comparative purposes. Yet proliferation of minutiae is not its own justification. Authors of research monographs ought to make it plain (in few words but lucidly) that they have given such amplitude of detail only toward

[4] Kluckhohn, The Place of Theory in Anthropological Studies, 1939.

the end of elucidating such and such larger questions. And from time to time in any field there should appear books or articles on a somewhat higher level of abstraction which suggest the pertinence of various constellations of data to the primary problems of human interaction. It is the candid opinion of this writer that such efforts by Middle American specialists have been pitifully few. Professor Tozzer has pilloried activity of the sheer fact-grubbing type,[5] but the problems which continue to be attacked in this field appear to be primarily of an informational order. Do researches which require large funds for their support require no social justification other than that of quenching certain thirsts for knowledge on the part of a relatively small number of citizens? If archaeologists and ethnologists have hardly begun to ask themselves the tough-minded query —so what?, evidence is not lacking that this question has occurred to research foundations and other sources of financial support. Personally, I suspect that unless archaeologists treat their work quite firmly as part of a general attempt to understand human behavior they will, before many generations, find themselves classed with Aldous Huxley's figure who devoted his life to writing a history of the three-pronged fork. In Middle American studies up to this time I have been unable to find much evidence of awareness of or interest in the relevance of research and publication to what Linton has asserted to be the prime task of all anthropologists: " . . . to discover the limits within which men can be conditioned, and what patterns of social life seem to impose fewest strains upon the individual."

One almost dares to say quite flatly: the industry of workers in this field is most impressive as is, for the most part, their technical proficiency in the field and the scrupulous documentation in their publications, but one is not carried away by the luxuriance of their ideas. Let me elaborate these considerations. In discussing the various types of intellectual activity carried on by scholars, I have found it convenient to distinguish the following hierarchy of abstractions: methodology, theory, method, technique. Each of these concepts is, of course, progressively more concrete. The category of methodology refers to the logical bases of all intellectual work; the category theory refers to the conceptual framework of a single discipline; the category method refers to the sheer analysis and ordering of data (as opposed to the formulation of abstract concepts in terms of which such ordering is carried on); the category technique refers

[5] Tozzer, Maya Research, 1934, p. 5.

to a highly concrete systematization of principles for dealing with a particular aspect of a particular subject. Thus methodology deals with the fundamental general problems: what evidence is admissible in the court of learning? in accord with what principles may relations be validly inferred between the various elements of such evidence? Theory, on the other hand, operates within a particular system: how can given sets of data best be conceptualized congruently with accepted principles of general methodology? As for the distinction between theory and method, Goring has expressed this with singular felicity:

> . . . we must pass to some extent from the strict and narrow confines of ascertained certainty into the wider latitudes of theory, where the laws which govern the imagination in the construction of ideas are more paramount than those which regulate the intellect in its analysis of facts. The interpreting of fact involves operations different and distinct from those by which facts are established—it involves work of synthesis and exposition, not of analysis and discovery.

Technique is distinguishable from method only in so far as method involves the interrelations and consistency of a number of techniques. For example, archaeological method encompasses a number of techniques such as surveying, photographing, field cataloging and the like. Such techniques emphasize the details of the expert method.

Now if the reader does not like the words with which I have labeled these four somewhat separable types of operations, let him substitute other words or symbols. It is also perfectly true that these categories interdigitate and overlap at various points in our concrete activities. Nevertheless I maintain that such discriminations are useful toward developing greater awareness of what is inevitably involved in the acts of anthropologists as scholars. And I suggest that the greater number of students in the Middle American field ignore the categories "methodology" and "theory" almost entirely in so far as one can judge from their published writings. If they use the word "theory" at all, they tend to use it as a pejorative synonym for "speculation." No anthropologist, however, can perform intellectual operations without some reference to the logics of scholarship in general and a theoretical system of premises and concepts pertinent to the data of anthropology. The practical question always becomes:

is the anthropologist conscious of begging methodological questions and of choosing one theoretical position rather than another? If the methodology and theory are almost wholly beneath the level of consciousness it is axiomatic that they are inadequate. For all aspects of intellectual procedure must be made explicit in order that they may be subject to criticism and empirical testing.

In respect of the operations by which facts are established Middle American studies appear to be relatively sophisticated. The methods and techniques through which analysis and discovery proceeds seem to be subject to rigorous scrutiny and to be advancing constantly. By comparison, the methodological and theoretical development appears stunted indeed. Dr. Vaillant has indicated his awareness of the inevitable dependence of data, technique, and method upon theoretical preconceptions.[6] In general, however, almost no realization of the dependence of one system of categories upon another is evident. The tradition is accepted; fundamental premises are not questioned, and development occurs only within the limitations imposed by the traditional premises and concepts. Even the Carnegie Institution's well-known and justly praised scheme for a many-sided attack by specialists drawn from varied disciplines is but an extension of the received system, an improvement of method by intensification and intellectual cross-fertilization.

No one, of course, has greater abhorrence of an archaeology which is on the intellectual level of stamp collecting than Dr. Kidder. In the Year Book of the Carnegie Institution he has insistently reaffirmed the necessity for "work of synthesis and exposition," for interpreting facts as well as collecting them. Little effort seems, however, to have been given to developing an explicit and consistent logical scheme for attaining these ends. Thus far the published record suggests that his staff are still predominantly preoccupied with answering questions of a factual order. Dr. Kidder might reply that until we have a considerably fuller control of the facts generalization would be premature and misleading. Certainly the history of New World archaeology during this century gives us cause for alarm lest more synthetic interpretations which have an utterly inadequate observational basis become crystallized as sacrosanct dogmas. But unwarranted and stark synthesis is not to be identified in too cavalier a fashion with theory which means, first of all, examination of overt and covert premises (postulates and assumptions) and the general

[6] Vaillant, Early Cultures of the Valley of Mexico, 1935, pp. 285 and 304.

problem of the conceptualization of discrete data. There are, I think, grounds for believing that anthropologists generally have not quite kept on the forward march to the scientific frontiers in this respect. In a scientific world which was dominated by the *simpliste* mechanistic-positivistic philosophy to which Karl Pearson gave a definitive statement in "The Grammar of Science," it is true that the word "theory" wasn't quite respectable. In my observation the greater number of anthropologists still feel that "theorizing" is what you do when you are too lazy, or too impatient, or too much of an arm-chair person to go out and get the facts.

But for the point of view that ratiocination can properly begin only after *all* the facts have been garnered and harvested by observation anthropologists will get little support from their colleagues in science. There are many in the so-called social sciences today who subscribe to the naïve view that their subjects have failed of attainment because of too much "theory," whereas the sciences of matter have achieved honor and glory by eschewing theory and relentlessly observing facts. There is truth, to be sure, in the latter belief and it is undoubtedly true that there has been too little devotion to this task in some branches of "social science." But who has ever *seen* gravitation? One sees bodies fall and the theory of gravitation serves in a very satisfying manner as an explanation of their falling. Since, however, an element of reasoning, an element of inference (of drawing a conclusion which was not observed but in terms of which observations "make sense"!) enters into the matter, gravitation is not fact but conceptual scheme. Similarly, "Boyle's Law," with which every schoolboy is familiar and which has come to stand (in that vulgarization of physics and chemistry which is the common property of educated persons today) as a sort of type instance of scientific law is far from having that character of straightforward *description* of observed uniformities which is ordinarily imputed to it. No, inference is not a mode of thought with which the "natural sciences" have been able to dispense. If anyone affirms that theory has no place in Middle American studies until some fabled day when our factual knowledge approaches completeness, let him be reminded of the words in the "Manifesto on Freedom of Science" which has recently been signed by nearly fifteen hundred American scientists, including most of the members of the National Academy of Sciences:

The charge that theory leads to a "crippling of experimental research" is tantamount to a denial of the whole history of modern physics. From Copernicus and Kepler on, all the great figures in Western science have insisted, in deed or in word, upon the futility of experimental research divorced from theory.

Since no science can progress without inference, it becomes of critical importance that inference should not proceed along lines which are haphazard or capricious or controlled by unconscious prejudice. Since probably no fact has meaning except within the context of a conceptual scheme, archaeologists need to give their attention to these conceptual schemes as well as to the methods and techniques in accord with which data can be most efficiently discovered and analyzed. One lesson which the history of science seems most clearly to teach is that no science has prospered until it has defined its fundamental entities. A system of theory in any science involves a small number of categories and elementary relations between them. In mechanics, for example, these are: mass, location in space, direction of motion, velocity of motion. It is a symptom of the immaturity of anthropology that the logical instruments, the choice between alternative categories has been scandalously neglected. Ask an archaeologist to set forth and justify his conceptual scheme. It is an induction from my experience that the betting odds are enormous against this having even occurred to him as a problem. But if more archaeologists had given systematic thought to the logical implications of one concept which they continually use ("typology"), the problem of pottery classification in various areas in the New World would not be such a welter of confusion. Anthropologists generally have troubled themselves very little with what their conceptual tools actually meant if reduced to concrete human behaviors. The principal explanation for the misunderstandings surrounding the "Q-Complex" is assuredly that the referent for "complex" has been most ambivalent. This may be but the prejudice of a social anthropologist, but I do feel that, of late, the situation in social anthropology is more encouraging. Linton has made what seem to me to be major contributions to the conceptual structure of social anthropology. And, within the field of Middle American studies, Redfield and his co-workers appear to have formulated what they are trying to do much more explicitly and realistically than their archaeological associates.

What has been said of concepts holds very largely for premises also in the Middle American field. Most of the premises are indeed assumptions (covert premises) or axioms (premises taken as self-evident and not requiring proof). Scientific experience suggests that reasoning so premised is more than usually dangerous and treacherous. When one reasons by enthymemes one is proceeding blindly— not by conscious choice between points of departure which (while it may not prove in the light of facts later available to have been the wisest alternative), is at last patent to the investigator and to others as a choice and hence the more open to detection as a possible fallacy in the argument. Implicit in the reasoning of some of the leading workers in this field may be detected many unanalyzed, far-reaching assumptions as to cultural stability; the mechanics of diffusion; relationships of race, language, and culture; poly- and monogenesis; and the like. As for axiomatic reasoning, may it not simply be said that we are as yet hardly in a position to regard any feature of human behavior as altogether self-evident? And yet we find, for example, some of the most undemonstrated beliefs as to instinctive human needs taken as perfectly trustworthy axioms. Mathematics and most sciences have found it more satisfactory to proceed by the method of postulates (stated premises). The method of postulates is the "if . . , then . . ." method. The scientist says, in effect, "The facts hardly enable us at present to make an absolutely clear-cut choice between the following alternative points of departure: . . . However, since all discourse must proceed from premises we must make a highly provisional selection. I shall choose premises A, B, . . X as my postulates simply because, on the whole, they seem to me most compendent with the available evidence. But all I assert for my thesis is that *if* future research supports the choice of these postulates, *then* my interpretation of the facts about to be discussed here should still hold true." In terms of what the psychoanalysts and others have taught us about the dangers of emotional identification with unconscious premises, the psychological advantages (and we should never forget in our scholarly work that we and our fellow scholars are always human beings!) of the method of postulates are tremendous.

In the writings of Middle American specialists I have found but little realization of the fact that all discourse proceeds from premises and that there should be some justification for the choice one makes between alternative premises. Even the very central issue seems hardly to have been grappled with. Are Middle American students interested in their data primarily as evidencing (to some extent at least) certain trends toward uniformity in the responses of human beings toward types of stimuli (environmental, contactual, biological, and the like) or are they primarily interested in their data as unique events, to be described and imaginatively recreated (in so far as possible) in all their particularity? Interests of both of these types seem perfectly legitimate—as opposed to the antiquarian interest which makes the collection of specimens an end in itself. It will be convenient and in conformity with contemporary usage to designate these two legitimate types of interest as "scientific" and "historical" respectively. The position of the leaders in this field can only be inferred for the most part. That of Tozzer,[7] Lothrop, Spinden, the Pennsylvania group, and most of the German scholars appears to be resolutely historical. Such a position seems to me quite defensible, but a reasoned justification of the stand would seem to be in the interests of clarification. Perhaps these are not, ideally, two distinct types of interest. The thesis that they are but two sequent phases of a planned research might even be maintained. Actually, however, it is an experiential generalization that material collected and published by the "historically" minded is seldom suitable for "scientific" analysis. A focus of interest upon events in their uniqueness, a concentration of effort upon recapturing the sequence of one specific set of events (rather than upon the elements which a class of events may have in common) is most unlikely to provide that quantitative basis for generalization which is scientifically essential. As a practical matter, then, choice rather than combination of premises, seems to be involved and one's choice of premise here very definitely has consequences for one's whole conceptual structure. It should also have consequences for method and techniques, for a method of discovering and analyzing facts should not be incongruous with fundamental premises and the related concepts which are to be used as instruments in synthesizing the facts.

The interests of Kidder and Vaillant appear to be verging upon the scientific, but a full discussion of this very critical question from them would assuredly be most helpful and welcome. Dr. Kidder has recently written: "Archaeology and history seek to picture man's past; ethnology and the other social sciences to record the

<hr />

[7] See, however, Tozzer, Prehistory in Middle America, 1937a, p. 338; and Tozzer, Review, 1937b, pp. 152 and 159.

conditions under which he lives today. Both groups gather and analyze data necessary for understanding the nature of man and the structure of the modern world." [8]

But are we to "understand the nature of man" through the reflections which the reading of history stimulates in the thoughtful person? Is the "structure of the modern world" to be revealed by flashes of intuition catalyzed by historical insight or by the inductive generalizations of science? A systematic and rigorous exposition of the conceptual means by which these admirable objectives can be achieved would seem useful. Possibly Dr. Kidder's insistence upon archaeology as history is simply with a view to giving "a time-backbone" to the data which are to be grist to the mill of the generalizing approach. If so, one can only applaud. However, the light in which the members of the Carnegie staff view various specific questions reveals fairly consistent historical rather than scientific interests. Take, for example, the problem of the end of the "Great Period" and possible evacuation of Peten and Usumacinta sites. The many references to this in the writings of this group indicate a desire to explain these phenomena in all their historical uniqueness rather than a wish to extract from the events whatever bears upon the recurring regularities in human behavior. At all events, one wants to know whether the work of the Carnegie Institution aims, to use Kroeber's phrases, at historical integrations in terms of sequences and larger culture wholes or at processual integrations in terms of conceptual constants. Is the cardinal intention to preserve phenomena intact as phenomena or "to decompose phenomena in order to determine processes as such?" The scientific attack would seem to me preferable. While taking account always of the circumstance that the processes which control events are imbedded in time as well as in space and in the structure of social forms, a primary interest in discovering the trends toward uniformity in human behavior under specified conditions will be, I feel sure, the more fruitful. Problems need to be formulated with a view to illuminating the generalities of human action (often inferentially through study of artifacts or other cultural products) by the searchlight of simple induction and the method of agreement and difference.

There are signs, fortunately, that archaeologists are coming to grips with the somewhat more abstract problems which bear upon

[8] Kidder and Thompson, The Correlation of Maya and Christian Chronologies, 1938, p. 493.

their studies. Surely a new epoch dawns when the professional journal of American archaeology publishes a leading article entitled "Function and Configuration in Archaeology." [9] Even earlier, Strong gave us his enlightened and enlightening essay "Anthropological Theory and Archaeological Fact." [10] But while one may agree wholeheartedly with him that anthropology ". . . is a broad, historical science concerned with the relationship of cultural and biological factors through time and space," one must insist in the same breath that the conceptual tools for determining this relationship have very largely yet to be forged. The very sophistication at the levels of method and technique makes the methodological and theoretical naïveté of Middle American studies stand out in shocking contrast. Surely, if the total structure is to be substantially founded and to have balance, methodology and theory must receive the same systematic, persistent, and rigorous treatment which has been accorded to method and technique. Factual richness and conceptual poverty are a poor pair of hosts at an intellectual banquet. A proper hunger for facts and an impatience for an answer to many burning factual questions must not result in a relative sterility and futility of effort. Such, at any rate, is the perhaps mistaken and certainly very humble (but also very honest) opinion of one anthropologist who is a layman in this specialized field.

[9] Steward and Setzler, Function and Configuration, 1938.
[10] Strong, Anthropological Theory and Archaeological Fact, 1936.

V

THE NATIVE LANGUAGES OF MIDDLE AMERICA [1]

J. Alden Mason *

THE ABORIGINAL languages of Middle America display no characteristics that differentiate them as a group from the other Indian languages of North and South America. Insofar as American languages possess any common traits or even tendencies that set them apart from the languages of the Old World, a former theory with little present support,[2] those of Middle America are typically American. The major problem is that of their relationships and classification (Table I, pp. 78–87).

In compiling a new classification of the native languages of Middle America one is confronted with two rather opposite schools of thought. One, the conservative, personified by Boas, insists that every language should be considered independent until its relationship to another is proved or strongly indicated by careful study, and objects to even hypothetical groupings on less certain evidence. Thomas and Swanton,[3] who distinguish thirty stocks in Middle America, and Rivet [4] with twenty-four, follow this school, at least in the present case. The more radical students see no objection to the tentative suggestion of fewer major groups, combining languages on grounds that include resemblance in morphological type, together with a certain

* Pennsylvania, A.B., 1907; California, Ph.D., 1911; now Curator, American Section, University Museum, University of Pennsylvania.

[1] In the preparation of this article, in addition to my thanks to my collaborator, Mr. Frederick Johnson, I wish to express my appreciation for advice, information, and criticism to: Manuel J. Andrade, Miguel O. de Mendizábal, Lawrence Ecker, Wigberto Jiménez Moreno, Paul Kirchhoff, Clyde Kluckhohn, A. L. Kroeber, Norman C. McQuown, Kenneth Pike, the late revered Edward Sapir, Robert J. Weitlaner, and B. L. Whorf. This does not imply that they sponsor all opinions herein expressed.

[2] Boas, Handbook, 1911.
[3] Thomas and Swanton, 1911; referred to in text as T&S.
[4] Rivet, Langues Américaines, 1924.

amount of lexical resemblance. Radin,[5] Schmidt,[6] Sapir,[7] and Whorf [8] might be assigned to this school.

The determination of linguistic relationship [9] is fraught with many difficulties and pitfalls. I believe it generally agreed that genetic relationships can be proved firmly only upon lexical grounds, or those of resemblances in morphological elements, with the establishment of probable original forms, and the deduction of phonetic laws of sound shifting. When languages far separated display such lexical similarities, generally accompanied by phonetic and morphological resemblances, the proof of common origin and original geographic propinquity is clear. On the other hand adjacent languages frequently show many words in common. If the resemblance is close and the words generally in certain, mainly modernistic, categories, the presumption is for borrowing. But there are several areas in North America where common phonetic and morphological peculiarities embrace a number of languages which show little apparent lexical resemblance. This may be the result of inter-influence. One of those regions is that of Oaxaca in southern Mexico.[10] Such resemblances in phonetic and morphological type form the main basis for most of the recent proposed larger linguistic phyla. While they do not in themselves afford proof of genetic relationship, it must be admitted that in several cases later careful studies have corroborated, on a lexical basis, some of the groupings first proposed on morphological and phonetic grounds.

Since, in addition to the slow change that even an isolated language would undergo, the borrowing of lexical, phonetic, and morphological traits from neighboring languages may have been extensive, it is obvious that genetic relationship between two apparently very different languages can be established only after very long and detailed study such as has been accorded to few American languages.

The influx of alien elements may be so great as to produce practically a mixed language; nevertheless I believe that sufficient study

[5] Radin, North American Languages, 1919. He suggests the classification of all the native languages of the United States and Canada, and some of those in Mexico, into three major groups. As few Mexican languages were considered, and since his groupings were admittedly highly hypothetical and many of them have since been abandoned, little attention has herein been paid to this article.

[6] Schmidt, Sprachfamilien, 1926.

[7] Sapir, Britannica, 1929.

[8] B. L. Whorf, personal correspondence concerning Macro-Penutian.

[9] Kroeber, Linguistic Relationship, 1913; Boas, Classification, 1929.

[10] De Angulo, Oaxaca Tangle, 1925.

would always show which is the basic, and which the borrowed, form. Kroeber says,[11] "I recognize only one criterion of relationship: reasonably demonstrable genetic unity. Either two languages can be seen to have been originally one, or they cannot be seen to have been one . . . there can be no such thing as half relationship." Boas [12] takes a different but not exactly opposite point of view: "If the view expressed here is correct, then it is not possible to group American languages rigidly in a genealogical scheme in which each linguistic family is shown to have developed to modern forms, but we have to recognize that many of the languages have multiple roots." Nevertheless classifications of languages on a genetic basis, if not advanced with any claim to finality, are of great value for the light they throw on the migrations of peoples. The present classification is proposed merely as representing the weight of present opinion; future researches will doubtless modify it greatly.

There could hardly be a more inauspicious time than the present for an attempt at a classification of Middle American languages with any claim to finality. Following decades of inactivity, with occasional reworkings of old vocabularies and grammars, a group of trained linguistic students is now investigating a number of Mexican languages at first hand. Especially is this true of Southern Mexico where studies are being made, or have recently been made, on Tarascan,[13] Totonac,[14] Mixtec,[15] Otomi,[16] Matlatzinca,[17] Chinantec,[17] Mayan,[18] Cuitlatec,[19] Huaxtec,[19a] Mazatec,[19b] Zapotec,[19c] Mixe,[19d] Nahuatl.[19e] Work has also been done on Yaqui [19f] and some

[11] Kroeber, Serian, 1915.
[12] Boas, Classification, 1929.
[13] Dr. Paul Kirchhoff, Sr. Wigberto Jiménez Moreno, Dr. Morris Swadesh, Mr. Maxwell Lathrop.
[14] Mr. Norman A. McQuown.
[15] Mr. Kenneth Pike, Dr. Lawrence Ecker.
[16] Dr. Lawrence Ecker; Dr. Jacques Soustelle, Otomi, 1937; Mr. Robert J. Weitlaner.
[17] Mr. Robert J. Weitlaner, Dr. Jacques Soustelle.
[18] Dr. Manuel Andrade, Sr. Alfredo Barrera Vásquez.
[19] Sr. Pedro Hendrichs.
[19a] Sr. Guy Stresser-Pean.
[19b] Mr. and Mrs. Jean B. Johnson.
[19c] Sr. Andrés Henestrosa, Miss Edith Mackie.
[19d] Mr. Miller.
[19e] Srs. Wigberto Jiménez Moreno, Dávila Garibi, Adrián León; Mme. Soustelle.
[19f] Dr. Lawrence Ecker, Mr. Jean B. Johnson.

other northern languages.[19g] When these researches are published they will doubtless modify some of the conclusions herein reached, though I hope they will corroborate most.

The linguistic complexity in Middle America is even greater than that in the United States. In Mexico alone Orozco y Berra [20] lists some seven hundred and twenty names *and synonyms* of tribes and small groups, and one hundred and eighty languages with as many more synonyms; sixty-two of these languages are listed as extinct.[21] Doubtless many of these differ only dialectically, if at all, but nevertheless the linguistic diversity is obviously very great. This great multiplicity is due mainly to the sedentary nature of the population, especially in southern Mexico. Here in particular are great areas, populated by Indians living in villages where Spanish is never used and known by only a few officials. It is claimed that Aztec is spoken by half a million natives today. It is in their vitality that the Indian languages of Mexico differ most from those of the United States. In the more arid and more sparsely settled regions of northern Mexico the natives and their languages met the same fate as those further north; in the northern two-thirds of Mexico, with the exception of small groups in the western mountains, the languages have disappeared, and the natives lost all tribal culture and solidarity. It is in these regions, naturally, that the languages covered the largest areas.

In the more sedentary and densely populated regions, on the other hand, just as in California, the languages occupy smaller areas, dialects often changing from village to village.

Despite the greater complexity of the languages in Middle America, much less modern scientific work has been done upon them than in the United States. On most we have only vocabularies made long ago by men without training in phonetics or linguistics, on many not even that much.

As in America north of Mexico, the history of Middle American linguistic research has been one of constant reduction in the number of proposed separate linguistic stocks. The first comprehensive attempt to classify, delimit and tabulate the languages of Mexico was made by Orozco y Berra in 1864. He classified sixty-nine languages in thirty-five groups into eleven families, and left sixteen other im-

[19g] Such as Opata and Varohio.
[20] Orozco y Berra, Geografía, 1864; referred to in text as OyB.
[21] Id., pp. 54–76.

portant languages unclassified.[21] Pimentel,[22] Leon,[23] Belmar,[24] and several other Mexican students followed him with detailed linguistic studies and systems of classification. The results of Brinton's [25] many studies were condensed in 1891 in his classification of all the languages of America. His brilliant acumen led him to suggest certain relationships that, neglected for many years, have recently been corroborated.[26]

Finally in 1910 Thomas and Swanton [3] produced their classic work, still the standard for English-speaking students, based on all the data then available, especially on Orozco y Berra for Mexico. They distinguished twenty-seven independent families, and three more of uncertain independence. The late Walter Lehmann's [27] monumental work on Central America and southern Mexico in 1920 was the next great landmark and formed the basis for the classifications of Rivet [4] and Schmidt.[6] Lehmann's many various suggestions and properly equivocal opinions permitted these two to draw very different deductions from his statements. Rivet made languages independent whenever uncertain, reaching a total of twenty-four independent groups, while Schmidt adopted Lehmann's every hint regarding relationships and, though making no exact tabulation, reduced them to about twelve.

The most recent well-known classification, by the late Edward Sapir,[7] in 1929, adopting the results of his (generally unpublished) and other modern linguists' studies, distinguishes twenty independent stocks, though he offers suggestions of possible connections that, if accepted, would reduce the number considerably. In the last few years linguistic maps of North America have been made at several large universities [28] in the United States, mainly based on this classification by Sapir. The only printed ones are three recently issued in Mexico [29] which incorporate some of the most recent and most certain unpublished deductions of the men at present working there.

---

[22] Pimentel, Cuadro, 1862–1864.
[23] León, Familias lingüísticas, 1902.
[24] Belmar, Lenguas indígenas, 1905.
[25] Brinton, American Race, 1891.
[26] Such as the relationship of Seri, Tequistlatecan and Yuman; in this connection see Kroeber, Serian, 1915.
[27] Lehmann, Zentralamerika, 1920.
[28] Especially Harvard and Yale.
[29] Jiménez Moreno (referred to in text as JM), Map, 1936; de Mendizábal and Jiménez Moreno (referred to as MyJM), Map, n.d.; de Mendizábal, Map, 1937.

The map of pre-Columbian Mexico [30] distinguishes fourteen families for Mexico alone; that of North America [31] ten for all Middle America, in addition to several small unlisted languages such as Tarascan, Chinantec, Cuitlatec and Guaicura-Pericú.[31a]

In the classification herein proposed I have tried to steer a conservative middle course, tentatively considering as independent all languages whose relationship to any other is not generally accepted, and at the same time indicating hypothetical and possible relationships and larger groupings, and even mentioning other suggestions generally not accepted. Doubtless there are inconsistencies to this general plan, and I fear that the "personal equation" may play a larger role than a dispassionate study should permit.

One of the difficult questions is that of linguistic taxonomy. I have tried to follow Whorf and Trager's [32] suggestion of classification into phylum, stock, family, language and dialect with a sub-division of each. The Mexican linguists prefer the nomenclature *grupo*, *rama*, *familia*, *division*, *tipo*, with their sub-divisions. With our present lack of knowledge it is impossible to classify these languages so that in the various groups every division will be of the same order of differentiation. A single language, supposedly independent, should theoretically be assigned to a phylum of its own, but to allow for possible later incorporation in another group it would be unwise at present to do so.

A number of new terms are proposed for groups which to date have been known only by linking the names of the component languages. I feel that this is preferable to a cumbrous hyphenated nomenclature; the invention of terms for newly proposed groups is a common linguistic practice. The names proposed are hybrids made up of elements of the names of the component languages.

Languages presumably extinct are marked with an asterisk, and instances of uncertainty, or more than usual uncertainty, denoted by parentheses and question marks. Synonyms are enclosed in parentheses. For brevity, T&S denotes Thomas and Swanton; OyB, Orozco y Berra; MyJM, the map of de Mendizábal and Jiménez Moreno; and JM, that of Jiménez Moreno.

[30] de Mendizábal and Jiménez Moreno, Map, n.d.

[31] Jiménez Moreno, Map, 1936.

[31a] de Mendizábal and Jiménez Moreno have prepared a revised map of pre-Columbian Mexico, not yet published, which has been shown at two recent scientific congresses.

[32] Whorf and Trager, Uto-Aztecan-Tanoan, 1937; footnote, p. 610.

It is naturally impossible to mention, even by merely giving the name in a table, all of the hundred and eighty "languages" of Mexico.[21] Many of them are known only by a brief mention in the account of an early historian or conquistador; no word is known and so they can never be classified. The recent linguistic map of prehistoric Mexico [30] locates thirty-two extinct and unclassifiable languages. Of the others, some are extinct, but early writers, especially priests, have left us grammars and vocabularies by which the genetic relationships may be determined. On the other hand there are many living languages, spoken by thousands of natives, of which not enough is known to permit of a classification that is much more than a guess.

With the exception of Tarascan, for which no cogent evidences for relationship with any other major group have been offered, it is quite possible that future studies will prove that all the languages of Middle America belong to four major phyla. The southern members of the Hokan-Siouan phylum are already well-known, either proved or rendered highly probable; all apparently belong to the Hokan-Coahuiltecan (Hokaltecan) sub-phylum. Waicurian belongs here, if anywhere.

Resemblances between Penutian, Uto-Aztecan (Utaztecan), Mayan, Mixe-Zoque-Huave (Mizocuavean), and Totonacan have often been pointed out, and their genetic relationship suggested. B. L. Whorf's recent unpublished critical studies have convinced him that the first four should be combined in a phylum which he terms "Macro-Penutian," consisting of Penutian, Azteco-Tanoan, and Mayan; the inclusion of Totonac is problematical. According to him there are similarities in structure and morphology, and historically traceable likeness in vocabulary, through definite intermediate steps, with regular sound laws and sound correspondences.[8]

According to Sapir [33] there is a general feeling that Otomi, Mazatec, Mixtec and Zapotec all hang together, a connection first suggested by Belmar, though without convincing proof. The same feeling is expressed by most of the linguists working in Mexico; the latter add Chinantec to the group. The membership of Chiapanec-Chorotega is generally accepted. Following Whorf's example we might term this unproved phylum "Macro-Otomanguean."

The fourth phylum consists of the languages of Panama and the Atlantic watershed of Costa Rica and Nicaragua, for which Chib-

[33] Sapir, personal correspondence.

chan affinities have often been proposed. This includes the possibly independent Mosquito-Sumo-Matagalpa (Misumalpan) group. The term "Macro-Chibchan" best fits this possible phylum. Geographically between Macro-Penutian and Macro-Chibchan lie the four adjacent tongues Xinca, Lenca, Jicaque and Paya, whose relationships are most controversial. [Editorial Note: The editors have used the spelling Mosquito, in deference to past usage and it is so spelled on the linguistic map in this volume. Dr. Mason and his colleagues are adopting the spelling Miskito, which will probably become the standard form. For the sake of editorial uniformity we did not accede to Dr. Mason's wishes, but we hereby acknowledge the validity of his position.]

This four-fold grouping being unproved and still controversial, it will not hereinafter be stressed, and the Middle American languages will be considered under the following seventeen groups, provisionally treated as independent.

These five phyla may be geographically grouped into three categories. Macro-Otomanguean and Tarascan are purely Middle American without apparent congeners outside of this area. Hokan-Siouan almost certainly, and Macro-Penutian probably, are primarily United States stocks whose southern outliers are found in Mexico. The Macro-Chibchan languages of Central America are outliers from South America; the South American aspect of the culture of the tribes speaking these languages indicates that the migration was not from north to south.

Sapir [7] suggests that the migration of the languages into Middle America took place somewhat in this order, from earliest to latest:

> Macro-Otomanguean
> Mosquito*-Sumo-Matagalpa   (Macro-Chibchan?)
> Mixe-Zoque-Huave   (Penutian?)
> Mayan   (Macro-Penutian?)
> Hokaltecan   (Hokan-Siouan)
> Hokan Proper   (Hokan-Siouan)
> Utaztecan   (Macro-Penutian?)

An attempt has been made [34] to correlate these phyla and their possible migration sequence with physical type and culture. While the results are intriguing and the ideas stimulating, they are admittedly highly problematical and controversial.

* See editorial note, above.
[34] Gladwin, Snaketown, 1937.

PROPOSED GROUPINGS OF MIDDLE AMERICAN LANGUAGES

(Table I, pp. 78–87)

A. HOKAN-SIOUAN
  1. Hokaltecan   (Hokan-Coahuiltecan)   (Page 78)
  2. Waicurian   (Page 79)
B.   3. TARASCAN   (Page 79)
C. MACRO-OTOMANGUEAN
  4. Otomanguean   (Pages 79–80)
  5. Mixtecan   (Page 80)
  6. Chinantecan   (Page 80)
  7. Zapotecan   (Page 80)
D. MACRO-PENUTIAN
  8. Utaztecan   (Uto-Aztecan)   (Pages 81–82)
  9. Mayan   (Pages 83–84)
  10. Mizocuavean   (Mixe-Zoque-Huave)   (Page 84)
  11. Totonacan   (Page 85)
E. (Unclassified)
  12. Xincan   (Page 85)
  13. Lencan   (Page 85)
  14. Jicaquean   (Page 85)
  15. Payan   (Page 85)
F. MACRO-CHIBCHAN
  16. Misumalpan   (Mosquito†-Sumo-Matagalpa) (Page 86)
  17. Chibchan   (Pages 86–87)

o. ATHABASKAN

All the linguistic maps of Mexico show Athabaskan groups in northern Mexico, both the true Apache, the * Jano and * Jocome, probably related to the Chiricahua Apache, in Chihuahua and Sonora, and the * Toboso further east in Coahuila. The latter may have been affiliated with the Lipan and Jicarilla Apache. Though they were there not long after the Conquest and in later years raided far south into central Mexico, a study of the earliest sources, especially the work of Sauer,[35] makes it very doubtful if their territory extended over the border in prehispanic days. This, coupled with the fact that there are no Apache today in Mexico, has impelled their removal from consideration in the present classification.

† See editorial note, p. 59.
* Extinct.
[35] Sauer, Distribution, 1934.

1. Hokaltecan

(*Synonyms:* Hokan-Coahuiltecan,[7] Zentralamerikanisch-pazifische Gruppe[6])

Since all the Middle American languages assigned to the Hokan-Siouan phylum fall into the Hokan-Coahuiltecan or Hokaltecan sub-phylum, the validity of the larger group, or of the United States members of the smaller group, need not concern us. The skeleton classification is taken from Sapir,[7] with details from JM,[31] and is generally accepted, though little proof has been published. The genetic relationship of the three Mexican sub-stocks in the Hokan proper stock may be considered as proved; that of the other two stocks is not so certain but is accepted by the majority of authorities.

The inclusion of Yuman in Hokan is admitted by all. Brinton's[25] belief that Seri is related to Yuman is now accepted,[11] but his similar opinion concerning Waicuri and Pericú is still an unproved possibility. Sapir's bracketing of Esselen with Yuman, and Salinan with Seri may be valid, or a little premature. There seems to be little linguistic variation among the Seri. Guayma, which was originally considered a Piman language, is apparently Serian; Upanguaima is a word of doubtful linguistic value.[35] Brinton's[25] brilliant idea regarding the connection between Yuman and Tequistlatecan or Chontal, a small isolated group far to the south in Oaxaca, is now generally accepted.[11]

The name "Supanec" is suggested to denominate the stock consisting of the languages of the Subtiaba-Tlapanec-Yopi group. Although "Subtiaba" is the better known name, the true and earlier term for the language seems to be "Maribio." These languages differ very slightly in spite of the geographical separation and, according to Sapir,[33] Subtiaba in Nicaragua differs hardly more than dialectically from Tlapanec in Guerrero, implying recent separation. Radin[36] thinks that the two dialects of Tlapanec, known as Tlapaneco and Tlapaneca, differ more than either does from Subtiaba. The name "Yopi" has disappeared; it was probably a synonym for Tlapanec. The Hokan relationship, universally accepted today, was

---

[36] Radin, Tlappanecan, 1933.

first indicated by Lehmann [37] and later proved by Radin [36] and Sapir.[38]

The composition of the Coahuiltecan family (Pakawan of T&S) has not been changed. Schmidt [6] brackets Coahuilteco and Come-crudo with Karankawa, Cotoname with Tonkawa, both other members of the Coahuiltecan stock. Its membership in the Hokaltecan sub-phylum has been demonstrated by Sapir [39] and is generally accepted, though Rivet [40] has expressed his personal reservations on the point.

In the State of Tamaulipas T&S locate and list three "independent" families, Tamaulipecan, Olivean, and Janambrian, all of which may be related to Coahuiltecan. Linguistically practically nothing is known of any of them. Swanton says [41]: "At present the only scrap of a strictly Tamaulipecan language (apparently meaning a language of that state—JAM) available is a corrupted bit of Maratino, from the central part of the state near the Gulf." He compares this Maratino fragment and comes to the decision that it is related to Coahuiltecan. As this is near the center of the "Tamaulipecan" area, the presumption is that all these languages were related to Coahuiltecan. JM and MyJM accept this in their recent maps.[29]

Regarding the Olive, Swanton further says [41] that they "were brought into this territory from somewhere in the interior of Texas by a Spanish expedition in the sixteenth century . . . nothing of their language is known to have been preserved." They therefore probably belonged to one of the linguistic families of Texas, probably to some member of the larger Coahuiltecan stock, and, even if not, they should be ruled out of present consideration on grounds of posthispanic arrival. In their maps JM and MyJM [29] list them as related to Huaxtec (Mayan), but they have retracted this viewpoint in their new unpublished map.

The Janambre and related Pisone are reported to have belonged to one family, and to have spoken a "particular" language,[42] surely insufficient grounds on which to assign them to an independent fam-

[37] Lehmann, Costa Rican Languages, 1910; Subtiaba Language, 1915; Central American Languages, 1920.

[38] Sapir, Subtiaba, 1925.

[39] Sapir, Coahuiltecan, 1920.

[40] Rivet, Langues Américaines, 1924, footnote 2, p. 613.

[41] Swanton, Northeastern Mexico, 1915, p. 19.

[42] Orozco y Berra, Geografía, 1864, p. 296.

ily. JM and MyJM leave them unclassified [29]; they may have been related to either of the neighboring languages, Tamaulipecan or Otomi, with the presumption, for geographical reasons, in favor of the former.

The Guachichil (see under Utaztecan) have sometimes been considered [30] related to the Coahuiltec. Lehmann [27] noted Hokan resemblances in Cuitlatec, Xinca, Lenca, and Jicaque.

2. * WAICURIAN

(*Synonyms:* Guaycura,[29] Waicuru,[6] Waikuri,[4] Guaicuru,[25] and other variants)

Regarding Waicuri, little need be added to Kroeber's [43] opinion:

The available information on this idiom, however, all goes back to one very tenuous source, the . . . description of Baegert. The few words contained in this do not look like Yuman or even Hokan; but they are too few and too specialized to allow of any certain conclusions. Unless new records from Lower California can be discovered, a final judgment as to the position of Waikuri will not be possible until the comparative study of the Hokan languages has progressed so far that they can be successfully measured against the fragments of this obscure tongue. Pending this decision, Waikuri must be regarded as of unproved affinities and therefore held tentatively distinct.

The Yuman connections of Waicuri were first suggested by Brinton,[25] and have been noted as possibilities by later writers who have, however, universally followed Kroeber's advice to consider it independent or unclassified.

T&S [3] offer good reasons for considering Pericú a language related to Waicuri. As no word of the language is known, the question will probably always remain unsettled. At the very tip of the peninsula, they may well have been an independent family—as Waicuri may also have been—and the famous discovery [44] of crania of an archaic type in their area and ascribed to them strengthens this possibility. We may be reasonably certain, at any rate, that if the Waicuri were not of Yuman, Hokan, or Hokaltecan affinities, the Pericú were not.

* Extinct.
[43] Kroeber, Serian, 1915, p. 290.
[44] Ten Kate, Presqu'ile californienne, 1884.

3. TARASCAN

(*Synonym:* Michoacano)

Though the Tarascan area is at present small, it is very variant from the rest of Mexico ethnologically and archeologically. Archeological remains of Tarascan type are found over a much wider area, and the ceramics so much resemble some from the early Archaic cultures of the Valley of Mexico that some authorities [45] believe that the latter peoples were related to the Tarascans. They seem, therefore, to have been an autochthonous people. The language is also very variant; no evidences of connection with any other language have been accorded serious consideration, though Belmar suggested relationship to Otomanguean,[46] and by all modern authorities it is accorded an independent position. Almost all other suggestions concern component stocks of the new hypothetical Macro-Penutian phylum. No subdivisions or dialects are known.

4. OTOMANGUEAN

(*Synonyms:* Otomi-Mangue-Gruppe,[6] Otomi,[4] Otomian [7])

One of the major classificatory changes of recent years has been the breakup and redistribution of the Zapotecan family of T&S, and the incorporation of some of its component languages, together with the Otomian and Chiapanecan families, in a larger group known as Otomangue. This name, first proposed by Robert Weitlaner, was adopted by Jiménez Moreno.[31] This reallocation is accepted by all recent authorities, but the correct grouping of the subdivisions is still very controversial. Three groups or families are generally recognized: Otomian, Popolocan, and Chorotegan, with the Trique language of uncertain affiliation.

The Otomian family apparently divides into three groups, Otomi, Matlatzinca and Pame. According to Soustelle [47] and Weitlaner [48] the three languages are equidistant, with Matlatzinca nearer to Otomi than to Pame, but with the latter showing marked resemblances to Matlatzinca. Matlatzinca was considered a family distinct from Otomi by OyB [20] and MyJM [30]; the former did not classify Pame. The present Chichimec is close to Pame and could pass as its dialect,

[45] Noguera, Antecedentes, 1935.
[46] Belmar, Tarascan, 1910.
[47] Soustelle, Otomi, 1937.
[48] Robert J. Weitlaner, personal correspondence.

according to Weitlaner [48]; in Conquest days the name Chichimec seems to have had a cultural rather than a linguistic connotation, and was applied to ruder groups of Otomian, Utaztecan, and possibly other linguistic affinities.[49]

The new Mexican linguistic maps [29] show an isolated group of Otomi in Jalisco, not noted by OyB or T&S. There seems to be little question of this, as verified by old documents; the question is whether they were brought there in early post-Conquest days.

Ocuiltec is now extinct in Ocuila, but its variation Atzinca is spoken in San Juan Acingo.[48] Tepehua, which was placed with Otomi by Schmidt [6] and Rivet,[4] has been determined to be related to Totonac,[50] in which family T&S [3] had previously properly placed it.

The group formerly called Mazatecan,[51] consisting of Popoloca, Chocho, Ixcatec, Mazatec and Trique, has been renamed the Popolocan family,[52] inasmuch as Mazatec is the least typical member of it. Trique is even more different although phonetically close, and has here been given a family of its own. The name Popoloca is an unfortunate choice since, like Chichimec [49] and Chontal, it has been applied to a number of distinct groups; it is a corruption of the Aztec word meaning "unintelligible," and was applied by them to any person speaking a foreign language.[53] The name has been retained herein, however, on grounds of precedent.[54]

The position of the so-called Mazatec of Guerrero and Tabasco is very doubtful; they may have nothing more than the name in common with the Oaxaca Mazatec. The probably extinct Guatinicamame are mysterious; they probably were related, as Lehmann [27]

[49] Thomas and Swanton, 1911, p. 41; Gonzalez Casanova, Chichimeca, 1930; Brinton, American Race, 1891, p. 129.

[50] Lawrence Ecker, personal correspondence.

[51] Mechling, Oaxaca, 1912.

[52] Gonzalez Casanova, Popoloca, 1925.

[53] Brinton, American Race, 1891, p. 147; Chontallis, 1892.

[54] In addition to OyB, Geografía, 1864; T&S, 1911; Lehmann, Zentralamerika, 1920; among many monographs on Otomanguean tongues may be mentioned the following, through the list, like subsequent ones, does not pretend to completeness or even to include all the most important works:

Otomi-Pame-Mazahua: Soustelle, Otomi, 1937; Schuller, Macaque, 1925; Pame, 1925; de Angulo, Chichimeco, 1933; Gerste, Chichimeques, 1891; Gonzalez Casanova, Chichimeca, 1930; Weitlaner, Ixtenco, 1933. Matlatzinca: Schuller, Quata, 1925. Popoloca-Chocho: Belmar, Chocho, 1899; León, Popolocas, 1905. Mazatec: Belmar, 1892; Brinton, 1892; Hansen, 1937. Trique: Belmar, 1897.

Languages of Puebla and Hidalgo: Lombardo Toledano, 1931; Rubio, Hidalgo, 1934. Chiapanec: Becerra, 1937. Mangue: Brinton, 1886; Spinden, Chorotegan, 1925.

believed, to the Mazatec, but it is not impossible that they were Chinantec.[48] Dr. Kirchhoff has just discovered some early sources that indicate that the Tolteca-Nonoalca were of Mazatec affinities as opposed to the Nahuatlan Tolteca-Chichimeca.

Schmidt [6] places Chinantec and possibly Olmec in the Popolocan family.

5. MIXTECAN

Although many authorities, including T&S,[3] combined Mixtec, Zapotec, and several other Oaxacan languages in one independent family, their relationship has always been, and still is, disputed. The three languages Mixtec, Cuicatec, and Amusgo have always been bracketed in a Mixtecan group,[51] accepted by most authorities, but apparently they differ very greatly, so much so that Rivet [4] accords each an independent position. The apparent degree of difference probably entitles each to a rating as a family, although apparently only one language is concerned in each; no dialects of Cuicatec or Amusgo are known, but OyB gives the names of eleven little-known dialects of the more extensive Mixtec.[55]

No recent studies to establish the true position of Amusgo have been made, but Weitlaner [48] believes that his recent unpublished studies on Cuicatec have made its relationship to Mixtec almost sure. Regarding the larger relationships, some of the linguists now working in Mexico feel that Dr. Lawrence Ecker's unpublished researches on Mixtec corroborate the general feeling that Mixtec, Zapotec, Mazatec and Otomi all hang together [48]; Ecker refers to the "Proto-Oto-Mixtec language." [50] [55a] A statement of Sahagun has just (1940) been interpreted as indicating that the Olmec were of Mixtec affinities.

6. CHINANTECAN

Chinantec,[56] which apparently consists of only one language without very variant dialects, is so different [10] from other surrounding languages that every modern authority except Schmidt [6] has either assigned it an independent position or left it unclassified. Its general spirit, however, is similar to most of the adjacent tongues, and it

[55] Orozco y Berra, Geografía, 1864, p. 57.

[55a] Since this article was written, Ecker's "Relationship of Mixtec to the Otomian Languages" has appeared in print.

[56] On Chinantec, see Bevan, 1938; González Casanova, 1925; Schuller, 1925; Brinton, 1892.

has long been felt that it will eventually be found to be related to Otomi, Mixtec and Zapotec. According to Ecker [50] there is a "strong general resemblance in phonetics and word-structure to Otomian, but few things in particular." Weitlaner, who has worked upon it, feels "sure that it will come into the (larger) Otomangue group," but also notes marked morphological resemblances to Tlapanec.[48]

7. Zapotecan

The languages of the Zapotec group [57] seem to show much less resemblance to the Otomian languages than do the Mixtecan languages.[48] The former bracketing of Mixtec and Zapotec was almost certainly unjustified, and there may be a question whether they are related at all. It is probable, however, that the general feeling that all these languages are related will eventually be justified. Chatino [58] seems to be clearly related to Zapotec, but the relationship of Solteco and Papabuco is not so certain.

8. Utaztecan

(*Synonyms:* Uto-Aztekan, Yuto-Azteca [29] and variants)

Utaztecan is the only stock of the Azteco-Tanoan sub-phylum with which we need be concerned. More solid studies, approaching the standards of Indo-European philology, have been done upon it than probably on any other American linguistic family, and its main divisions are better established and documented. These indicate, however, that great changes must be made in the former nomenclature and subdivisions. The researches of Sapir,[59] Kroeber,[60] Whorf [61] and Mason [62] have resulted in the abandonment of the old tripartite division into Shoshonean, Piman or Sonoran, and Nahuatlan (T&S [3] employed "Nahuatlan" to include the latter two). Whorf [63] now distinguishes eight families of the Utaztecan stock, of which five (Shoshonean) are in the United States. The other three, Taracahitian, Aztecoidan, and Piman, all include members of the old Sonoran or

---

[57] De Angulo and Freeland, Zapotec, 1933–1934; de Angulo, Linguistic Tangle, 1925.
[58] Boas, Chatino, 1913.
[59] Sapir, Nahuatl, 1913, 1915.
[60] Kroeber, Uto-Aztecan, 1934.
[61] Whorf, Uto-Aztecan, 1935; Sonoran, 1936; Aztec, 1937; Tanoan, 1937.
[62] Mason, Tepecano, 1917; Yaqui, 1923; Sonoran, 1936.
[63] Whorf, unpublished.

Piman group. The last, small, homogeneous family, the new Piman, is the most variant of all; the old name Piman was therefore most inappropriate.

The present classification and nomenclature are based on Whorf [61, 63] with additions from Sauer and Kroeber.[60] Sauer's [64] detailed studies of the groups of the Pacific coast and mountains of northwestern Mexico, most of them now extinct, have suggested the relationships for many or most. The Tarahumaran sub-family apparently consists of only one language without marked dialects. On the other hand there are a great many languages that seem to fall in the Cahitan sub-family, though apparently all have been long extinct except the Yaqui, Mayo, Varohio and Ocoroni; the groupings are based mainly on old statements or circumstantial evidence rather than on lexical data, and doubtless some languages are wrongly placed. But as there is little likelihood of new data turning up, the present classification will probably never be greatly altered. Tubar, only recently extinct, if really so, and Varohio may lean more towards Tarahumare, and Acaxee and Xixime towards Tepehuan.

In the mountain and coast region to the south, and the great central plateau to the east, no such careful studies as Sauer's have been made, and the question of relationship is much less certain. In the coastal region of Jalisco and Guerrero MyJM [30] list thirty extinct and unclassifiable languages. The larger and more important of these, such as Teul-Chichimec, Cazcan, Coca, Tecuexe, Colotlan, are apparently either Nahuatlan or Tepehuan, and possibly were divided between these. Cazcan is generally assigned to Nahuatlan and was considered closely related to Zacatec and Lagunero.[3] If Davila Garibi's [65] vocabularies of Cazcan and Coca are really attributable to these extinct tribes, they are but dialectically different from Aztec. Coca has always been linked with Tecuexe which is reported to have been a Mexican (Aztec) colony. Colotlan and Teul-Chichimec were probably closely related to Tepecan; a vocabulary collected by Boas [66] at Teul is certainly Nahuat, but may have supplanted an earlier tongue here.

Three languages occupied large areas in the central plateau: Zacatec, Lagunero or Irritila, and Guachichil or Cuachichil. The former two have always been considered as Nahuatlan, and related to each

[64] Sauer, Distribution, 1934; Population, 1935.
[65] Dávila Garibi, Coca, 1935.
[66] Lehmann, Zentralamerika, 1920, II, p. 1081.

other and to Cazcan. The Toltec-like ruins of La Quemada and Chal-chihuites in this region lend credence to this. The Guachichil problem is more difficult. The name resembles Huichol, early accounts connect the two, and the Huichol make long journeys to the former Guachichil country to gather peyote which does not grow in their present habitat. On the other hand, they are closely linked to the Cora linguistically and culturally as well as geographically, and it is difficult to conceive of them as having had their present culture under such different ecological conditions, or to have changed it so greatly after migration. Although most recent authorities have linked Huichol and Guachichil, MyJM [30] put Guachichil with Coahuil-tecan, and JM [31] wisely leaves it unclassified.

Immediately south of the Rio Grande, in regions formerly ascribed to the Apache, Sauer [35] locates the Concho, Suma and Jumano, who he believes were affiliated with the Opata.

Both the Nahuatlan sub-family and the Piman family, although covering great areas, have such little linguistic variation, as American languages go, that each might be considered to consist of only one language with marked dialects. Tepecan, the southernmost Piman tongue, is not exactly intelligible to a Papago, the northernmost, but the difference is probably not greater than that between Spanish and Italian.

The break-up of the Toltec "Empire" about the year 1000, the Aztec custom of establishing colonies for trade and control of subjugated peoples, and the similar Spanish practice with friendly colonists, especially the Tlaxcaltecs, spread Nahuatl groups all over Middle America, often supplanting more autochthonous languages.

The most variant of the Nahuatlan languages seems to be that of Pochutla [67] which Whorf [8] puts in a category by itself as opposed to the Aztec-Toltec group; he considers it very different from Aztec.

The most obvious characteristic of the languages of the Aztec group is the use of the phoneme *tl;* Pipil and certain other Nahuatlan languages employ *t* in its stead. Lehmann [27] therefore distinguishes the two groups as the "Nahuatl" and the "Nahuat." The latter seems to be more peripheral in northern Mexico and older in Central America, where enclaves of both are found as far as Panama. Lehmann is dogmatically confident that the language of the Toltec-Chichimec was Nahuat. Whorf [8] thinks that it was Nahuatl, basing his argument on the main grounds that "the location and place-

[67] Boas, Pochutla, 1917.

names of the 'Toltec' area suggest rather the Nahuatl group." The archeological and geographical evidence seems to me to support Lehmann more; Toltec place-names would naturally have become "aztecized" by the time of the Conquest.[68]

9. MAYAN

(*Synonyms:* Mayance,[69] Maya-Quiche [29])

The Mayan stock is unusually homogeneous both as regards geographical location and linguistic differentiation. It is really too unified for even the major divisions to deserve the rating of "families," and many of the so-called "languages" differ only dialectically. But they are so well known and group into so many categories that an extensive terminology is needed.

The standard classifications are those by Stoll,[70] Tozzer,[71] and Gates [69]; these differ considerably, as do those published by Rivet,[4] Jiménez Moreno,[31] and MyJM,[30] suggesting that all are based on insufficient study. Dr. Manuel Andrade, who has spent some years studying these languages and their affiliations, is not yet ready to propose a classification which, when offered, will doubtless supersede all others. Dr. A. L. Kroeber has recently finished a new grouping,[72] based on a study of Stoll's,[70] Sapper's,[73] and Berendt's [74] vocabularies, a pre-publication copy of which he kindly supplied, which forms the basis for the classification here given, and the following

[68] The bibliography of Utaztecan is quite large, especially in Aztec or Mexican grammars (artes). Far less has been published on the languages of Northern Mexico. Among these may be mentioned, in addition to those above:
General: Buschmann, Aztekischen, 1859; Sonorischen, 1864.
Tarahumar: Tellechea, 1826; Ferrero, 1920; Basauri, 1929; Nida, 1937.
Cahita: De Velasco (1737), 1890; Mason, Yaqui, 1923.
Opata: Lombardo, 1702; Smith, Heve, 1861.
Cora: De Ortega, 1732; Preuss, 1932, 1934; Gomez, 1935.
Huichol: Diguet, 1911.
Piman: Smith, 1862; Dolores, Papago, 1913, 1923.
Tepehuan: Rinaldini, 1743; Mason, Tepecano, 1917.
[69] Gates, Distribution, 1920; Mayance, 1932.
[70] Stoll, Guatemala, 1884.
[71] Tozzer, Maya Grammar, 1921.
[72] Kroeber, Culture Areas, 1939.
[73] Sapper, Mittelamerika, 1894.
[74] C. H. Berendt collected a great mass of material on the Central American languages, especially Mayan; this is now in the University Museum, Philadelphia. A catalog of the Berendt linguistic collection was published by Brinton, 1900, as well as much of the material at various times.

notes. He shows the relationships diagrammatically, with frequent overlapping, which cannot be done in a table.

Kroeber makes two main divisions into Lowland and Highland Mayan, placing the isolated and divergent Huaxtec in the Lowland family. By most authorities Huaxtec is accorded an individual place in a tripartite grouping, but it seems to be not so variant as heretofore thought. Since some "Highland" languages are now found in the lowlands and vice versa, possibly but not necessarily a result of recent migration, these geographical terms seem not well chosen and might lead culture-historians to unjustified conclusions; I have therefore taken the liberty to substitute "Mayoid" for Lowland, and "Quichoid" for Highland. A number of other new terms are also proposed: Choloid for Chol-Chontal, Chañabaloid for Tzeltal-Chañabal, Tzeltaloid for Tzeltal-Zotzil, Quichil for Quiche-Ixil, and Kekchom for Kekchi-Pokom.

Thus, according to Kroeber, the Chol-Chontal (Choloid) language of the Mayan group approaches the Tzeltal-Zotzil (Tzeltaloid) language of the Chañabal-Chuj (Chañabaloid) group, and these two might be considered as forming a fourth Chol-Tzeltal group of Maya Proper. (I avoid the name Chontal for the Chol-Chontal [Choloid] language; although the former name is better known it is likely to be confused with the Tequistlatecan Chontal.) Similarly Jacaltec shows affinities with both the Motozintlecan and the Chañabal-Chuj (Chañabaloid) groups and might be considered a member of either. Huaxtec and Chicomuceltec are rather similar and the nearest other relative to Huaxtec seems to be Chontal. Chicomuceltec seems to be very different from Mam, which apparently belongs to the Quichoid family, although of all the Quichoid languages it is closest to the Mayoid. The Quiche-Ixil (Quichil) and Kekchi-Pokom (Kekchom) groups seem to be most remote from the Mayoid family.

On this account the table has been arranged with Huaxtec first in the Mayoid family, and Mam first and Pokom last in the Quichoid. Choltí goes with Chortí in the Mayoid division, not with Pokom in the Quichoid; it is close to Chol and Chontal. Itzá is a slight variant of Yucatecan Maya, not on a classificatory par with Lacandon and Mopan. JM and MyJM [29] considered Olive (see Hokaltecan) akin to Huaxtec, but have changed their opinions on this point. The seven dialects of Mam were recognized in the Mexican census of 1930.[75]

[75] de Mendizábal, Map, 1937.

Two different languages seem to have been spoken in the region of Aguacatlan, as represented by Stoll's [70] vocabularies. Aguacatec I is Mayan; Aguacatec II is related to Zoque (see Mizocuavean).

As regards its wider relations, Lehmann [27] believes that Mayan is related to Mixe-Zoque-Huave, and both descended from a common parent. JM [31] accepts this to the extent of adopting a "Grupo Zoque-Maya." This relationship is accepted as highly probable by many or most linguistic authorities who would consider this hypothetical parent tongue on the line of descent from Proto-Macro-Penutian; but as proof has not yet been offered it is best to consider Mayan as tentatively independent. I understand that Sapir withdrew his suggestion [7] that Mayan might fit into the Hokan-Siouan framework. Schuller believed that Mayan, together with most other Central American languages, belongs with Carib-Arawak in one great phylum.[76]

10. MIZOCUAVEAN

(*Synonyms:* Mixe-Zoque Huave,[7] Mixe-Zoke,[4] Zoqueana,[30] Mexican Penutian [7])

Mizocuavean is suggested as a concise substitute for the cumbrous Mixe-Zoque-Huave. The relationship of Mixe and Zoque was recognized as proved by T&S;[3] the inclusion of Huave is now generally accepted. Suggested by Lehmann,[77] it was proved to general satisfaction by Radin.[78] Each of these three probably consists of only one language, the other forms not greatly variant. Ayuc is the native name for Mixe or Mije,[79] but the latter term is probably too well standardized for any change. The Popoloca of Puebla, given by T&S [3] as an enclave of Mixe, is now considered a branch of Otomanguean.

Lehmann [27] and others note resemblances between Mixe-Zoque and a number of other languages to the south. A vocabulary collected by Stoll [70] at Aguacatlan, Guatemala, known as Aguacatec II,

---

[76] Schuller, Carib-Aruac, 1919–20; Centroamerica, 1928.

The bibliography of the Mayan languages is most voluminous; those most important for the question of classification are noted above. See also Villacorta, Tecpan-Atitlan, 1934. The best grammar in English is that of Tozzer, 1921. A few recent articles of lesser importance are: Schuller, Ts'ots'il, 1925; K'ak'chiq'el, 1930; Becerra, Chontales, 1934.

[77] Lehmann, Forschungsreise, 1910.

[78] Radin, Huave-Mixe, 1916.

[79] Miller, Mixe, 1937.

and a part of one gathered by Sapper [73] at Tapachula on the Mexico-Guatemala Pacific border, termed Tapachultec I, show this especially strongly, and these are generally classified in the Mixe-Zoque family. Tapachultec seems to be a mixed language; the second part, Tapachultec II, is of unknown affinity.[80] Of the four principal languages immediately to the south, to be considered later, Xinca, with the tiny Pupuluca of Conguaco, is accepted by practically all recent authorities as related to Mizocuavean; some add Lenca, fewer include Jicaque, and Sapir [7] even suggests the inclusion of Paya.

Sapir worked rather intensively on the Penutian languages and his opinion [7] that the Mizocuavean languages belong with this group should be given great weight; this was later corroborated by Freeland.[81] Penutian languages in Mexico are not recognized by JM, but the Mizocuavean languages, together with Xinca and Conguaco, are linked with the Mayan languages in an independent Zoque-Maya group.[31] Lehmann [27] suggests that Aguacatec II may form the bridge between Mixe-Zoque and Xinca; he and Radin [78] also note resemblances between Mixe and Maya.

11. TOTONACAN

The linguistic position of Totonac is most uncertain; it may be as independent as Tarascan. Through the researches of Mr. Norman A. McQuown, at present studying it, we shall soon know. Resemblances have been noted with Mayan, Nahua, and Mixe; several writers have considered it a mixed or transition language between Mayan and Aztec. The former opinion that it is rather close to Mayan is certainly wrong; Whorf [8] states that it is extremely unlike Mayan. It will be noted, however, that the only languages with which connections have been suggested all fall in the hypothetical Macro-Penutian phylum; while Whorf does not definitely include Totonac in this phylum, he once [82] made this suggestion.

Tepehua, considered a branch of Totonac by T&S but transferred to Otomi by Schmidt [6] and Rivet,[4] is certainly, in the opinion of the Mexican linguistic group, closely related to Totonac.[83]

[80] González Casanova, Tapachultec, 1927.
[81] Freeland, Mixe, 1930.
[82] Whorf, Uto-Aztecan, 1935, p. 608.
[83] For bibliographies of Totonac see Schuller, 1930; Gropp, 1938; see also Christiansen, 1937.

Languages of Honduras of Doubtful Affiliations

12. Xincan

(*Synonyms:* Jinca, Sinca, Shinka and variants; Popoloco of Guatemala)

13. Lencan   14. Jicaquean   15. Payan

The affiliations of the Xinca, Lenca, Jicaque and Paya languages are so uncertain and controversial that for the present they had best be left unclassified or independent. There seems to be some sort of connection between all but the lexical differences are so great that no two of them can be linked. Schuller [84] insists that they, together with most of the other languages of Central America, including the Mayan, fall in his great Maya-Quiche-Carib-Arawak phylum. Lehmann [27] sees Hokan traits in all except Payan. (The Hokaltecan Subtiaba are nearby.)

Almost all agree, however, that the true affiliations lie between Mixe-Zoque (Mizocuavean) and Chibchan. It should be noted that this is also the region of the cultural boundary between North and South America. By some they are considered intermediate languages, bridges from Mizocuavean to Chibchan, and they may be true mixed languages with double or multiple roots. Sapir [7] sees Penutian tendencies in all of them, decreasing from Xinca to Paya, and Lehmann [27] believes that there is a demonstrable original relationship between Xinca, Lenca, Jicaque, and Mixe-Zoque, and suggests that Aguacatec II forms the bridge from Mixe-Zoque to Xinca. Xinca is therefore placed with Mixe-Zoque by almost all authorities, Lenca by many; Whorf [8] follows Sapir in putting both under Penutian.

On the other hand Lehmann [27] sees Chibchan tendencies in all, increasing from Xinca to Paya, and calls all but the first "Chibchan outliers"; Paya in particular is sometimes linked with Chibchan. On the basis of these very equivocal opinions of Lehmann's, Schmidt [6] places all four in his "Chibcha-Sprachen" as well as in his "Miskito-Xinca-Mischsprachen," and all except Paya in his "Mixe-Lenca Gruppe." JM [31] places Xinca in his "Grupo Zoque-Maya," and makes a separate "Grupo Paya-Lenca" with the comment "Nexo entre Zoque-Maya y Chibcha-Misquito?"

[84] Schuller, Centroamerica, 1928.

The affinities of the extinct Popoluca or Pupuluca of Conguaco, an enclave in Xinca territory, are uncertain.[85]

16. Misumalpan

(*Synonyms:* Miskito-Sumo-Matagalpa,[4, 7] Miskito-Matagalpa Sprachen [6])

The term Misumalpan is suggested as a concise synonym for Mosquito *-Sumo-Matagalpa. The genetic relationships of the three members are not close and almost as controversial as their relationship to Chibchan. Some authorities consider Matagalpan independent, others think Mosquitoan so, but as the stock is accepted by Sapir,[7] Rivet,[4] Schmidt,[6] and JM [31] we may follow suit. The very detailed subdivision is mainly from Lehmann [27] who has made by far the most careful study which has served as the base for all recent classifications. Lehmann believes that the tiny extinct group of the Chuchures at the northernmost point of Panama were Mosquitoan, as well as some littoral groups in Costa Rica; Lothrop [86] considers it possible that the Chuchures were Nahuan. Lehmann thinks Sumo-Ulua rather closely related to Matagalpa-Cacaopera.

Conzemius [87] believes that the Mosquito are a sub-group of the Sumo. The frequently mentioned Zambos are negroes who speak a polyglot jargon, and the Corn Islanders are very similar. Kabo is the standard Mosquito dialect of the missionaries. Baymunana may be a synonym for Baldam. Conzemius divides the Sumo into the following groups: Tawahka, Ulva, Panamaka, Bawihka, and Kukra. The relationships of the members of the Suman family are most uncertain; a great amount of borrowing has taken place and many of the languages are much mixed. Also the migratory movements have been great, both pre- and post-hispanic. It is likely that the Mosquito-Sumo were late immigrants to this region at a comparatively short time before the Conquest.

Lehmann [27] considers all these as "contact-zone mixed languages"

* See editorial note p. 59.
[85] On Xinca, Lenca, Jicaque and Paya see Conzemius, 1923, 1928–1929; Brinton, Xinca, 1884.
[86] Lothrop, Costa Rica, 1926.
[87] Conzemius, who has traveled widely with the Misumalpan and other natives of the Atlantic Coast of Nicaragua, Honduras and Costa Rica, has published a number of articles recently upon them in which he expresses his opinions regarding their linguistic relationships.

with a considerable Chibcha content. The Chibcha relationship with Sumo-Ulva seems to be clearer than with Mosquito and Matagalpa; though some deny it for any, the group is considered related to Chibcha by Lehmann,[27] Schmidt [6] and JM [31]; the latter places his "Familia Sumo-Misquito" in his "Grupo Chibcha-Misquito.[88]

17. CHIBCHAN

The Chibchan is a large stock with many subdivisions and languages, most of them in Colombia. As with the other major groups, only those languages in Middle America, which is considered to include Panama, are considered in the table. The Middle American Chibchan tribes are all basically South American in culture, and presumably rather late migrants from Colombia. There is no difference of opinion whether all the tribes named are Chibchan; the question is whether any or all of the Misumalpan group are related to them.

There are two very different classificatory systems, those of Lehmann and Rivet, so variant that no correlation is possible. That of Lehmann [27] has been here adopted as it was accepted by Schmidt [6] and JM,[31] and seems more reasonable on geographical grounds. Rivet [4] divides the Middle American Chibchans into three groups: a) Talamank-Barbakoa, including the Guatusan, Talamancan, Cunan and Barbacoan (Colombian) sub-groups; b) Dorask-Guaymi, including Murire, Changuina and Chimila-Tairona (Colombian); and c) Chibcha-Aruak, consisting of a number of Colombian languages and the Rama-Melchora of Nicaragua.

The proper classification of many of these dialects, especially the extinct languages, is of course uncertain. There are moreover a number of small unassigned groups or enclaves in this region, such as Cholo, Chiru, Escoria, Urraca, Nata, Paparo, and Chuchures; Lehmann believes that some of them are transition languages between Dorasque-Guaymi and Cueva-Cuna. Some may not be Chibchan. The modern Guatuso are probably descendants of, and synonymous with, the ancient Corobici.

Schuller [84] of course puts all Chibchan languages in his great Maya-Quiche-Carib-Arawak phylum.

The linguistic position of the Choco languages is very much in question. Though the differences are great, there are enough re-

---

[88] See Brinton, American Race, 1891; Musquito, 1891; Matagalpan, 1895; Conzemius, 1926, 1929, 1932; Heath, Miskito, 1913.

semblances for Lehmann [27] to consider them related to Chibchan; Rivet [4] calls them independent. As they barely extend over the Colombian border into Panama we may beg the question.[89]

Major Unclassified Languages

Cuitlatec. Although still spoken, and once an important language, not enough is known of Cuitlatec to classify it. Mr. Hendrichs has recently gathered material from the last surviving members of this group. According to Weitlaner,[48] there are certain semantic resemblances to Ocuiltec (Matlatzinca-Otomi), but morphologically it is quite different, having a Hokan-like appearance. Lehmann [27] also noted similar tendencies and inclined to place it in the Hokan group, but Rivet [4] claims Lehmann's authority for making it independent. T&S [3] had authority for terming it "confessedly a Nahuatlan tongue, a mere idiom of the Aztec." JM [31] and MyJM [30] wisely follow OyB [20] in refusing to classify it.

Olmec. Archeologically the quasi-mythical Olmec [90] were important. Lehmann [27] thinks they were related linguistically to Chocho-Popoloca (Otomangue); Schuller [84] refutes this, as early sources differentiated the two groups. Berendt thought it might be related to Chinantec. Most authorities consider them Nahuatlan, probably of Toltec affinities; JM [31] classes them as Nahuatl. It is just (1940) reported, however, that an obscure statement of Sahagun indicates that they were Mixtec.

Carib

In considering the present languages of Middle America the Carib must be taken into consideration, though they are post-hispanic. Deported by the British from the Lesser Antilles in 1797 to the island of Roatan they are now found along the northern coast of Honduras and in places on the coast of British Honduras. Much mixed with negro blood and termed "Black Caribs" they now number some fifteen thousand, most of them speaking a Carib jargon.

[89] For other references to the native languages of Central America, especially Costa Rica, see: Brinton, Güetares, 1897; Conzemius, Rama, 1930; Fernández Guardia and Ferraz, 1892; Gabb, Costa Rica, 1875; Gagini, Costa Rica, 1917; Gatschet, Central Amerika, 1900; Grasserie, Costa Rica, 1904; Herzog, Costa Rica, 1884; Lehmann, Costa Rica, 1910; Prince, Panama, Tule, 1913; Rivet, Amerique du Sud, 1911; Sapper, Mittelamerika, 1904; Schuller, Salvador, 1925; Centroamerica, 1928; Squier, Nicaragua, 1853; Authors, 1861.

[90] Valentini, Olmecs, 1883.

TABLE I: PROPOSED GROUPING OF MIDDLE AMERICAN LANGUAGES (Pp. 78-87)

1. HOKALTECAN

A. Phylum: Hokan-Siouan A1. Sub-phylum: Hokaltecan

B. STOCK	B1. SUB-STOCK	C. FAMILY	C1. SUB-FAMILY	D. LANGUAGE	D1. VARIETY	E. DIALECT
Hokan	Esselen-Yuman	Yuman	Cocopa	Cocopa		Cocopa (Cucupa)
						Kikima (Halyikwamai)
						?Alakwisa
						Kohuana (Cajuenche)
				Kamia		Kiliwi, Kamia-Diegueño
				Akwa'ala (Paipai)		
			*Cochimi	*Cochimi		*Laymon
	Salinan-Serian	Serian		Seri		*Salinero, *Tepoca
						*Guayma, *Upanguaima
	Tequistlatecan (Chontal)			Tequistlatec (Chontal)		
Supanecan (Subtiaba-Yopi-Tlapanec)				Supanec	*Maribio	*Subtiaba
						*Maribichicoa-Guatajiagua
					Tlapaneco Tlapaneca (*Yopi)	
*Coahuiltecan		*Coahuiltecan (Pakawan)		*Coahuiltec *Cotoname *Comecrudo *Carrizo		
?*Coahuiltecan		?*Tamaulipecan		*Tamaulipec		
?*Coahuiltecan		?*Janambrian		*Janambre		*Pisone

* Extinct.

2. WAICURIAN

(Possibly, A. Phylum: Hokan-Siouan A1. Sub-phylum: Hokaltecan)

B. STOCK	B1. SUB-STOCK	C1. SUB-FAMILY	D. LANGUAGE	D1. VARIETY	E. DIALECT
?Hokan		*Waicurian	*Waicuri		*Edu, *Didu, *Utciti, *Cora, *Monqui, *Aripa
			*Pericu		

3. TARASCAN

A. Phylum: (Independent ?)

Tarascan	Tarascan	Tarasco	

4. OTOMANGUEAN

A. Phylum: (Macro-Otomangue ?)

B. STOCK	C. FAMILY	C1. SUB-FAMILY	D. LANGUAGE	D1. VARIETY	E. DIALECT	E1. VARIATION
Otomanguean	Otomian	Otomian	Otomi	*Serrano, Mazahua		
			Matlatzinca (Pirinda, Matlaltzinca)	*Matlame, *?Quata	Ocuiltec	Atzinca
			Pame	Chichimec-Jonaz	*Tonaz, *Meco	
	Popolocan	Popolocan	Popoloca (Chocho) of Puebla			
			Ixcatec			
			Chocho (Chuchon, Popoloca of Oaxaca)			
		Mazatecan	Mazatec	Mazatec of Oaxaca, ?Guerrero, ?Tabasco, *?Guatinicamame		

Continued on following page.

*Extinct.

A. Phylum: (Macro-Otomangue ?) (continued)

B. STOCK	BI. SUB-STOCK	C. FAMILY	CI. SUB-FAMILY	D. LANGUAGE	DI. VARIETY	E. DIALECT
Otomanguean (continued)	?Triquean		Trique			
	Chorotegan	Chiapanecan	Chiapanec			
		*Manguean	*Choluteca (Chorotega)			
			*Mangue		*Diria, *Nagrandan	
			*Orotiña		*Orisi, *Nicoya	

5. MIXTECAN

Mixtecan	Mixtecan		Mixtec		Alta, Baja	
	Cuicatecan		Cuicatec			
	Amusgan		Amusgo (Amishgo)			

6. CHINANTECAN

Chinantecan			Chinantec		Hume, Wahmi, Ojitlan, Yolox	

7. ZAPOTECAN

Zapotecan			Zapotec	Northern Mountains	Cajono, Miahuatlan, Nexitza, Ixtepexi, Zapotec	Zaachila, Ocotlan, Etla
				Southern Mountains		
				Valleys	Tehuantepec	
			Chatino		*Papabuco, *Soltec	

*Extinct.

8. UTAZTECAN

A. Phylum: (Macro-Penutian?) A1. Sub-phylum: Azteco-Tanoan B. Stock: Utaztecan

C. FAMILY	C1. SUB-FAMILY	C2. GROUP	D. LANGUAGE	DI. VARIETY	E. DIALECT
Taracahitian	Tarahumaran		Tarahumare		
	Cahitan	Cahita	Cahita		Yaqui, Mayo, *Tehueco, *Cinaloa, *Zuaque
		Tepahue	*Tepahue, *Macoyahui, *Conicari, *Baciroa		
		Tahue	*Tahue, *Comanito, *Mocorito, *Tubar, *Zoe		
		Guasave	*Guasave		*Comopori, *Ahome, *Vacoregue, *Achire
	(Cahitan?)	Varohio	Varohio (Guarijia). *Chinipa, *Guasapar, *Temori		
		Acaxee	*Acaxee		*Tebaca, *Sabaibo
		Xixime	*Xixime		*Hine, *Hume, *Aibine
		Ocoroni	Ocoroni, *Huite, *Nio		
	Opatan	Opata	*Opata		*Batuc, *Nacosura
			*Eudeve (*Heve, *Dohema)		
		Jova	*Jova		
	(Opatan?)	Concha	*Concho		*Chinarra, *Chizo
			*Jumano, *Suma		
Aztecoidan	Coran	Cora	Cora		Huaynamota, *Zayahueco, *Coano
			*Totorame (*Pinome)		
		Huichol	Huichol (?*Guachichil) *Tecual		

* Extinct.

8. UTAZTECAN (continued)

C. FAMILY	CI. SUB-FAMILY	D. LANGUAGE	DI. VARIETY	E. DIALECT	EI. VARIATION
Aztecoidan (continued)	Nahuatlan	Nahuatl	Mexicano	Aztec	?*Desaguadero, ?*Sigua
				*Tepanec, etc.	
			?Meztitlanec		
		Nahuat	?**Toltec-Chichimec	Pipil	*Alagüilac
				*Nahuatlato, *Bagaces, *Nicarao, ?*Chuchures	
		Pochutla			
		?*Teco-Tecoxquin, ?*Sayulteca			
		?*Cazcan	?*Lagunero (**Irritila)		
			?*Zacateco		
		?*Coca	?*Tecuexe		
Piman		Piman	Pima Alto	Papago, *Piato, *Himeri	
			Pima Bajo	Nebome, *Ure, *Cocomacague	
		Tepehuan	Northern	Northern Tepehuan	
			Southern	Southern Tepehuan, Tepecan	
			?*Teul, ?*Colotlan		
		?*Vigitega			

* Extinct.

9. MAYAN

A. Phylum: (Macro-Penutian ?) B. Stock: Mayan

C. FAMILY	C1. SUB-FAMILY	C2. GROUP	D. LANGUAGE	D1. VARIETY	E. DIALECT	E1. VARIATION
Mayoid	Huaxtecan	Huaxtecan	Huaxtec		Potosino Veracruzano	
			Chicomuceltec			
	Maya Proper	Mayan	Maya	Yucatec (Maya)		Itza Icaiche Santa Cruz
				Mopan		
				Yucatec Lacandon		
			Choloid	Chontal of Tabasco		
				Chol	Chol (*Cholti) *Chorti Chol Lacandon *?Acala *?Toquegua *?Manche	
		Chañabaloid	Tzeltaloid	Tzeltal (Tzendal)		
				Zotzil (Tzotzil, *Quelene, Chamula)		
			Chañabal (Tojolabal)			
			Chuj			
		Motozintlecan	Jacaltec (*Subinha)			
			Motozintlec			

* Extinct.

9. MAYAN (continued)

C. FAMILY	C1. SUB-FAMILY	C2. GROUP	D. LANGUAGE	D1. VARIETY	E. DIALECT	E1. VARIATION
Quichoid			Mam	Mam	(Mam)	
					Coyotin	
					Taquial	
					Tacanec	
					Tutuapa	
					Tupancal	
					Tacana	
					Tlatiman	
		Quichil	Aguacatec I			
			Quiche	Quiche		
				Cakchiquel		
				Tzutuhil		
				Uspantec		
			Ixil			
		Kekchom	Kekchi			
			Pokom	Pokomam (Pokoman)		
				Pokonchi		

Unclassified, probably Mayan: Solomec, *Quehache, *Achis, *Poton (*Ponton, *Putum)

10. MIZOCUAVEAN

A. PHYLUM	A1. SUB-PHYLUM	B. STOCK	C. FAMILY	C1. SUB-FAMILY	D. LANGUAGE	D1. VARIETY	E. DIALECT
(Macro-Penutian ?)	(Penutian ?)	Mizocuavean	Mixe-Zoquean (Zoquean)	Mixe	Mixe (Mije, Ayuc, Ayook)		
	(Other suggested sub-phyla: Zoque-Maya, Mixe-Lenca)				Popoloca of Vera Cruz		Texixtepec Oluta Sayula
				Zoque	Zoque		Tapixulapan
						*Tapachultec I	
						*Aguacatec II	
			Huavean	Huave	Huave		

* Extinct.

11. TOTONACAN

A. PHYLUM	A1. SUB-PHYLUM	B. STOCK	C. FAMILY	C1. SUB-FAMILY	D. LANGUAGE	D1. VARIETY	E. DIALECT
(Macro-Penutian ?)	(Totonacan ?)	Totonacan	Totonacan	Totonacan	Totonac	Coast Papantla Sierra	Tatiquilhati ?Chacahuaxtli Tatimolo Ipapana
					Tepehua		

12. XINCAN

A. PHYLUM	A1. SUB-PHYLUM	B. STOCK	C. FAMILY	C1. SUB-FAMILY	D. LANGUAGE	D1. VARIETY	E. DIALECT
(Macro-Penutian ?)	(Penutian ?)	Xincan	Xincan	Xincan	Xinca		Sinacantan Xupiltepec Xutiapa
					?*Pupuluca of Conguaco		

13. LENCAN

A. PHYLUM	A1. SUB-PHYLUM	B. STOCK	C. FAMILY	C1. SUB-FAMILY	D. LANGUAGE	D1. VARIETY	E. DIALECT
(Macro-Penutian ?)	(Penutian ?)	Lencan	Lencan	Lencan	Lenca		Guaxiquero *Intibucat Opatoro Similaton Chilanga

14. JICAQUEAN

A. PHYLUM	A1. SUB-PHYLUM	B. STOCK	C. FAMILY	C1. SUB-FAMILY	D. LANGUAGE	D1. VARIETY	E. DIALECT
(Macro-Penutian ?) (Macro-Chibchan ?)	(Penutian ?) (Chibchan ?)	Jicaquean	Jicaquean	Jicaquean	Jicaque		Yoro Palma Lean y Mulia

15. PAYAN

A. PHYLUM	A1. SUB-PHYLUM	B. STOCK	C. FAMILY	C1. SUB-FAMILY	D. LANGUAGE	D1. VARIETY	E. DIALECT
(Macro-Chibchan ?) (Macro-Penutian ?)	(Chibchan ?) (Penutian ?)	Payan	Payan	Payan	Paya		

* Extinct.

16. MISUMALPAN

A. *Phylum:* (*Macro-Chibchan?*)   B. *Stock: Misumalpan* (*Mosquito†-Sumo-Matagalpa*)

C. FAMILY	CI. SUB-FAMILY	D. LANGUAGE	E. DIALECT
Mosquitoan	Mosquito	Tawira	Tawira (Tauira), Mam, Wanki, Baldam, Kabo
Suman	Ulva	Ulva (Ulwa, Ulua)	Ulva, *Prinzo, ?*Kukra (*Cookra), *?Guanexico (*Guaxenico)
	Yosko	Yosko	
	Sumo (Simoo)	Tawahka	Tawahka, Lakus, ?Coco, ?Wasabane, ?Pispis
		Panamaka	Panamaka, Karawala, Tunki
		Boa	
		Bawihka	
	(Unclassified)		Ku, Silam, Yasika, Dudu, Musutepes
(Mixed Mosquito-Sumo)			Bambana, Kiwahka, Tungla, Kukalaya, *Sumo-Sirpe
(Possibly Mosquito-Sumo)			Baymunana, ?*Chuchure
Matagalpan		Matagalpa	Cacaopera, *Matagalpa, *?Chato, *?Dule, *?Pantasma

17. CHIBCHAN

A. *Phylum:* (*Macro-Chibchan?*)   B. *Stock: Chibchan*

CI. SUB-FAMILY	D. LANGUAGE	DI. VARIETY	E. DIALECT
Rama-Corobici	Guatuso	*Corobici (*Corbesi)	Guatuso, *Corobici
	Rama	Rama	Rama, Melchora
	(Unclassified)		*?Tice, ?Catapa, *Uruy, *Turrin, *Pocora, *Xurru, *Gotane, *Cocora, Patica

* Extinct.
† See editorial note p. 59, in re Miskito.

17. CHIBCHAN (continued)

CI. SUB-FAMILY	D. LANGUAGE	DI. VARIETY	E. DIALECT
Talamanca	Güetar	*Güetar	
	Talamanca	Cabecar (Chiripo)	Tariaca, Pocosi
		Suerre (Turricia)	
		*Voto	
		Bribri	Bribri (Valiente), Talamanca, Viceita, Urinama
	Boruca	Boruca	Boruca (Brunca), *Quepo, *Coto, *Burucaca, *?Turucaca, *?Osa
	Terraba	Terraba (Tiribi)	Terraba, ?Tojar, ?Teshbi, ?Depso
Guaymi-Dorasque	Dorasque	*Dorasque	*Dorasque (*Torresque), ?Burica, Duy
		*Changuena	
	Guaymi	Guaymi	*?Muoi, *?Move (Valiente-Norteño), *?Murire (Bukueta-Sabanero), *?Muite
Cueva-Cuna		*Penonomeño	
		*Coiba	
		Cuna	Mandinga, Chucunaque, Bayano, Tule (Yule), Caimanes, San Blas
(Unclassified)			Tucurrique, Orosi, Estrella, Xorrhue; Ara, Lari, Uren, Zhorquin, Teluski, Zuri, Chaliva, Chumulu, Gualaca, Zegua

* Extinct.

VI

THE LINGUISTIC MAP OF MEXICO AND CENTRAL AMERICA

Frederick Johnson [*]

*(Note: The map under discussion may be
found on the inside back cover of the present
edition.)*

A "LINGUISTIC MAP" is a device by which the distribution of languages over a specified area may be shown. Depending upon a number of circumstances such a map may be more than this. Human speech is divisible into a number of orders which may, for convenience only, be arranged in the form of a classification. Linguistic classifications are arbitrarily imposed schemes based upon more or less superficial characteristics. Such arrangements do, in the end, permit little or no exception. Within the limits imposed by the act of classification and, curiously enough, by the technical ability of the printing profession, a linguistic map can suggest a classificatory system. Thus a map may present certain facts illustrating the knowledge of the relationship between the tongues whose distribution is indicated. A linguistic map is essentially a two dimensional approach to a three dimensional problem—the development and dispersion of languages. However the attempt to represent relationships by means of color and line convention supplies a thin and unqualified third dimension.

When a map is drawn which covers a large area or deals with a wide variety of languages it is obvious that some areas will be shown more accurately and in more detail than others. Some areas have been investigated more fully, and the early records of the people in one region are more complete or better known than those of others. Unfortunately it is not practical to indicate on the map the degree of completeness or trustworthiness of the many boundaries. It should also be borne in mind that in some cases the map must be simplified in order that it may be legible and that it may conform to the limita-

---

[*] Tufts, B.S., 1929; Harvard, Hemingway Fellow, 1930–1933; Assistant in Anthropology, 1931–1933, 1935; now Curator, Robert S. Peabody Foundation for Archaeology, Andover, Massachusetts.

tions of the printer. These restrictions appear at times to necessitate a misrepresentation of the facts.

Among the most instructive sources of information concerning the distribution of languages are preceding maps. These have to be used with discretion however. Frequently the period which they represent is not similar to that intended for the present map. It becomes necessary then to delve into the usually scanty knowledge of the migrations and relationships of the various groups. With some exceptions, the modern maps contain the nucleus of the situation. The greatest difficulty comes in trying to fit two overlapping maps together. No two maps of this sort agree, probably because of individual interpretations of incomplete information. In the case of the present map certain former decisions have been accepted but occasionally a new interpretation has been added to an already confused situation.

In spite of their unsatisfactory character, the documents are a never-ending source of information. However the necessary careful analysis has so many ramifications that an incomplete study can cause a great deal of confusion. In their partial or complete ignorance of linguistics as a whole the early writers frequently confused such things as linguistic and political boundaries, or the names of chieftains and those of tribes. Upon occasion, the early informants and interpreters were not selected with any care. All too frequently, carelessly gathered facts were used by the conquerors to describe the characteristics of peoples or even regions. The task of analyzing this material is a never-ending one and so we have to rely on what has been done and hope that, as in the past, careful local studies will eventually reduce the raw data to acceptable fact. Whenever time and facilities permitted some of the situations on the present map, about which little was known, were improved by a perusal of the documents. Without any question, more of such work would have improved many sections of the present map.

It is not fair to criticize the early documents for what we consider omissions. The Conquistadores supplied the kind of information which their patrons and governments believed was required by the circumstances. That this information varied with the abilities and interests of the various travelers and administrators is only to be expected. At the present time these early data are being put to uses for which they were never intended. The primary purpose of the early recorders in determining linguistic and tribal boundaries was for use in colonial-political machinations. If one group of natives could make itself understood by another group a statement to this effect was usually sufficient. The important question of slight but significant differences in Dialect or Variety was rarely if ever recorded by the colonial administrators. That they were probably ignorant of many of these details or of ways of recording them seems obvious, but even if they were not they rarely considered such differentiations important. In utilizing these records, linguists should exercise great caution.

At this task's outset it was necessary to decide upon a date, or perhaps better, a period of time which would be represented on the present map. It was decided that an attempt would be made to represent the aborigines in the regions where they were first discovered. As far as possible this map represents the linguistic distribution during the latter part of the sixteenth century. However, many enclaves in which various idioms were spoken were not recorded until after this time. These have been included on the map on the basis of their first record which is qualified by an analysis of the known movements of neighboring peoples. Upon occasion, cautious use of archaeological and ethnographical data has aided in solving the more difficult problems. The necessary inclusion of a date gives the map among other things a certain historical significance and so the spacial relationship between various groups acquires a considerable degree of importance. There are several instances where the location of groups on this map is based on the partly authenticated folk-history of the movements and relationships of peoples rather than upon the vague documentary references to them. Thus, if under certain conditions, the documents indicate that two groups, when discovered, were separated by a third and if a detailed study of their language, traditions, and culture indicates that they may have been separated by changes coincident with the Conquest, their boundaries have been modified until the two groups are shown in contact. This manner of locating groups is fraught with many dangers and, if used indiscriminately, would not be justifiable. However, where this method has been applied to the present map the proof seems to be at least as good as that provided by a strict adherence to equivocal information in the documents.

Most linguistic boundaries are continually shifting and there are some which have been in such a constant state of flux that it is well nigh impossible to record them with any degree of accuracy. In some cases the movements of the boundaries may, with some hesitation, be traced to the wanderings of small bands of people over sparsely populated expanses of land. Such a situation may easily account for some of the contradictory records which are encountered in the literature describing regions similar to northern Mexico. Other difficulties with shifting boundaries are exemplified by the little-known situation in Honduras and Nicaragua. Here apparently, drastic changes in the distribution of languages had begun before the Conquest through the shifting of the balance of power from one group to another.

The movements of linguistic boundaries in the more thickly settled sections of Central America were due to a variety of very complicated situations which existed even before the arrival of the Spanish. The comment by Lothrop [1] concerning the Maya applies also to the Aztec and other highly civilized nations. They were subject to extremely complicated movements of peoples which are analogous to those which have confused the present picture of Europe. The conquests of an area set up a vicious cycle of events which prevented the stabilization of any sort of permanent boundary lines. It is even possible that changes in ecological conditions contributed their share toward the general, though possibly ordered, complications.

The arrival of the white man upon the scene, with his new economic system, his primitive knowledge of ethnology, and his absolute conviction in his own righteousness, completely upset the aboriginal situation. The extent of the upheaval enlarges as one attempts to discover the region in which any one of a multitude of enclaves lived immediately before the Conquest. The influences of the intruders were not confined to the region in which they were stopping. The process which resulted in the domination of one group set up movements in contiguous groups, which modified the distribution of languages far in advance of the physical presence of the white man. By the time the Europeans arrived in a distant region to make the "first records" of the aborigines, their influence had preceded them and the picture had changed.

Cartographers of necessity must deal with the records of regions whose inhabitants were experiencing a period of unrest which wreaked havoc with their aboriginal status. It is small wonder that the records are frequently contradictory. In assembling data to locate boundaries, lists of towns in which a certain idiom is spoken are

[1] Lothrop, Maya Frontier, 1939, p. 42.

frequently found in the literature. In such cases it is possible to indicate a distribution by arbitrarily drawing a boundary half way between two towns. When, as frequently happens in sections like southern Mexico, two, or even three, dialects are spoken in a single town, the cartographer finds himself in a dilemma. Since the map dictates that a line shall be drawn, he breaks the dilemma by drawing lines which might represent a theoretical situation. Almost unjustifiable decisions concerning the location of boundary lines have to be made when a town in which a certain dialect is spoken is separated from its main group by several towns speaking other dialects.

In the final analysis, a linguistic boundary cannot be drawn accurately on anything but a map of the largest scale. No matter how carefully a line is drawn on a map it cannot represent the true situation. There are instances where political boundaries or topographic features have been pointed out as linguistic boundaries. In every instance which has been investigated carefully it was found that the supposedly separated languages were found on both sides of the reputed boundary. This rather well-known phenomenon may come about in at least two general ways. First, individuals, preserving their linguistic identity, move from one region to another regardless of political or other considerations. Second, speech being so easily adaptable to any situation, different Dialects or even Languages which are contiguous will frequently mix. Thus there is developed a jargon which is mutually intelligible to the neighboring peoples. A boundary line cannot be made to represent this situation faithfully.

One of the silliest sources of confusion which exists in the literature describing the characteristics of the aborigines of Central America is the question of terminology. From the time of the Conquest names have been applied to various orders of languages, to small enclaves, and to the larger divisions with an utter disregard of any system. This wanton spattering of terms has been perpetuated by archaeologists, ethnographers and other students. At the present moment there are numerous terms whose existence is justifiable but they have been used to describe everything from a detail of pottery decoration to some of the larger orders of linguistic classification. The time is coming, if really it has not been passed, when some semblance of order should be introduced into this chaos.

To hold up the present map as an example of the correct use of terms is, of course, absurd. However, it may be suggested that the nomenclature adopted is purely and simply linguistic and when corrected and amended it can act as a basis from which to proceed in some acceptable fashion. There will be bellicose notes made of the fact that a few of the more familiar terms, especially from the point of view of archaeology, are omitted from the map. This has been done with malice aforethought. In some cases the missing terms have been confused by linguists themselves so that at the present they can be applied to several idioms. In other cases linguistic terms have been preempted by archaeologists to such an extent that their linguistic significance is obscured. In arranging the terms in the classification a certain amount of definition was accomplished. In any case, wherever possible, ambiguous terms have been either redefined or exchanged for terms which could be defined more precisely. In developing the present nomenclature Dr. Mason and the writer carried on a discussion which attempted to discover the first appearance of a term and followed roughly its history to the present most common usage. The spelling of the terms has been established according to the unknown and unwritten rules of a non-existent lingua franca which may be understood by Spanish and English speakers. The result is purely a matter of opinion for which no brief can be upheld. It is unfortunate that a table showing the development of these terms cannot be included. Another point is perhaps worth mentioning. It is well nigh impossible to mention a language without thinking of the people who speak it. A language cannot exist unless there are, or were, people to use it. In discussing linguistic groupings and their distribution such questions as race or ethnographical considerations, including conclusions resulting from archaeological analysis, should be carefully segregated into their proper place.

Linguistic maps of Central America are relatively scarce. Thomas and Swanton [2] were the first to show the distribution of the languages of the whole region, that is, the territory lying between the Rio Grande and the Panama-Colombian border. In 1920 Walter Lehmann [3] drew and discussed at length a map which included all of the region except for a section of northern Mexico. This was

[2] Thomas and Swanton, Languages, 1911. These authors are textually abbreviated as Thomas.

[3] Lehmann, Zentral Amerika, 1920.

followed in 1924 by Rivet's map.[4] Schmidt's map was published in 1926.[5]

The first modern linguistic map dealing with a restricted area was published by Orozco y Berra in 1864.[6] This work illustrated and discussed the contemporary knowledge of the distribution of Mexican languages and it has exerted a profound influence upon all subsequent maps of the region. In spite of the importance of this practically pioneer work it was necessary, for the purpose of the present map, to refine much of this data. Fortunately a great deal of this analysis has been accomplished by contemporary students. The most recent attempt to illuminate the distribution of Mexican linguistics may be found in three very important maps.[7] On these a number of significant boundaries have been relocated and a number of previously unrecognized enclaves have been added. In addition significant classifications have been proposed. It is to be regretted that explanatory data does not accompany these maps.

Several other maps of restricted areas in Mexico have been published. These provide detailed information concerning local situations and, in the end, prove to be of inestimable value. Maps of regions south and east of Mexico are less satisfactory. A few local studies exist and for these we are thankful. On the whole however, treatments of wider scope are confined to Thomas[8] and the works which followed, particularly the critical treatise of Lehmann.[9] There is even more need at present for a comprehensive study of the languages spoken east of the Ulua River than for those found to the west. It is obvious that such a study will provide an outline and supply numerous details which will aid in understanding the results of the contact between Central American and South American peoples. The consequences of such an understanding will penetrate deeply into the fog which surrounds much of the present knowledge of Central American cultures. It is hoped that the few innovations and implications which are tentatively and timorously made here will indicate the possibilities of intellectual aggrandize-

[4] Rivet, Langues de l'Amérique Central, 1924.
[5] Schmidt, Sprachfamilien, 1926.
[6] Orozco y Berra, Geografía, 1864.
[7] Jiménez Moreno, Map, 1936. Mendizabal, Distribucion, 1937. Mendizabal and Jiménez Moreno, Map, no date. This source is textually abbreviated as Mendizabal and Jiménez and in footnotes is cited as Mendizabal and Jiménez, Map.
[8] Thomas and Swanton, Languages, 1911.
[9] Lehmann, Zentral Amerika, 1920.

ment, if not more tangible remuneration, as a reward for an attack upon this almost despised section.

From the time of Orozco y Berra down to the present day, linguistic maps have reflected the general tendency toward the reduction in the number of the larger categories in the linguistic classification. Running through the maps beginning with the first one presents a changing picture of the amalgamation of the many regions. In spite of these developments only slight changes have been made in the techniques used to represent the distribution and relationship of the many idioms. Usually the maps differentiate only Stocks, or some category of similar status, and they make no attempt to indicate more particular classificatory divisions. Such a method is certainly justifiable on technical grounds for the complications involved by a more detailed portrayal not only increase the expense of publication but involve the education of the unfortunate printer. To add that the attempt to indicate such details necessitates the almost unqualified acceptance of a tentative classification introduces another factor to the already confusing problem. In the present map I have carried the differentiation outlined by the classification as far as a compromise between expense and legibility would permit. Only a period of use will tell whether or not the venture has been worth while.

The classification which formed the basis for the development of the key has been amply described by J. Alden Mason in the preceding paper. If for no other reason than emphasis some of his remarks must be enlarged upon. The classification represents a compromise between several current opinions. The arrangement of the Languages under four major headings is as yet unproved and controversial. In some cases languages have remained independent when their relationship with any larger group could not be accepted. In other cases hypothetical relationships and even unproved suggestions of possible affinity with the larger groups have been tentatively indicated. To complete the map by superimposing a scheme, which admittedly is so hypothetical, is indeed rash. No matter how carefully this is done it gives the classification an air of finality which is utterly false. Linguistic affinities and relationships, as they are indicated on the map, are only as accurate as is the classification as a whole. In spite of these shortcomings the implications of the distribution of the numerous tongues, as they are shown in relation one to the other, are of sufficient interest to be important. The importance of the map will increase in proportion to the discretion and caution which is employed in using it.

This map could never have been drawn and the comments would indeed be empty if it were not for the extended discussions, searching criticisms and friendly advice of Dr. J. Alden Mason. Many others have contributed generously and patiently by answering a bombardment of lengthy queries, and many of the successful sections of the map are those which have been supplied by others. The unacceptable portions are due either to my ignorance of existing analyses or to bold assumptions which I have had the temerity to perpetuate.

To many people in the publishing world I owe an everlasting debt of gratitude. Oftentimes these men have given of their time and energy at their own expense in an almost vain attempt to initiate me into some of the innermost secrets of their fascinating profession. The reproduction of this map is a tribute to their generosity.

The present form of the key was evolved as Mason's classification was abbreviated and adapted to the problem of illustration. The structure of the classification is so searching in its analysis of the problem that it was deemed advisable to include at least six of its eleven categories in the key. The result of such an abbreviation was tempered by a number of modifications of the system made necessary by the arbitrary character of the map. Distribution is of primary importance and this could be shown by recording the location of Dialects and Languages. Families, Stocks and the larger categories are, on the other hand, important from the point of view of present conceptions of relationship. In view of this, the key had to be arranged in a fashion which would emphasize the distribution and at the same time illustrate any conclusions concerning linguistic affinity. If it may be granted that the key is successful the map may be read in two ways. First, it is possible to find the location of the boundaries enclosing enclaves in which established idioms were spoken. Second, various degrees of relationship which existed between the located groups may be discovered by analyzing the arrangement of conventions. By observing similarities or differences in these devices various degrees of affinity may be inferred. In the latter case, to read the map correctly, it is necessary to refer finally to the details of Mason's classification. Opinions arrived at through the perusal of the key must be qualified by the advantages or faults of its source.

EXPLANATION OF TYPE

The problem of differentiating four of the smallest categories in the classification was solved by the use of four styles of type. In printing a name on the map the status of the idiom represented is indicated by style of the type, regardless of the area which surrounds it or any other circumstance in the key.

LEGEND

Each of the four Phyla is represented by a distinct color. A fifth color has been used to designate Stocks whose affiliation with any of the four Phyla cannot be suggested. The Stocks included in the Phyla could not, for practical reasons, be indicated by some convention on the map. These have been included in the Legend simply for convenience. In cases where Stock and Family names were identical a single term has been used to designate both categories. Each Family has been indicated through the use of a convention which distinguishes it from its neighbors. The color in which this convention is printed indicates the Phyla to which it belongs. Thus the colored conventions found on the map will, when compared with those in the key, indicate the Family, Stock, and Phyla of each enclave.

COMMENTS

During the process of investigating the many problems which had to be solved before this map could be drawn, a considerable body of data was gathered together. Space does not permit an analysis of this voluminous information. The following comments are an abbreviated digest of some of these data which is offered as a partial explanation of some of the more important features of the map.

PHYLUM HOKAN-SIOUAN

Yuman Family

The various members of the Yuman Family have been located principally upon the authority of Jiménez Moreno.[10] Certain modifications in the distribution of the Kiliwa, Akwa'ala and neighboring tribes have been made on the authority of Meigs and Drucker.[11]

[10] Jiménez Moreno, Map, 1936.
[11] Drucker, personal correspondence, 1939.

Tequistlatecan Sub-Stock

This Sub-Stock has been put in parentheses in the Legend because the Family affiliations have not been determined. Its presence in this category is an exception.

The Tequistlatecan lived in the western part of the district of Tehuantepec and the eastern sections of the district of Yautepec in the state of Oaxaca. Thomas [12] says: "The area occupied by them is chiefly in the districts of Tehuantepec, Oaxaca, extending to Guerrero." Since no evidence of continuous distribution can be found, it is assumed that this statement refers to the two extinct enclaves of "Chontal (de Guerrero)" located by Mendizabal and Jiménez.[13] The above locations cannot be transferred to the present map with any degree of accuracy. The source for the statement by Orozco y Berra [14] that Tequistlatecan was spoken in the Department of Tlacolula cannot be found.

SUPANECAN STOCK

Since this Stock cannot be divided into Families it is treated as a combination of both in the Legend. The names of the Languages, Varieties, and Dialects which comprise this Stock will be found in the areas similar in color and convention to the box opposite *Supanecan*.

The Tlapaneco Variety has been shown heretofore as an enclave in east central Guerrero. Lehmann [15] added a second enclave to the southwest, including in it his Tlappaneca-Yopi. Jiménez Moreno and Mendizabal [16] delineate a region which includes the two enclaves located by Lehmann and in addition extends the distribution to the Pacific coast. Relying upon the accuracy of the Mexican maps the area of the Tlapaneco has been adapted to the present map.

The Subtiaba Dialect of the Maribio Variety was encountered by Ponce on the Pacific coast of western Nicaragua.[17] It is not possible to determine the inland boundary. Following Lothrop, the boundary between the Ulva and the Subtiaba has been fixed by the Los Maribios mountain range. Spinden [18] located them on the Plains of Leon, Nicaragua. This however probably refers to their possible former home.

The Maribichicoa Dialect was spoken by people in a restricted

[12] Thomas and Swanton, Languages, 1911, p. 58.
[13] Mendizabal and Jiménez, Map, n.d.
[14] Orozco y Berra, Geografía, 1854, p. 186.
[15] Lehmann, Zentral Amerika, 1920.
[16] Jiménez Moreno, Map, 1936; Mendizabal and Jiménez, Distribucion, 1937.
[17] Lothrop, Costa Rica, 1926, p. 12.
[18] Spinden, Chorotega, 1924.

locality, located by Oviedo [19] on the plains of Leon on the banks of the Guatajiguala River. In view of this information the location indicated by Lehmann [20] may be incorrect.

COAHUILTECAN STOCK

To conserve space the Stock and Family designations have been combined in the Legend. It is quite possible that the several idioms included in the Coahuiltecan Family may have been separate languages. The Coahuiltec, Cotoname, Comecrudo and Carrizo have been located on the present map principally on the authority of Swanton,[21] and Jiménez Moreno.[22]

The Tamaulipecan and Janambrian Families, only possibly divisions of the Coahuiltecan Stock, have been located in accordance with the same sources.

The western boundary of the Coahuiltecan-speaking peoples cannot be located with any degree of certainty. The general consensus of opinion, expressed in particular by Sauer,[23] is that they were probably neighbors of the Chizo. On some maps the Chizo are separated from the Coahuiltecan-speaking peoples by a tongue of Toboso, a people speaking a language closely related to Apache. Existing meagre data concerning these people is very unsatisfactory but it implies that probably this southern penetration did not begin until after the Conquest.

PHYLUM MACRO-OTOMANGUE

Otomian Family

Three enclaves of Otomi correspond with those which were originally located by Orozco y Berra. Mendizabal and Jiménez [24] have modified the boundaries of these groups and added details of their distribution.

The other four enclaves are new to the cartography of the Otomi Language, having been first suggested by Jiménez Moreno.[25] In reference to the location of an enclave of Otomi near the Pacific coast of Jalisco and Colima, Sauer [26] has written: "The existence of Otomi in there is highly probable. It is not only the customary reference

[19] Lothrop, Costa Rica, 1926.
[20] Lehman, Zentral Amerika, 1920.
[21] Swanton, Linguistic Position, 1915; Indian Tribes, 1932.
[22] Jiménez Moreno, Map, 1936.
[23] Sauer Correspondence, 1939.
[24] Mendizabal, Distribucion, 1937.
[25] Jiménez Moreno, Map, 1936.
[26] Sauer, Correspondence, 1939.

to the hill folk in the sixteenth century, but entirely independent sources refer to their speaking the Otomi language; indeed, it is possible that some remnants of an Otomi speech still exists in that section. . . ."

The other Languages belonging to the Otomian Family have been located according to Mendizabal and Jiménez.[27] These correspond to locations determined by other authors with the exception of Matlatzinca, which has been placed farther south. Three additional enclaves in which this Language was spoken have been added to its previously known distribution by Mendizabal and Jiménez.[28]

Unfortunately it was impossible to consult Soustelle [29] in time to include his information here. It is highly probable that the detailed data included in this fundamental work will necessitate a number of modifications on the present map. However if these changes are adopted they should be checked with information dealing with the neighboring regions.

Popolocan Family

It is impossible to ascertain with any degree of certainty the exact extent of the Popoloca Language in the south-central portion of the State of Puebla. The boundaries shown in Thomas [30] correspond to those drawn by Orozco y Berra.[31] These delineations agree with Mendizabal and Jiménez [32] only in the south-central section. In the present map the northern tongue and the western extension indicated by the latter author have been suggested. The eastern extension however has been shortened because there is evidence of a southerly penetration of Nahuatl-speaking people which brought them in contact with the Cuicatec speakers.[33] The situation is at present uncertain and will remain so until it is possible to determine more accurately the distribution and geographical relationship of the Popoloca and other Languages involved at some definite date.

The Ixcatec Language has been located differently by practically every author who has given it important mention. The territory indicated on the present map is adapted from Mendizabal and Jiménez and is comparable to the location in Lehmann.[34] It is based on some indefinite information combined with the apparent possibility that

[27] Mendizabal and Jiménez, Map.
[28] *Ibid.*
[29] Soustelle, Otomi, 1937.
[30] Thomas and Swanton, Languages, 1911.
[31] Orozco y Berra, Geografía, 1864.
[32] Mendizabal and Jiménez, Map.
[33] Thomas and Swanton, Languages, 1911; Mechling, Oaxaca, 1912.
[34] Mendizabal and Jiménez, Map; Lehmann, Zentral Amerika, 1920.

the Language was surrounded by Mixtec. That this is not satisfactory or even correct is obvious. Mechling and Weitlaner place the Ixcatec Language in Santa Maria Ixcatlan which is in the center of the area in which Mazatec is spoken.[35]

The Chocho Language has been located by Orozco y Berra in the Department of Coixtlahuaca which lies in the northwestern part of the state of Oaxaca.[36] This location has been substantiated by subsequent investigators with the exception of Mechling, who adds three towns in the Department of Teposcolula lying to the southwest.[37] Lehmann [38] says that Chocho was spoken in Puebla. The distribution on the present map corresponds to that given by Mendizabal and Jiménez.[39]

The town of Coixtlahuaca in the Department of the same name was, according to Mechling,[40] also inhabited by the Popoloco who spoke a closely related dialect. Another town in the Department of Coixtlahuaca, Santo Domingo Tepene, was also inhabited by the Popoloco. It was impossible to locate these specifically on the present map.

Mixtecan Family

The Mixtec Language was spoken over a large area in western Oaxaca and neighboring Guerrero. The distribution indicated on the present map is adapted from Mendizabal and Jiménez [41] but, except in detail, it differs little from the distribution given by previous authors. Mechling [42] notes that the Mixtec did not cover a continuous area. They were scattered among villages where Mazatec, Zapotec and Chinantec were also spoken. It is not known if this situation existed at the time of the Conquest.

Cuicatecan Family

The Cuicatec Language is located in the district of Cuicatlan in the northern part of Oaxaca. On all maps, excepting the ones published by de Angulo [43] and those recently published in Mexico, it is shown contiguous to Mixtec, Nahuatl, Mazatec, Chinantec, and Zapotec. Satisfactory references to these people are surprisingly meagre. The presence of so many neighbors is distracting. A study of the situation

35 Mechling, Oaxaca, 1912; Weitlaner, Correspondence, 1939.
36 Orozco y Berra, Geografía, 1864.
37 Mechling, Oaxaca, 1912.
38 Lehmann, Zentral Amerika, 1920, p. 903.
39 Mendizabal and Jiménez, Map.
40 Mechling, Oaxaca, 1912.
41 Mendizabal and Jiménez, Map.
42 Mechling, Oaxaca, 1912, p. 656.
43 de Angulo and Freeland, Zapotec, 1934.

resulted in a decision to perpetuate the southwesterly extension of the Chinantec. This necessitates ignoring the possibility of the Cuicatec-Zapotec contact. Apparently the Cuicatec had been living in this locality for a considerable length of time. De Angulo [44] and others believe that as a result of wars with the Mixtec their territory had been reduced to the present size. It is quite possible that the changes in boundaries were responsible for contradictory information regarding contacts with so many neighbors.

Amusgan Family

The Amusgo Language was spoken on the Pacific coast of eastern Guerrero and western Oaxaca. The distribution, adapted from Mendizabal and Jiménez [45] varies but little from that noted by previous authors.

Chinantecan Stock

This is another case where the reference in the Legend is a combination of the methods of designating Stock and Family. The recent available information concerning the Chinantec is only slightly more precise than that supplied by Orozco y Berra. [46] The Language was found in parts of the Departments of Tuxtepec, Ixtlan, Choapam, and probably the northern portion of Villa Alta in the state of Oaxaca. At the present time Mendizabal and Jiménez [47] are the only authorities who locate the southwesterly extension through the Departments of Ixtlan, Etla and Cuicatlan. Mechling [48] indicates that Chinantec was in contact with Mixe, Mendizabal on the other hand, draws a tongue of Zapotec separating Chinantec from Mixe. The extension of the Zapotec is substantiated by de Angulo. [49] In choosing the delineation of Mendizabal and Jiménez it is not assumed that the situation noted by Mechling is erroneous.

Zapotec Stock

Since there are no Family divisions in this Stock the designation for Stock and Family has been combined in the Legend. With the exception of the northern and northeastern boundaries no evidence has come to light in recent years to justify changes in the usual

[44] de Angulo and Freeland, Zapotec, 1934, p. 32.
[45] Mendizabal and Jiménez, Map.
[46] Orozco y Berra, Geografía, 1864.
[47] Mendizabal and Jiménez, Map.
[48] Mechling, Oaxaca, 1912.
[49] de Angulo and Freeland, Zapotec, 1934.

delineation of Zapotec territory. Tentative changes in the Chinantec territory have, in the north, separated the Zapotec from direct contact with the Cuicatec and Mazatec. Moving the northeastern boundary to the west, as Mendizabal and Jiménez [50] have done, indicates that the Zapotec were not in contact with the Popoloca de Puebla or the Chocho. Lack of detailed data makes it impossible to offer reasons for or against this change.

De Angulo [51] separates the Zapotec Language into three dialects. A distribution of these is indicated on the present map. This delineation may be taking liberties with available information, for the boundaries, as they are drawn, do not correspond exactly with the distribution noted by Angulo. If Mendizabal and Jiménez are correct it may be assumed that the differences between the maps is due to changes coincident with the advance of European civilization. The easterly tongue of Zapotec between Chinantec and Mixe may have existed before the Conquest. In following de Angulo's divisions of the Zapotec into dialects, this tongue becomes a section of "Zapotec of the Northern Mountains." There are no data to prove this rather bold assumption.

Another difficulty of the same nature has to do with the geographical relationship between the Zapotec, Chocho and Nahuatl. Following Mendizabal and Jiménez the northwestern boundary of the Zapotec is located at the southwestern corner of the Chinantec. De Angulo, showing a smaller area for the neighbors of the Zapotecs, carries the boundary to the southwestern corner of the Chocho, permitting a tongue of Zapotec to extend to the southern boundary of the Nahuatl-speaking people. It has been necessary to choose arbitrarily the source for these delineations and, since Mendizabal and Jiménez attempt a Pre-Spanish distribution and de Angulo possibly represents a more recent distribution, the formers' judgment has been selected. The wisdom, in fact the basis, for this choice rests upon the documentation of the Mendizabal and Jiménez map.

Thomas,[52] following a statement made by Orozco y Berra,[53] locates the Chatino Language in the Departments of Jamiltepec and Centro in Oaxaca. Orozco y Berra, in addition to mention of the departments, lists the towns in which Chatino was spoken. This author mentions a number of towns in the Department of Juquila and these correspond roughly to the locations from which vocabularies have been collected. Lehmann [54] restricts Chatino to an inland enclave which appears to

[50] Mendizabal and Jiménez, Map.
[51] de Angulo and Freeland, Zapotec, 1934.
[52] Thomas and Swanton, Languages, 1911.
[53] Orozco y Berra, Geografía, 1864.
[54] Lehmann, Zentral Amerika, 1920.

extend further north than is indicated in any other reference to it. He offers no explanation for this distribution.

De Angulo [55] locates Chatino "in a mountainous area bordering the Pacific Ocean." This distribution corresponds roughly with that given by Mechling, and it is supported by Boas [56] and Mendizabal and Jiménez. Since the testimony of recent vocabularies places Chatino in parts of the Department of Juquila it has been so located on the map. The question of the wider, more westerly and northerly distribution, mentioned by previous authors, can only be settled by the early documents.

Jiménez Moreno and Mendizabal and Jiménez do not record the Papabuco Dialect, neither is this to be found on the present map.[57] Lehmann locates an enclave in which this dialect was spoken and implies that it was synonymous with Chatino. The available data on the Dialect is so meagre that it seems wiser to follow Orozco y Berra and consider them unclassifiable. This Dialect, if it can be proved to be such, is now spoken only in Elotepec along with Chatino.

The Soltec Dialect is an obscure idiom which may be closely allied to Zapotec proper. The only satisfactory location for it is found in Mechling who places it in the District of Zancatlan, Oaxaca, in the southwestern part of the territory occupied by the Zapotec of the Valleys. It is obviously the modern distribution. Apparently nothing is known of their earlier home.

PHYLUM MACRO PENUTIAN

With the exception of the Nahuatlan Sub-Family and a few minor notes on the details of distribution, the various divisions of the Utaztecan Stock, as they are incorporated in the present map, have been copied entirely from Sauer [58] with some additions from Kroeber.[59] The careful and detailed work of Sauer together with the additional information offered by Kroeber is the best and most complete that is available at the present moment.

Aztecoidan Family

No one is aware of the indefinite and contradictory character of the information concerning the Guachichil Language (?) better than the author. There appears to be some doubt even that the name should

[55] de Angulo and Freeland, Zapotec, 1934, p. 35.
[56] Boas, Chatino, 1913.
[57] Jiménez Moreno, Map, 1936; Mendizabal and Jiménez, Map.
[58] Sauer, Distribution of Languages, 1934.
[59] Kroeber, Uto-Aztecan, 1934.

be given a significant place on the map. In spite of the fact that so little is known of it, there seems to be little doubt but what some language related to the Aztecoidan Family was spoken in the vast region to which this name has been applied. The extent has varied greatly during different periods in its history and a demarcation of the boundaries is but a guess, probably a bad one. The boundaries on the present map are adapted from Orozco y Berra and Thomas with modifications taken from Kroeber 1934 and Jiménez Moreno.[60] In spite of these sources, the boundaries must remain tentative until more complete information is obtainable.

In presenting the details of the distribution of the Nahuatlan Sub-Family the present map differs radically from most of the previous maps. The wide strip of territory extending westward along the Pacific Coast was first broken up by Lehmann.[61] Jiménez Moreno and Mendizabal and Jiménez have gone one step further.[62] Through the enlargement of some enclaves, notably the Cuitlatec, and by the identification of a number of extinct tribes whose languages are unknown, the Nahua distribution has been restricted to a number of localized enclaves. In other sections a number of enclaves have been added by Mendizabal and Jiménez. One hesitates to perpetuate these somewhat radical assertions of the Mexican cartographers presented as they were without documentary proof but, since recent work suggests the probability of their accuracy, they are offered here as plausible though unproved possibilities.

The Desaguadero and Sigua are two enclaves on the Caribbean Coast of Costa Rica in which some idiom of Nahuatlan was spoken. The dialect may have been either Aztec, Pipil, or some variant.

The Nahuat Language includes scattered enclaves. Several groups of Pipil have been identified. Innovations on the present map include a change in the eastern boundary to conform to the findings of Lothrop.[63] Since these decisions are based upon archaeological discoveries, as well as upon interpretations of early records, their use on a linguistic map must remain tentative. The enclave of Pipil in the northern part of Honduras south of Trujillo has been included tentatively. This group was located by Lehmann, but the proof of its existence is obscure and extremely doubtful.

The areas occupied by dialects such as the Nahuatlato, Bagaces and Nicarao have been located in their established regions. The only

[60] Orozco y Berra, Geografía, 1864; Thomas and Swanton, Languages, 1911; Kroeber, Uto-Aztecan, 1934; Jiménez Moreno, Map, 1936.
[61] Lehmann, Zentral Amerika, 1920.
[62] Jiménez Moreno, Map, 1936; Mendizabal and Jiménez, Map.
[63] Lothrop, Maya Frontier, 1939.

question which surrounds them involves the details of their linguistic relationship and the exact extent of their boundaries.

The location of Teco-Tecoxquin, an idiom whose place in the Nahua group is tentative, has been indicated by Mendizabal and Jiménez. Some difficulty is experienced in placing the enclave surrounded by Cora and Huichol in southern Tepic and northern Jalisco. The combined maps of Mendizabal and Jiménez, Sauer and Kroeber place the Teco-Tecoxquin immediately west of the Cazcan. The difficulty seems to lie in the determination of the Cora and Huichol boundaries. It is possible, if not probable, that a documentation of the Mendizabal and Jiménez map, which might supply dates for the boundaries given, would clarify the problem and prove that the present map is erroneous.

Our knowledge of the distribution of the Cazcan and Coca Languages, including the Tecuexe Variety, is at present incomplete. One Cazcan enclave, located by Kroeber has been modified by Mendizabal and Jiménez. This Language has been noted by Orozco y Berra and Thomas. The second enclave, to the west of the first Cazcan area, has been located by Mendizabal and Jiménez. Since the latter seem to have drawn their boundaries from Jiménez Moreno's work and also from Davila Garibi,[64] this group seems sufficiently well established. The possible difficulty with this location is the date which it represents. Because of difficulties with the different scales of the several maps and the lack of points of orientation in the Mendizabal and Jiménez map the boundaries of the area are by no means accurate; they simply indicate the existence of this idiom in this locality. The contact between the Cazcan and the Tecual may be of some historical interest.

The boundaries of the Lagunero on the west are established by the indefinite boundary of the Concho and the incompletely authenticated limits of the Tepehuan. The southern boundary along which they came in contact with the Zacatec and Guachichil is but tentatively located. Since the northern boundary is that of the practically unknown Coahuiltecan-speaking people even the dotted line on the present map is hardly justifiable.

The western boundary of the Zacatec Variety is determined by the eastern boundary of the Tepehuan. The eastern boundary is as indefinite as is the western boundary of the neighboring Guachichil. The boundary given has been adapted from Mendizabal and Jiménez and Kroeber, but this must be considered as tentative in the extreme.

There is considerable difficulty in distinguishing the boundary be-

[64] Davila Garibi, Idioma Coca, 1935.

tween the territories in which Tepecan and Tepehuan were spoken. On the basis of the Sauer and Kroeber maps the northern, eastern, and western boundaries have been tentatively established. The southern boundary of the Tepecan is even more indefinite. Their distribution, as well as that of their neighbors, the Cazcan, has not been completely studied. The boundary indicated by Mendizabal and Jiménez has been adapted to the present map.

Mayoid Family

The location of the Huaxtec Language has changed but little during the course of many delineations. The most recent, possibly important, modification of the boundary is found in Mendizabal and Jiménez [65] and has been incorporated in the present map. Heretofore Janambre has been shown separated from Huaxtec and now, with no reasons given, the two Languages are shown in contact along a section of the northern border.

The Chicomuceltec Language has been located by Mendizabal and Jiménez in the extreme southeastern part of Chiapas. This location has been adapted to the present map.

A variation of the Yucatec Variety of Maya, the Itza, was spoken in northern Yucatan, especially in the vicinity of Chichen Itza, until just before the Conquest. The people eventually moved to Flores, the present capital of the Peten. Because of several complications coincident with their migration it is not practical to locate them at the time of the Conquest. They have been placed in their Pre-Conquest habitat.

The divisions of the Yucatec-speaking Maya are relatively indistinct. Little or nothing is definitely known of the linguistic relationships of the Icaiche. They have been tentatively located in the environs of the town of the same name in southern Campeche. The Santa Cruz, closely identified with the Yucatec, were found around the Bahia Ascención in northeastern Yucatan. The Mopan have been located southeast of Lake Peten from information supplied by Thompson.[66]

The Yucatec-speaking Lacandon were the ancestors of the people who introduced this Variety into the valley of the Usumacintla River. All we know is that they originally came from the northeast, displacing people also called Lacandon, who, according to Thompson, spoke a Chol dialect. Since we know nothing of the original Yucatec speakers, they have been located tentatively simply to indicate their existence.

[65] Mendizabal and Jiménez, Map.
[66] Thompson, Chol Mayas, 1938, p. 582.

Thompson [67] has provided an excellent discussion of the distribution of the various groups who probably spoke Choloid Languages. The locations on the present map are adapted from this work. This author has seen fit to include the Chontal of Tabasco with the Chol speakers. While this is acceptable, it seems wise, in the presence of conflicting opinions, to suggest a slight difference in speech.

The inclusions of the Toquegua with the Chol may be ill-advised. Thompson seems willing to accept this identification but Lothrop [68] claims that nothing is known of their speech beyond the practical certainty that they spoke some Mayan tongue.

The Chañabal, and Tzotzil Languages have been located by Mendizabal and Jiménez. [69] The Chuj Language has been located by Thomas [70] and no subsequent data have shown reason for modification.

The areas in which the Motozintlec and Jacaltec Languages were spoken are rather indefinite. Motozintlec was probably common in extreme southeastern Chiapas and across the border in Guatemala. Jacaltec certainly was spoken in the northwestern corner of Guatemala, but its extent at the time of the Conquest is not clear.

Quichoid Family

The Mam Language and its Dialects occupied the southeastern section of Guatemala. A boundary for this language is indicated for convenience only; probably no definite one ever existed.

Aguacatec II is located by Lehmann and Mendizabal and Jiménez, who agree that it was related to Zoque. [71] Thomas and Rivet [72] include this Language with the Maya. It appears that the latter identification is slightly more justifiable.

The locations of the members of the Kekchom group have been adapted from Thomas, whose information has not been superseded. Slight changes in boundary have been made in order to indicate which groups were neighbors of the others.

The Pokom Language may consist of a single Variety, Pokoman, for Pokonchi seems to be very closely allied. Lothrop [73] has shown that almost certainly there were four enclaves of Pokoman-speaking Maya in El Salvador.

[67] Thompson, Chol Mayas, 1938.
[68] Lothrop, Maya Frontier, 1939.
[69] Mendizabal and Jiménez, Map.
[70] Thomas and Swanton, Languages, 1911.
[71] Lehmann, Zentral Amerika, 1920; Mendizabal and Jiménez, Map.
[72] Thomas and Swanton, Languages, 1911; Rivet, Langues de l'Amérique Centrale, 1924.
[73] Lothrop, Maya Frontier, 1939.

Mixe-Zoquean Family

The ideas regarding extent of the territory in which the Mixe Language was spoken have changed but little during the development of its literature. The names of Dialects which Rivet [74] obtained from Lehmann [75] could not be located on the present map because they could not be found on any available map.

Information concerning the existence of a language called Popoloca de Vera Cruz is scarcely more than a rumor. This language, or at least the people who are reputed to have spoken it, is mentioned by Rivet, but his record of it is not clear. It has been entered on the present map upon the authority of Mendizabal and Jiménez.

The territory in which the Zoque language was spoken has scarcely been changed on any map since Thomas. That indicated on the present map has been adapted from Mendizabal and Jiménez, who show modifications of the eastern boundary due to extensions of the territories occupied by the Chiapanec, Tzotzil, and Chol.

Opinions regarding Huave territory have changed but little during the course of various investigations. The boundaries on the present map are adapted from Mendizabal and Jiménez who indicate maximum easterly extension along the Pacific Coast of Oaxaca into western Chiapas.

TOTONACAN, XINCAN, LENCAN

These three Stocks have been included in the Legend as a combination of Stock and Family designation under the Macro-Penutian Phylum. It might have been more accurate to add these to the list of stocks grouped under "Unaffiliated Stocks," but there is some slight suggestion that they are related to the Macro-Penutian. The proof for the assumption that their affiliation with the Macro-Penutian is uncertain is not yet sufficient to permit profitable discussion.

Totonacan Family

Aside from minor variations in the boundaries and also with the exception of the encroachment of the Otomi enclave to the northwest, the area on the map in which Totonac was spoken remains practically identical with that originally drawn by Orozco y Berra.[76]

[74] Rivet, Langues de l'Amerique Centrale, 1924.
[75] Lehmann, Zentral Amerika, 1920.
[76] Orozco y Berra, Geografía, 1864.

Xincan Family

Concerning the Xinca Lothrop [77] says, "In the sixteenth century the Xinca dwelt on the southern side of Guatemala from the Rio de los Esclavos eastward to the present border of El Salvador and from the coast up into the high mountains."

On several maps the Xinca are shown to surround a small enclave most frequently located in the central and eastern part of their territory. The identification of this foreign group has varied with the whims of several investigators. Occasionally it has been shown as Lenca and, frequently, affiliation with the Xinca has been indicated. The first problem to be solved is, who are these people? The illusory term Popoluca has been applied to them and perhaps the term "Pupuluca de Conguaco" is more definitive. The scant references to this group give them a mythical character. Franz Termer, describing his discoveries during a recent sojourn in the region, wrote to Lothrop in June 1939, saying that the enigmatical Popoloca settled on the southern slope of the Moyuta volcano. He adds that they possibly spoke only a dialect of the Xinca Language. This possibility is cause for the inclusion of this group with the Xinca.

Lencan Family

That the Lenca inhabited a large part of Central Honduras, reaching to the Pacific at the Gulf of Fonseca, cannot be questioned. The actual boundaries are however difficult to determine. On the present map they have been determined by the limits of their neighbors. The western boundary is fairly well fixed by the eastern extension of the Maya. The other boundaries are simply arbitrary divisions between neighboring languages.

PHYLUM MACRO-CHIBCHAN

Justifiable criticism may be leveled at the choice of names used to distinguish the elusive and little-known linguistic units which comprise the Mosumalpan Stock. The use of these spellings, many of which are obviously of German derivation, is in tribute to Conzemius who has supplied by far the greatest amount of information concerning these people. This author has identified groups which it seems likely have not been mentioned in the English or Spanish literature and thus it seemed wise to use his terms throughout, rather than confuse the issue by attempting to Anglicize a few.

[77] Lothrop, Maya Frontier, 1939, pp. 42-43.

Mosquitoan Family

Conzemius [78] suggests the probability that the Mosquito were originally a subtribe of the Sumo. Conzemius [79] derives the present day Mosquito from a mixture of Sumo and slaves captured from a Portuguese ship wrecked in 1641. If such an incredible circumstance can be proved to be the truth, the separating of the Mosquito from the Sumo on this map, purporting to date at the time of the Conquest, would not be justifiable. However, since this testimony is so tenuous and the statements of a few linguists are to the contrary, they are enclosed by boundaries.

The separation of the various names on the map into Dialects is not wholly justifiable. The literature has not distinguished carefully between linguistic and political divisions. Inconsistently, the map here shows divisions which may be more important politically than linguistically. It is expected, however, that certain political divisions will be reflected in a careful linguistic classification.

The Mam are said to have occupied the region about the Laguna Caratasca. The boundaries of the region in which the Mam Dialect of the Mosquito Language was spoken are open to question. It is possible that the Mosquito have expanded since 1600, so impinging upon Paya territory. Also it is not impossible that both Languages were spoken in the same region. South of the Mam, at the mouth of the Wanks River, lived the Wanki. In recent times the Wanki have followed up the river as far as Bocay. Conzemius [80] identifies a group which lived on Sandy Bay which he calls Baldam. He says that they hardly differ from the Kabo and Tauira. The Kabo extended southward from Sandy Bay as far as the Rio Grande. The Tauira lived inland from the Kabo and between the Wanks and the Prinzapolca Rivers. The early inhabitants of the southern part of the Mosquito territory are barely mentioned. Authorities disagree concerning the actual limits. That selected for the present map represents the northern boundary of the Rama who, according to Lothrop,[81] now occupy an island in the Bluefields Lagoon. It is possible that this latter occupation is the result of a Post-Conquest migration to the north. It is impossible to determine the interior (western) boundary of the Mosquito because of the absence of data. On the present map the arbitrary boundary has been adapted from Thomas and Lehmann.[82]

[78] Conzemius, Miskito and Sumu, 1932, p. 17.
[79] Conzemius, Notes on Miskito and Sumu, 1929, p. 58.
[80] Conzemius, Notes on Miskito and Sumu, 1929.
[81] Lothrop, Costa Rica, 1926, p. 17.
[82] Thomas and Swanton, Languages, 1911; Lehmann, Zentral Amerika, 1920.

Suman Family

The Sumo occupied a large portion of Nicaragua and sections of El Salvador and Honduras. The many names for the apparently numerous groups of Sumo are confusing. In the case of the Yosko, as with other tribes, the only locations given are river valleys. The boundary lines have been added simply for convenience.

Matagalpan Family

The most definite information concerning the location of this group is that placing them in a region surrounding the town of Matagalpa, Nicaragua. There is no doubt that this language was more widely distributed but definite information concerning the extent is completely lacking. Conzemius [83] says that they formerly occupied the western region of the Mosquito Coast and he also cites the village of Cacaopera and Lislique in El Salvador where the Cacaopera Dialect was spoken. Lehmann [84] shows an extension of Matagalpan northwest to Danli in east central Honduras. An indication of this wider distribution for this Family might be wise. On the other hand, such a procedure would disrupt the distribution of the Sumo and perhaps Mosquito tribes, for which the information is only slightly more precise. The Sumo-speaking Boa, for instance, are said to have lived on the headwaters of the Rio Grande,[85] a statement which in itself is indefinite. However, this location might be interpreted as indicating a section of the territory said also to be occupied by the Matagalpa. It is obvious that the reason for this confusion is our lack of knowledge of the migrations of the many groups.

The implications of the greater distribution of the Matagalpan Language are interesting, perhaps quite important. On the one hand, a direct contact with the Lenca to the west should not be ignored and, on the other, the proximity to the Rama and other Chibchan speaking peoples is not without its significance. The implied separation of the Ulva from the Sumo should also not be forgotten.

CHIBCHAN STOCK

The situation in regard to the members of the Chibchan Stock to be found in southern Central America is deplorable. With the exception of the people in Costa Rica and the surrounding regions whose political and, to a considerable extent linguistic, affiliations were determined by Lothrop,[86] very little trustworthy information has been

[83] Conzemius, Notes on Miskito and Sumu, 1929, p. 57.
[84] Lehmann, Zentral Amerika, 1920.
[85] Conzemius, Miskito and Sumu, 1932, p. 15.
[86] Lothrop, Costa Rica, 1926.

published. In the great work of Lehmann [87] there is to be found a considerable amount of information but, unfortunately, this does not stand up under minute analysis. The author has confused the names of groups with those of caciques and other famous personages and also it appears that the information which he has obtained is not altogether complete. For the purposes of the present map this situation should have been investigated thoroughly, but time and resources did not permit. The present arrangement is essentially a combination of Lothrop and a preliminary analysis of Lehmann's work. It is to be hoped that further work in this area will completely clarify the situation.

UNAFFILIATED STOCKS

JICAQUEAN

Very little concerning the territory occupied by the Jicaque has been added to that indicated by Thomas.[88] The boundaries have been adapted from this map with slight modifications. Because of the location of the eastern boundary of the Maya, the western boundary of the Jicaque has been moved to the east of the Ulua River. It is recognized that the former has been drawn principally from the results of archaeological investigations, but until more substantial linguistic or documentary data are available, this will have to suffice. The restriction of the southeastern frontier is due to Lehmann's identification of a Lenca group in what Thomas indicated to be Jicaque territory.

PAYAN

The descriptions of the locations of the Paya are very confusing indeed. The only one which seems certain is the western boundary on the north coast, the Aguan River, and Conzemius 1928 adds that they did not extend beyond 86 degrees east of Greenwich. Nothing concerning the southern boundary can be found in the modern literature, and so the boundary on the present map has been arbitrarily drawn simply for convenience. The various authorities contradict themselves and each other in their attempts to locate the eastern boundary. Practically every one states that the Paya extended as far as Cabo Gracias a Dios or the Wanks River, but all maps draw the boundary at the Patuka River. Since the Mam division of the Mosquito are, upon reasonably good authority [89] reported as living in the region

[87] Lehmann, Zentral Amerika, 1920.
[88] Thomas and Swanton, Languages, 1911.
[89] Lehmann, op. cit.; Rivet, Langues de l'Amerique Centrale, 1929; Conzemius, Notes on Miskito and Sumu, 1929.

around the Laguna Caratasca, the western boundary of the Paya is left at the Patuka on the present map.

TARASCAN

The area in which this language was spoken was previously illustrated as more restricted than that shown on the present map. The enlargement of the boundaries is after Jiménez Moreno and Mendizabal and Jiménez.[90] The delineation of the western boundary, taken from the latter authority, is a radical departure from the previous ones.

[90] Jiménez Moreno, Map, 1936; Mendizabal and Jiménez, Map.

PART II
THE MAYA

VII

ARCHAEOLOGICAL PROBLEMS OF THE HIGHLAND MAYA

A. V. Kidder *

THE HIGHLANDS of Guatemala, here defined as those parts of the republic at an altitude of over 2,000 feet, extend, a rugged but continuous mass, the entire east-west width of the country. They parallel and rise abruptly from the narrow Pacific coast plain, edged by a line of lofty and geologically young volcanoes, some of which are still active. Behind these peaks and buried to the shoulders in ash thrown from them is an older, time-smoothed volcanic complex, its valleys filled basin-like with ash. To the north and northwest the highlands culminate in the still more ancient crystalline and metamorphic massif of the Cuchumatanes. Many short rivers flow directly to the Pacific from the southern volcanic rampart. The Atlantic drainage consists of much longer systems heading deep in the mountains: the Motagua, Polochic, and Sarstun emptying into the Caribbean; the Ixcan, Negro, and Cancuen uniting in the plains of Peten to form the Usumacinta and drain to the Gulf of Mexico. The climate above about 4,000 feet is temperate to cool.

The highlands occupy so strategic a position in the lower Cordilleran backbone of the continent, and between the Pacific coast plain and the great jungles of the Peten, that they must hold the key to many of the most important archaeological problems, not only of Guatemala, but of all Middle America. But because students have, until very recently, devoted the lion's share of their attention to the Maya ruins of the Peten and Yucatan, and to those of the more advanced cultures of central Mexico, the relatively unspectacular sites in these highlands have largely been neglected. The region, however, contains abundance of remains, few of which have been described and these, for the most part, rather superficially. There has been very little systematic excavation.

* Harvard, A.B., 1908; A.M., 1912; Ph.D., 1914; Austin teaching fellow, 1910, 1912–1914; Curator of North American Archaeology, Peabody Museum; now Chairman, Division of Historical Research, Carnegie Institution of Washington.

No trace of the pioneer tribes that drifted southward for the original settlement of South America has as yet come to light in the highlands, or, indeed, anywhere else between the Rio Grande and Panama. It is, of course, possible that this doubtless slow and long-continued series of migrations was confined to the Pacific coast. But the open uplands, while lacking the abundant fish-resources of the littoral, and perhaps also less well supplied with game, could hardly have failed to serve at least as a secondary route; and even if not used as a highway for travel, it would seem that some people must very early have eddied or been pushed into the mountain valleys—always granted that conditions therein were comparable to those of today. Uncertainty on that point makes present speculation as to ancient human occupancy hazardous, for we are woefully ignorant of the time factor in the volcanological history of the region, which may well have been rendered utterly uninhabitable, perhaps for centuries at a time, by the furious eruptions that repeatedly have blanketed the highlands with ash. Nevertheless, extremely significant information regarding early New World man may well be derived from the highlands. It therefore behooves all workers to be on the lookout for pre-ceramic remains and, if such be found, to enlist the aid of geologists for determination of their age.

Passing upward in time, the next archaeological problem upon which research in the Guatemala highlands may be expected to throw light concerns the rise of New World civilization. This phenomenon was explained by Spinden as follows: all the more advanced American cultures were based on maize; maize was derived from *teocinte*, a plant native only to Middle America; the oldest aboriginal farming culture, the Archaic, occurs in the Valley of Mexico; *ergo*, Indian civilization was born in, and spread out from, the latter region.

Spinden's hypothesis has been of great service in focusing attention upon a question of fundamental importance, but it involved several assumptions upon which subsequent consideration has thrown serious doubt. The Mexican Archaic, for example, has been shown by Lothrop and Vaillant to be much too highly developed to be a basically ancestral culture. It must have sprung from something simpler, and no evidence of such a forerunner has been found in the area. Another argument against Spinden's evaluation of the Archaic is that there is a sprinkling, in various later Middle American cultures, of traits apparently not derived from the Archaic. These, lumped by Lothrop and Vaillant pending identification of their actual source under the non-committal term "Q," they suspect to represent a northward drift of southern, possibly trans-Isthmian, influences. If this view be accepted, the Archaic can naturally not be held solely responsible for all post-Archaic developments. Furthermore, Spinden's interpretation of the rôle of maize may be incorrect. That cereal may not have been fathered by *teocinte*, but may have descended from a hitherto undiscovered, or possibly extinct, wild ancestor, perhaps native to South America. Again, the basic impetus of Indian progress could have been supplied by some other plant; and maize, coming under cultivation relatively late, might, because of its obvious value, have spread rapidly over both continents. In that case, the Middle American habitat of *teocinte* would lose significance as an indicator of the place of origin of New World civilization. Lastly, it is conceivable that Middle and South American developments had independent beginnings; and that maize, having stimulated the one or the other, eventually became common property by diffusion.

The foregoing review is necessary to make clear the bearings of Guatemala highlands archaeology upon the Archaic problem. For that region contains remains which, although their age relative to the Mexican Archaic is not clear, are unquestionably connected in some way therewith. These belong to the Miraflores culture, so called because first found at, and still best known from, the Finca Miraflores, a part of the great archaeological site of Kaminaljuyú, in the outskirts of Guatemala City. Miraflores is characterized by excellent pottery; polished red; polished black with delicately incised designs; Usulutan, a yellowish ware with wavy decoration in lighter colored lines. It also yields many hand-modeled clay figurines. As to its architecture, either secular or religious, all information is lacking. Miraflores pottery, although readily distinguishable from that of the Mexican Archaic, appears to belong to the same general prepolychrome horizon; and Miraflores figurines strongly resemble those from the Valley of Mexico.

The nature of the thus-evident relationship between Miraflores and the Mexican Archaic is a matter of much importance. Does Miraflores represent, as Spinden and Gamio held, a southward spread of the Archaic? Is it a contemporary manifestation of an early, widespread, autochthonous culture of the Middle American highlands? Or is it the outgrowth of a southern culture gradually working its way northward?

None of the above queries can at present be answered. But had we the detailed knowledge of the content and the development of Miraflores that Vaillant's splendid stratigraphic and analytical researches have given us of its Mexican congener, comparative study might yield reliable results. Work similar to Vaillant's must therefore be done in Guatemala, not only at Finca Miraflores, but throughout the highlands, as well as in Mexico south of the Valley. And investigators in all parts of Middle America should be on the alert for evidence of more primitive pre-Archaic, pre-Miraflores cultures. If such never come to light we shall be forced to postulate a South American origin, or to believe, with Gladwin, in a transplantation from the Old World.

Particular attention, in such search, should be devoted to those parts of the highlands not blanketed by patently recent deposits of volcanic ash. The Miraflores remains at Kaminaljuyú were laid down subsequent to the latest falls in that immediate vicinity, but Lothrop has reported material of comparable age, from beneath ash in Salvador. Thus, large parts of the southern highlands may have been uninhabitable during the period when Miraflores, if autochthonous, was passing through its developmental stages. If so, evidence of those stages may exist in areas less subject to the eruptions of the coastal volcanoes. One of several highland regions which might repay investigation is that about San Antonio Huixta on the northwestern slopes of the Cuchumatanes, for there, as Kempton and Popenoe have reported, *teocinte* is found in maximum abundance. However, the distribution of *teocinte* may likewise have been affected by volcanic activity. As in study of early man in the highlands, we are again hampered by our present ignorance of the age and extent of the ash falls.

We must leave in this most unsatisfactory state the question of Archaic-Miraflores ancestry, with its immensely important implications for New World prehistory. Continuing still further upward in time, we find ourselves in somewhat better case. For there can be little doubt that the presumably widespread, and apparently relatively uniform culture represented in the Valley of Mexico by the Archaic and in Guatemala by Miraflores, gave rise to the later Middle American civilizations. There is no evidence, beyond the presence of the somewhat nebulous "Q" traits, that, in fundamentals, their development was stimulated or shaped by influences from without. No abrupt cultural break is perceptible, nor any chronological hiatus. Vaillant, indeed, has followed Archaic up to the beginnings of Teotihuacan; and Ricketson, at Uaxactun, found deposits with Miraflores-like figurines lying directly below remains foreshadowing Old Empire Maya. The process, then, was seemingly the archaeologically familiar one of the crystallization, from a more primitive and more generalized forerunner, of a number of locally specialized higher cultures.

Future research will unquestionably show that this interpretation of our at present scanty data is over-simplistic. But, as did Spinden's hypothesis, it may serve to define specific problems, the most immediate of which concern the postulated growth, from the complex typified by Archaic and Miraflores, of the classic Maya and highland cultures.

It has long been inferred that Maya development resulted from a downward drift of maize agriculture into the Peten plains, where warm climate, abundant rainfall, and fertile soils favored production of larger crops than could be grown in the highlands. And Ricketson's discovery of Miraflores-like figurines in the deepest deposits at Uaxactun has reinforced this opinion. But proof is still lacking. It is, for example, quite possible that lowland agriculture, with manioc as the staple, worked up the tropical east coast from the Amazon-Orinoco region to foster early Middle American civilization; and that the subsequent discovery or introduction of maize allowed its spread into the highlands.

If there was a transference of culture either upward or down, its passage must have been by way of the northern slopes of the highlands. And the movement could not have been other than gradual. It is inconceivable that a stone-age people could quickly have conquered, for farming purposes, the Peten jungle; or that tropical methods of agriculture rapidly invaded the cooler, drier intermontane basins. The topographically transitional areas in the northern parts of Alta Verapaz, Quiché, and Huehuetenango may therefore be expected to yield evidence regarding the direction and the nature of any cultural drift which took place.

These areas also need careful investigation for determination of subsequent relations between the lowlands and the highlands. At present it would appear that Maya civilization burst suddenly into full flower in the Uaxactun-Tikal district of northern Peten, where we find the earliest stelae, bearing dates in the already perfected calendar, as well as the apparently oldest examples of the typical Maya vault. One must, however, be on guard against the common tendency to identify as the place of its origin the region where any given trait or complex is first discovered. And so one should not conclude too hastily that northern Peten was the hearth of classic Maya culture. Southern Peten is archaeologically next to unknown. Nor should the highlands themselves be disregarded. From that direction J. E. Thompson, R. E. Smith, and Anna Shepard are beginning to suspect that repeated waves of ceramic influence may have flowed into the Peten. The Maya calendar, too, would seem more likely to have come into being under open upland skies than in forested plains. The vault, however, as Gamio has pointed out, could hardly have developed in the seismic southern district, although the beginnings of stone architecture might have been made in the less disturbed northern highlands.

The trouble is that we know so little of highland archaeology. But that they hold the clue to much that is now obscure has been demonstrated by Carnegie Institution's recent work at Kaminaljuyú.

In tombs at that site were found vessels proving that the early Maya Old Empire (Tzakol ceramic phase of R. E. Smith) was contemporaneous with a well-developed stage of the Teotihuacan ("Toltec") culture of Mexico (Plate IV). Contemporaneity of Teotihuacan and Old Empire had already been suspected, on the basis of a few polychrome sherds collected by Linné at Teotihuacan, but at that time the succession of Peten pottery types was not sufficiently understood to permit determination of what Old Empire horizon was represented. The more abundant and positive data from Kaminaljuyú are accordingly of great value for interpretation of Middle American prehistory in upsetting the rather generally held belief that Teotihuacan was a post-Old Empire and Maya-inspired development. This in turn emphasizes the need for greater knowledge of Archaic-Miraflores, from which, it now appears, must have come the basic elements common to both Teotihuacan and Old Empire Maya.

Another vital problem toward whose solution highlands remains promise to contribute, is that of the correlation of Maya and Christian chronology. This, as has been pointed out in a recent paper by J. E. Thompson and the writer, depends upon connecting the ceramic phases of the Old Empire, datable in the Maya calendar, with the dendrochronologically dated cultures of southwestern United States. The Tzakol phase of the Old Empire has, through Kaminaljuyú, already been correlated with Teotihuacan. Further work in the highlands should also reveal the time relationship between earlier and later Peten phases and pre- and post-Teotihuacan cultures in central Mexico. That having been accomplished, studies in northern Mexico should complete the Peten-Southwest chronological linkage.

The Kaminaljuyú materials, both ceramic and architectural, indicate that, during Old Empire times, the southern highlands were much more closely connected with Mexico than with the Peten. One strongly suspects actual waves of influence from Mexico, but in this case again it is necessary to guard against too hasty conclusions based upon our prior knowledge of and greater familiarity with Teotihuacan and Monte Alban. The writer nevertheless believes, because of the apparently higher developments in Mexico, and because native chronicles seem to show that in the proto-historic period there occurred a succession of movements from that direction, that Mexican stimuli were preponderant in shaping the growth of the later cultures in the southern highlands (Pls. IV, V, XII, Fig. 25).

In other parts of the highlands, however, the situation may have been different. The writer has seen pottery from northern Huehuetenango that was surely Maya-inspired; and at Quen Santo is a typical Old Empire site with stelae dated at 10.2.5.0.0. and 10.2.10.0.0. In Alta Verapaz, as might be expected from its remoteness from Mexico and its accessibility to Peten, Maya ceramic influences are strong. The writer, however, can see no evidence for the mass migration from Peten into the highlands, at the close of the Old Empire, which has been postulated by certain students.

We have considered, so far, only contacts from the west and north. But in the east and to the south there existed cultures which, at one time or another, doubtless affected or were affected by those of the highlands. Of these, perhaps the most interesting is that which produced the remarkable sculpture of the Pacific coast plain.

All in all, the Guatemala highlands, subsequent to the Archaic-Miraflores era (and quite possibly even then), would seem to have been a meeting and mixing ground, rather than a mother of culture.

But, to continue the warning note, it should be remembered that this is often one's first impression of a little-understood area lying between regions whose remains are better known. In any case, however, there can be no question regarding the outstandingly great importance of highland archaeology, nor as to the need for its more intensive investigation, with a view to more precise definition of the content and geographic range of cultures of all periods.

Although the field is so nearly virgin that additional data of any sort are welcome, certain categories of information are particularly urgently required. As has already been stressed, we should know something about the age and extent of volcanological activity. Search should be made for pre-Miraflores remains; and as it is most desirable to have actually datable material from which to work backward, excavation should be done at Utatlan, Iximché, Mixco Viejo, and other sites known to have been occupied at the time of the Conquest. Finally, more intimate acquaintance with the antiquities of the Pacific coast is greatly needed, for there is good evidence that along the coast there passed, and in places there settled, groups of Nahua-speaking people: in early times the Pipil, later the colonizing Aztecs. And Pipil, presumably from the coast, settled in the Motagua Valley and Alta Verapaz. The range of the Pipil, at the time of the Conquest, is fairly well delimited. Pipil settlements can therefore doubtless be located, and their culture, of which we are as yet almost entirely ignorant, can be described. It will then probably be possible to determine whether that culture was wholly or in part imported from Mexico, or whether the incoming Pipil took over an earlier local culture. Could we find answers to these questions we would be supplied with very useful data bearing upon the general question of the race-language-culture relationship. The writer believes that, on the humbler levels at least, culture has normally tended to be more closely rooted to the soil than language, and that language has been more stable than race: in other words, that people pass readily from place to place, languages with greater difficulty, and culture most slowly of all. This, in the present state of our knowledge, is of course pure postulation, but the matter is obviously so vital for the historical interpretation of linguistic, somatological, and archaeological findings and, indeed, for all anthropological thinking, that we should take advantage of all such test cases as that of the Pipil.

This paper has concerned itself with the broadest of generalities, partly because of limited space, but principally because the literature of highland archaeology is so scanty and the conclusions of its writers are based so largely on materials of uncertain provenience and chronological association that present discussion of specific problems is futile.

VIII

ARCHAEOLOGICAL PROBLEMS OF THE LOWLAND MAYA

J. Eric S. Thompson *

FOLLOWING the first two decades of the present century, a period largely devoted to amassing and interpreting information on its most advanced elements, knowledge of Maya culture and a realization of its still unsolved problems have advanced very appreciably due to the more intensive studies made possible by the larger financial resources at the disposal of institutions working in the Central American field.

Whereas, for example, Tozzer's study of the ethnology of the Lacandons and Yucatec Mayas was practically the only thorough exploitation of that very important field prior to the third decade of this century,[1] for the last few years ethnological research carried on season after season by several investigators has enormously augmented our knowledge of this particular branch of Maya cultural history.

Building on the earlier and essential exploratory work, intensive excavation of individual sites is producing a fuller picture of Maya development, while the introduction of the technique of "dirt" archaeology, interpreted through the study of pastes in pottery, is supplying a warp of interchanged products and routes of communication into which the wefts of individual site histories can be inserted.

The purpose of this paper is briefly to summarize the most recent advances in the field and touch on certain outstanding problems. Largely owing to the more impressive surface remains, consisting of hierarchic traits as opposed to those of the underlying lay cultures, the Peten district of Guatemala and adjacent parts of British Honduras have been the center of most intensive excavation, but there was early a shift from unrelated studies of the more spectacular branches of Maya archaeology to an interpretation by means of the

* Cambridge, 1922–1925; now Archaeologist, Carnegie Institution of Washington.

[1] Tozzer, Mayas and Lacandones, 1907.

humble sherd and artifact, with the result that more is now known of the history of that one small region than of any other part of the Maya area. Concentration of effort in this small region has magnified its importance, in all probability previously over-estimated, as we shall see, in relation to the whole, but it has given us a yardstick for measuring in due course areas still unsampled. For that reason a brief outline of what has been accomplished there is essential to an understanding of the present status of Maya archaeology.

Supplementing the earlier excavations at Holmul[2] (Peten) which produced a stratified series of rich burials, ceramic sequences, which lead back from at least the end of the so-called Old Empire to underlying monochrome horizons, have been established at Uaxactun[3] (Peten) and San José,[4] Mountain Cow,[5] and Benque Viejo[6] (British Honduras). These monochrome levels, almost without doubt, precede any surviving dated stelae and the introduction of the corbelled vault, and were probably flourishing in the first half of Cycle 8.[7] There are reasons to believe that future work will carry the sequence farther into the past.

The associated pottery shows a very considerable diversity of form within each site, although scarcely suggestive of a recent adoption of this art. Furthermore, Miss Anna Shepard has discovered a marked variation in the tempering materials employed.[8] In the monochrome horizons at Uaxactun, sherd is the dominant temper. At San José it is crystalline calcite but with a substantial number of sherd-tempered sherds. The latter occur particularly in the rarer forms, but are entirely absent in the common or garden unslipped storage jar. At Benque Viejo red-ware sherds are overwhelmingly untempered but a fair proportion of unslipped ware was quartz tempered.

Such divergence of form and temper in the lowlands strongly argues against these monochrome horizons, which were clearly contemporaneous, having been the earliest in the Maya area. There are, indeed, hints that earlier ceramic phases will be found in the Guatemalan highlands.

[2] Merwin and Vaillant, Holmul, 1932.
[3] Ricketson and Ricketson, Uaxactun, 1937. R. E. Smith, Shape Analysis, 1936; Ceramics of Uaxactun, 1936.
[4] Thompson, San José, 1939.
[5] Thompson, Southern Cayo, 1931.
[6] Thompson, Reconnaissance in British Honduras, 1938.
[7] Smith and Smith, Excavations at Uaxactun, 1933; A. L. Smith, Uaxactun, 1934.
[8] Appendix A in Thompson, San José, 1939.

One important result of the establishment of these ceramic sequences is to divorce Maya history from the stela complex. It is now clear that the interval spanned by inscriptions on monuments bears no relation to the actual occupation of a site. Benque Viejo is a case in point. The one sculptured stela carries the date 10.1.0.0.0, 5 Ahau 3 Kayab(?), whereas the pottery, the earliest horizon of which may conceivably antedate the first phase at Uaxactun, indicates an occupation from early in Cycle 8, nearly 800 years earlier. Similarly, pottery types from Pusilhá, British Honduras, indicate an occupation long after 9.15.0.0.0, the date of the latest monument.

Dirt archaeology in the Peten and British Honduras has not only extended the span of occupation to well before the earliest surviving dated stelae, it has also produced evidence pointing to a post-stela occupation which in certain wares, such as Yucatecan slate, is linked with the tentatively defined Period of Mexican Contact.

Excavations at the above-mentioned Peten and British Honduras sites have established that a number of traits are either entirely absent or appear sparingly at the close of occupation, a horizon which, as noted, is probably post-stela. Among those occurring only as surface finds or on a very late horizon are: pottery spindle whorls, marble vases, Yucatecan slate ware, bark beaters, and flat metates at Uaxactun and San José, copper (one find) at San José only, small polished cuneate axes and pottery stamps at Uaxactun only, and in both cases very rarely. Yet several of these features have been reported with considerable frequency from various sites in British Honduras by T. Gann and others, and from Maya sites outside the Peten-British Honduras area. At Kendall, British Honduras, for example, caches yielded *inter alia* a number of finely carved jade ornaments (at all times rare in Peten-British Honduras lowland sites), fifteen polished axes, a cylindrical pottery stamp, but no eccentric flints such as are found so frequently in "Old Empire" caches.[9]

Again tripod metates with heads of animals in relief at one end have not been found at Uaxactun, Benque Viejo, San José or Mountain Cow, but occur in British Honduras sites.

In view of the absence below the latest levels of these various traits at our type "Old Empire" sites in the Peten and British Honduras, we can postulate that a lithic horizon, in which polished implements became common, and which replaced one in which implements were almost invariably chipped and metates displayed little variation, al-

[9] Price, Sittee River, 1897–1899; Gann, Maya Indians, 1918.

most coincided with the cessation of major activities at these sites. Unfortunately at the period when these collections from eastern British Honduras were made, scant attention was paid to pottery forms with the result that little is known of the associated ceramics, but a number of these pieces could scarcely have come from an "Old Empire" Peten site.[10] The absence of plumbate and typical fine orange pottery, turquoise, and gold, on the other hand, hint that these sites are not contemporaneous with the Mexican Period in Yucatan.[11]

This evidence, although inconclusive, of yet another horizon between the stela cult and the Mexican Period in Yucatan lengthens the sequence already established, and at the same time argues against the over syncopation of Maya history involved in the advocacy of a 10.10.0.0.0 correlation. The fact that the "Old Empire" was essentially a pre-neolithic horizon and the possibility that the Maya began to receive metal before polished stone was in general use are of considerable interest. Excavations at these Peten-British Honduras sites have supplied a great mass of trade material. Such late finds as Yucatecan slate ware, spindle whorls from the Huaxteca, ware with specular hematite in its red slip or paint (probably from the Guatemala-Honduras area) and marble vases (from the Uloa Valley) are evidence of wide-flung trade relationships, while imported wares and obsidian in the early deposits show that trade was not confined to the latest phases.

The Peten-British Honduras area has been unduly emphasized in this summary not because it would seem to be of overwhelming importance, but because it has been the scene of most active excavation.

Extension of digging to the highlands of Guatemala has had surprising results. The architecture, art, and mathematical genius of the Mayas of the "Old Empire" have focused attention on the lowlands. Nevertheless the Peten and adjacent regions were singularly ill-adapted for originating an indigenous culture owing to the exuberance of their flora and the scantiness of their natural resources. Indeed, the more that is learned of the relations of that region with other areas, the more it appears to have been a receiver rather than an originator.

[10] Gann, Maya Indians, 1918, Figs. 15, 16, 18, 21a represent forms not typical of the "Old Empire" ceramics.

[11] Vaillant, Chronology and Stratigraphy, 1935.

Of the handicaps of the rain forest much has been written, but little attention has been drawn to the extreme poverty in useful minerals and rocks of the Peten. Minerals are to all intents and purposes non-existent while the ubiquitous limestone formations yield only building stone and flint for tools.

On the other hand, the Guatemala highlands are rich in those minerals most prized by the Maya. Volcanic eruptions supplied them with the utilitarian obsidian, also a stone far superior to limestone for metates, and tuff, a temper superior to that of the lowland calcite because of the higher firing temperatures obtainable with it.

Iron pyrite, mercury, many varieties of igneous rocks and, in later times, metals were other advantages of the highlands not possessed by the lowlanders. Furthermore, the highlanders controlled the supply of quetzal feathers, presumably re-exported the much prized *Spondylus* shells of the Pacific, and may have had sources of jade at their command.

One would expect such wealth in primary products to be reflected in the material culture, and, instead of being, as generally pictured, a region without the Maya pale, such an area should have possessed cultures materially as wealthy as that of the Peten. Apart from architecture and stone sculpture that appears to have been the case.

The burials excavated by A. V. Kidder at Kaminaljuyú, immediately outside Guatemala City, are richer in a number of ways than any burial of the coeval Uaxactun II (Tzakol) and San José II horizons.[12] The wealth of jade in the former far exceeds anything found in a contemporaneous Peten burial. Marble vessels, although of a crude type, occur in the Kaminaljuyú burials, but in the Peten they do not appear until at least two centuries later, at the very close of occupation. The same is true of crystal beads, found at Kaminaljuyú but absent from Peten sites. Furthermore, the ability to fashion pottery statuary in the round had advanced to a considerable stage of perfection at Kaminaljuyú, whereas it was almost non-existent in the Peten. The abundance of shell work, iron pyrite mirrors, mosaic mirrors, etc., place these burials far ahead of anything of the same date yet found in the Peten. The slaughter of slaves to accompany their masters to the next world, a practice established by archaeology and confirmed in literature for the Guatemalan highlands, but seemingly absent in the lowlands, points to an advanced barbaric civilization.

[12] Carnegie Institution, Important Discovery, 1936.

It is, of course, true that those criteria by which we are prone to judge Maya culture—dated stelae, the corbelled vault and formalized art—are absent or poorly represented in the Guatemala highlands, but this complex was clearly something superimposed on the basic Maya culture which spread unevenly, and never reached in its entirety large parts of the Maya area. On the other hand, the writings of Román y Zamora, Ximénez and the authors of the *Popol Vuh* and the *Annals of the Cakchiquels*, to indicate but a few of the sources, depict as advanced and politically highly organized these highland regions which are now shown by archaeology to have possessed a rich material culture. The time has surely come to tone down this over-emphasis of lowland culture at the expense of that of the highlands.

Perhaps the most important result of work at Kaminaljuyú is the production of evidence confirming and broadening the cross-ties,[13] previously established at San José,[14] with classical Teotihuacan, in the Valley of Mexico (Plates IV–V). It is tempting to suppose that these contacts in the Guatemalan highlands were actually the result of Mexican invasion, and to link them with the Mexican ancestors of the rulers of the principal Maya highland tribes. In some features of social organization the Guatemalan highlands were closer to Central Mexico than were the Maya lowlands, yet the picture is confused by the Pipil invaders, who, if they are responsible for the many features attributed to them, are more likely to have derived from southern Vera Cruz.

The position of Yucatan and Campeche in Maya history is still undergoing changes. The discovery of early stelae and sherds of the Tzakol (basal flanged bowl horizon) in that region continues to emphasize its importance during the "Old Empire," and has completely falsified the former reconstruction which pictured Yucatan as uninhabited during the early centuries of Maya development (Plate I). The vexatious problems of the Itzas and the Xius are still unsettled, while Yucatecan ceramic sequences, burial customs, and types of artifacts still remain largely unknown. Exploration in recent years has brought to light a large number of important "Old Empire" sites in southern Campeche and Quintana Roo.[15] Some of these, notably

[13] Kidder and Jennings, Guatemala Highlands, 1937.
[14] Thompson, Maya Chronology, 1935, p. 69.
[15] Morley, Calakmul Expedition, 1933; Ruppert, Explorations in Campeche, 1934, Campeche Expedition, 1938.

Calakmul with 103 stelae, are of very considerable size. They serve to extend the area of advanced Maya culture, and partially close a gap between the well-explored Peten to the south and the Chenes country to the north. Exploration in southern Quintana Roo a quarter of a century ago revealed a number of cities, of which Rio Bec and Ramonal are the best known, with elaborate façades, magnificent veneer masonry, and unusual plans in which flanking towers played a conspicuous part.[16] More recent exploration has added to the number of these sites, and has produced much fuller architectural information, but as yet, no full report on this area has been published. Noteworthy, however, are the essential identity of this façade decoration with that of Chenes style, and the fact that these buildings are not as yet datable in terms of the Maya calendar. Stelae at these sites are uncommon, and the few yet reported are plain or indecipherable. A number of years ago it was claimed that these Rio Bec-Ramonal sites represented the transitional period between the "Old Empire" in the south and the renaissance in Yucatan.[17] At present, however, the tendency is to make pre-Mexican architecture at Chichen Itzá contemporaneous with late "Old Empire." Should that reconstruction be correct, there would be little room for a transitional phase. In any case very fine veneer and elaborate façade decoration are hardly ancestral features. Furthermore, there is extremely little in Rio Bec architecture that shows a Peten influence.

Exploration at Chichen Itzá has been concerned primarily with architecture. Following the discovery of superposition of late buildings with minor architectural and artistic changes in the Temple of the Warriors complex,[18] an earlier sequence has been established by the discovery by archaeologists of the Mexican government of an earlier and stylistically different building beneath the Castillo.[19] An earlier temple has also been found beneath the Casa del Adivino at Uxmal, incased pyramids have been reported from a number of sites including Copan, Holmul, Uaxactun, Piedras Negras, and Kaminaljuyú, while a buried temple is known to exist beneath the High Priest's Grave at Chichen Itzá. There should, therefore, be no lack of architectural sequences of this type, although their classification involves expensive excavation.

[16] Merwin, Southern Part of Yucatan, 1913.
[17] Spinden, Maya Dates, 1930.
[18] Morris, Charlot and Morris, Temple of Warriors, 1931.
[19] Carnegie Institution, El Castillo, 1937.

To the southeast the first sequence of ceramic types for the Uloa Valley has been expanded and a tentative framework for the Yohoa Valley established.[20] At Copan a succession of ceramic horizons, as yet incomplete, has been tentatively delineated, and much information on architecture, including superposed ball courts, has been amassed.[21] Farther south, in El Salvador, a start has been made in the extremely complex task of untangling the various cultures, and tentatively identifying them with linguistic groupings.[22]

Information on the non-hierarchic aspects of the southwest of the Maya area and the upper Usumacintla is practically non-existent, and until sampling has been carried out in that region, the general picture must remain unbalanced. Recent work has, however, added to our information on the hierarchic elements of culture in those areas, notably at Palenque, where later dates have partially bridged the gap between the previously known latest dates and the advanced architecture.[23]

Investigations in Maya architecture, like those of general Maya archaeology, have passed from general to specific problems. At Piedras Negras a sequence of stone buildings with thatching, concrete-and-beam flat roofing, and, finally, corbeled vaulting have been established.[24] Yet at Uaxactun the vault appears fully developed without any intermediate steps. If a series of stelae which serve to date structural changes are *in situ* there, the vault existed at Uaxactun about two centuries before it appeared at Piedras Negras.[25] Uaxactun, and to a much lesser extent, San José, have produced masonry type sequences. Illustrative of the complex currents of style diffusion is the fact that Benque Viejo late masonry strongly resembles Uaxactun, while late San José is close to what is presumably late at Tikal. Lines joining these pairs of sites cross each other. The important part played by non-vaulted structures perhaps throughout "Old Empire" history is every season more strongly confirmed.

In the north of the peninsula of Yucatan, Puuc and Chenes architectural styles have been more closely defined, and their distribution

[20] Strong, Kidder and Paul, Northwestern Honduras, 1938.
[21] Stromsvik, Copan, 1938.
[22] Lothrop, Central American Expedition, 1927, Southeast Frontier, 1939; Richardson, Maya Sculpture, 1938.
[23] Palacios, Inscripcion Descubierta, 1936.
[24] Satterthwaite, Logical Sequence, 1938.
[25] Smith and Smith, Excavations at Uaxactun, 1933; A. L. Smith, Uaxactun, 1934.

more thoroughly plotted.[26] It is becoming increasingly clear that architectural styles in this general region do not represent sequent stages in a single northward cultural movement, but that their differences are due to separate origins rather than to development from one stage to another.

The center from which the Puuc-Etzná-Xcalumkin complex diffused has not yet been found, although it might be southwestern Campeche, an archaeological lacuna.[27] At Cobá, northern Quintana Roo, on the other hand, architecture and art display very strong evidences of Peten origin with a later(?) influence from the East Coast.[28] It is evident that many cultural infiltrations have affected Yucatan.

Some advance has been made in determining the functions of some structures, notably ball courts and sweat houses,[29] while certain architectural motifs would seem to have been exchanged between the Peten and the Usumacintla Valley.[30] Excavations of house mounds and buildings supposedly not used primarily for religious purposes throw light on the border line between hierarchic traits and elements of the underlying lay cultures. It has been suggested that benches are indicative of a public, religious or civil, function for the structures that housed them, but at San José they occurred in one structure, at least, which presumably was for domestic use.

Examples of Maya art have been greatly increased by recent excavations. Frescoes at Chichen Itzá and Uaxactun and painted pottery from many sites have the added importance of increasing knowledge of the everyday activities and ceremonies of the people —a welcome counter balance to the overemphasis archaeology has given to the religious side of Maya culture. A recent study on the provenance of the Leyden plaque is indicative of the possibilities in the comparative treatment of minor details of sculpture.[31] The general problems of Maya art have, however, received little attention subsequent to the studies of Spinden [32] and Maudslay.[33]

In epigraphy and the related problems of Maya astronomy and

[26] Pollock, Architectural Survey, 1936.
[27] *Ibid.*
[28] Thompson, Pollock, and Charlot, Coba, 1932.
[29] Blom, Maya Game, 1932; Cresson, Sweat Houses, 1938.
[30] Satterthwaite, Sixth Piedras Negras Expedition, 1936.
[31] Morley and Morley, Leyden Plate, 1938.
[32] Spinden, Maya Art, 1913; Portraiture, 1916; Progress in Maya Art, 1917.
[33] Maudslay, Archaeology, 1889–1902; Some American Problems, 1912.

the correlation few solutions have received universal acceptance. Around the correlation question debate still rages, although now the emphasis has largely shifted from between correlations which would make 11.16.0.0.0 or 12.9.0.0.0 coincide with the arrival of the Spaniards to examination of the merits of the 11.16.0.0.0 correlation as opposed to one that would place the arrival of the Spaniards at about 11.3.0.0.0. In other words discussion now revolves not so much around whether to make Maya Old Empire dates 260 years later than under the 12.9.0.0.0 correlation, but whether they would not fit the ceramic and architectural evidence better if they were shifted yet another 260 years.

A new method of reading Yucatecan dates supposes that the Tun number and day Ahau frequently associated with Calendar Round dates indicate that the latter occur in the given Tun which in turn falls in a Katun ending on the given day Ahau. Such a method would fix many Yucatecan dates as firmly as if they had been given in the Long Count, but the material at present available is insufficient to prove or disprove the method.[34]

Stylistic changes in early "Old Empire" times have been generally accepted, but a chronological classification of Yucatecan glyph variations conflicts too seriously with rather generally approved reconstructions of Maya history to be universally endorsed at present.[35]

A mass of epigraphic material concerning such ritualistic features as world direction colors and deities which one would expect to find in "Old Empire" inscriptions eludes detection, and calendrical calculations still fail to show any relation to the sculptural subjects of the stelae on which they are given. The writer feels that in both cases the next decade will widen the scope of epigraphy's contribution to more general problems by establishing such ritualistic relations. Such few advances as have been made and universally recognized, as for instance the function of the Initial Series Introducing Glyph, are susceptible to mathematical proof. The recent publication of a large body of calendrical texts, in many cases accompanied by brilliant decipherments, has notably augmented study material.[36]

In Maya ethnology two main lines of research are being pursued. The first, a sociological approach, studies the effects of the impacts of European and native cultures in Middle America upon one an-

[34] Thompson, New Method, 1937.
[35] Beyer, Inscriptions at Chichen Itza, 1937.
[36] Morley, Peten, 1938.

other, their various fusions and the resulting contacts of mestizo culture, a series of unending and fluid adjustments. The second branch
of the study elevates the recording of elements of aboriginal culture
from a secondary to a primary aim and, therefore, concords more
closely with the more limited archaeological objective of recon-
structing aboriginal culture as it was prior to the arrival of the Spaniards.

The most sensational aboriginal survival to be rediscovered by the
ethnologist is that of the 260-day calendar in the Guatemalan highlands,[37] still integrated with many of its ritualistic, divinatory, and
social functions, but in many minor points, such as in house types,
pagan deities, trade routes and arts and crafts, studies of contemporary mixed cultures have yielded much information for repainting
the aboriginal picture.

Bridging the gap between modern ethnological work and archaeological projects, studies of the considerable mass of documents in
Maya and Spanish have added greatly to the reconstruction of both
the history and daily life of the Maya. Notable among these studies
are the translation of the Chilam Balaam of Chumayel [38] and the
discovery and publication of papers on the investigation of idolatry
in Yucatan by Diego de Landa and Diego Quijada.[39]

Linguistic research, insofar as it relates to historical reconstructions, seem to indicate that the Mayas of the Guatemalan highlands
have shifted very little from the areas they had occupied for many
centuries.[40] Such a conclusion, if verified, should check many an
ardent theorist who conjures up a migration to account for every
trait transmitted from one area to another.

Largely owing to adverse climatic conditions, physical anthropology is very much the Cinderella of Maya studies as far as archaeology is concerned, although the living Maya of Yucatan have been
thoroughly measured. The problem raised by Starr's studies of the
marked differences in cephalic and nasal indices between such linguistically and presumably culturally closely related peoples as the
Yucatecs and Tzotzil-Tzeltals,[41] is still untackled.

In reviewing the period of excavation that has followed that of

[37] La Farge and Byers, The Year-Bearer's People, 1931; Lothrop, Modern
Survivals, 1930; Termer, Ethnologie, 1930.
[38] Roys, Chumayel, 1933.
[39] Scholes and Adams, Diego Quijada, 1939; Scholes and Roys, 1938.
[40] Andrade, Linguistic Investigations, 1936.
[41] Starr, Physical Characters, 1902.

exploration one is struck by the lack of coordination of effort. A series of isolated intensive digs have been initiated at widely scattered centers with the result, for example, that we are still unable to fit Copan ceramics and architecture into the fuller picture revealed by work in Central Peten and British Honduras, while the architecture and much of the ceramic history of the southern highlands, Oaxaca, or of northern Yucatan are similarly unanchored.

Possessing, as we now do, a fairly full picture of the cultural history of the Central Peten and adjacent parts of British Honduras, it should be simple to work outward from that area in jumps of fifty to a hundred miles, which should yield material associated with already classified material as a control. Such a method of attack, already followed by Vaillant on the Mexican plateau with such conspicuous success, holds less chance of mistakes and should gradually increase our knowledge of Maya history. On the other hand, excursions into the unknown in widely separated localities without relevant data as control material are more likely to lead to misinterpretation of findings and, instead of gradually enlarging a clear picture of Maya development, leave us in the dark until the intervening areas have been dealt with. Furthermore, with such a method there is a risk that a sudden termination of archaeological activities in the Maya area might leave the intervening and therefore key areas untouched.

Another method of working from the known to the unknown, and one that has proved very successful in other archaeological fields, has not yet been tried in the Maya area. That is to establish through the presence of European artifacts horizons definitely datable in European chronology, and working back from them. In this manner Mixtec polychrome [42] and late Aztec pottery [43] have been dated by Spanish artifacts. Such a horizon exists on Wild Cane Cay, off the south coast of British Honduras, and must be present elsewhere.

One of the most encouraging features of the present approach to the problem of Maya archaeology is that despite the multiplication of lines of research, the inter-relationships between problems, everyday more evident, have been fully exploited. Ceramicists profoundly influence the conclusions of the epigrapher on the correlation question, the architect is called upon for his views on an historical reconstruction and art, ethnology and Maya literature contribute to elucidation of problems of Maya religion.

[42] Caso, Oaxaca, 1938, p. 53.
[43] Noguera, Templo Mayor, 1934, pp. 272–273.

The recent shift of emphasis from the hierarchic traits to the underlying lay elements is a healthy sign. It is broadening our concept of Maya culture from one in which only the highest manifestations of that culture were considered worthy of study, and has called a halt to the disregard, understandable in the pioneer exploratory phase of Maya archaeology, of those large areas which in speech and lay culture are Maya, yet lack those elements.

The field, too, has been widened, and thanks to the established connections with classical Teotihuacan and Mazapan,[44] any Maya historical reconstruction must now satisfy conditions in the Valley of Mexico before it can be accepted as a correct interpretation of facts in the Maya area. Southern Vera Cruz has recently been brought into the Maya historical framework, and it has been claimed that the earliest contemporaneous date in Middle America is found in this area.[45]

It is such broad problems that need fuller investigation. Their existence calls attention to what is perhaps the greatest defect of present-day studies in Middle American achaeology—over-specialization. The man who devotes himself to a single branch of Maya archaeology without a wide supplementary knowledge of the field as a whole can hardly hope to get from his narrowly channeled studies the wider implications, and must miss many leads from related fields of investigation. All such leads cannot be supplied by a fellow specialist to whom the conclusions are submitted, for they usually come only after one has "soaked" oneself in the problem for a long period and in the form of flashes induced, it would seem, by subconscious cerebration of the problem in hand. As long as this present tendency to specialization without a foundation of general knowledge continues, the prospects for the elucidation of Maya culture in its broadest sense, not merely a framework of architecture and ceramics, are not bright in proportion to the increased effort, and we of the present generation are in danger of evolving into technicians, not scholars, a retrogression from the standards set us by Tozzer and his generation.

[44] Linné, Teotihuacan, 1934; Vaillant, History and Stratigraphy, 1937; Thompson, San José, 1939.
[45] Stirling, Tres Zapotes, 1940.

IX

Maya Epigraphy

Sylvanus Griswold Morley *

IN THE BEGINNING of the present century the leading figures in Maya epigraphy were the Germans: Ernst Förstemann, Eduard Seler and Paul Schellhas; and the Americans: G. T. Goodman, C. P. Bowditch and Cyrus Thomas. The Englishman, Alfred P. Maudslay, whose monumental work on Maya archaeology in the "Biologia Centrali-Americana" contained the first accurate reproductions of the Maya inscriptions, and the Austrian, Teobert Maler, whose superb photographs of the Maya inscriptions in the "Memoirs of the Peabody Museum of American Archaeology and Ethnology," an equally admirable continuation of Maudslay's earlier work, were both still living. Finally, a fourth American, D. G. Brinton, had but recently died, having enriched the field with extensive contributions characterized by their brilliancy and by a quality almost of prevision. These were the nine wise men of Maya epigraphy.[1]

Maya hieroglyphic writing had been established as an original graphic system, which, though largely ideographic, yet held promise of containing a limited number of phonetic elements.

The three basic counts of the Maya inscriptions—the Initial Series, the Supplementary Series, and the Secondary Series—all had been recognized. The first had been identified by both Förstemann (1887) and Goodman (1897) as a diurnal count, proceeding from a fixed point of departure, practically identical in its operation to the Julian Period of modern astronomers, and the last as an additional diurnal count to be subtracted from, or added to the Initial Series date, as the case might be, in order to reach earlier or later dates. The first had been named the Initial Series by Maudslay because, when present, it

---

* Pennsylvania Military College, C.E., 1904; honorary Ph.D., 1921; Harvard, A.B., 1907; A.M., 1908; Associate in American Archaeology, Carnegie Institution of Washington.

[1] Full bibliographic citations are to be found in the author's *Inscriptions of Peten*, 1937–1938. Specific titles are listed in the bibliography of this volume.

almost invariably is to be found at the beginning of the inscription; the second had been called the Secondary Series by Bowditch because he found the numbers presented by this count to be secondary to, and usually counted from the Initial Series, or other Secondary Series connected therewith.

Bowditch had also named the glyphs of the second count above, the Supplementary Series. Although the meaning of this count was as yet undetermined, he had correctly surmised that it was in some way dependent upon the Initial Series for its meaning, in a sense was supplementary thereto, hence his name for it.

Förstemann had already published his brilliant studies upon the Maya codices, especially the "Codex Dresdensis," which latter he proved conclusively was an astrological treatise based upon extremely accurate observations of the apparent revolutions of the sun and Venus (the ancient Maya world was essentially geocentric) and the actual revolutions of the moon, together with eclipse data and tzolkin records, the latter used by the Maya priests in casting horoscopes. Finally, Förstemann worked out the essential features of the Maya Long Count (the Initial Series) as it appears in the "Codex Dresdensis" and demonstrated that all Maya dates were counted from the zero date, 4 Ahau 8 Cumhu.

Goodman, working independently and entirely without knowledge of Förstemann's researches, with different material altogether—the stone inscriptions—had duplicated Förstemann's discoveries as to the Long Count and its zero date, and, in addition, had identified the head-variant numerals; while his tables, "The Archaic Annual Calendar" and "The Archaic Chronological Calendar," though published more than four decades ago, still remain the student's indispensable tabular "short cut" for deciphering Maya dates.

Schellhas had already published his definitive study on the representations of the Maya deities in the three pre-Columbian Maya codices, and had identified the name-glyph corresponding to each.

Seler and Thomas, though their contributions to Maya epigraphy were less fundamental than the work of Förstemann, Goodman and Schellhas, nevertheless had done much to elucidate and amplify Goodman's earlier readings of the Copan, Quirigua, and Palenque dates. Both published commentaries on Goodman's decipherments with which, in the main, both agree. Seler's greatest contributions, however, lie not in Maya epigraphy, but in Mexican epigraphy, in which latter field he is easily the leader. Thomas' most illuminating observations were made in connection with the codices, in the decipherment of which he was second only to Förstemann.

The pioneer explorations of Maudslay and Maler and the brilliant interpretations of Brinton in the field of the native Maya literature have already been noted.

Bowditch, although he had published a number of shorter papers of great significance, had yet to write his magnum opus on Maya epigraphy, "The Numeration, Calendar Systems and Astronomical Knowledge of the Mayas." This appeared in 1910 and was a résumé of his investigations in this field during the two previous decades.

Recognizing the primary place of astronomy, or perhaps better of its less reputable half-sister, astrology, in the records of the ancient Maya, Bowditch epitomized in the title of his monograph the principal subject with which it dealt.

This work summarized all previous knowledge of Maya epigraphy. Following the inductive method of presentation, it leads from simpler to more complex material, each step being proved before the next is attempted. While too advanced for the needs of a beginner, Bowditch's monograph was the first general study of Maya epigraphy, and, together with the section on archaeology of the "Biologia Centrali-Americana" by Maudslay and Goodman and the Memoirs and Papers of the Peabody Museum by Maler and Förstemann, it still remains a primary source for the study of the Maya hieroglyphic writing.

Feeling the need for a more simple presentation of this complex subject, in brief a text book for beginners, the writer published "An Introduction to the Study of the Maya Hieroglyphs" in 1915, which, in effect, is a primer written for comprehension by high school students, to teach the first steps in Maya epigraphy. It contains little that is new, beyond the identification of the glyph for the hotun or period of 1800 days, aiming rather at meeting the more simple needs of a beginner in this field.

In 1915 the writer presented to the Fifth Pan American Scientific Congress held at Washington a paper entitled "The Hotun, the Principal Chronological Unit of the Old Empire" published in 1917. This established that the hotun or quarter katun period was the unit used by the ancient Maya in the erection of their stone monuments, i. e. at the ends of 1800- (hotuns), 3600- (lahuntuns) and 7200-day periods (katuns).

The following year he announced that the Supplementary Series was basically a lunar count, Glyph A indicating the length of the current lunar month, whether of 29 or 30 days, and Glyph C, the number of the last completed month in the lunar half-year, or eclipse period of five or six months.

Juan Martínez Hernández, the eminent Yucatecan antiquary, has been writing on the Maya codices and the Books of Chilan Balam since 1910. His profound knowledge of the Maya language, in which he has no equal, has made him peculiarly fitted to translate the archaic and ritualistic phraseology of the Books of Chilan Balam, practically all the ancient Maya learning that survived the Spanish Conquest. In 1926 he revived the Goodman correlation of Maya and Christian chronology, reaching a new point of contact between the two calendars one day later than that of Goodman.

R. C. E. Long published his first paper on Maya epigraphy in 1918, and since has been a frequent and versatile contributor to the field.[2] He has written on various phases of Maya chronology and the interpretation of specific Maya texts; he has discussed the correlation problem, the higher numbers in both the codices and inscriptions, the age of the Maya calendar and the dedicatory dates of different monuments. His observations are always well considered and merit careful study.

Two years later, in 1920, the writer published the first monograph of a contemplated trilogy on the chronology of the Maya inscriptions—"The Inscriptions at Copan"—which deals with the epigraphy of that site.

During the next decade, 1920–1930, the field widens and many new investigators appear.

Although Hermann Beyer, of the Department of Middle American Research of the Tulane University of Louisiana, had been writing about the Mexican calendar and hieroglyphic writing since 1910, he did not turn his attention to the Maya calendar and epigraphy until 1920. Since the latter date he has been an indefatigable and prolific investigator in this field, having published more than fifty papers on many phases of Maya epigraphy and several major contributions, including "Studies on the Inscriptions at Chichen Itzá." His most significant discovery has been the identification of the meaning of the variable central element of the Initial Series introducing glyph as the name glyph of the deity who was patron of the month in which the Initial Series terminal date falls. This, though first sug-

[2] See bibliography in Morley, Peten, 1939.

gested but subsequently rejected by Bowditch, has been of invaluable assistance to Maya epigraphers in checking readings of partially missing or effaced Initial Series, since each of the nineteen divisions of the Maya vague year of 365 days had a corresponding patron deity, whose name glyph was recorded as the variable central element of the Initial Series introducing glyph, and if this element does not agree with the month sign recorded, then either the reading suggested is wrong, or there is an error in the original text, the latter a very rare contingency.

Although Herbert J. Spinden published his first contribution on Maya archaeology in 1910, followed by many other articles and several books including his monograph "A Study of Maya Art" which is the standard authority in this field, it was not until 1920 that he began an intensive study of the Maya calendar and chronology, his conclusion thereupon being embodied in "The Reduction of Maya Dates" published in 1924; "Maya Inscriptions Dealing With Venus and the Moon" in 1928; and "Maya Dates and What They Reveal" in 1930. In the writer's judgment, Spinden's conclusions as to the Maya calendar and chronology are largely invalidated by the fact they are based upon the primary assumption that the Maya Long Count date 12.9.0.0.0 13 Ahau 8 Kankin fell in A. D. 1539, a correlation of Maya and Christian chronology now rejected by every other student of the subject save only Hans Ludendorff and Arnŏst Dittrich, and one, moreover, at variance with the best interpretation not only of the native documentary sources of the sixteenth and seventeenth centuries, but also of the dirt archaeology, especially the ceramic evidence.

Robert W. Willson of the Department of Astronomy at Harvard University published the results of his studies on Maya astronomy in 1924 as "Astronomical Notes on the Maya Codices." Willson, a leading authority on astronomy and especially on the motions of the heavenly bodies, brought to bear upon the subject a vast fund of the very type of astronomical knowledge which the ancient Maya possessed. He defined conditions which he believed to be essential to the successful solution of the correlation problem, and held that the table of eclipses in the Codex Dresdensis would ultimately lead to the correct alignment of Maya and Christian chronology. His death, while he was at the beginning of his studies, removed a valuable prospective contributor to this field.

Carl Eugen Guthe, Director of the Museums of the University of

Michigan, has devoted much time to the Maya lunar calendar, both in the codices ("A Possible Solution of the Number Series on Pages 51 to 58 of the Codex Dresdensis," 1921) and in the inscriptions ("The Maya Lunar Count," 1932). Guthe's most important contribution has been the discovery that the moon ages recorded by the Supplementary Series are probably based upon tabular rather than observational data, the latter as contended by Teeple, who first deciphered the moon-age glyphs.

In 1925, John E. Teeple, the distinguished chemical engineer, published the first of a remarkable series of papers on the Supplementary Series which established by mathematical proof that Glyphs C, D and E were the key signs, so to speak, of that count, the first two recording the current moon age—Glyph D being used when the moon age was below 20 days and Glyph E when it was above 20 days—and the third, Glyph C, giving the position of the last completed lunation in the lunar half year of five or six months. The latter discovery proved that Glyph C of the Supplementary Series presents the same sort of eclipse data in the inscriptions as Förstemann had found on pages 51 to 58 of the Codex Dresdensis nearly two score years previously.

Five other papers on the Supplementary Series and other phases of the Maya calendar followed in 1925–1928 and, having become a Research Associate of the Carnegie Institution of Washington because of these outstanding discoveries, Teeple published through that institution in 1930 the results of his previous investigations under the title of "Maya Astronomy." This scholarly monograph summarizes Teeple's researches in the Supplementary Series and the Maya Venus-solar calendar. He proposed here for the first time his "Theory of Determinants" which he explains as calendar corrective formulae, wherein by means of the Secondary Series, the 365-day calendar year was kept in harmony with the 365.24-day tropical year. Teeple's death on March 23, 1931 deprived Maya epigraphy of its most original contributor since Goodman.

In 1925, T. A. Joyce, deputy head keeper of the Department of Ceramics and Ethnography at the British Museum, published an analysis of the dates on the Hieroglyphic Stairway at Naranjo, "The Hieroglyphic Stairway at Naranjo, Guatemala," with which the writer finds himself largely in disagreement. Joyce believes the Hieroglyphic Stairway at Naranjo was dedicated at the close of the Great Period of the Maya Old Empire, whereas the writer feels that it dates from almost two centuries earlier, at the beginning of the Middle Period of the Old Empire.

Enrique Juan Palacios, the Mexican epigrapher, has been a constant contributor to this field since 1926. He has reported a number of new dates from the State of Chiapas (1926 and 1936) and discussed the correlation question (1932). After reviewing the evidence in the latter exhaustively, he favors the Goodman-Martínez Hernández-Thompson correlation.

In 1927, J. Eric Thompson announced a new correlation of Maya and Christian chronology, "A Correlation of the Mayan and European Calendars," the point of contact being five days later than that originally proposed by Goodman in 1905 and four days later than that proposed by Juan Martínez Hernández in 1926.

Since 1925, Thompson has been a continuous contributor to Maya epigraphy, as well as to the general field of Maya archaeology. His most important discovery in Maya epigraphy has been the determination of the meaning of Glyph G of the Supplementary Series. The writer, in his original study on the Supplementary Series, erroneously associated Glyph G with this count, but Thompson proved mathematically that the nine different forms of this glyph differ directly with the Initial Series, upon which they depend for their ninefold variation. In a paper outlining this significant discovery, "Maya Chronology, Glyph G of the Lunar Series," published in 1929, Thompson shows that the nine different forms of Glyph G are probably to be associated with the *bolon-ti-ku* of Maya mythology—the Nine Gods of the Underworld, which in turn are doubtless related to the Nine Lords of the Night of the Aztec pantheon. This discovery has proved a valuable check in the decipherment of Initial Series just as Beyer's discovery of the relationship between the variable central element of the Initial Series introducing glyph and the corresponding month date has also done. The Thompson and Beyer formulae have served either to confirm or to disqualify many doubtful readings of fragmentary Initial Series.

In 1930 Hans Ludendorff began the publication of a series of papers purporting to confirm the Spinden day-for-day correlation of Maya and Christian chronology, eleven of them having appeared to date. As previously noted, the writer believes the Spinden correlation to be incorrect, hence he also rejects the greater part of Ludendorff's findings, which are based directly upon that correlation and only derive their significance therefrom.

The last decade, 1930 to 1940, has produced few additional investigators in Maya epigraphy. In 1930 R. B. Weitzel published an article, "Maya Chronological System," and in 1935 two others, "Maya Moon Glyphs and New Moons" and "Maya Correlation Problem." He believes the moon ages in the Supplementary Series are tabular, as previously advanced by Guthe. He further holds that the day sequence between the Old and New Empire calendars is not a continuous series, in which he follows Teeple, and any correlation based thereupon is therefore open to serious doubt.

In 1933 Lawrence Roys wrote a report on the current status of the correlation problem, "The Maya Correlation Problem Today." While admitting, as indeed all other students of the correlation question have done, save Spinden, Ludendorff and Dittrich, that the problem is far from solved, Roys leans toward the Goodman-Martínez Hernández-Thompson correlation which equates the Long Count date 11.16.0.0.0 13 Ahau 8 Xul with A. D. October 20 to November 4, 1539 (Julian).

E. Wyllys Andrews has studied the Supplementary Series, concentrating on three signs, Glyphs X, Y and Z, and last two of which are restricted almost exclusively to the inscriptions at Yaxchilan. The first he believes to have been used to express the correlation between the synodical month count and the cyclical variations in the time of the rising and setting of the moon, which on the average rises 48 minutes later each day ("Glyph X of the Supplementary Series of the Maya Inscriptions").

More recently (1936) the German student, Arnŏst Dittrich, has come to the defense of the Spinden day-for-day correlation without, however, adducing any new evidence of a convincing character in support of it.

In 1939, the writer published "The Inscriptions of Peten," the second section of his contemplated trilogy on the chronological aspects of the Maya inscriptions. This covers the greater part of the Old Empire region, including its oldest centers: Uaxactun, Balakbal, Uolantun and Tikal.

Analyzing the foregoing brief summary of the progress that has been made in deciphering the Maya inscriptions, both on stone and in the codices, it is at once apparent that time in its various manifestations, the accurate record of its principal phenomena, constitutes the major content of Maya writing, a truth perceived by Förstemann, Brinton, Goodman and Bowditch half a century ago.

In so far as they have been deciphered, and we are now able to read perhaps as much as one third of the hieroglyphs, the Maya inscriptions and codices have been found to deal exclusively with the counting of time in one way or another: the length of the tropical year, the apparent revolutions of the planet Venus and its several phases—superior and inferior conjunctions, eastern and western elongations—lunations, eclipses and, to an essentially agricultural people, the all important corrections necessary to keep an official calendar year of 365 days in harmony with the tropical year of 365.24 days.

Furthermore, all our advances have been made along the chronologic-calendric front, just as all the major defeats have been suffered by those who have believed the Maya graphic system was basically phonetic, and have sought to "read" its different texts. From Bishop Landa's alleged alphabet, first published by the Abbé Brasseur de Bourgourg in 1864 down to the present day, all such efforts have failed to produce convincing results, some of the alleged "readings" in their vagueness rivalling the inconsequential, not to say fantastic messages unscrupulous mediums are wont to produce at will from the spirit world.

The astronomic-mathematic approach has brought us where we now are—namely to a knowledge of about one third of the characters employed in Maya writing, so that we can conservatively claim they no longer conceal from us the general tenor of their meaning as being chronological, astronomical and religious records.

But it must be admitted that the astronomic-mathematic approach has brought us almost to a dead end. From the first, of necessity, it was confined almost exclusively to those signs which have numerical coefficients, or if without them, to a limited number of signs which can be shown to derive their respective forms from their known relation to numerical sequences such as the nineteen divisions of the year, the Nine Gods of the Underworld, etc.

Only a very few signs having numerical coefficients now remain to be deciphered, and almost certainly no important numerical series.

But what of the remaining two thirds of the Maya hieroglyphs—those without coefficients—of what do they treat? and how may they be deciphered?

Answering the last question first, it would seem that the next step should be a careful analysis and classification on a purely objective basis, of the non-numerical glyphs, always with close attention to associated glyphs or groups of glyphs and always with direct reference to the nearest associated Long Count dates with the hope, born of previous experience, that the associated date may well supply a definite astronomic interpretation for the associated non-numerical glyphs.

Beyer has made a praiseworthy beginning at such a classification of the non-numerical glyphs at one site in his "Studies on the Inscriptions at Chichen Itzá" already mentioned, but this is only a beginning, and victories on this non-numerical front will be few and far between in their very nature, and moreover, less susceptible of conclusive proof.

Meanwhile Maya epigraphy badly lags for want of the certain identification of a single glyph denoting a place name. Even at this late date we do not know the hieroglyph for a single center of the Maya civilization, much less that for any of the different rulers of its many city states. This is in lamentable contrast to the situation in Aztec epigraphy where the name glyphs of hundreds of towns and scores of rulers in central Mexico have been identified, their specific meanings proved by accompanying Spanish or Nahuatl glosses written in Spanish script. But in Maya epigraphy as yet we have no such advantage and, indeed, the writer strongly doubts that any place names will ever be found in the Maya stone inscriptions.

These latter texts were highly specialized in character, what might perhaps be called current almanacs, recording the dedicatory date of each monument, the corresponding moon age and the calendar correction data necessary at the moment to bring the 365-day official year into harmony with the tropical year; but of history in the Old World sense, probably not a word will be found.

The ancient Maya indubitably recorded their history but not in the stone inscriptions. Aztec history has survived in a number of pre-Columbian Mexican codices, and rescripts of Maya history have been preserved in the so-called Books of Chilan Balam, native manuscripts dating from the Colonial Period, written in Spanish script, but of the three Maya codices that have come down to us, most unfortunately not one is historical in nature.

If not of history, then of what do the remaining undeciphered two thirds of the Maya stone inscriptions treat?

The writer has recently summarized his views on this matter in "The Inscriptions of Peten," which considered opinion he can do no better than to quote here:

While it is impossible to answer this question surely at the present time, one may perhaps hazard the guess that the remaining undeciphered glyphs deal with further ceremonial matters, perhaps such as offerings appropriate to specific religious festivals, the designation of lucky and unlucky days, the malevolent and benevolent deities of the ritualistic year, the name glyphs of the patron deities of the six different months of the lunar half-year, the glyphs for the different phases of the planet Venus, etc. Some of the glyphs as yet unknown undoubtedly represent deities; others perhaps the special kinds of offerings with which they were to be severally propitiated; and still others, the special rites with which they were to be worshipped—that is to say, more and more of ritual, of liturgy, of astrology and religion, and less and less of history in the Old World sense of personal and national records.

Amid this maze of speculation one fact alone stands forth, clear and unmistakable: Whatever may be the burden of the undeciphered glyphs, the Maya stone inscriptions from Copan in the extreme southeast to Chichen Itzá and Coba in the distant northeast from the Island of Jaina off the northwest coast of Yucatan to El Tortuguero in western Tabasco, and Tonina, Comitan and Chinkultic in the highlands of central Chiapas in the southwestern corner of the Maya area, *all tell the same story*, because everywhere within this vast region the undeciphered glyphs are *always the same*, recognizable in form though unknown in meaning. Whatever their significance may be, it is the same everywhere, that is to say, they must treat of matters common to all, such as a generally accepted astronomy and the common religious philosophy arising therefrom, and not of purely local matters. Throughout the Maya area, the undeciphered glyphs deal with an extremely limited subject matter and are essentially homogeneous.

X

CHRONOLOGY AND ASTRONOMY IN THE MAYA AREA

E. Wyllys Andrews [*]

T HE TRULY remarkable advances made by the Maya in mathematical and calendrical science have been described above by Dr. Morley. It has been further indicated that the focal center of religion and ceremonial life in this area was in the heavens, for the celestial bodies exerted direct control over the affairs of man. Through a study of their movements singly and in relation to each other, one could determine favorable times for the planting of crops, for the harvest or for any and all of the activities which formed the background of this agricultural civilization. For any evolved astrological practice an extremely precise knowledge of the periodicity of movement of the celestial bodies was essential. Their elaborate calendar and highly advanced mathematical knowledge were ideal tools in the attainment of such a goal—were, in fact, probably evolved mainly to fill this need. The only flaw in their equipment was an ignorance of fractions. Instead, they used the more cumbersome but equally effective equation. Thus, although they were unable to state that one lunation was equal to 29.53020 days, they achieved exactly the same end by using the equation $149L = 4400^d$, an estimate less than four ten-thousandths of a day in error. In the middle of the Old Empire, the Copan astronomers used the value 365.2420 days for the length of the tropical year as against the correct value for that time of 365.-2423. This is of exactly the same accuracy as our present Gregorian year, and much more accurate than the Julian Year (365.2500^d) used in Europe centuries after the Maya civilization had fallen into decay. In a paper of this size it would be quite impossible to summarize in any detail the various ramifications of Maya astronomical knowledge. This has been ably done in words understandable to the layman by the late Dr. John E. Teeple in his paper "Maya Astronomy." [1] In

---

[*] Harvard, A.B., 1938; graduate school, 1939—.
[1] Teeple, Maya Astronomy, 1931.

this paper we wish rather to show how the astronomical records of the Maya may be used towards the solution of a much broader problem, probably the most important single problem facing the New World archaeologist today.

The correlation of Mayan and European Calendars has as yet been accomplished with no certainty, but the field has been narrowed down to three general solutions. These solutions, named Ahau Equations by R. W. Willson,[2] define the difference between the statement of Maya days in terms of absolute chronology and the corresponding Julian day. The correlation evolved by Goodman and revived by Juan Martínez Hernández and J. Eric Thompson[3] expresses this difference as 584285; that evolved by Herbert Spinden[4] and supported by Hans Ludendorff and other German workers is based on the figure 489484; a later correlation with the value 626927 will be discussed at the end of this paper. Given any date in our own calendar with a supposed equivalent in the Maya system accompanied by a record of some astronomical phenomenon occurring on that Maya day—an obvious check on the veracity of the equation would be to determine if such a phenomenon actually did take place at the point in time indicated. In the inscriptions and codices we have a large body of such astronomical literature associated in varying directness with specific Maya dates. Were the delineation of phenomena more distinct and the association more specific, this alone could answer our problem; but such unfortunately is not the case. The two correlations receiving the most support at present are based on historical material which is briefly summarized in Kidder and Thompson.[5] In the following pages, we shall explain how the astronomical data may be used to test these correlations and how an attempt has been made to establish a correlation on the basis of these data alone.

The first and most specific body of material is known as the Supplementary Series, a series of glyphs almost invariably following Initial Series, stating the moon age on that date and placing the involved lunation in a pattern of lunar semesters. These glyphs and the manner in which they present the lunar data are clearly described on pp. 42–64 of Teeple. If this is a collection of actual lunar obser-

[2] Willson, Astronomical Notes, 1924.
[3] Cf. Thompson, Correlation, 1927.
[4] Cf. Spinden, Maya Dates, 1924.
[5] Kidder and Thompson, Chronologies, 1938.

vations, we have a splendid check on any proposed correlation. Thompson discovered that the actual moon age derived from astronomical tables via the Ahau Equation 584285 corresponded closely to the recorded moon ages of the monumental dates. The 489484 equation, he found, did not satisfy this condition, but was about 10 days off. A controversy then arose which is still in existence:

1. Was the lunar count from New Moon or some other phase?
2. Was it a series of actual observations or a series of extracts from a ceremonial lunar calendar which had accumulated several days' error?

The defenders of the 584285 equation believe the lunar count was from new moon and was a record of actual observations. To support this contention, Teeple offered the following:

1. Landa stated that the count was from the time the New Moon rises until it disappears.
2. Most primitive peoples count from new moon.
3. The Maya Venus count was from inferior conjunction; we should expect the lunar count by analogy to start at solar conjunction.
4. The Dresden Codex Eclipse Tables record solar eclipses (eclipses at New Moon); we should thus expect the lunar count to begin at this phase.

Guthe has quoted some interesting suggestions of J. Eric Thompson involving the form of the lunar glyphs.[6] If the lunar month was completed at full moon, we would expect Glyph C, expressing completed moons, to have a full rather than a crescentic moon sign. Glyph D, also having a crescentic moon sign, might indicate the count started at crescentic moon. Glyph E, he states, "should be a full moon, since at 20 days after new moon, the moon is considerably closer to full than to crescentic." This explanation seems not only invalid but unnecessary. The two occurrences of the crescentic form in the Supplementary Series are the two cases where the moon sign is only part of a glyph. Their reduction in size is easily accounted for by the necessity of placing them in a single glyph block with other elements. In the two cases where the moon glyph is the principal or only element, the "full" moon sign is used. As we know of no case in the inscriptions where the "crescentic" form occurs alone, we can justifiably assume that this "full" moon sign is nothing but *the* moon sign, and the crescentic type its reduced replica.

[6] Guthe, Lunar Count, 1932, pp. 272–273.

Thompson [7] has quoted Dieseldorff to the effect that the Kekchi say for new moon "the moon is dead." Sahagun further informs us that the Mexicans believed the moon dead around time of conjunction. Schulz [8] pointed out that the numerous death symbols such as crossed bones in the Dresden Codex eclipse tables might indicate a similar Maya belief. Cesar Lizardi Ramos [9] recently published a paper offering further evidence from an analysis of the forms of Glyph B of the Supplementary Series that the lunation died or ended at the time of its obscuration at Solar conjunction. As final evidence on this point, we mention Damian Kreichgauer's statement that in the Mexican Codices new light is portrayed as a young moon being freed from the "World Tree."

Teeple points out that the 1–3 day deviations on either side of a calculated pattern of lunations seem to occur entirely unsystematically. If that be true, clearly no formalized calendar was used. He is, however, certainly at fault in one matter. The Maya may not have used a formalized lunar calendar, but the Supplementary Series is surely not a record of actual observations. Ludendorff pointed out that if monuments were dedicated on hotun-endings indicated by the terminal date of the inscription, the moon ages must have been worked out in advance to enable the inscriptions to be carved on the stone monuments. In view of several explicit statements of early historians, it seems probable that these monuments were dedicated at festivals marking the ends of these five-year periods. The important question is whether the monumental statements closely represent the actual moon age on the date involved.

Spinden and Ludendorff attempt to fit the Supplementary Series evidence into the pattern of the Ahau Equation 489484, upon which Ludendorff's "Untersuchungen zur Astronomie der Maya" [10] are based. Could it be proved either that the lunar count was from new moon, or that its record corresponded with actuality, this correlation would have to be abandoned—for it locates lunar month beginnings at a point four days before actual full moon. Spinden claims the records were not those of actual observations, but lunar positions in an ancient lunar calendar which, inaugurated in the distant past, had accumulated an error of four days at the time of the monu-

[7] Thompson, Solar Year, 1932, p. 411.
[8] Schulz, Beiträge, 1936, p. 773.
[9] Lizardi Ramos, Glifo B, 1939.
[10] Ludendorff, Untersuchung, 1930–1937.

ments. With this adjustment, the lunar beginnings of the monuments correspond to actual full moons according to his correlation. This thesis has been worked out in great detail in Ludendorff's "Das Mondalter in den Inschriften der Maya." [11]

Ludendorff has offered a refutation for practically every point mentioned as contradicting his thesis. He points out that no new moon varies more than $0^d.6$ from a series of average lunations, so that the amplitude in possible variation is $1^d.2$ instead of the 4^d we find on the monuments. The remaining $2^d.8$ at least, we must assume, was error, and presumably the Maya with their astronomical ability could have made a closer approximation had they wished. He also points out that at single sites there is, over long periods of time, a uniformity in the deviation of the records from the series of average new moons. For example, in a definite group of cities during a definite period of time all the moon age statements are slow; then for a following period at the same sites all statements will be fast. Were the record observational, this would not occur. He answers Teeple's arguments on p. 227 as follows:

1. Landa's information might have come as an affirmative response to a leading question.
2. Certain primitive peoples do start their count from full moon.
3. The Venus illustration is unfair. No other point in the Venus cycle could be used except solar conjunction.
4. He claims in his Untersuchung Nr.2 that the Dresden tables might have been used for lunar eclipses. This has been confirmed by Guthe. Thus the inference that solar conjunction was the critical point in the lunar orbit breaks down.

Ludendorff claims that the lunar count was inaugurated about 450 B. C. and embodied the formula $149L = 4400^d$. This involves an error of $> 0^d.48$ per century, slightly over 4^d by the time of the monuments, and was certainly known to the Maya. But Teeple claims that this count was not introduced until 9.12.5.0.0. At this date, which marks the start of lunar uniformity in Old Empire Cities, Ludendorff believes the above formula was discarded in favor of the more accurate $405L = 11960^d$. This latter (involving the small error of $< 0^d.34$) Teeple claims was used before the period of uniformity; but it is rather difficult to visualize a people gradually increasing in proficiency discarding an accurate formula in favor of one less suitable.

[11] Ludendorff, Untersuchung Nr. 4, 1931.

We have then a picture of the lunar calendar lagging $0^d.4$ per century between 450 B. C. and the Period of Uniformity; then a change, after which it started to catch up at the rate of $0^d.34$ per century. The period in which we have hieroglyphic inscriptions is of sufficient length to allow us to notice this trend if it existed. Teeple claimed this could not be demonstrated, but Ludendorff devotes much of his moon age paper in proving (to his own satisfaction) that it can. He maintains that the deviation cannot be noticed in single inscriptions, but is evident in a comprehensive analysis. Because of their ignorance of fractions, the Maya could not express an exact lunation in a single number, but only as an equation or as a rough alternation of integers around an unstated fractional number. Their lunar calendar thus consisted of a series of inexact figures totalling to a correct multiple in the end: This could not be a steady alternation of 29- and 30-day declarations, but needed an occasional extra 30-day period. In the case of $405L = 11960^d$, there would be an extra 12^d if the alternation were even; so the series had to be made up of 215 30-day months and 190 29-day months. In such an irregular series, small errors crept in, but these were evened out at the end. The curve of variation from the "average sequence" called for by the formula actually meets the axis of the "average sequence" 11960^d. It is this very source of error, Ludendorff maintains, which conceals the trend of average variation from physical conditions.

In recent papers, R. P. C. Schulz discusses the correlation problem in the light of the Supplementary Series. He maintains that the Spinden Correlation fits better with the eclipse count which apparently began at the end of the period of uniformity,[12] and attempts to show that the other correlation does not locate the monumental new moons at actual new moon [13]; but in his comparison he uses the mean equation 584383 instead of the final Thompson figure 584285. This throws the entire lunar count two days behind new moon, and represents an unfortunate choice on the part of Schulz. Beyer recently arrived at the conclusion that the lunar count was from old light, and chose the equation 584284.[14]

Although the matter is by no means settled, the evidence of the Supplementary Series seems to favor a 584285 correlation. It is possible to understand how the Maya, for religious reasons, might retain

[12] Cf. Schulz, Korrelation, 1933 and Chronologie, 1935.
[13] Schulz, Beiträge, 1936, pp. 765–774.
[14] Beyer, Lunar Glyphs, 1937.

a lunar calendar despite an increasing accumulation of error. But why they should discard it, adopt another more accurate (as Ludendorff states they did at 9.12.5.0.0.)—and still retain the error which their older calendar had accumulated is hard to see. Again, the entire theoretical structure offered by Ludendorff was evolved not to explain the Supplementary Series, but to fit it into the pattern of a correlation it was endangering. We shall see later that much of Ludendorff's work in other branches of Maya astronomy has recently undergone very severe and apparently just criticism in both Europe and America.

Another body of astronomical data, on pp. 51–58 of the Dresden Codex, consists of tables falling in two general parts. The first is an arrangement of 405 consecutive lunations in groups of 5 and 6, the 5-moon groups being followed in the text by a picture. The tables total 11959^d, but 11960 was intended, as the second part of the tables contains a series of multiples of the latter number. This was the formula used at Palenque, although it was given there as $81L = 2392^d$. Finally, at the start of the table is an Initial Series. 9.16.4.10.8., which is very probably the starting date of the tables.

The tabular arrangement of the lunations has been much discussed. None doubt that the arrangement is such that each interval between groups represents an eclipse syzygy, but Guthe and others have shown that such an arrangement could be fitted into the actual eclipse pattern in absolute time in a number of different places and for this reason will not serve alone to correlate Maya chronology with ours. The arrangement is ingenious. Teeple explains on pp. 86–93 of his paper how, due to the close coincidence in length of three actual eclipse half-years and two tzolkins ($519.^d93$ as against 520^d), eclipses will follow for a long time around three days of the double tzolkin. Furthermore, after the interval represented by the tables as a whole, eclipses would be repeated on the identical tzolkin days. Assuming that the table was made to fit the actual pattern of any eclipse series, eclipses would occur only schematically at 11960^d intervals, for this value is some $0^d.122$ too large. After they had occurred on the original tzolkin day about 8 times, they would start to occur a day earlier. After falling on this second tzolkin day for approximately 8 times, they would lag another day. For the remainder of the series, they would fall on this third tzolkin day. The three tzolkin days on which the Dresden eclipses could fall are given one below the other under each eclipse interval.

After any eclipse series had run its course, eclipses would start to occur a whole lunation earlier—and this long-time correction is actually considered in the section giving multiples of the basic 11960^d. Under these larger intervals, three tzolkin days a lunation apart are declared, so that the main table may be corrected to apply over three of these overlapping eclipse series. In addition, two tzolkin days, staggered one half lunation are declared in the same synoptic table so that the data may be applied to lunar eclipse series. Schulz has discussed these eclipse series in relation to both correlations,[15] but in a later paper Noll-Husum has shown rather conclusively that the record fits the Ahau Equation 584285 much better than that of 489484.[16] As in the case of the Supplementary Series, the Ludendorff proof rests again on artificial calculations. This time he subtracts an assumed "constant" of 51 days in each calculation. This constant seems to be devised solely to meet the disparity between Spinden's chronology and the actual record, there being no declaration of the number in such a context either in the inscriptions or the codices.

Noll-Husum's most important suggestion covers the applicability of the tables to actual phenomena over immense periods. He points out that in the succession of these long-range eclipse series, "The nine little pictures with the 148^d intervals were, so to speak, the 'sliding' part of the table, and were slowly moved forward to the left" [17] in order to keep its arrangement in accord with actual phenomena. He even suggests this might have been done on a mechanical model. The practice is strongly indicated by the misplaced picture at interval No. 26, which actually occurs after a 177-day interval, whereas the total figure above, the tzolkin day, and the calculations following show it belonged after a 148-day interval, 1 lunation before. The brilliant suggestions of Mr. Noll-Husum have contributed much to our final decision on the correlation problem, and we must await with impatience the publication of further and even more decisive data promised in a supplementary note to his 1937 paper.

The start of the tables must obviously have been an eclipse syzygy. Furthermore, we know that, as the date 9.16.4.10.8. at Copan inaugurated an eclipse arrangement of lunations into semesters of 5 and 6 moons each, there must have been a node day within 18 days

[15] Schulz, Chronologie, 1935.
[16] Noll-Husum, Grundlegendes, 1937.
[17] *Ibid.*, p. 59.

after the corresponding 12-Lamat date in the same tzolkin (see Teeple, pp. 86–90, 104). The 584285 correlation places an eclipse syzygy exactly on 9.16.4.10.8., which ties in with the monumental data and the best of possible starting dates for the Codex tables. Furthermore, according to this correlation node day occurs some 17 days later, within the limits prescribed above. According to the 489484 equation, the nearest eclipse syzygy to 9.16.4.10.8. is 69 or 70 days away, and the nearest node day is 56 days before the 12-Lamat in question.

On pp. 24 and 46–50 of the Dresden Codex is a synoptic table of the synodical revolution of the planet Venus. Connected with it is the Initial Series 9.9.9.16.0., most probably its starting date. As we know from their construction that the tables started with a heliacal rising, we may assume that such a phenomenon must have occurred close to the above date. This condition is again met by the 584285 correlation. The Spinden formula, however, places the nearest Venus conjunction 280 days from the date—about as far as possible.

Spinden stresses supposed coincidences of dates in the inscriptions with actual equinoxes, solstices, and certain arbitrary points in his "Farmer's Year." Teeple pointed out that this "Farmer's Year" had no actual existence until it was invented by Spinden "to fit the supposed Christian dates." Neither have we evidence to assume that the solstices and equinoxes were considered important by the Maya. If they were, we would expect a considerable number of such coincidences to appear in a random sample to support any correlation. It would be well to remember Teeple's classical warning that by such a method we would be able to prove the Mayas celebrated Washington's Birthday or Yom Kippur.

Much attention of late has been attracted by a series of papers on this subject by Ludendorff.[18] He has translated a number of monumental dates into Christian chronology with the Spinden equation and examined the actual celestial configurations which obtained on those dates, finding numerous conjunctions of the planets with the sun, with themselves, and with bright stars near the ecliptic. He analyzes the results in his "Wahrscheinlichkeitsbetrachtungen" and reaches the conclusion that these dates were chosen because of extraordinary phenomena or groups of phenomena which occurred on them, i. e., that the Maya recorded in the inscriptions dates which were of unusual astronomical significance. This methodology has been ade-

[18] Ludendorff, Untersuchungen Nr. 7–10, 1933–1937.

quately discussed by Thompson,[19] and there is little we can add to his remarks. He found that Ludendorff had chosen a number of dates which had been wrongly read, and then demonstrated that the percentage of "significant" phenomena was actually higher on the incorrect dates than on the correct ones. After a recent examination of Ludendorff's mathematical discussion of his results in relation to the laws of probability, Noll-Husum had the following to say: "I can now venture to make a final statement: The Spinden correlation affords only accidental coincidences." [20] If the number of phenomena found on Ludendorff's dates is no more than would be expected on any date, and false dates offer more phenomena than correct ones, we cannot seriously consider his results as proof of the validity of Spinden's correlation.

Finally, we wish to discuss one more correlation. In 1927, P. Damian Kreichgauer published a correlation developed on purely astronomical grounds.[21] This uses the Ahau equation 626927, equating the Spanish conquest with the approximate Maya date 11.10.0.0.0., almost exactly two calendar rounds and 13 tuns later than the Thompson formula. The correlations we discussed above were evolved essentially from historical data, and for them our astronomical data acts as a valuable check. The Kreichgauer correlation, on the other hand, was derived solely from the latter and does not check completely with the historical material. It does agree with Landa's date of 12 Kan on July 16, 1553. Furthermore, it places a katun-ending shortly before 1542 (1538). But this was a Katun 12 Ahau instead of the 13 Ahau indicated by much conquest material. Although this fact weakens Kreichgauer's arguments, it by no means invalidates them completely. Any of the fragmentary data on the degenerate 16th Century calendar must be viewed with a certain amount of suspicion. Schulz comes to the conclusion in his 1936 paper that this correlation, completely ignored in the English literature, on astronomical grounds alone is the best thus far offered. It will therefore be well to examine the material offered in its support.

Kreichgauer assumes that: (a) 9.16.4.10.8. is the start of the Dresden eclipse tables, (b) 9.9.9.16.0. initiates the Venus tables and corresponds to a heliacal rising, (c) Landa's declaration that 12 Kan fell on July 16 was not over 5 days in error. We indicated above

[19] Thompson, Maya Chronology, 1936, pp. 83–91.
[20] Noll-Husum, Grundlegendes, 1937, footnote, p. 62.
[21] Kreichgauer, Anschluss, 1927, and Maya-Chronologie, 1932.

how eclipses occur in clusters of 20 at 11960^d intervals. These clusters, occurring at single points in the tzolkin, are separated by approximately 2300 years. In any table of eclipse calculations, therefore, the obvious starting point would be either the first or one of the first of such a cluster—thus the table would acquire a maximum span of validity. The problem then is to find an eclipse on a day 12-Lamat in actual chronology separated by some multiple of 260 days from the known position of 12-Lamat at the time of the conquest, which was the first or one of the first in its series, and which was separated by an interval of 48,488 days from a heliacal rising of Venus. Kreichgauer found that only the eclipse of August 7, 872, would answer all the above conditions.

To supplement this data, Kreichgauer found additional support in the Dresden Codex. Initial Series dates in the tables supposedly relating to Mercury, Mars and Jupiter corresponded to actual heliacal risings of these planets. Furthermore, 9.16.4.11.3 at the start of the table corresponds to the total lunar eclipse of August 22, 872, which was visible in the Maya area.

CONCLUSIONS

Both Kidder [22] and Vaillant [23] have pointed out that on archaeological grounds an 11.16.0.0.0. correlation is greatly preferable to one at 12.9.0.0.0. This preference might extend to an 11.3.0.0.0. solution, which Vaillant inferentially recommends. On these grounds alone, Kreichgauer's correlation at 11.10.0.0.0. might form an acceptable compromise between the latter two values.

The Spinden and Goodman-Thompson-Martínez Hernández correlations are based largely on 16th Century material, and their conformity with this data is therefore obvious. The Kreichgauer correlation disagrees sharply with much of this material, and the break in the calendar that he must assume seems improbable for a number of reasons.

We have seen that the 11.16.0.0.0. solution seems to pass reasonably well the astronomical tests. This 584285 equation places a new moon at the spot demanded by the inscriptions, places an eclipse syzygy at 9.16.4.10.8., and a heliacal rising of Venus near 9.9.9.16.0. On the other hand, the Spinden correlation may be reconciled with

[22] Kidder and Thompson, Chronologies, 1938.
[23] Vaillant, Chronology and Stratigraphy, 1935.

the astronomical data only after much highly unconvincing mathematical prestidigitation. It disagrees with the apparent record of the Supplementary Series; it places 9.16.4.10.8. 69 or 70 days before an eclipse syzygy; and, finally, it places 9.9.9.16.0. almost as far as possible from a Venus heliacal rising. The Kreichgauer correlation agrees strikingly with all astronomical data now on hand, but was created with this very purpose in mind. Were we more certain that the Maya were aware of the "Saros-groupings" of eclipses in clusters of 20 and certain that the actual starting point of the eclipse tables was at 9.16.4.10.8., this solution might be regarded as more firmly established. At present, these may be considered as merely highly probable assumptions.

In the final analysis, the Spinden correlation fails equally on archaeological and astronomical grounds and may probably be discarded. At present the Goodman-Thompson-Martínez Hernández Correlation may be considered as the foremost probability, being strongly supported by both archaeological and historical data, and agreeing reasonably well with our astronomical test material. If archaeological evidence, as it well may, makes a later correlation more desirable, we will probably have to assume a break in the Maya calendar. In that case, the Kreichgauer correlation has excellent astronomical backing, yet agrees sufficiently with historical data (i. e., makes July 19 = 12 Kan) to indicate a break for which an explanation might be forthcoming.

XI

DIFFUSION OF MAYA ASTRONOMY

Herbert J. Spinden *

AN ANSWER is sought to the following question: how fundamental
was the influence of the Mayas in ancient America? Obviously
in a short article the evidence bearing on this problem can only be
sampled. Suffice it to define briefly this Maya civilization itself, and
then to examine certain intimate acceptances of one or two remarkable Maya concepts by neighbors of alien speech.

It will, I think, be pretty generally admitted that the Maya Indians
had a high self-contained civilization, a truly primary civilization distinguished by strikingly original arts and sciences. They had their
own special system of hieroglyphs for inscribing texts on blocks of
stone and in paper books; their own notation of numbers in place
values; their own calendar and long-range chronological machine.
With clear means of record they evolved a true science of astronomy
which, being only human, they combined with a pseudo-science of
astrology. They erected lofty buildings of stone and rubble after
discovering how to make lime by burning limestone. As a further
development of this invention they used stucco as a plastic medium
in architectural decoration and also learned to paint in fresco. They
practiced city planning. In massive sculptures, generally subservient
to architectural effects, they cultivated a masterly style of decorative
realism. Through the ceramic, textile and lapidary crafts they found
continuous expression for everyday esthetics. Their government was
theocratic, but applied to city states rather than to a unified nation.
Their priest-kings are pictured as speaking through the masks of
gods. On death such men probably became gods in their own right
by apotheosis. In Maya religion the rule of the universe was divided
among beast gods and grotesque composite gods who gradually assumed the human face and figure. It seems that the drama of nature

* Harvard, A.B., 1906; A.M., 1908; Ph.D., 1909; Curator, Mexican Archaeology,
Peabody Museum, 1920–1929; now Curator, American Indian Art and Primitive
Cultures, Brooklyn Museum.

was partly explained by the conflict between a Jaguar God of the clear sky, the sun, the moon, the stars and the dry season, and a Serpent God of the clouded sky, the storm, the lightning, the rain and the wet season of the year. The planet Venus and, perhaps other planets as well, helped the Serpent God and was inimical to the Jaguar God.

This extreme specialization of the Mayas in intellectual and artistic matters emerged from the Archaic civilization which previously had accomplished the domestication of important American food plants and the stabilization of numerous Indian tribes into sedentary community life. Archaic figurines occur in the lowermost stratum at Uaxactun as proof of succession. Actually the difference between the personality of the far-flung Archaic culture and that of the Maya in their restricted territory is so great that transition becomes something of a miracle. But archeologists now find similar miracles elsewhere, observing how rapidly great national styles took form in Egypt, Mesopotamia and China out of the commonplace Neolithic.

There are no certain indications of animal gods and no stylized forms of animals in Archaic art, but the dead were buried ceremoniously and doubtless animistic beliefs were held. The nude female figurines—distributed from the Pueblo area of the United States to the Calchaquí area of Argentine—have been compared to other nude female figurines common in the Neolithic area of the Old World, and like these explained as fertility fetishes applied to agriculture. I believe Archaic art, as the index of Archaic civilization, was truly diffused in America from a single focus, but doubt that any important part of it was introduced by the first immigrants via Siberia and Alaska since American agriculture is so clearly an independent invention.

At any rate there came a time when Archaic art was suddenly cast aside in the small Maya homeland for something very different. Actually we cannot date any pottery object or stone sculpture of assured Maya design much before the time of Christ and no vaulted building until at least three centuries later.[1] Nevertheless, we must go back to the seventh century before Christ for the genesis of their calendar and to times almost as early for the invention of the instrumentalities of record.

Doubtless many persons regard Maya astronomy and mathematics as collateral products of a great civilization. But I think they should

[1] The Tuxtla Statuette is not of assured Maya design.

rather be regarded as the true cause and original ferment which produced those arts and ceremonies which now seem to us so wonderful. The accumulation of facts regarding intervals between celestial events, indispensable to a science of astronomy, requires method and time—much time. A celestial ephemeris can be kept before writing by tagged beads on strings. Such bead records would disclose in visual patterns a basic order in heavenly phenomena and lead to other recording devices.

Three important considerations affect the origin of the Maya civilization: first, the slow up-building of astronomical knowledge providing a new religious theme; secondly, the establishment of theocratic leadership, logically based on prestige coming from prophecy, etc.; thirdly, a heavy population, resulting from long social security which alone can explain the tremendous urban works. Arts of the Mayas before their urban stage were doubtless essentially Archaic and throughout their most brilliant period the Mayas were definitely in the Stone Age.

The change came with a rush, arts and ceremonies rising to a recondite complexity which made imitation practically impossible. It seems that the Mayas found no takers among their neighbors for the high science, philosophy and esoteric design which was theirs between the fourth and seventh centuries after Christ. Apparently no one of their neighbors could accept the Maya calendarial complex of day count, hieroglyphic writing and notation of numbers. Writing never existed among the Chorotega to the south of the Maya although ceramic influences were felt strongly enough. In the west and north the classical levels at Teotihuacan, ancient capital of the Toltecs, were similarly devoid of hieroglyphs. While some authorities have assumed the contemporaneity of Toltec and early Maya art, resting their argument mostly on pottery taken from a royal sepulchre at Holmul, recent enlarged collections of potsherds from Uaxactun, Piedras Negras, etc. give scanty support, if any, to Vaillant's Holmul sequence. It now seems likely that this famous deposit must be referred to the Intermediate Period. At that time the ancient science of the Mayas, along with their custom of dating monuments, was but slightly cultivated.

The full Toltec level is traceable throughout southern Mexico and northern Central America by the distribution of speech scrolls, a device not found on early Maya monuments in connection with human beings. These are seen in Teotihuacan frescos and on pottery apparently antedating hieroglyphical and calendarial records. Very similar ones are found in Toltec buildings at Chichen Itza and in connection with the earliest inscriptions at such non-Maya sites as Cerro de las Mesas, Tajin, Maltrata, Xochicalco, Monte Alban, Santa Lucia Cozumalhualpa, etc. These are ruins ascribed to tribes speaking languages distinct from the Maya and from each other. It appears that writing and the use of dates suddenly became universal in all territory contiguous to the Maya, except possibly in the south.

The answer to this enigma lies, I believe, in a revival of early Maya learning which took place between the tenth and thirteenth centuries after Christ, represented first of all by the Dresden Codex and secondly by inscriptions in the Red House at Chichen Itza. The dates in the Dresden Codex reach back into the first century before Christ. The last one corresponds to 950 A. D., ushering in an Eclipse Table and a Venus Table which give days coinciding with the required phenomena for an additional three centuries. The style of drawing is Maya, without evidence of metals, but there are a few Toltec details.

Quetzalcoatl, the Toltec king, priest, astronomer and culture hero extraordinary, is said to have gained the respect of the original inhabitants of Yucatan by his devotion to their traditional religious and scientific interests. There can be little doubt, I think, but that he reduced the Maya calendar and some of its appurtenances to a system of signs or ideographs which fitted all languages equally well. The use of dates and hieroglyphs, all pretty much of one style, became general among civilized nations following the time of Quetzalcoatl. He had started a year count in 1168 with a Day 1 Knife, giving its name to a Year 1 Knife, and in Year 2 Reed (1194–5) he instituted a New Fire Ceremony to be celebrated at intervals of 52 years. He died on April 5, 1208, and on April 13, eight days later, his soul arose in the east as the Morning Star. Perhaps this means he was immolated and then passed through apotheosis. Certainly April 5 and April 13, with April 9 halfway between them, are positions of great importance in the Venus calendar and the Farmer's Year during the First Empire of the Mayas. Also they were positions of great importance in the Venus calendar of the Mixteca during the thirteenth, fourteenth and fifteenth centuries, as we shall see from a survey of their dates and pictures.

While Seler, many years ago, thought that the calendar which the Spaniards found in general use among tribes distributed from Michoacan to Nicaragua might have originated among the Zapotecs, it can easily be shown now that such was not the case. It concerned a year consisting of 18 months having 20 days each, plus 5 days at the end, making 365 days in all without provision for leap year correction. The years were designated in cycles of 52 according to the days which fell in a certain key position and inquiry revealed that there was a cycle of 260 day names. This general calendar, complicated as it may seem, is really a simplification of the Maya time machine. It lacks several essential elements of the very exact mode of fixing time seen in the so-called Initial Series dates on Maya monuments of the First Empire. These Initial Series dates are three concurrent time counts in one, and beyond that require very special facilities in writing which the non-Maya nations did not possess.

I report concerning series of much emphasized dates in several Mixtec MSS. where the pictures disclose astronomical significance. These Mixtec dates can be converted rather easily into Maya ones by the simple device of locating the equivalent of the Mixtec year-bearer in the Maya month position 6 Muan. The Mixtec year begins 100 days before its year-bearer and runs 265 days beyond its year-bearer. Therefore, the first hundred and the last five days of the year make a double appearance. More serious than the choice which sometimes has to be made between two days of the same name in one year is the choice of the proper 52-year cycle. Once, however, a Mixtec date has been transcribed into one of its Maya equivalents others can be found readily enough. When an astronomical significance is disclosed in keeping with the pictures and the context it may be accepted tentatively or definitely as the case may be.

Let me illustrate: on page 47 of the Codex Vienna is a rather well-known picture of the grotesque Quetzalcoatl as Venus God supporting, Atlas-like, the starry sky and the waters above the sky (Fig. 6, *a*). The accompanying date is Year 10 House Day 2 Rain, the god himself bearing the designation Nine Wind. Now the last pre-Spanish position of the Year 10 House was 1489–90. We start our

---

Fig. 6

a. Codex Vienna (Vindobondensis), page 47, Quetzalcoatl as Venus God, 9 Wind, Date A, Year 10 House, Day 2 Rain.

b. Codex Vienna, page 48, The Venus God, 9 Wind descends from heaven and walks the earth. Date B, Year 6 Rabbit, Day 5 Reed.

c. Codex Vienna, page 10, The Venus God, 9 Wind operates a fire drill, Date M, Year 7 Reed, Day 4 Earthquake.

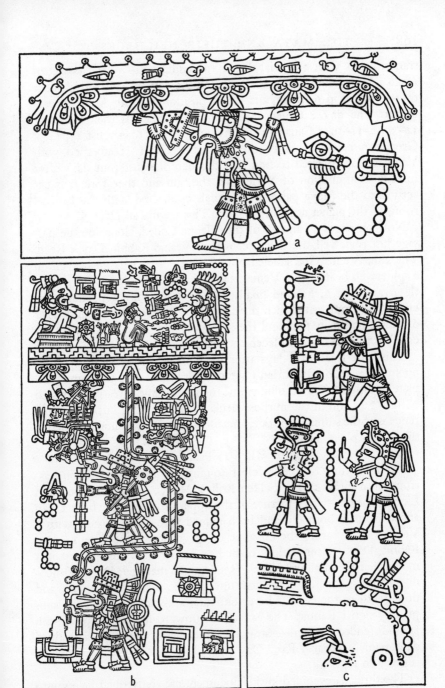

Fig. 6. (For description, see facing page.)

transcription with the trial Maya tun-ending 12– 6–12– 0– 0, 10 Ahau 3 Mol. Counting forward we find the day 10 Akbal, equivalent to 10 House, in 6 Muan, the Maya position for any Mixtec year-bearer. The day 2 Cauac, equivalent of 2 Rain, is then found at 12– 6–12–11–19, 2 Cauac 17 Pop, which reduces to August 25, 1489, Gregorian calendar. Since the picture is clearly concerned with Venus we are pleased to find that this date lies just four days after Inferior Conjunction of Venus and the Sun and therefore falls exactly into the Maya pattern for rituals connected with the heliacal rising of the planet as Morning Star. This I will call *Date A*.

Now on pages 47 and 48 of the Vienna Codex, alongside the passage just reviewed, are three records of Year 6 Rabbit, Day 5 Reed. The same Venus God labeled Nine Wind descends from heaven on a spiderweb bearing the Venus Staff, then he walks the earth in battle array (Fig. 6, *b*), and finally in a part I do not reproduce discusses with four seated men the cited date. The last pre-Spanish year 6 Rabbit began in 1498 and the next preceding one in 1446. In this case it is the next to last placement that fits.

This Date B is just 4 days after an Inferior Conjunction of Venus on June 23, 1446, Gregorian Calendar. Not only does this date completely support the adjoining one which I have already discussed both in fact and in the purpose declared by pictures, but the occurrence is at the summer solstice, anciently a position of importance for the Venus phenomena.

Date B: 12– 4– 8–15–13, 5 Ben 11 Pax, June 27, 1446.

We now turn to a very clear joining of three dates having astronomical interest. The Selden Roll, a Mixtec MS. in the Bodleian Library, begins with a picture of the uppermost heaven where a man and a woman, both old and both named One Deer, discuss with a Venus God wearing the costume of Quetzalcoatl the date Year 13 Rabbit, Day 2 Deer. Below eight heavens of stars are the crescent moon, half the sun, and Year 1 Reed (right margin), Day 1 Crocodile (left margin). Footprints run upward through the stars and downward to the earth where four men are seated around the simple day sign 1 Rabbit. The earth is an upward-looking serpent with jaws distended to form a straight angle. Below the earth is a third date, namely: Year 7 Reed Day 7 Reed. The text, greatly reduced, is given in Fig. 7, *a*.

The three dates joined in this document are transcribed below into

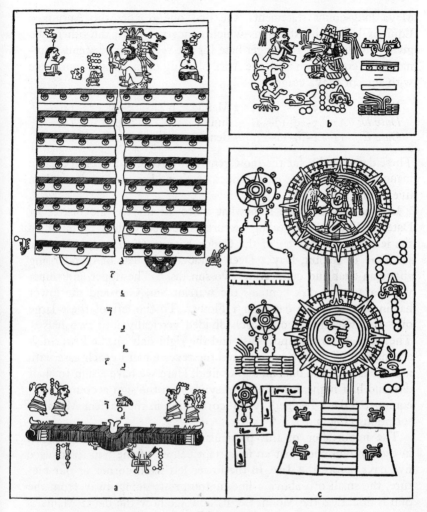

Fig. 7

a. Selden Roll; beginning, Venus God between man and woman above eight heavens
divided into night and day; Date C, Year 13 Rabbit, Day 2 Deer; at sides, Date D,
Year 1 Reed, right margin; Day 1 Crocodile, left margin; at bottom, Date E,
Year 7 Reed, Day 7 Reed.

b. Codex Vienna, page 38, Venus God, conversing with an eclipse demon; Date C,
Year 13 Rabbit, Day 2 Deer.

c. Codex Vienna, page 23, Altar with two solar disks over a blood stream; at left
two disks divided into night and day; Date C, Year 13 Rabbit, Day 2 Deer.
(Note: on original, blood spatters cover the stream.)

Maya long-count statements; the first one reaches the Autumnal Equinox but with extensions which concern Venus, the other two giving an older and a younger base for the regulation of Venus ceremonies in connection with the April planting of maize, in accordance with ancient Maya usage.

Date C:	12– 5– 9– 7– 7,	2 Manik	0 Zip,	Sept. 23, 1466.
Date D:	12– 5– 9–17– 1,	1 Imix	14 Ceh,	April 5, 1467.
Date E:	11–13–19–11–13,	7 Ben	1 Yax,	April 6, 1240.

These dates are by far the most generously recorded ones in Mixtec manuscripts, some 61 occurrences of them having been noted in five MSS. (Figs. 7, 8).

Let us now examine somewhat more attentively the matter of Date C. The most revealing picture associated with it is found on the left half of page 23 of the Codex Vienna (Fig. 7, *c*). Here we see Year 13 Rabbit, Day 2 Deer beside a red pillar of blood rising above an altar and connecting two sun disks. The upper and somewhat larger sun disk contains the warrior Sun God and the lower has in its center the day sign 1 Flower. To the left of these large orbs are two smaller ones each divided vertically into two halves. The left half on the upper disk and the right half on the lower disk are marked with the sun's rays and the reverse half in each case with numerous eyes and dots on a gray field. Here we have a sign for half day and half night, resembling in symbolism the sign accompanying equinoctial dates reached by my correlation in the ancient Maya inscriptions (Fig. 7, *c*).

The importance of this particular Autumnal Equinox is found in the circumstance that an important eclipse of the Sun took place five days before the date. In the lower left-hand corner of our picture, the small orb above a line of footprints going away from the Sun is doubtless the Moon. Let us now see how the day 2 Manik is intimately involved in important phenomena. Five days before 2 Manik gives us 10 Ik for the eclipse and it happens that $9 \times 260 + 5$ (1565 days) is an eclipse interval. Adding this number (4–6–0) to Date C we get another visible eclipse of the Sun, this time on 2 Manik. Making the same addition a second time we find that a third 2 Manik reaches exactly an Inferior Conjunction of Venus and the Sun this time on April 6, 1475. Again 5 days brings us to the syzygy of an invisible eclipse one day after Heliacal Rising of our planet.

12–5– 9– 7– 2, 10 Ik   15 Uo,   Sept. 17, 1466   Eclipse of the Sun.[2]
      5
12–5– 9– 7– 7, 2 Manik 0 Zip,   Sept. 23, 1466   Equinox.
  4– 6– 0
12–5–13–13– 7, 2 Manik 0 Mol,   Dec. 30, 1470   Eclipse of the Sun.[2]
  4– 6– 0
12–5–18– 1– 7, 2 Manik 0 Mac,   Apr. 6, 1475   Inf. Conj. of Venus.
      5
12–5–18– 1–12, 7 Eb   6 Mac,   Apr. 11, 1475   Eclipse of the Sun.

In my paper on Indian Manuscripts of Southern Mexico I have referred to Date D as follows [3]:

> The most conspicuous representations of Venus ceremonies are in connection with a day 1 Crocodile in a year 1 Reed. . . . Converting this recurrent Mexican date into Maya and then European equivalents, we find the most probable position in relation to Venus to be April 5, 1467, Gregorian Calendar. Here it coincides with the last visibility of the planet as evening star before an Inferior Conjunction with the Sun on about April 9, while a first visibility of the planet as morning star falls on April 13. This agrees very closely (the discrepancy may amount to 2 days) with the Venus dates associated with the great Toltec ruler Quetzalcoatl, who died or was sacrificed on April 5, 1208, and who was converted into the God of Venus when the planet made her first appearance 8 days later. This earlier phenomenon was also in a year 1 Reed, but the day of the apotheosis was 1 Reed instead of 1 Crocodile.

On the narrative side of the Codex Vienna, page VI, we see an historical personage, Lord Five Crocodile, father of the famous Mixtec conqueror Eight Deer, in connection with a star temple to which Day 1 Crocodile is attached (Fig. 9, c). In front of this temple are three dates, the last one being our Date D, and the others Year 6 Reed, Day 5 Reed and Year 10 Reed, Day 9 Reed. The year-bearers correspond to 1459, 1463, and 1467 or may be distant from them by one or more calendar rounds. The first one, if placed in 1459, strikes 6 days after the Heliacal Rising of Venus as Morning Star and 10 days after the Inferior Conjunction. This discrepancy is too wide for serious consideration. If, however, the date is put back one Venus calendar round into the past it fits almost perfectly, striking the fourth or fifth day after conjunction.

---

[2] These first two eclipses were visible in Mixtec territory (Oppolzer nos. 6357, 6365); the last one (no. 6376) was not visible.

[3] Spinden, Indian Manuscripts, 1933, p. 447.

Date F: 11–19–16– 7–13, 5 Ben 6 Mac, May 14, 1355.

Year 10 Reed Day 9 Reed, placed just four years after Date F, could only have reference to Superior Conjunction of Venus but it is unlikely that this position was ceremonially important. Adding one calendar round and four years to Date F we get an Heliacal Rising about five days after Inferior Conjunction and according to pattern:

Date G: 12– 2–13– 3–13, 9 Ben 6 Mac, May 1, 1411.

The calculations of Lord Five Crocodile form an interesting series of Venus dates for 1355, 1411, and 1467. Actually Date D, which plays such an important role, is less finely drawn than the others as far as Venus is concerned but Day 1 Crocodile also begins the permutation table for divining purposes.

It is a strange circumstance that one son of Lord Five Crocodile was sacrificed by another son on account of a second 1 Crocodile Venus date. I refer to the excoriation of Lord Nine Flower by Lord Eight Deer. In this case a long-drawn-out ceremony began on July 22, 1473, when we see the Venus staff carried by Nine Flower. On the actual day of the Heliacal Rising of Venus the staff was planted but the sacrifice itself did take place August 13, 1474, the second phase of the ceremonies beginning on August 7. I now think that the sign 9 Wind which follows 1 Crocodile is not a current date but instead the proper name Nine Wind, a common Mixtec name of the Venus God (see Codex Zouche or Nuttall, pp. 52, 53, and 69).

Date H: 12– 5–16– 8– 1, 1 Imix 19 Pop, August 31, 1473. The distance from Date D is $9 \times 260 = 2340$ days, also nearly equal to 4 synodical revolutions of Venus.

We now come to a fuller consideration of Date E. It can be found close to Venus phenomena for an unusually long time, at intervals of 104 years.

Of all these dates, however, April 6, 1240 is the closest to the ideal situation. At any rate there is supplementary evidence which seems to apply most forcibly to it. The next earlier possibility is better handled in the declaration Year 7 Reed Day 10 Vulture (page 43, Codex Zouche) as can be seen below where it reaches the Heliacal

---

FIG. 8

a. Lienzo of Yolotepec, central hieroglyph; Date E, Year 7 Reed, Day 7 Reed.
b. Codex Nuttall (Zouche), page 38, Venus God, Date E, Year 7 Reed, Day 7 Reed.
c. Codex Nuttall (Zouche), page 39. The personages One Rain and Seven Rain, departing from the crucial day, Date E, Year 7 Reed, Day 7 Reed.

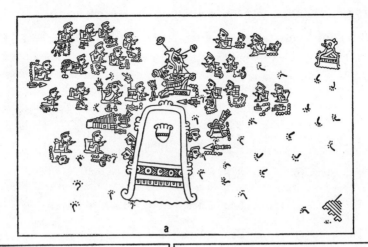

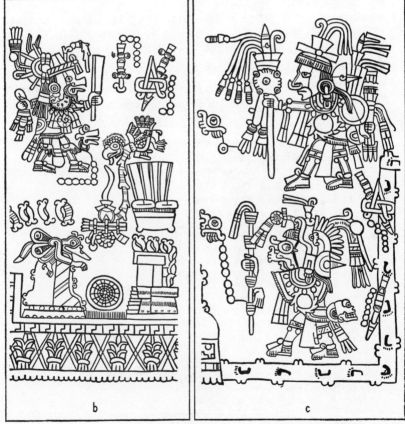

Fig. 8. (For description, see facing page.)

Rising of Venus three days after Year 7 Reed Day 7 Reed, and four days after the Conjunction.

DATE E: YEAR 7 REED DAY 7 REED

Maya Day	Gregorian Day	Inf. Conj. of Venus
10–18– 3– 5–13, 5– 5– 8– 0	7 Ben 1 Yax June 22, 928	June 28, 928
11– 3– 8–13–13, 5– 5– 8– 0	7 Ben 1 Yax May 28, 1032	May 30, 1032
11– 8–14– 3–13, 5– 5– 8– 0	7 Ben 1 Yax May 2, 1136	May 1, 1136
11–13–19–11–13, 5– 5– 8– 0	7 Ben 1 Yax Apr. 6, 1240	Apr. 1, 1240
11–19– 5– 1–13, 5– 5– 8– 0	7 Ben 1 Yax Mar. 12, 1344	Mar. 3, 1344
12– 4–10– 9–13,	7 Ben 1 Yax Feb. 16, 1448	Jan. 31, 1448

Date I: 11– 8–14– 3–16, 10 Cib 4 Yax, May 5, 1136.

This phenomenon took place before the Toltecs had conquered Chichen Itza but easily enough it may represent data upon which

---

FIG. 9

a. Codex Vienna, right half of page 43, and adjacent left half of page 44. Sequence begins in the lower left hand corner and travels between guide lines.

Date N, Year 2 Reed, Day 2 Reed.
Date E, Year 7 Reed, Day 7 Reed.
————, Year 4 Reed, Day 4 Deer.
Date D, Year 1 Reed, Day 1 Crocodile.
————, Year 3 House, Day 7 Rain.
Date D, Year 1 Reed, Day 1 Crocodile.
Date D, Year 1 Reed, Day 1 Crocodile.
Date D, Year 1 Reed, Day 1 Crocodile.
Date E, Year 7 Reed, Day 7 Reed.
————, Year 12 Knife, Day 2 Eagle.
Date E, Year 7 Reed, Day 7 Reed.
Date K, Year 10 Reed, Day 12 Eagle.

b. Codex Vienna, page 4; at right Date K, Year 10 Reed, Day 12 Eagle; at left, Year 6 Reed, Day 7 Deer.

c. Codex Vienna, page VI (Historical Side), Temple 1 Crocodile, Lord 5 Crocodile designated by sun headdress (hieroglyphic designation before and after this personage), and Venus dates:
Date F, Year 6 Reed, Day 5 Reed.
Date G, Year 10 Reed, Day 9 Reed.
Date D, Year 1 Reed, Day 1 Crocodile.

Fig. 9. (For description, see facing page.)

Quetzalcoatl worked and which possibly he presented in his Sacred Book. In keeping with it is the record of Year 2 Reed Day 4 Eagle on page 12 of the Codex Zouche. I make it:

Date J: 11– 9– 2– 5-15, 4 Men 3 Yax, May 2, 1144, again very close to ideal position.

On page 4 of the Vienna Codex is Year 10 Reed Day 12 Eagle. It transcribes to April 4, 1256, which falls seven days after Inferior Conjunction or if carried back another round of the Venus Calendar almost meets the ideal conditions of the Venus Table of the Dresden Codex (Fig. 9, *b*). I give the two possibilities:

Date K: 11– 9-10– 7-16,   12 Men 3 Yax, Apr. 30, 1152.
        5– 5– 8– 0
       11-14-15-15-16,   12 Men 3 Yax, Apr. 4, 1256.

In the same Venus family is a date recorded thrice in the Vienna Codex, pages 18, 44 and 45, namely Year 3 Reed Day 2 Herb. It reduces very nicely to the following position four or five days after Inferior Conjunction:

Date L: 11–16– 8– 5– 12, 2 Eb 0 Yax, Mar. 24, 1288.

Before reverting to further consideration of Date E I wish to call attention to another rather close record on Venus which marks the recession in the Maya year for two or perhaps three rounds of the Venus calendar. It is Year 7 Reed Day 4 Earthquake found on page 10 of the Vienna Codex in a passage which shows the Venus God "Nine Wind" operating a fire drill (Fig. 6, *c*). It is repeated on page 33 of the same MS with Venus associations again in evidence:

Date M: 12– 4-10– 8-17, 4 Caban 5 Chen, Feb. 1, 1448.

The day is, I believe, the next one after Inferior Conjunction; also it is 16 days in advance of 7 Ben 1 Yax in the last position given above on page 174. If, as I think, it is intended to cover the recession from April 6, 1240 of eight-year phenomena the allowance is somewhat in excess.

Date E is recorded not once but many times in association with Venus ceremonies. For instance, on page 38 of the Zouche Codex (Fig. 8, *b*) we see Venus God "Nine Wind" standing before this Year 7 Reed, Day 7 Reed. On page 39 of the same MS. (Fig. 8, *c*) we see "Seven Rain" and "One Rain," the latter bearing a Venus staff departing from the crucial day. In the Vienna Codex the Venus staff is stuck in a valley between two hills beside a trumpet shell (see Fig. 9, *a*) along with this date.

The Lienzo of Chicomostoc, in the Royal Ontario Museum,[4] Toronto, Canada, has in the lower left-hand corner a fine representation of the legendary place of origin called Seven Caves (Fig. 10). In the cave are two signs, 1 Reed and 9 Wind, which represent, I suppose, the Venus Gods Nine Wind and One Reed, the latter being the calendarial name of Quetzalcoatl. Above the cave is our Year 7 Reed Day 7 Reed. The Lienzo of Yolotepec or Amoltepec,[5] in the American Museum of Natural History, has this same Year 7 Reed Day 7 Reed beside the central hieroglyph and in two other places (Fig. 8, a). Abraham Castellanos believed that this Mixtec MS. dealt with a sort of astronomical congress. In view of the fact that the Mixteca had no way to mark a particular calendar round it is quite possible that well-known dates, far in the past, such as this one, were used as chronological bench marks.

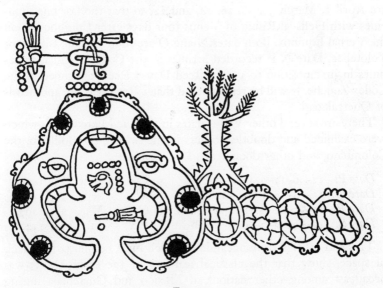

FIG. 10

Lienzo of Chicomostoc; Date E, Year 7 Reed, Day 7 Reed; and in cave, Days 9 Wind and 1 Reed.

Year 7 Reed Day 7 Reed may have started a vogue for the doubled name types. We find Year 2 Reed Day 2 Reed; Year 8 Reed Day 8 Reed; Year 1 Rabbit Day 1 Rabbit; Year 5 Knife Day 5 Knife, etc.

4 Rickards, Codex Rickards, 1913.
5 Peñafiel, Monumentos, 1890, Pl. 317.

The first two of these belong in a formal series of Venus dates eight and forty years after Year 7 Reed Day 7 Reed as follows:

Date E:	11–13–19–11–13,	7 Ben	1 Yax,	Apr.	6, 1240.
	8– 2– 0				
Date N:	11–14– 7–13–13,	2 Ben	1 Yax,	Apr.	3, 1248.
	8– 2– 0				
	11–14–15–15–13,	10 Ben	1 Yax,	Apr.	1, 1256.
	8– 2– 0				
	11–15– 3–17–13,	5 Ben	1 Yax,	Mar.	30, 1264.
	8– 2– 0				
	11–15–12– 1–13,	13 Ben	1 Yax,	Mar.	28, 1272.
	8– 2– 0				
Date O:	11–16– 0– 3–13,	8 Ben	1 Yax,	Mar.	26, 1280.

In the same succession of years the Inferior Conjunctions of Venus are April 1, March 30, 28, 26, 24, and 22, so that the last one coincides with Heliacal Rising of Venus four days after Conjunction on the Vernal Equinox. Both dates N and O are found on the Lienzo of Yolotepec. Date N is recorded 4 times in the Codex Vienna, sometimes in juxtaposition to year 7 Reed Day 7 Reed, and once in the Codex Zouche. It will be remembered that 1 Reed was the apotheosis of Quetzalcoatl.

There are several other Venus dates in the five Mixtec MSS. which were examined and doubtless others in the Selden, the Bodleian, the Colombino, and other documents. I merely list:

Date P:	12– 6–17–9–11,	13 Eb	10 Pax	June	13, 1494.
Date Q:	12– 4– 8–1– 2,	13 Ik	0 Uo	Sept.	20, 1393.
Date R:	12– 7– 2–6–18,	4 Eznab	11 Ceh	Mar.	25, 1499.
Date S:	11–19– 3–7– 9,	8 Cib	14 Pax	July	24, 1342.

This and other astronomical data, which must be omitted for lack of space, show that the classical learning of the early Mayas was broadcast among other nations of Mexico and Guatemala during the two or three centuries preceding the coming of the Spaniards.

XII

SOURCES AND METHODS IN THE STUDY OF MAYA ARCHITECTURE

H. E. D. Pollock *

SOURCES

IT WOULD be difficult to designate the precise start of the formal study of Maya architecture. It is, however, a simple matter to point to our earliest sources on the subject. These clearly occur in the first accounts of the discovery of Yucatan and the adjacent Mexican shore. As early as 1520 there appeared Juan Diaz's report of the Grijalva expedition of 1518, and in the following year Peter Martyr brought forth an account of the Córdoba voyage of 1517 that had resulted in the discovery of Yucatan. Both narratives reflect the wonderment of the Spanish at the size of the towns and their admiration of the houses and temples of stone, a form of construction they had seen nowhere else in the New World.

The appearance of these writings marks the beginning of a great outpouring of histories and narratives relative to the newly found territory of New Spain. As might be expected, they vary greatly as to content, accuracy, and point of view. The great Aztec center of Tenochtitlan, because of its wealth and power, absorbed the lion's share of attention, but it is probable that much that is recorded in regard to the Mexican culture is pertinent to the study of the Maya. At this place we must limit ourselves rather strictly to the subject in hand. It should be remembered, however, that the early sources hold much information that is not directly concerned with Maya architecture, but that is nevertheless of real value to the understanding of the building remains.

* Harvard, A.B., 1923; A.M., 1930; Ph.D., 1936; now Archaeologist, Carnegie Institution of Washington.

Sixteenth and Seventeenth Centuries

The narratives of Juan Diaz [1] and Martyr [2] are simple records of what the Spanish adventurers did and saw in the new land. If space permitted, it would be advantageous to quote Diaz's description of a community on the Island of Cozumel. This naïve yet factual account contains a certain breath of life—the picture of a living, functioning community—that is not found in the archaeologial remains. Such material is consequently important to the archaeologist in his attempt to arrive at the full meaning of the architecture.

The two great military leaders, Cortes [3] and Alvarado, [4] give us relatively little pertaining to the native structures. Bernal Diaz, [5] on the contrary, though a common soldier and writing many years after the conquest, describes the towns, the character of the houses, the temples, the temple furnishings, and even gives vague descriptions of architectural decoration, altars, sacrifices, and the native priests. All of these men are recounting first-hand experiences.

A different group of writers are those that came to the New World some years after the conquest but at a time when there was much that remained of native culture and tradition. Among such men may be mentioned Bienvenida, [6] Palacio, [7] and various authors of the Relaciones de Yucatan, [8] all of whom write at varying length of remains that were ancient even in their day. Two writers within this group stand out as exceptional—Landa, [9] from whose writing we gain so much of our knowledge of Maya culture, and Ciudad Real. [10] The former goes into considerable detail in describing examples of the ancient architecture, and even includes several crude drawings, while the latter has left an extraordinarily accurate and observing description of certain buildings at the ruins of Uxmal.

Lastly, there are the sixteenth-century historians, writing mostly from hearsay, occupied with too many matters to give much atten-

[1] Juan Diaz, Itinerario, 1858.
[2] Martyr, Orbe Novo, 1912.
[3] Cortes, Letters, 1908.
[4] Alvarado, Conquest of Guatemala, 1924.
[5] Bernal Diaz, True History, 1908–1916.
[6] Bienvenida, Carta, 1877.
[7] Palacio, Carta, 1860.
[8] Relaciones de Yucatan, 1898–1900.
[9] Landa, Yucatan, 1937.
[10] Ciudad Real, Relación Breve, 1872.

tion to Maya architecture, but nevertheless including material of value. Oviedo,[11] Las Casas,[12] and Gomara [13] are examples of the earlier part of the century, while Torquemada,[14] Herrera,[15] and García [16] were writing at the close of the period. Much of the earlier writing had been purely narrative in character, but in Torquemada and García we see a subjective point of view. They question origins, make comparisons with the Old World, and arrive at conclusions as to how, when, and why the native cultures arose in America. Herrera stands out as the great historiographer of the time. In his compilation of all available material relative to his subject, and in his attempt at a critical attitude in regard to sources, he approaches the methods of the modern historian.

By and large, the literary output of the seventeenth century was not up to the standard of the earlier period. There are, nevertheless, some valuable sources. Lizana [17] has left us a description of the ruins at Izamal, an account of certain religious practices, and something of native history and legend. The histories of Cogolludo [18] and Fuentes y Guzmán [19] are standard sources for Yucatan and Guatemala. The former gives some attention to the ancient remains, and discusses their purpose and the rites connected with them. The latter describes, and upon occasion illustrates, certain of the old native towns, but these descriptions have been proved to be highly inaccurate. The work of Avendaño [20] and Villagutierre [21] is important in providing information on that strange hangover of Itzá Maya culture that persisted in native state until the very close of the seventeenth century. Avendaño offers little in regard to the appearance of the Itza capital, but Villagutierre describes the temples, the idols, the furnishings, and certain rites and customs. The writing of these two men is akin to

[11] Oviedo, Historia General, 1851–1855.
[12] Las Casas, Historia de las Índias, 1877; Apologética Historia, 1909. It should be noted that no attempt is made at full bibliographic reference to the authors cited. Only representative works or works of value to the present study are given.
[13] Gomara, Historia, and Crónica, 1749.
[14] Torquemada, Monarchia Indiana, 1723.
[15] Herrera, Historia General, 1727–1730.
[16] García, Origen, 1729.
[17] Lizana, Historia de Yucatan, 1893.
[18] Cogolludo, Historia de Yucatan, 1867–1868.
[19] Fuentes y Guzmán, Historia de Guatemala, 1882–1883.
[20] Avendaño, Relación, 1696.
[21] Villagutierre, Historia Itzá, 1701.

that of the preceding century. They are the last of the sources dealing with unadulterated native culture, and they mark the close of an epoch.

Before going further, we may pause to note the character and relative value of the material we have considered. It is the work of these early men that is our contact with the old living culture. We have kept rather strictly to the architectural aspect of the accounts, but it should be stressed that these writings are replete with other material that is of indirect but real value to the study of architecture. Indeed, it is this other material—history, legend, myth, religion, social structure, and the like—that is the great contribution of the early sources, a contribution far more important than the simple description of buildings.

Eighteenth and Nineteenth Centuries

The eighteenth century seems not to have been prolific of material relative to our subject. It was, however, a period of importance to the general field of historical research. Not only was there an increased awareness of, and interest in, what had gone before, but there was a turn to the critical point of view in dealing with earlier records. In America, the conquest and submergence of the native civilizations were now two centuries gone, and men awoke to find that the remains of these cultures were fast disappearing. Before the middle of the century, we see in the great collection of Boturini [22] an appreciation of the value of aboriginal documents as sources for the pre-conquest history of Mexico. Boturini's collection was dissipated before his death, and his projected history never written,[23] but he stands as an enlightened figure in his effort to preserve the knowledge of the aboriginal civilizations.

Indicative of the time, although strangely contrasting, are the histories of Robertson [24] and Clavigero.[25] Both make the effort to assemble and sift all previous knowledge concerning the native cultures and the conquest. The former assumes a highly critical attitude and goes too far in questioning the accuracy of the early records, but his work is of value in the cry for observance of uncolored fact.

[22] Boturini, Idea, 1746.
[23] Veytia (Historia Antigua, 1836), who had access to Boturini's collection, produced a more limited work of this sort.
[24] Robertson, History of America, 1777.
[25] Clavigero, History of Mexico, 1817.

Clavigero knew his material better than Robertson and showed an avid interest in everything pertaining to the land, the people, and their history. Unfortunately, he did not possess sound critical ability in respect to his sources, with the result that much of his writing is highly colored and without basis in fact.

These eighteenth-century writers, so indicative of the changing attitude toward historical research, give little or no attention to the Maya. Toward the end of the century, however, there appeared a group of men whose work is directly concerned with that culture, and the architecture in particular. The work referred to is that of Ordóñez, Calderón, Bernasconi,[26] and del Rio [27] at the ruins of Palenque. The travels of these men, their descriptions of the remains, and the drawings of Bernasconi and del Rio,[28] mark the crude beginnings of archaeological field work. The writing of the first three is vague, purely descriptive, and pays no attention to the historical implications of the remains. Del Rio is more methodical in his description, and makes a sound comparison to the ruins of Yucatan, although he is utterly wild in looking to the Old World for origins. One hesitates to call this work scientific, but the attempt at factual description and graphic recording of remains is the start of correct archaeological procedure.

The nineteenth century opens with a truly great figure—Alexander von Humboldt.[29] During the years 1799 to 1804, this illustrious scientist and explorer made extensive travels in South America and New Spain, compiling a vast amount of data extraordinary in their range. Antiquities were but a part of his varied interests, and he gives brief attention to Maya remains. He stands, however, as a landmark in his diligent accumulation of data, in his unbiased presentation of material, and in his attitude toward the remains of antiquity as fragments of history.

The work of Humboldt was immediately followed by that of Dupaix and Castañeda,[30] and Palenque was once more the scene of their labors. The presumably straightforward description of Dupaix

---

[26] Muñoz, Calderón, Bernasconi, Palenque, 1783–1789. The reports of these men have never been published but are found in substance in Waldeck and Brasseur, Monuments Anciens, pp. 4–8, 1866.

[27] Rio and Cabrera, Palenque, 1822.

[28] The original del Rio drawings seem to have been lost, those appearing in the 1822 edition probably being the work of Castañeda (see below). See Kluckhohn, Palenque, 1935.

[29] Humboldt, Vues de Cordillères, 1810; Political Essay, 1811.

[30] Dupaix, Antiquités Mexicaines, 1834.

actually is none too accurate, but an encouraging note is some attention to building materials and methods of construction. The real
value of the work lies in the accompanying drawings by Castañeda,
the first of Maya architecture to be published, and the only ones
known to that time with the exception of the unpublished Bernasconi and lost del Rio copies.[31] The drawings are inclined to be interpretive and to reflect the impressions of the artist rather than
sticking to fact, a particular fault being the somewhat European
character given to the sculpture. They stand, however, as the first
pictorial record of Maya architecture.

The labors of del Rio and Dupaix lay in manuscript form a good
many years, and in each instance appeared with the work of other
men.[32] The dissertation of Cabrera,[33] which accompanied the del Rio
report, is of little value, but is of interest in stressing the importance
of the preservation of antiquities and early manuscripts, and in re-
ferring to the existence of a number of other ruins. Among the many
documents in conjunction with the Dupaix report may be mentioned those of Zavala,[34] Lenoir,[35] and Warden.[36] The first gives some
slight attention to matters of masonry and construction at the ruins
of Uxmal. The writing of Lenoir still looks mainly outside of America for origins and comparisons, but there is a suggestion of the
comparative method within Middle America, and he distinguishes
three ages, Palenque, Toltec, and Aztec, although with no particular
foundation for the assertion. Warden points out the unjustified belittling of Robertson, notes the existence of early and later peoples
and culture strata, and attempts accuracy in descriptive material.
Extraordinary in the modern note that it strikes is a report at this
time by Walckenaer, de Larenaudière, and Jomard.[37] These men
plea for an end of unfounded speculation, for exact recording, and
for adequate plans, drawings, and observations, that should thus
allow comparative work. They correctly distinguish the Central
American remains from those of Mexico.

Exploration and field work were also being carried on, notably by

[31] It will be remembered that the illustrations appearing with the del Rio account seem to be mainly the work of Castañeda.
[32] The Dupaix report was first published by Kingsborough in 1831, but re-
appeared three years later with the authors mentioned below.
[33] Rio and Cabrera, Teatro Critico, 1822.
[34] Zavala, Ushmal, 1834.
[35] Lenoir, Monuments Mexicains, 1834.
[36] Warden, Antiquités de l'Amérique, 1834.
[37] Walckenaer, de Larenaudière, Jomard, Amérique Centrale, 1836.

Galindo,[38] Waldeck,[39] and Friederichsthal.[40] The few extant drawings of the first are surprising in their fidelity and the avoidance of personal interpretation. Waldeck's work is a strange mixture of inaccuracy, unjustified restoration, over-drawing, and exaggeration, but in spite of this, the most detailed and ablest presentation of Maya architecture up to that time. While his writing is full of wild theories, he nevertheless makes comparisons within the Maya and Middle American areas, and mentions a culture sequence of Maya, Toltec, and Aztec. There is, unfortunately, but a brief account of Friedericksthal's travels. His work is of interest in the use of daguerreotype, but none of his views or drawings were published. He seems to have had an advanced point of view in his recognition of different epochs of construction, in his appreciation of the value of architectural comparisons, and in distinguishing the remains of Yucatan and Palenque from those of Mexico.

Up to this time Maya archaeology had been confined to a relatively small number of remains, but the two great journeys of Stephens [41] and Catherwood [42] changed completely this state of affairs. The explorations alone of these men would mark them as important figures in Maya archaeology, but the straight forward, uncolored description of Stephens, and the accurate drawings of Catherwood, assisted by the use of daguerreotype and camera lucida, left a work of immense value. Stephens' sound opinion, moreover, as to the indigenous origin of the ruins and their lack of tremendous age was of great importance at a time when there was so much loose thought on the subject. Catherwood's illustrations suffer through lack of clarity, and his working drawings are by no means adequate, but his concise statement in regard to architectural features and construction is far and away the best of his time.

Writers of the middle of the century worthy of passing mention are Carrillo,[43] Squier,[44] and Scherzer,[45] each of whom contributed brief descriptions of Maya remains. Far more important figures are

[38] Galindo, Mémoire, 1832; Copan, 1834; and in Walckenaer, etc., Amérique Centrale, 1836.
[39] Waldeck, Voyage Pittoresque, 1838; Waldeck and Brasseur, Monuments Anciens, 1866.
[40] Eyriès, Friedericksthal, 1841.
[41] Stephens, Central America, 1841; Yucatan, 1843.
[42] Catherwood, Views, 1844.
[43] Carrillo, Kabah, 1846; Zayi, 1846.
[44] Squier, Notes, 1855; States, 1858.
[45] Scherzer, Travels, 1857; Quirigua, 1936.

Charnay [46] and Brasseur de Bourbourg.[47] The former attained an accuracy in his plans and sections that was previously unknown, but most important of all he was the first to use photography and to take casts, a tremendous advance in technique. While Brasseur's work was mainly outside of the actual remains, he provides us with some descriptive material, notes the differences of architectural styles in different regions within the Maya area, and speculates on the functions of buildings. Finally, attention should be called to the work of Le Plongeon,[48] Bastian,[49] Habel,[50] and Rau.[51] Le Plongeon appears to have been the first to perform any considerable amount of excavation. His lurid imagination made his writing almost valueless, but the new material that appeared in his photographs, plans, and drawings was important. Bastian and Habel are mainly notable for their excellent publication of sculptures from Santa Lucia Cozumalhuapa, although the former wrote learnedly on aboriginal history. Rau's contribution dealing with the sculpture from the Temple of the Cross at Palenque is a masterly compilation of all material available on the subject.

It was during this period, and largely through the researches of Brasseur de Bourbourg, that the majority of documents of native Maya origin first received attention. The so-called codices,[52] aboriginal pictorial records, contain a good many examples of what appear to be representations of buildings. The style of presentation is so conventionalized that little can be gathered in regard to architectural form. It is barely possible, however, that examples of architectural decoration in the codices may be connected with deities associated with the buildings, and thus may serve as criteria in connecting archaeological remains with certain gods and religious practices. The various chronicles,[53] written documents in native Mayan languages but in Spanish script, make almost no reference to architecture or

[46] Charnay and Viollet-le-Duc, Cités et Ruines, 1863; Charnay, Ancient Cities, 1887.

[47] Brasseur, Histoire, 1857–1859; Ti-hoo, 1865; Mayapan, 1866; Waldeck and Brasseur, Monuments Anciens, 1866.

[48] Le Plongeon, Yucatan, 1878; Mayapan, 1881; Sacred Mysteries, 1886; Queen Moo, 1896; Salisbury, Le Plongeon, 1877; Isla Mujeres, 1878.

[49] Bastian, Cotzumalguapa, 1876; Steinsculpturen, 1882.

[50] Habel, Cosumalwhuapa, 1878.

[51] Rau, Palenque, 1879.

[52] Villacorta and Villacorta, Codices, 1930–1933.

[53] Brinton, Maya Chronicles, 1882; Cakchiquels, 1885; Villacorta and Rodas, Popol Buj, 1927; R. Roys, Chumayel, 1933.

construction of any sort. They deal mainly with native history, mythology, religious rites, and customs. In this respect they are of the same value to the study of architecture as the early Spanish sources.

Beginning with the books of Bradford [54] and Prescott,[55] there appeared a series of general works on American antiquities. They varied in the amount of attention given to Maya remains, and in no case presented new material. Such writers as Baldwin [56] and Short [57] contributed excellent ideas, however, in pointing out unknown areas, different epochs of the remains as between areas, different periods at the same site, and the position of architecture in the reconstruction of history. Ancona,[58] Carrillo y Ancona,[59] Orozco y Berra,[60] Nadaillac,[61] Chavero,[62] and Molina [63] should be mentioned as authors of such general works. By far the greatest was Bancroft,[64] whose gigantic compilation still stands as a reservoir of source material.

During these same years there was a group of men who turned their attention specifically to architecture. The writing of Viollet-le-Duc [65] is a classic example of sweeping conclusions based on little evidence. It is mainly of interest in treating the development of architecture as an evolutionary process, later forms growing out of, and retaining something of, earlier forms that in turn developed from prototypes. A striking contrast is Daly's [66] modern and comprehensive view of the position of architecture in historical research, the possibilities inherent in such studies, and the manner of approach. Works of lesser interest are those of Fergusson [67] and Peet,[68] the former touching upon the historical aspects of architecture, the latter stressing the evolutionary character.

[54] Bradford, American Antiquities, 1841.
[55] Prescott, Conquest of Mexico, 1843.
[56] Baldwin, Ancient America, 1871.
[57] Short, North Americans, 1880.
[58] Ancona, Historia de Yucatan, 1917.
[59] Carrillo y Ancona, Historia Antigua, 1883.
[60] Orozco y Berra, Historia Antigua, 1880.
[61] Nadaillac, Pre-historic America, 1884.
[62] Chavero, Historia Antigua, 1887.
[63] Molina Solís, Historia del Descubrimiento, 1896.
[64] Bancroft, Native Races, 1882.
[65] Charnay and Viollet-le-Duc, Cités et Ruines, 1863; Viollet-le-Duc, Habitations, 1876.
[66] Daly, Monuments du Mexique, 1864.
[67] Fergusson, History of Architecture, 1873–1876.
[68] Peet, Architectural Orders, 1882.

We must give brief mention to two writers at the end of this period, lasting to approximately 1885, who represented an important school of thought, although not primarily concerned with the Maya. Bandelier [69] and Morgan [70] revived the highly critical attitude seen in the writing of Robertson. As in the case of the earlier writer, they went too far in belittling the pre-Columbian civilizations. Morgan's work on building remains is a monument of faulty reasoning and wrong conclusions, in spite of his zeal for the bare truth. The thought of these men is nevertheless of definite importance in stressing the necessity of ethnological and sociological knowledge in the reconstruction of history, a truth equally applicable to the understanding of architectural remains.

Let us review briefly this period beginning with the eighteenth and extending over the greater part of the nineteenth century. Broadly speaking, the fundamental trend was the ever-increasing interest in the history of the aboriginal civilizations. This first became manifest in the collection and study of early documentary material, both native and European. Shortly after, we see men turning their attention to the material remains, and in their journeys and descriptive records we find the seed of archaeology. A combination of the critical attitude intent upon accuracy and the visualization of the remains as historical records brought this seed to fruition, but there remained the matter of evolving adequate methods and techniques to apply to the new science. In this connection, we see extensive exploration and the beginnings of crude excavation. There was an ever-growing body of descriptive and illustrative material, with increasing emphasis upon accuracy, and toward the end of the period the first use of photography. Along with discovery and recording, there were problems of interpretation. In the case of the Maya, men were struck with the importance of the building remains, and we see the start of the comparative method applied to matters of construction and design. The chronological significance of the ruins is made apparent through the recognition of sequent periods of construction and development of architectural style. Lastly, there is some small attempt to discover the function of buildings and to give them true meaning as parts of a once living culture. The period thus saw the problems outlined and the start of appropriate methods, but

---

[69] Bandelier, Art of War, 1877; Tenure of Lands, 1878; Sources, 1879; Social Organization, 1880; Romantic School, 1885.
[70] Morgan, Houses, 1881.

there was still much to be done in the latter respect and almost un-
limited possibilities in the matter of technique.

MODERN PERIOD

The first archaeologist in the Maya field that may be called modern was Alfred Maudslay.[71] His extensive explorations, combined
with some excavation, resulted in a large body of illustrative material
possessing of accuracy and excellence previously unknown. Not
only did the field work set a new standard, but the material was
superbly published, and it stands as the first of the major sources
dealing with Maya architecture. Maudslay was entirely modern in
his approach to the historical problem, appreciating the value of
combining early documentary material, geography, ethnology, linguistics, mythology, and archaeology in the recovery of history. It
is regrettable that he never carried out the detailed comparative work
that was contemplated.

Interest in Maya archaeology was increasing rapidly at this time,
and one name follows another in rapid succession. Two of the earliest workers in the field were E. H. Thompson [72] and Maler.[73]
Neither of these men possessed the sober and scholarly attitude of
Maudslay, but they contributed a large amount of new material,
much of which has never been published. Thompson's work is
highly variable in quality, but at its best includes accurate surveys,
careful records of excavation, and good photographs. He pays some
attention to prototypes and the general development of Maya architecture. Maler is notable for his great explorations and discoveries,
and for his superlative photographic record. His plans and drawings
are somewhat sketchy, and not always to be trusted, but his photographs gave a huge increase to the knowledge of architectural, sculptural, and inscriptional material.

A writer of different stamp than the above was Sapper,[74] primarily

[71] Maudslay, Explorations, 1883; Archaeology, 1889–1902; Central America,
1892; American Problems, 1912.

[72] E. H. Thompson, Labná, 1889; Labná, 1897; Xkichmook, 1898; Yucatan,
1904; Maya Arch, 1911; and short articles in Proceedings of the American Antiquarian Society, new series, vols. 4, 5, 8 (1888, 1889, 1893).

[73] Maler, Yukatekische Forschungen, 1895; Central Usumatsintla, 1901; Yukatekische Forschungen, 1902; Central Usumatsintla, 1903; Upper Usumatsintla,
1908; Peten, 1908; Peten, 1910; Peten, 1911.

[74] Sapper, Guatemala und Chiapas, 1895; Nordlichen Mittelamerika, 1895;
Mixco, 1898.

a geographer and ethnographer, but with an interest in the aboriginal remains. His field material consists of a relatively few sketch plans and drawings, but in his writing he brings to bear a point of view that we have seen only vaguely hinted at prior to this time. Using assemblage, orientation, construction practices, and broad matters of design, he classifies the remains into architectural types associated with ethnographic and linguistic areas. He further takes into account the effects of environment upon architecture, considers the nature and function of the ancient settlements and buildings, and suggests migrations, cultural associations, and intercourse of tribes as reflected in the architectural remains. Sapper's writings on these matters are unfortunately brief, but he offers a valuable approach to the subject.

In these same years Seler [75] was beginning his vast and varied researches on the native civilizations. His interests went far beyond Maya architecture, but he produced a great deal of work that bears directly or indirectly upon the subject. Seler went further than any previous writer in rounding out his field material with extensive research amongst the early documents and all that had been thought on the matter up to his time. He recognizes stylistic differences in the architecture, and takes account of stratigraphy as seen in building sequence, as well as regional variance arising through temporal or cultural factors. The most interesting aspect of his work is his strong cast toward mythology and religion which leads him to interpret architectural decoration and reach conclusions in regard to the dedication and possible function of buildings. He uses the architectural remains to construct elaborate theories of culture sequence, migrations, and general matters of history that rest on very insecure foundations, but in his approach, in his effort to interpret the use and meaning of the remains, his work is highly significant.

Excellent field reports were being produced at this time by Saville [76] and Gordon.[77] With the possible exception of Thompson's work at Labná, the excavations of these men at Copan constituted the first major attack of that sort upon any site in the Maya region (Plate II). The resulting publication was a careful record of operations and discoveries but lacking in comparative and interpretive data. Gordon later turned his attention to the art of the Maya. He

[75] Seler, Chaculá, 1901; Gesammelte Abhandlungen, 1902–1923; Palenque, 1915; Quetzalcouatl-Fassaden, 1916; Uxmal, 1917.

[76] Saville, Copan, 1892; Labná, 1893.

[77] Gordon, Copan, 1896; Copan, 1902; Chronological Sequence, 1904; Serpent Motive, 1905; Maya Art, 1909.

treated the subject from the aspects of symbolism and development, but recognized the effect of environment upon art and architecture. He was the first to attempt a general analysis of this sort although Maudslay had pointed out the value of the approach.

While the results of Maudslay's great labors were still being published, there appeared the second major work on Maya architecture. This was the result of Holmes's [78] brief trip to Yucatan and Mexico during the winter of 1895. For the first time, the architecture was treated as a distinct subject in a well rounded, logical manner. His survey was too rapid to lay stress on accuracy, but it is preeminent in graphic presentation with particular attention to the important matters of masonry and construction. Holmes makes the most of the comparative method, and readily visualizes the possibilities inherent in architecture as one of the major instruments of archaeology. His point of view was extraordinarily broad, for he thought in terms of the culture under consideration, and saw the need to relate the art and architecture to its authors and their civilization, in other words, to reconstruct the life and history of the times.

The turn of the century witnessed the work of several men that require brief mention. Gann [79] was carrying on explorations and excavations in British Honduras; Périgny [80] was exploring in the Peten and the Yucatan peninsula; Rickards [81] was photographing the ruins he visited in his travels through Yucatan, Tabasco, and Chiapas. None of the publications of these men were detailed architectural studies, but they brought forth a considerable amount of new material.

It is hardly possible to over-estimate the significance of the explorations, excavations, and researches of Tozzer [82] and Merwin.[83] The work is notable not only for the amount of new material that was produced but for new standards of accuracy and of fullness of information extracted from the remains. Following the sound beginnings made by Holmes, Tozzer organized his material so adequately that the majority of subsequent site descriptions and architectural studies have followed his form of presentation. The comparative

[78] Holmes, Mexico, 1895–1897; American Art, 1914–1919.
[79] Gann, Honduras, 1900; Honduras, 1905; Maya Indians, 1918.
[80] Périgny, Yucatan Inconnu, 1908; Villes Mortes, 1909; Nakcun, 1911; Amérique Centrale, 1911.
[81] Rickards, Mexico, 1910.
[82] Tozzer, Tikal, 1911; Northeastern Guatemala, 1912; Nakum, 1913.
[83] Merwin, Yucatan, 1913; Merwin and Vaillant, Holmul, 1932.

method was carried further than in previous work, and the highly important chronological information provided by the hieroglyphic inscriptions first came into use in connection with architectural studies.[84] Merwin followed Tozzer in most of these respects, and in addition contributed the first adequate stratigraphic sequences in architecture and pottery, a development of the utmost importance.

At this same time, Hewett [85] and Morley [86] were conducting excavations at Quiriguá. The work produced comparatively little architectural information, but on a smaller scale paralleled that of Tozzer and Merwin in showing sequence in building construction and dating of remains through hieroglyphic inscriptions. The brief publications include some restoration drawings of the architecture, a form of presentation that had been used in small degree by Maudslay and Merwin. While Morley's work is not primarily identified with the study of architecture, his extensive explorations, discoveries and decipherment of hieroglyphic texts have been of the greatest value in bringing forth new material and creating a chronological framework within which the architectural remains may be placed. Material of immediate value is seen in numerous maps of sites and plans of structures, in occasional details and photographs of buildings, in stylistic comparisons of sculpture, and in efforts to work out the relative time and direction of growth of certain sites, as well as specifically to date some of the remains. A number of his smaller papers, moreover, are directly concerned with architectural material.

In 1913 there appeared Spinden's [87] "Study of Maya Art," the third, and unquestionably the most important, of the major works on architecture. While this study is concerned with the analysis, interpretation, and development of Maya art in all its aspects, architecture is treated as a distinct subject and is focused against a more comprehensive historical background—cultural, aesthetic, and chronological—than occurs in any other work. Spinden gives a systematic discussion of the architecture, pointing out trends of development in design and construction, and making comparisons between the remains of various sites and regions. The underlying idea is the ar-

[84] Hewett and Morley (see below) were making use of inscriptions at the same time.

[85] Hewett, Guatemala, 1911; Quiriguá, 1912; Quiriguá, 1916.

[86] Morley, Uxmal, 1910; Ancient Temples, 1911; Quiriguá, 1913; Archaeology, 1915–1929; Tuloom, 1917; Copan, 1920; Peten, 1937–1938.

[87] Spinden, Copan, 1912; Maya Art, 1913; Maya Art, 1917; Ancient Civilizations, 1928.

ranging of the remains, monumental and architectural, in chronological sequence, based primarily on stylistic criteria, but controlled by known dates and other available historical data. The possibility of such an arrangement is founded on the concept of a more or less orderly evolution in art and architectural forms, and is an extension of the ideas noted in the works of Viollet-le-Duc, Peet, and to a lesser extent E. H. Thompson.

General works dealing with the aboriginal civilizations of Middle America, and containing relatively extensive sections devoted to the architecture of the Maya, appeared at this time under the authorships of Joyce [88] and Spinden. Such treatment developed no new material but gave a certain unity to the subject and tended to place the architecture in its complete setting against a background of culture and history.

Lastly, there is the work of Lothrop [89] on the remains of the eastern coast of Yucatan. Guided by the sound methods and accumulated knowledge that had preceded, he succeeded in presenting his material in more detail and as a better rounded whole than in any previous publication. The work is particularly notable in the adequacy of the illustrative material, including some restoration drawings, in the use of the comparative method to relate the remains to those of other regions, and in the handling of the cultural, chronological, and general historical aspects of the problem. It stands as the fitting conclusion to a period that was of such importance to the study of Maya architecture.

Once more we may pause for review. This period of approximately forty years, beginning near the end of the past century and extending over the first quarter of the present, is characterized by greater activity in research, by steady advance in technique, and by elaboration and better understanding of method. We note at this time the continuance of wide exploration, resulting in the discovery of many previously unknown remains. There was a rapid increase in the amount of published material, and it set a new standard of organization and presentation. Advances in technique and better methods were leading to the recovery of information that was not only more accurate, and more detailed, but that in its form and nature was of more value to the problems at hand. Adequate excavation was developing stratigraphy with its bearing on stylistic sequence and

[88] Joyce, Mexican Archaeology, 1914; Maudslay Collection, 1923.
[89] Lothrop, Tulum, 1924; Architecture, 1925.

chronology. Attention to matters of construction, architectural design, and decoration was providing material for adequate comparative studies. The unraveling of the Maya calendar and the decipherment of hieroglyphic texts were building up a chronological framework of tremendous value to the understanding of the architecture. The comparative method of studying the remains was undergoing refinement, and it was becoming apparent that this method offered several avenues of approach—the ethnographic, stressing cultural and environmental influences, and the developmental, stressing chronology, being prominent. Lastly, there is the first serious research on the identification and meaning of art forms in monumental and architectural decoration, and some furtherance of the attempt to discover the position and function of the remains in the old culture. The period mainly witnessed elaboration and refinement of the thought and methods of the preceding era. At the same time there came an increasing realization of the scope of the problem, and of the many forces that could and must be brought to bear in order to extract from the remains their true and full meaning as fragments of history.

1924–1939

The past fifteen years have witnessed an exceptional burst of activity in Maya archaeology. This is particularly notable in the intensive excavations at a few selected sites and in operations on a smaller scale at numerous other locations. Exploration, reconnaissance, and detailed survey have more or less kept pace with excavation. Literary research has gone on unabated. All of this labor has resulted in a very large body of new material and of old material reworked into more intelligible form. It is beyond the scope of this paper to attempt a consideration of all the work during these years. Much of it remains to be published, and a good deal has been brought forth only in preliminary form. We shall, therefore, confine ourselves to pointing out certain broad lines of endeavor that appear to be of particular significance to the study of Maya architecture.

The development of stylistic sequence through stratigraphy in the form of superimposed building remains is so well known a product of modern excavation that it can be passed over without comment. The importance of such reliable control in point of relative chronology has more than ever been emphasized by Smith's [90] proof of the

[90] A. L. Smith, Stelae, 1929; Ricketson and Ricketson, Uaxactun, 1937.

fallibility of dating buildings by means of presumably associated monuments. The dangers of any hypothetical scheme of architectural development has been brought out by Satterthwaite [91] in showing widely variant, although probably contemporaneous, forms of construction in adjacent regions and variant styles even within a region. It has become increasingly clear that the technical aspects of masonry and construction are extraordinarily reliable and sensitive criteria of chronological and cultural change. Nearly all of the recent work has paid strict attention to these matters, but the labors of Morris [92] and Roys [93] have been particularly valuable in describing, classifying, and analyzing principles of construction.

While there has been no broad survey of Maya art, specific examples have been subjected to detailed analysis, notably in the work of Charlot and A. Morris.[94] Hissink's [95] study of the façade mask, the first of the sort since Spinden's work, constitutes a course of research of the greatest importance to the understanding of stylistic changes in architecture. Along with Hissink, Tozzer [96] and Palacios [97] have contributed to the study of the subject matter of sculptural remains and have shown the possibility of recovering historical information from the art.

Definite advances have been made in unraveling the knotty problem of the uses to which buildings were put. For many years, the ball court was almost the only type of structure that could be assigned a specific function, and even then the distribution and cultural connections of these structures were incorrectly known. This fault has largely been corrected by Blom [98] and the remains have been given added meaning through information derived from documentary sources. Similar work has been carried on by Blom, Ricketson,[99] and Ruppert [100] in calling attention to the possibility of certain structures having served as observatories of astronomical phenomena.

[91] Satterthwaite, Expeditions, 1936; Roof Types, 1938.
[92] Morris, Charlot, Morris, Warriors, 1931.
[93] L. Roys, Engineering Knowledge, 1934.
[94] Morris, Charlot, Morris, Warriors, 1931.
[95] Hissink, Masken, 1934.
[96] Tozzer, Toltec Figures, 1930.
[97] Palacios, Mas Gemas, 1937.
[98] Blom, Ball-game, 1932. Also see Nordenskiöld, Changes in Material Culture, 1920, pp. 101–109.
[99] Ricketson, Astronomical Observatories, 1928; Notes on Observatories, 1928; Ricketson and Ricketson, Uaxactun, 1937.
[100] Ruppert, Caracol, 1935; and article in this volume.

Morley, Mason,[101] Cresson,[102] and Satterthwaite [103] have identified buildings as having been sweat houses, while the last has made progress in establishing the identity of certain questionable remains as temples, and in pointing out the ceremonial character of structures that might be considered domiciliary. Lastly, the writer [104] has attempted the association of one type of structure with a particular deity or religious cult.

There has been but one study embracing the architecture of the Maya and the cultures of Mexico as a whole. Using the comparative method, Marquina [105] traces cultural origins, spread, and development over a wide area. It is questionable if our knowledge is sufficient at present to give validity to such treatment, but it is of value in focusing attention beyond the local area, and in placing the Maya remains within the whole sweep of Middle American culture. Works of more limited scope, but treating Maya architecture as a whole, are those of Totten [106] and Conant.[107] These men view the remains from the standpoint of the history of architecture and are interested in the ruins as products of a little known but worthwhile school of the building art. They consequently touch upon the underlying philosophy of Maya art and architecture, an approach that has to some extent been followed by Vaillant.[108] Mention should be made of the splendid restoration drawings, for the most part unpublished, of Bolles, Russell Smith, and Proskouriakoff, a form of presentation that is of definite value to the knowledge of Maya architecture.

There have been a number of studies in recent years that have indirect bearing on the understanding of the ceremonial architecture. By no means all of these can be mentioned, but it seems particularly worthwhile to note the population studies of Smith [109] and Ricketson,[110] and the work on house mounds and residential sites by Wauchope [111] and Thompson.[112] It is obvious that we must know some-

[101] J. A. Mason, Sweat-Baths, 1935.
[102] Cresson, Sweat Houses, 1938.
[103] Satterthwaite, Unusual Type, 1936; Temple Buildings, 1937; Thrones, 1937.
[104] Pollock, Round Structures, 1936.
[105] Marquina, Estudio Arquitectonico, 1928.
[106] Totten, Maya Architecture, 1926.
[107] Conant, Maya Architecture, 1938.
[108] Vaillant, Native Art, 1928; Artists and Craftsmen, 1935.
[109] A. L. Smith, Map of Environs, 1929.
[110] Ricketson and Ricketson, Uaxactun, 1937.
[111] Wauchope, House Mounds, 1934; Maya Houses, 1938.
[112] J. E. Thompson, Cayo District, 1931.

thing of the composition, or at least the arrangement, of rural and urban populations in order fully to appreciate the character and significance of the ceremonial centers. Lastly, we should like to call attention to Tozzer's [113] critical review and Kidder's [114] broad visualization of the methods, position, and aim of archaeology in historical research. Orientation of this sort toward a broad objective is essential to the intelligent study of the architectural remains.

METHODS

In the preceding pages we have dealt with the sources that give rise to our knowledge of Maya architecture. We have been able to touch upon only a portion of the great amount of literature that has accumulated over the centuries, but it is hoped that the more important aspects of this material and the general trend of thought have been set forth. In this connection, we have noted the growth and development of methods suitable to architectural research, and we now may give some attention to the nature and use of these methods.

The study of architecture, as an archaeological procedure, is directed toward the recovery of history. It is founded upon the principle that the building remains reflect certain aspects and attributes of the culture or cultures that created them. Viewed in this light, the research is concerned with every phase of history, no matter how remote, that may find reflection in the remains. As a practical matter, procedure advances in a series of steps directed first toward a knowledge of the architecture and second toward the application of this knowledge to wider problems of history. At the outset we are confronted with the fundamental problem of identifying the remains with the builders and with what may be termed the inorganic phases of their civilization. Such questions deal with ethnic groups and cultures, geography and environment, chronology, construction, and design. Next in order, is the problem of relating the remains to the old living culture, of discovering the position, use, and function of the architecture in the life of the people. Lastly, there are the more remote questions, concerned primarily with broad problems of history but touching upon the architecture, such as social and religious structure, aspects of the intellectual life, as art, astronomy, and engineering, and a host of other matters that may to greater or lesser

[113] Tozzer, Maya Research, 1934.
[114] A. V. Kidder, Investigations, 1930–1938; Kidder and Thompson, Correlation, 1938.

extent be reflected in the remains. Research in the Maya field has largely been confined to the first part of the procedure, and we shall limit ourselves accordingly in the discussion that follows.

As indicated above, the study of Maya architecture is immediately concerned with the identity of cultures, with the contact and movement of cultures, and with an adequate chronology, exact or relative, that will give order to otherwise unrelated facts and events. It has developed in the course of our study that the comparative method is the procedure that is applied to the solution of such problems. This method deals with stylistic comparisons and may be applied to matters of construction, design, ornament, or the like. Similarities or dissimilarities of style arise through a variety of causes, such as time, environment, culture, and function of buildings. In any specific instance, these causes occur as unknown factors, and it is their evaluation and interpretation that lead to the solution of the problem.

Under these conditions, it is obvious that results will differ according to the stress laid upon one or another of the several unknown factors. We may, for example, explain stylistic differences as occurring through architectural development, i. e., time, and in doing so, tend to subordinate, or exclude, the elements of environment, cultural influence, and function. On the other hand, we may explain such differences as mainly cultural and subordinate, or exclude the possibilities of chronological, environmental, or functional factors having accounted for the stylistic dissimilarity. The handling of these problems is presumably determined by previous knowledge, and the accuracy of the resulting interpretation is logically dependent upon the control exerted by such external information and by due regard for all of the factors involved. These controls are of the utmost importance in the use of the comparative method, and their disregard has led to some unfortunate errors and inconsistencies in the study of Maya architecture.

This misunderstanding of the nature and use of comparative data is seen in the chronological interpretation of architectural remains on the basis of artificially selected and superficially arranged stylistic criteria. While it is a proved fact that stylistic sequences occur, they are valid only in so far as they actually have been determined as real sequences, through stratigraphy, calendrical inscriptions, or other chronological control. There are numerous causes that bring this about, but the fundamental reason lies in the caprice of man as creator, with the result that specific developments cannot be assumed or predicted. Any such artificial arrangement of Maya architecture is therefore hypothetical and without basis in fact. It involves the tacit assumption of a uniform origin and a homogeneity of lowland Maya culture that is far from proved, and disregards the obvious factors of environment, cultural contact and migration, and the varying function of buildings. Fortunately, there has been a pronounced tendency in recent years to recognize all of these factors and to avoid conclusions on the basis of stylistic sequences that are purely conjectural.

FUTURE RESEARCH

It is impossible to determine the direction and ramification of research over any considerable period in the future. Elaboration of method, new techniques, most of all, increased knowledge of the subject guide the work into channels that cannot be foreseen. We must, nevertheless, give constant thought to immediate problems. Our review of the past half century, and particularly of the last fifteen years, has indicated a number of directions in which research seems to be moving profitably. At this place we can touch upon only a few of the broader aspects of the problem.

The important question of field work must be dealt with in summary fashion. In spite of the valuable, at times spectacular, results that have come from intensive excavation, it appears that for the present emphasis should be on exploration, reconnaissance, and survey of a somewhat detailed nature. The reason for this, broadly speaking, is that we should have an inclusive, even though superficial, knowledge of the architecture as a whole before giving too much attention to the character and interrelationship of local forms. More specifically, surface material is not sufficiently well known in nature or distribution to justify the selection of specific sites for large-scale excavation or to allow the most profitable interpretation of the results of such work. It is true that we have knowledge of a good number of architectural types and styles, and have varying indication of their geographical extent, but there are large areas that offer little or no information. Indeed, it is probable that such relatively unknown regions equal or exceed those that are comparatively well known. It therefore seems that work of an extensive nature should receive the greater emphasis in the immediate future.

Secondly, there are the problems concerned with the use and interpretation of factual knowledge. This is a very broad field, and we shall mention only one approach, but it is important, and one that has been neglected in Maya research. The use of distribution maps is an established procedure, the value of which lies in the visual presentation of the geographical, and at times chronological, relationship of data within a single category, or the association of data within two or more categories. Almost fifty years have passed since Sapper made his studies of architectural types on an ethnographic basis, and there has been practically no work of the sort since his time.[115] We can recognize today at least a dozen distinctive styles of architecture within the Maya area, and possibly half as many more that may be distinct or merely variants of the major classes. In a few instances we have fairly complete knowledge of the geographical distribution, while in the case of the majority information is scant. It appears, however, that there are ample data to justify a tentative map of remains according to architectural style.

We cannot go into all the possibilities inherent in the procedure. A map of this sort would be a start in establishing stylistic areas and determining their border lines. It is obvious that the existence of widely different yet adjacent styles, intermediate and transitional styles, sharp border lines between areas, or the overlapping of areas are conditions that carry ethnic, cultural, chronological, and environmental implications. The procedure attains its maximum value in the application of distributions dealing with other forms of data—archaeological, cultural, linguistic, environmental, and the like. A single example is the association of architectural styles with linguistic and political areas. Such an association not only might assist in explaining stylistic variation but carries the implication of who the builders were, highly important information in placing the remains in their true cultural and historical setting.

Lastly, there is the problem of relating the architecture to the ancient culture, of determining its position and function in the life of the people. This, in a sense, is the ultimate goal of architectural research, and until the problem is solved, we cannot feel that the remains possess full meaning, or that they rest in their true historical setting. In recent years there has been some tendency to meet these questions. We have noted investigations concerned with the use of certain types of buildings and the function of particular groups of structures. We have remarked upon several indirect lines of research

---

[115] Villacorta and Villacorta (Arqueología Guatemalteca, 1927–1930) have to some extent followed this scheme of presentation.

that should lead to the better understanding of the character and function of the civic or ceremonial center. There has been some work on the identification of art forms and the interpretation of the subject-matter of sculptural and other decorative material, but on the whole, since the great labors of Seler, research has not run strongly in this direction. While we unquestionably can gain a certain amount of information from the design and functional character of structures, it is apparent that much of our knowledge must come indirectly through the early documentary sources that stand as a contact with the old, living culture. The approach is circuitous, for it is the material dealing with social organization, religious practices, mythology, and the like, rather than simple description of buildings, that should lead to the desired end. There is so much to be done in the recording and study of remains that these more distant problems may not seem pressing. It is nevertheless true that some thought should be directed into these channels, for without such knowledge, the remains are not truly intelligible as examples of the architecture, as products of the culture, or in the light of Maya history.

XIII

THE CORBELED ARCH IN THE NEW WORLD

A. Ledyard Smith [*]

THE CORBELED arch offers an interesting example of the tendency of widely separated peoples faced by similar needs and employing similar materials to arrive at closely comparable results. This type of arch was known in prehistoric times in various parts of both hemispheres: in the Old World in Greece, Egypt, Mesopotamia, India and Syria [1]; in the New World in the Maya area of Middle America, the Andean highlands of Peru, Bolivia and northern Argentina, and in dome-shaped graves in North Carolina, Tennessee, Ohio, Pennsylvania and the central Mississippi valley region [2] (Fig. 13, e). There seems no reason to believe that the corbeled arch of Eurasia and America had a common origin, nor does it seem likely on the basis of our present information that there was any connection between its occurrences in North, Middle and South America. These three areas in which the vault is found are widely separated: 1500 miles between those in South and Middle America, and some 1000 miles between those in Middle and North America. It is the purpose of this paper to discuss the corbeled arch in Middle and South America. Due to paucity of data on this subject in South America, the greater part of the following discussion will deal with the arch in Middle America.

In beginning, it may be well to define the term corbeled arch. According to Roys corbeling is the placing of a stone so that it projects beyond the one below it and a corbeled arch consists of two approaching series of many layers of stone so placed.[3] In association with this is also the principle of the cantilever, holding a stone firmly at one end so that the outer end is free and unsupported.

---

[*] Harvard, B.S., 1925; Graduate School, 1927–1928; now Archaeologist, Carnegie Institution of Washington.
[1] Gladwin, Excavations at Snaketown, 1937, Vol. II, p. 145.
[2] Thomas, Mound Explorations, 1894.
[3] Roys, Engineering Knowledge of the Maya, 1934, p. 34.

Origin of the Corbeled Arch in Middle America

The corbeled arch in Middle America in its early stages of development employed the principle of the cantilever to a far greater extent than it did later. Before the corbeled arch was used to roof buildings it was undoubtedly experimented with in small constructions. There is evidence of this in Uaxactun where the partial remains of a tomb were found in connection with constructions antedating the earliest known vaulted rooms. The upper part of the tomb had been removed but enough remained to show the beginning of an arch. It is the writer's belief that the corbeled arch in Middle America had its origin in the Department of Peten, Guatemala, in the region of Uaxactun and that it made its first appearance in buildings at the same time as the advent of the stela complex and Tzakol pottery,[4] the third pottery period in the Uaxactun ceramic sequence. At Uaxactun, where work has been carried on by Carnegie Institution of Washington for the past decade, there is strong stratigraphic evidence to support this belief in Structure A–V,[5] a palace type of construction which started from a small nucleus and developed through gradual accretion into a multichambered complex.

In order to understand the writer's reasons for associating the beginning of the vault in buildings with the stela complex and Tzakol pottery, it is necessary to give a brief picture of the development of Structure A–V. This complex started with a series of superimposed platforms which had supported houses of perishable material. The pottery found within these platforms and under the floors associated with them was of the Chicanel [6] or second ceramic phase at Uaxactun. The next development was the covering of these early constructions with a large platform supporting three truncated pyramids and their vaulted superstructures, which may well be the earliest vaulted buildings in the New World. Following this there was a sequence of vaulted rooms in Structure A–V covering a period of about five hundred years and showing a gradual development in vault construction. Of these four periods we are, for the present, interested only in the first. This period is characterized by an early type of vault and association with Tzakol pottery. The latter does

---

[4] See Chapter XVI.
[5] Smith, Carnegie Inst. of Wash., Year Books, 1932, pp. 97–100; 1933, pp. 92–95; 1934, pp. 82–86; 1935, pp. 115–118; 1936, pp. 115–117.
[6] See Chapter XVI.

FIG. 11. MAP OF THE MAYA AREA, SHOWING ARCHAEOLOGICAL SITES WITH AND
WITHOUT VAULTS

not occur before the first vaulted buildings. In Period I of the vaulted
chambers a number of additions were made, in the last of which
stands a stela with the date 9.3.10.0.0 (A. D. 508).[7] Buried under
earlier constructions than that associated with this stela, but later

[7] All dates correlated to the Christian Calendar in this paper are according
to the Goodman-Martínez-Thompson correlation.

than the first vaulted chambers, another stela was found in standing position with the early date 9.0.10.0.0 (A. D. 448). This makes a period of sixty years between the two monuments. There was just as much construction carried on between the erection of the first vaulted building and the 9.0.10.0.0 date as between 9.0.10.0.0 and 9.3.10.0.0. This being the case, the building of the first vaulted rooms in Structure A–V can be tentatively placed at 8.17.10.0.0 (A. D. 388). Of course this hypothesis rests on the assumption that the two monuments in question are in situ and that their dates are contemporaneous. Stylistically the dates are contemporaneous but due to the habit of the Maya of moving monuments from one place to another, the question of their being in situ is debatable. A discussion of the evidence which points to the original position of the stelae is too lengthy to take up here, but, having gone into all the possibilities, the writer feels there is very little doubt that they were found in situ. In further support of this early date for vaulted buildings is the discovery by Ruppert, at Balakbal, in southern Campeche, of an 8.18.10.0.0 (A. D. 408) stela standing in a vaulted structure.[8]

In view of the fact that the earliest dated stela in the Maya area is Stela 9 at Uaxactun,[9] 8.14.10.13.15 (A. D. 328), and that Tzakol pottery is definitely tied to the first appearance of vaulted buildings, it is not improbable that these three new features in Maya culture started at the same time and that their origin was in the region of, if not at, Uaxactun. What stimulated this advance in culture, it is at present impossible to say, but that it did occur in the first half of the fourth century A. D. is extremely probable.

DEVELOPMENT OF THE CORBELED ARCH IN MIDDLE AMERICA

The development of the corbeled arch is interesting. In its earliest stage it was very crude, the vault being composed of rough, unshaped, flat stones layed in a thick bed of mortar and smaller stone (Fig. 12, a). The soffit slopes were covered with a heavy layer of plaster leaving a very uneven surface. During the five hundred years of its use at Uaxactun, vault construction improved in appearance and strength. Large, well-cut stones, tailed deeply into the hearting, were used. These specialized vault stones had their exposed faces nicely dressed so that the application of a thin layer of plaster left a flat

[8] Ruppert, Explorations in Campeche, 1934, p. 93.
[9] Morley, The Inscriptions of Peten, 1938, Vol. I, p. 160.

even surface (Fig. 12, *b*). Up to this point the corbeled vault employed the principle of the cantilever, but in its later development in Yucatan this principle was in part lost by the introduction of the boot-shaped vault stone (Fig. 12, *c*). These highly specialized vault stones do not tenon back into the hearting to any such degree as did the earlier types, and the bearing surface of one stone upon the other is minimized. The result is that the function of these stones as a support is to a great extent lost, and they become a veneer for the cement hearting which holds them in place and carries the main strain. These boot-shaped vault stones are the best cut and dressed stones used in corbeled vaulting in the New World and even without a plaster finish offer a beautiful surface. The above sequence does not mean that all vaults constructed of rough or crudely shaped stones are necessarily early. Along the eastern coast of Quintana Roo even the very late vaults are made of crude masonry.

Types of Corbeled Arches in Middle America

The material used in the construction of the corbeled arch in various regions was naturally dependent upon the amount and character of the stone at hand. For the most part the stone supply in the Maya area was more than ample but its quality varied greatly. The builders took advantage of any favorable characteristics, and thus we find in the Usumacintla region the abundant use of thin slabs, the natural stone occurring split in this fashion. In other areas, such as the Peten, where this type of natural fracture does not occur, either rough uncut or well-cut and specialized stones were used. At Comalcalco in Tabasco, due to the lack of stone, the vaults were built of bricks burnt in open fires.[10] Almost as important as the stones used in the vaults was the lime cement in which they were set. The development of the use of lime cement in Yucatan to a point where it played an even greater part in vault construction than the stones themselves has been mentioned above.

It is not the purpose of this paper to take up the many technical details involved in the construction of the corbeled arch, but it does not seem out of place to mention briefly the inverted step at the spring, the use of wooden beams, and the diversity of shape. In its usual form the corbeled vault in the Maya area carries an offset or inverted step at its spring. Along the east coast [11] and in southern

[10] Blom and LaFarge, Tribes and Temples, 1926, p. 113.
[11] Lothrop, Tulum, 1924, p. 36.

Quintana Roo,[12] however, it is the exception rather than the rule, and instances of the vault without this offset occur sporadically throughout the Maya area.[13] Spinden, in an attempt to explain the use of the offset, says, "It seems probable that the vault was built over a wooden form, and the shoulder projection at the spring of the vault was to give a few inches leeway to permit the ready removal of the false work." [14] Since that time many vaults without the offset have been found. This, in addition to the fact that the vault did not need such support during its construction,[15] disproves this theory. If the offset at the spring had any structural purpose other than that of beginning the closing of the arch, it is yet to be explained.

The use of wooden cross beams set in the face of the vault is common throughout the Maya area although the arrangement varies greatly. The purpose of these beams has been and still is a problem. Thompson believed that they were a conventional survival of cross-beams in the Maya bush house or "ná" of Yucatan and served no useful purpose in the vault.[16] Roys points out that while there is little doubt that vaulted rooms bore the impress of a wooden predecessor, the cross beam undoubtedly did strengthen the vault.[17] In the water-way arch at Palenque stone beams are used instead of wood (Fig. 12, o).

Probably one of the most variable features of the corbeled arch in the Maya area is its shape. Figure 12 shows some of the most common as well as extreme shapes employed by the ancient builders. The soffit slopes may be flat, concave, or convex, the last being the least common, and the spring may start almost from the floor or close to the capstones, although its usual level is somewhere slightly above half the total height of the room. Of course, any shifting of the level of the spring changes the shape of the vault. End walls of vaulted chambers may be approximately vertical or conform to the side walls and soffit slopes of the vault proper. In the southern cities nearly vertical end walls are less common than in northern Yucatan where that type of end wall predominates.[18] The bottle-shape vault

---

[12] Merwin, Ruins of the Southern Part of the Peninsula of Yucatan, 1913, p. 111.

[13] Thompson, Pollock and Charlot, Ruins of Coba, 1932, p. 121.

[14] Spinden, Maya Art, 1913, p. 109.

[15] Roys, Engineering Knowledge of the Maya, 1934, pp. 69-70; Merwin, Ruins of the Southern Part of the Peninsula of Yucatan, 1913, pp. 112-113.

[16] Thompson, Genesis of the Maya Arch, 1911, pp. 501-516.

[17] Roys, Engineering Knowledge of the Maya, 1934, pp. 44-55.

[18] Thompson, Pollock and Charlot, Ruins of Coba, 1932, p. 121.

which occurs frequently along the eastern coast of Quintana Roo [19] also is found at Uaxactun (Fig. 12, *a*). Stepped vaults, which have the appearance of an inverted stairway (Fig. 12, *d-f*), are found throughout the Maya area but are seemingly more common in the Peten and Usumacintla cities than elsewhere; yet they occur at Cobá in northern Quintana Roo, at Tancah and Xelhá, along the eastern coast of Quintana Roo, and at Uxmal in Yucatan.[20] Arches that have an acute apex and no capstones are not common. The Caracol at Chichen Itzá contains such a vault (Fig. 12, *h*), as does also the vault shown in Figure 12, *g*, from the same site. In the latter the inverted V-shaped top was formed by flat stones leaning against each other. A vault similar to this has been found at Hatzcap Ceel.[21] The only difference here is that the course of stones directly below the apex does not project to form an overhanging step. At Comalcalco (Fig. 12, *j*) this same shape is arrived at, according to Blom, in the following manner: "Apparently . . . the interior half of the arch was built first, and the exterior half of the arch made to lean against the central core." [22] The elaborate trefoil arch is found at Palenque (Fig. 12, *i*). Figure 12, *l*, shows the form of the arch in a passageway at Tikal. Here there is an inset rather than an offset at the spring. An unusual arch from Chichen Itzá is shown in Figure 12, *k*. The stones in this arch were so cut that when they were laid up in the usual fashion they formed a semi-circle. A characteristic of the vaults in the Puuc

[19] Lothrop, Tulum, 1924, p. 36.
[20] For *Cobá*, see Thompson, Pollock and Charlot, Ruins of Cobá, 1932, p. 62; for *Tancah and Xelhá*, Lothrop, Tulum, 1924, Figs. 125 and 136; for *Uxmal*, Carnegie Institution photographic files.
[21] Thompson, Investigations in the Southern Cayo District, 1931, p. 254.
[22] Blom and LaFarge, Tribes and Temples, 1926, p. 109.

FIG. 12. EXAMPLES OF MAYA ARCHES

a. Uaxactun.
b. Uaxactun.
c. Uxmal.
d. Uaxactun.
e. Tikal.
f. Palenque.
g. Chichen Itzá. (After Holmes, Mexico, 1895.)
h. Chichen Itzá. (After Ruppert, Caracol, 1935.)
i. Palenque. (After Holmes, Mexico, 1895.
j. Comalcalco. (After Blom and LaFarge, Tribes and Temples, 1926.)
k. Chichen Itzá.
l. Tikal.
m. Labna.
n. Uxmal.
o. Palenque.

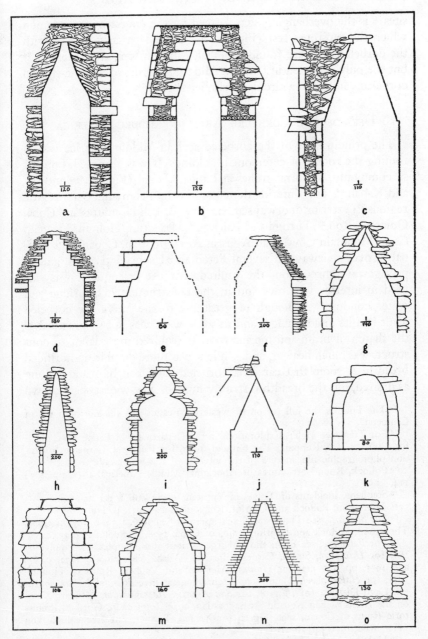

FIG. 12. EXAMPLES OF MAYA ARCHES (For description, see facing page.)

sites [23] is the overhanging step formed by the course of stones upon which the capstones rest (Fig. 12, *c*). Curved passages roofed with the corbeled arch are found at Tikal, Chichen Itzá, and Palenque,[24] but the only reported instance in Middle America of a dome-shaped corbeled vault is on a circular chamber at Aké.[25]

Uses of the Corbeled Arch in Middle America

The principal use of the corbeled arch in Middle America was in roofing the rooms of ceremonial buildings. It was also used, but not so commonly, in portal arches at Labna, Uxmal (Fig. 12, *m* and *n*), and Kabah [26]; over interior doorways in the Peten and Usumacintla regions [27]; exterior doorways at San José, British Honduras and Cobá, Quintana Roo [28]; in tombs at Palenque, Uaxactun, Holmul, Hatzcap Ceel (Mountain Cow), San Agustín Acasaguastlan, Copan, and Xacbal [29]; over stairways in several Peten and Usumacintla sites; and in passageways throughout the vaulted area. At Palenque it was also used in interior windows and in the construction of a bridge and water conduit.[30] Although of great use to the Maya the corbeled vault had its disadvantages and in some ways was not so practical as the thatch or beam and mortar roof. It required more labor to construct, was much heavier, and, while it was more durable, it sacrificed breadth. A room that carries a corbeled vault can be made as long as desired, but the breadth is strictly limited. The widest span known

---

[23] The Puuc is the hill region of western Yucatan and the northern tip of Campeche.

[24] For *Tikal*, see Maler, Explorations in the Department of Peten, 1911, p. 11; for *Chichen Itzá*, Ruppert, The Caracol, 1935; for *Palenque*, Carnegie Institution photographic file, picture of the interior of the waterway.

[25] Pollock, Round Structures of Aboriginal Middle America, 1936, pp. 113–114.

[26] Stephens, Incidents of Travel in Yucatan, 1843, Vol. I, pp. 399–400.

[27] Thompson, Pollock and Charlot, Ruins of Coba, 1932, p. 118.

[28] For *San José*, see Thompson, Excavations at San José, 1939, p. 26; for *Cobá*, Thompson, Pollock and Charlot, Ruins of Cobá, 1932, p. 70 and Fig. 35, *c*.

[29] For *Palenque*, see Blom and LaFarge, Tribes and Temples, 1926, pp. 180–188; for *Uaxactun*, Smith, Carnegie Inst. of Wash., Year Books, 1934, p. 85, and 1935, pp. 116–117; for *Holmul*, Merwin and Vaillant, Ruins of Holmul, 1932; for *Hatzcapceel*, Thompson, Archaeological Investigations in the Southern Cayo District, 1931, Fig. 8; for *San Agustin Acasaguastlan*, Kidder, Notes on the Ruins of San Agustin Acasaguastlan, 1935; for *Copan*, Gordon, Prehistoric Ruins of Copan, 1896, Fig. 2; for *Xacbal*, Termer, Zur Archäologie von Guatemala, 1931, pp. 10–11.

[30] Holmes, Archaeological Studies among the Ancient Cities of Mexico, 1895–1897, Fig. 47, *d*, and Figs. 65 and 66.

is in the Mercado at Chichen Itzá, where the far beyond average breadth of fourteen feet, eight inches (4.52m.) is attained. Even the strength of the vault was not always trusted, for we often find cases of secondary walls being used in an attempt to give added support, and it is exceptional to find a second story room built directly over a lower room, the usual practice being to build upper stories over a solid foundation. However, the high façades which resulted from the lofty vaults presented a splendid surface for the expression of Maya art in sculpture and stucco work, and in their temples and palaces the Maya evidently were willing to sacrifice interior spaciousness to exterior splendor.

Spread and Distribution of the Corbeled Arch in Middle America

In a recent article [31] Lothrop points out that the Maya probably settled in Guatemala, in both the highlands and lowlands, before Baktun 8 or the beginning of the Christian era. Whether they came from the south or the north is still a matter of speculation, but that they developed their classical culture after their arrival is accepted. It has already been shown that the corbeled arch played an important part in this cultural development and that it probably had its origin at the same time as the stela complex and Tzakol pottery in the region of Uaxactun, about the first half of the fourth century. Taking the sites at which both stelae and vaults are found, but bearing in mind the possibility that the stela complex may have spread more rapidly than the vault, we find that in about a century the use of the vault began to spread. To the south it reached Copan, to the north it spread to the Rio Bec sites of southern Campeche and Quintana Roo, up the east coast of Quintana Roo as far as Tulum and the inland city of Cobá, and to the west into the Usumacintla region. Before the end of the so-called Old Empire, around 10.3.0.0.0 (A. D. 889), the arch was also in northern Campeche and Yucatan and had found its way into all the general regions of the Maya area that it was to occupy.

In discussing the distribution of the corbeled arch in Middle America it can be said that it is limited to the Maya area. This area, which includes the states of Chiapas, Tabasco, Campeche, Yucatan and Quintana Roo in Mexico, British Honduras, most of Guatemala, and part of Honduras and Salvador, is roughly limited on the west

[31] Lothrop, Southeastern Frontier of the Maya, 1939, p. 43.

by the Isthmus of Tehuantepec. Its southeastern limit according to Lothrop [32] is shown in Figure 11.

Vaulted as well as some non-vaulted sites are shown on the map of the Maya area in Figure 11. While the map gives a fairly good picture of the general regions in which the vault is found, it is misleading in that it leaves great blank areas such as the northwestern corner of Guatemala, southeastern Campeche, and a great part of Quintana Roo. This does not mean that the arch was not in use in these areas, because it undoubtedly was, but merely that, due to lack of exploration or excavation, it has not been found. It should also be pointed out that while we can definitely say the arch was used at certain sites, it is impossible to be sure that it was not used at any site where excavation has not been complete. For this reason, in regions where the arch is common, sites in which it is absent have been put down only when sufficient investigation has been carried on to warrant it. In regions where the arch is absent only the more important sites have been indicated.

The peninsula of Yucatan as far south as Lake Peten in Guatemala, the Usumacintla region, and the lower Motagua and Copan Valleys are, with a few isolated exceptions, the regions to which the corbeled arch is confined. The most western use of the vault occurs at Comalcalco in Tabasco; the most southern in small chambers at Papalguapa and Asunción Mita,[33] in southeastern Guatemala. These last two sites are exceptions in that they lie outside the areas mentioned above. A possible explanation for the presence of vaults in that region is the occurrence of laminated stone, an ideal medium for their construction. Other vaults outside of the general areas where they are to be expected, occur in tombs at Xacbal [34] in the Department of Quiché and at San Agustín Acasaguastlan [35] in the Department of Progreso, Guatemala. It is possible that future excavation in the Guatemalan highlands may prove that the vault used in burials is not as exceptional as it now appears to be.

The corbeled arch has been reported at several places in Middle

[32] Lothrop, Southeastern Frontier, 1939, Fig. 3.

[33] For photographs of vaults at Papalguapa and Asunción Mita, see Carnegie Institution photographic files.

[34] Termer, Zur Archäologie von Guatemala, 1931, pp. 171–172. Seler, in Die alten Ansiedelungen von Chaculá, 1901, p. 44 and Fig. 29, describes two subterranean chambers with stone roofs at Uaxac-Canal as being possible vapor baths. I have not put this site down on the map as having a vault because from the drawings there does not seem to be any principle of corbeling involved.

[35] Kidder, Notes on the Ruins of San Agustín Acasaguastlan, 1935.

America outside the Maya area, but, due to the inaccuracy of early descriptions and the lack of evidence at the present time, these reports must be considered doubtful. Xochicalco and Monte Alban in Mexico, in the states of Morelos and Oaxaca, respectively, are two such cases. At Xochicalco corbeled domes have been reported in subterranean chambers and at Monte Alban the same type of construction in mounds, but Pollock,[36] in discussing these two instances, looks upon them with a great deal of skepticism. Marquina, in his "Estudio Arquitectónica Comparativo de los Monumentos Arqueológicos de Mexico," reproduces a drawing of the ruins of Toluquilla in the state of Querétaro done in 1880 which shows what appears to be a half vault, but it cannot be relied on.[37] Nuttall [38] suggests that portal vaults may have occurred on the Isla de Sacrificios in the harbor of Vera Cruz, but, as Spinden shows, this point cannot be regarded as settled.[39] Humboldt describes what may possibly be a mud brick vault at Cholula [40] but as far as the author knows no mention is made of it in modern literature. Finally, in her article on Tajin, Mrs. Spinden says, "Early drawings of temples at Tusapan and Huatusco, on which too great reliance cannot be placed, show high roofs of stone and mortar construction. Nebel describes the rooms surmounting the pyramid at Tusapan as vaulted, and the temple of Huatusco according to Castañeda's drawing has a sloping roof, while, within, the holes for cross beams are visible." [41]

Regions of the Maya Area in Which the Vault Does Not Occur

It has already been pointed out that, with the exception of the Motagua-Copan regions, the arch occurs only in rare instances south of Lake Peten-Itzá. In the highland region of Guatemala, although

---

[36] Pollock, Round Structures of Aboriginal Middle America, 1936, pp. 42–43, 64–65.
[37] Marquina, Monumentos Arqueológicos de Mexico, 1928, p. 26.
[38] Nuttall, The Island of Sacrificios, 1910, pp. 267–269. In a paper he read before the Twenty-seventh International Congress of Americanists, held in Mexico City in 1939, José García Payón mentioned the presence of a corbeled vault over a stairway in a passage in one of the buildings at Tajin Chico, in the State of Vera Cruz, Mexico.
[39] Spinden, A Study of Maya Art, 1913, p. 110.
[40] Humbolt, Vues des Cordillères et Monumens des Peuples Indigènes de l'Amérique, 1810, p. 29.
[41] Spinden, The Place of Tajin in Totonac Archaeology, 1933, pp. 230–231.

thickly populated by the Maya, the arch was not used. There are two possible reasons for this, the eruptive nature of the country, and Mexican influence. It is more than probable that long experience with an earthquake region advised the Maya against using the arch. Gamio [42] divides the highlands into two regions, the eruptive southern cordillera, and the sedimentary cordillera of the north. He points out that in the former no edifices of true architectonic character exist and gives Miraflores and Arévalo (Kaminaljuyú) as the archaeological centre of the region. In the sedimentary cordillera, he says, structures were built of heavy weight and relatively little height and that those at Quen Santo, Chaculá, Zaculeu, Utatlan, and elsewhere do not appear to have been effected greatly by earthquakes. It would appear from this that the extent of seismic action in various localities influenced the architecture of the ancient builders, for in the highly eruptive southern cordillera pyramids were not crowned with superstructures with masonry walls, while in the cordillera to the north, where there is much less danger of earthquakes, such superstructures are common.[43] The beam and mortar roofs which surely covered many of these buildings of the northern cordillera would be more adaptable to the region than the arch and more durable than thatch. These structures have a strong Mexican feeling and are probably a fusion of Mexican and Maya ideas.

It is possible to attribute the absence of the arch in the southeastern limits of the Maya area to influence from the south, but its nonoccurrence in southern British Honduras and the Pasión Valley, with one possible exception at Seibal,[44] is indeed strange and for the present must remain unexplained. Here we find in other respects typical Old Empire sites, many of which have early monuments associated with platforms and pyramids of cut stone. Lubantun, in British Honduras, has no stelae but the stone work in its substructure is of the best workmanship. Work has been carried on at Pusilhá and Lubantun by the British Museum without uncovering any vaults.[45] In the Pasión region the author has been to a number of sites, some

[42] Gamio, Cultural Evolution in Guatemala, 1926–1927.

[43] Examples of such superstructures are found at Xoch, Yolchonáp, and Rabinal. Drawings of the two former are on file at the University of Pennsylvania Museum; for the latter, see Maudslay, A Glimpse at Guatemala, 1899, pp. 101–104.

[44] Maler, Explorations of the Upper Usumacintla, 1908, p. 20.

[45] Gann, Discoveries and Adventures in Central America, 1929, p. 211.

of which are of considerable size, and feels that if these had used the arch at least some evidence should be found on the surface, for at even the smallest Usumacintla sites, there are almost always some remains that indicate its presence.

BEAM AND MORTAR ROOFS IN THE MAYA AREA

Beam and mortar roofs have already been mentioned as a possibility in the highlands. Evidence for this type of construction has been found at Mountain Cow, in British Honduras, by Thompson [46] and at Piedras Negras where Satterthwaite places it before the vault and suggests that it may be due to early Mexican influence.[47] He believes that the vault did not reach Piedras Negras until about the beginning of the seventh century,[48] a hundred years after the earliest stela at that site. If the vault arrived at Piedras Negras from the Uaxactun region it is possible that the beam and mortar roof, which was used at Uaxactun after the introduction of the vault,[49] may have found its way there from Piedras Negras. The beam and mortar roof is also found along the east coast of Quintana Roo where it has been suggested that its presence is due to Mexican influence.[50] Not enough work has been done to draw any conclusions, but it is always interesting to speculate. If we assume that the beam and mortar roof at Uaxactun was due to Mexican influence and bear in mind that it is found associated with Tzakol pottery which can be correlated with Teotihuacan,[51] we have a Mexican influence at Uaxactun in early Old Empire times. It is possible that it is this early influence that is seen on the east coast of Quintana Roo, an influence long before that which presumably penetrated from Yucatan. On the other hand, there is no reason why the beam and mortar roof could not be of Maya origin. True it is rarely found, but it is much more difficult to identify than the more permanent stone vault. Many in-

[46] Thompson, Investigations in the Southern Cayo District, 1931, Fig. 5.

[47] Satterthwaite (in a talk before the American Philosophical Society in Philadelphia, 1938).

[48] Satterthwaite, Notes on the Work of the Fourth and Fifth University Museum Expeditions to Piedras Negras, Peten, Guatemala, 1936, p. 85.

[49] Smith, Carnegie Inst. of Wash., Year Book, 1937, p. 136.

[50] Lothrop, Tulum, 1924, p. 36; Vaillant, Artists and Craftsmen in Ancient Central America, 1935, p. 33.

[51] Kidder and Thompson, The Correlation of Maya and Christian Chronologies, 1938, p. 508.

conspicuous mounds may well conceal the remains of buildings which once supported the beam and mortar roof.[52]

THE CORBELED ARCH IN SOUTH AMERICA

We have already pointed out that the most southern known example of the arch in Middle America occurs at Asunción Mita in the Department of Jutiapa, Guatemala. The most northern corbeled vault in South America of which the author has heard is found in the Utcubamba Valley in northern Peru, some 1500 miles to the south. In this immense intervening distance no vaults are known and independent invention in Middle and South America seems probable.

According to Nordenskiöld [53] the cantilever arch was not known in South America, but Lothrop points out that it was used from northern Peru to the Diaguita region in northwestern Argentine.[54] In other words, it had a range of over 1500 miles throughout the Andes. Its origin is unknown, but it does go back to the Chavin-Tiahuanaco horizon,[55] probably before 700 A. D., how much earlier only future investigation can decide.

As in Middle America, in South America the corbeled arch was put to various uses, but instead of being principally employed in roofing temples and governmental buildings it was used to a far greater extent in the houses of the common people. It was also used in doorways, portal vaults, niches, windows, bridges, and burials. The usual form of the vault when used as a roof was dome shaped, a form to date found only in Middle America at Aké. This type of vault, which is formed by a series of smaller and smaller circles of stones layed up until they leave only a small opening at the top closed by capstones, is stronger than a vault with straight sides. The reason for this is that the vault stones must be wedge shape to form a circle and thus have a horizontal arch action which prevents them from

[52] In Fig. 2 of his article, An Unusual Type of Building in the Maya Old Empire, and in Fig. 1 of another article, Notes on the Work of the Fourth and Fifth University Museum Expeditions to Piedras Negras, Peten, Guatemala, Satterthwaite indicates a combination of vault and beam and mortar roof. It is as if a normal vault were cut horizontally in half and the wide gap between the two sides was covered by beam and mortar construction. As far as is known this type of vault is unique.

[53] Nordenskiöld, Origin of the Indian Civilization in South America, 1931, p. 55.

[54] Lothrop, Coclé, 1937, p. 206, note 1.

[55] Olson, Old Empires of the Andes, 1931, pp. 10–11.

slipping inwards (Fig. 13, *a*). In some cases temples and houses in South America had rectangular vaults and here the identical principle as that of the vault in the Maya area was employed (Plate III, *a*). Vault stones often were layed in mud but the use of lime cement was unknown in South America.[56] The vault was much flatter than the high Maya vault, and only in the case of doorways were the exposed edges of the arch stones cut on a bevel so as to give a flat surface to the soffit slope.

A large percentage of the houses used by the common people in the mountainous country from northern Peru to the region of Lake Poopó in Bolivia had stone roofs. These houses were either round, square, or rectangular. Of the sierra of northern Peru, Olson says, "Certain villages are composed entirely of circular stone structures some ten to thirty feet in diameter with stone roofs of corbeled dome type. Other villages show both round and square houses with similarly domed roofs." [57] In the region of Lake Titicaca, Bennett [58] describes rectangular houses with corbeled vaults. One of these at the ruins of Macalaya was sixteen feet long, twelve wide and thirteen high (4.87 m. by 3.66 m. by 3.96 m.) and did not need any great thickness of wall to support the stone roof (Plate III, *c*). Houses with corbeled roofs also occur south of Lake Titicaca at Lake Poopó in Bolivia.[59] Excellent examples of the corbeled vault used in governmental buildings are found at the ruins of Pilco-Kayma on the Island of Titicaca (Plate III, *a*, and Fig. 13, *c*). The Inca doorway is considerably narrower at the top than bottom and in the more impressive structures had the exposed faces of the stones in the jambs cut on a bevel so as to form a smooth surface. Although these can hardly be called corbeled arches, they come very close to it in some cases (Plate III, *b*). Figure 13, *d*, shows the portal vault or gateway to the Fortress of Cuelape in the Utcubamba valley in northern Peru. The corbeled arch is used in niches at the ruins of the Iñak-Uyu on the Island of Koati [60] and in windows over doorways at the ruins of Maucallajta in the Department of Puno, Peru.[61] The Inca sometimes

[56] Kroeber, Cultural Relations between North and South America, 1930, p. 20; Nordenskiold, Origins of the Indian Civilizations in South America, 1931, p. 55.

[57] Olson, Old Empires of the Andes, 1931, pp. 10–11.

[58] Bennett, Archaeological Hikes in the Andes, 1933, pp. 165–166.

[59] Posnansky, Las Razas Interandinas, 1937, pp. 115–116.

[60] Bandelier, Islands of Titicaca and Koati, 1910, Plate LXXIV, 5.

[61] Inojosa and González, Exploraciones Arqueológicas en el Perú, Departmento de Puno, 1936, pp. 161 and 164.

built their bridges on the principle of the cantilever by projecting stones from either side and laying a single stone over the remaining space between.[62]

In northwestern Argentina the corbeled vault has not yet, to the author's knowledge, been discovered above ground, but it does occur in burials at La Paya in the Province of Salta (Fig. 13, *b*) and at Caspinchango in the Province of Catamarca.[63] In the highlands of Peru burials were placed in "chulpas" (Fig. 13, *a*). These are towers of stone or adobe, either square or circular, with conical roofs and a small chamber with a corbeled dome inside. Various uses have been suggested for chulpas but according to Means most of them were probably used as tombs.[64] They are plentiful in most parts of the Titicaca basin, the most southern examples being found at Pucará in Bolivia, some eighty-five miles south of La Paz. To the north they occur in the Department of Junin, Peru.

THE CORBELED ARCH IN NORTH AMERICA

In the first paragraph of this paper the writer referred to the description by Cyrus Thomas of the corbeled vault occurring in dome-shaped graves in North Carolina, Tennessee, Ohio, Pennsylvania, and the central Mississippi valley region (Fig. 13, *e*). In Bulletin 37 of the Bureau of American Ethnology, G. Fowke refers to vaults in Pike County, Missouri, described by Lewis C. Beck in 1823. Fowke points out that Beck's knowledge of these remains was probably

[62] Squier, Peru, Incidents of Travel and Exploration in the Land of the Incas, 1877, p. 432.

[63] For *La Paya*, see Ambrosetti, El Sepulcro de La Paya, 1902; for *Caspinchango*, Debenedetti, La Influencia Hispanica en los Yacimientos Arqueologicos de Caspinchango, 1921.

[64] Means, Ancient Civilizations of the Andes, 1931, pp. 200–202.

FIG. 13. VAULTED CONSTRUCTIONS IN SOUTH AND NORTH AMERICA

a. Chulpas at Mancallajta.
   (After Inojosa and González, Exploraciones, 1936.)
b. Tomb at La Paya.
   (After Ambrosetti, Sepulcro, 1902.)
c. Section of room with niche in ruins of Pilco-Kayma on the Island of Titicaca.
   (After Bandelier, Titicaca, 1910.)
d. The gateway to the fortress of Cuelape in the Valley of the Utcubamba.
   (After Olson, Old Empires, 1931.)
e. Grave in mound, Fish group, Allamakee county, Iowa.
   (After Thomas, Mound Exploration, 1894.)

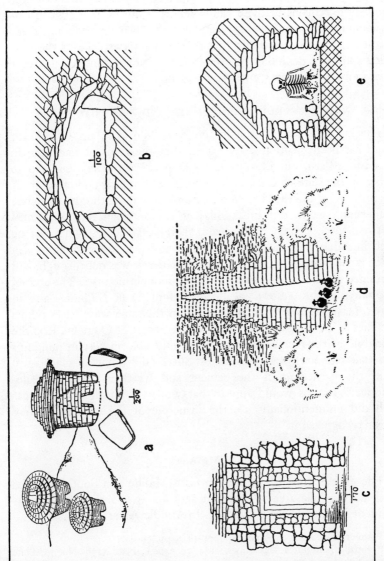

Fig. 13. (For description, see facing page.)

derived entirely from reports made to him. The accuracy of Thomas's report published in 1894 cannot be depended upon because it is difficult to distinguish fact and interpretation. As far as the writer knows, the remains of these vaults reported during the last century no longer exist, nor have any similar finds been reported in recent literature. It seems therefore that before the occurrence of the corbeled vault can definitely be established in North America we must have more proof than we have at present.

The True Arch in the New World

The use of the true arch in the New World in pre-Columbian times has been mentioned by Squier [65] at the ruins of Pachacamac near Lima, Peru, and illustrations by Dupaix [66] show its use at Monte Alban in the state of Oaxaca, Mexico. The former is undoubtedly of Spanish origin and the latter must be looked upon with little credence as no such construction exists today at Monte Alban. At Uaxactun,[67] Department of Peten, Guatemala, there is what resembles a true arch in a doorway cut through a wall. All that holds the stones in place is the mortar, which, before the doorway was cut through, had hardened and bound the masonry into a monolithic mass. The arched doorways in the western façade of Temple A at Nakum,[68] also in Peten, may possibly be accounted for in the same way. Roys points out that at Tulum and Tancah on the east coast of Quintana Roo the principle of the true arch was accidentally used in certain buildings but that true arch reactions almost surely did not take place until after the hardening of the cement and weather cracks had developed.[69] It thus would appear that while the aborigines on occasion did unintentionally use the principle of the true arch, they never recognized it.

Summary

The corbeled arch was used in both Middle and South America with a 1500-mile area in which it was not used intervening. Independent invention seems probable. In Middle America, where it was

[65] Squier, The Arch in America, 1871–1872, pp. 79–80.

[66] Dupaix, Antiquités Mexicaines, 1834, 2d exped., Plate xxvii, No. 76; Plate xxviii, No. 77; and pp. 21–22.

[67] Smith, Structure A–XVIII, Uaxactun, 1937, Plate 11, a.

[68] Tozzer, Nakum, Guatemala, 1913, pp. 167–168, Plate 40, 1.

[69] Roys, Engineering Knowledge of the Maya, 1934, pp. 78–80.

limited to the Maya area, it apparently had its origin in the region of Uaxactun about the first half of the fourth century A. D. along with the stela complex and Tzakol pottery. In South America in the Andean region it was used over a much greater area extending from northern Peru to northwest Argentina, but here its antiquity, to date, has not been traced beyond approximately the eighth century A. D. The use of the vault in the Maya area was confined to a great extent to governmental and religious buildings, whereas in the Andean region it was also used in the houses of the common people. It would seem from what is known that the corbeled arch was as widely, if not more widely, distributed in South America than in Middle America. The greater proven antiquity lies at present in the Maya area, but to call the corbeled vault in the New World the "Maya vault," as so often has been done, is not only misleading but may be giving the Maya credit for something they were not the first to invent.

XIV

A Special Assemblage of Maya Structures

Karl Ruppert *

GROUPING of structures in the Maya area has primarily been thought of as forming quadrangles or delineating courts. One specific grouping or arrangement which repeats itself a number of times seems worthy of note and must have played an important part in the Maya community. This arrangement was first noted by Blom in 1924 [1] in Group E at Uaxactun, but its widespread occurrence was not reported until 1934 [2] by the writer who had noted its appearance in a number of sites visited during reconnaissance in southern Campeche, southern Quintana Roo and northern Guatemala. Briefly this arrangement in its most stylized form consists of three small buildings on a single platform defining the eastern side of a plaza while on the western side of the plaza rises a large pyramidal structure (Fig. 14).

Blom was the first to suggest that the grouping at Uaxactun had some astronomical value and it does present tantalizing data. That the arrangement played an important part in the functioning of the community is indeed probable. Its great importance, however, is enhanced when the same arrangement of structures is encountered in other cities. Since the small buildings on the east side of the plaza are definitely not domiciliary and the pyramid on the west does not support a building the arrangement must be ceremonial or esoteric in function.

There are thirteen sites where this grouping occurs in almost pure form and six where it is less clear (Fig. 15). The questionable character of the latter sites arises from the three buildings on the east side of the plaza not resting on a single long platform (Fig. 18), the extremely small size of the group or the fact that the maps of the

---

* Arizona, B.S., 1920; George Washington, M.S., 1924; Harvard, M.A. 1928; now Archaeologist, Carnegie Institution of Washington.
[1] Blom, Report, 1924, p. 218.
[2] Ruppert, Explorations, 1934, p. 94.

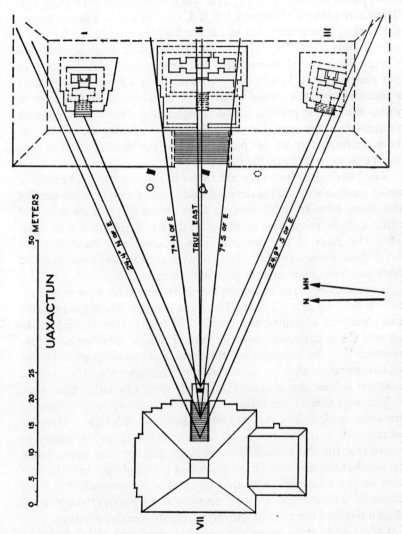

FIG. 14. UAXACTUN, GROUP E. THIS IS THE TYPE SITE FOR THE ASSEMBLAGE

site are so conventionally drawn that the orientation is due north and south.

So far the earliest known dated Maya city is Uaxactun and this is the type site for the grouping as it was first reported here (Fig. 14). The distribution is of interest for, if Uaxactun is taken as the center, the typical arrangement has so far not been located beyond a radius of 110 kilometers. The type site places the three small buildings on a single long low platform. This platform occurs in all but two of the nineteen sites. In addition two sites do not have a single large pyramidal structure on the west side of the court. The groupings in these cities should perhaps not be considered; yet they may represent variants. It is also true that when the three buildings are not on the same platform they are not placed in a row nor do they seem to conform in plan to those of the type site.

The buildings, where they are found in sufficiently good repair to make possible a somewhat detailed study, are of two or three parallel chambers, have an indentation in the outer wall at either side, and often a slight projection of the central part of the back wall (Fig. 16). The plans of the east buildings at Uaxactun, Naachtun and Uxul show great similarity. The last two are the best preserved and have much in common as to plan and elevation.

In some cases in the east grouping more than three structures may rest on the long east platform. The three primary structures however can readily be identified and usually rise higher than the others. In general other structures, like the three primary ones, are now represented only by mounds, but the former are usually small. In one or two instances they do appear as mounds higher than the primary ones but at least one of these (Oxpemul) faces east rather than west.

The west side of the plaza is defined by a single large pyramidal structure which does not support a building although a masonry platform or stela may rest on its summit. While it may definitely be stated that the three buildings on a single platform are never found on any but the east side of the plaza and the single pyramidal structure on the west, variations are suggested at some sites but the evidence is not clear and in such cases as at El Paraiso [3] the plaza is diminutive and the plan of the city is highly conventionalized.

Only one of these groupings has been excavated and only in the

[3] Ricketson, Uaxactun, 1937, p. 296, Fig. 192. At Honradez as shown on Merwin map, Peabody Museum, there are three structures on a platform defining the north side of a plaza.

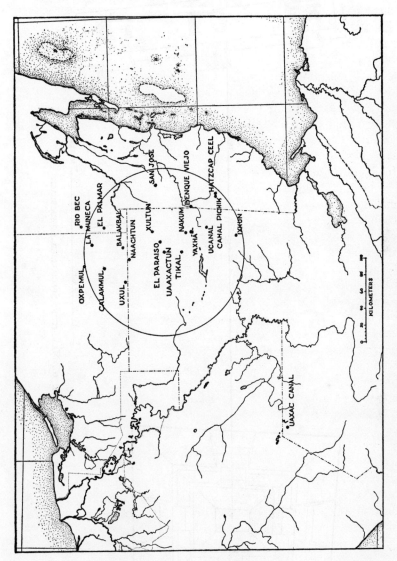

Fig. 15. Map of Maya Area Showing Distribution of Specialized Assemblages

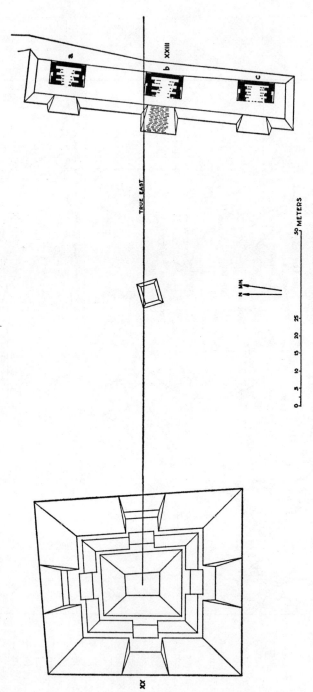

FIG. 16. NAACHTUN, SPECIALIZED ASSEMBLAGE

TABLE II

COMPASS BEARINGS OF SPECIAL ASSEMBLAGES OF MAYA BUILDINGS

DISTANCE FROM UAXACTUN Sites	Kilometers	VARIATION FROM TRUE E-W BEARING Sites	Reading	BEARING OF LONG AXIS OF EAST MOUND Sites	Reading	MOUND FORMING GROUPING East Mounds	West Mound	Map Reference
Uaxactun	0	Uaxactun	0° 57' S	Nakum	True North	I, A, 2	C	Tozzer 1913, Plate 32
Nakum	35	Naachtun	2° 21' S	Uxul	N 0° 10' E	XIII a, b, c	XI	Carnegie Institution, Unpublished
Yaxha	42	Uxul	3° 25' S	Uaxactun	N 1° 08' E	E-I, II, III	E-VII	Ricketson 1937, Page 107
Naachtun	45	Nakum	4° 40' S	Benque Viejo	N 2° 23' W	II, III, IV	VIII	Morley 1938, Plate 191, a*
Balakbal	52	Benque Viejo	5° 03' N	Hatzcap Ceel	N 5° 18' E	I, F, E	A	Thompson 1931, Figure 7
Uxul	60	Ixkun	6° 13' S	Naachtun	N 5° 24' E	XXIII a, b, c	XX	Morley 1938, Plate 206
Benque Viejo	64	Rio Bec II	7° 40' S	Ixkun	N 5° 08' E	X		Maudslay 1889-02, Vol. II Plate 67
Calakmul	78	Oxpemul	8° 37' S	Rio Bec II	N 7° 36' E	I	III	Carnegie Institution, Unpublished
Ixkun	92.5	Calakmul	9° 0' S	Balakbal	N 9° 03' E	VIII a, b, c	VI	Morley 1938, Plate 218
Cahal Pichik	93	Hatzcap Ceel	9° 05' S	Yaxha	N 10° 17' E	XIII	XV	Morley 1938, Plate 212*
Hatzcap Ceel	94	Yaxha	10° 15' S	Oxpemul	N 11° 21' E	V a, b, c	II	Carnegie Institution, Unpublished
Oxpemul	102	Balakbal	10° 15' S	Calakmul	N 12° 25' E	IV a, b, c	VI	Carnegie Institution, Unpublished
Rio Bec II	108	Cahal Pichik	15° 54' S	Cahal Pichik	N 14° 30' E	D, E, F	B	Thompson 1931, Figure 4

MAPS OF FOLLOWING SITES CONVENTIONALIZED, EAST MOUNDS NOT ON ONE PLATFORM, OR ASSEMBLAGE QUESTIONED

Tikal	22		Due East		True North	62, 63, 64, 66		Tozzer 1911, Plate 29
Xultun	29		13° 34' N		True North	VIII	XI	Morley 1938, Plate 190*
Ucanal	61		Due East		True North	Group B		Merwin, Peabody Museum
San Jose	81		0° 20' S			A-2, 3, 4	A-7	Thompson 1939, Figure 1
La Muñeca	91		6° 15' N			VI, VII, VIII XI		Carnegie Institution, Unpublished
Uaxac Canal	262		13° 44' N		N 10° 0' W	Temple Group B		Seler 1901, Page 48

* Published Scale Incorrect

case of two others are portions of the east buildings exposed. Where no faced walls are visible the survey of the group is more difficult and bearings taken are much less apt to be correct. The sites of Ucanal, Nakum and Tikal, which may have this grouping, are not considered as the maps have been so conventionalized that all structures have a true north-south bearing. Thus little value may be placed on this material when considering it for the bearings of the various buildings in the group. In examining a grouping for specific orientation, points must be chosen that may be used for all sites. It seemed advisable therefore to extend a true east-west line through the group with one point falling in the center of the west structure. When Uaxactun, the type site, is examined the east-west line from E–VII strikes the north jamb of the doorway of the middle east building (Fig. 14, E–II) which is 0°57' of the arch to the north of the center of the doorway.

Where no doorway is exposed, the center of the middle mound is taken as the point for measuring the angle. The greatest variation noted from true east is 15°54' south at Cahal Pichik, a site 93 kilometers southeast of Uaxactun (Fig. 17); at Naachtun, 45 kilometers southeast of Uaxactun, it is 2°21' south of east, but at Nakum, only 35 kilometers south, it is 4°40' south of east. Thus the distance from Uaxactun does not seem to have any proportional bearing on the amount of variation from true east (Table I).

An examination of the long axis of the east mounds shows a variation of from 2°23' west of north to 14°30' east of north. Only one site, Benque Viejo, falls west of north. There does not seem to be any relation to the bearing of the long axis and that of the east-west line.

Some important facts might be deduced if the arrangements could be assigned to the chronological period in which they were constructed. The Uaxactun complex was certainly erected not later than early in the 9th cycle. At other sites even though stelae may be found in the plaza, lack of excavation makes it impossible to suggest a date for the erection of the complex as there is no assurance of the contemporaneity of the structures and monuments. Even though most groupings have stelae associated with them there is a scarcity

---

FIG. 17. CAHAL PICHIK, SPECIALIZED ASSEMBLAGE

Greatest variation from true east-west bearing seen at this site.

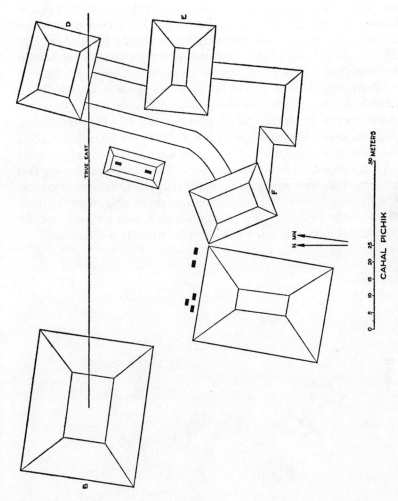

TRUE EAST

CAHAL PICHIK

N MN

0 5 10 15 20 25 50 METERS

Fig. 17. (For description, see facing page.)

of epigraphic material. It may, however, be said that these stelae carry dates ranging from early 9th cycle to early 10th cycle with no relation in time to proximity to Uaxactun or its orientation.

In considering Group E at Uaxactun in the light of an astronomical observatory it is of extreme interest to note how closely lines of site, as due east, and the north and south amplitudes of the sun, coincide with various points on the buildings. The station from which the observations may have been made is not known. Its position from the base to the top of the west mound would give an increase in the size of the arc in which amplitudes of the sun might fall.

When other similar groups are analyzed there is apparently no relation to any of the observational points made at Uaxactun, so that the possibility of the grouping having been used for astronomical observation is somewhat negated. It may, however, have been used in this manner at Uaxactun and if so may not some ceremony or ritual have developed with the observations. The other sites having this grouping may have given more attention to the ritual and ceremony attendant therewith. The general scheme of planning, with the three structures in a more or less easterly position, was retained, but the great rigidity to orientation was not adhered to as at Uaxactun.

FIG. 18

La Muñeca. This is a poor example of the assemblage, as the three structures on east side of the plaza are not on a single long platform, nor does west pyramidal structure conform to stylized type.

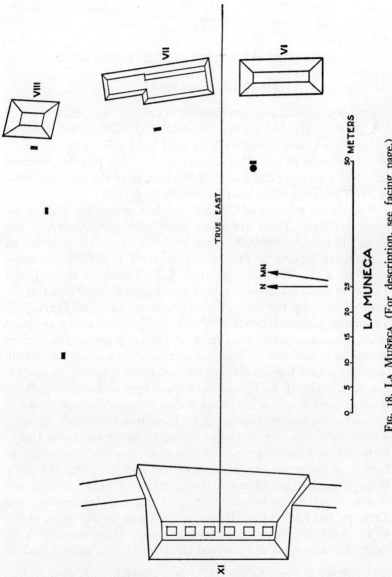

FIG. 18. LA MUÑECA (For description, see facing page.)

XV

DOMESTIC ARCHITECTURE OF THE MAYA

Robert Wauchope *

OUR KNOWLEDGE of pre-Columbian domestic architecture in the Maya area has reached the awkward but interesting developmental stage characterized by what used to be called growing pains. Its achievement of even this adolescence has been retarded, because definitely a younger and less attractive brother of the other branches of Maya research, it has been shamefully neglected.

Most earlier students of Central American prehistory ignored the subject entirely. There are a few exceptions, notably Sapper and Starr, and these, incidentally, were the only writers to comment on comparative aspects of the subject up until 1938. Other writers, however, E. H. Thompson in 1886, J. E. Thompson in 1931, and Tozzer in 1934, for examples, have stated in print their belief in the value of pursuing the study. Ricketson, Blom, LaFarge, Byers, J. E. Thompson, Gann, McBryde, Shattuck, Redfield, and others recorded modern house types in the course of various projects. Excavations in ancient house mounds prior to 1932 have been many but poorly recorded with a few exceptions, among which the work of Ricketson, A. L. Smith, J. E. Thompson, and Lothrop is outstanding. Ricketson in particular was interested in house mounds as one means of estimating the ancient population of Uaxactun, Guatemala. In 1932, Kidder, most of whose work had been done in the southwest United States where house types are so important, saw the possibilities of further investigation. As a result of the impetus given the study through his interest, intensive investigations of house mounds and sites were carried on by the writer at Uaxactun, Chichen Itzá, and Zacualpa, and Kidder himself excavated a house mound in the course of his work at San Agustín Acasauguastlan. More recently A. L. Smith has unearthed and restored an ancient house under Structure

* University of South Carolina, A.B., 1931; Harvard, A.M., 1933; graduate student, 1934, 1938; now Assistant Professor of Archaeology and Anthropology, University of Georgia.

A–V at Uaxactun. Kidder also suggested a survey of modern Maya houses, which was carried out by the writer in 1934. Since then Satterthwaite, Shook, J. E. Thompson, Steggerda, and others have volunteered information on house types observed by them in the course of other work.

One would expect that if we assembled the published reports of the researches mentioned above, we would have a large corpus of material to apply toward historical reconstruction. Actually, however, the significant data can be summarized in slightly over a hundred words! Challengingly interesting ethnological and archaeological problems have been formulated, tantalizing glimpses of the possibilities of future work are discernible, but (to risk carrying my growing pains metaphor *ad absurdum*) before our gangling problem-child can grow any taller we must put some archaeological meat on his skeleton.

All Maya houses, contrary to an assumption at one time, are not alike; we are beginning to realize that the differences between them are significant from historical, economic, and social points of view. Structurally speaking, only a few ways of building a house are possible with the materials available to the Maya. Indeed, we build our own frame houses along almost exactly similar principles. When we look for variations of historical or ethnological significance, we find the most important ones not in the framing of the superstructure but in substructure and ground plan. Platform substructures may or may not be used. Strangely enough, their use today is not governed by topography, nor are they otherwise functionally necessary. The low substructure was a feature of ancient houses at Uaxactun and many present-day Maya platforms duplicate these prehistoric ones (Fig. 19, *sub*). Among the house sites of Chichen Itzá, on the other hand, substructures were conspicuously absent. The modern Yucatecan platforms can scarcely be interpreted as mere survivals of an ancient custom, to which, as to many other customs, the Indian has clung. If it can be shown through excavation that the ancient Maya of Yucatan did not build house platforms, when and why was the practice temporarily discarded after the end of the stela epoch?

Ground plans are rectangular, square, rectangular with rounded corners, apsidal, or round (Fig. 19, *super*). The earliest houses studied were either apsidal (below Structure A–V at Uaxactun) or rectangular (in the environs of Uaxactun); surface sites at Chakantun, as-

signed by Lundell to the late occupation of the Peten after 1450, are
either apsidal or dumb-bell shaped; all prehistoric dwellings excavated in the Guatemala highlands (at Chukumuk and Zacualpa)
and one in the Baja Vera Paz (San Agustín Acasaguastlan) were
rectangular; thirteen undated prehistoric houses at Chichen Itzá and
other small habitations at Kabah and Sayil were probably rectangular. Sixteenth-century houses in Yucatan were probably rectangular,
yet Yucatecan dwellings have been prevailingly apsidal since at least
1843 and probably earlier. Other modern houses in the Maya area
are almost invariably rectangular. The square house with pyramidal
roof appears in the southwest highlands of Guatemala, concentrated
in the more isolated Indian villages such as the lake towns of Santiago
Atitlan, San Pedro de Laguna, San Lucas Toliman, and the Cakchiquel towns of San Sebastian to the west and Santa Apolonia to the
east. It also appears slightly north of this area among certain Tzeltal
groups of Chiapas. There is some evidence that it may be an older,
more aboriginal type than the rectangular. Apsidal dwellings turn
up again at Lake Pethá and Lake Izan in the Usamacinta region, and
among the Chontals of Tabasco. Rectangular houses with rounded
corners, which are probably the result of an attempt to build a
rectangular house on a basically apsidal framing, appear in Yucatan,
Campeche, and Quintana Roo in places where rectangular houses
either share with apsidal houses in frequency or outnumber them
(Tizimin, Catmis, and Campeche); they are found also in the Usumacinta, at Pantepec, two towns in northern Oaxaca, and two settlements in eastern Guanajuato. True round houses with conical roofs
occur at the Trique town of Chicahuastla, the coast settlements of
western Guerrero, among the Totonac in Vera Cruz and the Huaxtec of San Luis Potosí.

FIG. 19

SUPER: GROUND PLANS

a. Apsidal.   *c.* Rectangular.
b. Flattened ends.   *d.* Square.

SUB: ANCIENT AND MODERN SUBSTRUCTURES

a. Modern, Tizimin, Yucatan.   *f.* Ancient, Uaxactun, Guatemala.
b. Ancient, Uaxactun, Guatemala.   *g.* Modern, Lerma, Campeche.
c. Modern, Temax, Yucatan.   *h.* Ancient, Uaxactun, Guatemala.
d. Ancient, Uaxactun, Guatemala.   *i.* Modern, Cuilapa, Guatemala.
e. Modern, Valladolid, Yucatan.

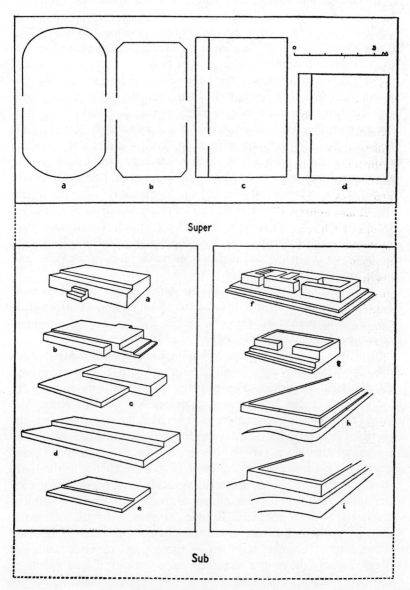

Super

Sub

FIG. 19. (For description, see facing page.)

In Yucatan and Campeche frequency of the apsidal plan seems to be in direct proportion to the incidence of pure Maya population, while the opposite is true of rectangular dwellings. When apsidal houses first appeared in Yucatan and whence they came are interesting questions, unanswerable at present because of the great lack of archaeological information and documentary house data for the period between the sixteenth and early nineteenth centuries. It is possible that round houses originated in the west and that apsidal houses were the result of easterners' attempts to copy round dwellings on a basically rectangular framing, but it is difficult to reconcile such a hypothesis with a very early occurrence of apsidal houses in the Peten. Most students of Maya prehistory would probably prefer to derive the many Yucatecan and the few scattered western apsidal dwellings from those of the Peten of stela epoch days. But here we are confronted with the difficulty that all ancient Yucatecan houses so far observed are apparently rectangular. Equally perplexing are problems of the origin and sequence of house plans in the Peten and in Mexico.

Our knowledge of ancient Maya houses is not limited to their imperishable substructures. It is bolstered by additional information gleaned from prehistoric frescoes, graffiti, and codices, by occasional references in early Spanish accounts, and by a fairly large amount of information gathered through technological studies of modern Maya dwellings, together with linguistic and as yet not well understood distributional evidences. The primary and prehistoric sources are sadly overbalanced by later and therefore less valid evidence. We know that ancient superstructures resembled, in a general way, the thatched huts built by the Maya today, but careful study of the latter shows that they vary widely in certain details which cannot always be attributed to environment (Fig. 20). Thatch methods are usually dependent on the materials available—an environmental conditioning. Wall types, while influenced to a certain extent by habitat, are not always so governed. Rubble masonry walls are most common in northern Yucatan where there is an abundance of building stone; adobe is almost standard in those parts of Guatemala and Mexico where the mud is at hand; wattle walls are found chiefly in southern Yucatan along the range of hills where suitable withes are plentiful. But in areas where all these materials are found, why do we encounter significant geographical distributions? In central Yucatan, for example, walls built of vertical poles are almost standard, yet

a

b

FIG. 20. MODERN MAYA HOUSES

a. Tizimin, Yucatan.   *b*. Sotuta, Yucatan.

one comes suddenly on districts or towns or neighborhoods, identical in environment, where all the houses have walls of horizontal wattle or vertical wattle. Here again is a problem yet to be solved; I have not been able to correlate the distributions with any particular social class, economic status, known event of history, or ancient province boundary. The same thing may be said of other features such as porches, penthouse sheds, door types, principles of house framing construction, and details like roof apex caps of clay (recently discussed by Linné), lashing patterns, and so on.

The reader may well be of the opinion that I am suggesting the possibility of too much significance in houses and house details. Every possible consideration is mentioned, not in the belief that they are all significant, but in order that future investigation may be conducted according to a methodical plan rather than by chance sampling. Such an approach is of necessity somewhat subjective and we should guard against its attendant dangers. I feel sure also that some anthropologists will classify studies of this kind as "atomistic research" and scorn it accordingly, but I consider the following quotation from Lowie's "History of Ethnological Theory" a sound reply:

"How intensively a particular problem shall be studied at a definite stage varies with the circumstances, precisely as does the decimal place to which a physicist shall carry his calculations. For certain purposes it suffices to characterize a dwelling as round; in Samoa a close analysis reveals that what is so described is not a true round structure at all, but a rectangular house with shortened middle section and terminal apses. Any inferences from the occurrence of "round" dwellings in Samoa are therefore fallacious. If technological and genealogical particulars of forbidding aspect loom large in modern monographs, they should not be interpreted as meaningless trivialities. They may be essential for the broaching of new problems, for the definition of the observed phenomenon itself.

Ethnologists are not always sufficiently conscious of the assistance rendered to them by techniques and concepts extraneous to their own discipline. Yet such dependence is no cause for abasement. . . ."[1]

Although detailed descriptions of Maya houses are very rare in early accounts, we have indirect ways of learning how the dwellings were constructed. Many of the early dictionaries, for example, con-

[1] Lowie, Enthnological Theory, 1937, pp. 253–254.

tain terms which refer to parts of the house. Through comparative linguistics, "linguistic palaeontology," we can describe fairly accurately the kind of house used at a time before the Maya-Quiché language branched into its present dialects, by assembling all the house terms which, though perhaps differing in sound today, are alike when translated literally into descriptive terms based on ideas totally unrelated to the house. As examples: an intermediate roof purlin is often called "road of the rat"; door or entrance, "mouth of the house"; roof bow, "toad's crutch"; ridgepole, "head of the house"; penthouse, "son of the house"; and mainpost, "leg of the house." If these slang expressions are found in any two languages that have been isolated from each other since their divergence from the old parent language stock, the expressions must have been given to the various house members before the language split into dialects, for it is incredible that the groups acquired the same odd terms by chance.

The results of domestic architecture studies have uses more far-reaching than historical reconstruction alone. They reveal information with social, religious, and psychological implication; a proper understanding of these may conceivably aid interpretation of future finds that indicate comparable conditions in ancient times. Communal labor and ownership, the division of house labor by sex and age and time, beliefs concerning the felling of house materials, new house ceremonies, and various attitudes and concepts connected with dwellings and their related structures serve as examples of the type of material to which I refer. Excavations of ancient domestic architecture interpreted in the light of what we know about the modern Indians (and what ethnology was recorded by early writers like Landa) might yield important information on average living conditions as revealed by such things as boundary walls and their social significance, finds indicating community trades, and the allocation of space within the house. I scarcely need add that one would skate over very thin ice in attempting conclusions along these lines. Again, since we know that Maya houses are occupied an average of a little more than a Maya generation, say twenty-five to thirty years, excavation of a series of house mounds whose total range of occupancy covers a complete ceramic period might enable one to discover the approximate length of that period in terms of years. The conditions for such an estimate would have to be perfect, for there are many pitfalls, notably the fact that houses were probably abandoned after not more than three deaths in the household, and the Maya practice of re-using old house sites for new dwellings and of converting habitations into burial mounds.

No chapter on Maya domestic architecture would be complete without a word concerning the New World application of the Vitruvian theory, which derives features of stone construction in temples from wooden house prototypes. I cannot go into all the aspects of this theory here other than to say that it has been invoked as an interpretation of temple profiles, ground plans, certain types of substructure, arches, cornices, vaults, half-columns and banded columns, lattice-work, "log-cribbing" façade decorations, hut-niches, veneer- and core-construction, and roofs carved in imitation of thatch. Undoubtedly the first temples were of wood or adobe, but for reasons (chiefly chronological) explained in a previous publication,[2] I consider it wiser to regard these resemblances between stone temples and wooden or adobe huts as due to the ancient architects' desire for distinctive decorative motifs based on bush-house characteristics, rather than as actual survivals of the original features of a prototypical temple.

A study of the sequence of prehistoric house types in Middle America not only would contribute to fuller understanding of Maya prehistory and the relations of the Maya proper with their neighbors to the west and south, but also has wider possibilities. I have already shown how, by means of linguistic as well as archaeological research, we might describe in some detail house construction at an early horizon. If, by the same processes, we should extend such knowledge southward to Costa Rica, Nicaragua, Panama, and South America, and northward through northern Mexico and Cuba to out Southwest and Mississippi Valley and Southern States, the possibilities of adding fundamental facts to New World prehistory seem promising. Waterman believes, for instance, that the round house was the original type introduced into the New World from Asia, that it is now found among the most primitive and isolated or marginal tribes, and that it has been replaced elsewhere by dwellings of rectangular plan.[3] This may have been the case, but there is far too little information now available upon which to base such a hypothesis. To do so, knowing as little as we know now, is to involve ourselves in an unwarranted evolutionary scheme by which all

[2] Wauchope, Maya Houses, 1938, pp. 149–151.
[3] Waterman, T. T., Architecture, 1931.

Indians in the New World either have or eventually will come to the conclusion, independently if not by diffusion, that the rectangular house is superior to the round. Even this idea is not too fanciful, for, as Pollock has pointed out, the materials with which the Indians built houses may have been instrumental in limiting the shape of the dwelling to the present prevailingly rectangular plan. Secondly, we know so little of pre-Columbian Indian history, or, for that matter, of post-Columbian Indian history, that we cannot know how isolated these so-called primitive tribes have actually been, or how long they have been in the places they now occupy. Again, the assumption that because certain tribes are more primitive than others they are nearer to the original cultural state in which they arrived from Asia is open to serious objections. It is difficult to imagine, for instance, the Lacandones, the Great Basin Shoshoneans, and the Tierra del Fuegians (to take three groups often classed as "primitive") sharing a material culture, or any other kind of culture, closest to that of the first Asiatics to arrive in the New World.

The real point I wish to make here, however, is that Waterman's goal is not too ambitious, given sufficient archaeological, historical, and ethnographical information. The fact that undertaking the solution of a problem of such magnitude is enormous is no reason to abandon it. In no other line of research are we much further advanced toward a complete reconstruction of its New World prehistory. Studies in domestic architecture have contributed much toward solution of anthropological problems in Egypt, the Aegean, the Danube, parts of Oceania and China, the southwestern and southern United States, and other areas. It would be very foolish indeed to ignore the aid they promise toward solving not only local problems in Central America but also much broader problems of New World anthropology.

XVI

Ceramics of the Peten

Robert E. Smith *

THE PETEN is located in the northern part of Guatemala and lies wholly in the humid tropics of the Caribbean coastal plain of northern Central America. For the most part it is densely forested. It has a marine limestone base rising only two or three hundred meters above sea level except for the occasional ranges of low hills running generally East and West and these rarely exceed 500 meters in elevation. The Peten is bounded on the north by the states of Tabasco and Campeche and the Territory of Quintana Roo, Mexico, on the east by British Honduras, on the south by the Departments of Izabal and Alta Verapaz, Guatemala, and on the west by the States of Chiapas and Tabasco, Mexico.

Such are the actual boundaries of the Department of Peten, Guatemala, but from an archaeological point of view it would seem advisable to forget these man-made arbitrary divisions and consider the Peten as an early Maya realm held together by a uniformity of topography, climate, language and culture. If this be admitted then the territory must be extended to include a considerable portion of the bordering states of Mexico and a part of British Honduras.

The main archaeological sites in this region from which representative pottery samples have been recorded are Uaxactun, Holmul, and Piedras Negras in Guatemala, and San José, Lubaantun and Pusilhá in British Honduras. Of these only two Uaxactun and San José have yielded a clear-cut and distinct sequence of cultures based on stratigraphy. A sequence was found at Holmul based not on successive archaeological deposits in the ground, but upon various vaults and disused rooms in two Maya structures. Piedras Negras finds have so far been restricted largely to surface material. This is also true of Lubaantun. Pusilhá on the other hand had a stratified deposit in a

* Harvard, A.B., 1922; now Archaeologist, Carnegie Institution of Washington.

cave, but the sequence was somewhat obscured by the fact that the debris was thrown in through a chimney thus forming curvilinear rather than horizontal or vertical strata.[1]

Manifestly, therefore, we must use Uaxactun and San José as our basis in establishing even tentatively the various Peten ceramic phases. Fortunately the sequences in these two sites coincide to a great degree, the major variance being that Uaxactun predated San José and the latter outlived Uaxactun. In view of the fact that the writer was closely associated with the analysis of the Uaxactun ceramic material and even though the San José pottery report has been published, it seems best to use the former exclusively in outlining the ceramic cultural development.

At Uaxactun four main ceramic phases were established. They were given the arbitrary names Mamom, Chicanel, Tzakol and Tepeu.[2] Mamom refers to the most ancient and Tepeu to the most recent cultural phase. Both Tzakol and Tepeu have been divided into early and late. The late subdivisions retain all of the early culinary forms but take on new shapes and designs in the decorated wares. The Mamom pottery was found in black dirt below all plaza floors,[3] having been dumped there to level the ground for the original plaza floor. It precedes masonry structures and probably carved stone stelae. It has been called archaic although it is neither a primitive (in the crude sense) nor an antiquated culture. The Chicanel material which follows immediately after the Mamom was located above the earliest plaza floor, often associated with the earliest masonry structures, usually low platforms. The Tzakol wares may be said to coincide with Uaxactun architectural Period I of the vault, and the Tepeu wares with architectural Period II of the vault.

OUTSTANDING WARES AND SHAPES FOUND IN THE FOUR
MAIN UAXACTUN CERAMIC PHASES

The Mamom Phase

Unslipped jars with flaring necks.
Daub ware jars with pinched lips.
Black ware jars with incising on shoulders.
Red ware plates with flaring sides.

---

[1] Joyce, British Honduras, 1929, p. 443.
[2] Smith, Ceramics of Uaxactun, Pamphlets I and II, 1936.
[3] Ricketson, Uaxactun, 1937, p. 224.

Red ware plates with horizontal grooving.
Red ware bowls with horizontal grooving.
Mars orange ware bowls.
Red or buff ware modeled figurines.
Tempering material used: Sherd 64%, Calcite 17%, Tuff 10.5%, Sherd and Calcite 7%, Miscellaneous 1.5%.

The Chicanel Phase

Unslipped jars with low flaring thick necks.
Red ware jars with short flaring necks.
Red ware wide everted lip plates.
Red ware thickened and out curved bowls.
Red ware basal angle bowls.
Cream ware labial flange dishes.
Brown ware lightly incised bowls.
Red ware jars with short flaring necks.
Tempering material used: Sherd 66%, Calcite 33%, Miscellaneous 1%.

The Tzakol Phase

Unslipped jars with great variety of lip treatment (some have closed spouts).
Polychrome jars with straight necks.
Orange ware basal flanged bowls (a few have open spouts).

Black ware basal flanged bowls plain or incised.
Polychrome basal flanged bowls (some have covers, a few have open spouts) (Plate IV, top and middle).

} most have ring base but some 3 cascabel feet

Orange to red ware bowls with rounded sides and either ring or ring stand bases.
Orange ware bowls with flaring sides (cache vessel).
Black ware tripod bowls (small solid feet).
Black ware tripod cylindrical bowls (slab legs as a rule) carving or plaster technic for decoration (Plate V).
Tempering material used: Sherd 1%, Calcite 42.5%, Tuff 53%, Miscellaneous 3.5%.

The Tepeu Phase

Unslipped jars with large orifice.
Red ware jars with flaring and rounded necks (some have handles).

Red ware bowls with rounded sides.
Polychrome bowls with rounded sides.
Red ware incurved lip bowls.
Brown ware incurved lip bowls.
Red ware incurved lip tripod dishes.
Red ware tripod plates with flaring sides.
Polychrome tripod plates with flaring sides.
Polychrome basal molding tripod plates.
Polychrome bowls with straight sides.
Polychrome cylindrical or barrel shaped vases.
Carved (fine) orange vases with pedestal bases.
Carved (fine) orange bowls with rounded sides.
Unslipped, often painted, moldmade figurines which are gener-
ally whistles and represent both humans and animals.
Tempering material used: Calcite 79.5%, Tuff 19.5%, Miscel-
laneous 1%.

It is not the purpose of this brief resumé to either analyze or summarize Uaxactun pottery. That has been done in several different
publications. The object of this paper is first to examine Peten ceramic
archaeology in general; second to trace the distribution of Uaxactun
shapes and wares through the Peten, and third to follow Peten-type
ceramics in other regions of Central America and Mexico.

The first step in a study of ceramic material is to know its
provenience. Mere knowledge of the site is not sufficient. One should
ascertain whether the pottery was recovered from a refuse dump,
from the fill of building construction, from the surface, or from a
grave. In most Peten sites pottery is found in the fill of temple walls,
in pyramid fill, and in the fill used in leveling off plazas. But at
Piedras Negras, possibly all along the Usumacintla river, few potsherds were used in masonry fill. This condition would lead one to
believe that the Maya Indians of this region either dumped their
refuse into the river or created extensive middens near-by. The practice of using refuse material as the rubble in masonry fill exhausted
most of the refuse dumps in Central Peten. The only middens that
remain at Uaxactun are those where the debris was thrown off the
edge of a plaza with the idea of extension. From these practical
dumps as well as from the pottery-mixed rubble in pyramids and
buildings great quantities of potsherds were taken and definite stratigraphy was established. It is also a fact that the ceramic sequence
obtained from the various levels in the refuse dumps agreed exactly

with the pottery series noted in a multiple pyramid complex,[4] and the ceramic order established in Structure A–V which has three main architectural periods of development.

Burials whether involving a simple grave, a cist, a crypt or a chamber might be accompanied by anywhere from one to thirty-five pottery vessels. It is interesting to note that the ceramic material found with burials is usually only of the finest and therefore insufficient for establishing a specific ceramic phase. It may be that an especially fine piece saved for generations was finally interred with some descendant of the original owner, or it may be that some handsome trade pieces, the precursors of a new style found their way into an important grave. It is even possible to find the old, the current and the precursor type in the same tomb. Therefore, it would seem a dangerous practice to set up a phase analysis on tomb evidence alone. A sequence of graves and the materials found within them often occurs but it is only a sequence and should not be used to define ceramic cultural phases at the site in question.

It is naturally the ambition of every archaeologist to find a means of dating excavated material. This desire appeared to be on the brink of realization when it was discovered that not only did Uaxactun harbor a series of dated stelae covering a period of 570 years but that it also disclosed stratigraphic sequences in pottery types, in burials and in details of architectural practice. If an association between a dated monument and either pottery or architecture could be established the problem was solved. Or was it? Somebody objected on the grounds that the stela might have been moved from its original position and that therefore the date would not be contemporaneous. Somebody else suggested that the date on the stela might refer to either past or future events. These suppositions may or may not be valid, but there is one way to find out whether or not the date on a stela is contemporaneous to the stairway within which it is set or to the pottery with which it is associated and that is to test the matter thoroughly. If it can be established in two or three different cases that monuments bearing dates within a certain span of years are always associated with certain pottery types and a specific style of architecture the problem will have been solved. Another method of tackling the time element is by means of the tree ring system. This is not practicable in the Peten because of the irregularity of tropical rainfall.

[4] Smith, Structure A-I, Uaxactun, 1937.

In tracing the distribution of ceramic shapes and wares throughout the Peten, we propose to review the matter phase by phase. Beginning with the Mamon phase, where outside of Uaxactun are examples of this culture found? With the possible exception of San José, British Honduras, Mamom pottery types have not turned up at any other Peten site. This does not necessarily mean that they do not exist elsewhere but possibly that not enough intensive digging has been done to find them. The Chicanel phase is well established at San José but otherwise it is so far unknown in the Peten region. The Tzakol phase on the other hand is abundantly represented from one end of the area to the other in such places as Piedras Negras,[5] Tayasal, Nakum,[6] Holmul,[7] San José and Baking Pot.[8] This is also true of the Tepeu phase wares and shapes, quantities of which are found at Piedras Negras,[9] Palenque,[10] Tayasal, Nakum,[11] Holmul,[12] Pusilha,[13] Baking Pot,[14] and San José.

Just what is meant by the statement, made above, that the Uaxactun Tzakol and Tepeu phases are abundantly represented at Piedras Negras, and elsewhere? Have these sites a complete duplicate collection of the pottery discovered in the Uaxactun Tzakol and Tepeu phases? The answer is no, but they have all or most of the basic or culinary shapes, the same techniques of decoration, and in a very broad sense the same types of design. The wares vary more than the shapes and this is especially true of the decorated wares. These are apt to differ as to paste and tempering ingredients, often vary as to the exact surface shade, and may offer different design patterns. The truth of the matter is that as one approaches the periferal cities of the Peten one encounters more variation and novelty. Central Peten appears to have been so far as is known relatively uniform in its ceramic art and it is really surprising that such outlying cities as

[5] Butler, Piedras Negras, 1935, Pls. VI, No. 8, VII, No. 17, VIII, Nos. 29, 34, 36, 37, 39, IX, Nos. 45, 59.

[6] Vaillant, Maya Ceramics, 1927, Fig. 250.

[7] Merwin and Vaillant, Holmul, 1932, Pls. 18 b, 19 f, 20 e, 21–26, 27 d, f, h, 28.

[8] Ricketson, Baking Pot, 1929, Pl. 17 b and c.

[9] Butler, Piedras Negras, 1935, Pls. V, Nos. 3–5, 9, 10, 13, 14, 15, VII, Nos. 7, 14, 15, VIII, Nos. 21, 22, 24, 26, 27, 30, 33, IX, Nos. 54–56, 61, 62.

[10] Vaillant, Maya Ceramics, 1927, Figs. 306 and 385.

[11] Vaillant, Maya Ceramics, 1927, Figs. 246, 247 and 249.

[12] Merwin and Vaillant, Holmul, 1932, Pls. 29–31.

[13] Joyce, British Honduras, 1929, Pls. XL, Fig. 1; XLI, Fig. 1 B, Fig. 2 B; XLIII, Figs. 4 and 5.

[14] Ricketson, Baking Pot, 1929, Pl. 17 a.

Piedras Negras and San José did not differ more definitely. It is quite obvious that they were influenced by other cultures and yet the Central Peten influence is strong. It is curious to note that both Piedras Negras and San José had a later ceramic phase than anything found at Uaxactun or for that matter almost any other site in Central Peten.

How far afield has the Peten ceramic influence traveled or where do we encounter Peten type pottery away from its natural habitat? It is too early to attempt to determine Peten influences but we can point out where pottery similar to that manufactured in the Peten has been found. Once again let us approach the matter phase by phase. There is no doubt that the early types of modeled clay figurines together with much of the pottery found in the Miraflores barranca are highly characteristic of the Mamom phase. The same types of early figurines are found all over the highlands of Guatemala, notably at Utatlan, Totonicapan, etc. as well as to the South in Honduras and Salvador, and with local variations to the Northwest in Mexico. The Chicanel phase shapes and wares have not been encountered outside of the Peten but they may well exist. Certain Tzakol shapes and decorative techniques have been discovered in the Alta Verapaz region at such sites as Chamá,[15] Coban and San Pedro Carcha. The same is true of the Quiché at such places as Utatlan and Zacualpa [16] but no Peten types whatsoever have turned up at Chukumuk or Chuitinamit on Lake Atitlán.[17] The grave material from Kaminaljuyú had a large percentage of Tzakol types but not so the pottery found in the building fill and general digging. Teotihuacan in Mexico appears to have been in rather close contact with the Peten during the Tzakol ceramic phase if similarity in pottery shapes and methods of decorating can be taken as a guide.[18] The Tepeu phase types have a somewhat different distribution. Several Tepeu shapes and certain Tepeu styles of design are to be found in the Alta Verapaz [19] at Chamá and Coban, some in the Quiché notably at Zacualpa.[20] Ceramic material from northern Quiché is even more strongly reminiscent of Peten pottery. Kaminaljuyú on the other hand appears to lack the Tepeu influence entirely. Finally

[15] Butler, Alta Verapaz, 1939, Pls. 2 *o*, *p*, and 9 *a*.
[16] Lothrop, Zacualpa, 1936, Fig. 32 *a* and *b*.
[17] Lothrop, Atitlán, 1933.
[18] Linné, Teotihuacan, 1934, Figs. 19, 21–29.
[19] Butler, Alta Verapaz, 1939, Pl. 10 *b*.
[20] Lothrop, Zacualpa, 1936, Pl. 5 *a* and *c*, and Fig. 34.

Peten wares assignable to the Tepeu phase at Uaxactun and to Period V at Holmul were found under stratigraphic conditions at Coba, Yaxuna, Kabah and Sayil in Yucatan.[21] These are the main sites and sections where pottery similar to that of the Peten is found in any quantity. Casual occurrence of Tzakol and Tepeu wares and shapes may have been recorded in Salvador, Honduras and in sections of Guatemala and Mexico other than those mentioned above. In the same way isolated types from various exterior sources occur in the Peten.

From this brief survey it is apparent that a considerable amount of trade existed in pottery vessels and other ceramic objects from the earliest times to the coming of the Spaniard. During the Uaxactun Mamom phase there appears to have existed a certain uniformity in figurine modeling throughout Central America and Mexico, but unfortunately next to nothing is known about the ceramic art concurrent with the manufacture of these early figurines. It is only in a few sites in Mexico, Uaxactun in Guatemala and Lake Yojoa in Honduras that this early material has appeared under stratigraphic conditions. At the time of the Chicanel phase at Uaxactun there may have been a cessation of trade between the Peten and the outside world. But whatever happened to trade during the Chicanel phase it certainly took on renewed vigor in the Tzakol period, and most of the associations point either south to Kaminaljuyú or northwest as far as Teotihuacan in Mexico. On the other hand during the Tepeu phase ceramic trends appear to have been north into Yucatan and southeast into Honduras and Salvador.

It will of course be realized that results of investigation in Peten ceramics and the problems arising therefrom cannot be dealt with satisfactorily in such meagre compass as that of the present paper. A complete illustrated work upon the pottery of Uaxactun is now in course of preparation and a volume dealing with the ceramics of San José has just been made available.[22] These publications will materially assist the student to a wider knowledge of the Peten ceramic field. Finally if a complete picture is to be obtained there would seem to exist a definite necessity for short intensive excavations at key sites within the Peten area radiating toward the north and south and at other points outside of the Peten area following these same directions.

[21] Roberts, Ceramics, 1935.
[22] Thompson, San José, 1939.

XVII

A POTTERY SEQUENCE FROM THE ALTA VERAPAZ, GUATEMALA

Mary Butler *

THE CORDILLERAS that run like a back-bone of the New World through North and South America divide the Highlands of Guatemala into a northern or Atlantic, and a southern or Pacific, drainage. The Alta Verapaz, an Atlantic province northeast of the country conquered by Pedro de Alvarado in 1524, was part of the area known to the Spaniards as Tezulutlan or the Land of War, and subdued at last when force had failed by Dominicans preaching the Gospel. The country is fertile and rugged, with a heavy rainfall and innumerable rivers, of which those in the northwest of the province drain into the Chixoy, one of the three streams that unite to form the Usumacinta, the great river that flows northwest across the base of the Yucatecan peninsula past early Maya cities to empty into the Gulf of Mexico. There is no doubt that contact by water between highlands and lowlands has its roots in a very distant past, and that study of a highland area as strategically placed as the Alta Verapaz should help to solve the problems of Maya archaeology.

A collection of archaeological material, carefully documented by Robert Burkitt and now in the University Museum, Philadelphia, which comes from two burial mounds at Chamá in the west of the province [1] and from ruins at Chipal, Kixpek, Tambor, Chihuatal, and Ratinlixul, sites farther west in the province of Quiché, provides a sequence of pottery types from the Chixoy drainage that has one foot in early and the other in late Maya history. On the

---

* Vassar, A.B., 1925; Radcliffe, A.M., 1930; Pennsylvania, Ph.D., 1936; now Director, Hudson Valley Archaeological Survey; Research Associate, University Museum, Philadelphia.

[1] For archaeological material from this area already published see: Burkitt, R., Highlands, 1930; Dieseldorff, E., Mayavölker, Vol. 1, 1926, Vol. 3, 1933; Seler, E., Guatemala, 1904; Alta Verapaz, 1908; Gordon and Mason, Pottery, 1925–1928; Spinden, H. J., Art, 1913; Termer, F., Archäologie, 1931; Villacorta and Villacorta, Arqueologia, 1930.

basis of stratigraphy and association, three main periods in the sequence can be established, and a possible fourth one:

TABLE III

PERIOD	SUB-PERIOD	DIAGNOSTIC
I	Chamá 1 Chamá 2	Black ware
II	Chamá 3 Chamá 4 = Chipal 1	Decorated cylinder jars
III	Chipal 2	Plumbate ware
IV?	Chipal 3	No plumbate, metal

Chamá is today a *finca* or coffee plantation northwest of Coban in a low-lying (elevation, 880 feet) fertile valley at the junction of the Tsalbhá and Chixoy rivers. The Kekchi-speaking Indians who live there are few in number, immigrants and descendants of immigrants from the colder Coban-Carchá area, but the quantity of potsherds found in the soil suggests a much larger prehistoric population. Two of the mounds built at Chamá by this earlier people provide the basis for Periods I and II of the sequence considered here. They are burial mounds A and B, in which apparent stratification coincides with change in types of funeral pottery.

PERIOD I

Black Ware—*Chamá 1,*

WARES: Black; Smoked (brown to black); Maroon; Red; Three-color Polychrome, *Chamá 2;* Household, unslipped.

SHAPES: Basic shape is the bowl, usually globular, with or without a collar (Fig. 21, *n, k*). Characteristic convex bevel or angle in the bowl side (Fig. 21, *m*). Tetrapod or four-legged bowl, Black, *Chamá 1* (Fig. 21, *c*). Flanged bowl with three and possibly four legs, Black; with ring base, Three-Color Polychrome, *Chamá 2* (Fig. 21, *p*). Cylinder jar with three slab feet, Smoked, *Chamá 2* (Fig. 21, *o*).

DECORATION: Incising, geometric, Black, Smoked, *Chamá 1* (Plate VII, *a, c*); naturalistic, Black, *Chamá 2* (Plate VII,

DECORATION: *b*). Grooving, Black, *Chamá 2* (Fig. 21, *i*); fluting, applied knobs and ridges, Smoked (Plate VII, *e; Fig. 21, b, k, l, o*); characteristic horizontal ridge at bend or bevel, knobbed four to six times in circumference (Fig. 21, *c, l*). Geometric polychrome painting in orange, red, and black, *Chamá 2*. (Pl. VIII, *a.*)

ASSOCIATIONS: *Chamá 1:* Pottery cylinder seal with crude cameo animal design, fine modelled pottery animal whistle (Plate X, *b, a*), but no mould-made figurines. Conventionalized zoömorphic(?) carved jades, round and tubular jade beads; obsidian flake knives; sandstone mirror backs. Extended burials. Probable trade pieces: two vessels of Costa Rica, one of Salcajá-Momostenango, type (Fig. 21, *h, g*).[2]

TABLE IV

Shape and Ware Frequencies in Period I

(See Fig. 21)

Fig. 21	a	b	c	d	e	f	g	h	i	j	k	l	m	n	o	p	Total
Blk.		2	2	1					2	1	2		2				12
S.	1							1	6	4	4		2		1		19
M., R.							2					1		1			4
P, 3-c																6	6
H.					1	2											3
Total	1	2	2	1	1	2	1	2	2	7	6	4	3	3	1	6	44
	CHAMÁ 1								CHAMÁ 1–2						CHAMÁ 2		

[2] Comparative material cited: *Quiché*—Lothrop, S. K., Zacualpa, 1936, Wauchope, R., Zacualpa, 1936; *Pacific Highlands*—Lothrop, S. K., Atitlan, 1933; *Central America*—Lothrop, S. K., Costa Rica, 1926, Vaillant, G. C., Playa de los Muertos, 1934; *Peten*—Merwin and Vaillant, Holmul, 1932, Ricketson, E. B., Housemounds, 1934, Uaxactun, 1937, Smith, R. E., Pottery Shapes and Decoration, 1936; *British Honduras*—Thompson, J. E., Archaeological Investigations, 1931; *Usumacinta*—Butler, M., Piedras Negras, 1935; *Mexico*—Vaillant, G. C., Mexican Correlation, 1938; Caso, A., Monte Alban, 1935, Oaxaca, 1938.

FIG. 21. VESSELS, PERIOD I

a–h, Chamá 1; *i–n*, Chamá 1–2; *o–p*, Chamá 2. Museum Catalogue Nos., all with prefix NA: *a*, 11198; *b*, 11249; *c*, 11251; *d*, 11211; *e*, 11155; *f*, 11166; *g*, 11159; *h*, 11230; *i*, 11179; *j*, 11223; *k*, 11176; *l*, 11224; *m*, 11200; *n*, 11226; *o*, 11175; *p*, 11217.

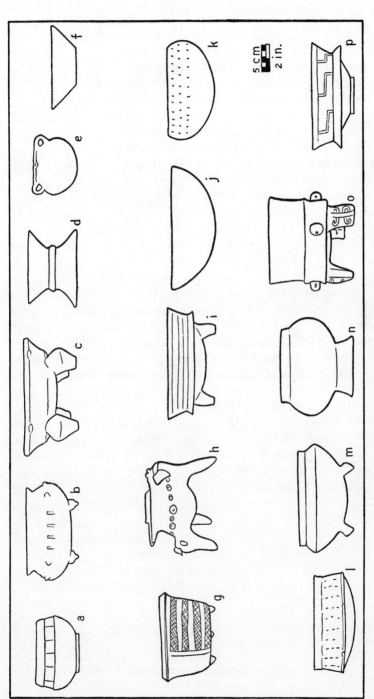

FIG. 21. (For description, see facing page.)

Mound B at Chamá supplies the material for Period I. It rises about six feet above the level of a hill-top of which it forms the eastern edge, and extends approximately fifty feet east and west, sixty-five feet north and south. It overlies, at a depth of six feet, a bed of packed stone resembling the fill used in stone-faced masonry, which rises from east to west in steps. The main step, twenty-four feet wide, lies under the crest of the mound, and on it were found a series of burials, one group lying on the stone pack, another above it within the angle formed by the two remaining walls of a burial chamber in the eastern end of the mound, a third group west and south of the chamber, and a fourth close to the surface of the mound. It would seem probable that the stone fill is all that remains of an original terracing of the hill-top, possibly for a building in the center, west of where Mound B now stands. With the decay or disuse of the building came the use of the wide terrace for burials and subsequent erection of a mound over them. The pottery from this underlying layer of burials is the group called *Chamá 1*. The building of the stone-lined burial chamber may have followed the building of the mound or may have been the occasion for it. Most of the pottery assignable to it is indistinguishable from that of *Chamá 1* and in marked contrast to that found with burials in the rest of the mound. It is therefore assumed that the use of the chamber for burials preceded that of the mound west and south of it, and the material associated with it is called *Chamá 2*.

While Period I pottery forms a well defined local group, we find even in *Chamá 1* links with other parts of the Maya area. Convex-beveled bowls appear in Uaxactun I and the tetrapod in the earliest levels of Maya pottery at Holmul in the Peten, Tzimin Kax in British Honduras, and Chukumuk in the Pacific Highlands. The latter is the only trait found at Chamá of the renowned Q-complex of early Central American culture elements. Equally important is the appearance in *Chamá 2* of the polychrome flanged ring-base bowl, the slab-foot cylindrical tripod, and the incised-snake globular bowl. Of these the first two establish contact with early levels in Peten-

---

FIG. 22. VESSELS, PERIOD II

a–h, Chamá 3; *i–l*, Chamá 3–4; *m*, Chamá 4; *n–q*, Chipál 1.
Museum Catalogue Nos., all with prefix NA: *a*, 11192; *b*, 11262; *c*, 11242; *d*, 11169; *e*, 11598; *f*, 11663; *g*, 11037; *h*, 11196; *i*, 11184; *j*, 11084; *k*, 11157; *l*, 11042; *m*, 11236; *n*, 11325; *o*, 11538; *p*, 11490; *q*, 11491.

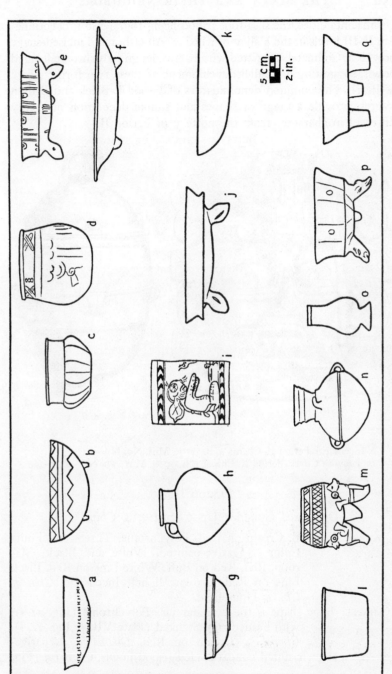

FIG. 22. (For description, see facing page.)

Usumacinta cities, the slab-foot tripod being found also in Teotihua-can II–III levels in the Valley of Mexico. An elaborated incised-snake bowl is at Chihuatal associated with parrot design polychrome flanged bowls, suggesting a parallel development of these two forms (Plate VIII, *a*). The common denominators of Period I, Black and Brown Wares, provide a range of shapes and simple decoration markedly different in character from the pottery of Period II.

a   b

FIG. 23

a. Incensario, Period II, Chamá 4, h. 37ᶜᵐ·; Mus. No. NA–11235.
b. Jar with Cover, Period II, Chipal 1, h. 95ᶜᵐ·, Mus. No. NA–11519–20.

PERIOD II

Decorated Cylinder Jar—*Chamá 3, 4, Chipal 1*

WARES: Smoked, Cream on Red, Polychrome, Three- and Four-Color; Negative-painted, White and Black; Ma-roon, Red, Red on Buff, White Line on Red, Black Line on Red; Brown [light]; Incensario, *Cha. 4-Chi. 1;* Household.

SHAPES: Basic shape is the cylinder jar: Polychrome (Fig. 22 *i*); with beaded rim, Smoked (Plate VII, *p;* Fig. 22, *l*), *Chamá 3;* Cream on Red, *Chamá 4.* Negative-painted concave-sided tripod bowls, *Chamá 3* (Fig.

22, *e*), and dishes, *Chamá 4* (Fig. 22, *j*). Disk indent on exterior base of negative-painted bowls, *Chamá 3*. Short-necked jars, often with gadrooned melon bodies, Smoked, Cream on Red, *Chamá 3* (Fig. 22, *c*); with a longer neck in Four-Color Polychrome. Lamp-chimney jars (Fig. 22, *o*) and effigy vessels (Fig. 23; Plate VI, *a-g, i, k*), Red, Incensario, *Cha. 4-Chi. 1*. Mouldmade animal head-, and cylinder foot-, tripods, Red, *Chipal 1* (Fig. 22, *p, q*).

DECORATION: Fine painting of human figures on cylinder jars in orange, red, black, and white, usually with black and white herring-bone border, is characteristic of *Chamá 3* (Fig. 22, *i*; Plates VI-*h*, VII-*o*, VIII-*c*). Three-Color Polychrome appears only on two *Chamá 3* pear-shaped jars, in geometric designs (Fig. 22, *d*; Plate VII, *m*). The bulk of the four-color designs can be arbitrarily divided into historical-ceremonial scenes and mythological personages, and the associated glyphs, on the basis of style, into descriptive and calendric, the first usually found with historical scenes and the second with mythological figures. Outline, black on cream, in simple floral design, *Chamá 3*, mythological, *Chamá 4* (Plate VII, *n, r*). Negative painting on light-weight fine vessels of simple geometric patterns in white against a black background (Fig. 22, *e*; Plate VII, *g-l*) appears in *Chamá 3* and continues through *4* with flattening of shapes and elaboration of design (Plate VII, *g, i*). A number of bowls have three broad vertical orange stripes painted over the design (Plate VII, *h*). Carved conventionalized glyph bands on neck of *Chamá 3* short-necked jars, as borders on Cream on Red *Chamá 4* cylinder jars decorated by incising or carving of fine naturalistic designs (Plate VII, *q, s, t*). Incised lattice design, *Chamá 3* (Plate VII, *f*), applied rows of pellets and incised-boss monkey heads, Smoked (Plate VII, *e*); spikes and notched fillet (Plate VI, *b, f, j, k*), Incensario, *Cha. 4-Chi. 1*. Effigy human and animal figures and heads, fine style:—as tripod vessel supports (Fig. 22, *m, p*; Plate VII, *d*), as vessel decoration (Plate VI, *a, c-e, g*), and as censer vessel and lid forms (Fig. 23; Plate VI, *b, f, i, k*).

ASSOCIATIONS: Fine mold-made pottery figurines (Plate X, *c-j*), low-relief plaques. Jades finely carved in human or animal heads and human figures in low relief; small anthropomorphic stone figures in the round in a vigorous crude style in marked contrast to that of the jades; round or tubular jade beads; obsidian flake knives, chipped flint knives or spear points; pyrites mirrors; oblong stone bark beater and large flakes of mica, Tambor. Bone tubes with carved ends. Extended burial, Chamá; seated burial in vaulted round or oblong chamber with side door, Chipal, Kixpek, Chihuatal, Ratinlixul; chamber showing elementary true vault, urn burial (Fig. 23, *b*), skeletal dedication offerings in pyramid piers, Chipal. Probable trade pieces: a pitcher (Fig. 21, *h*) and a polychrome lamp-chimney jar, both of Costa Rica type, from *Chipal 1;* a Chuitinamit red and white incised stepped-fret sherd at Chamá; White Line and Black Line on Red bowls(?) see below.

The two remaining groups of pottery from Mound B at Chamá, that from the west and south of the burial chamber, called *Chamá 3,* and that from close to the mound surface, called *Chamá 4,* show differences in type that are borne out by the stratification in material from Mound A, and from superimposed burial chambers in a mound at Kixpek.[3]

Mound A, also on a hill-top, is about sixteen feet high, ninety-five north to south, and at least fifty east to west. The northern and central parts of the mound are built of a pumice-stone sand, abundant locally, above yellow clay, while the southern side is, like Mound B, of earth with occasional stones and potsherds plentiful through it. Mound A was stone-faced, the top being finished in an oblong platform thirty by forty feet, running east to west, with a thirteen foot terrace to the south from which steps lead down to a plaza between A and another mound, E. Stones below the platform top-soil trace out the ground-plan of a small building, sixteen feet by six, lying east to west. Burials in Mound A were found only in the platform area, one group running under the platform retaining wall, another group below and around the building at a depth of about

[3] Cf. Dieseldorff, E., Mayavölker, Vol. 1, 1926, p. 25, Figs. 68–71, 83, 88.

TABLE V

SHAPE AND WARE FREQUENCIES IN PERIOD II

(See Figs. 21–24, Pl. VI)

	Fig. 24	Fig. 22																	Pl. VI									Fig. 23		Fig. 21		Total
	c	a	b	c	d	e	f	g	h	i	j	k	l	m	n	o	p	q	a/d	b	c	e	f	g	i	j	k	a	b	e	f	
S		2		4						7		1	5	1																		20
C/R				4						13*																						17
P		2			3		2	2		16		3	1																			29
N/P						3				2	8	5	3																			21
M/R		2	2												2	2	4	2	1	2				1								18
B	1												1																			2
H								2	2																					12	2	18
I																			2		2	2	3	2	1	2	2	1	3			20
Total	1	6	2	8	3	3	2	4	2	38	8	9	10	1	2	2	4	2	3	2	2	2	3	3	1	2	2	1	3	12	2	145
	CHAMÁ 3	CHAMÁ 3–4																	CHAMÁ 4—CHIPAL 1													

* 5 incised or carved; rest fragmentary.

two feet, and a third group near the surface, in and on the remaining stone-work of the building. As in Mound B, each group of burials was in turn disturbed by the next users of the mound who stacked the grave goods that bring bad luck to a robber, but took the stone of the burial chamber for their own use. Bone fell to pieces quickly in Mound A, but enough remains to show that the dead were, as in B, laid extended on the back, with a jade bead in the mouth.

The burials associated with the building are presumably later than those disturbed by it. These, in turn, could be considered later than the group beneath the platform retaining wall if we knew the latter to have been built earlier than its central structure. It seems probable, however, that the mound, already used for burial, was terraced and strengthened in preparation for erection of the building. The two groups of pottery in the body of the mound are therefore considered contemporary, and from resemblance to Mound B material are classed as *Chamá 3*, the surface group as *Chamá 4*.

From Chipal, colder country (6000') in the Cuchumatanes Mountains southwest of Chamá, comes pottery with strong local characteristics, of which the earliest deposits tie into the Chamá sequence. The site lies on a bench overlooking a ravine that drains into a tributary of the Chixoy. The groups of ruins there, A–F (B[4]), point to an extensive and sophisticated city. Its pottery, coming from stone-lined burial chambers, under-plaza cemeteries, and dedicatory deposits, is divided into three periods on a typological basis. While such a basis is a poor substitute for stratigraphy, it is strengthened in this instance by the appearance with more elaborate pot types of Plumbate, a distinctive ware apparently exported north from Salvador relatively late in prehistoric times. The pottery groups assigned to *Chipal 1* lack Plumbate Ware and show definite relationship to *Chamá 4* in Smoked, Cream on Red, Negative-painted, and effigy vessels.

Period II pottery is important both from the angle of local developments and that of outside contacts. Smoked Ware is the lineal descendant of that of Period I, distinguished from it by characteristic shapes, thin walls, hard, fine-textured surface, and a reddish, instead of a brown-to-buff, paste. It could be considered the basic ware of the period, since there is good reason to think that Smoked, Cream on Red, Negative-painted, and Polychrome were essentially the same ware differently finished. Negative painting of pottery, in which a design painted on a light slip is after firing left light against a dark background, is a trait distinctive in one local style of the early Maya city of Piedras Negras on the Usumacinta, in another of Chixoy Period II. A small negative-painted cylinder jar in Chixoy style has been found at Piedras Negras; negative-painted vessels from Holmul and Uaxactun in the Peten show Chixoy influence. It is, however, in *Chamá 3* polychrome cylinder jars, mould-made figurines, carved jades, and *Chamá 4* fine effigy vessels that Chixoy Period II establishes its kinship with the lowland cities. Polychrome cylinder jars, some showing Chamá influence, cylinder foot tripods, and figurines conforming to mould-made technique mark the late level at Uaxactun, similar cylinder jars and tripod belong to the last phase of Holmul, and cylinder jars and figurines are frequent at Piedras Negras. At the latter site, as in the Chixoy, polychrome seems to be succeeded by cut decoration. The replacing of polychrome painting on Chixoy cylinder jars by incising and carving as techniques for rendering fine figure designs shows a logical development of carved from painted wares and may well provide the source of inspiration for vessel carving in the Maya area.

At Chipal we find a local style characterized by vessels painted red over a buff slip. Any effigy portion of a vessel is left unpainted, forming a Red on Buff Ware. The characteristic shapes of lamp-chimney jar and animal-foot tripod are closer in affiliation to Central America than to the Maya area, and two types of Central American vessel have appeared at Chipal probably as trade pieces. A black geometric design occurs on a red bowl from Tambor, White Line on Red on the only *Chamá 3* effigy jar, on a Chihuatal bowl, and one with a pedestal base (Fig. 24, *f*) from Period III. These are probably trade pieces, possibly from the Pacific Slope, since White Line on Red Ware, so scarce in this collection, is common at Chuitinamit and known from other sites.

Period III

Plumbate—*Chipal 2*

WARES: Red, Brown (light), Fine Orange, Plumbate (silvery gray-green to orange glazed surface), Incensario, Household.

SHAPES: Elaboration of existing Chipal forms, such as doughnut jar, cylinder jar with rattle base (Fig. 24, *d*, *e*), and

SHAPES: animal-foot tripod with deep bowl (Fig. 24, *h*) or negative-painted or fine incised decoration. Long-necked jar, one spouted (Fig. 24, *c*; Plate IX, *l-n*); straight-sided bowl with round rattle feet, Orange, Buff (Fig. 24, *i*), one a grater bowl, Orange (Plate IX, *h*); tripod globular censer, Red on Buff; shoe vessel (Fig. 24, *k*, *l*).

DECORATION: Single polychrome (Plate IX, *n*), negative-painted, fine incised, and carved (Plate IX, *i*, Fine Orange) vessels show survivals of earlier techniques on Period III shapes. Characteristic of Period III are incising, Orange, Plumbate (Fig. 24, *i*, *j*); disk indent on jar shoulder, Orange (Plate IX, *m*); and abbreviated, often grotesque, figures applied to squat censers (Plate IX, *e*, *f*). Plumbate vessels take up the fine effigy shapes of Period II (Plate IX, *a-d*, *j*).

ASSOCIATIONS: One fine pottery figurine head, one crude modelled figurine-censer (Plate X, *g*, *i*). A small crude stone figure of a type common in the Highlands and two jades in the same tradition; jade beads, obsidian flake knives, pyrites mirrors, and an alabaster jar (Plate IX, *o*). Seated burials as Period II. Possible trade piece:—White Line on Red pedestal-base bowl (Fig. 24, *f*).

With Period III there is a wave of new influence in the Chixoy drainage in which emphasis in pottery is laid on texture and shape rather than on decoration. Effigy, except in Plumbate Ware, is confined to applied decoration, becomes stylized, and tends to crudity and vigor rather than fine representation. The contemporary appearance of fine effigy in Plumbate supports the suggestion that this ware comes from a southern periphery of the Maya area presumably reached late by fine style influence. Plumbate and Fine Orange Wares, characteristic of the period, tie in to the late phase of Maya history through their association with the Mexican Period in Yuca-

---

FIG. 24. VESSELS, PERIODS III AND IV

a–l, Period III; *m–p*, Period IV.
Museum Catalogue Nos., all with prefix NA: *a*, 11503; *b*, 11603; *c*, 11608; *d*, 11515; *e*, 11513; *f*, 11438; *g*, 11606; *h*, 11634; *i*, 11434; *j*, 11702; *k*, 11524; *l*, 11525; *m*, 11385; *n*, 11381; *o*, 11378; *p*, 11380.

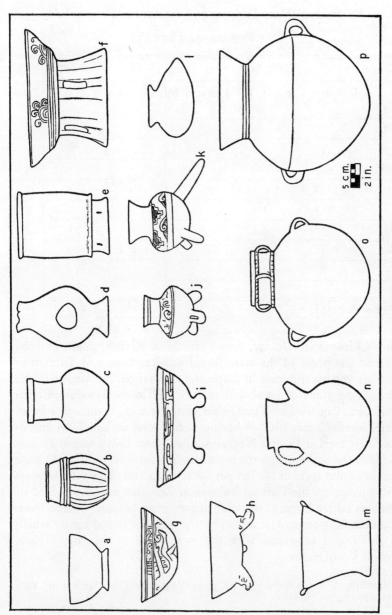

Fɪɢ. 24. (For description, see facing page.)

TABLE VI

SHAPE AND WARE FREQUENCIES IN PERIODS III AND IV

(See Figs. 22, 24, Plate IX)

Column groups — Fig. 24: a–p; Pl. IX: a–g; Fig. 22: o, q.

	a	b	c	d	e	f	g	h	i	j	k	l	m	n	o	p	a	b	c	d	e	f	g	o	q	Total
S		1						1																		2
C/R			2					1																		3
P								1																		1
N/P	2		2																							4
R	2			1	1	1			3	1														2	1	12
B		1					1																	1		3
FO			2					2			1															5
Pl.								1					1				1	1	1	1			2			8
I																					1					1
H												2		1	1	3						6				13
Total	4	2	6	1	1	1	1	6	3	1	1	2	1	1	1	3	1	1	1	1	1	6	2	3	1	52

tan.[5] Chixoy Fine Orange, found chiefly at Kixpek, might be considered one phase of the ware found in Vera Cruz and Yucatan in another version differing in shape and decoration, but similar in the identifying traits of color and texture and in the association with Plumbate. Chixoy Fine Orange has contacts with Usumacinta-Peten cities, similar carved bowls having been found at Yaxchilan and in the latest level at Piedras Negras; similar grater bowls late at Piedras Negras, and at Jonuta on the lower Usumacinta; carved Fine Orange jars in similar style in the last period at Uaxactun. This ware appears also further up the Chixoy drainage at Zacualpa in the province of Quiché, where it marks the later of two main periods. Contact with southern Mexico may be shown by the globular tripod censer which is also found associated with the shoe vessel in the late, Mixtec, Period V in Oaxaca.

[5] Lothrop, S. K., Zacualpa, 1936, pp. 36–41; Vaillant, G. C., in Merwin and Vaillant, *op. cit.*, pp. 79–81.

PERIOD IV

Metal-using, post-Plumbate—*Chipal 3*

WARES: Red, Smoked, Household.

SHAPES: Vessels with constricted neck and flaring rim (Fig. 24, *n, p*).

DECORATION: Applied grotesque effigy (Plate IX, *g*) with spotty over-painting in Red on Buff (1), White Line on Red (1).

ASSOCIATIONS: One crude modelled pottery bird whistle, one triangular flat stamp with cameo conventionalized bird design (Plate X, *k*). Jade beads; tiny greenstone celts; pyrites mirrors; obsidian flake knives, chipped arrow point, pair of ear spools (Plate XI, *a*); turquoise mosaic fragments. Shell beads and bracelets, some inlaid (Plate XI, *h, k, l*). Copper bells, rings, hair ornament [6] (Plate XI, *b, i, e, j, f*); gilded sheet metal; gold strips with holes in the ends, probably to be sewn on cloth, beads, and a small cup (Plate XI, *c, d, g*). Seated burial as II, III.

This period is tentative, since its pottery comprises only a handful of vessels, and it is defined primarily by negative evidence, the lack of metal in the Plumbate Period and the lack of Plumbate with the four finds of metal objects at Chipal. Only further work in the area can prove the value of this distinction or of the positive traits that seem to support it. While one of the four metal finds was by hearsay in a Period III censer, the other three were associated with vessels of which shape and decoration could be considered developments from Period III types. One Smoked jar (Fig. 24, *m*) was made

---

[6] Dr. William C. Root, of the Chemistry Department of Bowdoin College, has analyzed several specimens and reports on them as follows:—

2 copper bells: made of copper containing traces of silver and gold, cast by the *cire perdue* method, show traces of gilding. Comparative study so far done suggests that copper objects found in British Honduras and Tajumulco, Guatemala, are, like these from Chipal, made from metal originating in the highlands of Guatemala or Chiapas, not from Honduras or Salvador ores.

Gold band: made of gold and silver alloy with a small amount of copper, probably similar in composition to two gold discs found at Zacualpa (Lothrop, Zacualpa, 1936, p. 63, Fig. 68), and differing from gold plating on a clay bead found in the Department of Huehuetenango.

Gilded sheet metal: not analyzed but undoubtedly made from gold and copper alloy, gilded. Closely resembles specimens from Coclé, being probably an example of mise-en-couleur.

on a kabal,[7] a primitive substitute for a potter's wheel, used in Yucatan at the time of the Conquest, in which the pot rests on a greased disk revolved on a board by the feet of the potter who sits before it. This device, the only thing of the kind known in the pre-Columbian New World, was presumably invented late in Maya history because so few vessels show signs of its use. The presence of Plumbate in Mexico in the Chichimec Period and its absence in the following Aztec Period establishes a precedent for a Maya post-Plumbate period, though it by no means implies it.

Conclusions

The pottery under discussion, consisting of a selected group of burial vessels, forms a representative, not a comprehensive, collection. Nonetheless, though further work in the area is needed to correct or strengthen many of the distinctions traced here, the sequence and basic criteria of Periods I, II, III are checked by evidence from other parts of the Maya area and supported by the stylistic development of figurines and carved jades (Table III).

On the basis of the evidence presented, *Chamá 1* is considered as roughly contemporary with Uaxactun Ib, *Chamá 2* with Uaxactun II (Tzakol), Holmul III, and early Piedras Negras, *Chamá 3* with Uaxactun III (Tepeu), Holmul V. *Chamá 4–Chipal 1* bridges the gap between *Chamá 3* and the eleventh century A. D., *Chipal 2* and *3* the remaining five hundred years of pre-Columbian history. The question of absolute dating in the Maya area at the present time has been summed up by Vaillant in an article [8] in which the astronomical possibilities are checked against the known ceramic evidence in a series of four tables. Either the correlation of Table IV which would put the start of Chixoy I at the latest in the ninth century A. D., or that of Table III which pushes it back two hundred and sixty years, would satisfy the one chronological requirement of the Chixoy pottery. This is provided by the Plumbate Ware of Period III which belongs in Mexico to the Chichimec Period dated 1100–1300 A. D., and in Yucatan to the Mexican Period, 1191–1450 A. D. If Plumbate was exported from Salvador it would presumably have reached the Guatemala Highlands, on the direct route to both Mexico and Yuca-

[7] Mercer, H., Kabal, 1897.

[8] Vaillant, G. C., Maya Chronology, 1935. Vaillant's Chamá, I, II, III, and IV correspond to *Chamá 2* (I), *Chamá 3* (II, III) *Chamá 4–Chipal 1* (IV), as defined in this paper.

tan, sometime during the eleventh century. Therefore our present understanding of the position of Plumbate requires the beginning of Chixoy III to fall no later than the eleventh century A. D.

While the evidence on inter-city and inter-regional pottery trade is as yet only suggestive, relative quantity and position of types indicate the possibility of a wave of influence carrying fine effigy pottery from the Peten-Usumacinta cities into the Highlands having balanced the waves that carried fine figure painting on polychrome jars and, later, carved wares from Chamá into the lowland cities. Present frequency suggests a Highland center of distribution for the Fine Orange Ware considered here. Reversing the tendency that has considered similar traits in the Lowlands and Highlands to show diffusion from the former and therefore late arrival in the latter, Chixoy evidence implies late occupation of Usumacinta cities in the carved Fine Orange found at Piedras Negras and Yaxchilan.

Summing up Chixoy contacts with the country to the south, east, and west, we can say that Period I pottery shows some relationship to Chukumuk II, Period II to Chuitinamit, respectively early and late periods in the Pacific Highlands; that contact was maintained with the Costa Rica-Nicaragua area from Periods I–III, and that pottery, jades, architecture, and Period IV jewelry point to contact in all periods with central and southern Mexico. In view of the style contrast in Period III, it is interesting to note that the legendary arrival in the Highlands of the tribes powerful there at the time of the Conquest probably falls at the end of the eleventh century A. D.[9]

[9] Juarros, D., History, 1823, pp. 161–167; Lothrop, S. K., Atitlan, 1933, p. 67.

XVIII

THE ETHNOLOGICAL SIGNIFICANCE OF COPAN POTTERY

*John M. Longyear III** *

ORDINARILY, the ethnographical aspects of a ceramic complex —its distribution in time and space and relations with other centers of pottery manufacture both within and without its particular culture—become evident only after the sequences, forms and techniques of the complex are minutely defined. Pottery study in Central America has not yet approached so advanced a stage, but the fact that distinctive shapes and decorative styles abound in the region has enabled workers in this field to draw certain conclusions regarding ceramic distribution and trade. The increased investigations of the last few years have materially widened our knowledge of Maya ceramics, with the result that there are few localities at the present time from which reliable pottery data are lacking. One of the latest sites to come under intensive study is the Maya Old Empire center of Copan, in western Honduras (Plate II).

Among the projects included in the present work at Copan by the Carnegie Institution of Washington is the determination of pottery sequences and relations at that site, with the aim of eventual clarification of the southeastern Maya ceramic complex, of which Copan is a part. The sherd material from stratigraphic excavations is still being studied, and a final analysis is therefore impossible at this time. Certain indications of relations with other culture centers have, however, begun to appear.

As evinced by its pottery, Copan was in contact with three principal Central American regions. These were the southeastern frontier region of the Maya Empire; the Guatemala highland territory; and the Peten-British Honduras area.

The southeastern frontier of the Maya comprises all of Honduras west of a line slightly to the east of the Ulua River and Lake Yojoa

* Cornell, A.B., 1936; Harvard, Graduate School, 1936–1940; now Archaeologist, Carnegie Institution of Washington.

and all of Salvador west of the lower Lempa River.[1] It was with this area that Copan had many of its closest contacts. In the earliest levels of the latter site appears an abundance of Usulutan vessels with offset or grooved rims and tetrapod support—a form hitherto reported in quantity only from the Departments of Usulutan and San Miguel in Salvador,[2] although it is also found in early Ulua valley horizons [3] and in the first ceramic period at Chukumuk, in the Guatemala highlands.[4]

The polychrome period at Copan also shows affinities with that of Salvador. Bowls decorated with monkeys in black or red outline, often with a contrasting color filling the body, are common to both areas,[5] while vessels with painted conventionalized glyph bands and vertically compressed human figures, typical especially of Copan, have almost exact counterparts in collections from the environs of San Salvador.

Likenesses between central Honduras and Copan are not as strong as are those between Copan and Salvador. While the first-named region is represented at Copan by a few sherds of vases with the small slab feet, swollen lips and decoration typical of that area,[6] trade appears to have stopped there, for no Copan pottery is found in the Ulua-Yojoa drainage.

Copan evidently received much from the pottery of the Guatemala highlands. A few fine vases recovered from tombs and other ceremonial deposits of the Honduranian site display the mastery in color and line in painting the human figure that has made specimens from the Alta Vera Paz region famous for years (Pls. VI–VII).[7] More striking, however, are the numerous Teotihuacan types that appear to have reached Copan via Kaminaljuyú, a site just outside of Guatemala City. Several tombs in this latter center were investigated by Dr. A. V. Kidder of the Carnegie Institution, who found therein a pottery of distinctly Teotihuacan II–IV type (Plate IV, lower): tripod vases with covers and "al fresco" decoration, "eggshell orange" bowls [8] and "Tlaloc vases." [9] Of these, the first two have

[1] Lothrop, Maya Frontier, 1939.
[2] Lothrop, Salvador, 1927.
[3] Strong, Kidder, and Paul, Honduras, 1938.
[4] Lothrop, Atitlan, 1933.
[5] Vaillant, Maya Ceramics, 1927, Fig. 20.
[6] Vaillant, Maya Ceramics, 1927, Fig. 23.
[7] Gordon, Maya Pottery, 1925–1928.
[8] Called "thin orange" by Vaillant, "yellowish-red" by Linné.
[9] Linné, Researches at Teotihuacan, 1934; Kidder, A. V., Report, 1938.

also been found in fairly early Copan horizons. The tripod vases lacked the "al fresco" decoration, but otherwise there was no appreciable difference between the Kaminaljuyú, or for that matter the Teotihuacan specimens and those from Copan.

With the Peten-British Honduras region, Copan evidently had few ceramic contacts. These may well have been important ones, however, for the first polychrome pottery found at Copan for some time is composed of a few sherds from basal-flanged dishes—a form characteristic of and largely confined to the Peten region and British Honduras (Plate IV, upper). In later periods, a few sherds with "twist-and-bud" designs are reminiscent of Pusilhá.[10]

These relations between Copan and other areas are significant and, in at least one instance, startling. The similarity existing between Copan and Salvador pottery is well-known, and the absence of sherds from the former site in deposits of the Ulua-Yojoa region has been noted before, but the presence of Teotihuacan-derived Kaminaljuyú trade wares in early Copan horizons heretofore has never been suspected. Previously, Mexican pottery types reported from the southeastern Maya region and from Salvador in particular have been attributed to the Pipil, who migrated southward after the break-up of the Toltec Empire.[11] The Teotihuacan finds at Copan, therefore, have pushed back the time of Mexican influence in the southeastern Maya area several centuries and have given us new light on the wide extension of trade in these comparatively early times.

The early polychrome pottery from the Peten-British Honduras region is also of considerable interest, bearing as it does on the origin of Copan polychrome wares. Although the Peten material appears in Copan before any other polychrome pottery, the latter site did not follow it in either form or decoration, but suddenly acquired a distinctive style found nowhere else but in the southeastern Maya region. This abrupt appearance of a fully-developed type of pottery at Copan argues against its origin at that site, but further conclusions lie in the field of pure speculation at present. The Ulua-Yojoa drainage contains no Copan types and appears to have derived most of its own from Salvador, thus ruling it out of consideration as the birthplace of the Copan style and forcing us to turn to Salvador, where polychrome vessels in the decorative techniques of both the Ulua-Yojoa region and Copan are found. Did an invasion of Salvador styles

[10] Joyce, British Honduras, 1929.
[11] Lothrop, Salvador, 1927.

cut short the early Peten influence at Copan and determine the future trend of polychrome pottery at that site? This is a possibility, but only extensive stratigraphic excavation in Salvador can confirm or deny it.

Besides indicating that Copan polychrome was probably of extraneous origin, the recent investigations at this site have further shown that the idea of a high development of painting in life forms, long held as a characteristic of Copan, is largely mythical. The typical Copan polychrome is of poor quality, the decoration is executed in heavy, crude lines, and life figures when present are invariably distorted or poorly proportioned. The few vessels so far found at Copan with really excellent life painting have all been inspired by, if not actually imported from other regions. Most of them appear to be in the style of the Alta Vera Paz area (Plates VI–VII), while a few owe their technique to the Ulua-Yojoa or Salvador cultures (Plate XVII). Perhaps Copan's artistic talent was concentrated in stone carving to the detriment of pottery, for the stelae and altars of that site are as outstanding as its pottery is disappointing. In support of this suggestion, it is perhaps significant that many centers of the best Maya pottery—the Alta Vera Paz region, Holmul and the Rio Hondo drainage, Salvador, the Ulua valley—possess no correspondingly fine stone carvings.

Stratigraphic excavation at Copan has resulted in the abandonment or alteration of several ideas of long standing concerning the pottery of that site. On the other hand, these have been replaced by the partial knowledge of the many and far-flung influences operating there and the realization that Copan, far from being isolated in its location on the southeastern Maya frontier, was in contact with many of its contemporary centers of higher culture in Central America.

XIX

SKELETONS FROM THE CENOTE OF SACRIFICE AT CHICHEN ITZÁ

Earnest A. Hooton [*]

THE SACRED CENOTE of Chichen Itzá, Yucatan, has been one of the chief sources for romantic tales about the Maya.[1] The well was formed by the collapse of the roof of a cave over one of the underground rivers which burrow through the native limestone of Yucatan. Tradition had it that in the time of impending calamity, virgins were hurled into this natural well, along with precious possessions of many kinds. In 1909, Mr. Edward H. Thompson investigated this tradition by dredging the Sacred Cenote. Archaeology bore out tradition, since ornaments of copper, gold, and jade, together with many other objects, were brought up from the mud at the bottom. In addition, a number of skulls and other human remains were recovered that seemed to substantiate the ancient tales, until submitted to the examination summarized here.

The skeletal series from the Cenote at Chichen Itzá is too short and too diversified by age and by sex to warrant statistical elaboration, and I do not intend to publish here the raw data which would provide an altogether too lengthy, too expensive, and too unpalatable bill of fare for this volume. The collection consists, as measured, of 10 calvaria and 3 extra faces attributed to adult males, 8 putatively adult or subadult female calvaria, 7 calvaria of children between the ages of 10 and 12 years, and 14 more or less complete calvaria of younger children, mostly aged 6 years or less at time of death. There are, in addition: 2 paired and 6 odd femora, 2 paired and 7 odd tibiae, and 12 odd fibulae; 8 odd humeri, one complete pelvis, and 5 odd innominate bones. Thus the remains of at least 42 individuals are rep-

* Lawrence, A.B., 1907; Sc.D., 1933; Wisconsin, A.M., 1908; Ph.D., 1911; Oxford, B.Litt., 1913; Harvard, Instructor, 1913–1921; Assistant Professor, 1921–1927; Associate Professor, 1927–1930; now Professor of Anthropology; Curator, Somatology, Peabody Museum, since 1913.
1 Willard, Sacred Well, 1930; Herrera, Historia General, 1726–1730.

resented in this collection. All of the bones are in an excellent state of preservation and are of a dark grayish brown color, much like the coating of a stale chocolate cream.

It is commonly supposed that these bones represent the remains of sacrificial victims who were cast into the Sacred Cenote. All of the individuals involved (or rather immersed) may have been virgins, but the osteological evidence does not permit a determination of this nice point. Certainly, or almost certainly, 13 of the skulls belonged to adult males, and 4 of the 6 pelves represented. The males ranged in age from subadult (18–21 years) to old (55 years and over). Only one of the females was middle aged (35–54 years); of the other 7, 6 were young adults (21–34 years) and the other a subadult (18–20). There are 7 skulls of children between 10 and 12 years. Of the 14 skulls of younger children, 9 were estimated to have been aged 4 to 6 years, one 6 to 8 years, one 3–4 years, one 18 months. The other 2 were represented only by fragments.

All of the skulls show clear traces of artificial deformation, with the exception of 4 in the group of the younger children. One of these possibly undeformed skulls has a length-breadth index of 83.65. The others range from 93.51 to 98.67. Two of the adult male skulls and one subadult female skull also show indices ranging between 83 and 88. All of these show comparatively slight deformation. In the markedly deformed skulls the length-breadth indices range up to 113. The varieties of cranial deformation are so numerous that they are bewildering. Five skulls of children exhibit only plain occipital deformation. Seven skulls have frontal flattening combined with antero-posterior flattening of the occipital region. Nine skulls show a type of deformation which I call postero-vertical, because the post-auricular region of the skull appears to have been squashed downward. Six more skulls have this type of deformation combined with frontal flattening. Two combine frontal deformation with an annular constriction in the post-coronal region. While all of the adult male crania show frontal flattening, evidence of this type of deformation occurs in only half of the adult females and older children, and in but one of the young children. All degrees of deformation occur and the age distribution suggests that flattening was cumulative during the growth period of the individual. However, degree of flattening was probably conditioned also by the nutritional state of the subject and by variation in the nature and amount of artificial pressure applied. The effects of pressure would be more pronounced upon the less resilient crania of undernourished children. The probable agencies of deformation are: in the case of occipital flattening antero-posteriorly directed—cradle-boards or cradle pads; in the case of vertical flattening—the carrying of weights; for frontal flattening—the forehead bands to which were attached tump-lines. I should doubt that all of the combinations of head deformation were effected in the individual simultaneously by use of some general contraption. It is possible, of course, that the frontal bone was intentionally flattened by means of a board, but the extreme fronto-occipital type of deformation common among the Chinook was not observed in the Cenote series.

The cranial capacities, measured with the use of mustard seed by Hrdlička's method, are as follows: 10 males, mean 1310; 8 females, mean 1170; 7 children aged 10–12 years, mean 1180; 14 children aged 1½–8 years, mean 1154. These are, of course, small cranial capacities, but they represent the contents of small skulls. In the adult males the glabello-occipital length ranges from 152 mm. to 175 mm., the maximum breadth from 139 mm. to 163 mm., and the basion-bregma height from 118 mm. to 132 mm. Of course these diameters have been distorted by cranial deformation.

The crania are uniformly brachycephalic, and, although this condition is exaggerated by deformation, it obtains also in those few crania which seem unaffected by these influences. The breadth-height index is always so low as to classify the cranium as tapeinocephalic, but the height-length index ranges between orthocephaly and hypsicephaly, probably in accordance with the amount of vertical flattening present. The minimum frontal diameters are so frequently affected by frontal deformation that a calculated mean would be specious.

In association with the deformation of the skull vaults the zygomata are bowed outward, so that it is doubtful whether a mean dimension is representative. The range of this measurement in 9 adult male skulls is 133 mm. to 148 mm., and the mean 140.33 mm. The mean of the bizygomatic diameter of 6 female crania is 134.66 mm. The faces of the males were long; 5 total face heights average 122.8 mm., and 10 upper face heights 71.9 mm. The corresponding dimensions for females are: 3 total face heights 111.3 mm., 6 upper face heights 65.17 mm. The upper facial indices of the males are all mesene, ranging from 50 to 54.4. The faces of the females are relatively shorter, with a range from 42.11 to 51.88. Similarly, the children have upper facial indices ranging from euryene to mesene, with a strong predominance of the former category.

The mean orbital indices range quite erratically from chamae-conch, or low values, to hypsiconch, with the lower values more frequently observed in the adult male crania. Similarly, the nasal indices cover a range from relatively narrow (leptorrhine) values to the distinctly broad (chamaerrhine) types. The external palatal indices are also very heterogeneous, ranging from long, narrow to short, broad forms. All of the children, of course, have extremely short and relatively broad palates.

The gnathic indices suggest considerable facial prognathism in a number of individual crania, but it seems probable that the basion-nasion length in many cases has been diminished by cranial deformation.

It is impossible to present within the compass of this paper the many detailed morphological observations on this series of crania. In the male crania a sagittal elevation is rare; the supra-mastoid crest is moderately or well developed; the flat occiput sometimes has a moderate torus and sometimes a well developed external occipital protuberance. In the females and children the development of these features is attenuated. The serration of sutures attains medium development in but 3 of the males; in all other crania the pattern is simple. Wormian bones in the lambdoidal, temporo-parietal, or temporo-occipital sutures are present in all but 5 of the 34 crania (85.29 per cent). This is a very high proportion and may be attributed, no doubt, to growth disturbances caused in part by cranial deformation, in part perhaps by malnutrition. Two crania have Inca bones—one bipartite and the other tripartite. Both of these occur in crania of adult males. Two adult male skulls also show the pterion retourné (articulation of the temporal bone with the frontal in the pterion region). The other crania show narrow to very broad H-formed pteria. Parietal foramina are much more consistently present than in any American series I have previously observed. They are recorded as absent in but 6 of 35 crania (17.14 per cent). Retro-mastoid crania are usually multiple. Mastoids are of medium size in the males, usually small in the females and, of course, small or undeveloped in children. This series shows an unusual frequency of forked or bifurcated mastoid processes (7 crania, 20.00 per cent). The morphological features of the facial skeleton are in no wise remarkable. High nasal bridges are perhaps a little more common than in most American

Indian crania. In the adults suborbital fossae are usually poorly developed—a condition characteristic of Mongoloids—and the malars and zygomata are usually robust, especially in the males. Slight to very pronounced alveolar prognathism is observable in all of the adult crania.

The teeth of the adult skulls show considerable wear, frequent caries, and alveolar abscesses, with multiple ante-mortem dental losses. Two of the children's crania had one or more decayed milk teeth. Since the incisors had usually been lost after death, their form could not be observed. Of 4 crania in which the incisors were present, 3 had the shovel-shape. Three of the male adults had some slight development of a palatine torus. Of 13 adult crania in which the shape of the palate was observable, 5 had U-shaped palates, 3 parabolic, and 5 hyperbolic.

The base of the skull in this series presents the usual variations—nothing particularly worthy of note. Dehiscences in the floor of the auditory meatuses were observed in 3 of 10 adult male skulls, 2 of 8 adult female skulls, 4 of 7 children 10 to 12 years old, and 9 of 10 crania belonging to children 6 years or younger.

The most interesting feature of the series is the cranial pathology. In the youngest group of skulls 7 of 11 showed slight to very extensive osteoporosis. All of the 7 skulls of children 10 to 12 years exhibited the lesions of this disease. Healed, thickened, and cicatrized traces of this ailment may be observed in 3 of 7 adult female skulls, while one subadult shows the characteristic *cribra orbitalia* of the presumably incipient stages of the disease. In 6 of 10 male skulls pathological thickening of the skull vault was observed, usually in the bregmatic region. I have discussed and illustrated the osteoporosis of the Cenote crania in my monograph on the Indians of Pecos.[2] I know nothing more about the disease than I did in 1930. It seems to be a deficiency disease, active in children. The effects on the cranium are similar to those obtained by putting monkeys on a scorbutic diet. The disease may have been caused by dependence upon a diet consisting mainly of maize. An alternative suggestion is that it is due to hemolytic anemia. Dr. George D. Williams tried to find it in modern Yucatecan children of Maya stock, but was unable to identify it. Perhaps osteoporosis caused the downfall of the Maya civilization. I make a present of this idea to Maya archaeologists, who are perennially questing for an explanation.

[2] Hooton, The Indians of Pecos, 1930, pp. 316–319.

Three of the eight ladies who fell or were pushed into the Cenote had received, at some previous time, good bangs on various parts of the head, as evinced by old, healed and depressed circular lesions; and one female had suffered a fracture of the nose. One woman also had platybasia, a condition in which the skull base is pushed up into the cranial cavity. Two of the men had received head wounds which left depressed lesions. Altogether, it is suggested that the adult denizens of the Sacred Cenote may not have been generally beloved in their pre-sacrificial careers.

On the whole, these Mayas (if they were Mayas) seem to have been quite ordinary little brachycephalic Indians, unusually diseased and, in the case of the adults, somewhat inordinately battered. Their skulls were notably deformed, and one supposes that their abundant pathologies may have been a concomitant of their high cultural status.

The lengths of 4, probably male, femora suggest, on the basis of Manouvrier's tables, a range of stature from about 158 cm. to 167 cm., while 3 female bones indicate statures between 145 and 148 cm. Of course, these are little better than guesses, but, in any event, the adults in the Cenote were not tall. The usual morphological variations observed in Indian crania are recorded here. Thus various degrees of platymeria, platycnemia, femoral torsion, development of pilaster, variations of the gluteal ridge, and squatting facets occur. There are one well-preserved and quite typically male pelvis, and 5 odd innominate bones, 3 male and 2 female.

In general morphological and metric features it would not be difficult to duplicate this Cenote series in Pueblo crania from the Southwest or in Peruvian collections. Two of the more outstanding characteristics of the Cenote skulls—extreme and elaborate varieties of artificial cranial deformation and widespread osteoporosis—could also be matched in Peruvian series.

It is of considerable interest to ponder the fact that intentional artificial deformation of the skull in a people with hooked, beaky noses is associated with the development of high civilizations in two widely separated areas—the Near East and the Western cordillera of the Americas. It intrigues me to note that cranial deformation is conspicuous by its absence in Northeastern Asia, and, in fact, among the peoples of Asia who can be described from a racial point of view as Mongoloid, and that prominent, convex noses, although observable in Asia among mixed Mongoloid peoples, are absolutely incompati-

TABLE

DIGESTS OF MEASURE

CHICHEN ITZÁ,

	Adult Male			Adult Female	
	NO.	RANGE	MEAN	NO.	RANGE
Glabello-occipital length	10	152 −175	(164.50)	8	152 −165
Maximum width	9	139 −163	(155.22)	8	145 −162
Basion-bregma height	7	118 −132	(126.00)	7	110 −127
Minimum frontal diameter	11	85 −102	(95.36)	8	85 − 95
Menton-nasion height	5	120 −126	(122.80)	3	107 −114
Prosthion-nasion height	10	67 − 77	71.90	6	56 − 69
Maximum diameter bi-zygomatic	9	133 −148	140.33	6	132 −140
Bigonial diameter	4	99 −109	103.75	3	96 −100
Mean angle lower jaw	4	119 −130	123.75	3	117 −123
Height of symphysis	4	36 − 41	(38.00)	3	29 − 33
Bi-condylar width	4	85 −130	113.50	3	116 −118
Minimum breadth ascend-ing ramus	5	29 − 34	32.40	3	31 − 34
Height of ascending ramus	4	57 − 62	59.00	3	51 − 62
Condylo-symphsial length	4	100 −106	104.00	3	89 −109
Orbits-height					
Right	11	32.50− 40	35.09	6	32 − 37
Left	12	32 − 37.50	34.62	6	32 − 37
Orbits-breadth					
Right	11	38 − 46	(41.14)	6	38 − 41
Left	12	38 − 44	40.12	6	38 − 40.50
Nasal height	11	47 − 59	(52.18)	6	43 − 53
Nasal breadth	11	23 − 30	25.77	6	24 − 28.50
Basion-prosthion	6	94 −102	(98.83)	6	91 −108
Baison-naison	6	89 −101	(95.00)	6	89 − 98
Palate-external length	9	54 − 64	58.78	5	54 − 88
Palate-external width	9	64 − 76	(68.56)	5	65 − 71
Maximum circumference (above browridges)	7	488 −526	(502.57)	8	480 −496
Arc-nasion opisthion	7	231 −367	(321.43)	7	302 −340
Arc-vertical transverse	8	227 −331	(303.75)	8	290 −313
Thickness of left parietal above temporo-parietal suture	9	4.60− 8.50	5.73	8	4.60− 7.60
Cranial index	9	83.73−105.26	(94.87)	8	87.88−104.52
Height-length index	7	73.14− 81.58	(77.30)	7	71.79− 81.43
Height-breadth index	7	75.46− 93.53	(82.46)	7	70.99− 85.23
Facial index	5	82.31− 91.30	(86.59)	2	81.43− 83.09
Facial index upper	8	50 − 54.41	51.38	6	42.11− 51.88
Gnathic index	6	100 −109.68	(104.13)	6	96.94−117.39
Mean orbital index	12	80.49− 91.19	86.01	7	81.01− 92.50
Nasal index	11	42.37− 56.60	(49.85)	6	47.17− 58.14
Palatal index	9	104.92−133.33	(116.39)	5	115.52−129.63
Capacity, Hrdlička's method	10	1140−1400	(1310.50)	8	1070−1272

VII

MENTS AND INDICES

YUCATAN

MEAN	Child 10–12			Child 5–6		
	NO.	RANGE	MEAN	NO.	RANGE	MEAN
(158.25)	7	143 –152	(146.57)	7	131 –159	(144.86)
(152.12)	7	146 –163	(154.14)	7	133 –156	(146.71)
(117.71)	7	108 –128	(116.71)	3	96 –124	(112.00)
(90.50)	7	90 – 96	(93.43)	7	79 – 93	87.57
111.33	1	102	102.00	1	80	80.00
65.17	7	57 – 61	59.29	10	49 – 60	54.30
134.67	7	112 –126	(120.71)	12	103 –121	112.67
98.33	0	0	0	0	0	0
120.67	0	0		0	0	0
31.33	0	0	0	0	0	0
116.67	0	0	0	0	0	0
32.00	0	0	0	0	0	0
57.33	0	0	0	0	0	0
99.33	0	0	0	0	0	0
34.33	7	31 – 34	32.57	12	29 – 33.50	31.12
34.17	7	32 – 33	32.57	12	29.50– 35	31.50
39.33	7	36 – 39	37.21	12	33 – 37.50	35.08
39.08	7	35 – 38.50	36.50	12	33 – 37	34.88
48.17	7	42 – 50	45.00	12	34 – 43	38.12
(25.58)	7	22 – 24	(22.79)	12	19 – 29	21.29
96.17	7	81 – 91	87.57	6	78 – 89	84.50
92.83	7	84 – 90	87.00	6	74 – 91	83.50
55.80	7	43 – 51	47.57	7	40 – 45	42.43
67.80	7	60 – 67	63.00	7	56 – 61	59.00
(488.50)	7	460 –480	(471.14)	14	438 –476	(461.50)
(321.86)	7	300 –330	(309.86)	14	262 –337	(311.29)
(304.12)	7	296 –332	(308.43)	14	270 –307	(294.29)
5.46	7	3 – 4.60	3.79	14	2.60– 4.60	3.31
(96.23)	7	98.03–111.64	(105.24)	14	83.65–112.98	(99.91)
(74.83)	7	73.03– 88.28	(79.67)	8	68.57– 84.93	(75.72)
(76.99)	7	68.79– 83.56	(75.82)	8	66.21– 80.00	(75.35)
82.26	1	91.07	91.07	1	77.67	77.67
48.40	7	46.72– 54.46	(49.19)	10	46.43– 50.00	48.23
103.69	7	95.51–107.06	100.67	6	96.30–112.16	101.45
87.52	7	84.42– 93.06	88.46	12	82.64– 98.56	89.64
53.28	7	45 – 54.76	50.77	12	45.35– 74.36	55.99
121.60	7	117.65–139.53	132.71	7	134.09–143.90	138.89
(1169.62)	7	1115–1230	1180	14	960–1310	(1153.93)

ble with a full development of Mongoloid physical characters. I should say that neither these flattened heads nor those proboscis-like noses are, nor have been, at home in Mongoloid Asia. Perhaps the former have been squashed and the latter pulled out as an independent manifestation of Americanism, long after the undeformed and un-nasalized ancestors of the American Indian reached the New World by swimming the Bering Straits or hopping from stone to stone through the Aleutian Isles. If so, the evidence of the physical type of the Mayas suggests a long process of specialization and inbreeding and agrees with the highly evolved character of their culture. The Maya culture may have evolved *in situ*, and I am perfectly willing to let it go at that, and even to leave it there, but I think that the long, curved noses and the short, flat heads probably did not. I am inclined to think that the ancestors of the classical Mayas were not very different from the White hybridized type which we call Armenoid—hook noses from Henry Field's Iranian Plateau race, round heads from the good old Alpines—and inspired with similar aesthetic ambitions to improve their head form. Eventually they picked up some Mongoloid features—hair, pigmentation, cheek bones, et cetera. These may have been fairly recent accretions, because Mongolization is a late racial phenomenon in the Old World and probably still later in the New. It's a long, long way to Chichen Itzá, but the Roman-nosed god and the Long-nosed god both made it. Before them, perhaps, went the ancestors of the curious, Toda-like Lacandones, and after them may have come the lank-haired, slant-eyed Mongoloids. All of them may have journeyed together, but I doubt it. The elements were probably blended gradually. I do not think that the cities of the Maya Empires were much like New York.

XX

MAYA ETHNOLOGY: THE SEQUENCE OF CULTURES

Oliver La Farge *

PARTLY because of long, sad neglect, Mayan ethnology is still a young study, just beginning to flourish vigorously.[1] Now that it is getting a portion of the attention it deserves, it is timely to set forth certain considerations which should govern investigators in their approach to it.

Study of the Mayan tribes serves to illuminate several distinct problems, resulting in a pull of divergent interests likely to produce too great a concentration on a single aspect of the matter, to the detriment of understanding of that aspect as well as of the subject as a whole. To many students of the Maya, the greatest interest lies in what might be called the archaeo-ethnology, the detection among modern tribes of living survivals from before the Conquest, with their important bearing upon the archaeology of the region. To others, the various stages of acculturation and culture-conflict are most attractive, while there is always a certain amount of work done, here as elsewhere, as if the people studied were living *in vacuo*.

There is a tendency, with whatever approach, to over-simplify

* Harvard, A.B., 1924; A.M., 1929; Hemingway Fellow, 1924–1925.
[1] The new awakening of Mayan ethnology is strikingly shown by the literature. In more than half a century prior to 1930 one finds short papers, local, historical, and popular studies many of which do contain valuable source information, surveys such as Starr's Notes, 1901–1903, desk studies such as Brinton's Nagualism, 1894, but outright, major ethnological works based on field investigation are just about confined to Stoll's Ethnographie, 1884, Tozzer's Mayas and Lacandones, 1907, Gann's Maya Indians, 1919, and Sapper's work considered as a body. A list of Sapper's articles would make an outrageously long footnote, the more important are included in the bibliography. Since 1930 we have Thompson's Mayas of Southern and Central British Honduras, 1930, Termer's Ethnologie und Ethnographie, 1930, La Farge and Byers' Yearbearer's People, 1931, McBryde's Solola, 1933, Redfield and Villa's Chan Kom, 1934, and Bunzel's A Guatemalan Village, now ready for the printer. This burst of production was preceded and accompanied by a host of shorter papers by the same authors, Lothrop, Tax, Goubaud, and many others.

the problem, as if all we had to do were to segregate Spanish and pre-Columbian elements, while noting what parts of each culture had been overthrown by the other. This tendency overlooks the fact that the peculiar history of this area has produced a situation of great complexity, which the ethnologist must approach cautiously while maintaining, if possible, his intellectual balance between the various angles of interest in the subject.

The conflict which we see going on today is not a simple one of Indian versus Spanish, or Indian versus Spanish plus Machine [2] culture, but is in fact a clash between the Machine culture on the one hand, allied to a Spanish-American culture having its own individuality and itself in conflict with the Machine, and what I am calling the Recent Indian, a well-stabilized, complex culture containing certain elements which, although deriving from its predecessors, are not to be found among them. This conflict is the most recent of a series of stabilizations and clashes, a sequence without which present problems cannot be understood.

The placing of this sequence in time must be largely a matter of guesswork, since our record of conditions among the Mayan tribes in the past centuries is so extremely sketchy, their recorded history so nearly nil. Certain dates may be projected from fixed points in the history of the Republic and Viceroyalty of Guatemala, and it happens that a series of decrees and laws affecting Indian land tenure are particularly significant.[3] Somewhat arbitrarily, I am using these as pegs. From the Conquest until recently there has been a steady drive, with some reversals, to destroy the Indian ownership of large blocks of land which forms the physical and economic base of tribal solidarity and of freedom from the necessity to work for non-Indians. These steps and retrogressions, taken together with major historical developments, show the rising and falling pressure of non-Indian culture upon the tribes.

In developing this thesis I shall rely upon the evidence in the Cuchumatán district since this is best known to me personally. It can readily be seen, I believe, that in a general way the sequence for

[2] The term Machine culture best denotes the complex international culture now emanating from Europe, North America, and Japan as centers of aggression. Machines and machine-made goods, the elimination of local variations in dress, possessions, languages, and ideas, a new *Weltanschauung*, and an international, interdependent economy are its chief characteristics.

[3] I am indebted to Dr. Charles Wagley for pointing out the significance of these decrees and laws, and providing me with the references for them.

that district holds good for the Highland Maya in general, to a lesser degree for the inhabitants of the lowlands.

As indicated above, when one settles in a highland Indian village, one is confronted by a conflict between a combined Spanish-American and Machine culture, itself in some conflict, and a local culture conceived by the Indians themselves as being ancient beyond the memory of man, a smooth blend of diverse elements, beautifully integrated, and possessing factors not found in its predecessors.

The entrance of the Machine culture, with its outstanding feature of international economics, begins with the development of the export coffee industry by which Guatemala first entered world commerce on a large scale. Coffee exports in 1860 were inconsiderable; by 1873 they reached 150,507 quintals; ten years later 312,271 quintals were exported, 598,404 in 1893, 875,000 in 1916,[4] and since about 1890 coffee has comprised over eighty per cent of Guatemala's commerce, and sometimes over ninety.[5]

It is not likely to be mere coincidence that in 1877, under President Rufino Barrios, communal ownership of land was abolished, all lands henceforth to be held individually.[6] About this same time, the system of *mandamientos* was put into effect, under which the government contracted to supply labor to fincas, which it did by force. Thus to make the great reservoir of highland labor available, two methods were being used: plain force, and the destruction of the economic base which made possible the Indians' refusal to come down voluntarily. In 1894 the *mandamientos* were replaced by *habilitación,* or debt-bondage, abolished in 1934.[7]

During the last part of the 19th century, there was a steady, concerted movement, with government backing, to establish Ladino colonies in the fertile, lower parts of the Cuchumatán district, hitherto undisturbed Indian territory. The new townships of Quetzal, Barrillas, and Nenton were thus created, while the older village of Santa Ana Huista was "captured." A few Ladinos appeared in every village and every township. That such intrusion was unprecedented

[4] Sapper, Mittel-Amerika, 1927, pp. 61–63.
[5] *Ibid.,* and Tannenbaum, Whither Latin America?, 1934, p. 157.
[6] Decreto No. 170, Recopilaciones de Leyes Agrarianas, 1890, pp. 90–93.
[7] Sapper, Nördliche Mittel-Amerika, 1897, pp. 220–221. Perhaps because of his affiliation with the German planters, in the work cited and in his excellent Die Zukunft, 1905, Sapper is very mild in his treatment of the effects of *habilitación* upon the Indians. A stronger view is expressed in La Farge, Santa Eulalia (Ms), Chap. III.

within the memory of the Indians and bitterly resented, and that these people were rather independent at the time, is shown by the very clear tradition among them now of resistance to the labor conscription, of alcaldes and other local officials shot or imprisoned, and by the bloody uprising of San Juan Ixcoy, which was avowedly aimed against Ladino intrusion.[8]

Due to various circumstances, different tribes [9] have been affected by the new cultural invasion to different degrees. Thus at Santa Ana Huista, a relatively lowland township heavily settled by Ladinos, the Indians appear to have lost most of their special institutions, a large proportion of them have abandoned their costume, and in general they are merging into the Ladino level.[10] At Santa Eulalia, high in the mountains, one's first impression is that the Recent Indian culture remains almost undisturbed. Investigation showed the following major changes as a result of some sixty years of conflict: Loss of pottery making and women's weaving; simplification of marriage-barter and service; a modified but still distinctive costume; fines instead of more violent and clearly more ancient punishments for adultery and other offenses; an incomplete ceremonial organization; an economy based on agriculture but dependent upon wage-income for comfort.[11]

In attempting to form a dynamic picture of the present process, or to sift out the rich mass of material which illuminates the ancient ways, the observer must form an understanding of the Recent Indian culture before modification set in. Like the archaeologist, he must go below the surface to the preceding strata, moving with all the care demanded by the doubtful processes of speculation and reconstruction.

Guatemala dates her freedom from 1821; there was agitation and trouble in the Viceroyalty at least a decade earlier, and throughout Latin America it was clear that Spanish control was weak. The borders of the north were feebly guarded, and it is fair to say that the "internal frontiers" were in the same state. Up to the last, Spain took out gold and tribute where she could, but general conditions did not make it worthwhile to exploit all the difficult, agricultural

[8] Recinos, Huehuetenango, 1913, p. 207; Sapper, Indianeraufstand, 1898.

[9] Reasons for the use of the term tribe for units partially corresponding to the rural townships are set forth in La Farge, op. cit., Chaps. I and III. See also Tax, Municipios of the Midwestern Highlands, 1937.

[10] La Farge and Byers, Yearbearer's People, pp. 183–184. Cf. Sapper, Die Zukunft.

[11] La Farge, Santa Eulalia, passim.

country. There was little or nothing to be done with a large production of corn, wheat, cacao, or cattle if one had it.

I believe that it is possible to set aside the years 1800 to 1880 as the undisturbed period during which Recent Indian culture solidified itself in relative peace. After independence, government was tied up in war with Mexico, the revolt of Los Altos, the wars and confusions leading to the break-up of the United States of Central America so vividly portrayed by Stephens.[12] That writer is infuriating to an ethnologist, since caste and race prejudice barred him from making any but would-be humorous and contemptuous comments on the Indians, yet he does describe great areas of territory within which the authority of the central government was only vaguely felt; extremely primitive, Indian sections where today the Ladinos are firmly in the saddle. The feebleness of central and local governments towards the end of this period, and near freedom of the Indians on their own soil, is also brought out by the history of the Chamula Rebellion of 1868 in Chiapas.[13]

Of course there was a wide variation in the isolation of different groups, all must have been subject to the demands of occasional armies or bands of warring factions, and perhaps too great an umbrageousness called down a disciplinary expedition. Priests remained throughout the area, but judging by Stephens, they were not many, nor did they attempt with any energy to hold the Indians to orthodox Catholicism. Núñez de la Vega and Gage [14] depict an unremitting struggle against superstition and outright paganism two centuries earlier, but that struggle plainly died away with the loss of support from a powerful government.

The general picture is just what we should expect from present evidence and the known history of the following period: A long stretch of time during which a new culture was able to solidify. The type of complex evolved, and the wide variations within the culture in different sections, is nicely illustrated by the Mayan ceremonial calendar, with its interwoven non-Indian elements which now have become inseparable from it. As it exists today, this part survival, part adaptation has already undergone further changes due to the present transition, but in the main I believe that the calendar as known to the

---

[12] Stephens, Central America, Chiapas, and Yucatan, 1841.
[13] V. Pineda, Sublevaciones Indigenas, 1888.
[14] Núñez de la Vega, Constituciones Diocesanas, 1702; Gage, The English-American, 1928.

older, learned men, is much as it was at the end of the undisturbed Recent Indian period.

It is uncertain whether any part of the calendar survives among the modern Tzeltal; [15] at the height of the undisturbed period they seem to have had uinals and day-names without numbers.[16] Among the Kanhobal Indians of the Cuchumatanes both haab and tonalamatl survive, measures in part of practical time, more of ceremonial time, and for divination. The Yearbearer is of great importance. A generation or so ago the uinal names were probably in common use. The Momostecos and some other Quiché groups have the tonalamatl without the haab,[17] while at Santa Catarina Ixtlahuacán in the 1850's the haab and Yearbearers survived without numbers.[18] Sapper [19] records twenty Quiché day-names without numbers, connected with witchcraft and a nagualism which has the appearance of a union of a pre-Columbian "companion spirit" [20] with a European werewolf complex. This association is weak or non-existent in the Cuchumatanes.

Further variations could be cited, and paralleled in one element after another. Even such emphatically Mayan phenomena as these survivals of the calendar are united by the common possession of tinctures of Catholicism and Spanish culture which cannot be separated from them in studying them as living instruments today. Some of these can be clearly identified and weighed, such as the prayer to God before a divination. The proper day on which to pray to the patron saint offers a more dubious problem, with overtones and undertones requiring cautious consideration; and when, in the Cuchumatanes, we encounter an affiliation between Ahau, Elab (Oc), and the cross, we find ourselves in a confusion of survivals, adaptations, substitutions, and new growths which I, for one, dare not try to resolve.

Any attempt to understand this curious problem causes the ethnologist to dig deeper, into the preceding periods from which variations, similarities, and complexities arise. In 1720 the *encomienda* and *re-*

[15] Blom and La Farge, Tribes and Temples, 1927, Chaps. XV and XVI.
[16] E. Pineda, Descripción Geográfica, 1845.
[17] Lothrop, A Modern Survival, 1930, and Further Notes, 1929, pp. 14–20; Goubaud, The Guaxajip Bats, 1937; Spina, Quiché Calendar, 1870.
[18] Hernández Spina, Kalendaryo Concervado Hasta el Dia (Ms); Scherzer, Die Indianer von Santa Caterina Istlavacan, 1856.
[19] Sapper, Über Brujerie in Guatemala, 1925.
[20] Fuentes y Guzmán, Recordación Florida, 1882–1883, Vol. II, p. 45; Núñez de la Vega, *op. cit.*

partimiento system was abolished by the Spanish crown,[21] a setback to the long war against Indian land tenure. With it went pure forced labor, instead of which a system of debt peonage was set up. It is interesting and significant that at the end of the undisturbed Recent Indian period, the government had to go back to pure force with the *mandamientos* to obtain labor, before working around once again to the comparatively humane debt system. Obviously, the earlier peonage had ceased to work in a great part of the Indian country.

The system established in 1720 gave the Indian a bare chance to avoid working for the ruling caste, and an opportunity to live off his own, unencumbered land. Furthermore, in a general way this measure coincided with the beginning of weakness in Spanish internal administration in Middle America. The high tide of Conquest had ebbed, new exploitation required constantly greater efforts for smaller returns. In 1695 the last *entrada* against the Lacandones[22] was made, in 1696 de Vargas completed the reconquest of New Mexico. Despite constant news of French encroachments on that far, northern frontier, and the development of promising Indian alliances, the policy of expansion was abandoned and the efforts of the crown to defend the borders grew steadily feebler.[23]

At this time the different tribes had been under Spanish control for between a hundred and two hundred years. The control had been vigorous and alert, now it gradually relaxed. Troops to support the priests and outlying settlers became fewer, harder to secure, less well armed. The new decree not only made it more difficult to obtain Indian labor, but by increasing the cost discouraged exploitation of the land.

I suggest then, that during the eighty years following 1720 a slow transition occurred. Although characterized by the emergence into the open of long suppressed, Mayan practices and institutions, *it was not primarily a return to the older culture,* but a re-adaptation of the combined cultures into a form far more satisfactory to the people than had been possible before, leading, by the turn of the century, to the Recent Indian in full flower.

At the beginning of this period there were plenty of Mayan survivals in the true sense, ready to emerge to greater strength. A

---

[21] McBride, Land Systems of Mexico, 1923, Chap. III, and the section on Encomienda; Simpson, Administration of the Indians, 1934.

[22] Stone, Some Spanish Entradas, 1932.

[23] Thomas, After Coronado, 1935.

strong evidence of this is the important Quiché manuscript, *Cholbal K'ih*,[24] which includes two tonalamatls of tonalamatls, arranged with explanatory text in a manner distinctly remniscent of the codices. The greater part of this manuscript seems to have been written in 1722. A marginal note correlating 5 K'anil with March 13, 1770, may mean that the latter part of it was written later, or that it was still in use at that time.

Such a manuscript illustrates another factor typical of the confusing nature of the sequence problem. Under lively Spanish rule, mild literacy was kept up among the Indians, through the education of selected children for church purposes. This literacy they, in turn, used for perpetuating in secret some of the more complex portions of their ancient knowledge. With the slackening of Spanish control, such education dwindled to almost nothing. So far, we know of no example more recent than this of a written document for ceremonial use, other than the texts of certain dances. It is possible that the withdrawal of Spanish control and resultant decline of literacy, operated to some degree to cause the decay of pre-Columbian lore and practices long dependent on one or another form of writing.

By the time this first transition period began, the days of independence were only a remote tradition. Many practices had been entirely forgotten, such diverse elements as wool, wheat, and the worship of the Christian God had been completely absorbed. Most of what can be said about the period is guesswork, although in a much longer paper one could offer pretty good proof of some processes. Innumerable small and large factors, such as the rate of Spanish recession, the personalities of individual priests and individual Indians, influenced the local variants of the evolving Recent Indian culture, and however uncertain the details, a conception of the transition is necessary to understand what one observes today.

As remorselessly as in archaeology, digging backward takes one further back. Obviously, the first transition springs from its predecessor, which I am calling Colonial Indian. The conquest and thorough reduction of Guatemala ranges over a century following the fall of Utatlán in 1524. Some groups, such as the Choles, were incompletely subdued till 1695, the Lacandones never were really brought under, but in the main that first century covers the process of conquest, which was in itself a form of transition. At first the Indian nations

[24] Anonymous, Cholbal K'IH and Ahilabal K'IH (Ms).

had some recognition as such, their lords and kings some standing. It was possible for priestly nobles to write the *Popol Vuh* [25] and *Annals of the Cakchiquels*,[26] with vivid memories of the era just closed, and still conscious of their traditions and rights. All that ended soon enough, the *encomiendas* were established and by the time Gage travelled through the country in the 1630's, conquest was solidly established wherever he went. All his descriptions portray utter subjugation of the Indians, ranging from the virtual enslavement of those near the towns, to the humble, unpaid services rendered him as he passed through the Cuchumatanes. The difference between his description of this latter section, and that of Stephens, is worth noting. Both found the country wild, and inhabited only by distinctly primitive Indians, but in Gage's time they were very meek; two hundred years later they had defiance and evasion in their systems, and even today one would not find the humble deference that Gage received at Todos Santos, his "Cuchumatlán Grande."

The church was vigilant. Survivals of the older religion were harshly oppressed. The distinction between the two creeds was emphasized by the persecution of one. Mayan religious practices seem to have been associated with hostility to the conquerors and with the hope of rebellion, whereas in the 19th century, the religious revivals associated with Indian uprising are all within the frame of the new, compound Recent Indian religion [27] to which its followers generally refer as "Christianity."

This was the time of levelling and destruction. Few cultures are ever inert, degrees of change exist at all times. Here, change must have been most marked at the beginning, when men still remembered freedom and lost power. When no one could personally remember not worshipping God, the period may be regarded as beginning to set. Mayan practices, driven underground, were mutilated and must have been greatly changed in character. Many institutions and patterns were entirely lost, and new ones received. The resultant culture was artificial, since it irked the Indians who maintained it, and was conditioned by the necessity of submitting to the exactions of

[25] The Popol Vuh merits a whole bibliography of its own. Most readily available editions are: Brasseur de Bourbourg, Popol Vuh, 1861; Reynaud, Les Dieux, les Héros, et les Hommes, 1925; Villacorta and Rodas, Manuscrito de Chichicastenango, 1927.

[26] Brinton, The Annals of the Cakchiquels, 1885.

[27] V. Pineda, Sublevaciones, *passim;* Sapper, Nördliche Mittel-Amerika, p. 283.

their conquerors. It was the sifting out of raw material, and development of emotional attitudes, from which a later, far more comfortable culture was to be evolved.

We have fair material on the Colonial Indian period, and a good deal more on the civilization of the various nations when the Spaniards encountered them.[28] The diversity of this latter is striking. Thompson points out the appearance of a purely Mayan culture among the early Choles,[29] listing a series of characteristics strikingly similar to those of the Cuchumatán peoples today. I question his suggestion that all the elements lacking among the Choles, such as worship of idols, and formal, noble priests, are of Nahua derivation. From consideration of present day ethnology as well as the earlier material, I think that there may have been an ancient, wide-spread Mayan culture, which survived among provincial tribes and has colored the recent culture of certain groups, while in the great centres something much more elaborate and less democratic was evolved. This latter presumably interchanged influences with other centres even in early times, the picture being later confused by the known, Nahua invasions. It is impossible to go into the whole matter here, and in any case it belongs to the archaeologist. I only want to point out that the problem would be quite bad enough were we merely faced with the conflict, adjustment, alteration and readjustment of compound cultures within historic times, whereas we are faced as well with cultural diversity and sequences prior to the Conquest.

I suggest, then, a post-Conquest sequence which, for the Mayan highlands, may be approximated as follows:

1. *Conquest.* Occurring at different times from 1524 on, but mainly before 1600. This is a violent period, shattering the Indian cultural structure.

2. *Colonial Indian.* From the end of the Conquest period to about 1720, when the abolition of *encomiendas* and pure, forced labor, gave the Indians a better chance to take up a tolerable mode of life. During this period Spanish and Christian elements were absorbed wholesale and somewhat altered; many Mayan elements were destroyed or mutilated, others greatly changed.

3. *First Transition.* Roughly from 1720 to 1800; both dates are mere pegs, the latter a guess, for which a round number is preferable.

---

[28] Any attempt at giving even the outstanding sources would involve a vast bibliographic undertaking.

[29] Thompson, Sixteenth and Seventeenth Century Reports, 1938.

Slow relaxation of Spanish control, emergence of suppressed Mayan elements, integration of both Mayan and Spanish-Christian elements into a new pattern within which the Indian is comfortable, with the resulting development of entirely or partly new forms.

4. *Recent Indian—I.* 1800 to 1880. The ending date suggested is three years after the land laws: 1877 sounds too precise, 1880 roughly places the strong, new tide of intervention in Indian life. During this period the integration becomes a smooth blend; well stabilized, it has the individuality and roundness that mark any culture, and its continued evolution is in the form of growth out of itself, rather than in response to alien pressures.

5. *Recent Indian—II.* 1880.— The Machine age and the Spanish-American cultures invade the stabilized Recent Indian, conflict and acculturation begin, continuing in different sections at very different rates. The process is much gentler than the Conquest, and Recent Indian still largely survives.

I have indulged in an extremely doubtful historical reconstruction for the purpose of bringing out certain considerations of importance, whether one is interested in the study of acculturation, or in detecting Mayan survivals and Spanish elements. The sequences proposed, and the dating, are purely tentative; I am fully aware that they lack adequate proof; perhaps this whole thesis amounts to a simple warning, that analysis of the present Mayan Indian culture is not as simple as it seems.

PART III

THE NORTHERN NEIGHBORS OF THE MAYA

XXI

PATTERNS IN MIDDLE AMERICAN ARCHAEOLOGY

George C. Vaillant *

MEXICO does not show the varied patterns in cultural adjustment that so characterize the North American scene. Only in the north, a relatively unfavorable and underpopulated district, do we find traces of hunting, fishing, and nomadic farming groups. Some of these remains may represent early cultural adjustments, but others are more probably persistences of former patterns whose creators were pushed out from the more favorable zones in southern and central Mexico and in the southwestern United States. Many of the modern Indian groups with their remarkable linguistic diversity and low cultural development could very conceivably be similar survivals of primitive communities, who had never reached the high development of their more civilized neighbors and who had lived an isolated existence in inaccessible and unfavorable regions.

All over south and central Mexico there are many evidences of sedentary populations, dependent on agriculture and possessing a competent and adequate equipment of pottery, clay utensils, stone tools, and, therefore by inference, since archaeology depends on imperishable remains, an equivalent corpus of textiles, basketry, gourds, and other perishable goods. The difference in basic equipment does not differ markedly, but in style and form there is a great variability. In North America, wherever a regional culture succession has been laid down, one is conscious of a considerable development in technical equipment. The Mexican archaeological sequences, so far discovered, save in the north, show a fairly uniform culture level for meeting ordinary living demands. Since some of these evolutions, like that of the early cultures of the Valley of Mexico, apparently reach back a couple of millennia, it would seem that the sedentary agricultural village life was developed very early and the main tech-

* Harvard, A.B., 1922; A.M., 1925; Ph.D., 1927; tutor, anthropology, 1926–1927; Winthrop scholar, 1926–1927; now Associate Curator, Mexican Archaeology, American Museum of Natural History.

niques uniformly distributed, long before the North American groups were in a position to avail themselves of this manner of life. The potential contemporaneity of the earliest Hohokam levels with the earlier stages of Copilco-Zacatenco seems balanced by the latter's more skillful technical treatments of utensils.[1]

The higher aspects of Mexican culture do not tend so much to step up the quality of this basic living equipment, as to divert surplus energy and technical skill into material religious expression, such as in the simplest form, building a temple on a large adobe or rubble platform or, in its most complex manifestation, constructing an elaborate ceremonial precinct with stone buildings, equipped with stone idols. Often accompanying this elaboration of religious practice we see evidence of a calendric system, which in testifying obviously to intellectual achievement, looms very large in our evaluations of relative cultural development. On the other hand, from what we can glean from Spanish and native sources, governmental techniques were very low, each town or village being independent. The outward aspects of high Middle American civilization with its conversion of technical skill to ritualistic ends contrasts strongly with the Peruvian cultural pattern, wherein high technical abilities seem to be more widely spread among the population, government appears to embrace much larger groups of people, and the outward panoply of religious ritual is less markedly taking toll of the economic resources of the tribesmen.[2]

This distinction acquires further weight, when we contrast the cleavage between the two areas of high culture in North America, the Southwest and the Southeast with its northern periphery, both of which offer primitive examples of these fundamental differences in direction. In the fully developed Anasazi, technical achievement seems to be directed toward the life of the community and the kiva is not elaborated into a mighty temple. On the other hand, in the eastern woodland region, we find great platforms and burial mounds, surpassing the ritualistic architecture of the Southwest but accompanied by a surviving material culture that seems superficially inferior. The woodland agricultural pattern necessitated a mobile village or villages or else permanent domiciliary units sufficiently scat-

[1] Gladwin, Snaketown I and II, 1937; Vaillant, Early Cultures, 1935.
[2] Cf. Means, Civilizations of the Andes, 1931, with Joyce, Mexican Archaeology, 1914.

tered to permit the rotation of fields. Consequently, a rendezvous for establishing tribal solidarity would be more of a social necessity than in a permanent sedentary village, with its successive generations of communal living. It seems conceivable that the impression of unity which the ceremonial center gives to Middle American high culture and the effect of disunity presented by the stylistic variation in the area may be reconciled, if one concede the possibility that the sedentary pattern was established in many mountain valleys and later the idea of the temple cult was diffused to them.[3]

Such a discussion as the above reduces to overly simple terms a very rich history of cultural development which not only ramifies in many directions but also embraces the fates of many peoples. Mexican archaeology involves a whole series of local situations and the process of archaeological research moves from site conditions to those affecting the general area. However, a baffling condition is caused by the physiography of the country which confined settlement to the mountain valleys, set off by ranges of mountains, or else along the river valleys of the coast equally isolated by arid stretches or forests. Such regional isolation resulted in social units composed largely of independent towns only occasionally united by the loosest of bonds, and historical and cultural analysis becomes a bewildering process under such conditions. There is bound to develop an extreme discordance in the rhythms of local culture evolution, outside stimulation, and migrations either of people or of culture traits. Pottery has long been used to symbolize situations of this nature, since its method of manufacture and decoration reveal the subtle processes of change and influence as no other imperishable element available to the archaeologist. A very preliminary list of the local ceramic families of Middle America, each of which often includes several wares and may also be expressed in terms of recognizable local variations and time factors, gives a fantastic picture, even from the very preliminary state of research in this field.

Against this variegated pattern of local development we have relatively little to set in the way of an evolutionary time sequence. The Sinaloa excavations promise to yield much data on culture replacement and on ecological adjustment and development of technique within each culture pattern.[4] Excavations in the Valley of Mexico

[3] Wissler, American Indian, 1938; Linton, this volume, Chapter III.
[4] Kelly, Chametla, 1938; Ekholm, this volume, Chapter XXIII.

likewise produce the effect of situations involving both peoples and culture and throw much light on the development of the religious system.[5] A documentary background unparalleled in New World annals supplements and enriches the picture. At Cholula in Puebla the same sort of shift in emphasis is revealed,[6] but in Central Vera Cruz the element of gradual evolution is lacking in the archaeological record.[7] The excavation of Monte Alban in Oaxaca has yielded a long slow sequence wherein stylistic and religious evolution culminates in a sharp religio-cultural replacement.[8] In Yucatan we see something of the conflict between two well established religious and artistic patterns of Maya and Mexican origin.[9] However, Uaxactun, in the Peten district of Guatemala, is the one site which indicates a long-continued occupation of a highly ceremonialized site.[10] The neighboring site of Holmul in a reduced form reproduces the same sort of time span through the medium of stratified graves containing representative wares found at Uaxactun.[11] The more northerly site of San José, British Honduras, extends the history of the Peten Maya into more recent times.[12] On the highlands of Guatemala, careful site analysis shows cultural impact in ceramic terms, but less of the aspect of ceremonial development.[13] These long occupations produce a different type of information and lack the all important common denominator of exact dates. However, elements in these series may be grouped as coeval, even if exact interlocking of elements might involve adjustments of a couple of centuries as to the precise date.

The most varied pattern of culture occurs in the Valley of Mexico.[14] The first phase shows maximum occupation depths of 15 to 30 feet for the Copilco-Zacatenco phase, which was a competently developed sedentary culture with no visible traces of involved ceremonial equipment. It is important to remember that cotton was known in the early stages of this settlement. Copilco-Zacatenco is

[5] Vaillant, Correlation, 1938.
[6] Noguera, Altar de los Craneos, 1937. This Volume, Chapter XXII.
[7] Krickeberg, Totonac, 1922, 1928; Strebel, Alt-Mexiko, 1885–1889.
[8] Caso, Monte Alban, Exploraciones, 1932, 1935, 1936, 1938.
[9] Tozzer, Maya and Toltec Figures, 1930.
[10] Ricketson, O. G., and E. G., Uaxactun, 1937.
[11] Merwin and Vaillant, Holmul, 1932.
[12] Thompson, San José, 1938.
[13] Kidder, Thompson, Butler, Smith, R. E., give full citations in this volume.
[14] Vaillant, Early Cultures, 1935; Correlation, 1938.

replaced by Cuicuilco-Ticoman without discovered transitions. This culture is distributed through Morelos, Puebla and as far east as Central Vera Cruz and shows nascent traits of Central Mexican ceremonialism revealed both by single mounds and clusters of them and in the presentation of the fire god. This culture may have evolved outside the Valley of Mexico contemporaneously with Copilco-Zacatenco but within the Valley it is later and shows merely 10 to 12 feet maximum refuse beds. Cuicuilco-Ticoman is followed by the Teotihuacan culture, which is represented by the most imposing ceremonial precinct uncovered in Central Mexico. Its earliest phase shows a blend of Cuicuilco-Ticoman, west Mexican, and exclusively Teotihuacan elements. General material culture remains fairly stable, with a gradual stepping up of ritualistic presentation in stone carving, ceremonial pottery, and figurines, until with the introduction of the mold, individualized types of beings are represented. Tradition ascribes a closing date of 1000–1100 A. D. for this culture but its duration and inception are less precisely given, with estimates ranging from 500 to 700 A. D. This heavily ceremonialized culture is replaced by relatively simple groups, who made distinctive ceramic styles in the Chichimec Period. There is a gradual resurgence of temple architecture combined with the spread of Aztec ceramics, until the typically Aztec ceremonial and technical culture dominates the northern part of the Valley. The Aztec custom of cyclical destruction enables us to estimate the appearance of the culture in the mid-thirteenth century and its spread by the mid-fourteenth. The ceremonial elements of a carefully defined polytheism, the tonalpohualli, a 52-year cycle, and stylized picture writing stem from a common source seemingly centering in the Mixteca Puebla area. Tradition describes movements and strife between tiny tribes carried on under a closely unified religious system.

Mixteca-Puebla culture constitutes the fifth period at Monte Alban, when it blasts the earlier Zapotec ritual.[15] The distribution of this type of ceremonialism which is closely paralleled by the distribution of Plumbate ware from the south and fine orange from the north has very important implications.[16] Elements of this culture are found in the Cerro Montoso culture of Vera Cruz, the Mexican occupation of Chichen Itza, and reach as far east as Santa Rita in Brit-

[15] Caso, Estelas Zapotecas, 1928; Exploraciones, 1938; Ancient Jewels, 1932.
[16] Vaillant, Chronology and Stratigraphy, 1935.

ish Honduras, as far south as Salvador and Naco, Honduras in terms of objects and in terms of day names even as far as Nicaragua.[17] Northward several vessels from Guasave, in far distant Sinaloa, show ritualized presentations of gods in the Mixteca-Puebla manner, but the population there apparently rejected development of the pattern, since these forms occur in the earliest polychrome level and there is no evidence of platforms.[18] Four things are notable about the Mixteca-Puebla culture: its spread is shown mainly in terms of ritualistic presentation; there is evidence that much of the distribution was accomplished by movements of peoples; the movement seems datable as between 1100–1300; at Monte Alban and at Teotihuacan, this complex replaced in the first case directly and in the second case indirectly, stable individualized local cultures.

The new excavations at Tres Zapotes in Vera Cruz show that our knowledge does not nearly embrace the total of the high cultures of Middle America. We do know however that at one period in its history Teotihuacan was in contact with culture groups south of it and its own settlements were spread through much of the state of Mexico, Hidalgo, Morelos, Puebla, and perhaps into Vera Cruz.[19] The ceremonial evolution which took place, if strongly localized in its stylistic execution, may well have been stimulated from outside and in its last phases at Teotihuacan and at Azcapotzalco, when the ceremonial site seems largely to have been abandoned, influences in nature of ceremonial presentations and of trade pieces were streaming in from Oaxaca.[20]

The Zapotec culture prior to the Mixteca-Puebla intrusion, falls into two main divisions. The basic culture seems to have been the sedentary type, having figurines but with little evidence of ritualization. To this was grafted the idea of the ceremonial building complex, a curious free style sculpture with negroid-like faces (los Dansantes), a conventionalized writing involving symbols rather than a more directly representative of picture writing, a calendric system, and a tiger-faced divinity. In the second period Q complex ceramic forms, like the swollen tetrapod, the spouted vessel, high annular

[17] *Vera Cruz,* Strebel, 1885–1887; *Yucatan,* Vaillant, Maya Ceramics, 1927; Hidden History, 1933; *Santa Rita,* Gann, Mounds, 1900; *Salvador,* Spinden, Salvador, 1915; *Naco,* Strong et al. 1938; *Nicaragua,* Mason, this volume, Chapter V.

[18] Ekholm, this volume.

[19] Vaillant, Correlation, 1938.

[20] Linné, Teotihuacan, 1934; Noguera, this volume.

base and pot stands provide a new element. The third period discloses the disappearance of the negroid sculpture to be replaced by the more formal Zapotec stelae, the tiger god becomes more animal in appearance, a long nosed god and a human one come in especially in connection with urns accompanying burials. Fresco paintings involving concepts similar to those at Teotihuacan are made, but with glyphic elements in true Zapotec style. The fourth period shows a higher conventionalization of the urns, and during what seems to be a very long period, there is a slow decay in excellence of ordinary household objects.[21] The fact that the later stages of Zapotec Monte Alban and Teotihuacan show elements of connection argues that the periods of duration were not very far separated in the period before contact. This influence would not seem to have been achieved by migration but rather through trade and trait-borrowing mechanisms. Mr. Noguera's paper [21a] showing how these cultures were in actual contact on the Puebla frontier gives most convincing evidence. Where the Teotihuacan people seem gradually to have absorbed continuously ceremonial elements from higher cultures located elsewhere, the Zapotec apparently turned from one type of ceremonial presentation to another, involving a pronounced shift in stylistic values.

Reduction of the Maya situation to such simple terms as pottery typology, ceremonial architecture, calendar, and the stelae cult gives a picture somewhat different from the developmental situation we have observed previously. These are visible, on the basis of wares and styles, potentialities for the establishment of at least three unspecialized sedentary cultures, the Usulutan of Salvador, the Miraflores of the vicinity of Guatemala, and the Mamom of Uaxactun so closely affiliated to the Playa de los Muertos of Honduras. Q complex vessel forms strongly affect these regional ceramic families. A sophistication of one of these groups, shown chiefly in ceramic decoration, appears as an early horizon to the north in Holmul and British Honduras. Curiously this Holmul I phase has not as yet appeared at Uaxactun.[22]

[21] Caso, Exploraciones, 1932, 1935, 1936, 1938; Stelae, 1928; Batres; Monte Alban, 1902.

[21a] This volume, Chapter XXII.

[22] Smith, R., Ceramics, 1936; Shape Analysis, 1936; Ricketson and Ricketson, Uaxactun, 1937; Strong, Northwest Honduras, 1936; Popenoe, Playa de los Muertos, 1934; Lothrop, Salvador, 1927; Atitlan, 1933; Vaillant, Resemblances, 1932; Notes, 1930; Archaeological Setting, 1934; Merwin and V., Holmul, 1932.

Upon this basis the ceremonial center appears accompanied by a stepping up of techniques of manufacture and design. We find the establishment of regional ceramic families, along the Usumacintla, in Yucatan, in the Peten, at several points on the Highlands of Guatemala, in the Copan-Salvador area, in the Middle Motagua region, and at Lubaantun. Trade and local adaptation, invention and development, bring these wares, basically disparate from the point of view of ethnic identity, into various combinations of unity and disunity.[23]

The stelae cult with its unified method of counting time is found spread over the central portion of the area, with such notable exceptions as much of Yucatan, British Honduras and the Highlands. This wide distribution offers a curious parallel to the spread of the less complex ritualistic elements of the Mixteca-Puebla religious culture. The greater number of stelae and longest run of sequential dates seem to occur in the Peten region.[24] A transition from Mamom via Chicanel to Tzakol, the developed Peten Maya ceramic style, is to be detected at Uaxactun.[25] The simplest and presumably earliest Maya ceremonial structure Temple E–VII-sub is found at this same place, in which the most conspicuous ceremonial element is the tiger-faced mask which has affiliations toward Vera Cruz and Oaxaca, but which in its Uaxactun form has a relatively slight distribution in terms of the Maya area.[26] These two elements, the tiger god and the calendar, do not seem to be integrally related.

The next characteristic feature is the distribution of the Maya vault in connection both with temple and with domiciliary architecture.[27] This trait which has an intimate relationship with the stelae cult does not occur continuously distributed outside of the Maya-speaking area. Yet in northern Yucatan, there is a majestic architecture, obviously exhibiting Maya ceremonial features, without the Long Count cult, and accompanies a regional pottery in ware and form much more closely allied to the Monte Alban zone than to the Peten. Furthermore, the calendric system as recorded, is based on the Katun Count rather than the Long Count of the south. Now

[23] Vaillant, Maya Ceramics, 1927; Chronology and Stratigraphy, 1935; Thompson, 1939.

[24] Morley, Peten, 1938.

[25] Smith, R., Shape Analysis, 1936; Ceramics, 1936; Ricketson and Ricketson, 1937.

[26] Ricketson and Ricketson, 1937; Vaillant, Pre-Columbian Jade, 1932; Saville, Votive Axes, 1929. Stirling, Initial Series, 1940.

[27] Smith, A., this volume, Chapter XIII.

although traditionally in Maya research the Yucatan Short Count is an abridgement of the Long, it would seem possible that it could represent another variation of the whole calendric principle.[28]

Thus in the case of the Maya area instead of a unified culture or even a ceremonial culture, we have several distinctive elements, not an inextricably interlocked complex. There is a calendar system, a method of building, a concept of a ceremonial center, a possibly early ritualistic diffusion, all occurring against a ceramic distribution, suggestive of several basal cultures. East of the Maya country there is little trace of further passage of such traits; and one strikes late, competently developed, heavily stylized cultures with a very reduced expression of the ceremonial center idea in Maya terms excepting such sites as the Naco type which have strong tinges of the Mixteca ceremonial pattern.

To my mind such distributions suggest a specialized development of specific features by outlying peoples, who were freed from conflict by wide opportunity for movement and population expansion. Such high stylistic achievements do not necessarily imply basic invention. A common interest in the tonalamatl and astronomy might produce such variable expressions of the calendar as the Peten Maya, the Yucatan, the Zapotec, and the Mixteca-Puebla varieties.[29] A unified invention and distribution of one type should produce rather the effect of Mixteca-Puebla ceremonialism at a later date. Therefore, on this basis, it is difficult to see how a Maya community under the present conditions as revealed by archaeology, would create first and earlier by far than its northern neighbors, so peculiarly complex a ritualistic system and then would transmit only reduced elements of it, without producing a stronger Maya tinge in respect to material culture than we note now to the north. Rather I see in geographical terms a center or series of centers in southern Vera Cruz or in the archaeologically unknown Chiapas. Possibly Maya tribes occupied this region and were the inventors, but that I do not know. Certainly I do not see how the present Maya ceremonial complex can be very much earlier than the northern ones.

Traces of Mixteca-Puebla influence appear in northern Yucatan and Mexican influence affects the western border of the Maya area.

[28] Andrews, this volume, Chapter X.

[29] *Peten-Maya and Yucatan*, Kidder and Thompson, Correlation, 1938; *Zapotec*, Caso, Stelae, 1928; *Mixtec-Puebla*, Caso, Religion, 1937; Spence, Gods of Mexico, 1923.

In the Peten and on the Highlands this effect is reduced to an occasional vessel form, the revival of tripod support for vessels and an occasional graffito etched on a temple wall. At Kaminaljuyú on the Guatemala highland, in the Tzakol period of Uaxactun, and Holmul II–IV, there is a brisk intrusion of new forms suggesting Teotihuacan. At Kaminaljuyú, Teotihuacan III–IV fresco painting on cylindrical vases shows specific contact. So perishable an art would hardly be a product of trade. Perhaps it was brought in by some of the strays who set up the Toltec migration tradition in the south.[30]

Thus, on this basis, the more closely the chronologies of the three great centers of culture which have been sampled archaeologically can be integrated, the more plausible the stylistic and commercial relationships become. The events in this restricted zone of high ceremonial are probably not closely connected with such technical distributions as those of specialized weaving and dyeing techniques, cultivated food plants, and linguistic migrations. The unspecialized sedentary villages provide a good nuclear core for the absorption of such traits. Their social and economic development would bring greater versatility and skill in their execution. The following papers on relationships with South America show this situation much more clearly.

The question of population growth is an important factor and the unequal development of regional culture is probably closely bound up with this problem. Especially difficult for archaeology to answer are questions of cultural diffusion, since to symbolize through imperishable objects the potentialities of the total social and material culture requires a broad empirical basis, not yet available. Yet to estimate the direction of cultural development may simplify to some degree the welter of conflicting elements that constitute the archaeological materials for the reconstruction of culture's relationship to human history in Middle America.

I see six great stages in Middle America, (1) a period of basic distribution of hunting and gathering groups, (2) a long period for the domestication and cultivation of food plants, (3) a long phase for the development of permanent villages, the distribution of basic material equipment, and the resultant creation of local populations, (4) an overlapping phase wherein possible migrations of peoples with upland techniques spread into the lightly populated forest country (5) then a specialized distribution, back over the upland, of the

<hr>

[30] Thompson, San José, 1939; Kidder and Thompson, Correlation, 1938.

idea of the ceremonial center, and variations of the ritualistic social and material development that is so characteristically Middle American, (6) finally, that peculiar upheaval that saw the cultural and in many places, governmental dominance of Mixteca-Puebla culture, which repeated, perhaps, in terms of a relatively densely populated area, the same sort of expansion made by the Maya tribes into a relatively depopulated zone.

XXII

EXCAVATIONS AT TEHUACAN

Eduardo Noguera *
Translated and Condensed By
S. B. Vaillant

IN JUNE of 1936 there was brought to the attention of the Department of Prehispanic Monuments the discovery of a pre-Columbian building on the property of the Industrial School of Agriculture in Tehuacan, Puebla. During operations in connection with some drainage pipes on the said property, workmen stumbled on some large flagstones, which when removed, were found to cover a great hole that on further investigation proved to be a tomb. Accordingly, the directors of the school informed the Federal Office of Hacienda in Tehuacan from which word came to the Department of Bienes Nacionales and so in turn to the Department of Monuments.

Luckily the professors in charge of the school proceeded scrupulously to remove the objects which appeared on the surface, but in spite of taking proper pains, they were unable to collect certain data indispensable in this type of investigation. At any rate this first exploration was useful and necessary, for unless the objects had been removed immediately on discovery many of them would have been injured.

Since the water ran immediately over the tomb, a deposit was gradually accumulating within it and for this reason many of the objects remained hidden under the sedimentation. Thus when we renewed the excavations we were able to recover 35 more objects of pottery and other materials, and two human skeletons. All these specimens, placed temporarily in a hall of the Industrial School of Agriculture, are now in the National Museum (Plate XII, Figs. 25, 26).

* Harvard, special student, 1917–1920; now Chief Archaeologist, Department of Prehispanic Monuments, Instituto Nacional de Arqueologia e Historia, Secretaría de Educacion Publica, Mexico.

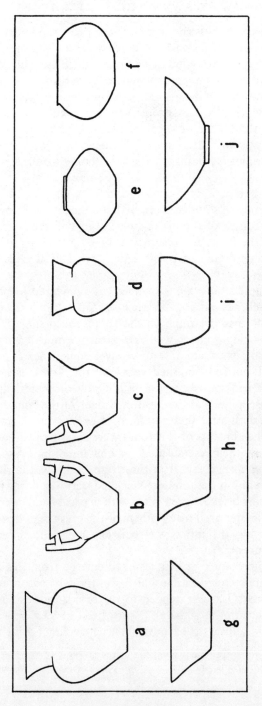

FIG. 25. VESSELS FROM TOMBS 1 AND 2, TEHUACAN

The discovery of this tomb was of the greatest importance. It is quite clearly a construction of Zapotec style and culture, well finished and consisting of a kind of vestibule which connects by a wide door with an antechamber. This antechamber forms the arms of the cruciform tomb; and it was here the human remains were found. The tomb proper is of vast proportions and contains two niches in each wall, with another of considerable size at the end. In none of these niches was any offering found, though we may assume there were some originally, perhaps of a destructible material which was not preserved.

The construction is of fine materials, of well cut slabs, and the lintels and jambs of the doors are of large blocks. In some portions can be seen remains of the plaster which lined all the interior, more especially on the floor; and one may assume that in its good days the tomb held some fresco of that religious symbolical character seen at Monte Alban.

A few months later a second tomb was discovered identical with the first, which proved the existence of Zapotec culture in the region. It is true that this tomb was in an advanced stage of destruction, its roof being gone as well as a great portion of its walls, but notwithstanding we were able to recover some fine pieces, among others some beautifully finished vessels of the Teotihuacan culture, one of which had step-shape legs and a row of typical little heads around its base as well as the head of a tiger in the round. Another similar vessel with a monkey's head in place of a tiger's appeared in fragments. The contents of this tomb were similar to those of Number 1, and show their resemblance and contemporaneity.

The most important aspect of these discoveries was in the class of objects recovered in the tombs. Associated with vessels of the purest Zapotec style of black or grey ware with vertical handles and typical Zapotec bowls, appeared many others of the great period at Teotihuacan proclaiming the intimate association and contemporaneity of the two cultures.[1]

Another important fact that seems to emerge from this discovery is that the Zapotec civilization which was thought before to be confined to eastern Oaxaca extended to hitherto unsuspected distances and reached even to these parts, far northeast of its supposed center. Here it would appear to have had constant contact with the civili-

[1] The list of these specimens is on file in the archives of the Department of Prehispanic Monuments, and the collection is in the National Museum.

zation of Teotihuacan and perhaps here, too, these great cultures exerted mutual influence on each other.

At the present, Tomb Number 1, since Tomb Number 2 was so destroyed, has been restored and preserved; and it is in the care of a deputy inspector resident in Tehuacan, while the objects removed from both tombs are on view in the National Museum.

The illustrations (Plate XII, Figs. 25, 26) show the specimens discovered in both tombs, the Zapotec vessels, including ollas with two

FIG. 26. INCISED GRAY WARE VASE, TOMB 1, TEHUACAN

vertical spouts, simple ollas, small vases with the God Tlaloc in relief, and bowls with incised and painted decoration, while Teotihuacan is represented by an even greater variety. Vessels of thin orange ware predominate, with incised and carved designs. There are also bowls of the same ware with cylindrical legs and vases of artistic value having smooth sides and crenellated legs and the base surrounded with tiny little heads, a detail typical of Teotihuacan. Two of these boast a sculpture in the round, one of a tiger, another of a monkey. Common also are small vases, with flat bottoms and conical or cylindrical legs, equipped with covers, as well as cups of brown ware, bowls of cream ware with a finely polished cerise slip, and others of less archaeological significance and inferior artistic value.

Along with the pottery objects were found in both tombs specimens of jade, such as a ring, discs, beads, and plaques, all destined for personal adornment. Knives, blades, and beads of obsidian as well as various ornaments of bone and shell occurred, to say nothing of stone metates, metalpilis, and polishers, but the most valuable thing archaeologically speaking, because of its rarity, was without doubt a little wooden idol, still in relatively good condition.

We were interested in trying to trace the cultural relations of this find to the neighboring of the Cholulan ceramic complex both in respect to its contacts and influences, as well as to the origins of Mixtec pottery. If, as this important discovery suggested, the Zapotecs and Teotihuacanos had lived in terms of intimate association in a region where the existence of neither great culture had hitherto been even suspected, it might be profitable to make a series of stratigraphic pits on the Tehuacan site. These would serve to supplement previous finds at Tepeaca and at the Barranca del Aguila in the vicinity of San Hipolito Xochitenango.

Accordingly, we chose a spot for our first excavations on the Rancho de San Francisco not far south of the church of El Calvario, which is half a kilometer from the Industrial School of Agriculture. Here stand several mounds, probably the former homes of the pre-Columbian inhabitants; and here we might logically expect to find rubbish heaps. Once the proper arrangements had been made with the owners, five pits were sunk, two in the open and three directly into the mounds. Another series of pits were made north of the church to sample the entire field between it and the Agricultural School. One excavation was on the west of the school itself near Tomb 1 and proved almost sterile (XIII). Another (XIV) was made near Tomb 2. Most of the pits were two meters square and were continued to a depth of one or two meters until tepetate was reached. A few trenches were also made near the tombs in the hope of encountering more burials, but without success.

The importance of the discovery of Zapotec tombs in previously unsuspected regions has already been stressed. The contents of the tombs as can be seen from the descriptions and illustrations prove clearly that we are dealing with manifestations of the Zapotec and Teotihuacan cultures themselves and not mere elements or influences. Indeed, it can be said for all practical purposes that the objects are half of one culture, half of the other. Thus it would seem that there are here the peripheral zones of both cultures, that in Tehuacan each had its frontier. Moreover, the importance of this region from the archaeological and historical point of view has always been recognized, since through here lay the old trade routes from Oaxaca to Vera Cruz and here the native traders and ambassadors must have met on their journeys to distant regions. Further along, Teotitlan del Camino must have been an important center for the continuous traffic of various products from many scattered markets.

Let us see now what the study of the pottery from the stratigraphic cuts reveals to us. The principal object of these excavations was to corroborate by stratigraphical digging the conclusions drawn from the material in the Zapotec tombs, that is, to observe with what intensity these cultures occur and which, if either, precedes the other in time.

Two principal types of pottery are to be found in Excavation I, which at first glance correspond to the vessels in the tombs. True, due to the tiny size of the sherds we can not be certain of the predominant shapes; but we can guess that they are ollas and bowls such as are common to Zapotec and Teotihuacan pottery. One ware, the grey, is perfectly fired, of great sonority and finely polished. The other, a rough brown, is well fired but unpolished.

We distinguish also in the brown ware various color tones from a dark to a reddish color, and in the russet group we find two distinct sub classes. The first is very rough and hard, porous and made from a sandy clay. The second, on the other hand, of which there is a smaller number, is well polished. On occasion it is difficult to distinguish between these fragments and the rough, due to a calcareous deposit adhering to some of them from the salts peculiar to the earth in which they lay buried. Decoration is almost absent, and when it does occur on the grey ware it consists of incision on the outer edge of the vessels by means of deep grooves (Fig. 27, Nos. 26–27); there is no painted decoration, although some sherds appear completely covered with brown or cerise paint. The brown pottery is undecorated and is for the most part coarse. The common forms are ordinary ollas and bowls, which indicates a utilitarian purpose. Scattered sherds occur of bowls and ollas covered with cerise paint. Other objects of pottery, like handles, legs, and figurines, are very rare; and the legs we found are all conical and short, and associated with the brown ware.

In Excavation II, the same brown and grey wares appear in various tones plus a third ware, black and perfectly polished. On some sherds, however, one surface is black and the other grey, tending to show a composition identical with that of the grey ware, the color being achieved by special firing and not by the application of a slip. The grey color occurs on the outer surface which suggests that it was caused by imperfect oxidation of the inner surface due to insufficient firing. The brown pottery suffers no change except that finely polished sherds are rarer than in Excavation I.

Due to the discovery of larger sherds in this cut we were better able to study the common forms and their decoration. In the grey pottery, some more finely polished than others, there occur wide mouthed bowls with reinforced or bevelled rims, as well as some with grooved necks, and incised decoration on the outer edge (Fig. 27, Nos. 23–27). The black pots are similar in shape to the grey, but perhaps smaller, with better executed and more varied decoration (Fig. 27, Nos. 1–8, 11–15; Plate XIII, Nos. 8–11) since besides the incision they have also designs carved before firing (Plate XIII, No. 14). The floors are straight, and in general the form is that of the complete bowls found in the tombs (Fig. 25).

In the brown or russet ware the most common form is an olla with a tall or slightly concave neck (Fig. 27, Nos. 19–22) but the lip is never rolled very much. There are also bowls, but not very many. The presence of only one Teotihuacan sherd suggest no occupation by tribes bearing that culture. The obsidian found is yellowish or grey, occurring in too small a quantity to be significant.

Excavation III produced abundant material, similar in most respects to that encountered in the other pits, except that the black ware predominates here. There occurred one fragment of an Archaic figurine in the lowest level. Also for the first time we find fragments of vessels the exterior of which is covered with white paint, with incised decoration penetrating this paint or slip (Fig. 27, Nos. 25–27). The consistency, appearance, and general technique show that this ware, too, is a product of the Zapotec culture.

The same types of pottery persist even in the lowest layers of the pit, with no appreciable change unless it be in the appearance of more black pottery or in the presence of less common forms; but it is clear that all the material is the product of one culture. Vessels with bevelled, incised rims occur in the same quantity. In the fifth cut we found a small cream colored sherd, incised and painted with a coarse

PLATE I

Earliest date now known in Yucatan (9.2.0.0.0.), 475 A.D., Thompson-Martínez correlation; carved on lintel at Oxintok, near Maxcanú. Courtesy of Carnegie Institution of Washington.

PLATE II

Hieroglyphic Stairway, Copan, Honduras. Reconstruction by Tatiana Proskouriakoff. Courtesy of Carnegie Institution of Washington.

PLATE III. VAULTED STRUCTURES IN SOUTH AMERICA

a. A chamber in the Palace of the Inca on the Island of Titicaca. (After Squier, Peru, 1877.)

b. An Inca House. (After Bennett, Hikes in the Andes, 1933.)

c. The Largest House of the Macalaya ruins. (After Bennett, Hikes in the Andes, 1933.)

PLATE IV. FOREIGN POTTERY TYPES FROM KAMINALJUYÚ, GUATEMALA

Upper and middle, Peten Polychrome, basal flange bowl.
Lower, Cylindrical vase, shape Teotihuacan style, decoration Maya.
Courtesy of Carnegie Institution of Washington.

PLATE V

Cylindrical Vase, Uaxactun, Guatemala. Tzakol Period. Courtesy of
Carnegie Institution of Washington.

PLATE VI. EFFIGY VESSELS AND CENSERS, ALTA VERAPAZ

Effigy Vessels and Censers, Period II. Polychrome Vase, Period II. *a, h*, Chamá 3; *b–e, i, k*, Chamá 4; *f, g, j*, Chipál 1. Museum Catalogue Nos., all with prefix NA: *a*, 11090; *b*, 11678; *c*, 11079; *d*, 11054; *e*, 11053; *f*, 11676–7; *g*, 11488; *h*, 11701; *i*, 11234; *j*, 11370; *k*, 11540. Fig. *h* after M. Louise Baker; *h*. 21cm.

PLATE VII. INCISED BLACK AND SMOKED WARES, NEGATIVE-PAINTED WARE, PERIODS I, II; DECORATED CYLINDER JARS, PERIOD II, ALTA VERAPAZ

a, c, Chamá 1; *b*, Chamá 2; *e, f, h, j–l, m–p*, Chamá 3; *d, g, i, q–t*, Chamá 4. Museum Catalogue Nos., all with prefix NA: *a*, 11255; *b*, 11216; *c*, 11227; *d*, 11236; *e*, 11077; *f*, 11240; *g*, 11301; *h*, 11070; *i*, 11585; *j*, 11690; *k*, 11089; *l*, 11596; *m*, 11069; *n*, 11068; *o*, 11221; *p*, 11041; *q*, 11587; *r*, 11075; *s*, 11693; *t*, 11588.

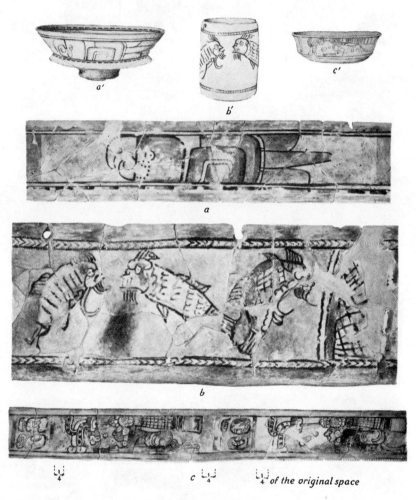

$\overset{\llcorner\lrcorner}{4}$ $\quad$ c $\overset{\llcorner\lrcorner}{4}$ $\quad$ $\overset{\llcorner\lrcorner}{4}$ *of the original space*

PLATE VIII. POLYCHROME DESIGN, PERIODS I AND II, ALTA VERAPAZ; AFTER
M. LOUISE BAKER

a, Chamá 2; *c*, Chamá 3; *b*, Chamá 4. Museum Catalogue Nos., all with prefix
NA: *a*, 11555; *b*, 11074; *c*, 11699. *a*, flange to rim, 8.5$^{cm.}$; *b*, h. 13$^{cm.}$; *c*, h. 5$^{cm.}$

PLATE IX. EFFIGY VESSELS AND CENSERS, PERIODS III AND IV, ALTA VERAPAZ

a–d, Plumbate vessels and lid, Period III; *e–f*, censers, Period III; *g*, White line on Red Jar, Period IV.

Decorated Vessels, Period III.

h, i, m. Fine Orange; *j, k*, Plumbate (*k*, showing admixture of Fine Orange clay?); *l*, Brown; *n*, Polychrome; *o*, alabaster.

Museum Nos., all with prefix NA: *a*, 11639; *b*, 11451; *c*, 11450; *d*, 11531; *e*, 11523; *f*, 11442; *g*, 11470; *h*, 11622; *i*, 11606; *j*, 11324; *k*, 11603; *l*, 11604; *m*, 11602; *n*, 11607; *o*, 11609.

PLATE X. POTTERY FIGURINES AND STAMPS, PERIODS I–IV, ALTA VERAPAZ

a, b, Chamá 1; *c–h,* Chamá 4–Chipál 1; *i, j,* Chipál 2; *k,* Chipál 3. Museum Catalogue Nos., all with prefix NA: *a,* 11160; *b,* 11263; *c,* 11351; *d,* 11208; *e,* 11352; *f,* 11358; *g,* 11353; *h,* 11571; *i,* 11461; *j,* 11451; *k,* 11388.

PLATE XI. JEWELRY, PERIOD IV, ALTA VERAPAZ

a, obsidian ear spool; *c, d, g*, gold; *b, e, f, i, j*, copper; *h, k, l*, shell. Museum Catalogue Nos., all with prefix NA: *a*, 11307; *b*, 11425; *c*, 11428; *d*, 11433; *e*, 11419; *f*, 11426; *g*, 11472; *h*, 11406; *i*, 11417; *j*, 11424; *k*, 11411; *l*, 11413.

a

b

PLATE XII

a. Black Vase, incised and painted.
b. Vase, Teotihuacan style, thin orange ware with decoration in relief, Tehuacan.

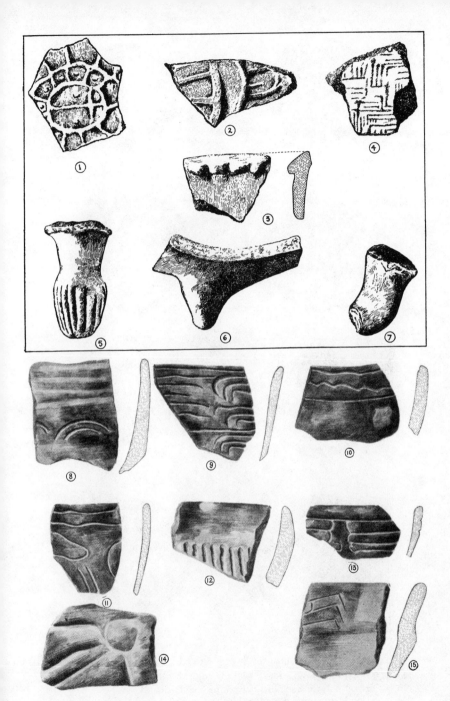

PLATE XIII. POTTERY FRAGMENTS FROM TEHUACAN

Nos. 1–3, sherds with stamped decoration.
No. 4, sherd with applied decoration.
Nos. 5–6, pot supports; No. 7, handle.
Nos. 8–15, incised sherds.

PLATE XIV. POLYCHROME BOWLS, GUASAVE, SINALOA, MEXICO

No. 1. Tripod polychrome bowl, figure dressed in feathers. Diam., 9¾ in.
No. 2. Tripod polychrome bowl, face in profile. Diam., 9½ in.
No. 3. Tripod bowl, brown on deep buff and incised. Diam., 8¼ in.
No. 4. Tripod bowl, red on buff and incised. Diam., 9⅛ in.
No. 5. Tripod bowl, black and incised (incisions whitened for photograph). Diam., 10 in.
No. 6. Tripod bowl, maroon on deep buff and incised. Diam., 9 in.
No. 7. Flat polychrome bowl, insect design. Diam., 9⅞ in.
No. 8. Tripod polychrome bowl. Diam., 7¾ in.

PLATE XV. POTTERY VESSELS, GUASAVE, SINALOA, MEXICO

No. 1. Tripod polychrome and incised jar. Height, 8⅛ in.
No. 2. Red jug. Height, 7⅜ in.
No. 3. Plain red bowl with nicked rim. Diam. of mouth, 8⅛ in.
No. 4. Red bowl with fluted modeling. Diam. of mouth, 7⅜ in.
No. 5. Shallow red-on-buff bowl. Diam., 9¼ in.
No. 6. Exterior of "Aztatlan Polychrome" bowl, incised white band. Diam., 9 in.
No. 7. Red-on-buff and incised pipe. Length, 6½ in.
No. 8. Red-on-buff cups, 2⅝ in., 2⅞ in.

PLATE XVI. POTTERY AND ALABASTER, GUASAVE, SINALOA, MEXICO

No. 1. Polychrome bowl. Diam., 6⅝ in.
No. 2. Polished black incised bowl. Diam., 7½ in.
No. 3. Tripod polychrome and incised bowl. Diam., 8¾ in.
No. 4. Tripod red incised bowl. Diam., 7 in.
No. 5. Tripod alabaster jar. Height, 7¼ in.
No. 6. Fluted alabaster bowl. Diam. of mouth, 3¾ in.
No. 7. Tripod white fluted jar. Height, 8 in.
No. 8. Parrot mask of pottery, white slipped. Diam., 6 in.

PLATE XVII

Polychrome Vase, Ulua Valley, Honduras. Courtesy of Peabody Museum, Harvard University.

PLATE XVIII. SCULPTURES FROM THE PACIFIC SLOPE OF GUATEMALA

a, b, c. Colossal heads from Monte Alto, Department of Escuintla, roughly 4 feet (1.20 meters) high.

d. Crude human figure from Monte Alto, 4 feet, 8 inches (1.40 meters) high.

e, e'. Crude human figure from Obero, Department of Escuintla, right profile and front, 3 feet, 5 inches (1.04 meters) high. Right profile and front.

PLATE XIX. SCULPTURES FROM SALVADOR AND THE PACIFIC SLOPE OF GUATEMALA

   a. Jaguar from Baúl, Department of Escuintla, Guatemala, approximately
5 feet (1.50 meters) high.

   b. Standard bearer figure from Santa Cruz Michapa, Department of Cuscatlan,
Salvador, approximately 3 feet (.90 meters) high.

c, c'. Human figure from La Flora, Department of Escuintla, Guatemala, 4 feet,
8 inches (1.40 meters) high. Right profile and front.

PLATE XX. POLYCHROME VASE WITH "PERUVIAN" DESIGN, CUICATLAN, OAXACA, MEXICO

Mixtec Culture. Museo Nacional de México. Photo, Carnegie Institution of Washington.

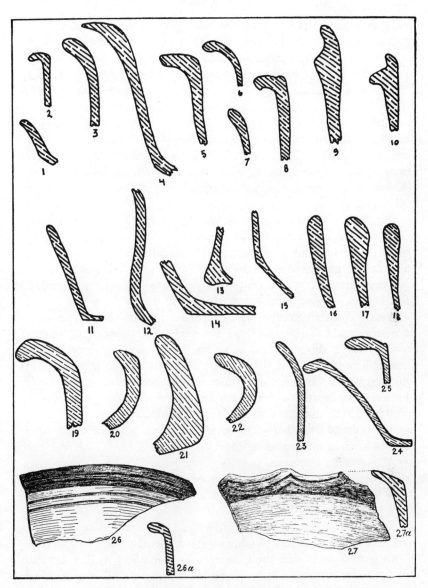

FIG. 27. POTTERY FRAGMENTS FROM TEHUACAN

Nos. 1–4, red clay; Nos. 5–9, gray clay.
Nos. 10–17, black pottery; Nos. 18–19, cream pottery.
Nos. 20–24, black clay; Nos. 25–27, white clay.

red paint that bears every sign of belonging to the Archaic culture (Plate XIII, No. 15). The brown ware is always the same, the rough type increasing in quantity and predominating in a wearisome fashion. Fragments also occur hard and beautifully fired, white and incised, which we consider a variety of the grey ware, but of better quality. The obsidian is whitish in the lowest cuts. In the material from excavation IV there is no variation. Although there were few sherds, these are similar to those found in previous pits. The discovery of one complete vessel, a grey ware olla, with a globular body and short concave neck, indicates to us one form for which the ware was used. A sherd of cream ware bore the mark of the petate or matting (Plate XIII, No. 4).

Excavation V produced the same types in similar proportions, only one piece standing out in the two cuts. This bore incised and grooved decorations, one before and one after firing. We found, also, two fragments of a stamped vessel bottom (Pl. XIII, nos. 1–2).

Excavation VI, north of the church, proved very productive, for here we found new types of pottery and even pottery of a different culture. Another little Archaic figurine body appeared, without doubt Vaillant's Type E [2] very well polished of orange ware with a slip, as well as an ear plug with one surface incised.[3] The presence of elements of this culture, even though it did not reach as far as this region, does suggest contact or at least trade between its bearers and the inhabitants of the Tehuacan region. Moreover, the discovery of only one Teotihuacan sherd in this pit and in some of the others demonstrates that there was no occupation or residence in this region by the Teotihuacanos.

At any rate, decorated pottery, be it incised or of stamped bottoms, occurs so rarely that it reaches only an insignificant percentage. The handles recovered are flat and wide, or of the projecting type, attached at one end only.

Excavation VII contributed a new type of pottery which had not previously been found and which is most abundant near the surface. This new ware is well fired, of dark brown ware, with a slip also dark brown. It occurs in bowls with or without rims, which when present are bevelled. There are also ollas with globular bodies, and one with grooves on the neck.

Vessels with stamped bottoms, of a yellowish clay, are more com-

[2] Vaillant, Ticoman, 1931, Pl. LXII.
[3] Vaillant, ibid., Pl. LXXXII.

TABLE VIII

TABLE OF PERCENTAGES OF THE MOST CHARACTERISTIC WARES IN THE EXCAVATIONS AT TEHUACAN

WARES	I	II	III	IV	V	VI	VII	VIII	IX	X	XII	XIII	XIV
Fine grey ware	9.27	11.92	10.60	22.04	17.35	28.15	18.23	25.57	12.36	28.17	20.96	17.31	23.46
Coarse grey ware	37.56	15.27	35.17	22.04	35.20	30.65	32.38	34.37	24.53	28.04	33.10	42.42	27.82
Fine brown ware	.4.75	4.26	0.56	6.10	9.18	7.38	6.15	6.53	8.25	3.65	5.01	6.67	8.24
Coarse brown ware	47.79	43.00	42.28	30.18	31.64	31.80	27.90	29.69	39.48	39.02	29.62	18.80	30.83
Black ware		25.51	12.10	19.66	6.63	2.01	6.35	3.67	14.43		11.30	14.68	7.14
Stamped ware							1.43						
Legs	0.72												

mon in cut 2; and here we found a pot leg slightly swollen at the end and covered with deep grooves (Plate XIII, No. 5). Four sherds of Teotihuacan thin orange ware appeared here, like the vessels discovered in the tombs, but from so small a number no conclusions can be drawn. Handles continue flat. There is a noticeably greater variety of brown ware in various shades, but due to the small size of the sherds no forms can be discerned.

The same types already reviewed occur in Excavation VIII, but more numerous than in the other pits are the Teotihuacan sherds. It will be remembered that we are now very close to Tomb 2 which had had some of its contents washed into the soil, a fact which explains the increase of this material without deducing an occupation.

We show in our tables neither the occurrence of these sherds nor of the white ware, for their number, two or three in each cut, in comparison with the great masses of Zapotec material makes it plain that only the latter is truly indigenous; and the others are merely an indication of trade or some religious pilgrimage.

Of excavations XIII and XIV only one cut could be obtained, since the earth was so shallow. The scant material nevertheless suggests homogeneity except for one small white sherd, well fired and different from the rest. A few more Teotihuacan sherds appear, whose presence has already been explained by the proximity of Tomb 2.

Although we are dealing here with only one culture and a single period as we shall show later, we have made the two following percentage tables to bring out the abundance of one ware in relation to the others and the variation in quantities as they occur in the several cuts.

The abundance will be noted in both tables of the coarse brown ware which must have been destined for storage and the like. This ware, as we have seen, is of a badly fired clay, rough in texture and simple in form, generally ollas and bowls for cooking. The great quantity is due to the fact that such vessels are the easiest to make and the most commonly used. There is an equal amount of rough grey ware, which served the same purposes as the brown but was better finished.

Of the wares which we can suppose were destined for other uses, as for example, the service of food (we found no fragments of urns or finely decorated vessels or even of any special form which might suggest ceremonial use), there exists a quite large quantity of fine grey ware. This is conspicuous for its bowls with bevelled rims,

TABLE IX

TOTALS AND PERCENTAGES OF THE SEVERAL WARES OF TEHUACAN

WARES	TOTALS	%
Fine grey ware	1013	16.61
Coarse grey ware	1859	30.51
Fine brown ware	369	6.05
Coarse brown ware	2229	36.57
Black ware	625	10.26
	6095	100.00

many of which are carved or grooved on the outside or have walls slightly inclined with the floor at an angle. Of the black ware, which is so similar to the grey, both in its composition and in the forms made, there was twice as much as of the fine brown. This ware was used to make simple vessels like rimless bowls, although the sherds are so small that the exact forms are difficult to ascertain.

Decoration, either on the rims of bowls or on the outside walls, is so rare that we made no mention of it in our tables. Its percentage is negligible.

Very valuable and important conclusions result from the study and excavations of this archaeological zone. At first the discovery of the two Zapotec tombs containing objects of certain Teotihuacan and Zapotec provenience made us suspect that we had found the impact of the two great cultures at their peripheral zone. Our first impression was that we were dealing with the frontiers of both cultures and that Tehuacan was the place where the two civilizations met and were bounded.

Actually, elements of the two cultures appeared in intimate association but of relatively recent date, as is proved by the type of clay used in these vessels and their peculiar forms. The presence of bowls and ollas of Teotihuacan thin orange ware, ollas with double spouts, incised bowls with sloping walls and flat bottoms, to say nothing of minor details, are enough to show that we are dealing with late elements in both cultures.

To confirm the discovery and the suppositions we had formed, we undertook the aforementioned excavations in an attempt to ascertain the relative proportions of the various wares and so to compare the density of the two cultures in the zone of Tehuacan.

However, the study of excavated material led us to surprisingly opposite conclusions. Actually the mass of sherds recovered, or at least all those large enough or definite enough in form for recognition as to period and culture, were alike. An examination showed us that we were dealing with homogeneous material, corresponding to the oldest period at Monte Alban, Period I according to Caso's excavations,[4] in that zone. The especial characteristic of this period is the peculiar shapes of the vessels, made of fine grey ware exactly like that we recovered in Tehuacan. If it is impossible, due to the shattered condition of our material, to reconstruct all the forms, we can at least observe that many of them have bevelled necks and rims, identical with those found at Monte Alban. This will be clear from a glance at our illustrations (Fig. 27, Nos. 24–27) and at Caso's material. These vessels and all the material of the aforementioned excavations we examined in the collections of the National Museum, and remained firm in our opinion.

Another conclusion resulting from our excavations is that neither the Teotihuacanos nor tribes bearing their culture ever lived in this place. The total absence of any Teotihuacan sherds except the few that were washed long ago out of Tomb 2 confirms this. The small number of Archaic sherds and figurines would lead us to draw the same conclusion with respect to these people, but the presence of even so few indicates trade relations between the Archaic and the Zapotec tribes in far off times. For whereas, as we have seen, the Teotihuacan sherds were washed into our upper cuts after the sacking and abandon of Tomb 2, i. e. in fairly recent times, the Archaic fragments are associated with the Zapotec material in our lowest cuts. We may assume then that they were deposited before the arrival of the Zapotecs or in the earliest days of their residence here. Since the figurine fragments are Vaillant's Type E of Ticoman [5] and consequently of the latest Archaic period, we can assume this to have been almost contemporaneous to Period II at Monte Alban.

Summarizing then, the data obtained in the excavations and in the discoveries at Tehuacan, we see the presence of two cultural periods, both of Teotihuacan and of the Zapotec. The most recent of the former and the middle of the latter are associated in Tombs 1 and 2.

[4] Caso, Monte Alban, 1935.
[5] Vaillant, *op. cit.*, Pl. LXII.

We observe also that the data assembled from our excavations indicate the presence of an early cultural phase of the Zapotecs which is in turn associated with one of the latest Archaic periods.

To confirm all this in the more extended excavations that are being carried out in the same territory, we must modify some of the conclusions reached in former studies. For it would seem that the cultural influences which later developed to constitute the famous Zapotec culture came from the north to the state of Oaxaca, where it reached its final flowering. This supposition tends to be confirmed in the chronicles, where we read clearly of the passage through Cholula of the Zapotecs and of their migrations to the south. This migration must have taken place when the Archaic civilizations were in their final phase while the culture of Teotihuacan was just emerging. Later the same Zapotecs, having left their traces in Tehuacan, went on to Oaxaca where they settled permanently and from where they extended, in all directions, their dominion and their influence. A group bearing this later culture reached Tehuacan, this time from the opposite direction, the south; and there felt the impact of the Teotihuacan peoples, who had by this time acquired distinguishing features, without this implying on the part of the latter any occupation of Tehuacan such as was made by the Zapotecs.

Furthermore, since we found no trace of the Mixtec nor the Mexican cultures which have been thought more recent, we may assume that the region remained unoccupied by any other tribe of new manners and customs, in spite of lying as it does on the path of the principal trade routes between Anahuac and Oaxaca, Soconusco and distant Yucatan. At any rate we hope that soon more prolonged excavations can be made in all the environs, so that we may know definitely all the events that took place in this territory.

XXIII

THE ARCHAEOLOGY OF NORTHERN AND WESTERN MEXICO

Gordon F. Ekholm *

INTEREST in the archaeology of Northern and Western Mexico
has quite naturally lagged behind that of the Valley of Mexico
and the regions to the south and east. It is a region which in comparison with those better known areas is relatively barren of the
kind of remains or of the historical associations which prompted
the earlier investigations. In archaeological research at the present
time, however, more emphasis is being laid on the problems concerned with the origins and early stages of the American civilizations, and the remains in peripheral regions achieve new significance. The importance of Northern and Western Mexico arises
specifically from its being a large intervening zone lying between
the higher civilizations of Middle America on one hand and the
cultures of upper North America on the other. A more complete
knowledge than we have of this region would undoubtedly help in
understanding the interrelations between North and South and thus
some of the outstanding problems of American prehistory.

By Western Mexico we may take to mean, roughly, the area included in the states of Michoacan, Colima, Jalisco, Nayarit, and
the southern portions of Guanajuato and Zacatecas. In archaeological
parlance this is commonly known as the "Tarascan Area," though for
no better reason than that the artifacts occurring in collections from
throughout the region have appeared to be basically similar to
those of Michoacan, the home of the Tarascan peoples at the time
of the Conquest. This inclusive and misleading use of the term
Tarascan will undoubtedly be modified when we know more of
the archaeology of the entire region. There are short descriptions

---

* Minnesota, B.A., 1933; graduate work, Minnesota, 1933–1935; Harvard, 1935–
1937; now field representative, American Museum of Natural History.

of a number of extensive mound areas,[1] some of which include pyramids and other large structures. There are a few reports of small excavations, and there are large collections of ceramics in a number of museums, in the main poorly documented. As far as I know there are published accounts of only three small stratigraphic excavations in this entire area,[2] the more recent investigations by Caso and Noguera having not yet been reported.

An architectural type peculiar to central Michoacan is the so-called Yacata, a T-shaped structure with a rounded end, all sides rising at a steep angle in large steps. These platform structures are made of coarse rubble interiors held in place by walls of broken rock laid flat and surfaced with a veneer of large stone slabs, such details of construction being unlike anything in Central Mexico. Objects of carved stone are not numerous and only of rather inferior workmanship.

We know more of the ceramics than of any other class of objects from the "Tarascan Area."[3] There was a great deal of modelling in clay, human and animal forms made simply as figures or modified in some way to form vessels. The realistic modelling of the bodies and, in the human figures, the wealth of detail of dress and of the various activities portrayed rank them among the finest things of this class in Middle America. There is a great variety of ordinary vessel forms including simple bowls, bowls with tripod and annular supports, large jars, and a few of a shape peculiar for Middle America—the so-called stirrup-mouth. Painted decoration is mainly of a single color, a red paint on a buff or brownish background. Until recently the only known locus of polychrome decoration has been the single site at Chupícuaro, Guanajuato,[4] but present investigations are showing that distinct types of polychrome wares are to be found in other localities as well. Practically all of the painted decorations consist of geometric figures, naturalistic designs occurring only rarely and on very small vessels.

While "Tarascan" archaeology is still generally characterized as

[1] Lumholtz, Unknown Mexico, 1902, Vol. 2, pp. 286–469; Galindo, Bosquejo de la Geografía Arqueológica del Estado de Colima, 1922.

[2] Caso, Informe Preliminar de las Exploraciones Realizadas en Michoacán, 1930; Noguera, Exploraciones Arqueológicas en las Regiones de Zamora y Pátzcuaro, Estado de Michoacán, 1931; Vaillant, Ticoman, 1931, p. 363.

[3] Noguera, Extensiones Cronologicó-Culturales y Geográficas de las Cerámicas de México, 1932.

[4] Mena and Aguirre, La Nueva Zona Arqueológica, 1927.

a single unit, it is obvious that thorough investigation will reveal a number of sub-cultures, each with its own sequence of time phases and exterior relationships. Such regional variations are suggested in the published data and are at the present time being substantiated by field investigation.

Likewise in regard to the outside relationships of the cultures of the "Tarascan Area" we can be only very vague. There are close resemblances between the ceramic decoration of Michoacán and that of the Matlatzinca area in the Valley of Toluca, but in regard to time relations or directions of influence nothing can be said as yet. The only definite connection with the cultures of the Valley of Mexico that has been pointed out is that apparently "Tarascan" influences are present in Teotihuacan I materials at Teotihuacan,[5] but there is a question as to whether this is an influence from the "Tarascan Area" or a similarity due to a diffusion westward of "archaic" traits which also went to form the Teotihuacan I culture.[6] The cultures of the "Tarascan Area" show very little relationship to those of the Oaxaca region, but then the archaeology of the intervening state of Guerrero is so almost completely unknown that it is impossible to say what the connections in this direction are. The possible cultural connections to the north and west we shall consider after discussing those areas.

The coastal region of Sonora and Sinaloa in northwestern Mexico is a long strip of low and at intervals fertile land that is probably the most likely route for the diffusion of agricultural peoples or of agricultural practices between Central Mexico and the region of the southwestern United States. From Nayarit to Arizona there is a route open to travel, unobstructed by any major geographical barriers, and, although much of the area is arid or unsuitable for agriculture, nearly all of the many river valleys contain excellent farming land.

Scholars from the University of California first recognized its importance and initiated work in this region according to a well-rounded program of related studies including geography, history, ethnology, and archaeology.[7] An archaeological survey of Sinaloa and northern Nayarit made by Drs. Sauer and Brand in 1930 dis-

[5] Noguera, Antecedentes y Relaciones de la Cultura Teotihuacana, 1935.

[6] Vaillant, A Correlation of Archaeological and Historical Sequences in the Valley of Mexico, 1938, p. 542.

[7] Ibero-Americana series, nos. 1–14, 1932–1938.

closed throughout this area a high culture of "Mexican" affiliations, especially characterized by its fine polychrome and incised pottery.[8] Then Dr. Isabel Kelly made excavations at two sites, at Culiacan and at Chametla,[9] the latter being near the larger town of Rosario somewhat south of Mazatlan. On the basis of sherd stratigraphy in rubbish mounds she has worked out a sequence of four time phases at each site, each characterized by a dominant complex of pottery wares. The four phases at Culiacan supposedly reach to the time of the Spanish Conquest while the sequence at Chametla is apparently earlier, the last two phases there corresponding to the two earliest at Culiacan.[10]

The historical accounts of the first Spanish explorations in this west coast country all agree that from Central Mexico through western Mexico to as far north as Culiacan the country was occupied by fairly high-cultured peoples, but that to the north of Culiacan there were barbarous peoples speaking other languages.[11] This historical information, plus the fact that no archaeological material of importance had ever been reported from the region to the north of Culiacan, led to the belief that the Culiacan River or possibly the Sinaloa River was the approximate northern limit of the "Mexican-like" cultures and that a gap existed between the cultures of Sinaloa and those of northern Sonora which represented an extension southward of the southwestern United States cultures. However, our survey of Sonora and northern Sinaloa made during the winters of 1938 and 1939 [12] does not substantiate the above theory but rather shows that the highly developed "Mexican" cultures extended at some time north of Culiacan to the Fuerte River and that there are prehistoric remains throughout Sonora, several of which may indicate a possible connection with the American Southwest. We shall discuss more fully the results of this recent survey as the detailed report will not be published for some time.

Excavations were made in a low mound near Guasave on the Sinaloa River in northern Sinaloa which disclosed it to be expressly a burial mound, the interments occurring both in large jars and as full-length burials surrounded by many fine pottery vessels and other

[8] Sauer and Brand, Aztatlán, 1932.
[9] Kelly, Excavations at Chametla, Sinaloa, 1938.
[10] Dr. Isabel Kelly has kindly allowed me to include here some as yet unpublished material.
[11] Sauer and Brand, *op. cit.*, p. 49; Sauer, The Road to Cíbola, 1932, p. 8.
[12] A survey sponsored by the American Museum of Natural History.

artifacts. The accompanying plates picture a number of ceramic pieces from this excavation which will serve to indicate the variety and artistic quality of the work of these people in the north of Sinaloa. Probably the most outstanding specimen is the tripod polychrome bowl, the interior of which is shown in Plate XIV, No. 1. This painting is a very sophisticated representation of a human figure completely costumed in feathers. It is a type of figure-painting which, as far as I am aware, is unlike anything on pottery from anywhere in Mexico but more closely resembles drawings in some of the Central Mexican codices. Some of the deepest burials in the mound and the vessels accompanying them appear to represent an earlier phase of culture, but the bulk of the material belongs to one time phase and is definitely affiliated with the Sinaloa cultures to the south. It belongs specifically to what Sauer and Brand and Kelly have termed the Aztatlan complex,[13] and it thus corresponds to the earliest phase determined at Culiacan. There is even a possibility that the decoration of vessels at this site is more complex and ornate than it is farther south in Sinaloa, but this impression may arise from the fact that our excavation at Guasave has yielded the only complete vessels belonging to the Aztatlan complex. However, we can tentatively conclude from this existence of the Aztatlan complex at Guasave, considerably north of Culiacan, with the apparently complete absence of the types of ware found by Dr. Kelly in the three later phases at Culiacan, that at some time considerably before the Conquest the higher-cultured peoples withdrew southward, supposedly because of pressure from more primitive tribes. (Pls. XIV–XVI).

A number of sites were found farther to the north on the Fuerte River yielding a red-on-buff and one style of polychrome pottery which fall readily into our Guasave series. The Fuerte River is apparently the northern limit of the "Mexican-like" cultures as we found no Sinaloa-like pottery anywhere to the north in Sonora in a fairly intense surface survey.

As a whole the Sinaloa cultures are definitely "Mexican" in affiliation. They have the complex of traits such as vessels with leg supports, peculiar elements of design, obsidian flake blades, and spindle whorls, a complex which is quite distinct, for instance, from the general Southwestern pattern. On the other hand, however, there is no

[13] Sauer and Brand, *op. cit.;* Kelly, Excavations at Chametla, Sinaloa, 1938.

stone architecture or sculpture, nor evidence of the elaborate ceremonial center, traits which are so characteristic of the "Mexican"
cultures. It seems that we must consider the Sinaloa complex to have
been a unit which developed in large part autochthonously and along
its own lines and to have received only moderate, possibly early,
but as yet undefined influences from some more highly developed
Middle American culture.

In my opinion there seem to be certain definable connections with
the plateau cultures, particularly the "Tarascan." Several sherds from
the Guasave site appear to be from stirrup-mouth and spouted vessels. Other similarities to traits common in the "Tarascan Area" are
urn burial, filed teeth, and a somewhat similar type of red-on-buff
pottery. Moreover, we have found with burials at Guasave the paint
remains of otherwise perishable vessels, the decorative technique of
which is comparable to that of the "cloisonné" ware from Chalchihuites as well as to the lacquer work of the present-day Tarascan Indians. The painted figure mentioned above has even more remote
affiliations, being without doubt related to certain art styles found
only in Central Mexico.

Following the earliest investigations in Sinaloa it was supposed
that the Sinaloa cultures would show their closest connections with
the coastal areas to the south,[14] but in her recently completed survey down the coast as far as the western border of Michoacan Dr.
Kelly has found that, although there is an island of Sinaloa-like culture in coastal Jalisco, there is none further south. The only other
alternative is to suppose that there were routes of travel and diffusion
of culture through the western rim of mountains from the plateau
to the coastlands, and, if this were so, the most logical route would
have been that of the pass used throughout historic times—through
the more open valleys which extend westward from Guadalajara to
Tepic. We have found fragments of Sinaloa-like pottery at Ixtlan in
Nayarit which lead us to believe that investigation there may prove
it to have been an important route in prehistoric times as well.

In the course of our recent survey there were found in Sonora
several significant hints as to the cultural connections between
Sinaloa and the Southwest. A series of sites located near the town of
Huatabampo on the lower Mayo River exhibits a culture which
seems to have been in certain basic traits Southwestern in affiliation.
The most characteristic pottery found at this site is a fine hard

[14] Kelly, op. cit., pp. 2, 42–43.

redware, the forms of which include small jugs, jars, and simple open bowls with occasionally a scalloped or wavy rim or an extension of one side of the lip to form a kind of scoop. No single sherd of the Sinaloa painted wares or of footed vessels was found. The location of these sites on old almost-obliterated courses of the Mayo River makes it appear that the remains are of considerable age, and this favors our opinion that the redware may possibly be affiliated with the early redwares of the Hohokam [15] or Mogollon [16] cultures of southern Arizona and New Mexico which they somewhat resemble. Such a connection would be borne out by several figurine heads found on the surface which appear to be related to those at Snaketown.[15] Also the finding of other sites in central Sonora where rectangular stone palettes and ridged three-quarter grooved axes occur is further evidence that elements of the Southwestern cultures extended far south into this region.

By several traits the culture at Huatabampo is also definitely related to the painted-pottery cultures of northern Sinaloa. Almost identical small red jugs of a peculiar swollen-neck shape (Plate XV, No. 2), as well as thin flat metates or milling-stones used with manos that extend over the sides, are found at both places. The evidence we have leads us to believe that the Huatabampo culture existed at an early period and that elements of it joined with later influences from the south to form the complex as we find it at Guasave; to the north it also had some as yet undefined connection with the Southwestern cultures.

Many other archaeological sites have been located in Sonora including a number of great shell heaps along the coast. In north central Sonora the Trincheras culture presents the most distinctive remains, to whose enigmatic question of dating we may be able to add some data from our small stratigraphic excavations. Concerning the numerous plainware sites which are fairly common throughout central Sonora we have as yet drawn no conclusions except that they are probably more Southwestern than southern in affiliation.

We might also mention here that several apparently pre-pottery sites were located in the survey, both on tributaries of the Mayo River. Few chipped implements were found, while there were a number of small flat-surfaced metates and corresponding small hand-

[15] Gladwin, Haury, Sayles, Gladwin, Excavations at Snaketown, 1937.
[16] Haury, The Mogollon Culture of Southwestern New Mexico, 1936; Haury, Some Southwestern Pottery Types, Series IV, 1936.

stones such as are characteristic of the Cochise culture in southern Arizona.[17] Furthermore, there is some indication that these artifacts are coming from deposits also containing remains of Pleistocene fauna.

The last great section we have to consider is that of Northern Mexico proper, including the area extending from the western slopes of the Sierra Madre Occidental to the Atlantic coast and approximately north of a line from Tampico to Guadalajara. We have considerable knowledge of the prehistoric remains existing in the northern part of this region and some of those in the south, but in the main this is the greatest terra incognita of Middle America.

The archaeology of the northwestern part of the state of Chihuahua is fairly well known, both in the accounts of the earlier writers, who described chiefly the large ruins of Casas Grandes,[18] and from the reports on several recent systematic surveys and analyses of the cultures.[19] The most outstanding remains to be found here are, of course, the large buildings made of great adobe blocks and the beautifully made polychrome and modeled pottery. On the basis of his survey and the study of a large collection of Chihuahua ceramics Sayles has outlined seven phases of cultural development which culminated in the Classic Casas Grandes or what he has called the Ramos Phase. This author, in general agreeing with Dr. Brand, concludes that all of the culture traits found in this Chihuahua region, except possibly one form of red-on-black pottery, can only be explained as a very late diffusion southward of Southwestern elements, specifically a combination of the Mogollon and Hohokam cultures.

To the south in the state of Zacatecas are the two important sites known as La Quemada and Chalchihuites. La Quemada,[20] a short distance to the southwest of the city of Zacatecas, has the appearance of being a fortress, situated as it is on the crest of a long rocky hill.

---

[17] Gladwin, Excavations at Snaketown: Comparisons and Theories, 1937.

[18] Guillemin Tarayre, Rapport sur L'Exploration Minéralogique des Régions Mexicaines, 1867, pp. 343–353.

[19] Sayles, An Archaeological Survey of Chihuahua, Mexico, 1936; Brand, Distribution of Pottery Types in Northwest Mexico, 1935; Carey, An Analysis of the Northwestern Chihuahua Culture, 1931; Bennett and Zingg, Tarahumare, 1935.

[20] Guillemin Tarayre, op. cit., pp. 358–391; Batres, Visita a los Monumentos Arqueológicos de "La Quemada," 1903; Noguera, Ruinas Arqueológicas del Norte de México, 1930.

The well-preserved ruins consist of many large rooms with massive stone walls, small truncated pyramids with steps up one side, and one non-truncated nearly true pyramid which is apparently unique in America. One room contains a number of round pillars constructed in the same manner as all of the architectural features at this site, of slightly worked flat slabs of rock well fitted together. Chalchihuites,[21] in western Zacatecas, is a smaller site the chief ruins being situated on a flat area but sharing many of the architectural features of La Quemada. Here again are found stairways, a room containing pillars, and, although no pyramids have been found, they may very well exist as all features at this site should be laid bare by excavation, and very little has been done. The masonry is of the same type as at La Quemada although here it appears to be somewhat cruder due to the predominant use of irregularly fractured igneous rock.

It is thus specifically in architecture that these two sites are "frontier cities," in that they are the northernmost extension of the massive building in stone which is so common to the higher civilizations of Middle America. The type of construction in which slightly worked slabs of rock are used appears to be related to that of Michoacan in the "Tarascan Area," a connection which is also borne out by the pottery.

The ceramics of La Quemada are hardly known, but we have good descriptions by Gamio of the pottery from Chalchihuites, and similar types seem to be represented at the two sites. A painted red-on-buff ware is most common at Chalchihuites, and it appears to be generically related to the red-on-buff of the "Tarascan Area." There are also an incised-incrusted and a so-called "cloisonné" ware, in the latter the design being carved in a thick layer of paint and the resulting hollows re-filled with pastel-colored pigments. A similar technique was used on the jars from Estanzuela and Totoate, Jalisco, and is still used in the modern lacquer work of the Tarascan Indians of Michoacan.

On the basis of the very limited information we have from these two sites, we can say only in general terms that they represent a northern periphery of the full Mexican complex and that they show certain specific connections with the cultures of the "Tarascan Area."

The most recent contribution to the archaeology of this section

[21] Gamio, Los Monumentos Arqueológicos de las Inmediaciones de Chalchihuites, 1910.

of northern Mexico was made by Dr. Mason[22] who surveyed the area in Durango to the north of Chalchihuites as far as the town of Zape, the latter being the location of another site which has been known for many years. He found a generalized type of Chalchihuites pottery to continue as far north as Zape, but there, although still basically "Mexican," the culture ". . . had become attenuated and peripheral, and had lost much of its fine quality." Although no investigation was made north of the region of Zape, Mason believes that the southern culture probably did not extend much farther north. From Zape it is about one hundred miles to the southernmost extension of the Chihuahua cultures as determined by Sayles, where no "Mexican" elements were observed. The assumption is that here a gap existed between the Southwestern and Mexican cultures.

This appears to be a clear-cut example of a complete separation of two distinct streams of culture, but I am disinclined to base any further generalization on such limited data. We must first know something of the relative ages of the two complexes and must at least have a survey of the intervening and neighboring areas to ascertain whether or not the remains of other and possibly earlier phases of culture do not occur which would bridge the gap.

It appears to me, too, that the question of whether or not Classic Casas Grandes pottery shows any Mexican influence in form and design is a matter of opinion unverifiable at the present time. In the effigy vessels of Casas Grandes I see a greater resemblance to those of the "Tarascan Area" than to those that occur in any part of the Southwest. It has been mentioned that the Casas Grandes hooded jars had no counterpart to the south, but I would point out their resemblance to the jars from Estanzuela in southern Zacatecas as pictured by Lumholtz which are quite similar even to the entire shape of the vessel. Such questions cannot be settled until intensive work is done in this central region of northern Mexico.

We know practically nothing of the archaeology of the state of Tamaulipas in the northeastern corner of Mexico, and, as Dr. Mason has recently pointed out,[23] investigations here will certainly prove important as through Tamaulipas and along the coast of Texas is the most likely route of diffusion between the cultures of the southern United States and Middle America. Large sites and pyramids are

---

[22] Mason, Late Archaeological Sites in Durango, Mexico, 1937.
[23] Mason, The Place of Texas in Pre-Columbian Relationships Between the United States and Mexico, 1935; Vaillant, Ceramic Resemblances, 1932.

known to exist in southern Tamaulipas,[24] supposedly belonging to the Huastec culture, the name being that of the people living in northern Vera Cruz and southern Tamaulipas at the present time and to whom all archaeological remains coming from northern Vera Cruz and Tamaulipas have been attributed. But, as in all parts of Mexico where our knowledge of the archaeology is scanty, it is mainly just the later more complex horizons that we know, and as the main waves of cultural diffusion through this region seem to have occurred at a fairly early time, it is only when investigations are carried out and the limits and depths of the cultures are known that we can say anything definite concerning the cultural link between Middle America and the southern United States.

From early times to the present much of northern Mexico has been occupied by primitive non-agricultural peoples who have left very little material with which the archaeologist can work. However, in Coahuila and in the valleys of the great Sierra Madre in western Mexico, there are many caves in which the usually perishable remains of these people are preserved. Unfortunately there has been very little scientific collecting of the material from these caves, and the textiles, basketry, and skeletal remains are rapidly being destroyed. One collection from Coahuila [25] indicates the importance of this area as the artifacts point to a cultural connection with the Basket Maker of Arizona and of the Big Bend area in Texas.

In the western mountains cave remains are numerous,[26] both of people who were cave-dwellers and of those who used the caves for burial. Such cave remains occur from the international border far down into Durango and represent cultures ranging from the simple Basket Maker level to those of more complex cliff-dweller stages. Especially in the North there appear to be certain definite relationships with corresponding cultures in the Southwest, but this is certainly only a part of the picture, and investigation of the entire mountain area will undoubtedly reveal links with the surrounding cultures in Mexico.

[24] Prieto, Historia, Geografía y Estadística del Estado de Tamaulipas, 1873.
[25] Studley, Notes Upon Human Remains from Caves in Coahuila, 1887.
[26] Lumholtz, Unknown Mexico, 1902.

XXIV

Pre-Pottery Horizon of the Anasazi and Mexico

Frank H. H. Roberts, Jr. *

THE PRE-POTTERY horizon in the Anasazi province of the Southwest consists of two phases, while in northern Mexico only one, the later, is represented. From a chronological point of view one seems to antedate all ceramics in the North and Middle American areas. The other probably precedes the practice of making containers of fired clay in only the Anasazi and northeast Mexican regions proper, being contemporary with earlier ceramic stages in districts farther south. The first group comprised simple hunting peoples dependent almost entirely on the chase for their maintenance. They did not remain long in one place but traveled wherever the animals moved in order to support themselves. The later peoples were semi-hunting, semi-agricultural in their habits and more settled in their mode of life. Thus far there has been little indication of any connection or relationship between the two. The time separating the periods when each was present in the area apparently was too long to warrant a hypothetical derivation of the later from the earlier inhabitants.

The first stage is characterized by two somewhat different complexes. One, represented by several sites and fairly extensive remains, occurs along the eastern margin of the Anasazi area, the other is known only from a single location on the extreme western frontier of the province. Future work may reveal that both were present in districts nearer to the local of subsequent developments, but as yet there are only suggestive traces in infrequent finds of single specimens comparable in some respects to components in the complex of one or the other. The western materials are those from Gypsum Cave in southeastern Nevada, the eastern are designated by the now familiar name of Folsom. Adjacent to each, although farther re-

* University of Denver, A.B., 1919; Harvard, M.A., 1926; Ph.D., 1927; Hemingway Fellow, 1924–1925; Assistant, 1925–1926; now, Archaeologist, Bureau of American Ethnology, Smithsonian Institution, Washington.

moved from the precincts of the Anasazi, are traces of other nomadic hunting peoples who probably had the same basic cultural pattern and date from approximately the same period. Possible affinities between them and the subsequent groups are even less likely than in the case of the inhabitants of Gypsum Cave and the Folsom men and for that reason discussion of their features is entirely beyond the scope of the present consideration.

Gypsum Cave contained relics of human handicraft, remains of the ground sloth, horse and camel bones. The scanty evidence on the nature of the cultural pattern merely sketches a broad outline from which many details are missing. Although they occasionally camped there over night, the people seemingly visited the cave solely for hunting purposes. Whether they occupied other places for longer periods is not known. During their brief sojourns at Gypsum Cave, however, they discarded or lost enough of their personal possessions to show that they were skilled in the manufacture of chipped-stone implements, were workers in wood, feathers, and sinew, and painted designs on their products, depending on various colored pigments to obtain the desired effects. For weapons they used the atlatl and foreshafted javelin. There is good basis for the assumption that they were familiar with the sloth and camel, but that they actually hunted and killed these animals was not convincingly demonstrated. Various bits of evidence suggest that such was the case as far as the sloth was concerned, yet the proof is not wholly satisfactory. That the people knew the horse is more debatable and despite the presence of bones in several levels the occurrences were not sufficiently clearcut to warrant belief that they did. It appears more likely that animal had passed from the scene just previous to the coming of the hunters.

Upper levels in the same cave yielded specimens attributable to the Anasazi. Some of these represent the earliest established stage of that pattern, the Basket Maker, and a general similarity between certain traits in that complex and some features in the materials from the older hunting group led to the suggestion that the latter may have been progenitors of the Basket Makers. All the evidence, however, is for a much older horizon and unless more convincing indications are found elsewhere postulation of such a relationship is not justified. The age of the Gypsum Cave deposits, that is of the early material, has been estimated at 10,000 to 11,000 years and if this dating is approximately correct the intervening millennia until the appearance of the first Anasazi, at about the beginning of the Christian Era, encompass too long an interval to warrant attempts to show a relationship on the strength of present evidence.[1]

The Folsom complex is also characterized by the association of man-made objects and bones from extinct species of animals, bison, mammoth, camel, and muskox. The main sites from which information on this group has been obtained are at Folsom, New Mexico, the type site for the identifying factor in the complex,[2] at several locations between Clovis and Portales, New Mexico,[3] in the Guadalupe Mountains in southeastern New Mexico,[4] and at the Lindenmeier ranch in northern Colorado.[5] The latter is well beyond the boundaries of the Anasazi, although influences from that province reached the district in later times as is shown by the finding of objects from the Classic Pueblo stage in caves near Sterling, Colorado, 90 miles east of the Lindenmeier site.

The cultural pattern of the Folsom people was based on the hunt. Although they may have supplemented their preponderant meat diet with occasional greens and wild seeds, there is no evidence to indicate any attempts at cultivation. Because the bulk of the Folsom material has come from open sites nothing is known about objects made from perishable things such as wood, skins, or vegetal matter. All that remains are articles of wood and bone. The complex consists of projectile points, several types of scrapers, a variety of cutting edges, drills, flakes with small sharp points that may have served to mark on wood and bone, well-made knives, large blades, sandstone shaft smoothers and rubbing stones of the same material, bone punches and awls, possibly bone points for projectiles, and carved bone "gaming pieces" and ornaments. Red and yellow ochres were used as sources of color. Most of the stone artifacts were chipped or flaked, there are no polished examples, and show that the lithic component in the material culture was mainly a flake industry, although tools of the core type, chiefly choppers and hand hammers, are found. The only forms that are sufficiently distinctive to serve as criteria for the complex are the characteristically fluted

[1] Harrington, Gypsum Cave, 1933.
[2] Figgins, Antiquity of Man, 1927; Roberts, Folsom Complex, 1935, pp. 3–6.
[3] Howard, Evidence of Early Man, 1935, pp. 79–123.
[4] Howard, op. cit., pp. 62–79.
[5] Bryan, Geology of the Folsom Deposits, 1937, pp. 139–152; Coffin, Northern Colorado's First Settlers, 1937; Roberts, Folsom Complex, 1935; Roberts, Additional Information on the Folsom Complex, 1936.

projectile points and fluted knife blades. Other items are so like those from later horizons that they cannot be considered indicative of Folsom, except when found in situ with bones from extinct animals or in association with the fluted forms.

There is no evidence on the type of weapons used. On the basis of the general theory that the atlatl and javelin were the oldest forms it is usually assumed that Folsom man depended on them when hunting or engaged in warfare. Many of the fluted points, however, are small enough to have been hafted on arrowshafts and shot from a bow and most of the larger examples do not exceed the weight and dimensions of stone points known to have been used on arrows by some of the later Indians. Furthermore, stone heads fastened to foreshafts set in javelins that unquestionably were thrown with the atlatl are no larger than some of the smaller Folsom specimens. Hence it is not possible to postulate, with any degree of certainty, from the points the kind of weapon on which they were used. There is good evidence that the bow and arrow reached the Southwest and other sections of the country in relatively late times, well along in the second stage of the Anasazi, and as a consequence it is taken for granted that Folsom man did not know it, yet it should be borne in mind that this is an assumption and not an authenticated fact.

The most significant occurrence of Folsom material, as far as the Anasazi is concerned, was that in Burnet Cave in the Guadalupe Mountains. At that place a fluted point, in association with bones from an extinct species of bison and an extinct species of muskox, was found near a hearth in a level several feet beneath a layer attributable to an early phase in the cultural pattern of that group.[6] Although there is some question about the age of peripheral Anasazi material in this region, as compared to that in more nuclear parts of the province, the Burnet Cave find does demonstrate that the big game hunters were present at a considerably earlier period. The general situation is suggestive of the Gypsum Cave setup and indicates a somewhat similar time lapse between the two groups.

The date for the Folsom horizon is placed at from 10,000 to 25,000 years ago with the belief on the part of many that it is closer to 25,000 than to 10,000. Here, as in the case of Gypsum Cave, the time involved appears too great for any hypothetical correlation with the Anasazi or other southwestern patterns. There are no skeletal remains definitely assignable to either the Gypsum Cave or the

[6] Howard, *op. cit.*, p. 78.

Folsom people. Hence there is no possibility of suggesting relationships on the basis of physical characteristics. Several finds purporting to be Folsom men attracted attention in recent years, yet in each instance identification rests on such flimsy evidence that acceptance is not warranted. In no case were there accompanying mortuary offerings or associated artifacts or faunal material. The mere presence of burials in the vicinity of Folsom sites or in deposits similar to those in which Folsom materials were found is not sufficient grounds to support the conclusion that they are the remains of Folsom people. This is particularly true when the interments are a number of miles away from the actual sites and in regions known to have been occupied at various times by different groups of later Indians.

Most indications for Folsom affinities point toward the Plains and the Southeast and subsequent developments are more likely to have taken place there than in the Southwest. There is, of course, a possibility that the similarities are more attributable to the basic nature of the hunting pattern than to an actual relationship and that the Folsom people, as well as some of the neighboring groups of approximate contemporaneity, may have drifted on south into Mexico as one of the earlier waves of migration and joined with others in giving impetus to incipient trends in that area. Thus far there is no evidence for any of these earlier peoples in the Mexican region, no Folsom points have been reported from south of the Rio Grande, so such a theory is purely speculative. The few finds that have been advanced as evidence of antiquity have been so convincingly refuted that at present no remains are known that can be regarded as comparable in age to Gypsum Cave, Folsom, or other North American complexes of that general period.[7] Lack of evidence in the current stage of investigations does not mean necessarily that there will be no discoveries of that nature. So little has been done in the north Mexican districts that there is almost no information about their archaeological manifestations. The problem may also be complicated by the fact that once the region of big game animals was left behind a certain change in cultural pattern was forced upon the people and they assumed more of the aspect of a food gathering group and their remains be more difficult to recognize as a result.

The second pre-ceramic phase, the Basket Maker horizon, rep-

[7] Martínez del Rio, Los Orígenes Americanos, 1936; Vaillant, Early Cultures, 1935, pp. 286–289.

resents the beginnings of the Anasazi pattern and is much better known than that of the preceding hunting peoples. The main center of development was in the Four Corners district where the states of Utah, Colorado, Arizona, and New Mexico meet, but traces of the complex are distributed sporadically over the province and peripheral variations occur beyond its southern and eastern boundaries and in the state of Coahuila. Materials from some of the caves in southern Chihuahua suggest a generalized form of the Basket Maker and may be an off-shoot from the same basic pattern, but at the present time there is not enough available information to attempt any correlation. Suggestion of the possibility of a relationship must suffice until there is more evidence on which to base conclusions.

The Basket Makers in their earliest recognized stage of development were in a state of transition between a nomadic, food-gathering hunting mode of life and a more settled style of existence in which agriculture was beginning to play an important part. The chief element in this addition to the economic pattern was maize. How this product, with the necessary knowledge on planting and cultivation, was obtained or whence it came is not known. There is little question but what it was introduced from the Mexican area and that it was transmitted through intermediary peoples, yet there is no information on the agents or avenues of diffusion. It was of great significance, however, because it provided the foundation on which the entire structure of ensuing cultural expansion rested.

The maize-growing industry, through its inherent nature, imposed a more sedentary existence on the people. During the planting season and the subsequent period lasting from the beginning of the ripening process until maturity and the crops were ready for use the people would not be able to wander far from their fields. As better methods of cultivation brought larger returns and produced surplus supplies storage places became necessary. With the harvest over and the grain stowed away there would be a tendency to remain in the vicinity of the food reserves both for the sake of convenience and as a matter of protection. Consequently the custom of roaming far and wide would decline and be replaced by the practice of remaining in restricted districts for longer intervals. A comparatively stable food supply and a more permanent place of abode gave opportunity for the development of new arts and industries and a broadening of the cultural pattern. That full advantage was taken of these favorable conditions is demonstrated by the growth in following periods.

Evidence for the Basket Makers is found in the lower levels of dry caves. The latter show that they served as temporary shelters and for storage places. In only a few examples were there accumulations of refuse, ashes and other debris indicative of continued occupation. For this reason it seems that the dwellings were erected in the open and because of their perishable nature little has survived to furnish information on their locations or general character. Traces of structures placed at the front of large open caverns where partial protection was provided by overhanging cliffs have been noted at a few sites. The evidence, such as it is, suggests a circular earth-lodge form of dwelling somewhat similar to the winter house of the Navajos, a habitation of poles covered with earth, but not enough was preserved to supply any specific details on methods of construction. Dug into the floors of most caves are circular or oval pits, many of them lined with stone slabs, that were the lower portions of granaries. Occasionally one is noted with a truncated pole, brush and plaster superstructure still in place over the pit, a form of construction that may have been carried over into house building, and several have been discovered filled with maize. The small, hard, yellow kernels, much like modern popcorn, being as bright and shiny as though only recently harvested.

The granaries frequently served in secondary capacities. Examples have been found lined with bark and grass, suggesting large nests, as though intended for sleeping places.[8] Many functioned as tombs for the dead and because of the custom of interring material objects, things used in life, with the deceased they now yield considerable information on the physical characteristics of the people and on their arts and industries. From the skeletal material comes evidence that the group was predominantly non-Mongoloid, that the people were short of stature and slender in build, that they were longheaded, and that they were the result of a blend of at least three basic strains, a racial mixture that took place prior to the migration from the Old World.[9]

The objects from the material culture show that the group was adept in the making of coiled baskets, twined-woven bags, ropes,

[8] Guernsey, Explorations in Northeastern Arizona, 1931, p. 114.
[9] Hooton, Indians of Pecos, 1930, pp. 355-362.

head bands, sandals, fur-cloth robes, short apronlike cord skirts for the women, game snares, and large nets for catching rabbits and other small animals. They had wooden planting sticks, curved sticks for use in dressing skins, wooden scoops for digging, and bone tools needed in weaving and work with hides. Articles for personal adornment consisted of a variety of beads made from stones of different colors, shells, seeds, and bones. Pendants were made from shells and stone, although the turquoise seems to have been unknown. There were feathered headdresses and feathered comblike hair ornaments. Weapons consisted of a foreshafted javelin hurled by means of the atlatl, short wooden clubs probably intended for fending, clubs fashioned from elk antlers, and stone knives.[10]

The Basket Makers had no true pottery but at about the end of their horizon, possibly in the transition from this stage to the one following, unfired vessels of clay that had been tempered with shredded cedar bark and grass were occasionally made. Many of these show the imprint of the baskets in which they were molded, both coiled and plaited forms being indicated, while a few suggest that they were fashioned entirely by hand. The walls or rims rising above the limits of the basket molds were formed with bands of clay and the vessels made without the aid of such supports were built up entirely through this early form of the coiling process. Other objects of unfired clay that made their appearance at approximately the same time were crude figurines of human females, small nipple-shaped objects of unknown purpose that might have been carrying basket representations for attachment to figurines, and models of bifurcated baskets. These, like the unfired pots, were prototypes for more elaborate forms in the subsequent stage and with the appearance of true ceramics they too were fired. It would seem that this complex of unfired clay articles represents the first impact of a new wave of influence that was sweeping into the area from the regions to the south. Present indications are that the influence was largely one of ideas rather than one produced by the transmission of actual objects because there is good reason to believe that the methods of manufacture were largely indigenous in development.[11]

The Basket Maker remains in peripheral parts of the province and in districts well beyond its borders are suggestive of the complex

[10] Guernsey and Kidder, Basket-Maker Caves, 1921; Guernsey, *op. cit.*, 1931.
[11] Morris, Beginnings of Pottery Making, 1927.

present in the main centers, but there are variations that can be attributed to cultural lag, to local modifications, and perhaps to influences from other sources. This is particularly true of the materials from the southeastern periphery in New Mexico and western Texas and from the caves in Coahuila. The latter appear unquestionably to belong to the basic Basket Maker, as shown by the skeletal remains [12] and various features of the material culture, yet there are differences sufficient to suggest that there may have been a separate center in this region and that developments were along similar, although not identical lines to those in the Anasazi centers. Being peripheral to both, the southeastern New Mexico southwestern Texas groups received influences from the two sources. There seems to have been a definite lag, however, in some cases. Comparative ages are not known. The Basket Makers in the Anasazi region are dated from the first through the sixth centuries A. D. on the basis of dendrochronology. Similar evidence is lacking for the peripheral and Coahuila remains. Hence it can only be assumed that they represent approximately the same chronological period. As a matter of fact sandals and woven bags from southeastern New Mexico through similarities and cross associations would place those remains on a level with the first pottery horizon farther north, although this outlying sector was still without ceramics. It is quite possible that there was a comparable lag with respect to the Coahuila center and the latter be on about the same time plane as the Anasazi. Cave materials from sites farther west in New Mexico are more in agreement with the main pattern and suggest closer correlation with the main centers.

The present picture, only a rough sketch at best, is that of a basic Basket Maker pattern spreading from the Four Corners region down across the Colorado Plateau, skirting along the Tularosa, Mogollon, and Mimbres Mountains and the headwaters of the San Francisco and Gila Rivers, and thence south into Chihuahua and Coahuila following the eastern fringes of the Sierra Madre for the most part. Indications for its presence in the west are not as definite and while it may have encompassed the Pacific slope of the cordillera the main suggestion in our present knowledge points toward the east. Influences from the Mexican area could have been transmitted through these people and thus reach the Four Corners center. In many respects this seems a more logical avenue for diffusion than that across

[12] Hooton, *op. cit.*, p. 238.

the desert regions south and west from the Anasazi province. Consideration of that phase of the subject, however, is more germane to the discussion of the Hohokam and Mexico and need not be dealt with here. The main contribution to the Basket Makers from Mexico was agriculture and, at a later date, the idea of pottery making and the production of figurines. The three did not reach the Anasazi as a complex, as some have stated, and the making of figurines did not persist through subsequent stages as it did in Mexico. There does not appear to have been any marked influence on other factors in the cultural complex. This may be due to lack of information or evidence for a comparable horizon farther south and future work in the latter region may demonstrate that many more Basket Maker traits were of Mexican origin. The question of a basic widespread Basket Maker pattern is involved and if, as has been suggested, the culture of the agricultural but pre-ceramic Mexicans was similar to that of the Basket Makers there will be the problem of determining what stems from that common background and what is to be attributed to diffusion and influence.

XXV

Mexican Influence upon the Indian Cultures of the Southwestern United States in the Sixteenth and Seventeenth Centuries

J. O. Brew *

THE ARCHAEOLOGY of that part of the United States known as the American Southwest has occupied the attention of students for the past sixty-four years. Numerous prehistoric sites have been excavated in Arizona, New Mexico, Colorado, and Utah and in peripheral areas surrounding these states. In the course of this work, which has disclosed the presence of at least two highly developed prehistoric cultures, the absence of evidence of any extensive connection with the high cultures of Mexico has continued to surprise the investigators. This absence is particularly noteworthy since it was originally supposed that the more advanced cultural traits of the area were derived from the south. Despite the original hypothesis, very few trade objects have been found which can be shown to have been manufactured in Mexico, and our studies seem to indicate that the rather extensive developments in architecture, ceremonialism, and the minor arts which we find in the Southwest between 500 and 1500 A. D. were largely indigenous. In the sixteenth century, however, this relative isolation was broken and the southwestern cultures came in contact with powerful influences emanating from the Valley of Mexico which brought about many significant changes in local modes of life.

The change did not arise from the northern expansion of the great American Indian cultures of Mexico but through the appearance in the Southwest of representatives of European civilization from the Spanish settlements in New Spain. Before the advent of the Spaniards, the higher cultures of the Southwest were existing in an advanced neolithic stage of development. Agriculture, with maize, beans, squash, and cotton, was well developed. The tools, however, were

* Dartmouth, A.B., 1928; Harvard, Thaw fellow, 1930–.

of wood, stone, and bone, and there were no domesticated animals except the turkey and the dog. The Spaniards brought metal tools, domestic animals, many new agricultural products, and a new form of ceremonialism, Christianity. The obvious superiority of many of these innovations led to immediate and enthusiastic adoption. Metal cutting tools easily superseded stone axes and knives, draught and riding animals revolutionized the economy and the relationships between the different groups, and sheep provided not only their wool as a new source of textile material but also a new and important addition to the food supply. The invaders brought the horse, ox, sheep, and pig. The most important of the new agricultural products were wheat, melons, and peaches.

The first appearance of the Europeans north of what is now the Mexican border was in 1539, when an expedition led by Fray Marcos de Niza and a Barbary Coast negro, Estevan, entered the present state of Arizona from Sonora and proceeded to the pueblo towns of Cibola of which Zuñi in western New Mexico is a modern survival.[1] This expedition was unsuccessful. Estevan, proceeding in advance against the orders of Fray Marcos was killed by the inhabitants of the Zuñi town of Hawikuh, and the Friar, fearful of approaching the town, contented himself with an observation from a distant hilltop and returned to Mexico City.

The report of Fray Marcos of the wealth and extent of the Cibola towns was enthusiastic and highly exaggerated. As a result, the viceroy Mendoza commissioned Francisco Vázquez Coronado to lead an expedition north. The new expedition set out from Compostela in Guadalajara with from 250 to 300 horsemen, 70 to 200 footmen, 300 to 1000 friendly Indians, and a liberal supply of baggage, extra horses, oxen, cows, sheep, and perhaps swine.[2]

Hawikuh was reached and taken after a battle on July 7, 1540. The remainder of the Zuñi towns surrendered immediately and the expedition continued its campaign which resulted in the discovery and subjugation of Acoma and many of the Rio Grande pueblos of New Mexico and the Hopi towns in what is now northeastern Arizona.[3]

The members of the Coronado expedition were pitifully disappointed at the poverty of the Pueblo villages and returned to Mexico

[1] Bandelier, Contributions, 1890.
[2] Hodge, Hawikuh, 1937.
[3] Winship, Coronado Expedition, 1896.

leaving two priests at Zuñi who were subsequently martyred. The report of this exploration was so discouraging that forty years passed before the Spaniards made any further efforts in this direction. Then, in 1581, an expedition entered the Pueblo country under the leadership of Fray Augustín Rodríguez (Friar Ruiz) who was accompanied by Fray Francisco López, Fray Juan de Santa Maria, and Francisco Sánchez Chamuscado in charge of a detachment of eight soldiers. Articles for trade and six hundred head of stock were taken along. This expedition followed a different route and came up the Rio Grande.[4] All three of the friars were killed and Chamuscado perished on the return journey.

More successful was the next expedition in the following year (1582). Fray Bernardino Beltrán, financed and accompanied by Antonio de Espejo, a prosperous merchant, followed the route of the Rodriguez expedition up the Rio Grande in an attempt to rescue the two friars of the previous expedition who were known to have been living when the surviving soldiers left New Mexico. These were found to have been murdered, but the Espejo expedition conducted intensive explorations into the Zuñi and Hopi region in a futile search for reputedly rich mining districts. This part of the expedition, too, was a failure, but much additional information about the inhabitants was obtained and, again, European artifacts and animals were distributed among the Indians.[5]

Up to this time the efforts of the Spaniards in the Southwest were purely exploratory. No successful attempts at colonization were made until the very end of the sixteenth century. An abortive colonizing expedition (the first) was led by Castaño de Sosa in 1590, with approximately two hundred people, including women. This expedition engaged in a battle with the inhabitants of Pecos pueblo, was recalled, and the leader arrested for unauthorized exploration. Following this was another purely exploratory party under the leadership of Leiva de Bonilla about which little is known and which seems to have passed through the Pueblo region and to have been cut to pieces by Indians presumably in the vicinity of what is now eastern Kansas.

In 1598, however, the Spaniards succeeded in colonizing in the Rio Grande valley near San Juan pueblo, north of the present Santa Fe, New Mexico, at the confluence of the Rio Grande and the Rio

[4] Gallegos, Relation, 1927.
[5] Luxan, Espejo Expedition, 1929.

Chama. The leader of the first colonization was Don Juan de Oñate.[6] Approximately ten years after the original settlement the government was moved from San Gabriel, which was across the river from San Juan pueblo, to Santa Fé. The latter city remained the capital of the province until annexation by the United States.

From this time on, the area under Spanish domination was gradually extended. Between 1610 and 1630 tribute was received in the Rio Grande from the Pueblo nations of Acoma, Cibola (Zuñi), and Tusayan (Moqui or Hopi).[7] Colonization continued in the fertile Rio Grande valley but elsewhere the penetration was largely religious. The avowed purpose of the Spanish expansion toward the north was two-fold, search for gold and search for souls. The religious side of the movement was led by the Franciscan Friars. When the promises of great mineral wealth were not fulfilled, the zeal of the friars was in a large measure responsible for the continuation of the colony. It is the tragedy of the Spaniards of New Mexico that they settled down to eke out a poor existence from farming and stock raising in valleys between mountains wherein the metals they sought lay undiscovered.

Oñate divided the country into seven mission districts and the first part of the seventeenth century saw rapid expansion of Franciscan activity. Although the figures cannot be thoroughly relied on, it is generally believed that there were eleven missions by 1617, thirty-three in 1630, and forty in 1680. These missions spread not only the gospel of Jesus Christ but also, and in some cases more successfully, the new cultural features brought from Europe. Even then contact with Mexico City was far from frequent. The distance was about 1500 miles, of which at least one third was semi-desert. Although special trips were made occasionally, the regular means of communication was the mission supply caravan. Mr. France Scholes, who has made an exhaustive study of the communications during the seventeenth century,[8] estimates that the caravan arrived in Santa Fe on an average of once every three years. A few luxury goods were carried by these caravans, but the largest part of the shipments consisted of hardware, arms and ammunition, clothing, and supplies (carpets, vestments, altar vessels, etc.) for the missions.

Most of our knowledge of this century and its trade comes from

[6] Bolton, Spanish Exploration, 1930.
[7] Scholes, Civil Government, 1935.
[8] Scholes, Supply Service, 1930.

the students of early Spanish-American documents, but some digging has been done in the ruins of the period. Hodge's History of Hawikuh has recently been published [9] and excavations have uncovered the church at Pecos and at Quarai in the Rio Grande region. The most recent archaeological investigation into seventeenth century remains is in the Hopi country of northeastern Arizona, farthest removed of all from the Santa Fe capital, where the Peabody Museum of Harvard University has been excavating the prehistoric and early historic pueblo at Awatovi near the end of Antelope Mesa.[10]

The site of Awatovi covers approximately twenty-five acres with an accumulation of ruined buildings and other occupational debris which sometimes attains a height of thirty feet. During extensive excavations in prehistoric sections of the town no Mexican objects have appeared. Digging in the seventeenth century town, however, has added materially to our knowledge of the Spanish Southwest and of the nature of the early contacts between native and foreign cultures.

The Awatovi mission was authorized in 1629 along with those at Acoma and in the Zuni country. Because of the distance from the capitol at Santa Fe, the author, who has charge of the Awatovi excavations, expected to find a small church and a rather make-shift establishment. Instead, at this outpost, which with the neighboring missions of Shungopovi and Oraibi was the most remote in all New Spain, the remains of three churches were found, two of which were over one hundred feet in length. One of the churches possessed a large transept and the architectural features, arrangements of baptisteries, sacristies, altars, etc., were liturgically correct. The priests lived in a well-built friary arranged in standard Franciscan fashion around the four sides of a courtyard or sacred garden. It is interesting to note the power of Franciscan formalism which produced in the rough materials of northern Arizona and by means of native labour an establishment as accurate and complete in major architectural details as might be expected in the ruder regions of contemporary Europe.

The mission of San Bernardino de Aguatobi was sacked and resident priests were killed in the Pueblo rebellion of 1680, when the concerted efforts of all the Pueblo Indian tribes expelled the Spaniards from New Mexico. The conquerors returned in 1692 and the

[9] Hodge, Hawikuh, 1937.
[10] Brew, Awatovi, 1937.

small third church at Awatovi was built subsequently in the east side of the original friary quadrangle. The fact that Awatovi alone, of all the towns of the Hopi country, reaccepted Spanish suzerainty and permitted the return of the priests probably played a part in its destruction in a civil war during the winter of 1700–1701.

The story of the original impact of the new culture upon the Indians of the Southwest is gradually being revealed by excavation and by continued research in early Spanish and Mexican archives. The nature of the first two centuries of European influence is reflected in the findings of the Awatovi Expedition. The sixteenth century was one of exploration and discovery when some features of Spanish civilization were introduced, but the actual contacts were few with many years intervening, and the total effect was relatively small. The seventeenth century was one of colonization and intensive missionary activity and marked the widest geographical extent of direct European influence until the advent of the North Europeans from the eastern United States in the middle of the nineteenth century. During the seventeenth century at Awatovi, with one side of the main plaza occupied by a large Franciscan establishment, the Indians had ample opportunity to observe and to experiment with the details of Spanish civilization. The profusion of peach stones and sheep bones in the houses and refuse mounds of the native seventeenth century town bears evidence that they seized upon and profited by the outstanding elements of the material side of the new culture. That the non-material or spiritual innovations did not fare so well is shown by the continued presence of native *kivas*, the subterranean Pueblo ceremonial chambers, and the strong survival to the present day of relatively pure native ceremonies with costumes and symbolism surprisingly similar to those shown on the many mural paintings discovered at Awatovi on the walls of prehistoric *kivas*. This is but one of many illustrations of strong eclecticism shown by the Pueblo Indians in their contacts with White civilization.

It is interesting that the only object of native Mexican manufacture found at Awatovi came to light in the sanctuary of one of the Franciscan churches, Church B. This was a small fragment of carved jade (Fig. 28). The maximum dimensions of the fragment are 4 cm. × 3.3 cm. and it is 1.5 cm. thick. It is apparently a fragment of an amulet in what is known to students of Middle American archaeology as the Oaxacan style, although their manufacture seems to have been widespread and not restricted to the region of Oaxaca.

Jade carvings of this type are illustrated and described in Lothrop's "Zacualpa, a Study of Ancient Quiché Artifacts," [11] an account of finds at the Maya site of Zacualpa, to the east of Chichicastenango in the upper drainage of the Motagua River in Guatemala. The following quotation will serve to identify the type. "The Oaxacan style is typified by . . . pieces [which] have faces in relatively high relief and are marked by use of the tubular drill. . . . With this implement

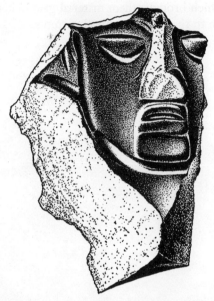

FIG. 28. OAXACAN CARVED JADE, FOUND AT AWATOVI, ARIZONA: ACTUAL SIZE

it is possible to cut not only circles but the arcs of circles, which evidently were made by tipping the drill at an angle so that only part of it touched the stone. Some of the specimens in this group may have been imported, but we believe most of them to have been manufactured locally. That the inhabitants of Zacualpa used the tubular drill is attested by the [an] unfinished object." The wide distribution of the manufacture of the Oaxacan type amulet prevents the establishment of the source whence the Awatovi specimen came. The discovery of the specimen in one of the Franciscan churches, however, suggests that it did not arrive in Arizona as an article of prehistoric

[11] Lothrop, Zacualpa, 1936.

Indian trade but that it was brought from Mexico by one of the priests.

In concluding this brief account of sixteenth and seventeenth century contacts between the Pueblo Indians of the Southwest and the Spaniards of Mexico, to the author the outstanding impression is not of the changes brought about, but rather the vigour with which the native groups resisted the fundamental changes to which they were exposed in the structure of their cultures and accepted only those new features which brought them material gain. These they adapted in large measure to their basic cultural patterns.

XXVI

MIDDLE AMERICAN INFLUENCES ON THE ARCHAEOLOGY OF THE SOUTHEASTERN UNITED STATES

Philip Phillips *

THERE must be something in the nature of Southeastern culture that impels students to seek its origins elsewhere. Lacking a chronology of its own, it is perhaps inevitable that its more advanced phases should appear as derived from outside sources. The Southwest, I believe, has passed through a similar experience—has only lately achieved a grudging independence from the Middle American hegemony. Will the Southeast be able to do the like? The extensive excavations now in progress throughout the Southern States will doubtless furnish the necessary time perspective, but one may predict that a large proportion of the more advanced and characteristic traits of Southeastern culture will still appear as exotic and we shall still be in search of their origins. And with better success, we may be sure, than has attended such efforts thus far.

The reasons for unsuccess lie, partly in the nature of Southeastern archaeology, which presents a complexity probably far more apparent than real, but not less in the manner of procedure, which, by singling out individual traits quite apart from their associations and general cultural setting, have at best merely produced similarities with other areas without throwing any light on the nature and extent of the implied connections.[1] The present effort, dealing with the possibilities of relationship between the Southeast and Middle America will, at the risk of prodigious oversimplification, attempt to avoid this criticism.

When we speak of Southeastern culture harboring influences from

* Williams, A.B., 1922; Harvard, M.Arch., 1927; Ph.D., 1940; now Assistant Curator, Southeastern Archaeology, Peabody Museum.
[1] Exception to the above statement must be made in favor of Vaillant's Ceramic Resemblances of Central and North America, 1932, which not only finds in the Mississippi Valley an association of Middle American traits, but attempts to account for their presence in that area.

Middle America, what do we mean? Not Southeastern culture generally, if there be such a thing, but rather a particular phase [2] of it, sometimes referred to as the "mound-building ceramic culture" of the Southeast. The expression is still imprecise, for upon investigation it becomes clear that the type of culture in question, though distributed pretty much throughout the Southeast, can be referred back to an axis lying along the middle and lower reaches of the Mississippi. Its clearest exemplification is to be found in the culture long recognized, and now classificatorily sanctified, as "Middle Mississippi." A brief description of this culture can be made to touch most, if not all, the supposed Middle American features in the Southeast, and will furnish at the same time something of an archaeological setting to the need for which I have just referred.[3]

Middle Mississippi is essentially a riverine culture based on bottom land agriculture, though to what extent agriculture dominated the economy is uncertain.[4] Its most conspicuous characteristic is the use of mounds as foundation platforms for "domiciliary" structures, generally speaking of religious or ceremonial nature. As a result of their function and the ubiquitous tendency to repeated rebuilding (itself a rather striking Middle American trait) Middle Mississippi mounds generally reveal upon excavation a series of super-imposed floors, post-mold patterns, fireplaces, etc. pertaining to the wooden structures at the various levels. A rectangular truncated pyramidal form seems to have been the fundamental type, sometimes elaborated by the addition of terraces or "aprons," ramps, and even stairways of clay or logs. The question of exterior finish is not without interest. Several recorded instances of mounds covered with a facing of stiff river clay would imply that they were kept clear of vegetation, that, in other words, clay was used architecturally in a manner

[2] Such words as "phase," "aspect," etc. as used in this paper are not to be taken in any classificatory sense. Not the least objection to the McKern system of classification is that it has usurped some of the most indispensable words in the archaeologist's vocabulary.

[3] The "oversimplification" mentioned above . . . I believe the majority of archaeological opinion would support the generalization, but it is not yet susceptible of proof. For classification of Mississippi culture, see Cole and Deuel, 1937, and the report of the Indianapolis Conference, listed in the Bibliography as Indianapolis Conference, 1935.

[4] Swanton is of the opinion that the river bottom occupation in the Southeast generally was earlier and on the whole less agricultural than that of the inland farmers, such as the Choctaw, who actually raised a surplus of corn for exchange with less favored neighbors. See Cultural Province of the Southeast, 1935, p. 377.

analogous to the stone veneer of Middle American pyramids. That such practice was general, however, is not indicated by existing evidence.

Mounds are characteristically grouped about a "plaza," not seldom with considerable formality of arrangement involving a consistent orientation approximate to the cardinal directions. An assemblage of this type bears striking resemblance to the plan of a small Maya site of the Great Period. Circumvallations, originally crowned by clay-covered stockades with projecting bastions, another Middle American trait,[5] are common but by no means universal.

Of house types and methods of construction generally, little is known. Most indications point to a simple rectangular single-roomed type of dwelling without specialized entrance or other features. Larger ceremonial houses or "temples" were not more elaborate. Construction seems to have been chiefly of a bent pole framework covered by cane, thatch or clay daub. Interior posts occasionally indicate a less flimsy rigid-frame type of construction.

The situation in respect to burial mounds (as distinct from domiciliary mounds containing incidental burials) is difficult to generalize. For the most part they do not occur, burials being in "cemeteries," or simply in and about the houses, or in the dump. When they do appear, it is seldom in unambiguous form, but rather as concentrations of interments made by placing the bodies on the surface and covering them with earth. The resulting accumulation becomes in course of time a low irregular elevation, without its becoming clear whether or not any deliberate mound-building intent was at work;—a very different sort of affair from the monumental tumuli of the earlier Hopewellian peoples of the Southeast. Burials are predominantly in the extended position, though secondary "bundle" burials are frequent and flexure occasional. Log tombs are sometimes encountered, and in the Cumberland district of Tennessee stone cist graves are the rule. Generally speaking, however, burials are casual, unelaborated, though usually well furnished with artifacts, particularly in the form of pottery.

Stone work, less important quantitatively than pottery, is not less highly developed. The usual assortment of points and other small implements in chipped stone need not detain us here. Larger chipped implements such as celts and adzes, and the specially characteristic agricultural tools generally described as "hoes" and "spades," are im-

[5] Beals, Comparative Ethnology, 1932, p. 110.

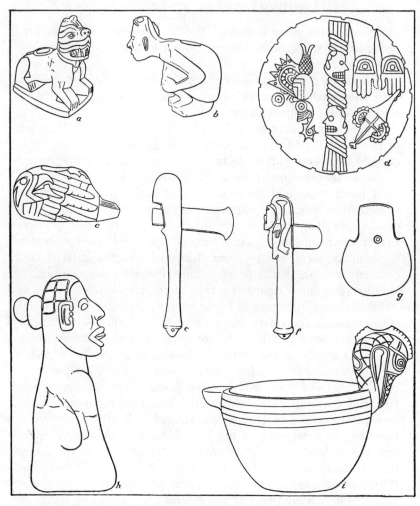

Fig. 29. Stone Implements Suggestive of Middle American Influence

a. Stone Pipe, Moundville, Alabama. (After Moore, Black Warrior River, 1905, Figs. 1–3.)
b. Stone Pipe, Moundville, Alabama. (After Moore, Black Warrior River, 1905, Fig. 132.)
c. Stone Pipe, Moundville, Ala. (After Moore, Moundville Revisited, 1907, Fig. 83.)
d. Stone Disc, Moundville, Ala. (After Moore, Black Warrior River, 1905, Fig. 5.)
e. Monolithic Ax, Etowah, Georgia. (After Moorehead, Etowah, 1932, Fig. 52a.)
f. Monolithic Ax, probably Tennessee. (After MacCurdy, Cult of Ax, 1916, p. 302.)
g. Stone Spud, Moundville, Alabama. (After Moore, Moundville Revisited, 1907, Fig. 90.)
h. Stone Statue, Etowah, Georgia. (After Moorehead, Etowah, 1932, Fig. 3.)
i. Stone Vase, Moundville, Alabama. (After Moore, Black Warrior River, 1905, Fig. 167.)

portant diagnostics of the culture. The culmination of flint work is seen in the beautiful long blades often cited as evidence of contact with Mexico. In polished stone the dominant ax form is the celt, which displays in addition to the normal rectanguloid form several elaborations of probable ceremonial significance. (Fig. 29, e–g).[6] Among these the monolithic ax, sporadic in appearance but pretty certainly of Middle Mississippi association, has excited considerable discussion, to which nothing can be added here, except to record agreement with Lovén's belief that an Antillean derivation is extremely unlikely.[7] Discoidals of all sizes, culminating in the large biconcave type prized by collectors, are highly characteristic but not especially revealing of remoter connections. More interesting are the large flat circular (rarely rectangular) "palettes," sometimes embellished with engraved designs in a style of which I shall have more to say presently (Fig. 29, d).[8] Among objects that might well qualify as minor sculpture may be reckoned the rare stone vessels with zoomorphic appendages (Fig. 29, i), the ruder "idols" (Fig. 29, h), and, of greater interest from our present point of view, the large stone effigy pipes (Fig. 29, a–c). The composite monster represented in Fig. 29, a, is of particular importance. Compounded of serpent, cat, possibly eagle, and (not impossibly) bat, this grotesque creature in whole or in part continually reappears in Middle Mississippi art. The Middle Americanist will be able to judge to what extent it is related to the bird-serpent-jaguar composite so widely distributed in Middle and South America.

Materials of bone, horn and shell are varied and abundant, but, generally speaking, of no great importance in the present connection. The exception is, of course, the highly characteristic development of engraving upon large marine shells or upon circular "gorgets" cut from them, a subject always to the fore in any discussion of the Southeast-Middle American problem. Among the more abstract and conventionalized figures are a number of motives of possible Middle American extraction. The Greek cross, a very common device in Middle Mississippi shellwork, has of course a world-wide distribution, but certain elaborations upon it, such as the guilloche

[6] MacCurdy was, I believe, the first to point out the evident ritual importance of the celt in the Southeast. See The Cult of the Ax, 1916.

[7] Lovén, Origins of Tainan Culture, 1935, p. 161.

[8] For the object itself, however, irrespective of decoration, the closest analogies lie with the palettes of the Hohokam of the Southwest. See Haury, Snaketown I, 1937, p. 121 et seq.

(Fig. 30, *l*) also found in Mexico and in late "Mexicanized" Maya, are not to be dismissed as lightly.[9] The scalloped disk (Fig. 30, *j*) has received some attention with a view to its possible calendrical significance. Unfortunately the number of scallops approximates, but in the majority of cases does not correspond to, the sacred 13, and the four arms of the central whorl become at times perversely three. The "woodpecker" type (Fig. 30, *k*) is interesting chiefly from the fact that the looped square from which the bird heads depend is said to be a common Mexican device.[10] Finally the spider (Fig. 30, *h*) is an emblem of Tezcatlipoca and as such appears frequently in Mexican art.[11] Its presence alone in the Middle Mississippi would excite little wonder; in conjunction with other factors of possible Mexican significance it acquires a certain importance.

In the anthropomorphic designs (Fig. 30, *a–g, i*) it is more a question of general stylistic tendencies than precise symbolic correspondences. Comparisons naturally center about the shell work of

[9] Morris, Warriors, 1931, Fig. 261 b.
[10] Holmes, Art in Shell, 1883, p. 285.
[11] Nuttall, Old and New World Civilizations, 1901, p. 44 *et seq.*

FIG. 30. SHELL GORGETS WITH FIGURES SUGGESTIVE OF MIDDLE AMERICAN INFLUENCE

a. Shell Gorget, Eddyville, Kentucky. (After MacCurdy, Shell Gorgets, 1913, Fig. 71.)
b. Shell Gorget, St. Marys, Perry County, Missouri. (After MacCurdy, Shell Gorgets, 1913, Fig. 70.)
c. Shell Gorget, New Madrid County, Missouri. (After Thurston, Antiquities, 1897, Plate 17.)
d. Shell Gorget, Etowah, Georgia. (After Moorehead, Etowah, 1932, Fig. 29.)
e. Gorget, Castalian Springs, Sumner County, Tennessee. (After Thruston, Antiquities, 1897, Fig. 247.)
f. Shell Gorget, Moundville, Alabama. (After Moore, Moundville Revisited, 1907, Fig. 97.)
g. Shell Gorget, Moundville, Alabama. (After Moore, Black Warrior River, 1905, Fig. 34.)
h. Shell Gorget, Perry County, Missouri. (After MacCurdy, Shell Gorgets, 1913, Fig. 67.)
i. Shell Gorget, Moundville, Alabama. (After Moore, Moundville Revisited, 1907, Fig. 98.)
j. Shell Gorget, Nashville, Tennessee. (After Holmes, Art in Shell, 1883, Pl. 55, No. 1.)
k. Shell Gorget, Mississippi. (After Holmes, Art in Shell, 1883, Pl. 58.)
l. Shell Gorget, Perry County, Missouri. (After MacCurdy, Shell Gorgets, 1913, Fig. 62.)

FIG. 30. (For description, see facing page.)

the Huasteca, which, though unquestionably similar in technique, is not, to my way of thinking particularly closely affiliated in style.[12] From a more general point of view, however, the manner of presentation, the bearing of the figures, particularly their sprightly dance-like attitudes, is inescapably Middle American, the nearest approach to the style perhaps being found in the codices. To account for this tendency without some sort of contact involves a terrific strain on the theory of "psychic unity."

In respect to the use of copper, the situation in Middle Mississippi is similar to what must have obtained in Mexico before the late introduction of higher metallurgical techniques from the south.[13] That is to say there was a familiarity with various cold-hammered techniques as well as the art of overlaying on other materials and the decorative, technique of repoussé. Thin plates, of use unknown, with elaborate designs in this medium are to be seen in Fig. 31. The rarity of such objects in the Southeast is proverbial and their occurrence is generally without precise archaeological association. Sufficient evidence, however, both external and internal links them with the Middle Mississippi culture. Aside from a slight superiority of finish there are no essential differences in subject matter and style from the shell engravings just referred to. Certain details such as the hand on jaw (Fig. 31, h) and the eye in hand (Fig. 31, i) point even more sug-

[12] Starr, Shell Gorget from Mexico, 1897; Holmes, Shell Ornaments from Kentucky and Mexico, 1903.

[13] Rivet and Arsandaux, Metallurgie Mexicaine, 1921, pp. 262–263.

FIG. 31. COPPER PLATES WITH FIGURES IN REPOUSSÉ, SUGGESTIVE OF MIDDLE AMERICAN INFLUENCE

a. Copper Plate, Etowah, Georgia. (After Moorehead, Etowah, 1932, Fig. 14.)
b. Copper Plate, Etowah, Georgia. (After Moorehead, Etowah, 1932, Fig. 15.)
c. Hair Ornament(?), Moundville, Alabama. (After Moore, Black Warrior River, 1905, Fig. 105.)
d. Copper Plate, Etowah, Georgia. (After Moorehead, Etowah, 1932, Fig. 16.)
e. Copper Plate, Malden, Dunklin County, Missouri. (After Fowke, Antiquities of Missouri, 1910, Pl. 18.)
f. Copper Plate, Henry Island, Alabama. (After Moore, Tennessee River, 1915, Fig. 52.)
g. Copper Plate, Etowah, Georgia. (After Moorehead, Etowah, 1932, Fig. 9.)
h. Copper Plate, Malden, Dunklin County, Missouri. (After Fowke, Antiquities of Missouri, 1910, Pl. 16.)
i. Copper Pendant, Moundville, Alabama. (After Moore, Moundville Revisited, 1907, Fig. 101.)
j. Copper Plate, Spiro Mound, Arkansas, University of Arkansas Museum.

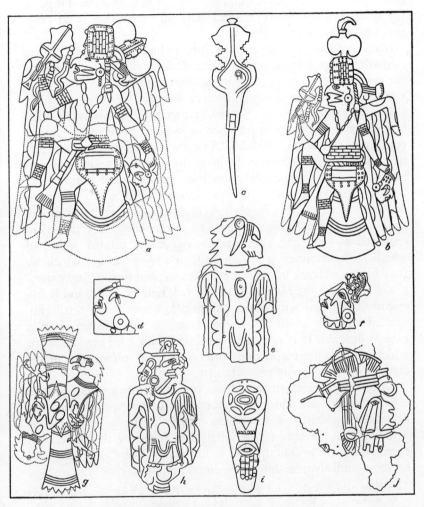

Fig. 31. (For description, see facing page.)

gestively toward Middle America, but to regard the plates as direct importations from Mexico, as some have done, seems altogether unwarranted. The few examples of Mexican repoussé I have seen show little similarity even in technique to say nothing of style. To go to the other extreme, however, and deny all connection is an exaggeration of scientific caution.

Middle Mississippi pottery is varied and highly developed relative to that of other Southeastern cultures. This is evidenced not only by the range of vessel shapes and decorative techniques, but also by the wide variety of uses to which pottery was put, as: pipes, figurines, ladles, rattles, pot supports, "anvils," trowels, ear-spools, beads, marbles, disks, etc. The mere presence of some of these minor objects contains a suggestion of Middle American influence, but more significant in this connection is the generally dominant position of pottery with respect to the total content of archaeological culture.

Wares include a *plain drab*, the common utility ware, with various decorative variants involving chiefly incision and punctation; *polished drab*, the dominant mortuary ware, occasionally incised or engraved (i. e. incised after firing); *red ware*; painted wares, of which the commonest is *red-on-buff*, or *red-and-white*, which by the addition of black becomes a *polychrome*; and finally "*lost color*," which may take the form of black on red, buff or white, and is frequently combined with direct painting.[14] A specialized textile impressed type, the so-called "salt-pan ware," is very characteristic in certain districts. It is not to be confused with cord-marked ware, which, though present in the more northerly manifestations of the culture, is not generally characteristic.

Generally speaking embellishment is marked by an emphasis upon elaboration of form and plastic adornment at the expense of surface decoration, which is on the whole extremely simple. So characteristic in fact is the tendency to vitalize all forms by the addition of theriomorphic elements that the name "Effigy Ware" has been used by some students to designate the entire complex.

[14] "Lost color" is the term first applied by W. H. Holmes to a decorative technique in which the design is executed in a stopping-out medium, after which the vessel is treated to an all-over coating of pigment. The stopping-out medium is then removed, leaving the design in the body color of the vessel. In brief, the *batik* method is adapted to pottery decoration. The fact that much of the "painted" pottery of the Middle Mississippi was decorated in this fashion is not yet generally recognized. To Max Uhle, I believe, belongs the credit of first calling attention to its presence. See Der mittelamerikanische Ursprung der Mound-builder und Pueblocivilisation, 1935, p. 679.

An adequate discussion of Middle Mississippi pottery from the point of view of possible Middle American connections would be many times the length of this paper. I can only indicate briefly a few of the points about which such a discussion would revolve. To begin with the companionship of drab, red ware and red-on-buff with polishing over the decoration finds a general parallelism in the early cultures of the Valley of Mexico and in the early phases of the Hohokam and Mogollon in the Southwest.[15] It would seem that Middle Mississippi pottery derives these most fundamental characteristics from a ceramic continuity that includes the cultures named. Unfortunately the problem is not as simple as that statement would imply. Thanks to the stratigraphic studies now being carried out by Ford and his associates in the Lower Mississippi, it is becoming evident that some of these wares, notably the red and painted types, have enjoyed a longer history in the Mississippi valley than first supposed. In other words, it cannot be held that this "standard association" of wares, however closely paralleled in other areas, was introduced into the Middle Mississippi in toto. Whether there was an earlier drive of influence, or whether such parallelism is merely the result of convergent evolution, will only become apparent with further knowledge of the local antecedents of Middle Mississippi. On the other hand, whatever their earlier history, there are good reasons for supposing that the spread of red and painted pottery within the Middle Mississippi itself was late, so late in fact as not to have reached some of the northern and eastern centers of the culture. In sites on the lower Ohio, and in the rich archaeological district around Nashville on the Cumberland, there is little or no red ware and the only decoration involving the use of pigment is in lost color. Southeast Missouri appears as an intermediate region in which a preliminary layout of design in lost color is reinforced by direct painting. In eastern Arkansas and western Mississippi, on the other hand, we get a clear dominance of direct painting over lost color. It would seem therefore that lost color is a separate problem, having nothing to do

---

[15] Haury, *op. cit.*, p. 229. "However, it is noticeable that as one goes back in time in Mogollon and Hohokam ceramics there is a convergence of characters, as plain and redware companionship, polishing over the decoration, and color and design similarities, which would tend to bring the two very closely together. For this reason it is suspected that they shared a common origin, or that the one inspired the other. If the former be true, the parent complex may not have been native to the Southwest but was widespread and one from which most, if not all, American pottery took its rise."

with the continuity mentioned above. The fact that it has not yet been reported from the Southwest encourages the supposition that it represents a direct importation from Middle America, where it enjoyed a wide distribution from early to late times.[16]

A second point has to do with a rather specialized type of decoration. Post-fired incision or engraving is primarily a Lower rather than a Middle Mississippi trait. It was used in the more southerly centers of the latter, however, generally without subsequent paint-filling, to produce designs of considerable interest here (Fig. 32). Similar in both subject matter and style to the shell and copper work already discussed, these designs show even more unequivocally their Middle American origin. This comes out particularly in the feathered serpent motive (Fig. 32, *f*, *g*, *l*) and the death symbols (Fig. 32, *a*, *d*, *e*, *i*), for both of which very close counterparts are to be found in Mexican art. The problem here is whether technique and style

[16] For the distribution of lost color, or negative painting as some prefer to call it, in Middle and South America, see Linné, Teotihuacan, 1934; Lothrop, Zacualpa, 1936.

Fig. 32. Designs from Jars Suggestive of Middle American Influence

a. Design from Jar, Wells, Mississippi. (After Brown, Mississippi, 1926, Fig. 279.)
b. Design from Bottle, Moundville, Alabama. (After Moore, Black Warrior River, 1905, Fig. 88.)
c. Design from Jar, Moundville, Alabama. (After Moore, Moundville Revisited, 1907, Fig. 67.)
d. Design from Jar, Moundville, Alabama. (After Moore, Black Warrior River, 1905, Fig. 147.)
e. Design from Painted Bottle, Franklin County, Mississippi. (After Holmes, Pottery of Eastern United States, 1903, Pl. 56, *b*.)
f. Design from Bottle, Moundville, Alabama. (After Moore, Moundville Revisited, 1907, Fig. 56.)
g. Design from Bottle, Moundville, Alabama. (After Moore, Moundville Revisited, 1907, Fig. 65.)
h. Design from Bottle, Moundville, Alabama. (After Moore, Moundville Revisited, 1907, Fig. 5.)
i. Design from Bottle, Moundville, Alabama. (After Moore, Black Warrior River, 1905, Fig. 63.)
j. Design from Jar, Moundville, Alabama. (After Moore, Moundville Revisited, 1907, Fig. 42.)
k. Design from Bottle, Moundville, Alabama. (After Moore, Black Warrior River, 1905, Fig. 22.)
l. Design from Pottery Bowl, near Augusta, Savannah River, Richmond County, Georgia. (After Holmes, Pottery of Eastern United States, 1903, Pl. 119.)
m. Design from Bottle, Moundville, Alabama. (After Moore, Black Warrior River, 1905, Fig. 9.)

Fig. 32. (For description, see facing page.)

were introduced together, or whether, as seems more likely, the style, already developed in another medium, found a technique ready to hand, in which case the significance from a purely ceramic standpoint would be slight.

The question of shapes must be entered into, unfortunately, in somewhat more detail. The reader is referred to Vaillant's excellent paper, already cited, in which on the basis of certain specialized shapes the author finds a strong connection between the Mississippi Valley and an early ceramic complex in Middle America known as influence "Q." [17] Vaillant does not deny the evidences already mentioned (shell work, copper repoussé, engraved decorations on pottery, etc.), but minimizes their importance, arguing that they represent a ceremonial infiltration for which a very few individuals may have been responsible, whereas the evidence of pottery shapes suggests to him a more fundamental and earlier drive of culture more Maya, or even pre-Maya, than Mexican. Since this idea is at variance with the conclusions toward which this paper is making, I am obliged to consider the point at length.

The shapes in question are as follows: (1) funnel-neck jar; (2) composite silhouette bowl ("cazuela"); (3) tripod support; (4) annular base; (5) spouted vessel ("teapot"); (6) spout handle ("stirrup-mouth"); (7) double-bodied vessel; (8) shoe-form pot; (9) effigies (both animal and human); (10) head vessel (human); (11) vessel with the head or features attached.

1–2. The funnel-neck jar and composite silhouette bowl are at home in the "Caddo" facies of the Red River, but are not characteristic of Middle Mississippi, therefore fall outside the scope of the present discussion.

3. Tripod support of vessels, particularly bottles, an important Middle Mississippi diagnostic, gives the strongest appearance of Middle American derivation, but not necessarily an early one, as Vaillant readily admits.[18] The possibility of a Southwestern origin,[19] however, must not be overlooked, nor the possibility of a local outgrowth from an earlier tetrapod, for whose existence we now have abundant evidence, following the line of development in Middle America.

4. The annular base is in better case than the tripod, since it is said

[17] Vaillant, *op. cit.*
[18] Vaillant, *op. cit.*, p. 13.
[19] Haury, *op. cit.*, Figs. 108, 109.

not to occur in the Southwest. The simplicity of the device, however, makes an independent invention by no means out of the question.

5. The teapot is a problem all by itself. Its extremely narrow distribution in the Middle Mississippi, coupled with demonstrable lateness in time would seem to argue strongly against derivation from an early horizon in Middle America. Furthermore, an extremely good case can be made out in favor of a local evolution from an animal effigy in which the tail becomes metamorphosed into a spout.[20]

6. The spout- or "stirrup"-handle, as it is called in Andean archaeology, could as well be derived from the Southwest as from Middle America, since its occurrence there is not more rare than in the Middle Mississippi. Again, if one prefers, a very plausible line of evolution can be supplied without going outside the Middle Mississippi area.

7. Against the double-bodied jar may be urged the double objection, that it occurs in the Southwest and is in any case a trait that could easily arise independently in separated areas.

8. The shoe-form has such a wide distribution in the New World generally, both early and late, that it is of significance as evidence for specific contacts. Examples are to be found in the Middle Mississippi with practically identical counterparts in both Southwest and Middle America.

9. The subject of effigies is too broad to be covered by a brief generalization. While undoubtedly many points of similarity between Middle Mississippi effigies and those of Q-influenced cultures of Middle America are to be found, in my opinion, the closest all-around affinities in style and treatment are with the Casas Grandes culture of Chihuahua, a purely Southwestern manifestation.

10. For one type of effigy, the so-called head vessel, in which the entire pot represents a human head, there is no counterpart in the Casas Grandes, I believe. But here again, as in the case of the teapot, an extremely limited distribution suggests a local specialization rather than introduction from an outside source.

11. Vessels with head or features attached, which I have called "rim effigy bowls," enjoy the widest distribution in the Southeast of any of Vaillant's Q-factors. It is the only trait of the lot that is

[20] Professor Dellinger has on exhibition at the University of Arkansas Museum a series of effigies from Eastern Arkansas illustrating this possibility in very convincing fashion.

clearly present in all sub-divisions of Middle Mississippi, and probably extends far beyond the limits of that culture, particularly in the
direction of the Southeastern States including Florida. It is evidently an old and fundamental Southeastern trait. Unfortunately for
Vaillant's hypothesis it is the one trait about whose Middle American
origin he is most in doubt. In view of its wide distribution east of
the Mississippi, he suggests that it may possibly go back to an Antillean prototype.[21]

From the foregoing it would seem that the case for contact with
the Q-complex, so far as Middle Mississippi is concerned, is not very
strong. A Middle American origin probably still remains the best
explanation for some of the traits listed by Vaillant (though in no
case, I believe, the *only* explanation) but their number is not great
nor are they of fundamental importance. Whether remotely sprung
from the Q-complex or not, it seems to me they do not constitute a
separate problem but may be sufficiently accounted for by reference to the same influences responsible for other Mexicanoid traits
already discussed in this paper.

Enough has been said to indicate the complex nature of Middle
Mississippi pottery and to suggest some of the problems involved.
Their solution will depend on further knowledge of the earlier complexes out of which Middle Mississippi evolved, at present one of
the principal archaeological blind spots in the Southeast. So far as
the present object is concerned, however, without that knowledge,
it is possible to say that Middle Mississippi pottery exhibits not a few
fundamental characteristics that point to the Southwest (or Middle
America, via the Southwest, if you prefer) and a smaller and in-
tensely interesting number of factors, for which some form of direct
contact with Middle America seems at present to be the only acceptable explanation.

Turning to the distribution of Middle Mississippi culture, we discover at once what a vague and unsatisfactory thing it is. At its
center, in the eponymous region, the Middle Mississippi Valley from
say the mouth of the Arkansas northward to the Missouri, it is sufficiently intense. Northward, up the Mississippi, Missouri, and the
Ohio, it fades with progressive attenuation into "Upper Mississippi"
and "Plains." There is a definite eastward extension into the Ten-
nessee-Cumberland area and across northern Mississippi and Alabama
into Georgia and Florida. Westward, however, from the flourishing

[21] Vaillant, *op. cit.*, p. 17.

centers in the lowland area of southeastern Missouri and eastern Arkansas, there is an abrupt termination—the Ozark upland was apparently an effective barrier in this direction. Southward, about the level of the Arkansas River the culture gives place to a number of manifestations loosely referred to as "Lower Mississippi." Their relationship to Middle Mississippi is still a matter for acrid controversy. It is sufficient for our purpose to note that few of the features for which a Middle American origin has been suggested above appear in the Lower Mississippi, and those that do are generally interpreted as a backwash from Middle Mississippi rather than a direct thrust from the south. Beyond the Lower Mississippi athwart the route to Mexico lies the Texas "cultural sink," hardly deserving that opprobium, except from the point of view of the transmission of culture from the south, of which, it is said, no traces are to be found.[22] In short the circumstances of distribution, so far as we know them, look decidedly unfavorable to the present thesis. I shall return to this point directly.

For chronology Middle Mississippi, unfortunately, depends on work done outside the central area. Wherever it has been found in stratigraphic relationship with other prehistoric cultures, as in central Illinois,[23] and at Macon, Georgia,[24] it clearly overlies them, and is overlain in turn by cultures of the early contact period. It has not yet been brought into relationship with the sound chronology worked out by Ford in Louisiana and Mississippi,[25] but there are strong indications that it will fall into the period immediately preceding the historic "complexes" (Choctaw, Tunica, Natchez and Caddo). In other words, Middle Mississippi seems to belong to the last phase of the pre-Columbian history of the Mississippi Valley, say roughly the interval between 1400 and 1700 A. D. Any connections it may have had with Middle America must be relegated, therefore, to this disgustingly late period.

This brings us to the final and most interesting question of all, to-wit: what was the nature of these contacts? We have reviewed the general aspects of distribution and found them unfavorable to any theory of migration or diffusion as generally understood. A further peculiarity of this distribution I have kept for discussion here. This

22 Mason, Pre-Columbian Relationships United States and Mexico, 1937.
23 Cole and Deuel, Rediscovering Illinois, 1937.
24 Kelly, Explorations at Macon, 1938.
25 Ford, Pottery of Louisiana and Mississippi, 1936.

is the fact that many of our supposed Middle American features far outrun the more fundamental aspects of Middle Mississippi culture. For example, the carved shell and repoussé copper of Etowah in Georgia and the recently discovered Spiro mound in eastern Oklahoma are remarkably similar to each other and to comparable material from Middle Mississippi sites such as Moundville, Alabama, yet neither are Middle Mississippi sites in any fundamental sense of the term. The usual explanation that these are examples of the far-flung influence of Middle Mississippi somehow fails to satisfy. I would suggest rather that these sites (and doubtless many others) have simply come under the same influence as Middle Mississippi, and that the influence in question is Middle American. Again, it will not have escaped the reader's attention that most, if not all, the traits involved in the present discussion have a religious or ceremonial background. We are evidently concerned with the transmission of a cult (or group of associated cults) rather than culture in a more general sense. For the purpose, hypothecation of a migration is not necessary; diffusion, in the sense of relayed borrowing, on the other hand, is not sufficient. Our contacts, however widely spread, would seem to have been fairly direct. There is not that attenuation with increase in distance generally associated with the idea of diffusion. As Vaillant has pointed out,[26] a relatively few individuals would have been sufficient as carriers of the new ideas. On the other hand, if trade most nearly meets the conditions, it must be confessed that of the nature of any such trade, or even its existence, we have not a scrap of information.[27] As an hypothesis, it derives its chief support, not from any positive evidence, but merely from the fact that all other explanations are so beset with difficulty.

However, it must be sufficiently obvious that questions such as the above must wait until we know something of the archaeology of the Middle Mississippi and its relations in time and space. I shall be satisfied if I have successfully indicated: (1) that Middle Mississippi, as now defined, shows among other "outside influences" a considerable number of characteristics that can only be interpreted as the result of more or less direct contact with Middle America; and (2) that although some of these features may have been inherited

[26] Vaillant, *op. cit.*, p. 11.

[27] Spinden imaginatively suggests a copper trade with the Lake Superior region, carried on under the aegis of Toltec warrior cults. See Indian Symbolism, 1931, p. 18.

from earlier cultures in the Mississippi Valley (and therefore may be regarded as only remotely Middle American in origin) the more unequivocal ones, and those that give the culture its special flavor, seem to have been introduced directly into the Southeast at a comparatively late time.

XXVII

Sequence of Culture in the Eastern
United States

Carl E. Guthe *

THE NATURE and variety of the archaeological remains in the eastern United States have been known for a long time.[1] The investigations carried on during the nineteenth century concentrated upon the preservation of the many forms of material objects encountered in the sites, and the general classification of the earthworks with which they were associated.

The most spectacular archaeological remains of the region were the earthworks. Their clearly artificial nature and the uncertainty of their history led to many speculations concerning their origin. The concept of the mound-builders became established in the public mind, based upon the assumption that all of the earthworks had been constructed by a people with a single culture, and that for some reason they had disappeared prior to the coming of the ancestors of the historic Indians. Historians and archaeologists today consider this concept completely obsolete. The archaeological records found associated with the various earthworks have proved beyond all doubt that these monuments were constructed by communities in many parts of the country which possessed widely varying cultures. The technical examination of the human skeletal remains found in and near the earthworks have shown conclusively that the builders were physically the ancestors of the historic Indians. It is entirely erroneous, therefore, to speak of the mound-builders as possessing a single culture, or as being a race distinct from the Indians.

At a relatively early date, the earthworks were classified for descriptive purposes into several general groups on the basis of their

* Michigan, B.S., 1914; Harvard, A.M., 1915; Ph.D., 1917; Austin teaching fellow, 1915–1917; now Director, Museum of Anthropology, University of Michigan.
[1] Squier and Davis, Ancient Monuments, 1848; Thomas, Mound Explorations, 1894; Shetrone, Mound-builders, 1930.

structure and use.[2] Domiciliary, or pyramidal, mounds occur more frequently in the southern part of the eastern United States. Conical, or burial mounds are very widespread, but are most frequent in the northern and central part of the area. Effigy mounds seem to be restricted almost entirely to the northern Mississippi Valley. There are a variety of inclosures. The best known of the ceremonial or geometric inclosures occur in the valleys of the Ohio River drainage. Throughout the region, forts are frequently found on hill tops. Another type of mound is the result of accretion of refuse rather than of intentional construction. Occasionally village sites may take the form of low, large mounds, and along the coast and some of the rivers, definite mounds are the result of continued occupation by communities using large quantities of shells. Such a classification is useful only in grouping earthworks objectively, and cannot serve to distinguish between the several cultures responsible for them.

About the turn of the century, in accordance with improved techniques and policies adopted in archaeological research generally, emphasis began to be placed more and more upon the cultural interpretation of the remains of this region. One major problem consisted, of course, in the identification and classification of the many archaeological complexes found in various parts of the Mississippi Valley, the Great Plains, and the eastern Coastal areas. In order that the relationships between these several complexes might be properly interpreted, it became essential to determine at least a relative chronology for them. Therefore, definite efforts were undertaken to obtain data upon both direct and indirect stratification in the many sites. The students working on the archaeology of the eastern United States today are concerned primarily with detailed studies of large sites, or groups of sites containing similar cultural complexes. Such studies are necessary in order that technical problems relating to the identification and classification of cultures may be solved, thus leading to a more exact knowledge of chronological contemporaneity or sequence of these data dealing with the history of the Indians living in eastern North America before the coming of the Europeans.

However, in spite of the existing apparent complexity of the archaeological problems of the area, it is possible to make some general statements with regard to what appears now to be the outline of this history.

The investigations carried on during the last fifty years by a large

[2] Thomas, Mound Explorations, 1894, pp. 29-32.

number of students working under the auspices of many different institutions have revealed that there once existed in the eastern United States a variety of cultures which can now be identified only archaeologically. The criteria on which these identifications are based are the construction of the earthworks, architectural features, burial customs, varieties of pottery, and the types of stone, bone, shell, clay, and metal weapons, utensils, and ornaments. A comparative study of the archaeological records of former Indian communities reveals that differences both in degree and in kind exist between them on the basis of these criteria. Certain criteria may remain relatively constant in a number of communities, while others may differ considerably. The extent and nature of this variation make it possible to assign communities to larger and smaller cultural groups. A detailed discussion of these variations is not pertinent to the subject under review. Suffice it to say that it is generally agreed that earthworks were apparently constructed by two great groups of cultures, called the Mississippi Pattern and the Woodland Pattern. The concepts of these two patterns should be considered only as working hypotheses, for it is entirely possible that, as further information is obtained, either or both of them may be divided into two or more patterns, and entirely new patterns may be established.

However, there are definite evidences in the eastern United States that the oldest records of the region are those of communities in which earthworks were unknown. The bluff dwellers of the Ozark region are known mostly by the remains which have been found in the rock shelters of southwestern Missouri and northwestern Arkansas, and as yet no positive relationship between mound construction and these cultures has been established.[3] Neither is there any direct stratigraphical proof that the bluff dwellers antedated either of the two mound-building culture patterns. However, definite evidence has revealed that in Georgia a non-mound building culture antedated some of the great earthworks there, and that in the Tennessee Valley, communities of shell-using people left great mounds of debris prior to the advent of those who constructed earthworks in that region.[4] In the northern part of the country, similar evidence for early cultures has been found, particularly in New York State.[5] It is, of course, impossible to place any definite antiquity in terms of

[3] Harrington, Bluff Dwellers, 1924.
[4] Webb, Wheeler Basin, 1939.
[5] Ritchie, Archaic Occupation, 1936.

calendar years upon these early cultures. Yet it is clearly recorded stratigraphically that cultures older than those of the builders of the earthworks existed in eastern North America.

By the very nature of the conception, it is impossible to define in detail the characteristics of either of the two great culture patterns responsible for the construction of the earthworks. Each is a generalization based upon an apparently recognizable association of fundamental cultural habits, held in common by literally thousands of archaeological communities distributed over a large geographical area.[6]

The people who used the Woodland Pattern apparently placed considerable emphasis upon stone implements of all kinds, and used bone and metal to a less extent. Their materials are characterized by a relative lack of ornamentation on pottery and implements, and a scarcity of ceremonial objects and ornaments, although polished stone ornaments of many shapes, often made of banded slate, are usually assigned to this pattern. Their houses must have been of very flimsy construction, because few remains of them have been found. They buried their dead usually in a flexed position, either singly or in groups, and heaped over the burials a mound of earth which was frequently of complex construction.

The peoples possessing a Mississippi Pattern seemed to place less emphasis upon stone materials, and used shell, bone, and metal to a greater degree. The pottery which they made varies considerably both in shape and in decoration, and there is an abundance of ceremonial objects and ornaments. Their houses were sturdy structures of posts and saplings, for some of which they built earthen foundations. These grew in size as the first house was destroyed or abandoned, and the foundation was increased and rebuilt for a new structure. Today these are known as domiciliary or pyramidal mounds. As a rule, the dead were buried in an extended position in cemeteries, and not in conical burial mounds.

It is inevitable that with the passage of time and as the result of diffusion and minor migrations, the various traits of these two patterns would react upon one another in a variety of ways in many parts of the area. As a result, a large number of archaeological culture complexes developed which reflected the characteristics of these great cultural patterns to varying degrees. Some of them, in the southern United States, like the cultures found at Etowah, in Geor-

[6] Deuel, Basic Cultures, 1935.

gia, belonged predominantly to the Mississippi Pattern, but did not lack traces of Woodland characteristics. Similarly, in the northern part of the area, such cultures as the Hopewell or the Iroquois appear to be related to the Woodland Pattern, but have strong Mississippi characteristics. The major problem which confronts each student of eastern United States archaeology today is to establish the exact relationship of the archaeological culture in which he is primarily interested to similar cultures, and to the great hypothetical patterns in terms of the specific archaeological traits on the basis of which its identity has been established.

In the light of such a complex archaeological situation, any conclusions drawn concerning the relationship of these cultures to those in other parts of the New World, and any deductions made with regard to chronological relationships, must be expressed with considerable caution and in general terms. Nevertheless, it does seem possible to record certain broad observations.

The existence of agriculture and particularly the use of maize, among the cultures which constructed earthworks in the eastern United States would lead to the opinion that some cultural contact must have existed between this area and the Middle American region. The custom of building pyramidal mounds tends to strengthen such a conclusion. Further justification is found in the presence of varieties of vessel shapes in the southwestern part of the Mississippi Valley which are reminiscent of similar shapes in Mexico and Central America,[7] and the use of elaborate designs (Figs. 29–32) on pottery, stone, and shell materials in the same region even as far east as Georgia.[8] The absence of many of the characteristic features of the archaeological cultures of the Southwest would lead to the assumption that this cultural contact took place over a route different from that followed by those who brought Central American traits to the Southwest.

However, in spite of the apparently fundamental character of these Middle American influences in the eastern United States, they probably arrived relatively recently. Reference has already been made to the existence of Indian communities in this region before the concept of construction of earthworks came into existence. Throughout the entire area, there may be found evidences of Woodland characteristics which show no apparent influence from the cultures to the

[7] Vaillant, Some Resemblances, 1932.
[8] Nuttall, Etowan, Mexican and Mayan Designs, 1932.

west and the south. These Woodland traits are less apparent in the southern part of the eastern North American area than they are in the northern part, due to the dominance of the Mississippi Pattern in the former section.

The earthworks constructed by the peoples of the Woodland Pattern are relatively simple except in those localities in which this custom was influenced by the more complex Mississippi Pattern. In certain parts of the Great Lakes region, European trade materials are associated with the simple Woodland burial mounds, showing that this relatively unmodified Woodland custom was still in use during proto-historic and possibly historic time.

The remains of communities possessing the Mississippi Pattern occur most frequently in the south, but extend northward into the Ohio Valley and even into the state of Wisconsin, where they become fairly rare, indicating a relatively late arrival of these customs in that section. In the south, among the Natchez, historic records state that these Indians were using domiciliary pyramidal mounds when visited by Europeans. Elsewhere in the region, European trade materials have been found in association with the Mississippi Pattern. In the Ohio Valley, similar trade materials occur in sites occupied by the Fort Ancient people, who possessed a culture which was apparently more closely related to the Mississippi than to the Woodland Pattern. While the evidence is still sporadic, there are nevertheless sufficient instances to indicate definitely that the custom of building earthworks existed in the eastern United States into proto-historic times, and in some localities into the historic period after the contact between the Indians and the Europeans.

Stratigraphical evidence on the relative chronology of these two great patterns has been obtained in the Ohio River basin. In several sites stratified deposits reveal that a simple Woodland Pattern was the first type of culture at the site.[9] The next culture recorded was one of the Hopewell group, which, in the opinion of some students, is one of the large number of archaeological cultures possessing mixed Mississippi and Woodland traits. The last of the cultures at these sites is predominantly Mississippi in character. In the southern part of the area, the Mississippi Pattern is more varied, and stratigraphical records of cultural changes have been found.[10] The assumption may therefore be made that the more elaborate Mississippi culture pattern

[9] Cole and Deuel, Rediscovering Illinois, 1937.
[10] Ford, Indian Village Site Collections, 1936.

is relatively recent, and was either introduced or developed in the southwestern part of the Mississippi Valley and diffused gradually from there northward and eastward, being modified as it spread by contact with the customs of the Woodland people it encountered. Within very recent years, dendrochronological studies have been made upon the timbers and charcoal fragments found in archaeological sites in the central and northern part of the area. While definite dates have not yet been announced, it is understood that these will probably fall within the last five centuries, thereby supporting the conclusions drawn from other evidence.

These statements upon the relative antiquity of the Indian cultures in the eastern United States which are associated with the earthworks cannot, by their very nature, be critical or definitive. Data upon detailed cultural relationships have been completely ignored in order to attempt to furnish a broad perspective upon the subject. While it is still impossible to present as definite a chronological outline for the history of the Indian cultures of this area as those which have been established for the Southwest and for Middle America, the research now in progress is such as to indicate that within another generation, in spite of the present apparent complexities of the problem, the essential factors of the history of the pre-Columbian Indian cultures of the eastern United States will be clearly formulated.

PART IV

THE SOUTHERN NEIGHBORS OF THE MAYA

XXVIII

ANTHROPOLOGICAL PROBLEMS IN CENTRAL AMERICA

Wm. Duncan Strong *

ETWEEN the southern borders of the Maya in Honduras and
the highland territories of the Chibcha in Columbia is a region rich in scientific potentialities for the anthropologist. In the dim
past the primitive ancestors of both high and low cultures in South
America moved southward down the ever narrowing backbone of
the cordillera or along the jungle-lined rivers of the isthmus. For untold centuries thereafter cultural stimuli were transmitted both north
and south through Central America between the great agricultural
civilizations that developed in South America and those to the north
in Oaxaca, Yucatan, and Mexico. Despite the highly individualized
characteristics of such southern and northern cultural peaks it must
be abundantly clear to the readers of this volume that those centers
shared much in common. Each had its own particular genius but
even our present incomplete distribution studies on both historic and
prehistoric levels reveal evidences of early and late contacts. Whether
by land or sea these cultural transmissions moved via Central America. We cannot hope to understand the processes leading to the
florescence of Inca, Chibcha, Maya, or Zapotec civilizations until we
know much more about the ethnology, linguistics, and archaeology of
Central America. Here, at the time of the conquest, flourished unique
cultures representing a blending of north and south. The present-day
survivors of these tribes and the buried material remains hold the key
to much that is both puzzling and significant in American anthropology. The field is rich and relatively unworked.

Even a fragmentary resumé of the present status of the major subdivisions of anthropology, in so far as they apply to Central America,
will indicate the almost unbelievable gaps in our present knowledge.

* California, A.B., 1923; Ph.D., 1926; now Associate Professor of Anthropology, Columbia.

Of the earliest migration from north to south there is abundant theoretical but no very convincing material evidence. At Rio Indio, just east of the Caribbean entrance of the Panama Canal, Linné describes the occurrence of crudely flaked flints at a site devoid of pottery.[1] This find, and a few similar occurrences, are significant but utterly inadequate to establish either the time or the exact nature of the cultures represented. They do suggest, however, that when early remains are sought for on any adequate scale they will be found even in this extremely difficult terrain. Doubtless the early movements through much of this jungle area were rapid, for human occupation of a tropical rain forest without manioc or similar cultivation is precarious. Further, as analysis of the material culture of any of the primitive tribes now occupying the area will show, non-perishable artifacts aside from pottery are rare. Hence this early evidence will be sparse. However, where stone for artifacts occurs and archaeological research by students trained to see flints or drab sherds as well as stelae is adequate, there is little doubt that our knowledge of these early human movements will increase. In a little-known area still full of unreported major ruins it is hardly surprising that the faint traces of wandering nomads rarely have been noted.

For similar reasons we as yet know little of the simpler cassava- or maize-raising peoples that antedated the historic civilizations of Central America. Here, again, the answer seems obvious—lack of scientific survey and stratigraphic testing in practically the entire central and southern portions of the area. So far, only one case of cultural superimposition has been reported in Salvador, two or three cases in northwestern Honduras, and one in the Pearl Islands almost four hundred miles to the south.[2] In Salvador, and in Honduras, the earlier horizons differ markedly from the later ones and in each case there are significant resemblances to early levels in Oaxaca, the Guatemalan highlands and the earliest-known Maya horizons. In the Pearl Islands, polychrome pottery associated with rectangular dwellings occurs above incised ware in round dwelling sites. The polychrome pottery, as Lothrop has pointed out, is identical with the almost historic pottery of Coclé, whereas Linné sees a resemblance between the earlier

[1] Linné, Darien, 1929, p. 52. Also see Lothrop, Costa Rica, 1926, Vol. 1, Part II, Chap. II.

[2] Lothrop, El Salvador, 1927, p. 173; Popenoe, D. H., Playa de los Muertos, 1934; Strong, Kidder, and Paul, Northwestern Honduras, 1938, pp. 45, 62, 105; Linné, Darien, 1929, p. 134.

incised ware and the Early Ancon ceramics from the coast of Peru.[3] The latter ware, recently found in a thick deposit at Chávin de Huantar, I believe to be one of the earliest-known ceramic horizons in Peru. Thus, despite the pitifully few stratigraphic excavations so far attempted, we already have early ceramic horizons in northern Central America related to basic Maya and Zapotec types in the north, and an early horizon in southern Central America at least suggesting an early ceramic type in Peru. In each case these underlying horizons share certain common characteristics. Between these two Central American datum points stretch some four hundred miles of territory wherein stratigraphic excavations have as yet hardly been attempted. Rich collections are available from several portions of this region but the vast majority of these are collector's items without scientific data. Thus, while we have a few distribution studies such as Lothrop's monumental "Pottery of Costa Rica and Nicaragua," and the descriptive reports of MacCurdy and Holmes in Chiriqui, we still lack objectively established culture sequences.[4] The careful work of Hartman in Costa Rica, like the remarkable Peabody Museum excavations in Coclé, are exceptions but here relatively late horizons seem to be represented.[5] It is obvious, therefore, that stratigraphic excavations based on potsherds and all associated artifacts are the paramount archaeological necessity in eastern Honduras, and all of Nicaragua, Costa Rica, and Panama.

Hand in hand with the establishment of prehistoric culture sequences must go the problem of isolating historic horizons. These must be known if we are going to unite the disparate findings of ethnology, linguistics, somatology, and archaeology into a meaningful anthropological presentation. In Costa Rica, Nicaragua, and Panama, Hartman, Lehmann, Lothrop, and others have made excellent general beginnings in this regard. Yet there is still a great need for careful

[3] Lothrop, Coclé, 1937, p. 32; Linné, Darien, 1929, p. 134; Strong, Ancon, 1925, pp. 152, 183. Correlation of Early Ancon ware with the Chávin de Huantar site, personal communication from W. C. Bennett. My belief in the relative antiquity of Early Ancon ware is based on its position and ceramic affiliations at that site.
[4] Lothrop, Costa Rica, 1926; MacCurdy, Chiriqui, 1911; Holmes, Chiriqui, 1888. Also see Osgood, Chiriqui, 1935, for a recent revision of the ceramic wares.
[5] Hartman, Costa Rica, 1901, 1907; Lothrop, Coclé, 1937. For northern Central America see Gordon, Ulua, 1898; Spinden, Chorotega, 1925; Strong, Northeastern Honduras, 1934, Bay Islands, 1935; Strong, Kidder, and Paul, Northwestern Honduras, 1938; Yde, Northwestern Honduras, 1938.

excavation at specific documented sites where stratigraphy and analysis may factor out the historic knowns from the prehistoric un-
knowns. In Honduras, the important site of Naco, mentioned by
practically all the early chroniclers, is a case in point. The significance of this site was stressed by Gordon in 1898. Since that time it
has been visited, or mentioned, by some half dozen archaeologists in
the region, yet, prior to 1936, no one had described even the ceramics
to be found there. This ware, found in association with Spanish artifacts, proved to be quite distinct from other Ulua-Chamelicon—Yojoa
types having a definite relationship to prehistoric Nahuatl horizons in
Mexico, finding significant similarities as far north as Chalchihuites
in Zacatecas.[6] Thus, archaeology here corroborated historical and
linguistic evidence, demonstrating that these late Nahuatl movements
can actually be traced for hundreds of miles on the basis of material
traits. There therefore seems no reason why this should not apply
equally well to many earlier ceramic horizons. Contact sites the
world over link the sequences of history with those of prehistory.
Acculturation can be observed in the material as well as the social
aspects of a culture. If anthropology is going to contribute its full
share to a dynamic interpretation of culture change it cannot continue to neglect such vital evidence.

Glaring as are the archaeological gaps in Central America they
seem relatively small when compared to the present pitiable status of
physical anthropology, ethnology, and linguistics. In regard to anthropometric measurements on the living we have data on a few
small native groups in Nicaragua secured incidentally on an expedition for simian specimens.[7] Despite the occurrence of numerous isolated Indian groups—relatively large in the south, small to the point
of vanishing in the north—little has been done to record the types.
Nor have any comparative studies of present-day national and purely
native population been made. On the north coast of Honduras live
Black Caribs of splendid physique and Mosquito "Indians" of pitiable
appearance though both are the result of similar if not identical
Indian-Negro miscegenation. Why should the immigrant Black Carib

[6] Strong, Kidder, and Paul, op. cit., Mason, Durango, 1937. Ceramics from
the important site of Tenampua have been similarly neglected. If the few unique
sherds secured by Squier, now in the American Museum of Natural History,
are characteristic, either Tenampua is not Lenca or else certain Lenca ceramics
differ markedly from the types now classified under that heading.

[7] Schultz, Nicaragua, 1926.

thrive while the once dominant Mosquito appears to degenerate in the same environment? These like innumerable other problems of human heredity and adaptation in the area remain untouched. Concerning the physical types of the carriers of the different prehistoric cultures in Central America we know equally little. In part this is due to the generally unfavorable conditions for preservation of human skeletal remains in humid environments. However, numerous burials have been found in certain river bank and beach sites.[8] These are usually fragile and require time-consuming and painstaking treatment if they are to be preserved. So far the very few archaeologists who have worked in Central America seeking chronology rather than specimens have been far too busy with their own specific problems to spend precious hours on each skeleton encountered. However, when the ceramic and other sequences are at least outlined there is no reason why physical anthropologists, following such archaeological leads, should not secure adequate skeletal samples from many horizons. When these are known as to physical type, when they can be compared to series of measurements on the surviving Indian groups on the one hand, and to large series of the present-day population in Central America on the other, biometric facts of importance are sure to emerge. For both historical anthropologist and human biologist such knowledge would be exceedingly important. It can still be obtained but the time is short. One must admit that there seems little promise at the moment that it will be obtained before looting, extinction, or assimilation have completed their effacing work.

At present the bulk of our ethnographic material concerning Central America is derived from historical sources. Oviedo, Gomara, Motolinia, Cereceda, Las Casas, Wafer, and many other early chroniclers left rich though incomplete accounts of the natives they encountered. These records have been more or less compiled by scholars of the last generation, notably Squier, Brinton and Bancroft. They have been basic to the work of all linguists in the area. More recently the early sources have been utilized most effectively by Lothrop and others to throw light on archaeological excavations in Guatemala, Salvador, Honduras, Nicaragua, Costa Rica and Panama. Each recent advance in Central American anthropology has revealed additional historical material to supplement the work of the investi-

[8] Strong, Bay Islands, 1935, p. 22, Pl. 2. Also see Strong, Kidder, and Paul, *op. cit.*, 1938, p. 41.

gator. Critical and exhaustive utilization of such sources is, and will remain, a *sine qua non* in the area. There is reason to believe that diligent search in the archives here and abroad will continue for some time to yield much important ethnographic material hitherto unutilized. Anthropologically minded historians and historical anthropologists have here a common meeting-ground. Meanwhile, it may be asked, what are the findings and prospects of direct ethnological research in Central America?

Modern ethnology has little to boast of in this region. In part this is due to historic circumstance, in part to neglect or pre-occupation elsewhere. The impact of sixteenth century European civilization on the native cultures of Central America was explosive and devastating. In practically all the higher centers the more complex manifestations of autochthonous civilization were rapidly obliterated, though the old racial strain and much of the basic economy persists today. Yet despite the prevalent hispanicization of the more densely populated areas, there are vast jungle and mountain regions where the displaced native life still follows the old patterns. Each year these cultural islands shrink before the rising tide of assimilation or extinction. Since these surviving groups represent all we may ever hope to know concerning the non-material cultures transitional between two great continents they constitute a direct challenge to field ethnologist and linguist. A handful of devoted European and Central American scholars have attacked this difficult problem but ethnologists or linguists from the United States have been few and far between.

In general, the native enclaves in Central America survive along the wilder eastern or Atlantic portion of the isthmus. They are far more numerous in the southeast, fewer or more acculturated in the northwest.[9] For extreme western Colombia and eastern Panama we have Nordenskiöld's study of the Cuna, and Gasso's account of the same people. Due to the inhospitality of much of this region and to the relatively large numbers of natives we may still hope for much more data from these groups. Farther to the west Johnson's researches among the Guaymí will help fill a large ethnological void that extends north to the border of Nicaragua and Honduras. The brief but vivid account of the Talamanca Indians secured by Gabb

[9] For certain of these ethnographic references see: Nordenskiöld, Indianerna, 1928; Gasso, Karibes, 1911; Johnson, this volume; Gabb, Costa Rica, 1875; Squier, Nicaragua, 1852, 1853, 1859; Lehmann, Zentral Amerika, 1910, 1920; Sapper, Ethnographie, 1901; and Spinden, Chorotega, 1925; Conzemius, Miskito-Sumu, 1932.

in the last quarter of the nineteenth century is one of the very few attempts to fill this hiatus. Gabb's population figures, plus his comments on culture breakdown, are not too encouraging in regard to present-day prospects for ethnology among these peoples. However, one can always remember another keen observer, Prince Maximilian of Wied, who, in 1833, stated that the Ohio valley mounds were already so badly looted that scientific archaeological research would be useless! Squier and Lehmann give much linguistic and some ethnographic information concerning various tribes of Nicaragua. Yet, in all this vast area, there is only one attempt at a complete monograph, namely Conzemius' slender but excellent account of the Sumu and Mosquito Indians. North of the Patuca river there are on record only ethnographic fragments. Squier makes a few remarks on Lenca ceremonials some eighty years ago; Sapper, in addition to vocabularies, records a considerable number of scattered ethnographic facts among many of these peoples, and Spinden has a few significant but tantalizingly brief comments on the marked South American characteristics to be found among the present-day Paya. Each one of these references is invaluable but one looks in vain for anything approaching a complete tribal account. Yet, in Honduras alone, there survive culturally primitive Sumu and Mosquito Indians on the Patuca and adjacent rivers; isolated, bark cloth-clad Jicaque enclaves in Yoro; and hispanicized but ethnically and linguistically interesting Paya Indians living in more than two pueblos in Atlantida. All of these, save possibly the Sumu, are readily accessible from the Honduras coast. The larger native populations to the south and east have already been mentioned. The recording of the ethnology and linguistics of these various native groups, living in wild and remote regions, constitutes a major and pressing problem in Central American anthropology. Environmental and linguistic barriers, combined with the repression enforced on the Indians by a half millennia of exploitation, makes this a terribly difficult assignment. It is not a task for immature or untrained investigators. Nevertheless it is a challenge that must be accepted now or never.

In regard to the major linguistic problems in our area the present situation verges on the absurd. Certain students derive some of the most important linguistic stocks in Central America from North America, others derive the same languages from South America. In each case the Central American languages in question are linked with important larger stocks in either the northern or the southern continents.[10] Sapir is one of the very few North American scholars in recent times to commit himself concerning these major linguistic problems. In bare outline form he has suggested that the Maya languages, may be offshoots from his enlarged Hokan-Siouan stock in North America. He also confirms the penetrating hypothesis made by Lehmann that Subtiaba in Nicaragua is related to certain Hokan languages in California, and suggests that Xinca and Lenca belong in his enlarged Penutian group to the north. Lehmann seems to favor a northern derivation for Mayan and Nahuatl, but connects the Lenca with the Chibchan stock and suggests a possible linguistic relationship between Chibchan and Arawak. He believes that Arawak peoples, or at least cultural influences, preceded the Chibchan peoples north into southern Central America. However, in both of the last cited hypotheses, he admits lack of adequate proof. Schuller, on the other hand, would connect the Maya directly with the combined "Carib-Arawak" stocks of the West Indies and South America. Herzog long ago suggested the possible affiliation of various Costa Rican and Honduran languages with the "Tupi-Carib" stocks in South America. Such a paradoxical situation is either pregnant with the possibility that the time is at hand when we can expect sweeping linguistic correlations between North and South America, or else it implies that the historical aspect of New World linguistic studies is in a bad way. Undoubtedly conservative linguists will decry most of the above major stock correlations as premature and based on inadequate evidence. In this regard it must be pointed out that, insofar as a non-linguistic anthropologist can observe, these crucially important problems have recently attracted surprisingly little attention among such specialists, at least in the United States. It is true that minor linguistic stocks are vanishing rapidly in both North and South America and need attention, but it must also be remembered that the few remaining Central American native groups represent languages that link the continents. If these precious facts are not skilfully recorded and integrated with the present evidence while there

[10] For the following linguistic references see: Sapir, Central and North American Languages, 1929; Lehmann, Zentral Amerika, 1910, 1920; Schuller, Carib-Aruac, 1919-1920, Centro America, 1928; and Herzog, Indianer-sprachen, 1884. The compendium of Thomas and Swanton, Indian Languages, 1911, remains the sanest introduction to this complex field. The present linguistic map, and the article by J. Alden Mason (this volume) brings this earlier study up to date. Lehmann's reports contain valuable archive, archaeological, and ethnographic references amidst the linguistic material.

is yet time we may as well resign ourselves to unending and probably futile speculation on one of the most important anthropological problems in all of Middle America.

It has been the purpose of this paper to point out various gaps in our anthropological knowledge concerning Central America. To those who are not familiar with the literature it may erroneously appear that our present corpus of material is all holes and no body. This is far from the case. Despite the fact that so much of our present information has been derived from the historian or, on the material side, from the collecting of attractive specimens, every scientist that has seriously approached the field has been amply rewarded. This is manifest in the present-day agreement between linguists, ethnologists, and archaeologists concerning the northern and westward extension of South American influences into aboriginal Central America. In 1891, Brinton drew this line across the isthmus on the Nicaraguan–Costa Rican border. Today there is general agreement that these southern influences were dominant westward as far as a line extending from the Bay Islands on the north to the Gulf of Fonseca on the south. Theoretical and conceptual formulations rise or change as factual knowledge increases. If the historical and factual approach has been emphasized here it is only because so much more data of this sort are vitally needed before significant generalizations can be drawn. Since the present-day cultures of Central America, plus the added European increments, stem in large part from the native background, any penetrating sociological analyses or psychological conceptualizations regarding modern problems must be based on the correlated findings of anthropology. There is a vast amount to be learned from the earlier civilizations with their unique adaptations to isthmian conditions. If this knowledge is secured while there is yet time it will yield scientific and practical dividends of far-reaching significance.

XXIX

THE ULUA VALLEY AND LAKE YOJOA

Doris Stone *

NORTHWESTERN Honduras is the pre-European meeting-ground
of various Central American cultures with the Maya. The
place of contact stretched from the Valley of Sula-Ulua south and
westward through Los Naranjos on Lake Yojoa and, by way of the
Copán valley, over into El Salvador. We can say with some confi-
dence that the extent of important Maya cities to the eastward ended
in the Sula-Ulua and in the region of Lake Yojoa. However, there
is strong reason to suspect that the Comayagua valley had a number
of Maya settlements.[1]

The Sula-Ulua valley often erroneously is called by the one word,
"Ulua." The Ulua river flows through a more or less narrow bed
from the place of its birth, in the present Department of Santa Bar-
bara, down through temperate mountain-lands, until it reaches the
wide plain of Sula in the rain-forest region of the coast. Here it blos-
soms in a broad, meandering line, banked by fertile, silty soils and
fed by a number of tributaries. And here—probably due to the very
richness of the earth—were located numerous cacao plantations and
at least one large city with evidence of decidedly Maya contacts.

Directly behind (that is, south) of the plain of Sula, and emptying
part of its waters into the Ulua river where the plain begins, lies the
Lake of Yojoa. This is an inland body of water, said to be the crater
of an extinct volcano, nestled in a picturesque setting of steep mountain walls. These literally appear to hem in the lake, except at the
northern portion. There the land lies flat—almost like a high plateau—
and the Rio Lindo or Blanco leaves subterraneously and flows,
through its own small valley, down the fairly gradual descent to the
plain of Sula, where it joins the Ulua in its journey to the sea. It is
through this same opening that the trade-winds come inland, bringing to the lake-margins rain and the freshness that bespeak good crops
and inviting sites for settlements.

---

* Radcliffe, A.B., 1930; now Associate in Archaeology, Tulane University.
[1] Hamy, Étude, 1896, pp. 10–11; also personal observation of the writer.

The bulk of pre-Columbian Honduran culture is Lenca. Lenca Indians and Lenca place-names were and are found in all parts of the interior, from Olancho through Comayagua, Gracias, and into El Salvador on the Pacific coast. In the region of Lake Yojoa, however, the Lenca met the Maya from the west. Also, in this neighborhood they were influenced by northeastern cultures coming up from the Caribbean sea.

At the northwestern end of Lake Yojoa is the site called Los Naranjos. This was an extensive city, with buildings of mortar and of stone, protected from the overflow of the lake by raised earthen mounds on which the buildings were located. The fairly flat, rich lands to the north and east offered ample ground for the agriculture which was needed to support such a city's populace. There are even the remains of a canal, which connected the lake with some of the more remote low fields. Los Naranjos, as a city, has many Maya features. There are the same temple-plans, inner and outer rooms with stone-step approach that are prevalent at Copan and other Maya towns of the period. There is even the Maya feature of altars placed before stone monuments. But, as far as Naranjos goes, here ends its similarity to Maya settlements. The stelae are heavy—more like massive stone sculpture than slender monoliths. The design is a single element, a man or a serpent, not the usual Maya figure on a monument crowded with conventionalization and hieroglyphic dates.

This combination of culture-traits, those of the Maya mingling with those of an "outside" civilization, is evidenced further by the pottery (Plate XVII). The building-form bespoke Maya, but the ceramics show a combination of Lenca and Maya. Innumerable pots have been dug up at this site. Most of them were found either in a large, flat area stretching northeast from the city or at a place called "Aguacate" about four and a half miles to the east. Many of these vessels are Lenca in form, although a large class is the usual plain, cylindrical Maya vessel. The designs on these pots generally are concerned with a conventionalized water-fowl. This is Lenca, with perhaps a touch of Paya influence. The Maya designs usually present one of three subjects. One is the morning star—conventionalized as in the Dresden codex; others are the serpent and various glyphforms. Most interesting are the combination-pieces, where the water-fowl motif appears with monkeys or Maya-like men—and the "glyph" blocks. These are obviously inspired by functional Maya glyphs which the artist either did not understand, or from which he derived the physical shape, adding his own conventionalized design inside it. These combination types are found in the Sula-Ulua valley in Comayagua, in the valley of Olancho, and in the eastern part of Salvador, all places associated with the Lenca.

In addition to the Maya and Lenca influences at Naranjos, there is the slighter but nonetheless important element of the Pipiles, seen in ceramics. One of the most important Aztec gods was Tlaloc, the rain-god. It is to be expected that his prestige would travel far, particularly among agricultural people. This deity appears in the Lake Yojoa-Ulua region. In both these sections there is a class of vessel having as a decorative subject the Mexican rain-god Tlaloc. It is interesting to observe that Tlaloc does not appear on pots that are Maya in shape, but only on those which are Lenca—that is, on the shapes common to Lenca territory, such as has been outlined above.

Concerning Lake Yojoa, there is no historical evidence available; concerning the Sula-Ulua, the information is scant but significant. At the time of the Spanish arrival, this was a section crowded with Indians. According to their usual methods, the conquerors immediately placed the land under the *repartimiento* and *encomienda* systems. The result was the destruction of thousands of Indian lives—and virtual eradication of the aboriginal population. The document allotting the lands in the *repartimiento* has been preserved. It is dated 1536.[2] Also of importance is the deed of the founding of San Pedro Sula in the same year. San Pedro exists today as the principal city in the Sula-Ulua region. According to this particular document the jurisdiction of San Pedro extended from the River Xagua to the mines of San Lucas on the River Chambazula.

This is more than just an allotment of land to Spanish lords. It includes, curiously enough, a region unified both in archaeological artifacts and in language. Significant also is the fact that the strip of coastal territory in the west, which one might think would come under this allotment, is ignored. This terrain stretches from the present boundary of Guatemala to Omoa, in Honduras. It was occupied in ancient times by a geographically separate people: ". . . the nation of Toqueguas, who were between the rivers Techin and Motagua . . ."[3] Their influence is bound up more with the east coast of Guatemala than with Honduras.

---

[2] Bobadilla, Monografía, 1936.

[3] Bobadilla, *op. cit.*, pp. 180–181. Also see Fuentes y Guzmán, Recordación Florida, 1882–1883.

We can dismiss the west, therefore, and turn to the eastern portions of the Sula plain. Here, by the sea, is the section known as Atlantida, with the Valley of Yoro lying in the hills behind it. This valley, and the part of Atlantida from the Xagua river westward, the Spanish grouped with the people of the Sula-Ulua region.

The portion of Yoro south of the range which separates it from Atlantida slopes gently westward to the Ulua basin, and to the sea. In various historical documents, we find the inhabitants of this area called "Sula Indians." The same manuscripts speak of the aborigines of the Sula-Ulua valley as "Sulas" or "Zuras." It is an important fact that the historic peoples of western Yoro and the bulk of the aborigines of the Sula-Ulua spoke the same language. This still is in use in certain sections, and it differs both from the Lenca of the interior and the Paya of the coast.

This Sula language erroneously has been called "Xicaque." It is true that some of the present inhabitants of Yoro apply this term to themselves—but "Xicaque" was used all through the early history of Honduras as a *termo provincial* to designate warrior-pagans. The word "Xicaque" as such is a Mexican word, a corrupt form of the Mexican word "Chicatic." [4] This has a number of meanings, among which is the following significant definition:

chicatic = cosa rezia y fuerte o persona anciana. [5]

Xicaque, then, was a term applied by the Mexicans and in turn used by the Spaniards to signify the "former or older inhabitants" of a region. These Spaniard conquerors had come to Honduras from Mexico, and were used to Mexican, not Honduran, dialect. It was quite normal for them to adhere to what was to their ears the commonest-sounding tongue. Hence the term "Xicaque"—and hence the application of this name to the people who later came to their attention as pagans, fighters, or subjects to be conquered.

Still in the department of Yoro, but east of the Yoro valley, are the headwaters of the Aguan river, which has the largest river-basin east of the Ulua. This was the home of the Paya Indians, who dwelt along the Aguan banks and spread over to the Patuca river, and north to the sea. The Paya even inhabited the Bay Islands of Honduras, within easy reach of the Ulua. They spread along the coast and up the Sula valley, where archaeological evidence of their culture is found

---

[4] Vásquez, Chronica, 1716, vol. 2, p. 411.
[5] Molina, 1880, Part 2, Folio 19 *verso*.

today. And there is the legend prevalent around Choloma near the Chamelicon telling of an ancient Paya chieftain in the region.

The culture of the Paya is characterized broadly by the term, "simplicity"—that is, a utilization of the natural objects surrounding them, with only the slightest possible degree of abstract conventionalization. This attitude is entirely different from the Maya, whose highly complex pattern of life was reflected in an overgrowth of design-conventionalization, and a strong sense of *horror vacui* affecting not only their ceramics and their sculpture, but also their dwelling-places and mode of living. It is easy, therefore, to distinguish a Maya from a Paya artifact, on this basis of inherent style.

The Paya culture bears a decided relationship with certain Central American tribes who dwelt to the south, namely the now-extinct Guetar of Costa Rica and related groups of the eastern coast of Nicaragua. Probably the most characteristic Guetar feature to be found among the Paya are the pots with designs applied in relief. Traces of this southern culture are prevalent in Honduras on the Bay Islands and around Guaimoretta lagoon. Definite elements of this culture also are to be found in the Sula-Ulua district.

The Maya, it must be remembered, are the very latest comers into this region—so late that their speech was found in use when the Spaniards arrived,[6] and Maya elements remained purer and less absorbed by the Ulua population than intrusions of Lenca, Paya, Costa Rican, or even occasional Mexican traits.

Naturally, a territory as rich in artifacts as the Sula-Ulua would be expected to yield some sort of building-sites. Only one such place, however, has been exposed. Up to August, 1936, the locality known as Travesia apparently was only a cow-pasture, a portion of a large banana-plantation. It had been turned over to cattle because of the number of small rises or mounds, thought to be burial-mounds of the ancients, and used in part by the present-day inhabitants as a cemetery. The great 1936 flood of the Ulua river caused the removal of the overseer's house to a safer location. The place chosen was one of the pasture hillocks. All of these mound-tops had remained free of water, and it was soon discovered that the whole group had an artificial drainage to the north. During the laying of the house-foundation, it became apparent that instead of a "graveyard" here were

[6] Probanza, 1533. Photo Ms. of original in the Archivo General de Indias, Justicia 1005, Número 3, Ramo 1. Also Lothrop, The Word Maya and the Fourth Voyage of Columbus, 1927, p. 363.

buried stone buildings. Further excavations showed that Travesia covered an extensive area, and was what might be called a "sacred city," judging from the number of temples and prayer-mounds revealed.

Travesia formerly had been known by the Indian name "Chumba." In a report written by an early Spanish governor—Don Alonso de Contreras—in 1582, Chumba (in addition to a number of other places whose names survive as plantation-names today) was stated to be a "pueblo" or "town" as distinct from the term "cuidad" or "city" applied to San Pedro.[7]

There are several very interesting points in regard to this place. One is the complete absence in early reports of any stone building in this area. If the Spaniards had observed the imposing stone structures excavated recently, it seems reasonable to suppose that they would have made serious comment. So Travesia may have been abandoned at the time of their arrival.

Connected archaeologically with Travesia are the ruins on the summit of Palenque Hill—the highest single rise in the Sula Plain. The word "palenque" is archaic Spanish, signifying "fortification" or "fortified site." Palenque Hill, therefore, must have been known to the conquerors: if not actually by its buildings, then by its Indian reputation. On the very top was a large platform of stone covered with stucco. This platform is surmounted by a rise of similarly worked, balustraded stairs. From the top of this construction, one can obtain a magnificent view of the entire Sula-Ulua—even to the gorge whence the Ulua river enters the plain of Sula—and the conjunction of the Ulua with both the Comayagua and Lindo rivers. One can see the Chamelicon river, after it has left its own valley, paralleling the Ulua northward. Visible, too, is the easy approach from Yoro, and, on clear days, even the waves of the Caribbean sparkle in the distance. Signal-fires burned from Palenque's top would speak their message for leagues, and its occupation would be of inestimable value to warrior peoples. In addition to the large platform, a number of similar, but smaller, edifices are built into the western side of the hill near the top, giving a better view of the Ulua's approach from the interior.

In Travesia, however, there is no sign of war. There are temples, prayer-mounds, stelae, cache mounds, and a large stone-lined pit or "room" with two small inner walls, the whole buried deep in the

[7] Bobadilla, *op. cit.,* p. ii.

earth. This in itself is a puzzle, but gives evidence of having been of sacrificial significance from the many burned-clay and cinder patches it contains and one small jaguar skeleton plus the remains of an obsidian sacrificial knife.

We cannot identify Travesia as belonging to any one culture. It is a mixture, like most of the remains of ceramics or stone in this area. However, we can isolate the interesting points of Travesia and from these make a summary that is applicable to the entire Sula-Ulua culture.

Whether the Sula Indians, as such, had buildings of stone, we cannot say. In Paya territory, however (in the vicinity of Guaimoretta), is a group of mounds bordering a rectangular area and interspersed through this section only on parallel lines. No work has been done here, but the plan of the site is obvious. The mounds at the lowest level of Travesia, outside the Quadrangle, are similarly placed. Also, near Bonito farm, in the present Department of Yoro, but near the headwaters of the Aguan—and, therefore, still in Paya country—Dr. W. Duncan Strong [8] found mounds arranged rectangularly, with stone-lined pits the purpose of which is unknown.

In respect to the "pit-room" at Travesia, one very important discovery must be mentioned. In the first yard of dirt removed from the pit was the head of a small clay figurine, the lower portion of which was uncovered only a few inches deeper. It is a "Playa de los Muertos" figure. A plait falls down the black of its neck, and it is clad in a loincloth resembling a wide belt with woven pattern. The finding of this figure in the top layer of Travesia suggests either that "Playa de los Muertos" figures were being made at the last period of this city, or that later inhabitants had preserved more ancient specimens.

Attention should be drawn also to another interesting find. In the space between two stucco-covered blocks of the prayer-mound that crosses the Quadrangle of Travesia were 30 wedge-shaped stones, each about a yard in length. Only one of these stones was decorated by notches, giving it the appearance of a conventionalized Christmas-tree. The stones had been piled around a fire, and the remains of ash and cinders lay two feet deep in the center, about two feet from the ring of stones. The exact purpose of these stones we do not know, but they are reminiscent of stonework in the country of the Payas.

Two bas-reliefs were attached to the wall of a small temple of the

[8] Strong, Bay Islands, 1935, p. 11.

latest period in Travesia. These figures were very crude. To a degree, they are comparable to Mexican interpretations of Tlaloc. Lenca influence also shows up at Travesia. A whistle excavated on the temple steps, for instance, was similar to figurine whistles found among the Lenca as far away as El Salvador. There are numerous pots of Lenca type from the cache mound and also specimens identical with the stone balls found by Dorothy Popenoe at Tenampua in the Comayagua valley.[9]

Last, but most obvious, come traces of the Maya. The buildings and the latest prayer-mounds are made of dressed stone, definitely a Maya feature. The great majority of mounds composing Travesia—not burial or cache mounds but the stone pyramidal mounds which flank the original rectangle—bear no evidence of dressed stone. The same is true of the "pit-room." The smallest temple excavated is Maya in plan, however, similar to the least elaborate structures in Copan, and has the remains of a red and blue fresco. The mounds comprising the main group all are late, of dressed stone, and built around a quadrangle—another distinctly Maya feature. Significant, too, is the presence of sherds with Maya figures in relief, found on the top level of the Quadrangle, as are two west-coast *spondylus princeps* shells, which the Maya held sacred and used as one of their media of exchange. All of this, coupled with ceramics identifiable as Maya, such as pot-forms, designs, and large clay mold-made heads, speaks for itself, strengthening the historical evidence of language, and of Maya trading-canoes that frequented the Ulua for loads of "cacao de Mico," reputedly the best chocolate of Central America, which grew in profusion in the Sula plain.

We must also consider a group of three-legged pots having white slips and red formalized designs. The legs of these pots are narrow and generally pointed, as if they might be conventionalized faces. These pots, found in the Sula-Ulua valley and also both in the Aguan and in the Olancho regions, offer such definite evidence of "outside" influence that they had best be put in the category of mixed-trait pieces, and not designated as a "pure Ulua" product. The cache mound at Travesia, also, yielded "foreign" specimens. From here came a rising inner-handle of a type which belongs to a shallow class of bowl peculiar to this region. These are supported by three peg-legs, and are unpainted, although sometimes a border of "thumb-nail" pattern surrounds the rim. The outstanding feature is the handles.

[9] Popenoe, Tenampua, 1928.

There are two of these, and they rise from the exterior of the bowl. Heavy at the base, these handles often have a weeping old woman, sometimes with one hand to her head, and one at her side. The body-features usually are crudely executed, but the wrinkled ancient face perpetually is one of grief. This type of handle has been found over a widespread area, such as Teotihuacan and Tres Zapotes, Vera Cruz. A definitely "Ulua" vessel is the legless "interior bird-pot." This has a light-orange background, with the design in the inside center of the bowl, and a decorative band around the interior rim. The design is the same water-fowl observed at Lake Yojoa, but is executed only in rough outline. Occasionally, a monkey replaces the bird. The colors are black and red, with, at times, white.

Other "Ulua" elements, not actually found as yet at the site of Travesia but recorded in burials not far distant, are the curious open-mouthed figurine whistles (which sometimes do not whistle but evidently were made in accordance with ceremonial form) and the double animal (one on top the other) figurine whistles. The open-mouth whistles differ from those of Lenca origin in that they are never of a complete person, and generally are two-headed, combining an animal with what may or may not be a human head.[10]

The magnificent marble vases from the Sula-Ulua are famous, and comprise the most widely appreciated groups of artifacts from this region. Their use appears to have been ceremonial, and they show an outgrowth from the influences of divers peoples. The marble vases, however, have emerged as a distinct localization, a product peculiar to and bound up with the civilization of a set area, the Sula-Ulua. Many have been found with burials close to Travesia.

To this pattern of "Ulua" belong the elements cited above. In this small, rich field we have to take into consideration the various and dissimilar peoples who made the region their home at one time or another. From this conglomeration, we can list the Paya, the Lenca, the Maya, and the Mexican as being those who—in combination at different times with the Sula—formed the mélange which has created the culture today called "Ulua."

[10] The open-mouth whistle has been noted by Dr. Lothrop in Nicaragua. See Lothrop, Costa Rica, 1926, Fig. 167 and Pl. 132. The double-animal whistles occasionally occur in Costa Rica. See Lothrop, op. cit., Pl. 191, Fig. f.

XXX

NON-MAYA MONUMENTAL SCULPTURE
OF CENTRAL AMERICA

Francis B. Richardson *

S AVE for the Maya area, our present knowledge of Central American archaeology is superficial compared to that of northern Middle America.[1] Specific archaeological data are rare with the exception of those emanating from a few scattered and restricted areas in the Guatemala highlands, northwestern Honduras, Nicaragua, Costa Rica, and Central Panama.[2] Preliminary reconnaissance during the past century from Colombia to, and including, the Pacific coast of Guatemala leaves much to be desired in the initial archaeological procedure of determining the general nature and distribution of remains. Data are therefore insufficient, and at times questionable. Linguistic research, together with early Spanish historical accounts, has contributed much toward establishing sixteenth century tribal territories, but these have not yet been correlated surely with cultural distributions. Chronological relationships are also obscure.

In spite of this unsatisfactory state of our knowledge, the examination of the field from a specialized approach, namely, monumental sculpture, suggests various problems and tentative conclusions. Monumental sculpture throws no light on the early stages of culture, an all-important question in American archaeology. It helps, however, to define the geographical limits of culture areas, and to clarify the

* Harvard, special student, 1936–1937; now Archaeologist, Carnegie Institution of Washington.

[1] Dr. S. K. Lothrop very kindly supplied much information and many helpful suggestions which have been included in this paper. The term "Central America" is used in its political sense, including therefore Guatemala, British Honduras, El Salvador, Spanish Honduras, Nicaragua, Costa Rica and Panama. "Middle America" includes Central America plus Mexico but exclusive of the Antilles.

[2] No attempt will be made to include a large bibliography. Those desiring excellent comprehensive bibliographies for *Panama*, see Lothrop, Coclé, 1937; for *Costa Rica*, see Lothrop, Costa Rica, 1926; for *Nicaragua*, see Lothrop, Costa Rica, 1926; for *Honduras*, see Yde, Honduras, 1938. There are no extensive bibliographies yet published for Guatemala and Salvador.

chronological relationships between them. The following comments are limited to those pieces of stone statuary too large to be moved any considerable distance, and which, therefore, may be considered representative of a culture in their immediate vicinity. Due to limitations of space, not all examples can be considered.

GUATEMALA

Archaeological remains on the slopes of the continental divide and the adjoining lowlands of the central Pacific coast of Guatemala have long been attributed to the Pipil, a Nahua-speaking tribe which reputedly migrated from Mexico after a drought in the early eleventh century A. D. Lothrop [3] points out that this Pipil migration continued to western Salvador, that it was the third wave of population in that area, and that the preceding inhabitants were Maya and Ikomagi. Historical, linguistic and archaeological indications partially support this contention. However, remains on the central Pacific slope of Guatemala give little indication of a former Maya occupation. The monumental sculptures within this area fall into three distinct categories: 1) Colossal stone heads in the round; 2) Crude human figures in the round, usually seated cross-legged; 3) Stone slabs with bas-relief carving.

The stone heads are found at Baul, Monte Alto, and El Palmar [4] (Plate XVIII, a–b). In size they range from an approximate diameter of 3 feet (1 meter) to at least 14 feet (4.3 meters) and in every case but one are human. The exception is a conventionalized jaguar head at Monte Alto (Plate XVIII, c). At Baul the head is associated with mounds; at Monte Alto there is no association with architecture, but two large heads, one human and one jaguar, and two crude human figures are aligned north and south. No information other than that obtainable from a photograph is available about the stone head at El Palmar.

The closest parallels to this class of sculpture appear at La Venta, Tabasco, Mexico, and at Tres Zapotes, Vera Cruz, Mexico.[5] The similarity lies in the colossal size of the heads, as no other single major

---

[3] Lothrop, Southeastern Frontier, 1939, p. 44.

[4] For *Baul*, see Dieseldorff, Religion, 1926, Tafel 28, No. 155; Waterman, Western Guatemala, 1924, pp. 349–350, Fig. 4. For *Monte Alto*, see Villacorta, C. A., Descubrimento, 1938; Villacorta, J. A., Prehistoria, 1938, photograph on p. 27. For *El Palmar*, see Anonymous, Album Grafico, 1936.

[5] For La Venta, see Blom, Tribes, 1926, pp. 84–85, Fig. 76. For Tres Zapotes, see Seler, C., Tuxtla, 1922, Plate VI; Weyerstall, Mounds, 1932, pp. 31–32, Fig. 3.

trait is common to all examples, but there is a tantalizing stylistic suggestion of that school of South Mexican sculpture tentatively isolated under the term Olmec.[6] It is perplexing, however, to note the marked resemblance between the jaguar head from Monte Alto and numerous masks on Structure E-VII sub at Uaxactun.[7] This building is in the heart of the Maya Old Empire and in all probability dates from before the beginning of the ninth cycle, approximately 450 A. D.[8]

The crude human figures seated cross-legged, usually devoid of clothing and ornamentation, have been reported from only two sites, Obero (Plate XVIII, e and é) and Monte Alto [9] (Plate XVIII, d). It appears that these figures are the product of the same people who carved the large stone heads, as at Monte Alto they both are found together, and, more significantly, are in orientation with each other. As in the case of the heads, moreover, the seated figures find their closest stylistic resemblance at La Venta.[10] On the basis of certain features of La Venta sculpture, Blom [11] is inclined to attribute these ruins to the Maya, but it seems that La Venta has closer relationships with the culture of the Pacific slope of Guatemala, reputedly of Mexican origin.

The third type of Pacific slope sculpture, stone slabs with bas-relief carving, is found almost exclusively at Santa Lucía Cozumalhuapa, with isolated examples at Baul, Palo Verde, Chocolá, Castillo, and Los Tarros.[12] They reach a height of 12 feet (3.66 meters) and are usually carved on one side only. There is little doubt that these relief carvings are of Nahua inspiration. They are characterized by human and anthropomorphic figures, a modification of the Diving

[6] For *Olmec* style, see Vaillant, Bearded Mystery, 1931, Pre-Columbian Jade, 1932, By their Arts, 1939; Saville, Votive Axes, 1929; Stirling, Initial Series, 1940; Andrews, Related Sculptures, 1939.

[7] Ricketson, Uaxactun, 1937, pp. 76–87, Figs. 42–50.

[8] Throughout this paper Christian dates are based upon the Goodman-Martínez-Thompson correlation.

[9] Other examples of this classification of sculpture come from the Pacific coast of Guatemala, but their exact provenience is unknown.

[10] Blom, Tribes, 1926, p. 89, Figs. 79 and 80.

[11] Blom, Tribes, 1926, p. 90.

[12] For *Santa Lucía Cozumalhuapa*, see Habel, Cozumalwhuapa, 1878; Strebel, Cozumahualpa, 1901; Seler, C., Mexiko und Guatemala, 1900, pp. 242–247 and Pl. XLIV. For *Baul*, see Burkitt, Two Stones, 1933; Waterman, Western Guatemala, 1924. For *Palo Verde*, see Seler, C., Mexiko und Guatemala, 1900, pp. 235–242. For *Chocolá*, see Carnegie Institution Sculpture File. For *Castillo*, see Burkitt, Two Stones, 1933; Carnegie Institution Sculpture File. For *Los Tarros*, see Habel, Cozumalwhuapa, 1878, pp. 16, 65; Eisen, Sculptures, 1888.

God, human sacrifices, skulls, speech scrolls, Aztec day signs, and the eagle-tiger complex presumably of northern origin. Morley [13] dismisses the possibility that a disputable seventh cycle Maya Initial Series date of 27 A. D. on a bas-relief at Baul represents a contemporaneous recording. He further points out that on stylistic grounds the sculpture is basically more Nahuatl than Mayan. This Baul stela is also the only bas-relief sculpture on the Pacific slope that does not fall stylistically into the general current of such carvings in that area. Minor sculptural details as well as the human figure on the front of the Baul stela can virtually be duplicated in certain Zapotec carvings. All sites with relief sculpture lie in a relatively restricted area on the slopes of the volcanoes, while the great heads and the crude human figures are concentrated in the lowlands, but penetrate into the foothills.

The above sculptures all possess northern affinities. Presumably the colossal heads and crude human figures are the product of one and the same people. There is a distinct possibility, however, that the relief carving should be credited to a different Nahua source. Certain Middle American cultures not only passed through but took root on these slopes. Their routes of migration, their geographical distribution and their chronological sequence are now obscure. Two monumental sculptures that stand apart from the above three classifications on the Pacific slope are a human figure from La Flora (Plate XIX, c and c') and a squatting jaguar from Baul (Plate XIX, a). Neither one falls stylistically into any main group of Middle American sculpture. The figure from La Flora, however, is vaguely reminiscent of certain sculptures from San Agustín, Colombia, in northwestern South America. [14] Stylistically, this figure is unique as it may represent the only echo of South American monolithic carving that reached Mexico, Guatemala, Salvador or Honduras. This suggested relationship is not too close but if one searches for affinities, the La Flora figure fits more readily into the northern South American rather than the Mayan, Mexican, or Central American sculptural complex. The importance of the Pacific slope of Guatemala, especially in relation to Highland and Salvadoranean archaeology, cannot be overemphasized as it must hold the key to much that is now perplexing.

[13] Morley, Peten, 1938, Vol. I, Chapter 2, Section 1, pp. 129–134 and Fig. 3.
[14] Preuss, Monumentale, 1929 Pls. 1, 23, 29, no. 2, 42, no. 1, 60, no. 2; Walde-Waldegg, San Agustin, 1937, Pl. VIII, no. 2.

Large stone sculptures are found scattered through the Guatemala highlands. The only considerable concentration, however, is at the ruins of Kaminaljuyú, where the sculptures have been classified by Lothrop into three distinct categories: [15] (1) Crude Group; (2) Early Maya Group; (3) Late Maya Group.

For the following reasons Lothrop regards examples of the "Crude Group" as earlier than those of either Maya group, and of "great age":

(1) Their stylistic affiliation with two sculptures found at Copan in the foundations of Stelae 5 and 4 (Fig. 37) (9.14.0.0.0 and 9.17.12.13.0?), 711 and 783? A. D.

(2) The stylistic relation of these Copan pieces to sculptures from Nicaragua of Chorotegan workmanship, and hence to the Tuxtla statuette.

(3) The association of the "Crude Group" at Kaminaljuyú with "Archaic" pottery.

If the above stylistic relationships and associations exist, it necessarily suggests a pre-Maya culture influencing a relatively large geographical area. This earlier civilization would have to be firmly established to distribute the suggested relationships so widely. Present-day archaeological indications in Central America neither substantiate nor refute the existence of any such civilization.

The stylistic similarity between the Kaminaljuyú "Crude Group" and the two Copan sculptures may well exist, but that they are early carvings is not conclusive. As has been pointed out, the interrelationship of cultural influences affecting the Guatemala highlands must await future work. Nevertheless, it can be stated that at Kaminaljuyú, when outside penetrations are recognized, the association is with the north and west rather than the south and east.

EL SALVADOR

In Salvador, no examples of monumental sculpture have yet been reported north or east of the Rio Lempa save for fragmentary pieces from Quelepa.[16] The few examples known come from the western section of the country. Large jaguar heads carved on oval and disc-shaped boulders are found scattered through the Departments of

[15] Lothrop, Arevelo, 1926a. For photographs of sculptures from Kaminaljuyú (Finca Arevalo), see Villacorta, J. A., Arqueología, 1927, pp. 36–48.

[16] Photographs of the fragmentary pieces of sculpture from Quelepa are in the possession of Dr. S. K. Lothrop.

FIG. 33. (For description, see facing page.)

FIG. 34. STONE JAGUAR HEADS FROM WESTERN SALVADOR

a. Exact provenience unknown.
b. Cara Sucia, Department of Ahuachapan.
Both specimens are now in the National Museum, San Salvador, and are approximately 2 feet (.60 meters) high.

Santa Ana and Ahuachapan, notably at Ahuachapan, Cara Sucia, El Congo and El Limón (Figs. 33, 34). At Tazumal, on the outskirts of the modern town of Chalchuapa, there were formerly three large sculptures: a stela with a figure and glyphs on each side,[17] and two "chacmool" type figures.[18] A typical "standard bearer" figure (Plate XIX, *b*), originally from Santa Cruz Michapa, Department of Cuscatlan, is in the possession of Dr. Salazar of San Salvador. Further, Squier [19] reports a carving, presumably in bas-relief, "eight feet long by four feet broad" at Opico, Department of San Vincente. He states that it is "true Mexican style, representing probably a prince

[17] Lothrop. Southeastern Frontier, 1939, Fig. 2.
[18] Weber, Salvadors, 1922, Fig. 39a and b; 42.
[19] Squier, Central America, 1858, p. 341.

FIG. 33. STONE JAGUAR HEADS FROM WESTERN SALVADOR

a. El Congo, Department of Santa Ana.
b. Finca El Limón, Department of Santa Ana.
c, d. Exact provenience unknown.
e, f. Ahuachapan, Department of Ahuachapan.
c is now in the possession of Dr. Alfonso Quinones, San Salvador, while *d, e,* and *f* are in the National Museum, San Salvador. They vary in height from 2 to 3 feet (.60 to .90 meters).

or warrior." Finally, Habel [20] mentions "two sculptured heads of colossal size" near two mounds in the vicinity of Sonsonate, Department of Santa Ana, and three more monoliths in a plain near the same town, stating that "two of them represented gigantic heads" and that they were all "more or less buried in the ground, the third so much as to obscure the design upon it."

The Salvador jaguar heads (Figs. 33, 34) not only illustrate an interesting series in design development but imply a chronological sequence. Conventionalism may or may not precede naturalism in art evolution. Not knowing under what circumstances most of the heads were found, it remains uncertain in which direction the suggested development took place. A clue as to age is that one partially eroded jaguar head resembling the conventionalized example from El Congo (Fig. 33, a) was found in the fill of a mound in the outskirts of Chalchuapa on Finca Casa Blanca and must therefore antedate it. The naturalistic examples are in a finer state of preservation which may indicate a later phase. The evidence of evolution from conventional to naturalistic is necessarily inconclusive. Assuming, however, that this was the case, the three main developments in technique are (1) from in the round to bas-relief, (2) from irregular to symmetrically shaped stones, and (3) from incised to high to low relief carving. If, however, the evolution is reversed the technical developments must necessarily be also.

These jaguar heads, although smaller than the heads from the Pacific slope of Guatemala, find their closest parallel with them, though the colossal jaguar head from Monte Alto (Plate XVIII, c) is the only one that bears a resemblance to the Salvador examples. If this similarity proves sound, the Salvador jaguar heads must be considered the product of the same culture that produced the human and jaguar heads of Guatemala as well as the crude human figures. Spinden [21] states that these jaguar heads are probably of the period of bas-relief carving at Santa Lucía Cozumalhuapa. That this colossal stone head complex existed in the Departments of Santa Ana and Ahuachapan, Salvador is indicated by Habel's reports, and conversely, that the Cozumalhuapa bas-relief complex did not is in turn indicated by the total absence of reports of any such sculptures in this area.

The presence of an unmistakable chacmool and standard bearer

[20] Habel, Cozumalhuapa, 1879, p. 32.
[21] Spinden, Salvador, 1915, p. 472, Fig. 77.

figure in Salvador again points to a cultural seepage from Mexico. These two types of carvings are found at Chichen Itzá and have been assigned to the period of Mexican influence at that site. The occurrence of chacmools in Middle America [22] vividly illustrates a discrepancy between the distribution of sculpture types and tribal territories,[23] as they are found from central Mexico to central Costa Rica. It should be noted, however, that their concentration appears to be Mexican as in Central America they have been reported only from Quirigua in Guatemala (Fig. 35, b), Amatlan in Honduras, Tazumal in Salvador, León in Nicaragua, and Las Mercedes in Costa Rica [24] (Fig. 35, a). The stela at Tazumal may be of Maya rather than Nahua inspiration. If so, what significance is there in the presence at that site of such a carving and a chacmool, a demonstrably late type of sculpture?

HONDURAS

For such a potentially fertile archaeological area as Honduras it is surprising how many gaps there are in our knowledge. Somewhere within its borders there presumably was a meeting and overlapping of traits commonly attributed to northern and southern cultures. Where and to what extent this took place is impossible to say with any degree of accuracy. Excellent work has recently been done in the Bay Islands and in northwestern Honduras to the exclusion of the remaining portions of the country. What little is known concerning the north and south coasts, and the central sections has been pieced together from meager reports. These date from the middle of the nineteenth century up to more detailed, but inadequate reconnaissance undertaken during the past twenty years.

Monumental sculptures in Honduras, exclusive of Maya Old Empire material, are not only rare, but are widely dispersed, and possess no apparent cultural unity. Isolated examples have been reported from Copan, La Florida and Quesalteca (Quesailica) Department of Copan, in the Ulua Valley, the Lake Yojoa district, the Comayagua Valley, the Bay Islands, Zacate Grande Island, and on the north

[22] Tozzer, Time, 1927, Fig. 4.
[23] Thomas and Swanton, Indian Languages, 1911.
[24] For *Quirigua*, see Saville, Vandalism, 1892. For *Amatlan*, see Tozzer, Time, 1927, Fig. 4. For *Tazumal*, see Weber, Salvadors, 1922, Fig. 39a and b. For *Leon*, Spinden informed the author that a chacmool from Nicaragua is now in a park in Leon.

coast.[25] Due to this lack of concentration of sculptural material in Honduras only a few specimens will be mentioned in conjunction with material from other areas.

NICARAGUA

In Nicaragua archaeological attention has been focused upon sculpture and pottery found upon numerous islands in Lake Managua and Lake Nicaragua and in the long but narrow strip of land between the lakes and the Pacific. Particular attention has been paid to the Islands of Zapatero and Ometepe. Future archaeological investigation in the Pacific area of Nicaragua should be directed towards correlating remains with linguistic and historical records.

The sculptures within this area have been assigned to the Chorotega, a group of linguistically related tribes of uncertain affinities.[26] They fall into two main groups, numerically approximately equal; those with and those without an animal or reptilian form in conjunction with a human figure.[27] No other large group of related Central American sculptures carved in the round, and there are but few carvings in bas-relief from this region, achieve such naturalism

[25] For *Quesalteca*, see Lothrop, Reconnaissance, 1917. For *Ulua Valley*, see Gordon, Uloa Valley, 1898, pp. 11 and 12, Fig. 4. For *Lake Yojoa* district, see Yde, Preliminary Report, 1936; Strong, Northwestern Honduras, 1938, pp. 102–105, Pl. 16, Nos. 1, 2, and 3. For *Comayagua Valley*, see Squier, Central America, 1858, pp. 130–133. For *Bay Islands*, see Strong, Bay Islands, 1935, pp. 129–135, Plate 32, No. 2; 33. For *Zacate Grande*, see Rivas, Monografía, 1934. For *North Coast*, see Morley, *Archaeology*, 1918. Spinden, Culture Area, 1925, Fig. 4.

[26] Lothrop, Stone Statues, 1921.

[27] For a comprehensive bibliography on sculptural material from Nicaragua, see Lothrop, Costa Rica, 1926, Vol. 2, Appendix I. The following items are the main sources plus recent references not included in Lothrop's bibliography: Arguello, Zapatera, 1926; Bovallius, Antiquity, 1866; Bransford, Researches, 1881; Carnegie Institution Sculpture File; Centro América, Penzacola, 1924; Centro América, Antigüedades, 1924a; Centro América, Expedición Científica, 1926; Squier, Nicaragua, 1852; Sultan, Engineer, 1932.

FIG. 35. SCULPTURES FROM GUATEMALA, HONDURAS, AND COSTA RICA

a. Chacmool from Las Mercedes, Department of Limón, Costa Rica. Now in the possession of the American Museum of Natural History, New York.
b. Chacmool from Quirigua, Department of Izabal, Guatemala. Now in the possession of the Museum of the American Indian, Heye Foundation, New York.
c. Crude human figure from La Florida, Department of Copan, Honduras, 2 feet, 8 inches (.80 meters) high. Right and left sides.

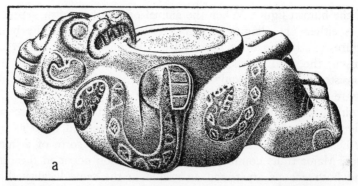

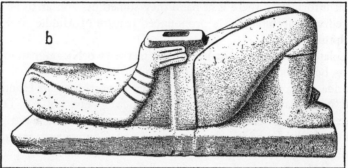

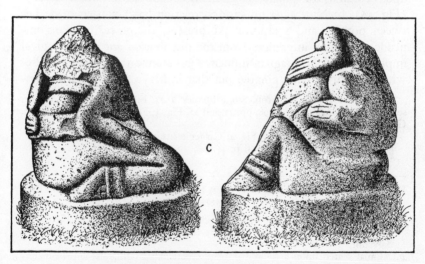

Fig. 35. Sculptures from Guatemala, Honduras, and Costa Rica
(For description, see facing page.)

of the human figure. When the animal or reptilian form is present, it is either (1) clinging to the back or shoulders of the human figure, (2) resting upon the head of the human figure, or (3) enclosing the head of the human figure within its jaws. The most consistent feature of sculpture without the animal form is a nude figure seated or standing upon a pedestal, column, or pillar. This position, moreover, is not uncommon in the other group. Occasionally in both groups the human figure has suspended from its neck or held in its hand an appendage, usually in the form of a human face. Major traits common to one classification occur in the other, and both groups are found associated in the same locality. From what information there is at hand they sometimes appear to be associated with architecture, a pronounced feature of Middle American sculpture.

Isolated statues more or less similar to the two Nicaraguan groups have been reported from near Comitan in southern Mexico, La Florida (Fig. 35, *c*) and the Ulua Valley in northwestern Honduras, and Nacasola in northwestern Costa Rica [28] (Fig. 39, *b*). To the above localities where Nicaraguan characteristics may have penetrated should be added the Department of Ocotepeque, Honduras, and the Guatemala Highlands, as human and animal figures perched upon columns or pillars occasionally occur within these areas [29] (Fig. 36). In Nicaragua no sure correlation has yet been made between pottery and sculpture. At present, therefore, it seems imprudent to draw inferences from the distribution and chronological implications of Nicaraguan influence in ceramic remains found elsewhere. Lothrop [30] has pointed out that in Maya and Mexican sculp-

[28] For *Comitan*, see Lothrop, Stone Statues, 1921, Fig. 69. For *Ulua Valley*, see Gordon, Uloa Valley, 1898, pp. 11 and 12, Fig. 4; For *Nacasola*, see Cabrera, Guanacaste, 1924.

[29] Ricketson, Tzalcam, 1936, Fig. 4; Carnegie Institution Sculpture File.

[30] Lothrop, Stone Statues, 1921, p. 311.

FIG. 36. SCULPTURES FROM SOUTHWESTERN HONDURAS AND THE GUATEMALA HIGHLANDS

a. Jaguar seated upon a pillar from the Department of Ocotepeque, Honduras; 4 feet, 2 inches (1.28 meters) high. It is now at Quinta Elena, Chalchuapa, Salvador.

b. Animal seated upon a pillar from the Guatemala Highlands; approximately 5 feet 3 inches (1.60 meters) high.

c. Jaguar seated upon a pillar from the Guatemala Highlands; approximately 3 feet, 4 inches (1.02 meters) high.

FIG. 36. SCULPTURES FROM SOUTHWESTERN HONDURAS AND THE GUATEMALA HIGHLANDS
(For description, see facing page.)

ture where the "alter ego" motif occurs it differs from that of Nicaragua in that the "body is characteristically an animal within the jaws of which appears a human head." This indeed is generally true, but not universally so. At Chichen Itzá Maudslay [31] illustrates two examples of a feathered serpent, the jaws of which enclose the head of a standing human figure, while the serpent body hangs down the back of the warrior. Lothrop further points out that two Nicaraguan sculptures, the Tuxtla statuette, and numerous Nicoya jadeite pendants all possess a common characteristic, an appendage that covers the mouth. A similar appendage appears on a presumably late sculptured head from Copan.[32] Thus, penetration of monumental sculpture of Chorotegan type to the north of Nicaragua is apparently sporadic.

At La Florida, Honduras there is a human figure crouching upon a pedestal with an animal clinging to its back (Fig. 35, c). As both the animal and human heads have been severed from their respective bodies it is impossible to tell whether the former enclosed the latter within its jaws or not. Lothrop [33] shows that this figure is in all probability a direct result of Nicaraguan influence, and establishes the presence of Chorotegan characteristics in direct contact with the Maya area. Whether this northern penetration of southern sculptural traits preceded, coincided with, or followed intensive organized Maya occupation in this area is debatable. It has been suggested that it was the earlier, due to stylistic similarities between Nicaragua–La Florida sculptures and the two previously mentioned figures found in the foundations of Copan stelae and which they therefore must antedate (Fig. 35, c, 37). This stylistic relationship, however, appears insecure for the following reasons:

(1) There is no "alter ego" motif on the Copan figures, which we have seen is one of the basic characteristics not only of the La Florida figure but of Nicaraguan sculpture in general.

(2) The Copan figures are not resting on a pedestal, column, or pillar, the other predominating trait of Nicaragua–La Florida sculpture.

(3) The Copan figures have collars or necklaces, appear clothed, and one of the two has feather ornaments on its body, while nudity is practically universal in Chorotega sculpture.

[31] Maudslay, Biologia, 1889–1902, Vol. III, Pl. 45.
[32] Carnegie Institution Sculpture File.
[33] Lothrop, Stone Statues, 1921, p. 314.

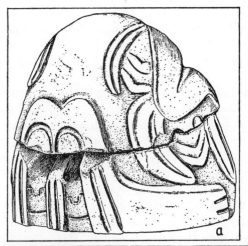

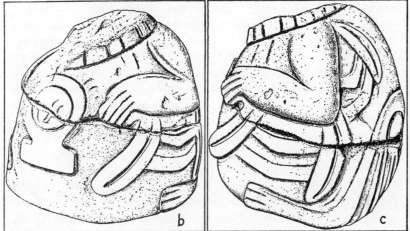

Fig. 37. Crude Human Figure from Copan, Department of Copan, Honduras;
Found in the Foundations of Stela 4 (9.17.12.13.0?), 783? a.d.

a. Back and right side.
b. Front and left side.
c. Left profile.
Height approximately 4 feet (1.22 meters).

(4) One Copan figure has an appendage suspended from its neck but of a different type from those of Nicaragua.

(5) The Copan figures are merely delineated upon a boulder, while no such type of carving has as yet been reported from Nicaragua or La Florida.

(6) The figure from the foundations of Stela 4 is carved in the unmistakable green-tinged stone of the Copan Valley and is too large to have been imported any considerable distance. The one found under Stela 5 has been lost.

What, then, do these two Copan sculptures represent for they certainly are far removed from traditional Maya carvings at Copan, and it is unlikely that they are the results of a contemporaneous neophyte sculptor? They must have been carved before the Maya acquired the skill in carving which is represented in their well known sculptures at Copan. Can they be correlated with Usulutan ware, a presumably early non-Maya ceramic horizon found in early Copan deposits? [34] Are they the first horizon of Maya carving or do they represent some other early culture in the Copan Valley? The feather ornaments on one of the figures suggest a Maya origin, as sculptures to the south are barren of this almost universal Maya characteristic. If they were not rediscovered by them, the later Maya inhabitants, if dates can be relied upon, would have had to keep one figure 275 years before using it in the foundations of a stela and the other, 350 years. Students who are searching for possible early stone carving in Central America should not overlook these two sculptures.

It has been suggested further that the "Crude Group" of sculptures found at Kaminaljuyú in the Guatemala highlands is stylistically affiliated through the two Copan statues to the La Florida figure and hence to Nicaraguan sculpture. If the stylistic association between the two Copan figures and the Nicaragua–La Florida sculpture is not accepted, the Kaminaljuyú "Crude Group" bears no relationship to, and is not to be associated with, the Nicaragua material. It is the author's belief that that is the case.

[34] Lothrop, Pottery Types, 1927; Lothrop, Atitlan, 1933, pp. 47–51.

FIG. 38. SCULPTURES FROM CHONTALES, NICARAGUA

a, a'. Human figure from Copelito, now in a Managua park. Height approximately 4 feet, 6 inches. (1.37 meters).

b, b'. Human figure from La Libertad, now in the possession of Mr. Vaughan, Finca San Francisco. Height approximately 5 feet, 4 inches (1.63 meters).

FIG. 38. (For description, see facing page.)

When, then, were these classical Nicaraguan or Chorotegan sculptures carved if one disassociates them from the two early Copan pieces? Can there be chronological significance in the fact that metal and glass artifacts are found in the same localities as so-called Chorotegan sculpture, that many of the monolithic sculptures are found standing, that most of them are in a good state of preservation, and that at the coming of the Spaniards in the sixteenth century the Chorotega, to whom these sculptures have been attributed, were occupying that section of Nicaragua? Again one must complain about the dearth of responsible and expository archaeological data from many sections of Central America. It seems unlikely, however, that these Nicaraguan sculptures could have been carved before or during the period when the Maya civilization flourished at Copan.

Occasional reports have established the existence of aboriginal remains scattered along the western slopes of the Cordillera Amerrique, Department of Chontales, east of Lakes Managua and Nicaragua.[35] Little attention has been paid to ceramics or to the extent and distribution of mounds in Chontales, but the more spectacular sculptures have attracted some curiosity and comment. Moreover, an interesting situation arises regarding the sculptures. They form a uniform, independent group differing greatly in detail and execution from the classical Nicaraguan statues discussed above. All are carved on a round shaft of stone with little attempt at giving form to the human figure (Figs. 38, 39, *a*, *c*). The technique is low relief applied to a three rather than a two-dimensional surface, a rare procedure in Middle America. The forearms are characterized by being placed across the torso, one above the other, while the legs are usually flexed. On the head is a coronet or fillet sometimes crowned with a complete miniature animal. This treatment of the "alter ego" motif differs greatly from the Nicaraguan sculptures previously discussed in that the animal form resting upon the head of classical figures is of mammoth proportions, and is only the head of the animal which protrudes far out in front of the human figure. The complete miniature animal found on Chontales sculpture is however not unlike Costa Rican animal representation. Some of the Chontales figures hold scepters, clubs, or spears in their hands, a Nicaraguan feature

[35] Belt, Naturalist, 1874; Boyle, A Ride, 1868; Crawford, Nicaragua, 1895; Sequeira, Chontales, 1938. Mr. Sequeira has recently conducted excavations at Copelito which is one of numerous sites in Chontales reported by him and his daughter. The two illustrated sculptures from Copelito were discovered by him and removed to Managua.

Fig. 39. Sculptures from Chontales, Nicaragua, and Costa Rica

a. Human figure from Copelito, Nicaragua, now in the possession of Doña Josefa, Vda. de Aguierre, Managua. Height approximately 5 feet (1.50 meters).

b. Human figure with "alter ego" motif from Nacasola, Department of Guanacaste, Costa Rica. Height approximately 8 feet (2.40 meters). (After Cabrera, Guanacaste, 1924.)

c. Human figure from El Silencio, Nicaragua. Height approximately 5 feet (1.50 meters).

confined to this region. Another characteristic not found elsewhere is incised detail strongly suggestive of textile representation. This textile motif is most vividly portrayed on the back of a figure from Copelito now in Managua and unfortunately almost half encased in a cement foundation (Fig. 38, *a, a'*).

As no group or class of sculptures in Middle America north of Nicaragua bears striking resemblances to the Chontales figures, one is forced to look to the south. Costa Rican sculptures provide few similarities, but from Central Panama Verrill and Lothrop illustrate carvings at Rio Caño, Province of Coclé, strongly reminiscent of the Chontales statues.[36] Further, it should not be overlooked that there is a possibility of a connection between the sculptures of Chontales and those of Callejón de Huailas in Peru.[37]

When these Chontales monoliths were carved and by whom must remain unanswered for the time being. A clue as to age may be gleaned from their excellent state of preservation. Such sharpness of detail as illustrated in all known examples and especially on the breast ornament of the figure from El Silencio, now in the possession of Dr. Joaquín Gómez of Managua (Fig. 39, *c*), hardly argues for many centuries of exposure to a tropical climate. Suffice it to say that they comprise a uniform group, isolated in an unexplored area, that they bear little resemblance to, and may be considered independent of, classical Nicaraguan sculptures, and that they fall into the southern rather than the northern sculptural complex.

Turning our attention to how the above condensed sketch of monumental sculpture fits into the general monolithic complex in Middle and South America, one is faced with an array of contradictory and puzzling data. The Baul stela and the Tuxtla statuette, both bearing extremely early dates, are found in the only areas where colossal heads and crude human figures occur, namely, southern Mexico and the Pacific slope of Guatemala and Salvador. Aside from the dates there is little reason to suspect that the heads and figures were carved previous to or even contemporaneously with the Maya Old Empire, but rather are the result of later Nahua developments and penetrations to the south. That these Mexican penetrations postdate the Maya Old Empire is indicated by historical evidence and by

---

[36] Verrill, Coclé, 1927; Lothrop, Coclé, 1937, Fig. 17.

[37] For illustrations of sculptures from Callejón de Huailas, see Tello, Peru, 1929; and Tello, Wira-Kocha, 1923. There are literally hundreds of sculptures from this area of which only a handful have been published.

numerous types of smaller stone carvings, presumably late material, common to southern Mexico and the Pacific area of Guatemala and Salvador. The author is in complete accord with Morley in his belief that the Baul stela does not represent a contemporary recording in the Maya system of notation. Why cannot the early date on the Tuxtla statuette be a similar inscription? Why do identical appendages exist on the mouths of the Tuxtla statuette and two Nicaraguan sculptures which the author believes postdate the Maya Old Empire? Finally, why does the jaguar head at Monte Alto bear such a marked resemblance to unquestionably early sculptures at Uaxactun? Solutions to these questions must await the future. Viewed in the light of monumental sculpture, however, the Maya neither gave to nor received much from other known Central American sources.

On the other hand, the three main groups of sculptures on the Pacific slopes of Guatemala and Salvador appear to be a direct result of Mexican influence. To these three groups of Mexican inspired sculptures should be added the chacmool and the standard bearer figure from western Salvador. South and east of Salvador there are no groups of sculptures that can be readily attributed to a northern source, other than two previously mentioned chacmool types from Nicaragua and Costa Rica. Concentrations of Mexican sculptured traits in Central America are confined therefore to the Pacific area of Guatemala and Salvador.

Jumping farther south to Nicaragua, the next locality where a focus of sculptural activity occurs, we find two horizons, one in Chontales, the other on the lake islands and in the strip of land separating the lakes from the Pacific. The classical Chorotegan sculptures on the lake islands present no clear, well-defined affinities. In conception, detail and execution they are quite barren of northern Middle American characteristics. They may be a highly localized development of a monolithic germ spreading up the Isthmus from northern South America. The type of "alter ego" motif and the modified monolithic shaft would tend to support this suggestion.[38]

---

[38] A. Kidder II, in Chapter XXXIII of this volume, discusses the chronological aspects of the alter ego motif and its penetration into Middle America. For South American examples, see Jijón y Caamaño, Cultural, 1930; Nordenskiöld, L'Amazone, 1930, Pl. XLa, b, and c, XLI; Preuss, Monumentale, 1929, Pl. 75; Schmidt, Peru, 1929, p. 152. Notice particularly the similarity in the unnatural humpback effect of a figure from South America (Preuss, Monumentale, 1929, Pl. 25, No. 3) and one from Punta de Las Figuras, Island of Zapatera, Nicaragua (Bovallius, Antiquities, 1886, Plate 23).

The Chontales sculptures fit more readily into the southern complex than do the classical Chorotegan carvings. Bas-relief technique applied to a monolithic shaft, textile representation, position of the arms, objects held in the hand, and other minor details are common to both Chontales and northwestern South America.[39] Although it is by no means conclusive that these two sculptural horizons in Nicaragua are a direct result of southern impetus, one is forced to accept that possibility.

Many existing ideas of the origin, development and interrelation of Central American cultures are sure to be revised in the future. Archaeologists have devoted their energies in large part to the more pretentious material remains existing to the north and south of the areas here discussed. The material one has to deal with, therefore, is totally inadequate for the formulation of definite conclusions. Contradictions, discrepancies, and a smattering of knowledge concerning the aboriginal remains abound on all sides. The focusing of activities on the areas to the north and south is an essential procedure, but more attention will have to be paid to Central America for a fuller understanding of the development and interrelationship of Middle and South American archaeology. In time definite links will be established between the two continents. A step in that direction has already been made through recent excavations in Panama. It is quite possible that in the next decade or so Middle and South American archaeologists, to understand and interpret their own work, will have to be on more intimate terms with what are at present two independent fields of research.

---

[39] Preuss, Monumentale, 1929, Pl. 21; Schmidt, Peru, 1929, p. 570; Perez, Tierra Dentro, 1937, Lamina XIII; Tello, Peru, 1929, Fig. 45.

XXXI

South America as Seen from Middle America.

Samuel K. Lothrop *

THE ANTHROPOLOGICAL contacts between Central America and South America since these regions were occupied by man constitute a complex problem which is far from solution. This problem has been examined previously by various scholars who, each assuming different viewpoints, have arrived at diverse conclusions. The present study is not an attempt to reconcile conflicting ideas but rather to enumerate them and to illuminate the constantly growing body of fact which ultimately should yield a solution.

At the outset we may point out that the southern continent gives evidence of long occupation by man. Physical type, linguistic complexity and cultural manifestations, although perhaps less fully recorded, appear no less varied in South than in North and Central America. Furthermore, it is clear that many and important inventions were made to the south as well as to the north of Panama.

In North America in recent years a rapidly growing body of evidence has come to light indicating that man existed on a paleolithic hunting plane, together with now-extinct animals, in times so remote that they must be measured by geological evidence.[1] Similar discoveries in southern Patagonia have shown that ancient hunting peoples had reached the Straits of Magellan as long as 5000 years ago, where they ate such animals as the extinct aboriginal horse.[2] These facts in both continents, however, are the result of isolated finds, which lack chronological and stratigraphic continuity. Hence at present they cannot be linked with more recent manifestations of culture. The foundations from which the higher civilizations of the

* Harvard, A.B., 1915; director, Peabody Museum Central American expedition, 1917; Ph.D., 1921; John Harvard fellow, 1921; research associate in Anthropology, Peabody Museum, 1920, 1933–1938; now assistant curator of Middle American Archaeology, Peabody Museum.

[1] MacCurdy, Early Man, 1937. Also Gladwin, Snaketown, Part II, 1937, Chap. IV.
[2] Bird, Antiquity of Patagonia, 1938.

New World sprang are still obscure, and today in neither continent can we safely postulate an age of more than 2000 years for the remains of any people living on an agricultural and ceramic plane.[3]

The Populating of South America

It is generally agreed among anthropologists that North America was peopled from Asia as the result of successive waves of migration across Bering Strait. It is also conceded that several physical types are represented, which are rarely encountered as a pure strain in the New World. The same physical types and their blends are found in South as well as in North America. The most widely held opinion is that tribes who had settled in the northern continent were pushed to the south by later arrivals and eventually crossed the Isthmus of Panama. The possibility is entertained, although without great conviction, that the Antilles may have served as stepping stones for a primitive migration by sea. It is even claimed that various elements in the population of South America crossed the wide waters of the Pacific in boats, braving the contrary currents and winds. In this study we shall consider only the most probable, the Isthmian route.

An examination of the topography, vegetation and climate of Panama and the adjacent territory reveals a singularly and surprisingly difficult approach to South America today. Although the Isthmus has often been crossed from ocean to ocean, we can find no record of any white man who has passed by land through the jungles between the Panama canal and Colombia since the days of the Conquistadores who then found much of the land in cultivation. Even the stalwart individual who rode his horses from Buenos Aires to Washington some years ago was constrained to pass this jungle stretch by sea.[4] Costa Rica also is a barrier to travel. At present, to our knowledge, there are only two routes south from the transcontinental railroad: the suggestively named *camino de los muertos*,[5] which follows the rugged continental divide to frigid elevations of nearly 12,000 feet, and a "trail" we have travelled through the jungles of the Atlantic coast, discernible only to the eye of a Talamancan Indian. Dire necessity alone would force primitive people to attempt

[3] Gladwin, *op. cit.*, pp. 38–39.

[4] Tschiffely, Buenos Aires to Washington, 1923; Tschiffely's Ride, 1933.

[5] This trail and the jungles below it are described in Tschiffely's Ride, 1933, pp. 224–233.

the passage of such regions, especially if the difficulties of travel were enhanced by lack of geographical knowledge.

If the possibility of southward migration by sea is entertained, it probably took place along the Atlantic coast of the Isthmus and up the rivers which drain the inter-Andean valleys of Colombia. Of the Pacific coastal waters between Panama and Ecuador a recent voyager in a small boat states: "head winds, heavy precipitation, rough seas, roadsteads widely open to windward . . . combined to make the cruise hurried, uncomfortable, and hazardous." On one stretch of the coast, "rollers that follow one another in rapid succession sometimes begin, even in calm weather, out of sight of the low shore. Violent tidal currents, rips, white water shoals, and dangerous flotsam of forest wreckage, which includes countless trunks of large trees, give the whole area a well earned sinister repute." [6]

Granted these unfavorable conditions, how was South America populated? There seem to be two answers: that migration took place by sea or that the climate has changed. The former can neither be proved nor disproved but, in our opinion, it is improbable that vessels capable of ocean navigation existed at the remote epoch of which we write. The question of climatic change, however, we shall examine.

The road of migration from Asia to North America has been controlled by the spread of glaciers which have periodically opened and closed it. Geologists believe that interglacial barriers were absent in North America some 70,000 years ago, again about 40,000 years ago and thirdly from about 20,000 years ago to the present. During the last glaciation it is believed that the air temperature was lowered until about 8000 to 6500 B. C. and that the level of the sea was reduced between 83 and 93 meters (272 and 305 feet) as a result of evaporation.[7] If then we can postulate the presence of man in North America before the last glaciation, we have in the ice sheets a mechanism which would crowd him to the south and, at the same time, ameliorate the difficulties of travel in that direction. The probability that South America was peopled in this fashion will be greatly increased if the presence of man in North America before the last advance of ice can be definitely determined. Studies of glacial clays,

[6] Murphy, Littoral of Pacific, 1939, pp. 2, 14.
[7] Antevs, The Last Glaciation, 1928, p. 81; Climate and Early Man, 1937, p. 125.

as yet unpublished, indicate that the so-called Folsom culture flourished towards the end of the last glacial period.

At the present time no trace of early migration to South America has been detected in the Isthmian region by archaeology except in Nicaragua, where footprints have been discovered in mud-flows correlated by geologists with the first eruptions which eventually built up the existing chain of volcanoes.[8] In Costa Rica and Nicaragua we discern the presence of an agricultural, pottery-making population at a much later period, which, owing to the presence of objects traded from Salvador, may be correlated in part with the late Maya and Pipil cultures.[9] No remains have been unearthed in Panama to which an age of more than two or three centuries before the Spanish conquest can be given.[10]

GROWTH OF PRIMARY CULTURE IN SOUTH AMERICA

This subject has been ably treated in detail by Nordenskiöld [11] and we shall confine ourselves to certain comments related to our problem. In the first place, it is demonstrable that the American Indian has repeatedly made mechanical inventions and has domesticated food plants and animals of fundamental importance to his existence. This is acknowledged because many culture traits are confined to the New World or to a particular part of the New World. South America as a whole exhibits admirable adaptation to environment and has contributed her full share of inventive genius.

In the development of higher cultures the most important step is marked by the invention or adoption of agriculture. In this respect South America perhaps outranks Middle America, for botanists in recent years have detected important centers of domestication in Colombia, Peru, Chile and the highlands of Brazil. In Peru alone over seventy plants of economic value were cultivated, including cotton and tobacco. Many important South American food plants have never been transplanted in other regions. Among these are ulluco (*Ullucus*), oca (*Oxalis*), anyu (*Tropaeolum*), yautia (*Xanthosoma*), llacou (*Polymnia*), arracha (*Arracacia*), achira (*Canna*), jataco (*Amaranthus*) and quinoa (*Chenopodium*).[12]

[8] Lothrop, Costa Rica and Nicaragua, 1926, Chap. II.
[9] *Ibid.*, Pl. LXIX, Fig. 281, p. 396.
[10] Lothrop, Coclé, Part I, 1937, p. 202.
[11] Nordenskiöld, Origin of the Indian Civilizations, 1931.
[12] Merrill, Plants and Civilizations, 1937, p. 40.

Nordenskiöld [13] has listed some sixty-five culture elements found in the temperate zones of both North and South America but occurring sporadically or not at all in the intervening regions. These are presumably traits not adapted to life in the tropics. He concludes that this situation may have been created by migrations which passed the tropics so rapidly that knowledge of traditional culture was retained or that slowly migrating groups successively adapted their culture to climates of the sub-arctic, temperate, tropic and again the temperate zones. In the latter case, it appears that similar needs under comparable living conditions have produced similar cultures.

EXCHANGE OF PRIMARY CULTURE

The question of cultural exchange between the Americas may be divided into two categories, in one case dealing with a large body of primitive traits whose history is still shrouded in the remote past, in the other instance embracing more advanced aspects of culture which archaeology has clothed to some extent with chronology. We deal first with the former.

We have already pointed out that the American Indian possessed marked ability to make inventions and to adjust himself to his environment. While unyielding in many instances to external influence and clinging tenaciously to inherited culture patterns—our Pueblo tribes well exemplify this—at times the Indian has acquired new ideas and forms of culture with avidity. Classic examples of rapid acculturalization are the spread of the horse in both North and South America [14] and the dispersion of hens throughout South America so rapidly that they reached Peru before Pizarro.[15]

The examples of diffusion we have cited occurred in historic times and the manner in which they took place is fairly well understood. A point we would emphasize about them is that they did not involve mass migrations, merely the usual interchange between neighbors. The wide dispersion in earlier times of complex cultural traits such as the rubber ball game, which was known from Paraguay to Arizona and also in the Antilles, or the arrow sacrifice, which was practised from Nebraska to Peru, and also of many agricultural

[13] Nordenskiöld, Origin of Indian Civilizations, 1931, Table I.
[14] Wissler, Influence of the Horse, 1914; Nichols, Horse of the Pampas, 1939; Nordenskiöld, Deductions, 1922, Chap. III.
[15] Nordenskiöld, Deductions, 1922.

products may have taken place more slowly but in an equally un-dramatic way.

During the period when basic traits such as agriculture were spreading, presumably long before the Christian era, the climate of Panama probably was even more of a barrier to travel than it is to-day. We have remarked that the original settlement of South America perhaps was aided by glaciation in other regions, attended by lowering of the oceans and a cool climate. In the period from 5500 to 2000 B. C., however, geologists believe that the temperature was warmer than at present.[16] This no doubt fostered the growth of vegetation and facilitated the domestication of plants; yet it would increase the difficulties of travel in the tropical forests of Panama, presumably at the very moment when basic inventions were passing through the Isthmus.

Whatever the mechanism, however, it is unquestionable that in the Americas inventions did take place long ago, that plants were domesticated and, in many cases, knowledge was exchanged between the continents. As a result there arose a series of local communities, villages supported by agriculture and doubtless loosely governed. From this common base arose in later times the great theocratic states of Middle America and Peru, but the simpler cultures per-sisted beside or even within them in many localities until the Spanish conquest.

THE HIGHER CIVILIZATIONS

Great diversity of opinion exists as to the origin and interdepend-ence of the higher civilizations of Middle and South America. It is obvious to all, however, that both basic concepts and the more ad-vanced inventions, such as weaving, pottery, metallurgy and archi-tecture, were shared in common by the two areas. The question is then: why is this so? The answers which have been given in general fall into two schools of thought, one based on a theoretical single origin and the other on a multiple origin for the higher cultures.

The hypothesis of single origin is well exemplified by Dr. H. J. Spinden's "Archaic theory" which at one time seemed exceedingly plausible and was widely accepted. Dr. Spinden [17] believed, as a re-sult of the discovery of deeply stratified remains in the Valley of

[16] Granlund, Die Geologie, 1932, p. 169.
[17] Spinden, Origin . . . of Agriculture, 1917.

Mexico, that the most ancient pottery could be correlated with the original discovery of agriculture and that a maize-pottery complex could be traced, on the basis of certain pottery and figurine types, from Mexico southward to the Amazon and Peru. This theory today, however, is no longer tenable, largely as the result of painstaking excavation carried out by Dr. and Mrs. G. C. Vaillant [18] in Mexico, who have demonstrated that the Early or Archaic culture in Mexico was not in fact a single phase but that it was the complex result of a growth of centuries. Furthermore, the Vaillants have shown that the far-from-primitive most ancient remains probably are less than 2000 years old and therefore long removed from the beginnings of agriculture. Recently Dr. Wendell C. Bennett has demonstrated that the Peruvian ceramic types which Dr. Spinden linked with Mexican were in fact a late manifestation of Chavin culture and therefore not necessarily of great age.[19]

A more complex concept of the origin of the higher cultures is advanced by Dr. Max Uhle,[20] largely on the basis of comparisons in pottery types and stone carving. Dr. Uhle believes that all manifestations of Andean culture were derived from Middle America, for the most part as the result of actual migration. In his earlier studies, Uhle postulated principally Mayan sources but in more recent publications he recognizes Chorotegan and Archaic strains, which in turn he relates to the Maya. Uhle's hypothesis will be criticised by many on the ground that they fail to see the likenesses in the objects he compares. The writer, for instance, does not believe that the Tello stela from Chavin "differs in nothing from the known pillars of Maya origin in Copan, Quirigua and other similar ruins," nor that the "glyphs" on the monolithic gateway at Tiahuanaco have a "close resemblance" to Maya glyphs.[21] These are matters of opinion, but Uhle's hypothesis is also open to criticism on factual grounds, chiefly for his failure to correlate Mayan chronology with that of Peru. If this is done, some of his postulated migrations become impossible or took place in the reverse direction. The chronology Uhle evolves for Panama,[22] based on the theory

[18] Vaillant, Early Cultures, 1935.

[19] Personal communication.

[20] Uhle, Principios de civilización, 1920, Influencias Mayas, 1922, Orígines centroamericanas, 1922a, Civilizaciones Mayoid, 1924, Civilizaciones Panameños, 1924a, Desarrollo, 1930, Civilizaciones de Manta, 1931.

[21] Uhle, Principios de Civilización, 1920, pp. 46-47.

[22] Civilizaciones Panameños, 1924a, pp. 192-193.

that each of the ten principal pottery types listed by Holmes and MacCurdy represents a separate civilization, will not bear the light of critical examination. Professor J. Jijón y Caamaño,[23] working on comparable lines, has reached comparable results regarding Ecuador, which Uhle [24] finds acceptable. Jijón envisages four waves of migration from the north into South America. The first is represented by Uhle's primitive fishing culture at Arica and by the Fuegians; the second he believes was an offshoot from the Archaic culture of the Valley of Mexico, producing Proto-Panzaleo I in Ecuador; the third wave was Chorotegan, creating Proto-Panzaleo II and, with Maya influence blended, the cultures of Chavin and Tiahuanaco; the final migration, he claims, was Mayan. Jijón's comparisons are open to the same general objections we have made in regard to Uhle's. We will discuss later the probability of Mayan penetration in South America as seen by students of the Mayan area.

Dr. Paul Rivet has published an elaborate discussion of the growth of the Andean civilizations.[25] Rivet believes, as does the writer, that culture in South America rests primarily on a common base whose source lies in the Amazon and Orinoco basins; he envisages migratory waves from the lowlands, each of which brought specific aspects of culture to the highlands, where they underwent further development. In addition, he believes that an invasion from Central America not only introduced culture traits from that area but spread the Colombian metallurgical techniques over Peru. Uhle at one time apparently held similar opinions, for in a paper written nineteen years ago [26] he states his conviction that migrations had reached the Andean region from the east and he specifically mentions Arawak. Kroeber,[27] in criticism of Rivet's theory, points out that it deals with personally selected culture elements "and its specific applications to Peru fit the facts unsatisfactorily."

The most recent, thorough and dispassionate discussion of relationships between Central and South America has been written by Dr. A. L. Kroeber, who reviews both general archaeological backgrounds and the specific traits which may indicate cultural exchange.

[23] Marea Cultural, 1930.
[24] Civilizaciones de Manta, 1931.
[25] Rivet, Civilisations Sud-américain, 1925.
[26] Uhle, Principios de Civilización, 1920, p. 44.
[27] Kroeber, Cultural Relations, 1930, p. 19.

Kroeber [28] notes a Mayoid strain in the art of Chavin, also possible Mexican influence in the terraced pyramids of the Chimu and various other minor resemblances between the two regions. His general conclusion is that "Mexico and Peru, where they are alike, differ from the intervening regions not in possessing culture material that is lacking there, but in having carried the degree of its development farther." The cultural peaks of Mexico and Peru represent then "a finer form or more intensive organization or expression of the common Middle American material." At the same time he advocates a critical examination of Chavín art by specialists in the Maya field.

The present writer is of the opinion that the key to understanding of the higher cultures in the New World may lie in the expansion of the Arawak tribes, whose original home seems to have been in the Orinoco basin. Starting untold centuries ago, Arawak groups have spread in all directions, with sufficient momentum to carry some across the Antilles to the tip of Florida and others southward to Bolivia, Paraguay, Argentina and Chile. The Arawak tongue is the most widely dispersed of any in the Americas as speech is classified at present.

Did the Arawak expansion penetrate Central America in times early enough to influence the building of the higher cultures? We think it quite possible. We suggest that the Arawak afford a logical explanation in part for the existence of the "common Middle American material" recognized by Kroeber, that they offer a possible mechanism for the spread northward in early times of such typically South American traits as manioc, coca, the blow gun and the rubber ball game. Furthermore, Arawak art is essentially curvilinear and, as known in isolated areas, for instance in the Antilles, it affords a common base from which specialized styles such as Maya, Coclé, Marajó and Chavin might alike have sprung. Arawak speech has been recorded in many places but not in Central America. Outstanding students of language,[29] however, claim that several Central American tongues, including Maya, contain an Arawak element and it seems possible that the Maya may be an offshoot of this stock or that they embody an Arawak ingredient.

The preceding paragraphs should not be considered an attempt to prove that the higher New World cultures sprang from a single

[28] Kroeber, *op. cit.*
[29] Schuller, Zur sprachlichen Verwandtschaft der Maya–Qu' itšé mit den Carib-Aruác, 1919–1920; Lenguas Indígenas, 1928.

source, but rather to point out part of the material which may be incorporated in them. It is also evident that a second outpouring from South to Central America is represented by the Chibcha who, in the Sixteenth century, occupied much of Panama and Colombia, part of Ecuador and most of the Atlantic coast of Central America, where the culture was distinctly of South American type. If the Lenca, Paya and Jicaque of Honduras are Chibchan dialects, as Lehmann believes,[30] and if they also may be classed as Penutian, as suggested by Sapir,[31] then we have for the first time a direct linking of North and South American tongues, the significance of which is still to be determined. What the Chibcha contributed culturally to the typical Central American tribes has not been fully worked out, but their influence has been noted as far north as the highlands of Guatemala.[32]

We have examined the question of northward migration from the point of view of ethnography. Let us now consider commerce. At the end of the Sixteenth century both the Inca and Aztec governments were at the apogee of their political power and territorial expansion, with the result that unusual facilities for intercontinental trade had come into existence. We have elsewhere explained [33] how this took place and have pointed out actual products of this trade: emeralds and gold from Ecuador in Coclé; presumably South American emeralds in the loot of Mexico; gold ornaments from Coclé and Colombia at Chichen Itzá in Yucatan; Peruvian goldwork in Guatemala and Oaxaca in Mexico.[34] In the case of Guatemala and Oaxaca it appears that individual travellers may have accomplished the entire journey to or from Peru because complex pottery traits, the whistling-effigy double-jar [35] and the well-known interlocking fish-pattern,[36] have been copied in the local clays and pigments of the north (Plate XX). These are features unlikely to have been invented twice but which, once seen, might easily have been imitated.

In Panama and southern Central America, in the opinion of the writer, there is a distinct Peruvian artistic strain which appears in pottery and metal designs, chiefly from Coclé and the Chorotegan

[30] Lehmann, Zentral Amerika, 1920.
[31] Sapir, American Languages, 1929.
[32] Lothrop, Zacualpa, 1936, p. 100.
[33] Lothrop, op. cit., pp. 74-75.
[34] Ibid., Fig. 68, b; 71, a, c; Coclé, 1937, Fig. 181, Table XII.
[35] Lothrop, op. cit., Fig. 92.
[36] Joyce, Mexican Archaeology, 1914, Fig. 41.

area.[37] In Peru these forms may be dated as post-Tiahuanco. Their presence farther north may be attributed in part to infiltration by land across Ecuador and Colombia and in part to trade by sea, of which there is historical record in the Sixteenth century.

Metallurgical processes also have almost without exception reached Mexico and Central America from the south. In Peru it is possible to place approximate but early dates on the invention of several different techniques. In the Maya area metal objects of foreign styles begin to appear only at the end of the Old Empire period (*ca.* 850 A. D.). A few specimens in late Teotihuacan style have been found in Mexico. Dr. Caso's excavations at Monte Alban should date the appearance of metalwork in southern Mexico.

A curious feature of the Central and South American material mentioned in the previous paragraphs is that in each instance an actual object or trait has been moved to the north. On the contrary, no actual objects of Central American manufacture have ever been recorded in South America although many cultural traits and a traffic in shells may be noted. At the same time, we have historical records indicating that northern peoples of Nahua extraction were pushing southward from Mexico: the Pipil of Guatemala and El Salvador, the Nahuatlato, Nicarao and Desaguadero of Nicaragua, the Bagaces of Costa Rica and the Sigua of Panama.[38] Regarding the culture of these groups, the writer can state from historical records and first-hand observation that in all cases beyond the Lempa River in El Salvador they had abandoned anything recognizable as Mexican except their religion and speech and, in western Nicaragua and northwestern Costa Rica, some rare polychrome pottery patterns. Instead they adopted the manner of living practised by their neighbors, Chorotegan and Talamancan tribes, probably as a result of intermarriage. In other words, the southward drift of the Nahua from the Twelfth to the Sixteenth centuries did not, so far as we know, influence South American culture and by its nature could not be expected to do so.

If we are to look for Mayan traits in the material culture of South America, there are several factors which must be considered. Obviously, if Mayan art influenced Andean art there must have been some definite form of contact which made this possible. Trade does

[37] Lothrop, Coclé, 1937.
[38] Lothrop, Costa Rica and Nicaragua, 1926, pp. 5–11; El Salvador, 1927, pp. 192–197, 216–217.

not afford an adequate explanation because we know that imperishable objects of Mayan manufacture rarely crossed their own frontiers. Among thousands of pottery vessels from Nicaragua which have passed through the writer's hands only one was obviously Mayan and there is only one other on record [39]; among tens of thousands of specimens from Costa Rica only one jar may possibly be Mayan.[40] Nothing at all which beyond argument must be of Mayan manufacture is known from Panama or South America.

The suggestion has been made by Uhle and others that not only Mayan art but Mayan tribes actually reached Peru by sea. To be sure, we know that for some time before the Conquest voyages were made from Yucatan to the gold-manufacturing lands of the Isthmus, both because there is documentary evidence [41] and because actual products of that trade have been found in Yucatan and late Old Empire cities.[42] On the other hand, there is no positive evidence (and we find it difficult to believe) that, at the very moment when the classical Old Empire cities were being founded, certain Mayas for unknown reasons sailed to far-away Panama, crossed the Isthmus, built new vessels amid insalubrious and presumably hostile surroundings and then navigated the unknown Pacific far to the south. We may also point out that in Yucatan large canoes and marine scenes are represented in frescoes during the Mexican period (1191–1437 A. D.), at which time we know there was trade with the south, but they are absent from Mayan art of more ancient eras.

Chronology also has a story to tell. In Peru we have various archaeological sequences to which an assumed but widely accepted chronology is linked by inference. In the Mayan area there is an absolute chronology, based on native inscriptions, which is joined to our time count, however, by inference. There are two correlations which have astronomical backing, differing merely by 260 years. In other words, we can place dates fairly accurately in our own chronological system and exactly in the Maya time count for many centuries and we know in part the development of material culture during this epoch. If, then, one accepts the normal Peruvian chronology and wishes to derive such Peruvian styles as Chavin, Nasca and Early Chimu from the Maya, the material used for com-

[39] Lothrop, Costa Rica and Nicaragua, 1926, Fig. 281, p. 396.
[40] Ibid., Pl. LXIX.
[41] Peralta, Costa Rica, 1883, p. 117.
[42] Lothrop, Coclé, 1937, Fig. 201; Zacualpa, 1936, pp. 71–72.

parison cannot be classical Maya because it is not old enough, but only the most ancient and stylistically divergent finds at such sites as Cahal Cunil, Copan, Holmul and Uaxactun. This material such students at Jijón and Uhle have failed to utilize or discuss.

We must conclude our remarks on the same uncertain note with which we began: archaeologists have not yet assembled enough data to determine aboriginal intercontinental relationships in the New World on a generalized basis; so-called expert opinion differs widely. At the same time, evidence is constantly coming to light which shows that an interchange of specific ideas and occasionally of actual commodities took place through the Isthmus of Panama.

XXXII

THE PHILOSOPHIC INTERRELATIONSHIP BETWEEN MIDDLE AMERICAN AND ANDEAN RELIGIONS

Philip Ainsworth Means *

PRELIMINARY APOLOGY

To one who for twenty years has not studied Mexican and Central American religions the suddenly imposed duty of examining these cults for the sake of discovering possible philosophical affinities between them and Peruvian religions is very onerous and laden with appalling complexities.

For one thing, there is too much source-material: in the pre-Spanish codices and in the post-Spanish codices, in the writings of the Spanish commentators and in those of modern scientists; and, to make matters worse, these kinds of source-material contradict one another fully as often as they corroborate.

Therefore, all that the present writer has been able to do is to select as best he could from the jumbled mass of data a few salient points which seem to illustrate the whole subject and which at the same time seem to offer grounds for comparison with analogous points concerning the religions of ancient Peru.

MEXICAN AND CENTRAL AMERICAN RELIGIONS

In the earliest discernible period of sedentary culture in Mexico and Central America—that is, in that archaic period when agriculture, the arts, architecture, and so on, had made their beginnings—religion must have had correspondingly inchoate forms of modality and of expression. We may assume, without violence to verisimilitude, that the objects then worshipped were things visible to all men but mysterious to all men none the less, largely because they were but imperfectly understood. Among them would be such things as the sun and other heavenly bodies, the rain, plant-life, animal-life,

* Harvard, A.B., 1915; A.M., 1917; Associate in Anthropology, Peabody Museum, 1921–1924, 1932–1933.

and a great array of similar natural objects which clearly had important bearing on the well-being of mankind. We may also assume that a great number of humbler deities abounded which concerned small groups rather than the people at large. These would be family or tribal gods, animistic or fetichistic in character for the most part.

For obvious reasons we can do no more than guess as to the nature of the rites pertaining to these early cults. We may safely assume, however, that down to the time when material culture was beginning to shift from the archaic phase into the earliest archaeologically definable quasi-historical phase, religious cults concerned themselves mainly with natural phenomena which, although more or less personified, were served with relatively simple rites by the elders of the people who had not yet become a professional class of priestly officiants.

In other words, we may suppose that, down to the opening centuries of the Christian era,[1] the peoples of Mexico and Central America were worshippers of innumerable gods, some localized and others generalized, who ranged from mere fetiches revered by a few individuals up to personifications of great natural phenomena who were worshipped over wide areas. That adoration had a direct and popular mode of expressing itself without the intervention of a definite priestly class is altogether likely, but not susceptible to proof.

Afterwards, however, during period after period, priestcraft waxed until it attained to amazing power over the minds of the people and over all that pertained to the forms of worship. Native art and tradition, and also modern scientific studies, agree in informing us that, from the earliest quasi-historical period, at Teotihuacan and elsewhere in Mexico and in Yucatan and Guatemala, down to and even beyond the time of the Spanish conquest, the people were held fast in spiritual and moral slavery to an enormous and baleful priesthood serving a confused throng of fearful gods.[2]

No subject is so intricate, so confused, and so confusing as that of Middle American religion as it is made known to us by the sources indicated above. Here one can mention only a few of its chief char-

---

[1] Vaillant, Archaeological Setting, 1934, Early Cultures, 1935b, Chronology, 1935a; Popenoe, Playa de los Muertos, 1934; Thompson, Mexico before Cortes, 1933; Tozzer, Chronological Aspects, 1926; Gann and Thompson, History of the Maya, 1935.

[2] Tozzer, Maya and Lacandones, 1907; Means, Centro-America y Sud-America, 1917.

acteristics. In general one may say that the personalities of its deities are far from clear-cut and that their functions and attributes overlap and conflict in such a manner as to indicate that, although theology had long since become aristocratic rather than popularistic, theological ideas, even among the priesthood, were far from being settled and definite. At the same time, the prevalence of excessive elaboration in all things pertinent to the appearance and functions of the gods, and also the oppressive and horrible universality of human sacrifice in their honor, are eloquent of the sinister dominance of a priestly caste which systematically terrorized the people for the sake of the gods.

It is not for a moment suggested that the Mexican priests slaughtered thousands of men yearly only for the fun of the thing. There was a philosophic concept underlying human sacrifice: The gods made man, and man must repay them for the privilege of life by yielding up his'own life-blood so that they may have the sustenance which they require.[3]

In the light of this dogma—obviously a priestly fabrication—one can understand the bloody nature of pre-Spanish Mexican religion. To take a specific example we may consider the peculiarly Aztec cult of Huitzilopochtli, God of War, whose great temple in Tenochtitlan was dedicated by Ahuitzotl in 1486, on which occasion tens of thousands of captured warriors were immolated.[4]

To the certainly frenzied, and perchance sadistic, minds of Aztec priests it seemed right and logical that the God of War should be nurtured on hearts torn from the breasts of warriors. Yet we should remember that Huitzilopochtli was held also to be a sun-god, born from the womb of Mother Earth every morning, fighting his way to dominance in the heavens during each day, and dying every night.[5]

One suspects that the solar aspect of Huitzilopochtli was the original one and that, before the theologians got hold of it and warped it out of shape with extraneous matter, this cult was as gentle and benignant as sun-cults elsewhere. Or, as Dr. Vaillant has suggested to me in talk, Huitzilopochtli may have begun as a hunting-god, being afterwards metamorphosed into the terrible war-god for whose

[3] Caso, Aztec Religion, 1937, p. 12; Thompson, Mexico before Cortez, 1933, p. 168.
[4] Alexander, Latin-American Mythology, 1920, pp. 58–59; Caso, Aztec Religion, 1937, pp. 12–14.
[5] Caso, Aztec Religion, 1937, pp. 12–14; Thompson, Mexico before Cortez, 1933, pp. 153–156.

belly prisoners must be captured in war and later slain and eaten by the priests.

Similar sinister perversions of originally benign cults into pejorative theological frenzies could be traced by the dozen, in the Mexican religions alone. Altogether different from the bulk of the god population was Quetzalcoatl, whose counterpart among the Mayas was Kukulkan, both names meaning The Feathered Serpent. In one aspect Quetzalcoatl was God of the Winds, and as such he seems to have been associated with all the cardinal points of direction. Moreover, he was said to have arrived in Mexico from a mysterious land called Tlapallan beyond the eastern ocean and to have made his first home in Mexico at Tollan. He was early worshipped at Teotihuacan, where his superb temple still impresses all who see it. Later his enemy, Tezcatlipoca, drove him to Cholula where an immense pyramid-temple was reared in his honor. At the end of his life in Mexico, among whose people he introduced many useful arts, sciences, and industries, he went away over the eastern sea, using for a ship a raft of serpents. Departing, he promised that he would return with some of his own kind.[6]

In Quetzalcoatl-Kukulkan we have the one benevolent Middle American divinity, and the one whose cult was the least bloody. Upon his personality and career the Spaniards seized after the Conquest, covering it with new details such as his having a white and bearded countenance. Some Spaniards even identified him with the Apostle Saint Thomas.[7] On the whole, however, it is more rational to believe that Quetzalcoatl was an unusually wise and kindly man, perhaps a king of Tollan, and certainly a "genius," who, after benefiting the Mexicans, passed away and was afterwards remembered as a culture-hero god.

The Maya deities and those of lower Central America were far less fearsome than those of Mexico. For the most part they were animal-gods to whom sacrifices other than human were made. Even the major gods, Itzamná among the Mayas and Votan in Guatemala and southwards, were free from the insatiable thirst for human blood which marked their Mexican compeers.[8]

[6] Caso, Aztec Religion, 1937, pp. 14–20; Alexander, Latin-American Mythology, 1920, pp. 66–71, 88–89.
[7] Alexander, Latin-American Mythology, 1920, pp. 66–67.
[8] Alexander, Latin-American Mythology, 1920, pp. 131–142; Thompson, Mexico before Cortez, 1933, pp. 157–164; Gann and Thompson, History of the Maya, 1935.

The most impressive and admirable aspect of Middle American religion, and the one most rich in true philosophy, is the calendrical. That it was shaped by the same priests who inexorably moulded the ghastly dogmas and cults which we have mentioned constitutes a great paradox. Even a modern astronomer must be filled with wonder when he contemplates the intricate and precise calculations set forth in remarkable hieroglyphs, the minute observations of the heavenly bodies, and all the other processes whereby the priests of ancient Mexico and Yucatan attained to that lordly wisdom whereupon they based their astoundingly accurate measurements of time.[9]

Calendrical lore, however, and the hieroglyphic science in which it found expression seem never to have reached farther south than Nicaragua. To this point we shall revert later. For the moment it suffices to say that the preliminary processes leading to their perfecting must have begun many centuries before Christ. Therefore, it is unlikely that any mass-migration from Central America southwards which set out during the last five centuries before Christ could have failed to carry with its other cultural baggage the germs at least of the hieroglyphic and calendrical sciences. Yet not a trace of them do we find beyond Nicaragua.

ANDEAN RELIGIONS

What little we know of the more advanced Peruvian religions prior to about A. D. 600 we glean from the art of the Early Chimu and Early Nazca cultures in, respectively, the northern and the southern halves of the Peruvian coast. We know not whether these cultures came thither already well grown or whether they sprang up from some variant of the archaic culture. At any rate, their peoples had innumerable animal-gods, some of which, to judge by the portrayals of them in art, were definitely hostile to man. We have, however, no indication that their worship was based upon the dogma that man must feed the gods with his own blood. At the same time, other deities are evidently bearers of gifts to man, and so, in spite of their bizarre shapes, they have a benign appearance. In general it

[9] Bowditch, Numeration, 1910; Morley, Introduction, 1915, Copan, 1920; Spinden, Maya Art, 1913, Ancient Civilizations, 1928, Maya Dates, 1930; Goodman, Maya Dates, 1905; Thompson, Civilization of the Mayas, 1927, Correlation, 1927a, p. 102, Maya Chronology, 1937; Martínez Hernández, Paralelismo, 1926, Significación Cronológica, 1928.

may be said that these early coast gods are not unlike their congeners in the more southerly parts of Middle America. It is possible that in this we have evidence of the comparatively close proximity of a common source within the archaic horizon; but this is mere conjecture.[10]

The summation of the art of the next great cultural period of Peru, i. e., that of Tiahuanaco (ca. 600–1100), is to be seen on the relief frieze of the celebrated Monolithic Gateway at Tiahuanaco near the southern end of Lake Titicaca. Aesthetically, this design is much further advanced in conventionalization than are the arts of the coast already mentioned. The central figure of the frieze is usually identified with the Creator-God, Viracocha. Portrayed with almost complete lack of realism, he stands upon a step-sided pyramid adorned with conventionalized condor-heads. In his four-digit hands he grasps a spear-thrower and a quiver containing javelins. His square and austere face has large round eyes from which tears course downwards, and his headdress consists of an elaborate fringe of out-raying tabs each of which terminates either in a decorative circle or else in a conventionalized puma-head. On either side of the Viracocha-figure there are twenty-four minor figures arranged in three horizontal rows of which the top and bottom rows show men with crown-like headdresses and with robes that look like wings while the middle row consists of partly anthropomorphized condors. All forty-eight figures are rushing towards the central figure bearing weapons before them. The lowest part of the design consists of decorative motifs including faces like that of Viracocha and also condor-heads.

The whole composition, marked by a great degree of formalism, is rigidly balanced and symmetrical. The delicacy of its execution is impressive, but it is unlike anything in the art of Middle America. Obviously it was intended to set forth religious beliefs as to the nature of which, however, we can only guess. Perhaps it is a safe conjecture that Viracocha, standing upon the earth and reaching upwards to the sky, is sending his tears to water the soil while the attendant figures, men and condors, rush forward to give him their homage and support.[11]

[10] Means, Ancient Civilizations, 1931, Chap. III.

[11] Schmidt, Kunst und Kultur, 1929, pp. 357–364, and *passim;* Lehmann and Doering, Kunstgeschichte, 1924, pp. 15–17, 28–30; Stuebel and Uhle, Ruinenstaette, 1892, *passim;* Joyce, Weeping God, 1913; Means, Ancient Civilizations, 1931, Chap. IV.

If this interpretation be valid, we have here a monument representing a wholesome and beautiful nature-worship. Certainly, there is nothing frenzied or cruel in it. Instead, there is a rich and, for us, esoteric symbolism involving the Supreme Being as a rain-giver and his relations with the creatures of earth. True, the forms in which the concept is set forth are clearly the result of priestly influence; but that influence has been exercised in a manner widely different from that of Mexico.

The religion of the Incas—Peru's last native dynasty—and of their subjects is better known to us than that of any earlier period for the reason that many Spaniards saw it still functioning when they entered the land and described it for us. Later, after the official establishment of Christianity, various ecclesiastical writers were shocked to find a vast array of widely varying pagan cults still strongly surviving throughout the country. The horrified descriptions of these cults which the good Fathers drew up constitute, paradoxically enough, the chief means whereby knowledge of them has been preserved to modern times.[12]

The religious situation under the Incas may be summed up by saying that there were two chief strata of cults. The one consisted of a vast series of animistic, fetichistic, and perhaps totemic cults widely dispersed among the people. They were concerned with innumerable and varied things such as animals, vegetation, springs, rivers, strange rock-formations, mythological persons (sometimes regarded as "ancestors"), and so on. Collectively, these objects of worship were called *huacas* (holy things) in the language of the Incas. There is no doubt that most of the huaca-cults were very ancient and that they were deeply rooted in the hearts and minds of the people. In general they were simple, unphilosophical, and harmless cults built around naturalistic concepts and served by crude rites and by sacrifices of fruits and of animals and of food.

The second stratum of religions under the Incas was the peculiar property of the ruling caste in the earlier reigns of that dynasty. It consisted of the richly ritualistic worship of the Sun, the Moon, and other super-terrestrial deities. It was, in effect, the State Church, and its High Priest was always a near kinsman of the Sapa Inca, Sole-and-Supreme Inca, or Emperor. Inti, the Sun, and Mamaquilla, Mother Moon, were regarded both as brother and sister and as hus-

[12] Arriaga, Extirpación, 1621; Avila, Narrative, 1873.

band and wife; from them, so the people were taught, the Incas descended, if not carnally, at any rate spiritually.[13]

In this last element of alleged descent from divinities of the sky we find in the Incas of Peru a wide divergence from the religious philosophy of Mexico and Middle America. In those northern regions there was no earthly dynasty which ventured to claim ancestors so august as these beneficent gods whom the Incas hailed as their progenitors. We may, therefore, consider that the concept of divine descent, whether carnally or spiritually, was in its final form a peculiarly Peruvian idea without trace of influence from the northern regions. Or, if we prefer, we may hold that the Sun and the Moon were originally the huacas of the Inca family, the totemic ancestors of the imperial caste; but, even so, they were totems altogether higher pilosophically than all other totems and consequently they owed nothing to such totems as regards their evolution into divine ancestors.

A much-neglected fact concerning Incaic religion is this: Although the Incas themselves were a great military dynasty among whom warfare was profoundly honored and by whom it was brought to a high state of scientific perfection, and although the earlier dynasties of the Andean area were likewise experts in and devotees to warfare, none of the Andean peoples ever—so far as we now know—envisioned a God of War. In this we see a striking evidence of the philosophical gulf between the religions of Middle America and those of the Andean area.

As their empire expanded from its homeland in Cuzco, spreading in all directions by grace of a combination of warfare with diplomacy, the Incas encountered more and more of the local huaca-cults which had existed from time immemorial. With characteristic sagacity they incorporated the huaca-cults into the pantheon of their State religion, giving to each one a minor but honorable place and part in the many ceremonies which filled the *huata* or ceremonial year of their empire. This broad-mindedness, coupled with the non-

[13] Garcilaso, Commentaries, Pt. I, Bk. II, Chaps. I and IV; Sarmiento de Gamboa, History of Incas, Chap. XXXVII, and *passim;* Santa Cruz Pachacuiti-yamqui Salcamayhua, Account, 1873, pp. 67–120, and *passim;* Cieza de León, Chronicle, Pt. II, Chaps. XXVIII and XXIX; Markham, Incas, 1910, *passim;* Alexander, Latin-American Mythology, 1920, Chap. VII, *passim;* Jijón, Religion, 1919; Means, Ancient Civilizations, 1931, pp. 417–422; Joyce, South American Archaeology, 1912.

deification of war, displays the vast difference between the Middle American warfare-to-get-victims-for-the-gods and the Andean warfare-to-bring-the-unenlightened-into-Incaic-civilization. In other words, the Middle Americans fought in order to obtain human food (prisoners of war) for their gods and the Andeans fought in order to distribute as widely as possible the benison of their admirable type of culture.

The *huata* was based on the equinoxes and on the solstices, four periodically recurring solar moments which were well understood, and the twelve moon-months were nicely adjusted to the solar year by means of special additional days. The *huata* began with the autumnal equinox, in June, and each of its months had appropriate festivals in which the State religion of the Sun and all the huaca-cults took their allotted parts. Ritual observances, including sacrifices of animals and libations of maize-beer, but only very rarely—if ever—entailing loss of human life, made up an impressive body of ceremonials, many of them performed in the public squares of cities and towns, others in the Sun-Temple before large assemblies of the elite.[14]

The astronomical lore upon which the Incaic huata was based was infinitely less intricate and profound than that of the Mexicans and the Mayas. For one thing, it completely lacked even rudimentary forms of hieroglyphic science. By means of shadow-casting towers called *sucanca*, and by means of gnomons carved in large boulders called *intihuatana*, the Peruvians arrived at an understanding of the equinoxes and of the solstices. As did the Mexicans, the Peruvians ascribed to the equinox a special importance. They realized that at noon on an equinoctial day no tower or gnomon would cast a shadow. Therefore, they held that at that moment the Sun would descend among them, and they prepared to celebrate the event with appropriate ceremonies. Mrs. Nuttall went to great pains to point out how the equinoctial "descent of the sun" was observed with rejoicings in all the civilized parts of tropical America.[15] In this parallel we cannot, however, claim to see proof of any direct contact between the different regions. It was simply a question of all the

[14] Baudin, Formation de l'Elite, 1927, and L'Empire, 1928; Means, Ancient Civilizations, 1931, pp. 367-385.
[15] Garcilaso, Commentaries, Pt. I, Bk. II, Chaps. XXI-XXIII; Cieza, Chronicle, Pt. II, Chap. XXVI; Nuttall, Sobre un Monumento, 1932.

tropical peoples becoming aware of an easily perceived phenomenon in nature.

Thus, on astronomical knowledge far more rudimentary than that of the Mexicans and the Mayas, the Incaic Peruvians based their solar year. They probably had, moreover, no concept of series of years building up into cycles such as the Middle Americans had. Nor are we told that each individual year had its special name in Peru as it did in Middle America. From all this one must conclude that the Peruvians had a much less well-developed sense of time than did the learned class among the Middle Americans. True, the late Baron Nordenskiöld sought to establish certain *quipu-cuna*, or knotted-string records, as proofs of a longer time-sense; but, in this case, the great Swedish scientist fails to carry conviction to one's mind.[16]

It is in the field of pure reasoning that the Peruvians, in the person of the greatest of the Incas, Pachacutec (fl. ca. 1400–1448), soared to philosophic heights far above those reached by any other native American thinkers. That unequalled ruler called a conclave of all the Sun-Priests to Cuzco in order that they might deliberate upon the tenets, dogmas, and rites of the State Church. After they had done so, he suddenly asked them if they could not conceive of a God even higher and more powerful than the Sun. On their declaring that they could not, Pachacutec adumbrated for them the concept of an eternal, immaterial, omnipotent, and endlessly good Supreme Creator God, Viracocha or Pachacamac. Thus the great Inca formulated a lofty monotheism which became the special faith of the Inca caste in his day and afterwards. The Sun-Cult remained, however, the State religion as far as the people were concerned.[17]

The beautiful, pondering, wistful supplications to Viracocha which have come down to us from late Incaic times are fully as admirable as the finest things of the sort from ancient Mexico. Even the poet-king Nezahualcoyotl never surpassed them. Yet, aside from a deeply pensive melancholy which marks them all, it cannot be said that these compositions display any philosophic interrelationship between the religious ideas of the peoples in the two great civilized regions of ancient America.

[16] Nordenskiöld, Calculations, 1925; Locke, Ancient Quipu, 1923, pp. 31–32, where he shows that quipus probably were not used for calculations.

[17] Means, Ancient Civilizations, 1931, pp. 427–428, where the chief sources are cited in full, including: Cabello de Balboa, Cobo, Cieza de León, Garcilaso, and Sarmiento de Gamboa.

Conclusions

We have very little evidence as to the quality of such religious ideas as were carried southwards from Middle America by the primordial migrants. It is probable that when we shall have learned more about the distribution of the archaic types of culture we shall gain also more data concerning the religious elements in them. In the meanwhile we may note that the complete absence in South America of even the most rudimentary forms of hieroglyphs and of inscribed calendars is a sure indication that the migrant stream must have left Middle America before writing even began to be evolved there.

From this point we may go on to say that after the putative archaic culture had arrived from the North—by land or by sea or by both—it slowly developed in its Andean habitat without further influence from outside. In so doing Andean culture rested, as did Middle American culture, on an archaic base; but, unlike Middle American culture, it never developed such tangibles as writing, and it did evolve a number of elements peculiar to itself, chief among them a veritable genius for imperial political organization far surpassing anything of the kind in the North.

In the realm of religion, also, the Andean folk shaped their own beliefs and rites, doing so in a manner altogether different in spirit and in content from that of the Middle Americans. Therefore, the quest for religious ideas common to both regions must be made in the stratum of religious cults which is most nearly common to both regions, namely in the rude and humble local cults of Middle America and in the analogous huaca-cults of Peru, both of which undoubtedly trace back to an archaic horizon, and both of which survived until after the Spanish conquest side by side with the later and higher cults which were fostered, but in such divergent ways, by the priesthoods of the two regions. Only when these archaic and popular cults shall have been thoroughly explored shall we begin to have an understanding of the philosophic interrelationship of Middle American and South American religions.

XXXIII

South American Penetrations in Middle America

Alfred Kidder II *

THE DETERMINATION of pre-Columbian penetration from South America into Middle America is an historical problem, depending for solution upon a detailed knowledge of the ethnography and archaeology of both regions, and particularly of the chronological relationships of early archaeological phases. Although there are numerous traits of culture common to both Middle and South America, in most cases the place of origin is uncertain. It is reasonable to suppose that an interchange of ideas, techniques and actual objects had been going on for many centuries prior to the Conquest. Some of the later introductions into Middle America are undoubted. Further in the past, however, it becomes increasingly difficult to find satisfactory evidence for the time or place of origin of given traits, and the direction of dispersal from a center. Thus the question of penetration, viewed broadly, entails the entire problem of the origin, development and history of the higher cultures of the New World.

At present we know that the higher cultures of Mexico and Central America were established on a firm basis of agriculture many years before the beginning of the Christian era. Datable remains of that period are lacking, it is true, but nothing can be more certain than that the early history of the Maya, for example, covered many centuries before the inscription of the Tuxtla statuette. In the Andean and Amazonian areas absolute chronology is still very uncertain. Sequences have been established in Peru and Bolivia, beginning with full-blown, markedly specialized cultures thought to date from the first half of the first millennium A. D. Just as certainly as the classical Maya of the Old Empire were preceded by years of development, so were the extraordinary phases which we know as Tiahuanaco, Chavin, Nazca and Chimu.

* Harvard, A.B., 1933; A.M., 1935; Ph.D., 1937; Assistant in Anthropology, 1933–1935; now Instructor and Tutor in Anthropology, Harvard, and Research Associate, Peabody Museum.

In Middle America no remains of great absolute age have been discovered. There is no evidence as to the nature of the non-agricultural forerunners of the later people. South America, however, has produced such remains, at the extreme southern tip of the continent.[1] As in the case of North American finds of undoubtedly even greater age, the Patagonian remains provide a mark to shoot at, a gap to fill and a respectable period for the development and growth of a local, that is, a South American, group of cultures. For many years Central America has been regarded by most Americanists as the giver of the fundamentals of New World neolithic life. There are many reasons why final judgement on this point should be suspended, not the least of which is the evidence from Patagonia, suggesting that the Indians had already passed through more favourable regions at an early date, and that some presumably remained there.

The fact that we can actually demonstrate remains of man in South America to be earlier than anything else yet known from south of the Rio Grande is no proof, of course, that the beginnings of higher culture were made in the southern continent. On the other hand, the still-persistent faith in the Central American origin of agriculture and associated neolithic arts cannot now be accepted without reserve for various reasons.

In the first place, maize has generally been considered the plant which provided the Indians with the means of achieving a higher culture. This is undoubtedly true, but it was probably not the *first* plant brought under domestication in all areas. As Thompson [2] suggests, there is a distinct possibility that manioc was cultivated before maize. Manioc is the great root staple of the warm regions of South America, botanically indigenous to the Amazon region. It spread presumably at a fairly early date into Middle America as far as Mexico and was in use on the Peruvian coast in the earliest horizons. There are a number of other plants not used in Middle America, such as the potato, quinoa and a number of root crops important in the Andes which may have provided a very early impetus toward higher culture, as strong as that which maize undoubtedly did produce. Multiple independent beginnings of New World agriculture are distinctly probable.[3]

Maize has generally been considered in the past to be of Central

---

[1] Bird, Antiquity and Migrations, 1938.
[2] Thompson, South America, 1936, p. 14.
[3] Sauer, Agricultural Origins, 1936, p. 288.

American botanical origin and to have been first domesticated there, but now these theories are both open to question. Peru was suggested as a centre of domestication some years ago and various investigators have considered certain specialized but fundamental types to be of South American origin.[4] The most recent botanical evidence has supported, if not proved, the idea that South America is the original home of maize and that Middle America was not concerned in its first domestication.[5] These factors all suggest the possibility that the basic ideas of domestication and concurrent first steps toward civilization were made in South America. Whether this is true wholly or in part, South America is placed in a favourable position for cultural give-and-take with Middle America as far into the past as archaeological knowledge has led us.

There is no doubt that such give-and-take took place across the Isthmus of Panama. The direction, however, in which traits and trait complexes were diffused is often uncertain on account of lack of archaeological and distributional data. It is quite obvious that a given trait or complex cannot be traced from place to place unless its centre of dispersal can be determined. This is only possible provided its distribution in time and space points definitely to a given area.

This is rarely the case. Since this section deals with South American penetrations in Middle America, emphasis here is naturally greater upon those traits which are thought to have originated and spread from south to north. It must not be forgotten, however, that northern South America received a great deal from Central America at the same time.

One of the most striking evidences of South American penetration, possibly representing a series of actual small migrations, is afforded by linguistics. The Chibcha language of Colombia and northern Ecuador spread into Central America possibly as far as Honduras. The Xicaque and Paya groups of Honduras, the Mosquito, Sumo, Ulva, Rama and Matagalpa of Nicaragua are, almost certainly, to be considered Chibchan in speech. All the tribes of Costa Rica and Panama, excepting the Chorotega, Subtiaba and certain small enclaves of Nahuatl speakers, were definitely of Chibchan origin (see linguistic map). "The Isthmian population in the sixteenth century presumably represented the latest immigration from the south-

[4] Sauer, *op. cit.*, p. 289.
[5] Mangelsdorf and Reeves, Origin of Maize, 1938.

ern continent," according to Lothrop.[6] Schuller [7] has suggested that Maya may be linguistically affiliated to Carib and Arawak, but this is completely uncertain at present.

Coupled with that of language there is ethnographic evidence to demonstrate the introduction of South American culture into Middle America. Chibchan groups in the regions just mentioned had fundamentally South American cultures.[8] This does not imply that they may be compared trait for trait with any given South American group, nor that their cultures were potpourris of exclusively South American traits.

There is general agreement, from the evidence of distribution, sometimes backed by archaeological evidence of antiquity, that the following traits and customs had their origin in South America. Some are northwestern South American, some Amazonian, some Andean.

Among food plants, manioc and the pineapple are certainly southern, probably Amazonian. Coca, chewed with lime in the Isthmian region, apparently never penetrated beyond the present limits of Nicaragua. Its botanical home lies in the region of the eastern slopes of the Andes. The custom of excessive intoxication on ceremonial occasions, current among many of the Middle American tribes from Honduras to Panama, is paralleled by similar excesses among South American groups in the northern, Amazonian and Andean areas.

Hunting ducks by means of allowing them to become accustomed to calabashes floating on the surface of the water and then hiding the head under a calabash cover and seizing the duck by the legs may have penetrated to Chiriquí from South America and even to Mexico.[9]

It is difficult to be sure whether house types of any sort in Central America owe their introduction to outside sources. The tree house and the house on piles are generally considered South American traits,[10] but environment may produce a need for such structures leading to their erection without outside stimuli. Such houses are common in northwestern South America [11] and occur sporadically in southern Central America. Round houses with vertical walls, found

<hr/>

[6] Lothrop, Coclé, 1937, p. 202.
[7] Schuller, Verwandschaft, 1919–1920.
[8] Mason, Observations, 1938, pp. 306, 311.
[9] Nordenskiöld, Origin, 1931, p. 43.
[10] Nordenskiöld, op. cit., p. 71.
[11] Nordenskiöld, Changes, 1920, Map 1.

in Panama,[12] are undoubtedly of South American origin. Communal houses noted among the Guetar of Costa Rica, a Chibchan tribe, are also very probably of southern origin. The wooden seat was in use in Central America as far north as Central Mexico, but its distribution points to a South American centre of dispersal.[13]

One element of household furnishing, the hammock, was certainly invented in South America and spread to Middle America. Its South American distribution [14] is exceedingly wide, while in Middle America it probably did not penetrate to the Maya area, but was apparently introduced in rather late times by Chibchan groups.

Certain elements of dress, the beaded pubic apron, the penis cover or tying up of the penis, found as far north as Costa Rica, and clothing of bark cloth, found as far north as Honduras, appear from their distribution to be South American. The same is true of such ornaments as pig tusk necklaces (known outside of South America only in Central Panama) and ear rods, as distinguished from more compact ear plugs.

Among weapons there is no doubt that the dart thrower or *atlatl* and probably the bow were introduced into South America from the north in very early times, but the blowgun was almost certainly invented in the New World in South America.[15] In southern Middle America it was used sporadically with poison darts and also as a sort of pea shooter; in the latter manner its distribution extends to Central Mexico. In South America, however, the distribution is extremely dense in the upper Amazon area [16] and, as Dixon has shown, many stages in its development from a simple to a complex instrument made of several parts can be traced.

Another weapon, demonstrably very old on the Pacific coast of South America, is the pierced stone club head, a plain doughnut-shape or star-shape ring. These were in use in Early Chimu times, and became widespread throughout the Andean area. Clubs of this sort were not generally used beyond the Nicoya Peninsula in Costa Rica, but they do occur in northern Jalisco in Mexico, and in the Bay Islands of Honduras.

One of the most interesting elements of possible South American

[12] Lothrop, *op. cit.*, Fig. 5.
[13] Nordenskiöld, Origin, 1931, p. 71.
[14] Nordenskiöld, Changes, 1920, Map 3.
[15] Dixon, Building of Cultures, 1928, pp. 121–124.
[16] Nordenskiöld, Ethnography, 1924, Map 7.

origin, which may be of relatively great antiquity, is the general use of rubber and especially the playing of rubber-ball games. In the Amazon area enema syringes of rubber were probably invented, but their use did not spread outside of South America. Ball games, however, had an enormous distribution in pre-Columbian times, from the Chané of the Paraguayan Chaco to the Hohokam of Arizona [17] and into the Greater Antilles. The striking feature of this distribution is the fact that in nearly all areas where the game was played the rules prohibited the use of the hands, limiting the players to striking the ball with head, hips or knees. Courts, often very elaborate among the Maya and Mexicans, were apparently developed in Middle America and were also used in Santo Domingo and Puerto Rico. Nordenskiöld,[18] followed by Lothrop,[19] believed the game to have been invented by the Arawak, in South America, presumably in the southern Amazon drainage, just north of the Chaco, and to have spread from South to Central America, culminating in the elaborate ritual of the Aztec "tlaxtli." Lothrop [20] suggests there is reason to believe that an "Arawak cultural stratum existed in northern Central America in very early times before the growth of such cultures as the Maya," and that perhaps later incursions of the same stock reached Panama.

The hypothesis that Arawak influence spread the ball game to Middle America is most interesting in view of recent evidence that the game, or courts always associated with it, were used by the Old Empire Maya. However, in view of the wide distribution and known antiquity of the game outside South America it is probably unsafe to commit oneself at present as to its place of origin. Although undoubtedly very ancient in South America, and quite possibly invented in the Amazon region where rubber is abundant, there is, as yet, no proof that this is so.

The higher Middle and South American cultures share certain traits of religion and sacrifice, usually associated primarily with Mexico and particularly with the Aztec. However, as Lothrop [21] has pointed out, there are many close parallels between the Chibcha of Colombia and the Aztec. Both groups practised two forms of human sacrifice; in one the heart was extracted, in the other the victim

---

[17] Haury, Ball Courts, 1937a; Rubber Ball, 1937b.
[18] Nordenskiöld, Changes, 1920, pp. 101–109.
[19] Lothrop, Coclé, 1937, p. 27.
[20] Lothrop, op. cit.
[21] Lothrop, Pottery of Costa Rica, 1926, p. 64.

was trussed up and killed with arrows or sprears, the blood flowing onto the ground. In both areas, selected captives being prepared for sacrifice were regarded as divine. Children were sacrificed to insure rainfall in both areas. In modified form these practices extended as far as Peru or farther south, and in the north, sporadically, into southern North America. Lowie [21a] has recently noted close parallels between the Aztec and the Tupinamba of Brazil in the treatment of captives to be executed. Lothrop [22] notes that human sacrifice traditionally was not introduced among the Nahua until the middle of the eleventh century. He concludes: "It is therefore quite probable that the idea is essentially a South American one, taken over and developed by the Nahua, especially the Aztec."

There are many parallel details of religious belief and practice shared by the Chibcha and the Mexicans; these, like human sacrifice, occurred in the intervening area. Men dying by sacrifice or in war and women dying in childbirth were regarded as sure of fortune in the next world. A priestly class whose members were trained for a period of years was common to both areas. The belief in a bearded white culture hero, Quetzalcoatl of the Aztec, Kukulcan of the Maya, Bochica of the Chibcha of Colombia and probably also Viracocha of the Peruvian Indians is a widespread conception, but its origin is impossible to assign to any area. The same is true of such concepts as the double-headed serpent, the interlocking fish or serpent and crested jaguar or crocodile demon, common to South and Middle American art, and of myths such as that of the revolt of utensils and weapons against their human masters, common to Mexico and Peru.[23]

There is one practice, probably of a religious character, common to both Middle and South America, of demonstrably great antiquity in the southern continent. This is the taking, preserving and displaying of trophy heads. The practice was apparently very common in Peru in the earliest archaeological phases of the coast, Early Nazca and Early Chimu, and, as is well known, its South American distribution is extensive. Nordenskiöld [24] points out that the practice was apparently both relatively rare and late in Mexico, whereas, among the Colombian Chibcha, heads were placed in front of temples. It

[21a] Lowie, South American Parallels, 1938.
[22] Lothrop, *ibid*.
[23] Krickeberg, Parallelen, 1928.
[24] Nordenskiöld, Origin, 1931, p. 69.

seems quite possible that taking and displaying of trophy heads may have had its origin in South America. It may also be connected with human sacrifice, already suggested as of possible southern origin, and the flaying of bodies. The latter practice is best known in connection with the Mexican cult of the god Xipe, in which flayed skins were worn, as was done also in Nicaragua by the Maribio.[25] Flayed human skins were used on the coast of Ecuador, however, stuffed with straw and displayed either in or in front of temples on the Manabi coast.[26] Skins of captives were similarly stuffed and displayed in highland Ecuador and the Cauca valley of Colombia. Although there is no evidence for the antiquity of flaying comparable to that for trophy heads, there is a marked possibility that human sacrifice, flaying and trophy-head taking originated in South America as a complex and spread to Mexico where certain features were greatly emphasized by the Aztecs. As in the case of the rubber ball game and many other traits it is at present impossible to be certain of a centre of dispersal.

Mortuary practices have been of little value in tracing American culture origins. The basic methods are so widespread that it is again impossible to do more than suggest that certain types of disposal of the dead appear to be South American. From the evidence of distribution, and certain antiquity [27] in South America, most students believe secondary urn burial to be of South American origin. If this is actually the case, it must have been among the earliest cultural introductions from the south into Middle America, for its distribution there is widespread and as early as the Old Empire of the Maya, at least. It is also common in southeastern North America.

Cremation, however, appears to have penetrated only sporadically into South America from the north.[28]

Preservation of bodies is undoubtedly a very old trait in South America, especially on the Pacific coast in Peru and Chile, where optimum conditions obtain. However, in northwestern South America preservation of the bodies of chiefs and important individuals by fire drying or by removal of the viscera followed by crude embalming was not uncommon, and apparently these practices spread

[25] Lothrop, Pottery of Costa Rica, 1926, p. 84.
[26] Verneau and Rivet, Ethnographie, 1912–1922, p. 49.
[27] Nordenskiöld, Changes, 1920, pp. 184–195, Map 16; Linné, Darien, 1929, pp. 212–216; Lothrop, Indians of Paraná, 1932a, p. 128.
[28] Linné, op. cit., Map 14.

into Middle America in late times,[29] probably through the agency of Chibchan-speaking groups such as the Guetar who apparently used the embalming method.[30]

Whether there is any historical connection between the Peruvian practice of supplying mummy packs with false faces in the form of masks of wood, metal, clay or leather, and the Mexican Tarascan method of applying a false head to the pack containing the cremated remains of chiefs, represents one of the peculiarly difficult problems raised by other Mexican-Peruvian parallels. Some of these have been indicated above; others are primarily archaeological.

Archaeology should be in a position to throw more light on the problems of cultural origins and penetrations than either ethnography or linguistics. However, the potentialities of archaeological research in Middle and South America have scarcely yet been realized, far less fully, or even half, exploited. With full ethnographic data it is possible to estimate the relative age of certain aspects of culture, but at present this approach is becoming less and less possible as primitive groups become acculturated and dispersed. The ultimate solutions of the basic problems expressed here are bound to be contributed by archaeology, aided by geology, paleontology, botany and other natural sciences.

At present we can only speculate on the question of ultimate origins, although we have indicated that there is much evidence pointing to the possibility that South America may have contributed far more than is generally supposed to the beginnings of higher culture in the New World.

Our present archaeological knowledge is limited almost exclusively to fully developed, and in most cases relatively very late, phases. Aside from the recent finds of great antiquity in southern Patagonia [31] or from marginal areas such as Tierra del Fuego, no definite pre-ceramic and presumably pre-agricultural phases have been discovered south of the United States. Furthermore, even the simplest agricultural cultures of Middle and South America must be the product of long developmental stages. It is apparent, then, that although present knowledge makes it possible to trace with some assurance the development and direction of the spread of certain

[29] Linné, *ibid.*, pp. 236–237.
[30] Lothrop, *op. cit.*, p. 81.
[31] Bird, Antiquity, 1938.

techniques in stone carving, pottery and metallurgy, all these belong to the higher cultures and are relatively not very far removed in time from the sources of historical information.

There have been a number of theories current in the past dealing with South American origins. Those of Spinden, Uhle and Jijón y Caamaño in particular have postulated Middle America as the source of southern culture. These theories, which deal exclusively with the evidence of fully developed, and often very late phases, are premature. It cannot be denied that many traits of Middle American origin reached South America; we may now examine some which presumably travelled in the opposite direction, and attempt to correlate them with known linguistic and ethnographic penetrations.

In Peru and Bolivia the oldest relatively dated cultures are those of Early Nazca and Paracas on the south coast of Peru; Early Chimu on the north coast of Peru and Tiahuanaco, Chavin and related phases of the Bolivian and Peruvian highlands. In the early period metal was already known and extensive trade was apparently carried on between coast and highland. Tiahuanaco culture in its classic form in the Lake Titicaca basin was apparently the culmination, artistically, of a very widespread culture whose influences were dispersed over great areas of Peru, Bolivia, Chile and in attenuated form much farther to the north. The period which followed was characterized by a second extreme localization of styles which persisted even under Inca dominance.

Archaeology in Ecuador and Colombia so far has served only to demarcate local areas marked by particular styles. Chronology, except by inference, has not been established. There is reason to believe that the remains at San Agustín, in southern Colombia, are older than the classic Chibchan of Bogotá, since nothing is said of the great monoliths of San Agustín by the first Spaniards who passed through this region. Stylistically these statues resemble Peruvian and Bolivian stone work of the middle period of the Peruvian culture sequence.

Throughout most of the rest of South America there is not even such evidence as this, although in Venezuela stratigraphic archaeology has been done.[32]

The situation in southern Middle America is little better; in spite of its continguity to the absolute dating system of the Maya, cross

[32] Bennett, La Mata, 1937; Kidder II, Ms. thesis.

dating has not been successful outside the Maya area. Lothrop [33] has examined the archaeology of Costa Rica and Nicaragua and has demarcated two general regions of the greatest importance. Western Nicaragua and western Costa Rica as far south as the Nicoya Peninsula, the Pacific area, is characterized chiefly by culture of Central American affiliation, especially in pottery. The principal wares are polychrome, exhibiting marked Maya and Mexican traits both in shape and in design. The highland area, east of the Gulf of Nicoya, the north central highlands and Atlantic coast of Costa Rica, is marked by "a culture which extended southward, with local modifications, into Colombia and Ecuador." [34] This region is closely linked archaeologically to the Chiriqui region of Panama, and extends to the north as far as the Bay Islands of Honduras.[35] At the time of the Conquest most of both regions was inhabited by Chibchan speakers, but the Nahuatl Nicarao and the Chorotega inhabited the Central American-affiliated Pacific area of Nicaragua.

This exceedingly brief sketch must serve as a background for the following discussion of certain aspects of culture which appear to have penetrated into Middle America from the south and east. It has seemed best to discuss separate categories and weigh the total evidence in conclusion rather than to attempt an areal analysis.

Architecture presents few direct, specific parallels between Middle and South America. The large pyramidal substructures of Mexico and Central America somewhat resemble the huge adobe platforms, sometimes pyramidal or crowned by pyramids, found on the Peruvian coast, and the smaller stone-faced pyramids of the north highlands of Peru. Such resemblances are probably due to common origin, as Kroeber [36] has pointed out, but, as in the case of many other traits common to Middle and South America, it is still impossible to affirm more than this. The same may apply to the corbeled vault, so highly developed by the Maya (Chapter XIII) and so crude in the southern Andes. Here it probably came into use much later than in the Maya area, and the impression is strong that Andean vaults were invented locally.

The mosaic arabesques of the walls of Mitla, in Oaxaca, have been compared to similar geometric arabesques in adobe, characteristic of

[33] Lothrop, op. cit.
[34] Lothrop, ibid., p. 89.
[35] Strong, Bay Islands, 1935.
[36] Kroeber, Cultural Relations, 1930, p. 200.

Peruvian coastal sites. There is a possibility that such arabesques represent a late Peruvian influence in southern Mexico, which presumably reached this region by way of the Pacific coast and may have been responsible for the introduction of certain metallurgical techniques as well.

Both in Middle America and in the Andean area, stone sculpture was often associated with buildings and mounds. Outside of the Maya and Mexican regions sculpture was represented primarily by carved monoliths. The concept of erecting such monoliths is undoubtedly very old. Although styles vary locally to a considerable degree, statues found from Tiahuanaco, in Bolivia, to Nicaragua, all appear to belong to a complex free of Maya influence and quite possibly of southern origin.

Certain groups of these statues are particularly significant. Those from the region of Lake Nicaragua,[37] late in date, are usually full human figures bearing animals on the back which often enclose the human head in the jaws. As Lothrop points out, this is not a trait of Maya-Mexican art, in which the usual depiction of this sort is that of a full animal figure holding a human head in the jaws. Lothrop feels that these statues tend to throw the Pacific area in which they occur into the general current of Central American archaeology, and this is certainly indicated by the evidence of pottery from the region. However, the human figure bearing an animal on the back with the animal head projecting over the human brow is a feature of many of the statues of San Agustín [38] and in modified form of the statues from farther south in Ecuador,[39] the north highlands of Peru [40] and the Titicaca basin.[41]

In South America the animal on the back and the animal headdress is a very ancient motif, found in Early Nazca, Early Chimu and at Tiahuanaco.[42] Certain Early Nazca vessels (Fig. 40) illustrate the use of a fox skin as a headdress, with the fox head capping the wearer's brow. These headdresses have actually been found at Paracas.[43] Nordenskiöld [44] pointed out that the "alter ego" repre-

[37] Bovallius, Nicaraguan Antiquities, 1886; Lothrop, Pottery of Costa Rica, 1926, pp. 91–94, Pl. IV–VII.
[38] Preuss, San Agustin, 1929, Pls. 8, 18, 19, 34, 55, 75.
[39] Jijón y Camaño, Marea Cultural, 1930, p. 116, Lam XVI.
[40] Tello, Antiquo Peru, 1929, Figs. 40–45.
[41] Valcarcel, Personaje Mítico, 1932.
[42] Nordenskiöld, Origin, 1931, Fig. 81.
[43] Yacovleff and Muelle, Fardo Funerario, 1934, Figs. 19, 20.
[44] Nordenskiöld, Origin, 1931, p. 63, Fig. 7.

FIG. 40. POLYCHROME VASE, NASCA
(After Yacovleff and Muelle, Fardo Funerario, Fig. 20, pp. 127–128.)

sentation still persists among the Chocó. On the basis of the known antiquity and distribution of this concept, it seems quite likely that the Lake Nicaragua statues are the result of South American influence.

Recently recorded statues from the Chontales district of Nicaragua (see pp. 411–414, Figs. 38, 39) strongly resemble a Coclé, Panama statue,[45] some of the cruder southern Colombian pieces,[46] some of those of the Callejón de Huaylas in northern Peru and some of the cruder examples from the Titicaca basin. These do not belong to the marked "alter ego" group although some have low animal headdresses (Fig. 39 *a, c*). The inter-resemblance is general, but the treatment of eyes, nose, head bands and the frequent presence of carved details suggesting textile representations and of clubs or sceptres appears significant. In view of the fairly continuous distributions of these crude statues there is good reason to believe them of common

[45] Lothrop, Coclé, 1937, Fig. 17.
[46] Perez de Barradas, 1937, Lam XII.

origin. Whether this was in South America it is impossible to be certain, but this style seems to be older there than in Central America. Just how the whole monolithic complex we have sketched is related to the Maya development of stone carving and the cruder work of southern Mexico and Guatemala is indeterminate at present.

Some years ago Kroeber [47] suggested that the stone carving of Chavín, exclusive of the Raimondi monolith, might display certain analogies with Mayan sculpture. He indicated the desirability of a comparative analysis by competent Mexicanists; this has not been made, but it does not seem that the similarities between Maya or Mexican styles and the style of Chavín are specific enough to suggest close relationship.

Graves and tomb construction as distinguished from certain burial practices mentioned above suggest a link between Middle and South America. Lothrop [48] points out that the Highland region (the Atlantic side) of Costa Rica and Nicaragua is characterized in general by rectangular stone cist graves. These are similar to the deep graves of Chiriquí (the Chiriquian archaeological province is closely related in other respects to the Highland area of Costa Rica and Nicaragua). Deep level graves of Chiriquí are undoubtedly related to the deep and often rock cut shaft graves of Colombia and Ecuador, which in turn are probably related to the wood and adobe walled tombs of the Peruvian coast and the stone cyst graves of the northern highlands of Peru. Linné [49] has demonstrated that deep level graves are relatively old in Colombia; in view of the Chibchan population of the Atlantic region of Costa Rica and Nicaragua it would seem likely that graves of this sort had been introduced from South America. Deep level graves extend to the north as far as the Totonac area of Mexico in fairly continuous distribution.

Pottery, always an important diagnostic in archaeology, indicates certain fairly definite cultural penetrations from South to Middle America and *vice versa*. However, it is still unsafe to consider any of these as bound up with the introduction of the making of pottery or of any complex of higher culture from one area to the other. The complexity of the problem of the interchange of influences mirrored in pottery styles is greatly increased not only by lack of chronological and often regional data, but also by possibilities of inde-

[47] Kroeber, Cultural Relations, 1930, pp. 16–17.
[48] Lothrop, Pottery of Costa Rica, 1926, Vol. 2, pp. 288–289.
[49] Linné, Darien, 1929, pp. 261–217, Map 13.

pendent developments and the presence of dozens of highly localized styles. These factors have limited students to the definition of certain broad trends, based on particular ceramic aspects.

The Highland area of Costa Rica and Nicaragua has produced a pottery complex exhibiting certain relationships to the Pacific area and hence to Central America in polychrome ware, but is chiefly characterized by Chiriquian and South American analogies in simple Painted, Monochrome and Appliqué Wares.[50] The historic inhabitants of this area were the Chibchan Guetar; Lothrop[51] feels that all the known archaeological material from this region is assignable to them. The same general archaeological complex reached the Bay Islands of Honduras. Strong[52] states that it is to the Highland wares of Costa Rica and Nicaragua that Bay Island Monochrome wares exhibit the closest similarity and suggests connection through the agency of Chibchan people. Specific elements in the Highland area exhibiting South American relationships have been summarized by Lothrop.[53] Many of the traits involved, such as the annular base, gourd-shaped vessels with human face on the neck, tripod vessels, applied modelled decorative elements, certain figurine types and design motifs cannot be placed definitely as to origin.

Tripod vessels, for example, have usually been assigned to Middle America on account of their dense distribution[54] and antiquity in that region. Forming a part of a complex in Highland Costa Rica and Nicaragua, Panama and northwestern South America as they do, their presence in Costa Rica and Nicaragua may well represent a re-introduction into southern Central America in late times. On the other hand, the profusion of small modelled decorative elements found on many wares of northwestern South America, the Greater Antilles and extending up the Atlantic coast as far as the Bay Islands of Honduras probably represents an actual penetration into Middle America. The same is almost without doubt true of negative painting or the lost-colour technique, involving the use of wax to cover areas not to be coloured. Lothrop[55] has summarized the distribution of negative painting from its sporadic occurrence as far south as Paracas, on the south coast of Peru, to Mexico. The greatest age is

[50] Lothrop, Pottery of Costa Rica, 1926, pp. 411–413.
[51] Lothrop, ibid., p. 392.
[52] Strong, Bay Islands, 1935, pp. 166–167.
[53] Lothrop, op. cit., pp. 407–410.
[54] Linné, Darien, 1929, pp. 111–113.
[55] Lothrop, op. cit., pp. 409–410.

probably represented at Paracas, although whether this is older than the middle of the Old Empire period of the Maya, from which some pieces date, is open to question. Greatest density of distribution is centred in Colombia and Ecuador, followed by Chiriquí and Costa Rica. Far less is to be seen from Peru, where it is concentrated in the north and is related to that of Ecuador. Specimens from the Maya area and Mexico are very rare. Lothrop does not regard the question of origin as settled, but states that the evidence seems strongly in favor of northwestern South America. If this is true Lothrop's earlier statement [56] that negative painting "is to be re-garded as the great contribution of northwestern South America to New World ceramics" is equally true.

There are certain typically Peruvian pottery shapes which have been found sporadically in Central America, usually north of the Costa Rica–Nicaragua area. Examples are the half-effigy double whistling jar found at Zacualpa, Guatemala,[57] Chimu in style but of local manufacture and the whistling jars of south central Mexico.[58]

A painted fish design in unmistakable Nazca style but on a vessel of non-Nazca shape has been reported from the Pacific coast of Guatemala.[58a]

Lothrop regards such unusual pieces as the indirect result of trade, and as we shall see in connection with metallurgy, there is consider-able evidence for trade between such distant points as Mexico and Peru in pre-Columbian times.

True metallurgy, as distinguished from the use of cold hammered native copper or meteoric iron, must be regarded as the greatest in-vention of the South American Indians and the one major technique which they without doubt contributed to Middle America.

At the time of the Conquest knowledge of metallurgy had spread over the Andean area, as far south as north central Chile, and as far as northwestern Mexico in Middle America. Every evidence points to Peru or Bolivia as a centre of origin, for metal was known to the earliest cultures yet discovered in Peru. Lothrop [59] has provided a recent summary of the origin and distribution of metallurgical techniques. His Table VI in the Coclé report shows the techniques

[56] Lothrop, Pottery of Costa Rica, 1926, p. 410.
[57] Lothrop, Zacualpa, 1936, Fig. 92.
[58] Noguera, Altar, 1937, p. 18, Figs. 15–23.
[58a] Dieseldorf, Kunst und Religion, 1933, Pl. 53, Fig. 141.
[59] Lothrop, Coclé, 1937, pp. 66–72.

which were known to the various early cultures. Hammering and embossing of gold, characteristic of Early Nazca, was apparently the first step in a long series of developments which entailed the discovery of copper, silver and tin, the knowledge of alloys, and such processes as welding, annealing, casting, plating by various methods, soldering, inlaying and engraving.

Nordenskiöld [60] has shown that bronze was probably not discovered until late Tiahuanaco times or after, but that what may be described as a copper age preceded its invention. From the distribution of bronze objects and the presence of nearby tin sources it is clear that the invention was made somewhere in the southern Andes of Peru or Bolivia. Knowledge of metallurgy must have passed early to Ecuador and Colombia. This region became a definite secondary centre of development. Only in Ecuador and southern Colombia was platinum used in the manufacture of jewelry. In Colombia, especially among the Quimbaya of the Cauca valley, casting à cire perdue was done with such skill as to place the work of these people second only to those of Oaxaca. The goldwork of the Isthmian region is closely related stylistically and technically to that of Colombia.

The spread of metallurgical techniques in Central America north of Costa Rica must have been relatively late, for there is virtually no metal in the Maya area until late Old Empire times, and that of foreign manufacture. In Mexico there are no archaeological traces of metal until post-Toltec times. Lothrop has shown [61] that at Coclé, Panama, goldwork of immediately pre-Conquest date incorporates a number of elements of form and design very ancient on the Peruvian coast, thus indicating a lagging penetration of traits from the south into Middle America.

Trade was undoubtedly of great importance in the spread of metallurgy; Arsandaux and Rivet [62] point out that the Mexicans must have learned the process through contact, presumably coastal, with the people of Ecuador and Peru, for there is no early history of metallurgy in Mexico and no development in the adjacent Maya area by which they could have been influenced.

It is well known that trade was extensive in late pre-Columbian times; Aztec traders had reached Panama; in the Isthmus knowledge

[60] Nordenskiöld, Copper and Bronze, 1921.
[61] Lothrop, Coclé, 1937, p. 203.
[62] Arsandaux and Rivet, Metallurgic, 1921; Nouvelle Note, 1923.

of the Inca and the wealth of the Inca Empire was current, while at
the same time traders were travelling up and down the Ecuadorean,
Colombian and Peruvian coasts.[63] The similarity of Mexican metal
forms, especially of axes and of thin non-functional copper axes,
used as money, and common in Oaxaca, to Ecuadorean and originally Peruvian types is a strong indication of direct contact. These
axe forms are lacking in lower Central America.

Lothrop [64] has published a résumé of the question of trade in connection with metallurgy and describes certain definite trade objects.
The best known are probably the small gold figures of Colombian
and Panamanian manufacture found in the Sacred Cenote at Chichen
Itzá in Yucatan.[65] Two objects of very probable Peruvian manufacture were found at Monte Alban, one a golden crown with a
golden plume inserted in it of typical Late Chimu style.[66] An earlier
example is a gold plaque, almost certainly of Peruvian manufacture,
in a style combining features of Chavin and Middle Chimu metal
art, found at Zacualpa, Guatemala. This object dates from the final
phase of the Maya Old Empire, before metal was being wrought by
the Maya or the Mexicans.

The sum total of evidence from all sources points to definite South
American penetrations into Middle America, but as yet their nature
and extent are in most cases ill-defined. Linguistics, ethnography and
archaeology indicate a strong, relatively late influx of Chibcha speaking people advancing through Panama and extending a fundamentally
South American type of culture up the Atlantic coast and highlands
of Costa Rica and Nicaragua as far as the Bay Islands of Honduras.
It is as impossible to draw sharp lines of demarcation between northern and southern cultures in this area as it is to do so wherever cultural fusion has taken place. As we have seen, many traits of probable
or possible South American origin have penetrated far beyond the
areas of Chibcha speech. At the same time Middle American traits
have influenced the southern continent. It must be admitted, however, that present evidence is so far from complete that only in a
few cases, such as metallurgy, is there little or no chance for a complete reversal of existing general ideas. The earlier, fundamental as-

[63] Lothrop, Navigation, 1932b.
[64] Lothrop, Zacualpa, 1936, pp. 61–76.
[65] Lothrop, Coclé, 1937, Fig. 201.
[66] Lothrop, Zacualpa, 1936, Fig. 71.

pects are still lost in antiquity. We have indicated some possibilities, but they are only that at present. The history of their origins and dispersals will require the concentrated attack of specialists in a dozen fields of anthropology and the natural sciences.

XXXIV

Conclusions: The Present Status of Americanistic Problems

A. L. Kroeber *

IT HAS FALLEN to my lot to try to assemble a review of some of the wider problems concerning America as a whole. Alfred Tozzer's work has been predominantly concerned with Mexico and Central America. It is therefore fitting that most of the contributions in this volume should deal with the same field or with problems partially connected with it. However, the volume covers a wide range geographically, and in physical anthropology, linguistics, and ethnology in addition to its archaeological core. It seems wiser to begin with the more general problems, and work gradually to the specific ones.

RACE

The origin and history of the native American race constitute one such larger problem, happily dealt with by Howells. He distinguishes two types of interpretative theory which superficially may seem very similar but in fact are not. The first, represented by the point of view of Hooton, explains the historical racial situation in native America as due to the interactions of a number of racial strains originating outside of America, and in large part in unknown but presumably distant regions. Whether these strains be conceptualized under committal terms like Australoid or non-committal ones like pseudo-Australoid may be important as a detail, but is only a detail. In either case an element is postulated which is remote and relatively elusive in terms of its history.

The contrasting view toward which Howells leans also poses several strains through whose interactions the racial picture of America is to be understood, but inclines to derive these elements

* Columbia, A.B., 1896; A.M., 1897; Ph.D., 1901; now Professor of Anthropology, University of California.

from the area of northern, eastern, and central Asia at a period prior to the development of the more highly specialized populations in this area, such as the modern Chinese and Mongols. If I understand Howells correctly, he does not attempt to exclude wholly the possibility of some subsequent influences from these specialized Mongolic peoples; but in the main he would derive the several American components from an already somewhat differentiated but not yet highly specialized block of East Asiatic populations probably containing some Caucasoid but no Negroid or Australoid ingredients. The general set of this picture would presumably not be very different from that advanced by Czekanowski, even though the picture would remain more fluid and less committed to specific findings.

As between the two points of view, that of Howells has the advantage of going less far afield, both geographically and racially, in its primary assumptions with which its hypothesis operates. It is, however, possible to go one step farther and to seek the origins of the several American elements within America itself, at least in considerable measure. Obviously, one would not wish to commit himself in advance to so narrow an assumption as that man entered America only at one time and as a single pure race, and that all differentiation was subsequent. It is rather a matter of allowing for a fairly heavy ingredient of internal differentiation on American soil in addition to already existent differentiation at the time of immigration. This point of view possesses the advantage over that of Howells which the attitude of Howells possesses over that of Hooton, namely that it makes fewer assumptions; or at any rate smaller and less far-flung assumptions.

Nor does such an attitude necessarily bring us back outright to the Hrdlička opinion that the American race is essentially a unit. Where Hrdlička has gone too far in the opinion of most anthropologists is in oversimplifying the situation, in his somewhat impatient sweeping aside of all minor American differentiations as being nearly insignificant, or in at most recognizing a differentiation into a few broad-headed and long-headed, or tall and short strains. It is obviously possible to admit that there is considerable differentiation among the native American populations and yet to believe that these differentiations occurred in considerable part on American soil, and in part either contemporaneously or previously in the nearer portions of Asia; bringing in hypothetical pseudo-Australoids, Caucasoids, and the like, only as a last resort when forced by the facts. Such an explanation or working hypothesis would at least seem to make the minimum of assumption.

One feature which characterizes the interpretations just reviewed is that in the last analysis they all contain a definitely subjective element. The Czekanowski school may be an exception: Its operations are highly technical, its published demonstrations scattered, and it is difficult to know, at any rate for one who is not himself a working physical anthropologist, how far the elements with which this school operates are really determined empirically or whether they also contain a subjective factor of mere opinion. However, as for the other views at any rate, it is clear that whether we start with concepts like a pseudo-Australoid type or like a primitive unitary American race developed in northeast Asia, the primary concepts are fundamentally based on subjective judgments, even though secondarily reinforced by masses of technical evidence. This need not be construed as a damning criticism. All phenomena connected with man and his history seem to demand a greater or less degree of intuitional judgment if they are to be dealt with understandingly; and a good intuition, which proves to be supported by the majority of the facts without forcing, does definitely carry us forward. It certainly has until now been difficult in the field of physical anthropology to make much progress by pure empirical work with the element of subjective judgment entirely eliminated. The argument, in short, is not against subjectivism, but in favor of the perpetual recognition of how great a part is really played in larger interpretations by the subjective factor. This recognition is perhaps particularly important in physical anthropology because its anthropometric techniques are likely to give a spurious impression of a high degree of objectivity in all its procedures.

For the same reason Howells' readiness to base his interpretations partly on appearance features which are not revealed by the conventional measurements, is to be welcomed rather than deplored. This is *de facto* a commoner procedure among physical anthropologists than is commonly avowed. It must also be remembered that admitting similarities between Indonesians and South Americans not revealed by the measurements is indeed subjective, but a subjectivism based on direct contact with the phenomena, often of many years' steeping in them. In short, it is subjectivism in the realm of perception, as compared with the subjectivism of reasoning, which is bound to loom larger in proportion as we develop theories of origins and other broad opinions. The perceptual intuitions of the professional scientist are likely to be worth more than those of the layman or amateur precisely because they are based on prolonged and systematic experience with phenomena; whereas his intuitions in the field of reasoning are likely to differ much less from the reasoning of the layman. The same, of course, holds in linguistics and cultural anthropology.

LANGUAGE

When it comes to linguistics we have Mason's sane review of the difficult attempts to classify the languages of Mexico and Central America, and Strong's complaint that either anthropologists are failing to avail themselves of the results of linguistic study or that Mexican and Central American linguistics is in a bad way as regards the historical findings which the cultural anthropologist most wants from it. The latter seems to be true, in the main. Also the reasons are not far to seek. Linguists are few and competent ones are fewer. For a generation past there has been a growing and healthy emphasis on exact recording and exhaustive analysis of individual languages. This tendency is not only desirable in itself through providing more precise and complete knowledge, but has been reinforced by the recognition that comparative studies might be done later, whereas with many dying languages the exact descriptive data had to be got now or never. This attitude in turn tended to become a habit or fashion, until some of our linguists came to see their descriptive analyses as an end in itself, and the sole end; or at most hoped to make some contribution of theoretical import through their particular analyses.

Any historical inquiry into unwritten languages is necessarily comparative. In the main the ethnologist or archaeologist wants for his own purpose only the historical results of linguistic work. The reason he has not had more such results proffered him is that in the Americanistic field comparative study, apart from frank guesses or prophecies, has been relatively rare in recent decades. On the other hand, what the archaeologist and ethnologist frequently fail to realize is that comparative linguistic work is extremely time consuming, and that only too often the linguist does not receive due recognition for his labors because cultural anthropologists fail to distinguish between sound and flimsy interpretations.

As a matter of fact, there are two kinds of comparative findings which the linguist can make. The first consists of what may be called the simple frontal attack by inspection. It leads to much quicker results, can make some use even of mediocre material, and leads to reliable results in the simpler situations but not in the more remote or problematic ones. This was the only method used by Powell in his famous classification of fifty years ago, and that it was a well-done job is clear from the way in which it has stood the test of time and is still the basis for most of the groupings commonly accepted and used by cultural anthropologists. Essentially this method is that of setting side-by-side what may be alike, and deciding, on common-sense inspection made without preconceived bias, which groups emerge as alike and which segregate off as unlike. No highly technical apparatus is needed. Powell was not a trained linguist, nor were Henshaw and most of his other collaborators who made the assemblages of the data for him—these data, incidentally, having never been published, although the comparisons were abundantly corroborated by all subsequent workers. In fact, Powell did not ever group together any two languages which have since been divorced by trained linguists. The reverse is true: He kept apart languages or groups of languages which even in his time there was reasonable warrant for believing to be genetically related, and which linguists now unanimously accept as having had a single origin. Shoshonean, Sonoran-Piman, and Aztec form the outstanding instance, but by no means the only one. In short, the frontal method sooner or later reaches situations in which the evidence is not wholly conclusive; and in all such situations Powell leaned back conservatively.

The second method is what may be called the reconstructive, and consists in applying the methods which were first developed in connection with the establishment of Indo-European. Under this method inspectional similarities are disregarded as being superficial and misleading in a certain proportion of cases. Similarity is regarded as being real similarity only when it is established by repetitive and regular recurrences of the fundamental elements, namely sounds in their context. These sound shifts or equivalences, once they prove to occur among three or more languages, in turn generally provide a basis for inferring the direction of change, and ultimately the sequence of changes. One language, for example, in regard to a particular sound element, has evidently departed secondarily from the three or four others with which it forms a closer unit within a larger group. Such a finding in turn enables one not only to reconstitute the former condition of the sound in question, but to determine whether the unit agrees with the majority of other units in the larger group and is therefore primary, or whether it represents a change and is secondary, the secondary differentiation of the divergent idiom within the unit thereby really becoming tertiary. In this way—the actual process is sketched only in barest outline—one finally constructs original Indo-European, original Uto-Aztecan, or what not, with a picture not only of its sound-elements but of its words. This picture of course, being reconstructive, is wholly inferential, and can never be absolutely proved or tested for its validity unless some ancient document were by a miracle to be recovered.

However, the reconstructed original language is not merely an end in itself. The comparative linguist now retraces his steps and uses his reconstituted original or ideal language as a point from which to work backward and help him to elucidate more sharply the historical changes which occurred as it differentiated into a series of languages. On this return journey he gains greater sureness in proportion as he leaves his inferential constructs behind him and returns toward the present and its mass of actual speech phenomena. Actually, of course, the process is a never-ending one. His reconstructed original language helps him to understand better not only the history but the present condition of the actually given languages he is operating with; and from this in turn he can correct and sharpen his formulation of the inferred original language.

It is evident that this reconstructive procedure calls for the finest analysis and a great amount of labor.

Beyond the inspectional approach and the reconstructive approach there is no other real method of dealing with linguistic relationship. Anything else that there may be resolves itself fundamentally into intuitional guessing. The intuitions may be penetrating and many of the guesses may be right, but they do not constitute proof. Languages which have been demonstrated as historically related almost invariably show a great many structural features in common. That is, their basic morphological patterns prove to be alike much as the lexical content proves to be alike. Consequently, if there are cases in which two or a series of languages show definite resemblances of morphological pattern, there is always the possibility that further analysis may also show similarities in their words and in their sound equivalences, even though the more superficial inspectional method has as yet failed to reveal any outstanding resemblances and the more fundamental reconstructive method has not yet been applied. It is this procedure which underlies a good part of Sapir's famous classification. Essentially what Sapir is doing when he connects Hokan and Siouan, or Chinook and Penutian, is to perceive structural resemblances which appear to him to work out into a coherent pattern beyond the scattered and random; and on the basis of this to predict that when sufficient analytical comparison of the content of these languages shall have been made, especially by the reconstructive method, it will turn out that genetic relationship will be demonstrable.

From one point of view such a procedure is nothing less than forecasting. From another, it amounts to a defining of problems which are worthy of attack because they hold out some hope of yielding positive productive results. The procedure has therefore a certain justification and value, provided it is understood for what it really is, and provided it is employed by a personality that is highly sensitive, perceptive, and balanced. It is in no sense whatever a definable or controllable method of science or scholarship.

The danger of the procedure is that its prophecies may be mistaken, especially by non-linguists, for proved or probable findings. Tremendous havoc can be worked when archaeologists or ethnologists begin to build structures of inference on Sapir's brilliant but flimsy gossamer web of prophecies as if it were a solid foundation. Gladwin's use of the Sapir scheme in "Snaketown" is an example.[1]

---

[1] Boas's objection to the Sapir procedure is based on a conviction that at present intelligent gathering of new material is more urgent than understanding of its relationships; in part also on a lack of interest in anything as reconstructive as all more remote relationships must be; and in part presumably on a generic distrust of intuition in scientific work. He has advanced as a counter-argument the fact that structural features may spread between originally unrelated languages by contact and a sort of diffusion. The contrary is usually assumed by Indo-Europeanists and other students of Old World languages. There are some evidences that Boas may be right to a certain extent. Nevertheless, all indications as yet are that such transfer of morphological pattern across the lines of relationship will prove to account at most for only a minority fraction of all structural features. Obviously, if the transfers emphasized by Boas were at all general, the Sapir method of intuition would be wholly deprived of validation, because Sapir would in that case be construing resemblances due to secondary assimilation as indicative of primary and genetic relationship. The consensus of opinion seems to be that it is not an all-or-none situation but a question of degree, with the majority of basic pattern features not due to secondary transfer, and therefore valid for prognosticatory utilization in the Sapir manner.

A pertinent case is furnished by Algonkin. Algonkin in the older sense as Powell used it as a well-defined family universally accepted by all students as having sprung from a single origin. With this Sapir united Kootenay, Salish, Nutka, Kwakiutl, Yurok, and Wiyot to form an extended or super-Algonkin, also having a common origin. There have been no serious reconstructive com-

If now we review what has actually been accomplished in the comparative study of North American languages since Powell, it is quickly apparent that it is very little. The inspectional method has pushed certain relationships into the realm of very high probability, especially relationships between small languages situated at no great distance from one another. In this category, for instance, are the Hokan and Penutian groupings of Dixon and myself. These, however, represent rather modest findings; there is nothing startling or upsetting about them. The average cultural anthropologist probably finds them to be only expectable in view of a glance at the map. Any linguist who will have no traffic with the inspectional method under any circumstances, and will accept only findings demonstrated one hundred per cent by the reconstructive method without remainder, of course is at liberty to disregard even these modest findings. As soon, however, as the closely contiguous California Penutian languages are left behind, and one compares them with, say, Kus in

---

parisons in support of this view and only very fragmentary inspectional ones, and those of small bodies of selected materials. On the other hand, it is plain that these half-dozen groups of languages are surprisingly similar in their basic pattern; for instance, in the way in which words are built up polysynthetically from two or more stems plus an even greater number of affixes which often have concrete meaning. One specific example of this particular polysynthetic tendency would be the use of numerals in combination with classifying elements denoting shape or material. One cannot really concern himself with the fundamental structural plan of these six or seven groups of languages without being impressed with the number and strength of such similarities. To explain these similarities as due to contact diffusion would by all ordinary linguistic experience to date make it expectable that we should also find similarity in content; but of this there is as yet little evidence: If there is content similarity, it is heavily disguised. There are also extraneous considerations which weigh against the contact-diffusion explanation, especially the geographic distribution of the languages in question. One would have to assume that diffusional influences were at work between the large block of recognized Algonkins in the East, a corridor through Kootenay and Salish, and a narrow and interrupted ribbon north and south along the Pacific Coast to Nutka, Kwakiutl, Yurok, and Wiyot; also that the influences had extended over this highly irregular territory but not elsewhere. It does seem, therefore, valid to infer that these structural resemblances will prove to mean something as to original connection when sufficient work shall have been done.

In that case we could also expect to find that the several groups either were very remotely and anciently connected, with tremendous subsequent alteration among themselves; or that they would prove to be highly variable in detail within the frame of a basic pattern; and in any event we should know what their changes had been. Until we do know this last, any conclusion is obviously hypothetical. In short, the Sapir judgment in this case, and no doubt in many others, constitutes a tenuous but brilliant working hypothesis whose only positive value should be its stimulation toward the working out of problems which hold productive promise.

Oregon, the inspectional method begins to leave us in the lurch: we get some, but not too many, superficially apparent resemblances. A step farther to Chinook, which Sapir also unites, and inspectional resemblances have disappeared altogether, not to mention that the structural pattern also seems heavily different. Obviously, we shall not be very sure whether Kus belongs with California Penutian, and shall remain in complete doubt whether Chinook does, until an intensive study by the reconstructive method has been made.

Now the amount of work done by the reconstructive method in America is surprisingly small. In the Old World we have well-founded comparative philologies not only for Indo-European but for Semitic, Hamitic, Bantu, Finnic, Sinitic, Malayo-Polynesian, and others. In America we have real beginnings only for Algonkin (in the old narrower sense) and for Uto-Aztecan, in the first case by Michelson, Uhlenbeck, and Bloomfield, with some participation by Sapir, and for Uto-Aztecan an excellent but incomplete foundation by Sapir, carried farther by Mason and Whorf. What might fruit-fully be done with Siouan was shown more than forty years ago by Dorsey—in four pages—but there has been no follow-up. On Athabascan, Sapir and younger men stimulated by him have done excellent spadework in spots, but there is not even an attempt to deal in a preliminary way with the group as a whole. To expand it into a larger Na-Dene by the inclusion of Tlingit and Haida is stimulating and quite likely correct, but it would be of far greater historical importance if we knew something of the internal relationships of the enormous Athabascan group. Eskimo cannot be treated comparatively until we have at least a few accurate data on the Pacific Eskimo dialects, which appear to constitute one sub-group as against the Arctic dialects; not to mention Aleutian. No degree of exact analysis of Eastern Eskimo dialects alone can ever give us linguistic conclusions of wider historical import. It is unnecessary to cite further instances of default. Strong is quite right when he speaks of American linguistics as being in a bad way as regards what it has to offer the culture historian.

How far it may be the duty of the linguist to try to provide the cultural anthropologist with what the latter feels he needs, is something about which two opinions, or a whole series of shades of opinion, may easily be held. Certainly, intensive analyses of particular languages must be the very foundation of all proper and sound linguistic work. On the other hand the situation is different from that in Europe. There a linguist is such in his own right, is classified as a philologist, holds a position as such, and is expected first of all to serve the interests of his branch of philology; anything more which he extends to historians of culture is a gratuity and a favor. In North America, however, nearly all the men working on American languages are first of all anthropologists; Bloomfield is the one outstanding exception. They have been trained in anthropology as well as in linguistics, received their degrees in anthropology, and usually hold their positions and make their living as anthropologists. It may therefore be presumed that they owe more to cultural anthropology than do their European colleagues. It cannot be said that they have paid their debt liberally, with the exception of Sapir's Greek gift of his classification, which is proving something of a Pandora box to the hastily optimistic.

The other side of the picture is this: If American linguists owe something to American cultural anthropologists, the latter also owe them something. The least that might be expected of them is a somewhat greater self-reliance—a foregoing of the feeling that an understanding of language and linguistic evidence is a high mystery reserved to a few of the elect, upon whom everyone else is dependent for what the elect may dole out, which is then accepted as a final authoritative gift from heaven. If our linguists are also anthropologists, it is because linguistic phenomena are in their nature interwoven with cultural phenomena and both together constitute anthropology. If that is so, the relation should be two-way. It may be too much to ask every ethnologist or archaeologist to be also a competently productive linguist in his own right. It does not seem to be too much to ask that he should understand what linguistics is really about, what its methods and criteria are, and what is better and worse in it. In that event, if the small number of linguists remained so swamped by the vast mass of their material as to be able to make only tantalizingly slow historical progress, the cultural anthropologist would at least have the recourse left open to him of trying to answer in a preliminary way some of the questions to which he feels he needs answers. If these provisional answers proved to be suggestive but inaccurate, they would presumably stimulate the professional pride of the linguists into correcting and improving them. I am not recommending this as an ideal procedure; but there is no reason why a cultural anthropologist who has waited ten or twenty vain years for a documented linguistic opinion as to whether two languages are probably related or probably not related, should not use his common sense and the inspectional method at least far enough to give himself some kind of an answer. If he does not, it is because he is imperfectly trained or lazy or under a bogey fear.

Mason, like Tozzer, is linguist, ethnologist, and archaeologist in one, and has not shrunk from his task of attempting a review of the historic relations of the languages of Mexico and Central America. He has had tough going because of poverty of materials—poverty of quality especially and also of sound preliminary digestion by predecessors. For some languages it remains necessary to use data secured in the sixteenth, seventeenth, and eighteenth centuries, even though the idioms are still living. Except in some measure for Uto-Aztecan, Mason has had to rely altogether on the inspectional method and on the opinions of others who have inspected or sometimes just guessed. In balancing these opinions and utilizing the qualitatively inadequate material he seems to have shown due conservatism. It is only to be hoped that better and fuller data will soon be forthcoming in sufficient quantity to replace his findings by equally good judgments based on superior materials. The corps of workers now studying native languages for the Mexican Government ought soon to provide such a basis. On the mere matter of distribution of the languages, wholly apart from questions as to which are and which are not related, the documentary studies of Jiménez Moreno and Kirchhoff give evidence of how much remains to be done and can still be done. For considerable parts of Mexico our linguistic maps have been based on pure guesswork, and hasty guesswork at that, while authentic information was lying unused not only in archives but in printed books. For Central America conditions have presumably been no better.

One slight caution may be voiced, even though it concerns only a point of terminology. Mason has in part adopted and in part coined syncopated words like Hokaltecan, Taracahitian, and Otomanguean. There is a certain convenience in such truncated abbreviations. I have myself had a hand in fathering "Penutian," which is an equally arbitrary compound. Many of the new compounds, however, represent merely an opinion, and they are being introduced in considerable number, bearing a form similar to that of names of proved families. It is to be hoped that the unwary cultural anthropologists will not bandy these shiny new counters about as if they were validated coin of the realm instead of merely provisional tokens whose right to currency remains to be determined by their general acceptance.

ETHNOLOGY

Ethnography is the branch of anthropological research which must of necessity be conducted most differently in Latin America and north of the Rio Grande. Tozzer's study of the Lacandon was the first modern ethnographic study of a people south of the Rio Grande who had managed to keep themselves relatively free from the impact of Iberian civilization through the centuries. Such tribes are however relatively few in South America, and very few north of Panama. In most of Latin America there is a much larger Indian population which is generally backward but no longer primitive. It is usually Christian, often fitted into the political institutions of the country, and always into the economic ones. Even where the Indians are bilingual or still mainly speak their native idiom, they no longer possess a native culture but instead live in a hybrid one. The active process of acculturation is so far behind them that they do not remember it, let alone the pure indigenous culture which preceded it. Conditions for ethnographic research are therefore thoroughly different from those in the United States and Canada, in most of which the native population is relatively insignificant in numbers and economically, but has received the heavy impacts of higher civilizations so recently that some parts of the native culture are usually still alive, and nearly the whole of it remains fairly well preserved in the memories of old individuals—sometimes astonishingly well preserved and even clearly conceptualized. North American ethnographic studies have consequently tended to aim at essentially static descriptions of the native cultures at the last moment of their independent survival; or in the past decade or so have sometimes been "acculturation studies"—analyses of the morbid dissolution processes active during the late decomposition of the native culture. Neither of these approaches is in general feasible in Latin America: The Indian cultures are neither native nor dying; they are almost invariably well hybridized and usually healthy.

To understand these Indian cultures of Latin America it is obviously necessary to know as thoroughly as possible the two streams of ingredients of which they are composed. Inasmuch as these have generally been intermingling for four centuries, the approach cannot but be historical if results are to have any real significance. No doubt a more historical approach would have bettered the quality of much ethnographic field research done in North America, and

would have prevented a certain shallowness of representation, besides forestalling certain reconstructions which suffer from neglect
of such civilized historical influences as did occur and are recover-
able. All in all, however, these historical influences—historical being
used in its stricter, narrow sense—other than contemporary ones,
constitute a very much smaller factor than in Latin America. There
the ethnographic attack demands first of all a genuinely adequate
knowledge of Hispanic-American civilization, not only in its present-
day form but since the beginning of contact and conquest.

Most ethnologists, especially if their previous work has been done
among United States or Canadian Indians, are unaccustomed to the
use of historical documents and temperamentally disinclined to learn
the use of them. They have generally read a few of the more notable
and familiar voyages of exploration, but are reluctant to master and
comb the totality of the historical literature, even where this does
not involve burrowing in unpublished archives. Swanton is an honorable exception, but for that very reason stands almost alone. Kees-
ing's recent study of the Menominee shows how fruitful the documentary approach can be, even when the objective is cultural analysis
rather than formal history. Latin Americans working in their own
field have shown much more appreciation of the significance of
historic material, but on the whole have tended to remain somewhat handicapped by want of ethnographic field experience and
consequent lack of development of the points of view resulting from
such experience. Their work, even where not merely belletristic but
genuinely historical, has too often lacked a factor which ethnographers elsewhere regard as indispensable.

It is therefore gratifying that La Farge's paper in the present volume has made an attempt to bridge the gap between our preserved
knowledge of the purely indigenous cultures and the cultures of the
present-day Indian populations as they lie open to fresh and first-hand
investigation on the spot.

La Farge tentatively distinguishes five stages in the Central American region. Up to nearly 1600 he recognizes the period of Conquest
and consolidation of the new order. From a little before 1600 to
about 1720 was the Colonial period. In this the subjugated Indians
were under strict control and there were everywhere great losses
of native culture material. By about 1720 the power of the central
Spanish government had weakened, the *encomienda* and *reparti-*

miento were abolished, a system of debt peonage began to grow up between the Indians and the governing class, but on the whole the Indians had their first chance at some measure of partial independence socially and industrially. In this Transition period there was a re-emergence of native elements of culture, but no return to the old cultures as such. There was also loss of a mild degree of literacy which had sprung up immediately after the Conquest and continued through the Colonial period; and with this loss the production of chronicles and other documents written by Indians for Indians also tended to cease. Toward 1800, as the Spanish power began to crack, and thereafter in the period of revolution for independence, the Indians escaped farther from control, and the locally varying hybrid cultures which had begun to emerge during the preceding Transition period had a chance to solidify in a first Recent period until about 1880. From then on, La Farge recognizes a second Recent period, in which the influence of the machine age began directly or indirectly to reach the Indian communities. In this contemporary stage their local cultures were being affected less by control from the central national government than by involvements of the Latin American countries in the scheme of European and North American industrialism.

La Farge's reconstructed outline of these four centuries is presented tentatively and without dogmatism. It is extremely important because, so far as I know, it is thoroughly novel. It may need considerable modification, and he is the first to recognize that it certainly needs enormous supplementing. But on the whole his construct seems sound as well as original, and ought to open up entirely new paths. It is fitting that this pioneer contribution to Central American ethnography should have been made in a volume composed in honor of the worker whose Lacandon study was equally original.

ARCHAEOLOGY

Archaeology constitutes perhaps the largest block in Alfred Tozzer's manifold work. It is certainly in the archaeology of Mexico and Central America that he has given intensive training to the largest number of new investigators and successors. Archaeology is also the most obtrusive variety of anthropological material presented by these countries. It is therefore natural that the larger number of the present contributions deal with either Mexican–Central American archaeology itself or its external relations. So great is the mass of material that it must be considered under several heads.

1. First among these is the set of problems that concern the antiquity of man and native culture in America. It is now generally accepted that wherever we have been able to work out continuous archaeological sequences, as in parts of Mexico and our own Southwest, these carry us back about two thousand years but no more. The older views which placed the first discovered stages in the second millennium b. c., or even earlier, seem no longer able to withstand criticism. In Peru also, though an absolute chronology is still altogether lacking, conservative estimates incline to see the whole course of known development as having taken place since the beginning of the Christian era.

In the same decade which has seen this limitation imposed on dead-reckoning or consecutive archaeology, there has also occurred the discovery of another set of data which, though still highly imperfect, suggest a much higher antiquity. The Folsom type discoveries are outstanding in this group of data, and are surrounded by a cluster of more sporadic ones. What gave these new data their greatest interest was the fact that they showed undoubted human artifacts in association with extinct species of mammals. These animals not forming part of the historic American fauna, it had become customary to assume them as not having existed in the hemisphere during the Recent geological period, and to label them as Pleistocene—which they undoubtedly were, though this fact, of course, does not preclude them from having also extended into the Recent. The general tendency therefore was to interpret these Folsom and other new finds as terminal Pleistocene, and to ascribe to them an age of ten thousand to twenty thousand years. There seemed the more warrant for this as there was a certain amount of supporting geological evidence—lake beds, varves, cave deposits, and the like. Unfortunately, authenticable human skeletal remains from these early discoveries have not yet come to light, so that one line of pertinent evidence is wholly lacking.

Whatever the age of the Folsom and analogous finds, it is clear that a decisive and perhaps long gap separates them from the earliest remains which can be put into continuous archaeological sequence. This is unfortunate, but it must be admitted and should be emphasized. Any attempt to treat the archaeology of a given American region since the Folsom manifestation as if it were a consecutive story, smears over the fact that the hiatus may be much longer than either the Folsom period or the later period on which we have data. Such a treatment cannot but produce an appearance of knowledge which is illusory and which invites the building of wholly speculative bridges that quickly tend to run into fantasy.

Another consideration of importance is that while these artifact finds associated with now-extinct animals may be definitely Pleistocene, and may in some cases be actually twenty thousand years old, we have as yet no conclusive proof in any one case of such an age. There is certainly no reason to believe that around ten thousand years ago any sudden and decisive geological or climatic changes occurred which simultaneously wiped out a considerable number of species. It is inherently much more reasonable to believe that some species became extinct within what was still unquestionable Pleistocene time; others with the specific ending of the Pleistocene, if such a point can be fixed; and that still others lingered on into the various phases of the Recent, some for perhaps two thousand years, others for five thousand, a few possibly for eight thousand.

Furthermore, there must be a very definite possibility, until specific negative evidence is forthcoming, that some of these species came to an end not due to climatic alterations but at the hands of man himself. In an earlier stage, while man's numbers were few and his arts and weapons undeveloped, these species may have continued to live alongside him without serious molestation. Once better equipped and organized, Indian tribes may well have put an end to piedmont bisons, horses, camels, mastodons, and mammoths; possibly in a very few centuries, in a given terrain. After all, it is the large game animals which most quickly succumb entirely to man once he is in position to hunt them effectively. It seems at least conceivable that horses or extinct bisons or elephants maintained themselves, at least in certain districts, very nearly until the beginning of our consecutive archaeological record; perhaps even into its beginning. One thinks in this connection of Uhle's elephant-pottery association in Ecuador, and wonders whether the Maya sculptures which have been controversially claimed to represent both elephants and toucans may not also be the product of the traditional recollection of actual proboscidians only a few centuries before. This is not a matter which can be pressed, because the evidence is too slender. But it is a possibility which can be kept in mind.

The earlier date, the longer span, have an inherent attractiveness to most human minds. Where they are supported by evidence which has withstood searching critical inquiry, they must be accepted. Where evidence of such positiveness is lacking, it is certainly wiser to keep estimates in suspense, or even to lean toward the smaller ones. So long as there is a real possibility that some of the associations of human artifacts with extinct animals may be no more than three thousand years old, it is certainly not wise to build interpretations on the contrary possibility that some of them may be twenty thousand years old.

One other consideration has been brought out clearly by Roberts in the present volume. The whole artifact inventory at all known Folsom type sites cannot be distinguished from the stone inventory of later sites, he says, except for the channeled Folsom points themselves. At any rate there are no consistent definable differences. This means that the whole concept of a Folsom culture boils down to two criteria: the single type of chipped point with channeling, and the association with varying extinct species whose date of extinction we do not know. This is really extremely slender evidence on which to erect even pseudo-historical constructs of culture successions. What we really have in the whole matter of origins of native American culture is a point represented by the Folsom finds floating free somewhere in time, a subsequent gap which may be anywhere from one thousand to eighteen thousand years long, and then two thousand years of archaeologically evidenced continuity in a few limited regions where conditions have been unusually favorable for recovery and interpretation.

2. Unusually interesting are situations in which the historical problem is limited by an apparent "must" factor, as in the papers by Kidder, Linton, and Ricketson. If such an imperative, whether positive or negative, can be established, a problem is likely to be simplified and an answer to be nearer. The question, however, always remains whether such an imperative is really binding. When Kidder, for instance, believes that the transfer of tropical agriculture from lowland to highland, or in the reverse direction, cannot have been effected rapidly, we are, no doubt, all inclined to agree in principle. We are not, however, in a position to estimate what rapid or slow might mean in terms of years or centuries. We can also not be sure that in certain cases the transfer did not take place with relative rapidity. All that is really meant by Kidder's conclusion is that the

environmental difference would interpose a barrier which ordinarily would make diffusion slower than it would be within a continuous environment. The absolute time required for the process might in the most favorable instances be actually quite brief, in other instances long or even perpetual.

Similarly with Linton's interesting suggestions as to the influence exerted by the varying exhaustibility of soils, and by sufficiently or insufficiently balanced diets. These recall Sauer's interesting suggestions as to the effect of friable soils and the possibility of multiple centers of plant domestication. In the abstract such considerations must be accorded considerable weight. Actually, however, each possible instance must be subjected to careful analysis. In other words, the factors in question are likely to be not really "musts" but "mays." A preliminary bird's-eye view of the phenomena may indicate that such a factor can well have had considerable influence on the whole; yet it may have failed to be operative in certain cases. The danger is in stretching a prevalence into a universal. All experience leads us to expect very few universals or even near-universals in history. Moreover, in proportion as a factor does appear to have been operative nearly universally, the exceptions to it also become significant because they indicate the presence of unusually strong counter-influences. Detailed case-by-case analyses are therefore called for if interpretations are not to become vitiated over-generalizations which more and more approach formulas.

One check is offered by the ability of generic factors to integrate with a variety of other factors in their applicability to particular historic situations. For instance, when Linton suggests that the Southwest came to lack a religious center of the type of a mound or temple because the cornfields in the arid Southwest could be successfully cultivated for an indefinite number of years or even generations, whereas the soils in Mexico and the eastern United States wore out, fields must therefore be rotated, and the tribe could consequently retain unity only by integrating itself around a religious center, we are unquestionably face to face with an interesting and perhaps important idea; but to accept it outright as the principal factor at work would be simplistic. The case of the Iroquois indicates that a high degree of communal integration can be achieved with a minimum of physical expression in a religious center. On the other hand there would be nothing to prevent the Pueblos from having accepted or developed the idea of a religious center for its own sake even though the nature of their soils permitted them to carry on their cultivation in close proximity to their towns. In short, the total pattern of each culture, its whole set of tendencies, must be searched before we can commit ourselves to an explanation. New suggestions like these by Linton are fruitful precisely because they add a new consideration to the older ones. They become dangerous only when they are pushed too one-sidedly by minds insistent on simple explanations in a field whose phenomena are almost invariably complex.

3. Relations of North and Central America with South America remain a perpetual problem because an indubitable generic similarity of the cultures of the two continents is balanced by the fewness of provable specific connections. Kidder II, Lothrop, A. L. Smith, and Vaillant all touch upon this problem. Vaillant's paper will be further discussed below. Smith's thesis is that, while the corbelled arch occurs both in Mexico and the Andean region, separate origins are indicated because of differences in structure and function and by a geographic gap in continuity as well as probably in time. One cannot but be impressed by this conclusion as sound. The time difference, however, must be regarded as still extremely tentative. Maya specialists seem to differ more than ever in their chronologies, and as for Peru, we have as yet no excavating specialists beyond Uhle, Tello, and Bennett, and no chronologies whatever that are more than guesswork. If the published illustrations are reliable, Smith is quite right that the usual form of the arch in Peru was a dome, which is likely to present fewer constructional difficulties than the semi-cylindrical vault. On the other hand some of these domes spring from a central pillar as well as from the circular walls, which fact introduces a new principle. Also the placing of a dome on a rectangular set of walls involves structural considerations which need elucidation. St. Sophia in Constantinople is still a landmark in the history of architecture because of the success with which it met this problem on a large scale. It may be a much simpler problem when the scale of construction remains small. But clear understanding of how the structural problem was actually met in the Andes is desirable.

Lothrop, as always, is stimulating, but it seems that a few of his suggestions must be used with reticence. For instance, his opinion that the expansion of the Arawak may furnish the key to an understanding of the higher New World cultures is entirely legitimate, provided it is regarded only as an opinion. Specific supporting evidence seems almost completely lacking; it is not really provided by the geographical distribution *per se* of the Arawak languages. They are so situated, it is true, that they might conceivably have influenced both the Andean region and Mexico; but this is not saying that they did seriously influence both. Unfortunately, we cannot explain the development of culture in Mexico and Peru by attaching this to any one given ethnic entity in either area, still less by an influence from one such entity upon the other area. It is therefore perhaps natural to look for the determining factor in a *tertium quid* lying outside both areas; and for this the Arawak are conveniently situated. In the last analysis, however, the opinion involves the explanation of the nearer at hand and better known by the remote and less known. It may be true none the less; yet its present extremely hypothetical character should be kept in mind.

In calling attention to indications of intercontinental trade, especially in the regions surrounding the Isthmus, both in his present paper and previously, Lothrop has rendered important service. I cannot however but feel that the evidence needs buttressing both by analysis and in quantity. Some of the resemblances seem subjectively precarious. Others, like the interlocking fish pattern, rest on minimal specimen material which appears not to have been duplicated and might represent an error, as of locality attribution. The strongest evidence as yet is of long-distance trade in natural materials, such as shell species; but we know from instances elsewhere, such as dentalia on the Northwest coast and shells in the Southwest, that trade in materials may extend much farther than traceable influence of customs or styles. Lothrop's own re-affirmation of the suddenness with which Mayan influences to the South cut off must also be considered. This would not of course prevent coastwise influences from South America reaching Oaxaca; but it is a complication in a picture which might otherwise be construed too simply.

Finally, there is the question of metallurgy in Mexico. That Isthmian gold and gold techniques were introduced as far as southern Mexico now seems well established. There is however a recent tendency, manifest several times in the present volume, to a wholesale attribution of all Mexican metallurgy to late-period introduction from South America. It seems well to remember that the indications in favor of this view are incomplete, largely because our knowledge of Mexican metallurgy is still lamentably deficient. When we shall have more, and more exact, data on this Mexican metallurgy, it is quite likely that its South American origin will be confirmed. For the

present, however, it seems wise to remember that we have only preliminary indications, and that full data might conceivably write an
entirely new story.

4. Relations of Mexico with the Southwest are dealt with by
Ekholm and Roberts. The latter limits and defines the relation of
early Anasazi to Mexico but skirts more or less around the intervening Hohokam culture. Ekholm, besides discovering, in a region more
northerly than heretofore known, a rich manifestation of the developed west Mexican coast culture which has only recently come to
light and which bears obvious though generic relations to central
Mexico, also reviews the area between the northern frontier of this
new culture and the southern limit of specific Hohokam. In this
intervening region of comparatively low archaeological development he finds to date a relative absence of relations southward and
rather little of specific relations northward with the Hohokam. I
continue to feel more positively about the latter half of this situation, and to recognize a larger area, comprising Sonora as well as the
Gila drainage, as constituting fundamentally a unitary development
including a local efflorescence around the Gila. In short, our retrieved
data are so overwhelmingly from Arizona that it may be that we are
inclined to construe the scattering evidences from north Mexican
soil as not Hohokam in affinity, because they are not specific Hohokam. If this view is correct, what is chiefly needed besides further
data from Sonora is a widening of our conceptual frame of Hohokam, or let us say Hohokamoid. Much the same may be true as regards Mogollon, which Nesbitt and Kidder have recently questioned
as really representing a radically different stem of development. They
seem justified, in view of the extreme paucity of features as yet attributed to Mogollon. The generic probability seems much greater
that Mogollon will prove to be a not very highly differentiated local
or temporal phase of either Hohokam or Anasazi.

5. Of the eastern United States and its relations with Mexico,
Guthe and Phillips have dealt. The latter finds that relatively unequivocal Mexican influences are recognizable in the eastern United
States in the manifestation currently called Middle Mississippi, and
that this influencing was probably comparatively late in time and
gave to Middle Mississippi its special flavor. Interpretative caution
has been so characteristic of Eastern archaeology that the decisiveness
of this finding is refreshing. It is the expression of a commitment of
opinion by a specialist which cannot but appear gratifying to one

who, though not qualified by experience to speak with authority in this field, has, nevertheless, been increasingly impelled toward subjective conviction to the same effect. There is one fly in the ointment, and for this Phillips is not responsible: There seems to be no adequate or tangible definition of the Middle Mississippi culture. Apparently Eastern archaeologists are fairly well agreed as to what they mean by the term, but they vary somewhat in the degree in which they construe it as an areal or temporal or content manifestation. It is evidently, like Lower Mississippi, Hopewellian, and Woodland, an empirically derived concept which possesses considerable validity and perhaps overwhelming validity, but which as yet lacks precise definition both of its core and its peripheral manifestations. Obviously, it is hardly likely that such definition can be made satisfactorily except in terms of the interrelated or interacting manifestations. In other words, its final justification must be in terms of the total picture east of the Rocky Mountains. This picture no one of the archaeologists of the eastern United States has yet found himself ready to be responsible for, either in incisive outline or in detail. The task is evidently not an easy one, due to the nature of the material as well as the nature of most of the earlier work of exploration. Undoubtedly some sort of a picture or interpretation is gradually forming in the minds of some of the Eastern archaeologists, especially through the medium of their repeated group conferences. These, however, help the outsider very little; and in return the outsider is not yet in position to bring his special resources to bear upon the clarification and solution of the Eastern problem. Phillips has made a convincing finding of the relation of one of the Eastern elements to an outside element; but this finding will obviously have only a limited significance until someone sees more clearly the interrelations of the several elements in the East, and can convey his understanding intelligibly and with at least preliminary evidential support. The time seems ripe, if not overripe, for someone who knows Eastern archaeology to have the courage of his scientific convictions. As long as everyone continues to regard cautious holding back as the primary virtue, there will be relatively little fundamental progress in the total Eastern field. The now established taxonomic method of attack is an honest attempt at an honestly founded classification, but only that. In spite of its breadth it is not a historic interpretation, nor an attempt at such an interpretation.

6. Questions of chronology, that is, of absolute dating, continue to

occupy a large place in Mexican archaeology. However, emphasis on them obviously is shifting. This is shown in the papers by Spinden, Thompson, and Morley. The first not only adheres to his original conversion of Maya time into our time, but continues to see an absolute chronology as the cardinal problem for Mexico and by extension for the whole New World. Thompson leans toward a later conversion date, but chiefly argues that the problem is one of sequences which should be elucidated from as many angles as possible. Morley is rather noncommittal on specific conversions or correlations of time, though retaining his interest in inscriptional data.

What really confronts us here is the difference between an essentially unitary approach through calculations derived from inscriptions and the adjustment of these to astronomical data, on the one hand; and a multiple approach on the other, in which inscriptions, calculations, and astronomy together form only one of several lines of evidence, the establishment of sequences by excavations being reckoned as at least equally important. One reason for the growth of the latter attitude undoubtedly lies in the fact that the once hoped-for agreement by the calculatory method has not been achieved. The trend has in fact been toward tentative acceptance of an absolute correlation two and a half centuries later than the original Spinden-Morley one, with some inclinations to make the shortening as much as five centuries. It is of course impossible for any non-specialist to judge as between these opinions. Nevertheless, it is clear that as long as difference of opinion among the specialists is augmenting, as compared with fifteen or twenty years ago, the outsider is bound to feel that no water-tight method has yet been achieved.

Any correlation method deals with three kinds of evidence. The first consists of documentary statements made in the past. So far as these were made about the Maya and Mexicans by Europeans, they seem to be very few and not in entire agreement. The majority of documentary statements merely embody in written form the legendary trends of natives in Guatemala, Yucatan, and Mexico; and these also are not in clear agreement, else the problem would long ago have been solved unanimously.

The second line of evidence is the application of calculations, and in this the element of proof by reasoning looms large. We have learned increasingly to distrust results in which the rational element outweighs the phenomenal one. Solutions by this method tend to elicit a quick and strong appeal; but in proportion as counter-reasonings grow up, the sense of conviction is lost. It is easy for a discoverer to remain convinced of his view, but the ability of findings to retain the conviction of others is dissipated as dissent and argument grow.

The third line of evidence is astronomical. As a matter of pure method, this should be decisive on the ground that it is objective. However, the pertinence of the astronomical evidence in the Maya problem is not as simple and clear-cut as might be wished. It is a question of how well a relatively small Maya scheme fits a very much larger and richer astronomical scheme of data; and in the determination of this there is possibility of different selections, and therefore of a subjective factor. Added to this is the fact that archaeologists in general do not themselves control the astronomical data, are therefore dependent upon astronomers' opinions as to the size of the subjective element, and consequently remain skeptical except when their particular favorite scheme happens to be corroborated.

All in all, the rational-astronomical approach comes pretty close to attempting to cut the intricate Gordian knot with one deft and powerful stroke, and then interpreting the prehistory not only of Mexico but of the whole hemisphere by orienting its manifold parts with reference to this one decisive finding. This in turn tends to mean that the larger solutions have already been found, and that there is left only the filling-in of the grand outline with details. Such a view might be true; but it would not be very stimulating. It is not likely to be very favorably received when a mass of new exploratory data on ceramics, architecture, and local culture sequences generally fits only imperfectly into the grand cardinal construct. There has been a vast mass of new data accumulated since the Spinden-Morley correlation chronology was first set up, and apparently the new mass and the chronology do not fit very well. Hence the tendency for the non-correlationists to depend more and more upon their own findings, irrespective of where these lead them. Thompson's attitude is of particular significance in this connection, because he is one of the very few workers who thoroughly control both the chronological and the specific archaeological evidence.

It need hardly be said that one whose knowledge of the specific Maya material is little more than that of a layman, is not qualified to pass judgment as between the several chronologies. I hope that I have not given the impression of leaning more toward one than toward another. In fact, my unconscious bias would presumably be

TABLE

Spanish Conquest

Mexican influence		Chipál 3		
Plumbate		Chipál 2		

10.3.0.0.0				
Maya Great Period		Chipál 1 Chamá 4		Uaxactun Late 3 (Tepeu)
Painted and Carved Vases				Middle 3
		Chamá 3	Holmul 5	Early 3

9.15.0.0.0 Full Maya Period			Holmul 4	
Local Styles	Kaminal- juyú	Chamá 2	Holmul 3	Uaxactun 2 (Tzakol)
Thin Orange Ware			Holmul 2	

8.14.0.0.0	Miraflores	Chamá 1	Holmul 1	
Pre-Ceremonial Period				Uaxactun 1b (Chicanel)
				Uaxactun 1a (Mamom)

* With additions and modifications by the editors.

X

SEQUENCES COMPARED *

Benque Viejo	Mountain Cow	San José	Chichen Itzá	Monte Alban	
		Santa Rita		Monte Alban 5	Aztec 2–4
			Chichen Itzá 2		Aztec 1
					Mazapan
		San José 5			
Benque Viejo 4	Mountain Cow 5	San José 4		Monte Alban 4	Teotihuacan 5
Benque Viejo 3	Mountain Cow 4	San José 3			
					Teo. 3–4
Benque Viejo 2	Mountain Cow 3	San José 2		Monte Alban 3	Teo. 2
					Colima with Thin Orange
	Mountain Cow 2			Monte Alban 2	Teo. 1 Ticoman
Benque Viejo 1b	Mountain Cow 1	San José 1		Monte Alban 1	Copilco-Zacatenco
Benque Viejo 1a					Early Zacatenco

toward the older chronology because it appears, or once appeared, to promise the greatest fixity of conviction. It is only possible for the outsider to try to understand the fundamental methods of thought which are being applied to this set of problems, and on the basis of such understanding to incline toward one view or the other, or to hold decision in abeyance. That for the next decade more exploration and more precise exploration are a desideratum will probably be conceded by everyone. If the new data strengthen the older and longer correlation, so much the better: We shall return to it with renewed conviction after a temporary wavering. If otherwise, we shall simply start fresh, undaunted by the realization that a piece of road which we were once inclined to believe was already traversed still lies ahead.

7. In any event there is a mass of local archaeology which remains to be done, whatever our decision as to chronology. The largest single block of papers in this volume deals with Mexican and Central American archaeology of this sort. Nor does the word local mean that the significance of results is narrowly circumscribed. Every well-done piece of local archaeology inevitably ties up with others as soon as enough of these have been done, and then becomes part of a larger inferential construct. Contributions of this sort, which go beyond the merely descriptive and actually face problems of inter-local relationships within the larger area, are those by Butler, Kidder, Noguera, R. E. Smith, and Thompson.

I have tried to tie these together, along with an unpublished Colima finding by Kelly, in a little table. Much to my gratification, this stimulated the editors into a more ambitious attempt in which they added the Holmul, Benque Viejo, Mountain Cow, San José, Monte Alban, and Valley of Mexico series, as well as a generalized Maya date sequence. This new table, IX, replaces my original one.

The editors have, in fact, gone further, and in Table X have provisionally correlated ceramic sequences from Louisiana to Peru and from 100 to 1600 A. D. This second table extends in parts beyond my knowledge, and for Peru somewhat beyond my convictions, which I have so far succeeded in keeping fluid, both as to the time relations of certain local series and as to absolute dating. It is, however, a satisfaction to have furnished the occasion for a correlation at once so specific and comprehensive as this one.

8. Finally there is the approach to archaeology through formulation of the basic or primary patterns revealed in its accumulating

data. Of this Vaillant's contribution is a striking and important example, whether or not one agrees with all its findings. The method is one of trying to discern general trends in the exceedingly multiple phenomena, and from these trends to work back to the generic factors which have been chiefly operative. There can be no doubt that Vaillant's formulation does give some explanation for the fact of high-level and low-level local cultures being interspersed so intimately in most of the Mexican–Central American region. It also accords well with the trend of historic facts, as exemplified for instance by the circumstance that, only fifty years before Cortés, Tlatelulco, a mere mile or so north of the central plaza of Tenochtitlan, remained "independent" enough to "revolt" against the Aztec "empire" after this had extended its sway or influence hundreds of miles away.

It is also of interest that Vaillant tries to draw into his problem the non-temple-building habit of the American Southwest. He differs from Linton in that he sees the reason for this not in the specific environmental factor of the character of southwestern soils but in the propensity for Pueblo technical achievement to be directed toward "the life of the community," that is, toward purposes concerning units or families within the community, rather than toward visible embodiments of the religious sentiments of the community as a totality. In passing to the eastern United States, it is true, Vaillant agrees with Linton: A mobile or scattered village was enforced by the necessity of rotation of fields, so that a central set of permanent religious structures was necessary for the maintenance of tribal integration. However one may react to this interpretation—and I for one am unsure, or at least not ready to admit it as the factor outstanding in importance over all others—it does seem encouraging that we have progressed far enough along for interpretations, as different as those of emphasis on the geographic underlie and the primary culture pattern trend, to have met.

A volume like this, then, is a tribute to the personality who has become its occasion, not only because of the new knowledge and new conclusions embodied in its pages, but as an example of the degree to which the different strands and methods of anthropology are after all interrelated in a larger whole.

TABLE XI

1700	SOUTH-EAST U.S.	SOUTH-WEST U.S.	MEXICO	OAXACA
1600		Pueblo V		
1500	Natchez Tunica		Aztec 4	
1400	Coles Creek	Pueblo IV	Aztec 3	Monte Alban 5
1300	Troy-ville		Aztec 2	
1200	Marks-ville	Pueblo III	Aztec 1	
1100			Mazapan	
1000	Tche-functe	Pueblo II	Teotihua-can 5	Monte Alban 4
900			Teo. 4	
800		Pueblo I	Teo. 3	
700				Monte Alban 3
600		Basket Maker III	Teo. 2	
500			Teo. 1	
400		Basket Maker II	Cuicuilco Ticoman	Monte Alban 2
300				
200			Copilco-Zacatenco	Monte Alban 1
100			Early Zacatenco	

* By the editors. Southwest Dates from tree-rings; other dates according to Lothrop, Vaillant and others.

HIGH-LAND MAYA	LOW-LAND MAYA	PERU NORTH COAST	PERU SOUTH COAST	PERU SOUTH HIGH-LAND	
		Late Chimu plus Inca	Late Ica plus Inca		1500
Chipál 3		Inca Conquest		Inca	1400
		Late Chimu	Inca Conquest		1300
Chipál 2	Chichen Itzá 2			Inca Conquest	1200
		Black-White	Late Ica		1100
Chipál 1 Chamá 4	San José 5	Red	Middle Ica II	Decadent Tiahuanaco	1000
	Uaxactun 3 San José 4 Holmul 5	Tiahuanaco	Tiahuanaco		900
Chamá 3	San José 3	Gallinazo Chavin II	Nazca Y Nazca B	Chiripa Pukara	800
		Early Chimu B		Classic Tiahuanaco	700
Chamá 2 Kaminaljuyú	San José 2 Holmul 2–4 Uaxactun 2				600
		Early Chimu A	Nazca X Nazca A		500
Chamá 1	Holmul 1				400
		Chavin I		Early Tiahuanaco	300
	Uaxactun 1b				200
Miraflores	Uaxactun 1a				100

provisional estimates in 1940, according to Kroeber, Thompson, Bennett, Wylly,

Adan, Elfego
1922.   Los Cuicatecos Actuales (Anales del Museo
                         Nacional de Arqueología, Historia y Et-
                         nología, 4a. Época, vol. 1, pp. 137–154,
                         Mexico).

Alexander, Hartley Burr
1920.   Latin-American Mythology (The Mythol-
                         ogy of All Races, vol. 11, Boston).

Alvarado, Pedro de
1924.   An Account of the Conquest of Guatemala
                         in 1524 by Pedro de Alvarado. Edited
                         and translated by Sedley J. Mackie (Docu-
                         ments and Narratives concerning the Dis-
                         covery and Conquest of Latin America,
                         no. 3, The Cortes Society, New York).

Ambrosetti, Juan B.
1902.   El Sepulcro de La Paya (Anales del Museo
                         Nacional de Buenos Aires, serie 3, vol. 1,
                         pp. 119–148, Buenos Aires).

———
1933.   The American Aborigines. (*See* Jenness, D).

Amsden, M.
1928.   Archeological Reconnaissance in Sonora
                         (Southwest Museum Papers, no. 1, Los
                         Angeles).

Ancona, Eligio
1917.   Historia de Yucatán desde la Época mas
                         Remota hasta nuestros Dias (4 vols.,
                         Mérida and Barcelona).

Andrade, M. J.
1936.   Linguistic Investigations (Carnegie Institu-
                         tion of Washington, Year Book, no. 35,
                         pp. 134–136, Washington).

Andrews, E. Wyllys
1934.   Glyph X of the Supplementary Series of
                         the Maya Inscriptions (American An-

491

492   BIBLIOGRAPHY

thropologist, n.s., vol. 36, pp. 345–354, Menasha).

1939. A Group of Related Sculptures from Yucatan (Carnegie Institution of Washington, Contributions to American Anthropology and History, no. 26, Publication no. 509, Washington).

de Angulo, Jaime
1925. The Linguistic Tangle of Oaxaca (Language, vol. 1, pp. 96–102, Menasha).

1933. The Chichimeco Language (International Journal of American Linguistics, vol. 7, pp. 152–194, New York).

de Angulo, Jaime, and Freeland, L. S.
1933–1934. The Zapotecan Linguistic Group (International Journal of American Linguistics, vol. 8, pp. 1–38, 111–130, New York).

Anonymous
1890. Recopilaciones de Leyes Agrarianas (Guatemala).

Anonymous
1936. Album Gráfico-Homenaje al Señor Presidente Constitucional de la República General don Jorge Ubico. Quetzaltenango.

Anonymous
MS. Cholbal K'ih and Ahilabal K'ih (Museum of the University of Pennsylvania, Berendt Collection, no. 58). [Copied by C. H. Berendt as a single document under the title "Calendario de los Indios de Guatemala." Location of original unknown. Photographic copies have been made by William Gates and by the Museum. MS. Translation by Rudolph Schuller, edited by Oliver La Farge and J. Alden Mason, in the possession of the Museum.]

Antevs, Ernst
1928. The Last Glaciation (American Geographic Society, Research Series, no. 17, New York).

1937.   Climate and Early Man in North America
                         (Early Man, MacCurdy, G. G., ed., pp.
                         125-132, Philadelphia and New York).

Anthony, H. E.
1928.   Field Book of North American Mammals.
                         New York, London.

Arguello, L. P.
1926.   Excursión a la Isla Zapatera (Centro Amé-
                         rica, Año 3, num. 29, January 15, 1926,
                         Revista Mensual del Sagrado Corazón de
                         Jesús, Granada).

Arriaga, Father Pablo José de
1621.   Extirpación de la Idolatría del Perú. Lima.

Arsandaux, H., and Rivet, P.
1921.   Contribution à l'Étude de la Metallurgie
                         Mexicaine (Journal de la Société des
                         Américanistes de Paris, n.s., vol. 13, pp.
                         261-280, Paris).

1923.   Nouvelle Note sur la Metallurgie Mexicaine
                         (L'Anthropologie, vol. 33, pp. 63-85,
                         Paris).

————   Atlas of Meteorology. London.
1899.

Aubin, J. M. A.
1885.   Mémoires sur la Peinture Didactique (Mis-
                         sion Scientifique au Mexique et dans
                         l'Amérique Centrale: Recherches Histo-
                         riques et Archéologiques. Premiere Partie
                         —Histoire. Paris).

Avendaño y Loyola, Andres de
1696.   Relación de las Dos Entradas que Hize a la
                         Conuersión de los Géntiles Itzaex, y Ce-
                         haches (MS. in the Newberry Library,
                         Chicago. See Means, 1917, pp. 103-174, for
                         translation of greater part).

Avila, Father Francisco de
1873.   A Narrative of the Errors, False Gods, and
                         other Superstitions and Diabolical Rites in

which the Indians of Huarochiri lived in Ancient Times. (XVI Century.) Translated and edited by Clements R. Markham (Hakluyt Society, London).

Aynesworth, K. H.

1936.   Biographic Studies of 21 Skulls of the Central Texas Indians (Bulletin of the Central Texas Archaeological Society, no. 2, pp. 30–34, Waco).

Baldwin, John D.

1871.   Ancient America, in Notes on American Archaeology. New York.

Bancroft, Hubert Howe

1882.   The Native Races (5 vols., San Francisco).

Bandelier, Adolphe F.

1877.   On the Art of War and Mode of Warfare of the Ancient Mexicans (Tenth Annual Report of the Peabody Museum of American Archaeology and Ethnology, vol. 2, pp. 95–161, Cambridge).

1878.   On the Distribution and Tenure of Lands, and the Customs with Respect to Inheritance, among the Ancient Mexicans (Eleventh Annual Report of the Peabody Museum of American Archaeology and Ethnology, vol. 2, pp. 385–448, Cambridge).

1879.   On the Sources for Aboriginal History of Spanish America (Proceedings, American Association for the Advancement of Science, no. 27, pp. 315–337, Salem).

1880.   On the Social Organization and Mode of Government of the Ancient Mexicans (Twelfth Annual Report of the Peabody Museum of American Archaeology and Ethnology, vol. 2, pp. 557–699, Cambridge).

1885.
The Romantic School in American Archae-
ology (New York Historical Society,
New York).

1890.
Contributions to the History of the Southwestern Portion of the United States (Papers of the Archaeological Institute of
America, American Series, no. 5, Cambridge).

1910.
The Islands of Titicaca and Koati. New
York.

Barradas
1937.
See Perez de Barradas, 1937.

Barrett, S. A.
1933.
Ancient Aztlan (Bulletin of the Milwaukee
Public Museum, vol. 13, pp. 1–602, Milwaukee).

Basauri, Carlos
1929.
Monografía de los Tarahumaras (Secretaría
de Educación Pública, México).

Bastian, A.
1876.
Die Monumente in Santa Lucia Cotzumalguapa (Zeitschrift für Ethnologie, vol. 8,
pp. 322–326, 403–404, Berlin).

1882.
Steinsculpturen aus Guatemala (Veröffent-
lichungen der Königlichen Museum zu
Berlin, Berlin).

Batres, L.
1902a.
Exploracions in Escalerillas Street, México.
México.

1902b.
Exploraciones de Monte Albán, México.
México.

1903.
Visita a los Monumentos Arqueológicos de
"La Quemada," Zacatecas. México.

1904.
Exploraciones en Huexotla, Texcoco, y El
Gavilán, México. México.

Baudin, Louis
1927. La Formation de l'Élite et l'Enseignement de l'Histoire dans l'Empire des Inka (Revue des Études Historiques, 93rd year, pp. 107–114, Paris).

1928. L'Empire Socialiste des Inka (Institut d'Ethnologie, vol. 5, Paris).

Beals, Ralph L.
1932. The Comparative Ethnology of Northern Mexico before 1750 (Ibero-Americana: 2, University of California, Berkeley).

Becerra, Marcos E.
1934. Los Chontales de Tabasco (Investigaciones Lingüísticas, vol. 2, pp. 29–36, México).

1937. Los Chiapanecos (Investigaciones Lingüísticas, vol. 4, pp. 214–253, México).

Belmar, Francisco
1892. Ligero Estudio sobre la Lengua Mazateca. Oaxaca.

1897. Ensayo sobre la Lengua Trike. Oaxaca.

1899. El Chocho. Oaxaca.

1910. El Tarasco y sus Relaciones con las Lenguas de la Familia Mixteco-Zapoteco-Otomi (Proceedings, XVI International Congress of Americanists, 1908, pp. 611–625, Wien).

Belt, Thomas
1874. The Naturalist in Nicaragua. London.

Bennett, Wendell C.
1933. Archaeological Hikes in the Andes (Natural History, vol. 33, pp. 163–174, New York).

1934. Excavations at Tiahuanaco (Anthropological Papers, American Museum of Natural History, vol. 34, part 3, New York).

1936. Excavations in Bolivia (Anthropological Papers, American Museum of Natural History, vol. 35, part 4, New York).

1937.   Excavations at La Mata, Maracay, Vene-
                               zuela (Anthropological Papers, American
                               Museum of Natural History, vol. 36, part
                               2, New York).

Bennett, Wendell C., and Zingg, R. M.
1935.   The Tarahumara. Chicago.

Berendt, C. H. Copyist MS. See Anonymous.

Beuchat, Henri
1912.   Manuel d'Archéologie Américaine. Paris.

Bevan, Bernard
1938.   The Chinantec; vol. 1, The Chinantec and
                               their Habitat (Instituto Panamericano de
                               Geologia e Historia, pub. no. 24, Tacu-
                               baya, México).

Beyer, Hermann
1937a.   Lunar Glyphs of the Supplementary Series
                               at Piedras Negras (El México Antiguo,
                               vol. 4, pp. 75–82, México).

1937b.   Studies on the Inscriptions of Chichen Itza
                               (Carnegie Institution of Washington, pub.
                               no. 483, Contribution no. 21, Washing-
                               ton).

Bienvenida, Lorenzo de
1877.   Carta de Lorenzo de Bienvenida a el Príncipe
                               don Felipe Dándole Cuenta de Varios As-
                               untos Referentes a la Provincia de Yucatán
                               (Cartas de Indias, pp. 70–82, Madrid).

Bird, J.
1938.   Antiquity and Migrations of the Early In-
                               habitants of Patagonia (Geographical Re-
                               view, vol. 28, pp. 250–275, New York).

Blackiston, A. H.
1906.   Ruins of the Cerro de Montezuma (Ameri-
                               can Anthropologist, n.s., vol. 8, pp. 256–
                               261, Lancaster).

Blom, Frans
1924.   Report on the Preliminary Work at Uaxac-
                               tun, Guatemala (Carnegie Institution of

Washington, Year Book no. 23, pp. 217–219, Washington).

1932.   The Maya Ball-Game *Pok-ta-pok* (called *tlachtli* by the Aztec) (Tulane University, Middle American Research Series, pub. no. 4, pp. 485–530, New Orleans).

1936.   The Conquest of Yucatan. Boston.

Blom, Frans, and La Farge, Oliver
1926–1927.   Tribes and Temples (Middle American Research Series, no. 1, Tulane University, 2 vols., New Orleans).

Boas, Franz
1911.   Handbook of American Indian Languages; Introduction (Bureau of American Ethnology, Bulletin 40, vol. 1, pp. 5–83, Washington).

1911–1912.   Album de Colecciones Arqueológicas (Publicación de la Escuela Internacional de Arqueología y Etnología Americanas, México).

1912.   The History of the American Race (Annals of the New York Academy of Sciences, vol. 21, pp. 177–183, New York).

1913.   Notes on the Chatino Language of Mexico (American Anthropologist, n.s., vol. 15, pp. 78–87, Lancaster).

1917.   El Dialecto Mexicano de Pochutla (International Journal of American Linguistics, vol. 1, pp. 9–44, New York).

1929.   Classification of American Indian Languages (Language, vol. 5, pp. 1–7, Menasha).

1933.   Relationships between Northwest American and Northeast Asia (Jenness, Ed., The American Aborigines, pp. 357–370, Toronto).

1938. The Mind of Primitive Man (2nd edition, New York).

Bobadilla, P. H.
1936. Monografía Geográfica e Histórica de San Pedro Sula. IV Centenario de su Fundación, 1536–1936. San Pedro Sula.

Bolton, H. E.
1930. Spanish Exploration in the Southwest, 1542–1706 (Original Narratives of Early American History, New York).

Boturini Benaduci, Lorenzo
1746. Idea de una Nueva Historia General de la América Septentrional. Madrid.

Bovallius, C.
1886. Nicaraguan Antiquities. Stockholm.

Bowditch, Charles P.
1910. The Numeration, Calendar Systems and Astronomical Knowledge of the Mayas. Cambridge.

Boyle, F.
1868. A Ride Across a Continent. London.

Bradford, Alexander W.
1841. American Antiquities and Researches into the Origin and History of the Red Race. New York.

Brand, Donald D.
1935. Distribution of Pottery Types in Northwest Mexico (American Anthropologist, n.s., vol. 37, pp. 287–305, Menasha).

Bransford, J. F.
1881. Archaeological Researches in Nicaragua (Smithsonian Contributions to Knowledge, vol. 25, Washington).

Brasseur de Bourbourg, Charles Étienne
1857–1859. Histoire des Nations Civilisées du Mexique et de l'Amérique-Centrale (4 vols., Paris).

1861. Popol Vuh. Le Livre Sacré et les Mythes de l'Antiquité Américaine. Paris.

1865. Essai Historique sur le Yucatan et Description des Ruines de Ti-hoo (Mérida) et d'Izamal, etc. (Archives de la Commission Scientifique du Mexique, vol. 2, no. 1, pp. 18–64, Paris).

1866. Rapport sur les Ruines de Mayapan et d'Uxmal au Yucatan (Mexique) (Archives de la Commission Scientifique du Mexique, vol. 2, no. 3, pp. 234–288, Paris).

Brenner, Anita
1931. The Influence of Technique on the Decorative Style in the Domestic Pottery of Culhuacan (Columbia University Contributions to Anthropology, vol. 13, New York).

Brew, J. O.
1937. The First Two Seasons at Awatovi (American Antiquity, vol. 3, pp. 122–137, Menasha).

Brinton, Daniel G.
1882. The Maya Chronicles. Edited and translated by Daniel G. Brinton (Library of Aboriginal American Literature, no. 1, Philadelphia).

1885a. The Annals of the Cakchiquels (Library of Aboriginal American Literature, no. 6, Philadelphia).

1885b. On the Xinca Indians of Guatemala (Proceedings, American Philosophical Society, vol. 22, pp. 89–97, Philadelphia).

1886. Notes on the Mangue Dialect (Proceedings, American Philosophical Society, vol. 23, pp. 238–257, Philadelphia).

1887. On the So-called Alagüilac Language of Guatemala (Proceedings, American Philosophical Society, vol. 24, pp. 366–377, Philadelphia).

1888.   On the Chane-abal (Four-Language) Tribe and Dialect of Chiapas (American Anthropologist, n.s., vol. 1, pp. 77–96, Washington).

1891a.   The American Race. New York.

1891b.   Vocabularies from the Musquito Coast (Proceedings, American Philosophical Society, vol. 29, pp. 1–4, Philadelphia).

1892a.   Observations on the Chinantec Language of Mexico and on the Mazatec Language and its Affinities (Proceedings, American Philosophical Society, vol. 30, pp. 22–30, 108, Philadelphia).

1892b.   On the Chontallis and Popolucas; a Contribution to Mexican Ethnography (Proceedings, VIII International Congress of Americanists, 1890, pp. 556–564, Paris).

1892c.   On the Mazatec Language of Mexico and its Affinities (Proceedings, American Philosophical Society, vol. 30, pp. 31–39, Philadelphia).

1893.   The Native Calendar of Central America and Mexico, A Study in Linguistics and Symbolism (Proceedings, American Philosophical Society, vol. 31, pp. 325–328, Philadelphia).

1894.   Nagualism. A Study in Native American Folklore and History (Proceedings, American Philosophical Society, vol. 33, pp. 11–73, Philadelphia).

1895.   On the Matagalpan Linguistic Stock of Central America (Proceedings, American Philosophical Society, vol. 34, pp. 403–415, Philadelphia).

1897.   The Ethnic Affinities of the Güetares of
                        Costa Rica (Proceedings, American Phil-
                        osophical Society, vol. 36, pp. 496–498,
                        Philadelphia).

1900.   Catalog of the Berendt Linguistic Collection
                        (Bulletin, Free Museum of Science and
                        Art [University Museum], vol. 2, pp. 203–
                        234, Philadelphia).
Brown, C. S.
1926.   The Archaeology of Mississippi (Mississippi
                        Geological Survey, University, Missis-
                        sippi).

Bryan, Kirk
1937.   Geology of the Folsom Deposits in New
                        Mexico and Colorado (Early Man, Mac-
                        Curdy, G. G., ed., pp. 139–152, Philadel-
                        phia).

Bryan, K., and Cady, R. C.
1934.   The Pleistocene Climate of Bermuda (Amer-
                        ican Journal of Science [5], vol. 27, pp.
                        241–264, New Haven).

Bulletin 28
1904.   Mexican and Central American Antiquities,
                        Calendar Systems, and History, Papers by
                        Seler and others (Bureau of American
                        Ethnology, Bulletin 28, Washington).

Bunzel, Ruth
MS., n.d.   A Guatemalan Village.

Burkitt, R.
1930.   Explorations in the Highlands of Western
                        Guatemala (The Museum Journal, Uni-
                        versity of Pennsylvania, vol. 21, no. 1,
                        Philadelphia).

1933.   Two Stones in Guatemala (Anthropos, vol.
                        28, pp. 9–26, Vienna).
Buschmann, J. C. E.
1859.   Die Spüren der Aztekischen Sprache. Berlin.

1864.   Grammatik der Sonorischen Sprachen. Ber-
                        lin.

Butler, M.
1935. Piedras Negras Pottery (Piedras Negras Preliminary Papers no. 4, The University Museum, Philadelphia).

Cabello de Balboa, Miguel
1576–1586. Miscelanea Antártica MS., dating about 1700–1725, in New York Public Library.
Cabrera, V. M.
1924. Guanacaste. San José.

Carey, H. A.
1931. An Analysis of the Northwestern Chihuahua Culture (American Anthropologist, n.s., vol. 33, pp. 325–374, Menasha).

Carnegie Institution of Washington
1936. Important Maya Discovery in the Guatemala Highlands (Carnegie Institution of Washington, News Service Bulletin, vol. 4, pp. 53–60, Washington).

1937. El Castillo, Pyramid-Temple of the Maya God Kukulcan (Carnegie Institution of Washington, News Service Bulletin, vol. 4, pp. 105–116, Washington).
Carrillo, P.
1846. La Estatua de Kabah (Registro Yucateco, vol. 4, pp. 16–18, Mérida).

1846. Zayi (Registro Yucateco, vol. 4, pp. 61–64, Mérida).

Carrillo y Ancona, Crescencio
1883. Historia Antigua de Yucatán. Mérida.

Caso, A.
1927. El Teocalli de la Guerra Sagrada. México.

1928. Las Estelas Zapotecas. México.

1930. Informe Preliminar de las Exploraciones Realiazadas en Michoacán (Anales del Museo Nacional de Arqueología, Historia, y Etnografía, 4a. Época, vol. 6, pp. 446–452, México).

1932a.	Monte Alban, Richest Archaeological Find in America (The National Geographic Magazine, vol. 62, pp. 467–512, Washington).

1932b.	Reading the Riddle of Ancient Jewels (Natural History, vol. 32, pp. 464–480, New York).

1932c.	Las Exploraciones en Monte Albán, Temporada 1931–1932 (Instituto Panamericano de Geografía e Historia, pub. 7, México).

1935.	Las Exploraciones en Monte Albán, Temporada 1934–1935 (Instituto Panamericano de Geografía e Historia, pub. 19, México).

1937.	The Religion of the Aztecs. Mexico.

1938.	Exploraciones en Oaxaca. Quinta y Sexta Temporadas 1936–1937 (Instituto Panamericano de Geografía e Historia, pub. 34, Tacubaya).

Caso, A., with Rubin de Borbolla, D.
1936.	Exploraciones en Mitla, Temporada 1934–1935 (Instituto Panamericano de Geografía e Historia, pub. 21, México).

Catherwood, Frederick
1844.	Views of Ancient Monuments in Central America, Chiapas and Yucatan. London.

Centro America
1924a.	Antigüedades de la Isla Penzacola (Centro América, Año 1, num. 9, May 15, 1924, Revista Mensual del Sagrado Corazón de Jesús, Granada).

1924b.	Antigüedades Nicaraguenses (Centro América, Año 2, num. 15, November 15, 1924, Revista Mensual del Sagrado Corazón de Jesús, Granada).

1926.   Seis Horas en los Teocalis del Zonzapote;
                        Diario de la Tercera Expedición Científica
                        del Colegio Centro América a La Isla de
                        Zapatera (Centro América, Año 3, num.
                        34, June 15, 1926, Revista Mensual del
                        Sagrado Corazón de Jesús, Granada).

Cereceda, Andrés de
1889.   Relación (In: Fernández, 1889).

Charnay, Désiré
1887.   The Ancient Cities of the New World.
                        Translated by J. G. and H. S. Conant.
                        New York.

Charnay, Désiré, and Viollet-le-Duc, E. E.
1863.   Cités et Ruines Américaines (1 vol. text and
                        atlas of plates, Paris).

Chavero, Alfredo
1887.   Historia Antigua y de la Conquista (in Riva
                        Palacio, México a través de los Siglos,
                        vol. 1, Mexico and Barcelona).

Christiansen, L. G.
1937.   Totonaco (Investigaciones Lingüísticas, vol.
                        4, pp. 151–153, México).

Churchill, Awnsham and John
1732.   A Collection of Voyages (3rd edition, vol. 2,
                        pp. 501–628, contains "The History of the
                        Life and Actions of Admiral Christopher
                        Columbus" by Ferdinand Columbus, Lon-
                        don).

Cieza de León, Pedro de
1864.   The First Part of the Chronicle of Peru.
                        (XVI Century.) Translated and edited by
                        Clements R. Markham (Hakluyt Society,
                        London).

1883.   The Second Part of the Chronicle of Peru.
                        Translated and edited by Clements R.
                        Markham (Hakluyt Society, London).

Ciudad Real, Antonio
1872.   Relación Breve y Verdadera de Algunas
                        Cosas de las Muchas que Sucedieron al

Padre Fray Alonso Ponce en las Provincias de la Nueva España (Collección de Documentos Inéditos para la Historia de España, vols. 57–58, Madrid).

Claflin, W. H.
1931.   The Stalling's Island Mound, Columbia County, Georgia (Papers, Peabody Museum of American Archaeology and Ethnology, vol. 14, no. 1, Cambridge).

Clavigero, Francesco Saverio
1787.   The History of Mexico. Translated by Charles Cullen (2 vols., London).

1817.   The History of Mexico. Translated by Charles Cullen (3 vols., Philadelphia).

Cobo, Father Bernabé
1890–1893.   Historia del Nuevo Mundo. Edited by Marcos Jiménez de la Espada (4 vols., Sevilla).

Codices

Codex Borbonicus
1899.   A Pre-Columbian Codex, preserved in the Library of the Chamber of Deputies, Paris (Leroux, Paris).

Lienzo de Chicomostoc
MS.   Unpublished Mixtec MS. in Royal Ontario Museum, Toronto (*see* Rickards, 1913).

Codex Colombino (Codex Dorenberg)
1892.   Plates 1–12 (Antigüedades Mexicanas, publicadas par la Junta Colombina de México, México).

Codex Dresdensis (Dresden Codex)
1880.   Die Maya-Handschrift der Königlichen Bibliothek zu Dresden; herausgegeben von Prof. Dr. E. Förstemann. Leipzig.

Codex Florentino
1905.   *See* Sahagun, 1905.

Codex Magliabecchiano, XIII-3
1904.   Manuscrit Mexicain Post-Colombien de la
                            Bibliothéque Nationale de Florence. Re-
                            produit au Frais du Duc de Loubat. Rome.

Codex Mendocino (Codex Mendoza)
1938.   Codex Mendoza. Edited and translated by
                            James Cooper Clark (3 vols., London).

Codex Nuttall (Codex Zouche)
1902.   Ancient Mexican Codex, belonging to Lord
                            Zouche of Haryworth. Introduction by
                            Zelia Nuttall (Peabody Museum of Amer-
                            ican Archaeology and Ethnology, Cam-
                            bridge).

Codex Selden, No. 1
1830.   Kingsborough, Antiquities of Mexico (vol.
                            1, Codex 5, London).

Codex Selden, No. 2
1830.   Kingsborough, Antiquities of Mexico (vol.
                            1, Codex 6, London).

Codex Telleriano Remensis
1899.   Commentary by E. T. Hamy (Loubat Edi-
                            tion, Paris).

Tribute Roll of Montezuma
1890.   A Pre-Columbian Codex Preserved in the
                            Museo Nacional, México (in Peñafiel, A.,
                            Monumentos del Arte Mexicano Antiguo,
                            vol. 2, pls. 228–259, México).

Codex Vaticanus 3738 (Vaticanus A) (Rios)
1900.   A Post-Colombian Codex Preserved in the
                            Library of the Vatican, Rome (published
                            by le Duc de Loubat, Rome).

Codex Vaticanus 3773 (Vaticanus B)
1896.   A Pre-Colombian Codex Preserved in the
                            Vatican Library (published by le Duc de
                            Loubat, Rome).

Codex Vindobonensis (Vienna)
1929.   Codex Vindobonensis Mexic. I. Facsimile.
                                 Text by Walter Lehmann and Ottokar
                                 Smital. Vienna.
Lienzo of Yolotepec
1890.   Mixtec Manuscript in the American Museum
                                 of Natural History (published in Peñafiel,
                                 A., Monumentos del Arte Mexicano Anti-
                                 guo, vol. 2, pl. 317, México).
Coffin, Roy G.
1937.   Northern Colorado's First Settlers (Colo-
                                 rado State College, Ft. Collins).
Cogolludo, Diego López
1867–1868.   Historia de Yucatán, escrita en el Siglo XVII
                                 (2 vols., Mérida).
Cole, F.-C. and Deuel, T.
1937.   Rediscovering Illinois; Archaeological Ex-
                                 plorations in and around Fulton County.
                                 Chicago.
Coleman, A. P.
1926.   Ice Ages Ancient and Recent. New York.

Collins, H. B.
1932.   Excavations of a Prehistoric Indian Village
                                 Site in Mississippi (Proceedings of the
                                 United States National Museum, vol. 79,
                                 art. 32, Washington).
Conant, Kenneth
1938.   Maya Architecture (MS. in the Peabody
                                 Museum of Harvard University, Cam-
                                 bridge).
Conzemius, Eduard
1923.   The Jicaques of Honduras (International
                                 Journal of American Linguistics, vol. 2,
                                 pp. 163–170, New York).

1926.   On the Aborigines of the Bay Islands (Pro-
                                 ceedings, XXII International Congress of
                                 Americanists, vol. 2, pp. 57–68, Rome).

1927.   Los Indios Payas de Honduras (Journal de
                                 la Société des Américanistes de Paris, n.s.,
                                 vol. 19, pp. 245–302, Paris).

1928. Los Indios Payas de Honduras (Journal de la Société des Américanistes de Paris, n.s., vol. 20, pp. 253–360, Paris).

1929a. Notes on the Miskito and Sumu Languages of Eastern Nicaragua and Honduras (International Journal of American Linguistics, vol. 5, pp. 57–115, New York).

1929b. Die Rama-Indianer von Nicaragua (Zeitschrift fur Ethnologie, vol. 59, pp. 291–362, Berlin).

1930. Une Tribu Inconnue du Costa-Rica; les Indiens Rama du Rio Zapote (L'Anthropologie, vol. 40, pp. 93–108, Paris).

1932. Ethnographical Survey of the Miskito and Sumu Indians of Honduras and Nicaragua (Bureau of American Ethnology, Bulletin 106, Washington).

Cortes, Hernando
1908. Letters of Cortes. Translated and edited by F. A. MacNutt (2 vols., New York and London).

Crawford, J.
1895. The Archaeology of Nicaragua (The Archaeologist, vol. 3, Waterloo, Indiana).

Cresson, F. M.
1938. Maya and Mexican Sweat Houses (American Anthropologist, n.s., vol. 40, pp. 88–104, Menasha).

Cushing, F. H.
1896. Exploration of Ancient Key Dwellers' Remains on the Gulf Coast of Florida (Proceedings, American Philosophical Society, vol. 35, no. 153, pp. 329–432, Philadelphia).

Daly, César
1864. Note Pouvant Servir à l'Exploration des Anciens Monuments du Mexique (Archives

de la Commission Scientifique du Mexique, vol. 1, no. 1, pp. 146–161, Paris).

Dauterman, C. C.
1938.

The Pottery Yard Stick at Monte Alban (Scientific Monthly, vol. 46, pp. 157–165, Lancaster).

Dávila Garibi, J. I.
1935.

Recopilación de Datos acerca del Idioma Coca y de su Posible Influencia en el Lenguaje Folklórico de Jalisco (Investigaciones Lingüísticas, vol. 3, pp. 248–302, México).

Debenedetti, Salvador
1921.

La Influencia Hispánica en los Yacimientos Arqueológicos de Caspinchango (Revista de la Universidad de Buenos Aires, vol. 46, pp. 745–788, Buenos Aires).

Deuel, Thorne
1935.

Basic Cultures of the Mississippi Valley (American Anthropologist, n.s., vol. 37, pp. 429–446, Menasha).

Díaz del Castillo, Bernal
1908–1916.

The True History of the Conquest of New Spain. Translated by A. P. Maudslay (Hakluyt Society, 5 vols., London).

Díaz, Juan
1858.

Itinerario de la Armada del Rey Católico à la Isla de Yucatán, en la India, el año 1518, en la que Fue por Comandante y Capitán General Juan de Grijalva. Edited by J. García Icazbalceta (Colección de Documentos para la Historia de México, vol. 1, pp. 281–308, México).

Dieseldorff, E. P.
1926–1933.

Kunst und Religion der Mayavölker (vols. 1, 2, Berlin; vol. 3, Hamburg).

Diguet, Léon
1898.

Note sur Certaines Pyramides des Environs d'Ixtlan (Mexique) (L'Anthropologie, vol. 9, pp. 660–665, Paris).

1899.

Rapport sur une Mission Scientifique dans la Basse-California (Nouvelles Archives des

Missions Scientifiques, vol. 9, pp. 1–53, Paris).

1905. Anciennes Sépultures Indigènes de la Basse-Californie Méridionale (Journal de la Société des Américanistes de Paris, n.s., vol. 2, pp. 329–333, Paris).

1911. Idiome Huichol (Journal de la Société des Américanistes de Paris, n.s., vol. 8, pp. 23–54, Paris).

Disselhoff, H. D.
1932. Note sur le Résultat de Quelques Fouilles Archéologiques faites à Colima (Mexique) (Revista del Instituto de Etnología de la Universidad Nacional de Tucumán, vol. 2, pp. 525–537, Tucumán).

Dittrich, Arnošt
1936. Die Korrelation der Maya-Chronologie (Abhandlungen, Preussischen Akademie der Wissenschaften, Phys.-Math. Klasse, no. 3, Berlin).

Dixon, R. B.
1923. The Racial History of Man. New York.

1928. The Building of Cultures. New York.

Dolores, Juan
1913. Papago Verb Stems (University of California Publications in American Archaeology and Ethnology, vol. 10, no. 5, Berkeley).

1923. Papago Nominal Stems (University of California Publications in American Archaeology and Ethnology, vol. 20, no. 2, Berkeley).

Dupaix, Guillelmo
1831. Viages de Guillelmo Dupaix sobre las Antigüedades Mejicanas. The Monuments of New Spain. Reproduced by Lord Kingsborough (Antiquities of Mexico, vol. 4; vol. 5, pp. 207–343; vol. 6, pp. 421–486, London).

1834. Antiquités Mexicaines (text and plates, Paris).

Durán, D.
1867, 1880. Historia de las Indias de Nueva-España (XVI Century) (2 vols., and atlas, México).

Ecker, L.
1939. Relationship of Mixtec to the Otomian Languages (El Mexico Antiguo, vol. 4, nos. 7–8, pp. 209–240, Mexico).

Eisen, G.
1888. On Some Ancient Sculptures from the Pacific Slope of Guatemala (Memoirs of the California Academy of Sciences, vol. 2, no. 2, San Francisco).

Emerson, R. A.
1935. A Preliminary Survey of the Milpa System of Maize Culture as Practised by the Maya Indians of the Northern Part of the Yucatan Peninsula (Mimeograph, Cornell University, Ithaca).

———
1936. Essays in Anthropology presented to Alfred Louis Kroeber. Berkeley. (See Lowie.)

Eyriès
1841. Les Monuments de l'Yucatan, par M. le Chevalier Emmanuel de Friederichsthal (Nouvelles Annales de Voyages, vol. 92, pp. 291–314, Paris).

Fassig, O. L.
1913. Hurricanes of the West Indies (Monthly Weather Reviews, supplement no. 487, Washington).

Fergusson, James
1873–1876. A History of Architecture in All Countries (4 vols., London).

Fernández, León
1889. Historia de Costa Rica durante la Dominación Española, 1592–1821. Madrid.

Fernández Ferraz, Juan
1892.   Nahuatlismos de Costa Rica. San José de
               Costa Rica.

Fernández Guardia, Ricardo, pub. Fernández, L.
1892.   Lenguas Indígenas de Centro América en el
               Siglo XVIII según copia del Archivo de
               Indias (Proceedings, IX International Con-
               gress of Americanists, San José de Costa
               Rica).
Ferrero, H. José
1920.   Pequeña Gramática y Diccionario de la Len-
               gua Tarahumara. México.
Fewkes, J. Walter
1907.   Certain Antiquities of Eastern Mexico
               (Bureau of American Ethnology, 25th An-
               nual Report, Washington).

1924.   Preliminary Archaeological Explorations at
               Weeden Island, Florida (Smithsonian Mis-
               cellaneous Collections, vol. 76, no. 13, pp.
               1–26, Washington).
Fewkes, Vladimir J.
1937.   Aboriginal Potsherds from Red River, Mani-
               toba (American Antiquity, vol. 3, pp. 143–
               156, Menasha).
Figgins, J. D.
1927.   The Antiquity of Man in America (Nat-
               ural History, vol. 27, pp. 229–239, New
               York).
Ford, James A.
1936.   Analysis of Indian Village Site Collections
               from Louisiana and Mississippi (Anthro-
               pological Study No. 2, Department of
               Conservation, Louisiana Geological Sur-
               vey, New Orleans).
Fowke, Gerard
1910.   Antiquities of Central and Southeastern Mis-
               souri (Bureau of American Ethnology,
               Bulletin 37, Washington).

Franco Inojosa, José Maria, and González, Alejandro
1936.   Exploraciones Arqueologicas en el Perú, De-

partamento de Puno (Revista del Museo Nacional, vol. 5, pp. 157–183, Lima).

Freeland, L. S.
1930.

The Relationship of Mixe to the Penutian Family (International Journal of American Linguistics, vol. 6, pp. 28–33, New York).

Friederichsthal, Emmanuel de
1841. *See* Eyriès.

Fuentes y Guzmán, F. A. de
1882–1883. Historia de Guatemala o Recordación Florida (Siglo XVII) (2 vols., Madrid).

Gabb, William M.
1875. On the Indian Tribes and Languages of Costa Rica (Proceedings, American Philosophical Society, vol. 14, pp. 483–602, Philadelphia).

Gage, Thomas
1928. The English-American, A New Survey of the West Indies, 1648. Edited with an introduction by A. P. Newton (The Broadway Travellers Series, London).

Gagini, Carlos
1917. Los Aborígines de Costa Rica. San José de Costa Rica.

Galindo, Juan
1832. Mémoire adressé à M. le Secrétaire de la Société de Géographie de Paris (Bulletin de la Société de Géographie, vol. 18, no. 114, pp. 198–214, Paris).

1834. Report of the Scientific Commission Appointed to Make a Survey of the Antiquities of Copan, etc. (in Morley, The Inscriptions at Copan, appendix 11).

Galindo, M.
1922. Bosquejo de la Geografía Arqueológica del Estado de Colima (Anales del Museo Nacional de Arqueología, Historia, y Etno-

grafía, 4a Época, vol. 1, pp. 165–178, México).

Gallegos, Herman
1927.

The Gallegos Relation of the Rodriguez Expedition to New Mexico, 1581–1582. Translation (Historical Society of New Mexico, Publications in History, vol. 4, Santa Fe).

Gamio, Manuel
1910.

Los Monumentos Arqueológicos de las Inmediaciones de Chalchihuites (Anales del Museo Nacional de Arqueología, Historia, y Etnografía, 3a. Época, vol. 2, pp. 469–492, México).

1921.

Text for Album de Colecciones Arqueologicas (F. Boas), Mexico.

1922.

La Poblacion del Valle de Teotihuscan (3 vols., Mexico).

1924.

The Sequence of Cultures in Mexico (American Anthropologist, n.s., vol. 26, pp. 307–322, Menasha).

1926–1927.

Cultural Evolution in Guatemala and its Geographic and Historic Handicaps. (Art and Archaeology, vol. 22, pp. 203–221; vol. 23, pp. 17–32, 71–78, 129–133, Washington).

Gann, Thomas
1900.

Mounds in Northern Honduras (19th Annual Report, Bureau of American Ethnology, part 2, pp. 655–692, Washington).

1905.

The Ancient Monuments of Northern Honduras (Journal of the Royal Anthropological Institute, vol. 35, pp. 103–112, London).

1918.

The Maya Indians of Southern Yucatan and Northern British Honduras (Bureau of American Ethnology, Bulletin 64, Washington).

1929.　　　　　　　　　Discoveries and Adventures in Central
　　　　　　　　　　　America. New York.

Gann, Thomas, and Thompson, J. Eric
1935.　　　　　　　　　The History of the Maya. New York.

García, Agustín
1927.　　　　　　　　　Informe sobre las Ruinas de La Quemada
　　　　　　　　　　　(Boletín de la Secretaría de Educación
　　　　　　　　　　　Pública, vol. 6, no. 4, México).
García, Gregorio
1729.　　　　　　　　　Origen de los Indios de el Nuevo Mundo,
　　　　　　　　　　　e Indias Occidentales. Madrid.

García de Palacios　　　See Palacios.

Garcilaso de la Vega, el Inca
1869.　　　　　　　　　The First Part of the Royal Commentaries
　　　　　　　　　　　of the Incas. (XVI–XVII Century.)
　　　　　　　　　　　Translated and edited by Clements R.
　　　　　　　　　　　Markham (Hakluyt Society, 2 vols., Lon-
　　　　　　　　　　　don).
Gassó, Leonardo, P. S. J.
1911.　　　　　　　　　La Misión de San José de Narganá entre los
　　　　　　　　　　　Karibes (República de Panamá) (Órgano
　　　　　　　　　　　Oficial en España de la Obra de la Propa-
　　　　　　　　　　　gación de la Fé, vol. 19, Barcelona).
Gates, William
1920.　　　　　　　　　The Distribution of the Several Branches of
　　　　　　　　　　　the Mayance Linguistic Stock. Appendix
　　　　　　　　　　　to Morley, S. G. The Inscriptions at
　　　　　　　　　　　Copan (Carnegie Institution of Washing-
　　　　　　　　　　　ton, pub. no. 219, Washington).

1932.　　　　　　　　　The Mayance Nations (The Maya Society
　　　　　　　　　　　Quarterly, vol. 1, pp. 97–106, Baltimore).
Gatschet, Albert S.
1900.　　　　　　　　　Central-Amerikas Sprachstämme und Dia-
　　　　　　　　　　　lekte (Globus, band 57, pp. 81–84, Braun-
　　　　　　　　　　　schweig).
Gerste, P. A.
1891.　　　　　　　　　La Langue des Chichiméques (Revue des
　　　　　　　　　　　Questions Scientifiques, vol. 30, pp. 81 ff.,
　　　　　　　　　　　Brussels).

Gladwin, Harold S.
1929.   The Red-on-buff Culture of the Papagueria
         (Medallion Papers, no. 4, Globe, Ari-
         zona).

1937.   Independent Invention versus Diffusion
         (American Antiquity, vol. 3, pp. 156–161,
         Menasha).

Gladwin, Harold S., and Associates
1937.   Excavations at Snaketown (2 vols., Medallion
         Papers, nos. 25–26, Globe, Arizona).

Gómara, Francisco López de
1749.   Historia de las Indias, and Crónica de la
         Nueva-España. Edited by A. Gonzáles
         Barcía (Historiadores Primitivos de las
         Indias Occidentales, vol. 2, Madrid).

Gómez, P. Aniceto M.
1935.   Estudios Gramaticales de la Lengua Cora
         (Biblioteca Lingüística Mexicana, I; In-
         vestigaciones Lingüísticas, vol. 3, pp. 79–
         142, México).

Gonzáles Casanova, Pablo
1925a.   Los Idiomas Popolocas y su Clasificación
         (Anales del Museo Nacional de Arqueo-
         logía, Historia, y Etnografía, 4a. Época,
         vol. 3, pp. 497–536, México).

1925b.   Vocabulario Chinanteca; Notas sobre la
         Lengua Chinanteca (Anales del Museo
         Nacional de Arqueología, Historia, y Et-
         nografía, 4a. Época, vol. 3, pp. 103–108,
         México).

1927.   El Tapachulteca No. 2, sin Relación Cono-
         cida (Revista Mexicana de Estudios His-
         tóricos, vol. 2, pp. 18–26, México).

1930.   Un Vocabulario Chichimeca (Proceedings,
         XXIII International Congress of Ameri-
         canists, New York, 1928, pp. 918–925,
         New York).

Goodman, J. T.
1897.   The Archaic Maya Inscriptions. London (in Maudslay, A. P., 1889–1902).

1905.   Maya Dates (American Anthropologist, n.s., vol. 7, pp. 642–647, Lancaster).

Gordon, G. B.
1896.   Prehistoric Ruins of Copan, Honduras (Memoirs, Peabody Museum of Harvard University, vol. 1, no. 1, Cambridge).

1898.   Researches in the Uloa Valley, Honduras (Memoirs, Peabody Museum of Harvard University, vol. 1, no. 4, Cambridge).

1902.   The Hieroglyphic Stairway, Ruins of Copan (Memoirs, Peabody Museum of Harvard University, vol. 1, no. 6, Cambridge).

1904.   Chronological Sequence in the Maya Ruins of Central America (University of Pennsylvania, Transactions of the Department of Archaeology, vol. 1, parts 1–2, pp. 61–66, Philadelphia).

1905.   The Serpent Motive in the Ancient Art of Central America and Mexico (University of Pennsylvania, Transactions of the Department of Archaeology, vol. 1, part 3, pp. 131–163, Philadelphia).

1909.   Conventionalism and Realism in Maya Art at Copan (Putnam Anniversary Volume, Anthropological Essays, pp. 191–195, New York).

Gordon, G. B., and Mason, J. A.
1925–1928.   Examples of Maya Pottery in the Museum and Other Collections (The University Museum, Philadelphia).

Goubaud, Antonio
1937.   The Guaxajip Bats, an Indian Ceremony of Guatemala. (Translation from Anales de la Sociedad de Geografía e Historia de

Guatemala, vol. 22, no. 1, 1935, Centro Editorial, Guatemala).

Gower, Charlotte D.
1927.

The Northern and Southern Affiliations of Antillean Culture (American Anthropological Association, Memoir 35, Menasha).

Granlund, Erik
1932.

De Svenska Högmossarnas Geologi (Sveriges Geologiska Undersökning, Arsbok 26, No. 1, Stockholm).

Grasserie, Raoul de la
1904.

Les Langues de Costa Rica et les Idiomes Apparentés (Journal de la Société des Américanistes de Paris, n.s., vol. 1, pp. 153–187, Paris).

Greenman, E. F.
1932.

Excavation of the Coon Mound and an Analysis of the Adena Culture (Ohio Archaeological and Historical Quarterly, vol. 41, no. 3, Columbus).

Gropp, Arthur E.
1938.

A Bibliography of Totonac Linguistic Materials (The Hispanic American Historical Review, vol. 18, no. 1, pp. 114–126, Baltimore).

Guernsey, S. J.
1931.

Explorations in Northeastern Arizona (Papers, Peabody Museum of American Archaeology and Ethnology, Harvard University, vol. 12, no. 1, Cambridge).

Guernsey, S. J., and Kidder, A. V.
1921.

Basket-Maker Caves of Northeastern Arizona (Papers, Peabody Museum of American Archaeology and Ethnology, Harvard University, vol. 8, no. 2, Cambridge).

Guillemin Tarayre, E.
1867.

Rapport sur L'Exploration Minéralogique des Régions Mexicaines (Archives de la Commission Scientifique du Mexique, vol. 3, pp. 173–470, Paris).

Guthe, C. E.
1920.

A Possible Solution of the Number Series on Pages 51–58 of the Dresden Codex (Papers, Peabody Museum of American Archaeology and Ethnology, Harvard University, vol. 6, no. 2, Cambridge).

1932. The Maya Lunar Count (Science, n.s., vol. 75, pp. 271–277, Lancaster).

Habel, S.
1878. The Sculptures of Santa Lucia Cosumalwhuapa in Guatemala (Smithsonian Contributions to Knowledge, vol. 22, art. 3, Washington).

Hamy, E. T.
1896. Étude sur les Collections Américaines (Journal de la Société des Américanistes de Paris, n.s., vol. 1, pp. 1–31, Paris).

1907. Croyances et Practiques Religieuses des Premiers Mexicains. Le Culte des Dicux Tlaloques (Ernest Leroux, Paris).

1922. Algunas Observaciones sobre la Distribución Geografía de los Opatas, de los Tarahumares y de los Pimas (Anales del Museo Nacional de Arqueología, Historia, y Etnografía, 4a. Época, vol. 1, pp. 93–98, México).

Hann, Julius
1897. Handbuch der Klimatologie. Stuttgart.

1903. Handbook of Climatology. Vol. 1 (general). Translated by R. De C. Ward. New York and London.

Hansen, Florencia
1937. Report on the Mazateco dialect; Morphology and Grammar (Investigaciones Lingüisticas, vol. 4, pp. 144–147, Mexico).

Harrington, M. R.
1920. Certain Caddo Sites in Arkansas (Museum of the American Indian, Heye Foundation, Indian Notes and Monographs, New York).

1922.   Cherokee and Earlier Remains on the Upper Tennessee River (Museum of the American Indian, Heye Foundation, Indian Notes and Monographs, New York).

1924.   The Ozark Bluff-Dwellers (American Anthropologist, n.s., vol. 26, no. 1, pp. 1–21, Menasha).

1933.   Gypsum Cave, Nevada (Southwest Museum Papers, no. 8, Los Angeles).

Harshberger, J. W.
1911.   Phytogeographic Survey of North America. Leipzig and New York.

Hartman, C. V.
1901.   Archaeological Researches in Costa Rica. Stockholm.

1907.   Archaeological Researches on the Pacific Coast of Costa Rica (Memoirs of the Carnegie Museum, vol. 2, no. 1, Pittsburgh).

Haury, Emil W.
1936a.   Some Southwestern Pottery Types (Medallion Papers, no. 19, Globe).

1936b.   The Mogollon Culture of Southwestern New Mexico (Medallion Papers, no. 20, Globe).

1937a.   Ball Courts (H. S. Gladwin and others, Excavations at Snaketown, vol. 1, pp. 36–49; Medallion Papers, no. 25, Globe).

1937b.   A Pre-Spanish Rubber Ball from Arizona (American Antiquity, vol. 2, pp. 282–288, Menasha).

Heath, George Reinke
1913.   Notes on Miskito Grammar and on Other Indian Languages of Eastern Nicaragua (American Anthropologist, n.s., vol. 15, pp. 48–62, Lancaster).

Heilprinn, A.
1887.   The Geographical and Geological Distribu-
                tions of Animals (International Scientific
                Series, vol. 57, New York).
Hernández Spina, Vicente
MS.   Kalendaryo dencervado hasta el dia por los
                sacerdotes del sol en Ixtlavacam, Pueblo
                decendiente de la nacion Kiché . . .
                Santa Catarina Ixtlavacam, Agosto 12 de
                1854 (Berendt Collection, Museum of the
                University of Pennsylvania, Philadelphia).
Herrera, Antonio de
1726–1730.   Historia General de los Hechos de los
                Castellanos en las Islas i Tierra-Firme del
                Mar Océano (5 vols., Madrid).
Herzog, Wilhelm
1884.   Ueber die Verwandtschafts beziehungen der
                Costaricensische Indianersprachen mit
                denen von Central- und Sud-Amerika
                (Archiv für Anthropologie, vol. 16, pp.
                623–627, Braunschweig).
Hewett, Edgar L.
1911.   Two Seasons' Work in Guatemala (Bulletin
                of the Archaeological Institute of Amer-
                ica, vol. 2, no. 3, pp. 117–134, Norwood,
                Massachusetts).

1912.   The Excavations at Quirigua in 1912 (Bul-
                letin of the Archaeological Institute of
                America, vol. 3, no. 3, pp. 163–171, Nor-
                wood).

1916.   Latest Work of the School of American
                Archaeology at Quirigua (Holmes Anni-
                versary Volume, Anthropological Essays,
                pp. 157–162, Washington).

Heye, G. G., Hodge, F. W., and Pepper, G. H.
1918.   The Nacoochee Mound in Georgia (Mu-
                seum of the American Indian, Heye
                Foundation, Contributions, vol. 4, no. 3,
                New York).

Hill, A. T., and Wedel, W. R.

1936.   Excavations at the Leary Indian Village and Burial Site (Nebraska History Magazine, vol. 17, pp. 2–73, Lincoln).

Hissink, Karin

1934.   Masken als Fassadenschmuck. Untersucht an alten Bauten der Halbinsel Yukatan (Sammlung Heitz, Akademische Abhandlungen Kulturgeschichte, 3d. ser., vol. 2, Strassburg).

Hodge, F. W.

1937.   History of Hawikuh. Los Angeles.

Holmes, W. H.

1883.   Art in Shell of the Ancient Americans (Second Annual Report, Bureau of American Ethnology, pp. 179–305, Washington).

1888.   Ancient Art of the Province of Chiriqui, Colombia (Sixth Annual Report, Bureau of American Ethnology, pp. 13–187, Washington).

1894.   Caribbean Influences in the Prehistoric Art of the Southern States (American Anthropologist, o.s., vol. 7, pp. 71–79, Washington).

1895–1897.   Archaeological Studies among the Ancient Cities of Mexico (Field Columbian Museum, Anthropological Series, vol. 1, no. 1, Chicago).

1903a.   Aboriginal Pottery of the Eastern United States (20th Annual Report, Bureau of American Ethnology, Washington).

1903b.   Shell Ornaments from Kentucky and Mexico (Smithsonian Miscellaneous Collections, vol. 45, pp. 97–99, Washington).

1906.   Certain Notched or Scalloped Stone Tablets of the Mound Builders (American Anthropologist, n.s., vol. 8, pp. 101–108).

1914–1919.   Masterpieces of Aboriginal American Art
                                          (Art and Archaeology, vol. 1, pp. 1–12,
                                          91–102, 242–255; vol. 3, pp. 70–85; vol. 4,
                                          pp. 267–278; vol. 5, pp. 38–49; vol. 8, pp.
                                          348–360, Washington).

1916.   Holmes Anniversary Volume, Anthropo-
                                          logical Essays. Washington.

Hooton, Ernest A.
     1930.   The Indians of Pecos Pueblo, a Study of
                                          their Skeletal Remains (Department of
                                          Archaeology, Phillips Academy, Andover,
                                          Massachusetts, Cambridge).

     1931.   Up from the Ape. New York.

     1933.   Racial Types in America and their Relations
                                          to Old World Types (American Aborig-
                                          ines, Jenness, D., ed., pp. 131–163).

Howard, Edgar B.
     1935.   Evidence of Early Man in North America
                                          (Museum Journal, University Museum,
                                          University of Pennsylvania, vol. 24, nos.
                                          2–3, pp. 61–175, Philadelphia).

Hrdlička, Aleš
     1898.   See Lumholtz, C., and Hrdlička, Aleš

     1901.   A Painted Skeleton from Northern Mexico,
                                          with Notes on Bone Painting among the
                                          American Aborigines (American Anthro-
                                          pologist, n.s., vol. 3, pp. 701–725, New
                                          York).

     1903.   The Region of the Ancient "Chichimecs,"
                                          with Notes on the Tepecanos and the Ruin
                                          of La Quemada, Mexico (American An-
                                          thropologist, n.s., vol. 5, pp. 385–440, Lan-
                                          caster).

     1923.   Origin and Antiquity of the American In-
                                          dian (Annual Report of the Smithsonian

Institution for 1923, pp. 481–494, Washington).

1926. The People of the Main American Cultures (Proceedings, American Philosophical Society, vol. 65, pp. 157–160, Philadelphia).

1935. Melanesians and Australians and the Peopling of America (Smithsonian Miscellaneous Collections, vol. 94, no. 11, Washington).

1937. The Minnesota "Man" (American Journal of Physical Anthropology, vol. 22, pp. 175–200, Philadelphia).

Humboldt, A. de
1810. Vues des Cordillères, et Monumens des Peuples Indigènes de l'Amérique. Paris.

1811. Political Essay on the Kingdom of New Spain. Translated by John Black (4 vols., London).

Hydrographic Office, U.S. Government
1938. Central America and Mexico Pilot. Monthly Weather Charts. Washington.

Ibero-Americana Series
1932–1938 Ibero-Americana Series, nos. 1–14 (University of California, Berkeley). *See also* Beals, Kelly, Sauer, under author reference.

Indianapolis Conference
1935. A Symposium upon the Archaeological Problems of the North Central United States Area (Report issued by the Committee on State Archaeological Surveys. Division of Anthropology and Psychology. National Research Council, Washington, n.d.).

Inojosa, José Maria Franco, and González, Alejandro
1936. *See* Franco Inojosa and González, 1936.

Ixtlilxochitl, F. de Alva
1891–1892.   Obras Históricas (XVI Century); Relaciones, vol. 1; Historia Chichimeca, vol. 2. Mexico.

James, Preston E.
1922.   Koppen's Classification of Climates (Monthly Weather Review, Feb. 1922. Washington).

Jenness, D. (editor)
1933.   The American Aborigines. Their Origin and Antiquity. Toronto.

Jijón y Caamaño, Jacinto
1919.   La Religión del Imperio de los Incas. Quito.

1930.   Una Gran Maréa Cultural en el N.O. de Sud América (Journal de la Société des Américanistes de Paris, n.s., vol. 22, pp. 107–197, Paris).

Jiménez Moreno, Wigberto
1936.   Mapa Lingüístico de Norte- y Centro-América (Museo Nacional, México).

Johnston, W. A.
1933.   Quaternary Geology of North America in Relation to the Migration of Man (The American Aborigines, Jenness, D., ed., pp. 9–45).

Jones, C. C.
1873.   Antiquities of the Southern Indians. Particularly of the Georgia Tribes. New York.

Jones, J.
1876.   Explorations of the Aboriginal Remains of Tennessee (Smithsonian Contributions to Knowledge, no. 259, Washington).

de Jonghe, E.
1906.   Le Calendrier Mexicain (Journal de la Société des Américanistes de Paris, n.s., vol. 3, pp. 197–227, Paris).

Joyce, Thomas A.
1912.   South American Archaeology. New York.

1913. The Weeping God (In "Essays and Studies Presented to William Ridgeway," pp. 365–375, Cambridge, England).

1914. Mexican Archaeology. London.

1916. Central American and West Indian Archaeology. London.

1923. Guide to the Maudslay Collection of Maya Sculptures (casts and originals) from Central America (British Museum, London).

1925. The Hieroglyphic Stairway at Naranjo, Guatemala (Proceedings, XXI Congress of Americanists, Göteborg, 1924, pp. 297–304, Göteborg).

1927. Maya and Mexican Art. London.

1929. Report on the British Museum Expedition to British Honduras (Journal of the Royal Anthropological Institute of Great Britain and Ireland, vol. 59, pp. 439–459, London).

Juarros, Domingo
1823. A Statistical and Commercial History of the Kingdom of Guatemala in Spanish America. Translated by J. Bailey.

Kelly, A.
1938. A Preliminary Report on Archaelogical Exploration at Macon, Georgia (Bureau of American Ethnology, Bulletin 119, pp. 1–68, Washington).

Kelly, Isabel T.
1938. Excavations at Chametla, Sinaloa (Ibero-Americana: 14, Berkeley, California).

Kidder, A. V.
1916. The Pottery of the Casas Grandes District, Chihuahua (Holmes Anniversary Volume, Anthropological Essays, pp. 253–268, Washington).

528 BIBLIOGRAPHY

1930–1938.   Reports on Investigations of the Division of Historical Research (Carnegie Institution of Washington, Year Book nos. 29–37, Washington).

1935.   Notes on the Ruins of San Agustín Acasaguastlan, Guatemala (Carnegie Institution of Washington, pub. no. 456, pp. 105–120, Washington).

Kidder, A. V., and Jennings, J. D.
1937.   Guatemala Highlands (Carnegie Institution of Washington, Year Book no. 36, pp. 9–10, Washington).

Kidder, A. V., and Thompson, J. E.
1938.   The Correlation of Maya and Christian Chronologies (In: Cooperation in Research, Carnegie Institution of Washington, pub. no. 501, pp. 493–510, Washington).

Kidder, A., II
1937.   Archaeological Investigations in Venezuela (MS. Thesis Submitted in Partial Fulfillment of the Requirements for the Degree of Doctor of Philosophy at Harvard University).

Kingsborough, Edward King, Lord
1831–1848.   Antiquities of Mexico (9 vols., London).

Kluckhohn, Clyde
1935.   A Note on the Source of the Drawings in the del Rio Volume on Palenque (Maya Research, vol. 2, pp. 287–290, New York).

1939.   The Place of Theory in Anthropological Studies (Philosophy of Science, vol. 6, pp. 328–344, Cambridge).

Koppen, W.
1918.   Klassification der Klimat nach Temperatur Niederschlag und Jahreslauf (Petermann's Mitteilungen, vol. 64, pp. 193–203, 243–248, Gotha).

BIBLIOGRAPHY 529

Koppen, W., and Geigen, R.
1936. The Climates of North America (Handbuch der Klimatologie, vol. 2, part 5, translated by R. de C. Ward, C. F. Brooks, A. J. Connor, Berlin).

Kreichgauer, Damian
1927. Anschluss der Maya-Chronologie an die Julianische (Anthropos, vol. 22, pp. 1–15, San Gabriel Mödling).

1932. Über die Maya-Chronologie (Anthropos, vol. 27, pp. 621–626, San Gabriel Mödling).

Krickeberg, W.
1918–1922, 1925. Die Totonaken (Baessler Archiv, vol. 7, pp. 1–55; vol. 9, pp. 1–75, Berlin. Spanish Translation, México, 1933).

1928. Mexikanische–Peruanische Parallelen ("Festschrift, Publication d'Hommage offerte au P. W. Schmidt," pp. 379–393, Vienna).

1937. Berichte über Neue Forschungen zur Geschichte der Alten Kulturen Mittel-Amerikas (Die Welt als Geschichte, 3 Jahrgang, pp. 194–230, Stuttgart).

Kroeber, A. L.
1913. The Determination of Linguistic Relationship (Anthropos, vol. 8, pp. 389–401, San Gabriel Mödling).

1915. Serian, Tequistlatecan and Hokan (University of California, Publications in American Archaeology and Ethnology, vol. 11, no. 4, Berkeley).

1930. Cultural Relations between North and South America (Proceedings, XXIII International Congress of Americanists, New York, 1928, pp. 5–22, New York).

1934. Uto-Aztecan Languages of Mexico (Ibero-Americana: 8, Berkeley).

1936.   Essays presented to Alfred L. Kroeber. *See* Essays, 1936, Lowie, 1936.

1939.   Cultural and Natural Areas of Native North America (University of California, Publications in American Archaeology and Ethnology, vol. 38, Berkeley).

Kroeber, A. L., and Waterman, T. T.
1931.   Source Book in Anthropology. New York.

La Farge, Oliver
1926–1927. *See* Blom, Frans.

MS.   Santa Eulalia, a Cuchumatán Indian Village, Guatemala (MS.).

La Farge, Oliver, and Byers, D. S.
1931.   The Yearbearer's People (Middle American Research Series, Tulane University of Louisiana, no. 3, New Orleans).

Landa, Diego de
1937.   Yucatan before and after the Conquest. Translated with notes by William Gates (Maya Society, pub. no. 20, Baltimore).

Las Casas, Bartolomé de
1877.   Historia de las Indias (Biblioteca Mexicana, 2 vols., México).

1909.   Apologética Historia de las Indias (Historiadores de Indias, vol. 1; Nueva Biblioteca de Autores Españoles, vol. 13, Madrid).

Lathrop, J., and Maxwell, D.
1937.   Report on a Partial Study of the Tarascan Dialect (Investigaciones Lingüísticas, vol. 4, pp. 111–129, Mexico).

Lehmann, W.
1909.   Methods and Results in Mexican Research (Translated by Seymour de Ricci from Archiv für Anthropologie, vol. 6, pp. 113–168, Paris).

1910a. Beitrage zur Kenntnis der Indianersprachen Costa Rica's nach eigenen Aufnahmen (Proceedings, XVI International Congress of Americanists, Wien, 1908, pp. 627–644, Wien).

1910b. Ergebnisse einer Forschungsreise in Mittelamerika und México, 1907–1909 (Zeitschrift für Ethnologie, vol. 42, pp. 687–749, Berlin).

1915. Über die Stellung und Verwandtschaft der Subtiaba-Sprache der Pazifischen Küste Nicaraguas und die Sprache von Tapachula in Südchiapas (Zeitschrift für Ethnologie, vol. 47, pp. 1–34, Berlin).

1920. Zentral-Amerika (2 vols., Berlin).

1938. Die Geschichte der Königreiche von Colhuacan und Mexiko (Quellenwerke zur Alten Geschichte Amerikas, Ibero-Amerikanischen Institut, Berlin).

Lehmann, W., and Doering, H.
1924. Kunstgeschichte des Alten Peru. Berlin.

Lehmann-Nitsche, Robert
1928. Coricancha, el Templo del Sol en el Cuzco. La Plata, Argentina.

Lenoir, Alexandre
1834. Parallèles des Anciens Monuments Mexicains avec ceux de l'Égypte, de l'Inde, et du Reste de l'Ancien Monde (Antiquités Mexicaines, vol. 1, part 2, div. 1, Paris. See Dupaix, 1834).

León, Nicolás
1903. Familias Lingüísticas de México (Anales del Museo Nacional de México, 1a. Época, vol. 7, pp. 279–335, México). (Table reprinted in Investigaciones Lingüísticas, vol. 1, pp. 116, 117, México, 1933.)

1904.   Los Tarascos. México; continued in Anales del Museo Nacional, 2a. Época, vol. 1, pp. 392–502, 592 (México, 1903), and vol. 3, pp. 298–479 (México, 1906).

1905.   Los Popolocas (Conferencias del Museo Nacional, Sección de Etnología, no. 1, México). (Also in Anales de Museo Nacional, 2a. Época, pp. 103–120, México, 1905.)

Le Plongeon, Augustus
1878.   Archaeological Communication on Yucatan (Proceedings, American Antiquarian Society, no. 72, pp. 65–75, Worcester).

1881.   Mayapan and Maya Inscriptions (Proceedings, American Antiquarian Society, n.s., vol. 1, part 2, pp. 246–282, Worcester).

1886.   Sacred Mysteries among the Mayas and the Quichés, etc. New York.

1896.   Queen Moo and the Egyptian Sphinx. New York.

Lilly, E.
1937.   Prehistoric Antiquities of Indiana (Published by the Indiana Historical Society, Indianapolis).

Linné, S.
1929.   Darien in the Past (Göteborgs Kungl. Vetenskaps-och Vitterhets-Samhalles Handlingar, Femte Följden, Series A, vol. 1, no. 3, Göteborg).

1934.   Archaeological Researches at Teotihuacan, Mexico (The Ethnographical Museum of Sweden, New Series, pub. no. 1, Stockholm).

Linton, R. L.
1924.   North American Maize Culture (American Anthropologist, n.s., vol. 26, pp. 345–349, Menasha).

1926. The Origin of the Skidi Pawnee Sacrifice to the Morning Star (American Anthropologist, n.s., vol. 28, pp. 457–466, Menasha).

Lizana, Bernardo de
1893. Historia de Yucatán. Devocionario de Ntra. Sra. de Izamal y Conquista Espiritual (Museo Nacional de México, México).

Lizardi Ramos, César
1939. El Glifo B y la Sincronología Maya-Christiana (In press).

Locke, L. Leland
1923. The Ancient Quipu, or Peruvian Knot Record (American Museum of Natural History, New York).

Lombardo, Natal
1702. Opata Grammar. Mexico.

Lombardo Toledano, Vicente
1931. Geografía de las Lenguas de la Sierra de Puebla (Universidad de Mexico, vol. 3, no. 13, pp. 14–96, Mexico).

Lothrop, S. K.
1917. Reconnaissance Trip to Honduras and Guatemala (Unpublished notes now deposited with the Peabody Museum, Harvard University, Cambridge).

1921. The Stone Statues of Nicaragua (American Anthropologist, n.s., vol. 23, pp. 311–319, Lancaster).

1924. Tulum (Carnegie Institution of Washington, pub. no. 335, Washington).

1925. The Architecture of the Ancient Mayas (Architectural Record, vol. 57, pp. 491–509, New York).

1926a. Pottery of Costa Rica and Nicaragua (Contribution, Museum of the American Indian, Heye Foundation, vol. 8, 2 vols., New York).

1926b. Stone Sculptures from the Finca Arevalo, Guatemala (Indian Notes, Museum of the American Indian, Heye Foundation, vol. 3, no. 3, pp. 147–171, New York).

1926c. La Centinela, an Inca Ruin on the Coast of Peru (The Independent, vol. 116, pp. 13–16, Boston).

1927a. Pottery Types and their Sequence in El Salvador (Indian Notes and Monographs, Museum of the American Indian, Heye Foundation, vol. 1, no. 4, pp. 165–220, New York).

1927b. The Museum Central American Expedition, 1925–1926 (Indian Notes, Museum of the American Indian, Heye Foundation, vol. 4, pp. 12–33, New York, 1930).

1927c. The Word Maya and the Fourth Voyage of Columbus (Indian Notes, Museum of the American Indian, Heye Foundation, vol. 4, no. 4, New York).

1929. Further Notes on Indian Ceremonies in Guatemala (Indian Notes, Museum of the American Indian, Heye Foundation, vol. 6, no. 1, pp. 1–25, New York).

1930. A Modern Survival of the Ancient Maya Calendar (Proceedings, XXIII International Congress of Americanists, New York, 1928, pp. 652–655, New York).

1932a. Indians of the Paraná Delta, Argentina (Annals of the New York Academy of Sciences, vol. 33, pp. 77–232, New York).

1932b. Aboriginal Navigation off the West Coast of South America (Journal of the Royal Anthropological Institute, vol. 62, pp. 229–256, London).

1933. Atitlan. An Archaeological Study of Ancient Remains on the Borders of Lake Atitlan, Guatemala (Carnegie Institution of Washington, pub. no. 444, Washington).

1936. Zacualpa. A Study of Ancient Quiche Artifacts (Carnegie Institution of Washington, pub. no. 472, Washington).

1937. Coclé. An Archaeological Study of Central Panama (part 1, Memoirs, Peabody Museum of Harvard University, vol. 7, Cambridge).

1939. The Southeastern Frontier of the Maya (American Anthropologist, n.s., vol. 41, pp. 42–54, Menasha).

Lovén, S.
1935. Origins of the Tainan Culture, West Indies. Göteborg.

Lowie, R. H.
1937. The History of Ethnological Theory. New York.

1938. A Note on South American Parallels to Maya and Aztec Traits (American Antiquity, vol. 4, pp. 157–159, Menasha).

Lowie, Robert L. (editor)
1936. Essays in Anthropology Presented to Alfred Louis Kroeber. Berkeley.

Ludendorff, Hans
1930–1937. Untersuchungen zur Astronomie der Maya, Nrs. 1–10, with various sub-titles (Sitzungsberichten der Preussischen Akademie der Wissenschaften, Phys.-Math. Klasse, Berlin).

Lumholtz, C.
1900. Symbolism of the Huichol Indians (Memoirs, American Museum of Natural History, vol. 3, part 1, New York).

1902. Unknown Mexico (2 vols., New York).

1912.   New Trails in Mexico. New York.

Lumholtz, C., and Hrdlička, Aleš
1898.   Marked Human Bones from a Prehistoric
                         Tarasco Indian Burial Place in the State
                         of Michoacan, Mexico (Bulletin, Ameri-
                         can Museum of Natural History, vol. 10,
                         pp. 61–79, New York).

Luxán, Diego Pérez
1929.   Expedition into New Mexico made by An-
                         tonio de Espejo, 1582–1583. Translated by
                         G. P. Hammond and Agapito Rey (Qui-
                         vira Society Publications, vol. 1, Los An-
                         geles).

McBride, G. McC.
1923.   Land Systems of Mexico (Research Series,
                         American Geographical Society, no. 12,
                         New York).

McBryde, Webster
1933.   Sololá, a Guatemalan Town and Cakchiquel
                         Market-Center. A Preliminary Report
                         (Tulane University of Louisiana, Middle
                         American Research Series no. 5, Pamphlet
                         no. 3, New Orleans).

MacCurdy, G. G.
1911.   A Study of Chiriquian Antiquities (Mem-
                         oirs, Connecticut Academy of Arts and
                         Sciences, vol. 3, New Haven).

1913.   Shell Gorgets from Missouri (American An-
                         thropologist, n.s., vol. 15, pp. 395–414,
                         Lancaster).

1916.   The Cult of the Ax (Holmes Anniversary
                         Volume, Anthropological Essays, pp. 301–
                         315, Washington).

MacCurdy, G. G. (editor)
1937.   Early Man. Philadelphia and New York.

McKern, W. C.

1937.   An Hypothesis for the Asiatic Origin of the Woodland Culture Pattern (American Antiquity, vol. 3, pp. 138–143, Menasha).

1939.   The Mid-Western Taxonomic Method as an Aid to Archaeological Culture Study (American Antiquity, vol. 4, pp. 301–313, Menasha).

Maler, Teobert

1895.   Yukatekische Forschungen (Globus, vol. 68, pp. 247–259, Braunschweig).

1901.   Researches in the Central Portion of the Usumatsintla Valley (Memoirs, Peabody Museum of Harvard University, vol. 2, no. 1, Cambridge).

1902.   Yukatekische Forschungen (Globus, vol. 82, pp. 197–230, Braunschweig).

1903.   Researches in the Central Portion of the Usumatsintla Valley (Memoirs, Peabody Museum of Harvard University, vol. 2, no. 2, Cambridge).

1908.   Explorations of the Upper Usumatsintla and Adjacent Region: Altar de Sacrificios; Seibal; Itsimte-Sacluk; Cankuen (Memoirs, Peabody Museum of Harvard University, vol. 4, no. 1, Cambridge).

1908.   Explorations in the Department of Peten, Guatemala, and Adjacent Region: Topoxté; Yaxhá; Benque Viejo; Naranjo (Memoirs, Peabody Museum of Harvard University, vol. 4, no. 2, Cambridge).

1910.   Explorations in the Department of Peten, Guatemala, and Adjacent Region. Motul de San José; Peten-Itza (Memoirs, Peabody Museum of Harvard University, vol. 4, no. 3, Cambridge).

1911.   Explorations in the Department of Peten, Guatemala. Tikal (Memoirs, Peabody Museum of Harvard University, vol. 5, no. 1, Cambridge).

Mangelsdorf, P. C., and Reeves, R. G.
1938.   The Origin of Maize (Proceedings of the National Academy of Sciences, Vol. 24, pp. 303–312, Lancaster).

Markham, Sir Clements R.
1910.   The Incas of Peru. New York.

Marquina, Ignacio
1928.   Estudio Arquitectónico Comparativo de los Monumentos Arqueológicos de México (Secretaría de Educación Pública, México).

Martínez Hernández, J.
1926.   Paralelismo entre los Calendarios Maya y Azteca. Mérida, Yucatán.

1928.   Significación Cronológica de los Ciclos Mayas. Mérida, Yucatán.
Martínez del Rio, Pablo
1934.   Las Pinturas Rupestres del Cerro Blanco de Covadonga (Durango) (Anales del Museo Nacional de Arqueología, Historia y Etnografía, 5a. Época, vol. 1, pp. 43–66, México).

1936.   Los Orígenes Americanos. México.

Martyr d'Anghera, Peter
1912.   De Orbe Novo. Translated and edited by F. A. MacNutt (2 vols., New York and London).
Mason, J. Alden
1917.   Tepecano, a Piman Language of Western Mexico (Annals, New York Academy of Science, vol. 25, pp. 309–416, New York).

1923.   A Preliminary Sketch of the Yaqui Lan-
            guage (University of California Publica-
            tions in American Archaeology and Eth-
            nology, vol. 20, pp. 195–214, Berkeley).

1929.   Turquoise Mosaics from Northern Mexico
            (The Museum Journal, Museum of the
            University of Pennsylvania, vol. 20, pp.
            157–175, Philadelphia).

1935a.   Mexican and Maya Sweat-Baths (University
            Museum Bulletin, vol. 6, pp. 65–69, Phila-
            delphia).

1935b.   The Place of Texas in Pre-Columbian Re-
            lationships between the United States and
            Mexico (Bulletin of the Texas Archaeo-
            logical and Palaeontological Society, vol.
            7, pp. 29–46, Abilene, Texas).

1936.   The Classification of the Sonoran Languages
            (Essays in Anthropology presented to
            A. L. Kroeber, pp. 183–196, appendix by
            B. L. Whorf, pp. 197–198, Berkeley).

1937a.   Further Remarks on the Pre-Columbian Re-
            lationships between the United States and
            Mexico (Bulletin of the Texas Archaeo-
            logical and Palaeontological Society, vol. 9,
            pp. 120–129, Abilene, Texas).

1937b.   Late Archaeological Sites in Durango, Mex-
            ico, from Chalchihuites to Zape (Twenty-
            fifth Anniversary Studies, Philadelphia
            Anthropological Society, vol. 1, pp. 127–
            146, Philadelphia).

1938.   Observations on the Present Status and Prob-
            lems of Middle American Archaeology
            (American Antiquity, vol. 3, pp. 206–223,
            300–317, Menasha).

540 BIBLIOGRAPHY

Maudslay, A. C. and A. P.
1899.   A Glimpse at Guatemala and Some Notes on
                   the Ancient Monuments of Central Amer-
                   ica. London.

Maudslay, A. P.
1883.   Explorations in Guatemala, and Examination
                   of the Newly-Discovered Indian Ruins
                   of Quirigua, Tikal, and the Usumacinta
                   (Proceedings of the Royal Geographical
                   Society, n.s., vol. 5, pp. 185–204, London).

1889–1902.   Archaeology (Biologia Centrali Americana,
                   4 vols. plates, 1 vol. text, London).

1892.   The Ancient Civilization of Central America
                   (Nature, vol. 45, pp. 617–622, London).

1912.   Some American Problems (Journal, Royal
                   Anthropological Institute, vol. 42, pp. 9–
                   22, London).

Mead, Charles W.
1916.   Conventionalized Figures in Ancient Peru-
                   vian Art (Anthropological Papers, Amer-
                   ican Museum of Natural History, vol. 12,
                   no. 5, New York).

1932.   Old Civilizations of Inca Land, 2nd edition,
                   revised by Roland Olson (American Mu-
                   seum of Natural History, Handbook Se-
                   ries, no. 11, New York).

Means, Philip Ainsworth
1917a.   Las Relaciones entre Centro-América y Sud-
                   América en la Época Prehistórica (Bole-
                   tín, Sociedad Geográfica de Lima, vol. 23,
                   pp. 152–170, Lima).

1917b.   History of the Spanish Conquest of Yucatan
                   and of the Itzas (Papers, Peabody Museum
                   of American Archaeology and Ethnology,
                   Harvard University, vol. 7, Cambridge).

1928. A Survey of Ancient Peruvian Art (Transactions, Connecticut Academy of Arts and
Sciences, vol. 21, pp. 315–442, New Haven).

1931. Ancient Civilizations of the Andes. New
York and London.

Mechling, William H.
1912. The Indian Linguistic Stocks of Oaxaca,
Mexico (American Anthropologist, n.s.,
vol. 14, pp. 643–682, Lancaster).

Medina de la Torre, F.
1934. Monumentos Arqueológicos en el Oriente
del Estado de Jalisco (Boletín de la Junta
Auxiliar Jalisciense de la Sociedad Mexicana de Geografía y Estadística, vol. 9,
pp. 217–226, Guadalajara).

Mena, Ramón, and Aguirre, Porfirio
1927. La Nueva Zona Arqueológica (Chupicuaro,
etc.) (Revista Mexicana de Estudios Históricos, vol. 1, pp. 55–64, México).

de Mendieta, G.
1870. Historia Ecclesiástica Indiana (XVI Century). México.

de Mendizábal, Miguel O.
1937. Distribución Geográfica de las Lenguas Indígenas de México, conforme al Censo de
1930 (por Municipios) (Map) (Departamento de Asuntos Indígenas, México).

de Mendizábal, Miguel O., and Jiménez Moreno, Wigberto
n.d. Distribución Prehispánica de la Lenguas Indígenas de México (Map) (Secretaría de
la Economía Nacional; Departamento de
Arqueología del Museo Nacional, México).

Mercer, H. C.
1897. The Kabal, or Potter's Wheel of Yucatan
(Bulletin, Museum of Science and Art,
University of Pennsylvania, vol. 1, pp. 63–
70, Philadelphia).

Merrill, E. D.
1937.   Plants and Civilization (Independence, Con-
                          vergence and Borrowing in Institutions,
                          Thought and Art, Harvard Tercentenary
                          Publications, Cambridge).
Merwin, R. E.
1913.   The Ruins of the Southern Part of the Pen-
                          insula of Yucatan with Special Reference
                          to Their Place in the Maya Culture (MS.
                          Thesis in the Library of Harvard Uni-
                          versity, Cambridge).

Merwin, R. E., and Vaillant, G. C.
1932.   The Ruins of Holmul, Guatemala (Memoirs,
                          Peabody Museum of Harvard University,
                          vol. 3, no. 2, Cambridge).
Miller, W. S.
1937.   La Lengua Mixe o Ayuc (Investigaciones
                          Lingüísticas, vol. 4, pp. 130–133, México).
de Molina, A.
1880.   Vocabulario de la Lengua Mexicana. Leip-
                          zig.

Molina Solis, Juan Francisco
1896.   Historia del Descubrimiento y Conquista de
                          Yucatán. Mérida.
Moore, C. B.
1905.   Certain Aboriginal Mounds of the Black
                          Warrior River (Journal of the Academy
                          of Natural Sciences, Philadelphia, vol. 13,
                          pp. 125–244, Philadelphia).

1907.   Moundville Revisited (Journal of the Acad-
                          emy of Natural Sciences, Philadelphia, vol.
                          13, pp. 337–405, Philadelphia).

1908.   Certain Mounds of Arkansas and Mississippi.
                          Part I, Lower Arkansas River. Part II,
                          Lower Yazoo and Lower Sunflower
                          Rivers, Mississippi. Part III, The Blum
                          Mounds, Mississippi (Journal of the Acad-
                          emy of Natural Sciences of Philadelphia,
                          vol. 13, pp. 481–600, Philadelphia).

1909. Antiquities of the Ouachita Valley (Journal of the Academy of Natural Sciences of Philadelphia, vol. 14, pp. 7–249, Philadelphia).

1910. Antiquities of the St. Francis, White and Black Rivers, Arkansas (Journal of the Academy of Natural Sciences of Philadelphia, vol. 14, pp. 255–362, Philadelphia).

1911. Some Aboriginal Sites on Mississippi River (Journal of the Academy of Natural Sciences of Philadelphia, vol. 14, pp. 367–476, Philadelphia).

1912. Some Aboriginal Sites on Red River (Journal of the Academy of Natural Sciences of Philadelphia, vol. 14, pp. 483–640, Philadelphia).

1913. Some Aboriginal Sites in Louisiana and Arkansas (Atchafalaya River, Lake Larto, Tensas River, Bayou Macon, Bayou D'Arbonne in Louisiana; Saline River in Arkansas) (Journal of the Academy of Natural Sciences of Philadelphia, vol. 16, pp. 7–99, Philadelphia).

1915. Aboriginal Sites on Tennessee River (Journal of the Academy of Natural Sciences, Philadelphia, vol. 16, pp. 169–422, Philadelphia).

Moorehead, Warren K.

1928. The Cahokia Mounds (University of Illinois Bulletin, vol. 26, no. 4 [Includes observations printed in vols. 29, no. 35, and 21, no. 6], pp. 1–176, Urbana).

1929. The Mound Builder Problem to Date (American Anthropologist, n.s., vol. 31, pp. 544–554, Menasha).

1932. Explorations of the Etowah Site in Georgia (Department of Archaeology, Phillips Academy, Andover, New Haven).

Moreno, M.
1931. La Organización Política y Social de los Aztecas. Universidad Nacional de México Autónoma. Sección Editorial. México.

Morgan, Lewis H.
1881. Houses and House-life of the American Aborigines (Department of the Interior, Contributions to North American Ethnology, vol. 4, Washington).

Morley, F. R., and Morley, S. G.
1938. The Age and Provenance of the Leyden Plate (Carnegie Institution of Washington, pub. no. 509, Contribution no. 24, Washington).

Morley, Sylvanus G.
1910. A Group of Related Structures at Uxmal, Mexico (Archaeological Institute of America, American Journal of Archaeology, 2nd series, vol. 14, no. 1, pp. 1–18, Norwood).

1911. Ancient Temples and Cities of the New World (Bulletin of the Pan American Union, vol. 32, pp. 453–468, 627–642, 863–879, Washington).

1913. Excavations at Quirigua, Guatemala (National Geographic Magazine, vol. 24, pp. 339–361, Washington).

1915. An Introduction to the Study of Maya Hieroglyphs (Bureau of American Ethnology, Bulletin 57, Washington).

1915–1929. Archaeology (Carnegie Institution of Washington, Year Book, nos. 14–28, Washington).

1917a. The Hotun as the Principal Chronological Unit of the Old Empire Maya (Proceedings, XIX International Congress of Americanists, Washington, 1915, pp. 195–201, Washington).

1917b. The Ruins of Tuloom, Yucatan (American Museum Journal, vol. 17, pp. 190–204, New York).

1918. Archaeology (Carnegie Institution of Washington, Year Book, no. 17, Washington).

1920. The Inscriptions at Copan. Washington (Carnegie Institution of Washington, pub. no. 219, Washington).

1933. The Calakmul Expedition (Scientific Monthly, vol. 37, pp. 193–206, New York).

1935. Guide Book of the Ruins of Quirigua (Carnegie Institution of Washington, supplementary pub. no. 16, Washington).

1937–1938. The Inscriptions of Peten (Carnegie Institution of Washington, pub. no. 437, 5 vols., Washington).

Morris, Earl H.
1927. The Beginnings of Pottery Making in the San Juan Area: Unfired Prototypes and the Wares of the Earliest Ceramic Period (Anthropological Papers, American Museum of Natural History, vol. 28, part 2, New York).

Morris, E. H., Charlot, J., and Morris, A. A.
1931. The Temple of the Warriors at Chichen Itza, Yucatan (Carnegie Institution of Washington, pub. no. 406, Washington).

Motolinía (de Benavente, T.)
1914.   Historia de los Índios de la Nueva España (XVI Century). Barcelona.
Muñoz Camargo, D.
1892.   Historia de Tlaxcala. México.

Muñoz, Juan Bautista, Calderón, José Antonio, Bernasconi, Antonio, and others
1783–1789.   Expediente Relativo al Descubrimiento de las Ruinas del Palenque e Informes Referentes a ellas, etc. (Copies of MSS. in the Peabody Museum of Harvard University, Cambridge).
Murphy, R. C.
1939.   The Littoral of Pacific Colombia and Ecuador (The Geographic Review, vol. 29, no. 1, New York).
Myer, W. E.
1928.   Two Prehistoric Villages in Middle Tennessee (41st Annual Report, Bureau of American Ethnology, pp. 485–614, Washington).

Nadaillac, Marquis de
1884.   Pre-Historic America. Translated by N. d'Anvers. New York.
Nelson, N. C.
1933.   The Antiquity of Man in America in the Light of Archaeology (The American Aborigines, Their Origin and Antiquity. Edited by Diamond Jenness, pp. 87–130, Toronto).
Nichols, M. W.
1939.   The Spanish Horse of the Pampas (American Anthropologist, n.s., vol. 41, pp. 119–129, Menasha).
Nida, Eugenio A.
1937.   The Tarahumara Language (Investigaciones Lingüísticas, vol. 4, pp. 140–144, México).
Noguera, Eduardo
1930a.   Decorative Aspects of Certain Types of Mexican Pottery (Proceedings, XXIII In-

ternational Congress of Americanists, New York, 1928, pp. 85–92, New York).

1930b. Algunas Características de la Cerámica de México (Journal de la Société des Américanistes de Paris, n.s., vol. 22, pp. 249–310, Paris).

1930c. Ruinas Arqueológicas del Norte de México, Casas Grandes (Chihuahua), La Quemada, Chalchichuites (Zacatecas) (Publicaciones de la Secretaría de Educación Pública, México).

1931. Exploraciones Arqueológicas en las Regiones de Zamora y Patzcuaro, Estado de Michoacán (Anales del Museo Nacional de Arqueología, Historia y Etnografía, 4a. Época, vol. 7, pp. 89–103, México).

1932. Extensiones Cronológico-Culturales y Geográficas de las Cerámicas de México (Contribución al XXV Congreso Internacional de Americanistas, La Plata, Argentina, 1932, México).

1933. Objetos Procedentes de Ojitlán, Oaxaca (Boletín del Museo Nacional de Arqueología, Historia y Etnografía, 5a. Época, vol. 2, pp. 45–46, México).

1934. Estudio de la Cerámica Encontrada donde Estaba el Templo Mayor de México (Anales del Museo Nacional de México, 5a. Época, vol. 1, pp. 267–281, México).

1935. Antecedentes y Relaciones de la Cultura Teotihuacana (El México Antiguo, vol. 3, nos. 5–8, pp. 1–81, México).

1937a. El Altar de Los Cranios Esculpidos de Cholula. México.

1937b.   Conclusiones Principales Obtenidas por el Estudio de la Cerámica Arqueológica en Cholula (Mimeograph, México).

Noll-Husum, Herbert

1937.   Grundlegendes zur Zeitbestimmung der Maya (Zeitschrift für Ethnologie, vol. 69, pp. 54–63, Berlin).

Nordenskiöld, Erland

1920.   The Changes in the Material Culture of Two Indian Tribes under the Influence of New Surroundings (Comparative Ethnographical Studies, no. 2, Göteborg).

1921.   The Copper and Bronze Ages in South America (Comparative Ethnographical Studies, no. 4, Göteborg).

1922.   Deductions Suggested by the Geographical Distribution of Some Post-Columbian Words Used by the Indians of South America (Comparative Ethnographical Studies, no. 5, Göteborg).

1924.   The Ethnography of South America Seen from Mojos in Bolivia (Comparative Ethnographical Studies, no. 3, Göteborg).

1925.   Calculations with Years and Months in the Peruvian Quipus. Gothenburg, Sweden.

1928.   Indianerna på Panamanäset. Stockholm.

1930.   L'Archéologie du Bassin de l'Amazone. Paris.

1931.   Origin of the Indian Civilizations in South America (Comparative Ethnographical Studies, no. 9, pp. 1–76, Göteborg).

Núñez de la Vega, Francisco

1702.   Constituciones Diocesanas del Obispado de Chiapas. Rome.

Nuttall, Zelia

1901.   The Fundamental Principles of Old and New World Civilizations (Papers, Peabody

Museum of American Archaeology and Ethnology, Harvard University, vol. 2, Cambridge).

1910.   The Island of Sacrificios (American Anthropologist, n.s., vol. 12, pp. 257–295, Lancaster).

1932a.   Comparison Between Etowan, Mexican and Mayan Designs (Moorehead, Exploration of the Etowah Site in Georgia, pp. 137–144, Department of Archaeology, Phillips Academy, Andover, New Haven).

1932b.   Sobre un Monumento en Monte Albán de Gran Importancia (Contribución al XXV Congreso Internacional de Americanistas, La Plata, Argentina, 1932, México).

Olson, Ronald L.
1931.   Old Empires of the Andes (Natural History, vol. 31, pp. 3–22, New York).

Orozco y Berra, Manuel
1864.   Geografía de las Lenguas y Carta Etnográfica de México. México.

1880.   Historia Antigua y de la Conquista de México (4 vols. and atlas, México).

de Ortega, P. Joseph
1732.   Vocabulario en Lengua Castellano y Coro. México. (Reprinted in Tepic, 1888.)

Osgood, C.
1935.   The Archaeological Problem in Chiriqui (American Anthropologist, n.s., vol. 37, pp. 234–243, Menasha).

Oviedo y Valdés, Gonzalo Fernández de
1851–1855.   Historia General y Natural de las Indias, Islas y Tierra-firme del Mar Océano (4 vols., Madrid).

Palacio, Diego Gárcia de
1860.   Carta Dirijida at Rey de España, año 1576
                         (in Squier, Collection of Rare and Orig-
                         inal Documents and Relations, no. 1, New
                         York).

Palacios, Enrique Juan
1928.   En los Confines de la Selva Lacandona (Con-
                         tribución al XXIII Congreso Internacional
                         de Americanistas. Secretaría de Educación
                         Pública, México).

1932.   Maya-Christian Synchronology or Calendric
                         Correlation (Middle American Research
                         Series, pub. no. 4, pp. 147–180, New Or-
                         leans).

1936.   Inscripción Recientemente Descubierta en
                         Palenque (Maya Research, vol. 3, pp.
                         3–17, New Orleans).

1937.   Mas Gemas del Arte Maya en Palenque
                         (Anales del Museo Nacional de Arqueolo-
                         gía, Historia y Etnografía, 5a. Época, vol.
                         2, pp. 193–225, México).

Parsons, E. C.
1936.   Mitla, Town of Souls. Chicago.

Payón, J. García
1936.   Zona Arqueológica de Tecaxic-Calixtla-
                         huaca, Part I (Departamento de Monu-
                         mentos, México).

Peabody, C.
1904.   Exploration of Mounds, Coahoma County,
                         Mississippi (Papers, Peabody Museum of
                         American Archaeology and Ethnology,
                         Harvard University, vol. 3, no. 2, Cam-
                         bridge).

Pearce, J. E.
1932.   The Archaeology of East Texas (American
                         Anthropologist, n.s., vol. 34, pp. 670–687,
                         Menasha).

Peet, Stephen D.
1882.

The Origin of the Architectural Orders
(American Antiquarian, vol. 4, pp. 303–
322, Chicago).

Peñafiel, A.
1890.

Monumentos del Arte Mexicano Antiguo
(3 vols., Berlin).

Pepper, George H.
1916.

Yacatas of the Tierra Caliente, Michoacan,
Mexico (Holmes Anniversary Volume,
Anthropological Essays, pp. 415–420,
Washington).

Peralta, M. M. de
1883.

Costa Rica, Nicaragua y Panamá en el Siglo
XVI. Madrid.

Pérez de Barradas, J.
1937.

Arqueología y Antropología Precolombinas
de Tierra Dentro (Ministerio de Educación Nacional, Publicaciones de la Sección de Arqueología, no. 1, Bogotá, Colombia).

Périgny, Maurice de
1908.

Yucatan Inconnu (Journal de la Société des
Américanistes de Paris, n.s., vol. 5, pp. 67–
84, Paris).

1909.

Villes Mortes de l'Amérique Centrale (Tour
du Monde, n.s., vol. 15, pp. 445–480,
Paris).

1911.

Les Ruines de Nakcun (Journal de la Société des Américanistes de Paris, n.s., vol.
8, pp. 5–22, Paris).

1911.

Mission dans l'Amérique Centrale, 1909–
1910. Les Ruines de Nakcun (Nouvelles
Archives des Missions Scientifiques et Lit-
téraires, n.s., part 4, pp. 1–15, Paris).

Pimentel, Francisco
1862.

Cuadro Descriptivo y Comparativo de las
Lenguas Indígenas de México. México.
(Other editions 1874–1875, 1903.)

Piñeda, Emeterio
1845.

Descripción Geográfica de Chiapas y Soconusco. México.

Piñeda, Vicente
1888.

Historia de las Sublevaciones Indígenas, Gramática de la Lengua Tzeltal y Diccionario
de la Misma. Chiapas.

Plancarte, F.
1893.

Archaeologic Explorations in Michoacan,
Mexico (American Anthropologist, o.s.,
vol. 6, pp. 79–84, Washington).

Pollock, H. E. D.
1936a.

The Architectural Survey (Carnegie Institution of Washington, Year Book no. 35,
pp. 122–125, Washington).

1936b.

Round Structures of Aboriginal Middle
America (Carnegie Institution of Washington, pub. no. 471, Washington).

Pomar, Juan Bautista
1891.

Relación de Tezcoco (Nueva Colección de
Documentos para la Historia de México,
J. García Icazbalceta, ed., vol. 3, México).

Ponce, Alonso
1873.

Relación Breve y Verdadera de Algunas
Cosas de las Muchas que Sucedieron al
Padre Alonso Ponce en las Provincias de
la Nueva España, siendo Comisario General de aquellas Partes . . . Escrita por
dos Religiosos, sus Compañeros. Madrid.

Popenoe, Dorothy H.
1928.

Las Ruinas de Tenampua. Tipografía Nacional, Tegucigalpa.

1934.

Some Excavations at Playa de los Muertos,
Ulua River, Honduras (Maya Research,
vol. 1, pp. 61–85, New York).

Posnansky, Arthur
1937.

Antropología y Sociología de las Razas In-
terandinas y de las Regiones Adyacentes
(Instituto "Tihuanacu" de Antropología,
Etnografía y Prehistoria, La Paz, Bolivia).

Potter, W. B.
1880.

Archaeological Remains in Southeastern Missouri (St. Louis Academy of Science, Contributions to the Archaeology of Missouri, Salem).

Prescott, William H.
1843.

The Conquest of Mexico (3 vols., New York).

Preuss, K. Th.
1929.

Monumentale Vorgeschichtliche Kunst (2 vols., Göttingen).

1932.

Grammatik der Cora-Sprache (International Journal of American Linguistics, vol. 7, pp. 1–84, New York).

1934.

Wörterbuch Deutsch-Cora (International Journal of American Linguistics, vol. 8, pp. 81–102, New York).

Price, W. H.
1897–1899.

Excavations on Sittee River, British Honduras (Proceedings, Society of Antiquarians of London, vol. 17, pp. 399–444, London).

Prieto, Alejandro
1873.

Historia, Geografía y Estadística del Estado de Tamaulipas. México.

Prince, J. Dyneley
1913a.

A Text in the Indian Language of Panama-Darien (American Anthropologist, n.s., vol. 15, pp. 298–326, Lancaster).

1913b.

Grammar and glossary of the Tule Language of Panama (American Anthropologist, n.s., vol. 15, pp. 480–528, Lancaster).

Probanza
1533.

Probanza. Photo MS. of Original in the Archivo General de las Indias. Seville.

Putnam, F. W.
1878.

Archaeological Explorations in Tennessee (Eleventh Annual Report of the Peabody

Museum of American Archaeology and Ethnology, Harvard University, vol. 2, pp. 305–360, Cambridge).

1909.   Putnam Anniversary Volume, Anthropological Essays. New York.

Radin, Paul
1916.   On the Relationship of Huave and Mixe (American Anthropologist, n.s., vol. 18, pp. 411–423, Lancaster).

1919.   The Genetic Relationship of the North American Indian Languages (University of California Publications in American Archaeology and Ethnology, vol. 14, part 5, Berkeley).

1920.   The Sources and Authenticity of the History of the Ancient Mexicans (University of California Publications in American Archaeology and Ethnology, vol. 17, no. 1, Berkeley).

1933.   Notes on the Tlappanec Language (International Journal of American Linguistics, vol. 8, pp. 45–72, New York).

Rau, Charles
1879.   The Palenque Tablet in the United States National Museum, Washington, D.C. (Smithsonian Contributions to Knowledge, no. 331, Washington).

Raynaud, Georges
1925.   Les Dieux, Les Héros et les Hommes de l'Ancien Guatemala, d'apres le Livre de Conseil. Paris.

Recinos, Adrián
1913.   Monografía del Departamento de Huehuetenango, República de Guatemala. Guatemala.

Redfield, Robert
1930.   Tepoztlan. Chicago.

Redfield, Robert, and Villa R., Alfonso
1934. Chan Kom, a Maya Village (Carnegie Institution of Washington, pub. no. 448, Washington).

Reed, W. W.
1923. Climatological Data for Central America (Monthly Weather Review, vol. 51, pp. 133–144, Washington).

Relaciones de Yucatán
1898–1900. Relaciones Histórico-Geográficas de las Provincias de Yucatán (Colección de Documentos Inéditos Relativos al Descubrimiento, Conquista y Organización de las Antiguas Posesiones Españoles de Ultramar, 2nd series, vols. 11 and 13, Madrid).

Reville, Albert
1884. The Native Religions of Mexico and Peru. Translated by Philip Wicksteed. New York.

Rickards, Constantine George
1910. The Ruins of Mexico. London.

1913. Notes on the Codex Rickards (Journal de la Société des Américanistes de Paris, n.s., vol. 10, pp. 47–57, Paris).

Ricketson, E. B.
1934. Notes on the Pottery of the House Mounds of Uaxactun (in Wauchope, R., House Mounds of Uaxactun, Guatemala, Carnegie Institution of Washington, Contributions to American Archaeology, no. 7, Washington).

1937. Uaxactun, Guatemala, Group E, 1926–1931. Part II: The Artifacts (Carnegie Institution of Washington, pub. no. 477, Washington).

Ricketson, O. G., Jr.
1928a. Report on the Excavations at Uaxactun (Carnegie Institution of Washington, Year Book no. 27, pp. 307–312, Washington).

1928b.   Astronomical Observatories in the Maya
                              Area (Geographical Review, vol. 18, pp.
                              215–225, New York).

1928c.   Notes on Two Maya Astronomic Observa-
                              tories (American Anthropologist, n.s., vol.
                              30, pp. 434–444, Menasha).

1929.   Excavations at Baking Pot, British Honduras
                              (Carnegie Institution of Washington, pub.
                              no. 403, Contributions to American Ar-
                              chaeology, vol. 1, no. 1, Washington).

1936.   Ruins of Tzalcam, Guatemala (Maya Re-
                              search, vol. 3, pp. 18–23, New Orleans).

Ricketson, O. G., Jr., and Ricketson, E. B.
1937.   Uaxactun, Guatemala, Group E, 1926–1931.
                              Part I: The Excavations; Part II: The
                              Artifacts (Carnegie Institution of Wash-
                              ington, pub. no. 477, Washington).
Rinaldini, Benito
1743.   Gramática, Diccionario y Catecismo de la
                              Lengua Tepehuana. México.

del Rio, Antonio and Cabrera, Paul Felix
1822.   Description of the Ruins of an Ancient City,
                              Discovered Near Palenque. London.
Ritchie, W. A.
1936.   New Evidence Relating to the Archaic Oc-
                              cupation of New York (Researches and
                              Transactions of the New York State
                              Archaeological Association, Lewis H.
                              Morgan Chapter, vol. 8, no. 1, Rochester).

Riva Palacio, Vicente, Editor
1887–1889.   México a través de los Siglos (5 vols., México
                              and Barcelona).
Rivas, P.
1934.   Monografía Geográfica y Histórica de la
                              Isla del Tigre y Puerto de Amapala.
                              Tegucigalpa.

Rivet, Paul
1911.   Les Familles Linguistiques du Nord-Ouest
            de l'Amérique du Sud (L'Année Lin-
            guistique, vol. 4, pp. 117–155, Paris).

1924a.   Langues de l'Amérique Central (Article in
            Les Langues du Monde, Meillet, A. and
            Cohen, M., eds.; Collection Linguistique
            Publiée par La Société de Paris, vol. 16,
            pp. 629–638, Paris).

1924b.   Langues de l'Amérique du Sud et des An-
            tilles (Article in Les Langues du Monde,
            Meillet, A. and Cohen, M., eds.; Collection
            Linguistique Publiée par La Société de
            Paris, vol. 16, pp. 639–707, Paris).

1924c.   Langues de l'Amérique du Nord (Article in
            Les Langues du Monde, Meillet, A. and
            Cohen, M., eds.; Collection Linguistique
            Publiée par La Société de Paris, vol. 16,
            pp. 607–628, Paris).

1925.   Les Éléments Constituifs des Civilisations du
            Nord-Ouest et de l'Ouest Sud-Américain
            (Proceedings, XXI International Congress
            of Americanists, part 2, pp. 1–20, Göte-
            borg).

Rivet, P., and Arsandaux, H.
1921.   Contribution a l'Étude de la Métallurgie
            Mexicaine (Journal de la Société des
            Américanistes de Paris, n.s., vol. 13, pp.
            261–280, Paris).

Roberts, Frank H. H., Jr.
1935.   A Folsom Complex: Preliminary Report on
            Investigations at the Lindenmeier Site in
            Northern Colorado (Smithsonian Miscel-
            laneous Collections, vol. 94, no. 4, Wash-
            ington).

1936.   Additional Information on the Folsom Com-
            plex: Report on the Second Season's In-

558 BIBLIOGRAPHY

vestigations at the Lindenmeier Site in Northern Colorado (Smithsonian Miscellaneous Collections, vol. 95, no. 10, Washington).

Roberts, H. B.
1935.

Ceramics (Carnegie Institution of Washington, Year Book no. 34, pp. 126–127, Washington).

Robertson, William
1777.

The History of America (2 vols., London).

Robles, Carmen Alessio
1929.

La Región Arqueológica de Casas Grandes, Chihuahua. México.

Rock, Fritz
1924.

Altamerikanische Kulturbeziehungen zwischen Nord-, Mittel-, und Süd-Amerika (Proceedings, XXI International Congress of Americanists, part 1, pp. 200–211, The Hague).

Román y Zamora, J.
1897.

Repúblicas de Índias. Idolatrías y Gobierno en México y Perú antes de la Conquista (Colección de Libros Raros y Curiosos que Tratan de América, vols. 14 and 15, Madrid).

Roys, Lawrence
1933.

The Maya Correlation Problem Today (American Anthropologist, n.s., vol. 35, pp. 403–417, Menasha).

1934.

The Engineering Knowledge of the Maya (Carnegie Institution of Washington, pub. no. 436, Contributions to American Archaeology, no. 6, pp. 27–105, Washington).

Roys, R. L.
1933.

The Book of Chilam Balam of Chumayel (Carnegie Institution of Washington, pub. no. 438, Washington).

Rubio, Dr. Horacio
1934.

Distribución Geográfica de las Lenguas Aborígines en el Estado de Hidalgo (Investigaciones Lingüísticas, vol. 2, pp. 37–54, México).

Ruppert, K.

1934a. Explorations in Campeche (Carnegie Institution of Washington, Year Book no. 33, pp. 93–95, Washington).

1934b. Explorations in Campeche (Carnegie Institution of Washington, Year Book no. 33, p. 218, Washington).

1935. The Caracol at Chichen Itza, Yucatan, Mexico (Carnegie Institution of Washington, pub. no. 454, Washington).

1938. Campeche Expedition (Carnegie Institution of Washington, Year Book no. 37, pp. 18–20, Washington).

Sahagún, Bernardino de

1905. Codex Florentino, illustrations to Sahagun's Historia General (Codice Florentino, vol. 5, Madrid and Florence).

1932. Historia General de las Cosas de Nueva España. Books 1–4 trans. by Fanny Bandelier. Nashville.

1938. Historia General de las Cosas de Nueva España (5 vols., México).

Salisbury, Stephen, Jr.

1877. Dr. Le Plongeon in Yucatan (Proceedings, American Antiquarian Society, no. 69, pp. 70–119, Worcester).

1878. Terra Cotta Figure from Isla Mujeres (Proceedings, American Antiquarian Society, no. 71, pp. 71–89, Worcester).

de Santa Cruz Pachacuti-yamqui Salcamayhua, Juan

1873. An Account of the Antiquities of Peru. Translated and edited by Clements R. Markham (Hakluyt Society, London).

560 BIBLIOGRAPHY

Sapir, Edward

1913.
Southern Paiute and Nahuatl, a Study in Uto-Aztekan. Part I (Journal de la Société des Américanistes de Paris, n.s., vol. 10, pp. 379–425, Paris).

1914–1919.
Southern Paiute and Nahuatl, a Study in Uto-Aztekan. Part II of Sapir, 1913 (Journal de la Société des Américanistes de Paris, n.s., vol. 11, pp. 443–488, Paris).

1915.
The Nadene Languages, a Preliminary Report (American Anthropologist, n.s., vol. 17, pp. 534–558, Menasha).

1920.
The Hokan and Coahuiltecan Languages (International Journal of American Linguistics, vol. 1, pp. 280–290, New York).

1925.
The Hokan Affinity of Subtiaba in Nicaragua (American Anthropologist, n.s., vol. 27, pp. 402–435; pp. 491–527, Menasha).

1929.
Central and North American Languages (Encyclopedia Britannica, 14th edition, vol. 5, pp. 138–141, New York).

Sapper, Carl

1895a.
Altindianische Ansiedelungen in Guatemala und Chiapas (Veröffentlichungen aus dem Königlichen Museum für Völkerkunde, vol. 4, pp. 13–20, Berlin).

1895b.
Altindianische Siedelungen und Bauten im Nordlichen Mittelamerika (Globus, vol. 68, pp. 165–169; pp. 183–189, Braunschweig. Translated in Annual Report of the Smithsonian Institution, 1895 [1896], pp. 537–555, Washington).

1897.
Das Nördliche Mittel-Amerika. Braunschweig.

1898a.   Die Indianeraufstand . . . im Juli 1898, in
            San Juan Ixcoy, Guatemala (Interview
            with Dr. Sapper, Globus, vol. 74, p. 199,
            Braunschweig).

1898b.   Die Ruinen von Mixco (Guatemala) (Inter-
            national Archiv für Ethnographie, vol. 11,
            pp. 1–6, Leiden).

1901a.   Beträge zur Ethnographie des Südlichen
            Mittelamerika (in: Petermann's Mittei-
            lungen, vol. 47, part 2, Gotha).

1901b.   Speise und Trank der Kekchi-Indianer
            (Globus, vol. 80, pp. 259–263, Braun-
            schweig).

1904.   The Independent States of Yucatan (Bureau
            of American Ethnology, Bulletin 28, pp.
            623–634, Washington).

1905a.   Der Charakter der Mittelamerikanische In-
            dianer (Globus, vol. 87, pp. 128–131,
            Braunschweig).

1905b.   Der Gegenwartige Stand der Ethnographi-
            schen Kenntnis von Mittelamerika (Ar-
            chiv für Anthropologie, n.f., vol. 3, pp.
            1–38, Berlin).

1905c.   Die Zukunft der Mittelamerikanischen In-
            dianerstämme (Archiv für Rassen- und
            Gesellschafts-Biologie, vol. 2, pp. 383–421,
            Berlin).

1906.   Chols and Chorties (Proceedings, XV In-
            ternational Congress of Americanists, Que-
            bec, part II, pp. 423–465, Quebec).

1913.   Die Mittelamerikanischer Vulkane. Gotha.

1925a.   Los Volcanes de la América Central. Halle.

1925b.   Über Brujerie in Guatemala (Proceedings, XXI International Congress of Americanists, Göteborg, 1924, pp. 391–405, Göteborg).

1927.   Mittel-Amerika, Ein Praktischer Wegweiser für Auswanderer, Planzer, Kaufleute, Lehrer (Studien über Amerika und Spanien, no. 3, Halle).

1932.   Klimatkunde von Mittelamerika (from W. Koppen and R. Geigen, Handbuch der Klimatologie, pp. 31–38, Berlin).

Sarmiento de Gambóa, Pedro
1907.   History of the Incas. (XVI Century.) Translated and edited by Clements R. Markham (Hakluyt Society, London).

Satterthwaite, L., Jr.
1936a.   Notes on the Work of the Fourth and Fifth University Museum Expeditions to Piedras Negras, Peten, Guatemala (Maya Research, vol. 3, no. 1, pp. 74–91, New Orleans).

1936b.   The Sixth Piedras Negras Expedition (Bulletin, University Museum, vol. 6, no. 5, pp. 14–18, Philadelphia).

1936c.   An Unusual Type of Building in the Maya Old Empire (Maya Research, vol. 3, no. 1, pp. 62–73, New Orleans).

1937a.   Identification of Maya Temple Buildings at Piedras Negras (Twenty-fifth Anniversary Studies, Philadelphia Anthropological Society, pp. 161–177, Philadelphia).

1937b.   Thrones at Piedras Negras (University Museum Bulletin, vol. 7, no. 1, pp. 19–23, Philadelphia).

1938. Evidence for a Logical Sequence of Roof Types on Maya Buildings at Piedras Negras (Science, vol. 88, p. 504, Lancaster).

Sauer, Carl Ortwin

1932. *See* Sauer and Brand, 1932b.

1934. The Distribution of Aboriginal Tribes and Languages in Northwestern Mexico (Ibero-Americana: 5, Berkeley).

1935. Aboriginal Population of Northwestern Mexico (Ibero-Americana: 10, Berkeley).

1936. American Agricultural Origins: A Consideration of Nature and Culture (Essays in Anthropology in Honor of Alfred Louis Kroeber, pp. 279–297, Berkeley).

1939. Correspondence.

Sauer, Carl, and Brand, Donald

1931. Prehistoric Settlements of Sonora, With Special Reference to Cerros de Trincheras (University of California Publications in Geography, vol. 5, no. 3, Berkeley).

1932a. Aztatlan, Prehistoric Mexican Frontier on the Pacific Coast (Ibero-Americana: 1, Berkeley).

1932b. The Road to Cibola (Ibero-Americana: 3, Berkeley).

Saville, Marshall H.

1892a. Explorations on the Main Structure of Copan, Honduras (Proceedings, American Association for the Advancement of Science, no. 41, pp. 271–275, Salem).

1892b. Vandalism Among the Antiquities of Yucatan and Central America (Science, vol. 20, no. 517, New York).

1893.   The Ruins of Labná, Yucatan (The Ar-
                     chaeologist, vol. 1, pp. 229–235, Water-
                     loo).

1894.   The Plumed Serpent in Northern Mexico
                     (The Archaeologist, vol. 2, pp. 291–293,
                     Waterloo).

1899.   Exploration of Zapotecan Tombs in South-
                     ern Mexico (American Anthropologist,
                     n.s., vol. 1, pp. 350–362, New York).

1900a.   A Shell Gorget from the Huasteca, Mexico
                     (American Museum of Natural History,
                     Bulletin, vol. 13, pp. 99–103, New York).

1900b.   Cruciform Structures Near Mitla (Bulletin,
                     American Museum of Natural History,
                     vol. 13, pp. 201–218, New York).

1901.   Mexican Codices, a List of Recent Reproduc-
                     tions (American Anthropologist, n.s., vol.
                     3, pp. 532–541, New York).

1907–1910.   The Antiquities of Manabí, Ecuador (Con-
                     tributions to South American Archaeol-
                     ogy, The George G. Heye Expedition,
                     2 vols., New York).

1909.   The Cruciform Structures of Mitla and
                     Vicinity (Putnam Anniversary Volume,
                     pp. 151–190, New York).

1916.   Monolithic Axes and their Distribution in
                     Ancient America (Contributions, Museum
                     of the American Indian, Heye Founda-
                     tion, vol. 2, no. 5, New York).

1920.   The Goldsmith's Art in Ancient Mexico (In-
                     dian Notes and Monographs, Museum of
                     the American Indian, Heye Foundation,
                     New York).

1922.   Turquois Mosaic Art in Ancient Mexico (Contributions, Museum of the American Indian, Heye Foundation, vol. 6, New York).

1925.   The Wood-Carver's Art in Ancient Mexico (Contributions, Museum of the American Indian, Heye Foundation, vol. 9, New York).

1928.   Ceremonial Axes from Western Mexico (Indian Notes, Museum of the American Indian, Heye Foundation, vol. 5, pp. 280–293, New York).

1929.   Votive Axes from Ancient Mexico (Indian Notes, Museum of the American Indian, Heye Foundation, vol. 6, pp. 266–299, 335–342, New York).

Sayles, E. B.
1936a.   Some Southwestern Pottery Types, Series V (Medallion Papers, no. 21, Globe).

1936b.   An Archaeological Survey of Chihuahua, Mexico (Medallion Papers, no. 22, Globe).

Scherzer, Karl
1856.   Die Indianer von Santa Catarina Istlavacan; ein Beitrag zur Kulturgeschichte der Urbewohner Central Amerika. Vienna.

1857.   Travels in the Free States of Central America: Nicaragua, Honduras and San Salvador (2 vols., London).

1936.   A Visit to Quirigua. Edited by Frans Blom (Maya Research, vol. 3, pp. 92–101, New Orleans).

Schmidt, M.
1929.   Kunst und Kultur von Peru. Berlin.

Schmidt, P. Wilhelm
1926.   Die Sprachfamilien und Sprachen-kreise der Erde. Heidelberg.

566   BIBLIOGRAPHY

Scholes, F. V.
1930.   The Supply Service of the New Mexican
             Missions in the Seventeenth Century (New
             Mexico Historical Review, vol. 5, pp. 93–
             115, 186–210, Santa Fé).

1935.   Civil Government and Society in New Mex-
             ico in the Seventeenth Century (New
             Mexico Historical Review, vol. 10, pp.
             71–111, Santa Fé).

Scholes, F. V., and Adams, E. B.
1939.   Don Diego Quijada, Alcalde Mayor de
             Yucatan, 1561–1565 (Biblioteca Histórica
             Mexicana de Obras Inéditas, vols. 14 and
             15, Mexico).

Scholes, F. V., and Roys, R. L.
1938.   Fray Diego de Landa and the Problem of
             Idolatry in Yucatan (Carnegie Institution
             of Washington, pub. no. 501, pp. 585–620,
             Washington).

Schuchert, Charles
1935.   Historical Geology of the Antillean-Carib-
             bean Region or the Lands Bordering the
             Gulf of Mexico and the Caribbean Sea.
             New York and London.

Schuller, Rudolf
1919–1920.   Zur Sprachlichen Verwandschaft der Maya-
             Qu'itse mit den Carib-Aruac (Anthro-
             pos, vol. 14–15, pp. 465–491, San Gabriel
             Mödling).

1925a.   La Lengua Chinanteca del Estado de Oaxaca,
             Mexico (Anales del Museo Nacional de
             Arqueología, 4a. Época, vol. 3, pp. 185–
             191, Mexico).

1925b.   La Lengua Ts'ots'il (International Journal
             of American Linguistics, vol. 3, pp. 193–
             218, New York).

1925c. Primera Contribución al Estudio de las Lenguas Indígenas de El Salvador; Dialecto de Chilanga, Departamento de San Miguel (Revista de Etnología, Arqueología y Lingüística, vol. 1, pp. 127–135, San Salvador).

1925d. Quíenes Son los Indios Quatas? (Revista de Etnología, Arqueología y Lingüística, vol. 1, pp. 111–112, San Salvador).

1925e. Review of his "Gramática . . . Pame" (with miscellaneous important remarks on languages related to Otomi) (Revista de Etnología, Arqueología y Lingüística, vol. 1, pp. 143–148, San Salvador).

1925f. Sobre la Filiación Étnica y Lingüística de los Indios Macoaques (Revista de Etnología, Arqueología y Lingüística, vol. 1, pp. 113–119, San Salvador).

1925g. La Única Gramática Conocida de la Lengua Pame (Secretaría de Educación Pública, Departamento de Antropología, México).

1928. Las Lenguas Indígenas de Centro América con Especial Referencia á los Idiomas Aborígenes de Costa Rica. San José de Costa Rica.

1930a. Beitrag zur Bibliographie der Sprache der Totonaca-Indianer (International Journal of American Linguistics, vol. 6, pp. 41–42, New York).

1930b. Breve Contribución a la Bibliografía del Idioma K'ak'ciq'el, Dialecto Maya-K'ičé de Guatemala (International Journal of American Linguistics, vol. 6, pp. 37–40, New York).

568   BIBLIOGRAPHY

Schultz, Adolph H.
  1926.   Anthropological Studies on Nicaraguan In-
                 dians (American Journal of Physical An-
                 thropology, vol. 9, pp. 65–80, Philadel-
                 phia).
Schulz, R. P. C.
  1933.   Zur Korrelation des Mayakalenders mit der
                 Europäischen Zeitrechnung (Zeitschrift
                 für Ethnologie, vol. 65, pp. 396–399, Ber-
                 lin).

  1935.   Zur Chronologie der Maya (Zeitschrift für
                 Ethnologie, vol. 67, pp. 49–68, 321–331,
                 Berlin).

  1936.   Beiträge zur Chronologie und Astronomie
                 des Alten Zentralamerika (Anthropos, vol.
                 31, pp. 258–288, San Gabriel Mödling).
Seler, C.
  1900.   Auf Alten Wegen in Mexiko und Guate-
                 mala, Reiseerinnerungen und Eindrücke
                 aus den Jahren 1895–1897. Berlin.

  1915.   Die Huaxteca Sammlung des Königliches
                 Museums für Völkerkunde zu Berlin
                 (Baessler Archiv, vol. 5, pp. 98–135, Leip-
                 zig und Berlin).

  1922.   Alterthümer des Kanton Tuxtla im Staate
                 Veracruz (Festschrift Eduard Seler, pp.
                 543–556, Stuttgart).
Seler, Eduard
  1901.   Die Alten Ansiedelungen von Chaculá im
                 Districte Nenton des Departments Hue-
                 huetenango der Republik Guatemala. Ber-
                 lin.

  1902–1923.   Gesammelte Abhandlungen zur Amerikani-
                 schen Sprach-und Alterthumskunde (vols.
                 1–5, Berlin).

1904.   Antiquities of Guatemala (Gesammelte Abhandlungen, vol. 3; Bulletin 28, Bureau of
American Ethnology, Washington).

1908.   Alterthümer aus der Alta Vera Paz (Gesammelte Abhandlungen zur Amerikanischen
Sprach-und Alterthumskunde, vol. 3, pp.
670–687, Berlin).

1915.   Beobachtungen und Studien in den Ruinen
von Palenque (Einzelausgabe aus den Anhandlungen der Königl. Preuss. Akademie
der Wissenschaften, Phil.-Hist. Klasse, no.
5, Berlin).

1916.   Die Quetzalcouatl-Fassaden Yukatekischer
Bauten (Einzelausgabe aus den Anhand-
lungen der Königl. Preuss. Akademie der
Wissenschaften, Phil.-Hist. Klasse, no. 2,
Berlin).

1917.   Die Ruinen von Uxmal (Einzelausgabe aus
den Anhandlungen der Königl. Preuss.
Akademie der Wissenschaften, Phil.-Hist.
Klasse, no. 3, Berlin).

Sequeira, David and Helena
1938.   Notes on Archaeological Work in Chontales
and Ometepe, Nicaragua (Unpublished
notes in the possession of the Carnegie Institution of Washington).

Setzler, F. M.
1933.   Pottery of the Hopewell type from Louisiana (Proceedings, United States National
Museum, no. 2963, vol. 82, article 22, pp.
1–21, Washington).

Shelford, V. E. (Chairman)
1926.   Naturalist's Guide to the Americas (Published by the Ecological Society of Amer-
ica, Durham and Baltimore).
            1. Mexico—E. W. Nelson and E. A. Gold-
man

    2. Guatemala—W. Popenoe
    3. British Honduras—K. P. Schmidt
    4. Honduras—K. P. Schmidt
    5. Salvador—P. C. Standley
    6. Nicaragua—L. Griscom
    7. Costa Rica—L. Griscom
    8. Panama—E. A. Goldman and J. Zetek

Shetrone, H. C.
1930.   The Mound-Builders. New York.

Short, John T.
1880.   The North Americans of Antiquity. New York.

Simpson, L. B.
1934.   Studies in the Administration of the Indians in New Spain (Ibero-Americana, no. 7, Berkeley).

Smith, A. Ledyard
1929a.   Report on the Investigation of Stelæ (Carnegie Institution of Washington, Year Book no. 28, pp. 323–325, Washington).

1929b.   Report on the Map of Environs of Uaxactun (Carnegie Institution of Washington, Year Book no. 28, pp. 325–327, Washington).

1932.   Uaxactun (Carnegie Institution of Washington, Year Book no. 31, pp. 97–100, Washington).

1933.   Excavations at Uaxactun (Carnegie Institution of Washington, Year Book no. 32, pp. 92–95, Washington).

1934.   Uaxactun (Carnegie Institution of Washington, Year Book no. 33, pp. 82–86, Washington).

1935.   Uaxactun (Carnegie Institution of Washington, Year Book no. 34, pp. 115–118, Washington).

1936.   Uaxactun (Carnegie Institution of Washington, Year Book no. 35, pp. 115–117, Washington).

1937a.   Structure A-XVIII, Uaxactun (Carnegie Institution of Washington, pub. no. 483, Contributions to American Archaeology, no. 20, pp. 1–27, Washington).

1937b.   Uaxactun (Carnegie Institution of Washington, Year Book no. 36, pp. 135–137, Washington).

Smith, Buckingham
1861.   A Grammatical Sketch of the Heve Language. Translated from an unpublished manuscript (J. G. Shea's Library of American Linguistics, no. 3, New York).

1862.   Grammar of the Pima or Nevome (J. G. Shea's Library of American Linguistics, no. 5, New York).

Smith, R. E.
1936a.   Preliminary Shape Analysis of the Uaxactun Pottery (Carnegie Institution of Washington, Guatemala).

1936b.   Ceramics of Uaxactun: A Preliminary Analysis of Decorative Technics and Design (Carnegie Institution of Washington, Guatemala).

1937.   A Study of Structure A-I Complex at Uaxactun, Peten, Guatemala (Carnegie Institution of Washington, pub. no. 456, Contributions to American Archaeology, vol. 3, no. 19, Washington).

Sorre, Max
1928.   Geographie Universelle, vol. 14 (Mexique et América Central). Edited by de la Blache, Vidal and Gallois. Paris.

Soustelle, Jacques
1937.   La Famille Otomi-Pame du Mexique Central (Institut d'Ethnologie, no. 26, Paris).

Spence, Lewis
1923.   The Gods of Mexico. London.

Spina, H.
1870.   Quiché Calendar (Boletín de la Sociedad
                         Económica de Guatemala, Diciembre de
                         1870. Guatemala). So cited by Brinton,
                         Native Calendar, 1893, pp. 17–18. This
                         may be Hernández Spina, author of the
                         MS. Kalendaryo cited above.

Spinden, E. S.
1933.   The Place of Tajin in Totonac Archaeology
                         (American Anthropologist, n.s., vol. 35,
                         pp. 271–287, Menasha).

Spinden, H. J.
1911.   An Ancient Sepulcher at Placeres del Oro,
                         State of Guerrero, Mexico (American An-
                         thropologist, n.s., vol. 13, pp. 29–55, Lan-
                         caster).

1912.   The Chronological Sequence of the Princi-
                         pal Monuments of Copan (Honduras).
                         (Proceedings, XVII International Con-
                         gress of Americanists, Mexico, 1910, pp.
                         357–363, Mexico).

1913.   A Study of Maya Art, Its Subject Matter
                         and Historical Development (Memoirs,
                         Peabody Museum of American Archaeol-
                         ogy and Ethnology, Harvard University,
                         vol. 6, Cambridge).

1915.   Notes on the Archaeology of Salvador
                         (American Anthropologist, n.s., vol. 17,
                         pp. 446–487, Lancaster).

1916.   Portraiture in Central American Art
                         (Holmes Anniversary Volume, pp. 434–
                         450, Washington).

1917a.   Recent Progress in the Study of Maya Art
                         (Proceedings, XIX International Congress

of Americanists, Washington, 1915, pp. 165–177, Washington).

1917b. The Origin and Distribution of Agriculture in America (Proceedings, XIX International Congress of Americanists, Washington, 1915, pp. 269–276, Washington).

1924. The Reduction of Mayan Dates (Papers, Peabody Museum of American Archaeology and Ethnology, Harvard University, vol. 6, no. 4, Cambridge).

1925. The Chorotegan Culture Area (Proceedings, XXI International Congress of Americanists, Göteborg, 1924, pp. 529–545, Göteborg).

1928a. Ancient Civilizations of Mexico and Central America (Handbook Series, American Museum of Natural History, no. 3, 3rd edition, New York).

1928b. Maya Inscriptions Dealing with Venus and the Moon (Buffalo Society of Natural History, vol. 14, no. 1, Buffalo).

1930. Maya Dates and What They Reveal (Brooklyn Institute of Arts and Sciences, vol. 4, pp. 1–111, Brooklyn).

1931. Indian Symbolism (Introduction to American Indian Art, part 2, Exposition of Indian Tribal Arts, New York).

1933. Indian Manuscripts of Southern Mexico (Annual Report of the Smithsonian Institution for 1933, pp. 429–451, Washington).

Squier, E. G.

1852. Nicaragua, Its People, Scenery, Monuments (2 vols., New York).

1853.   Observations on the Archaeology and Eth-
                         nology of Nicaragua (Transactions,
                         American Ethnological Society, vol. 3,
                         part 1, pp. 85–158, New York; reprinted,
                         1909).

1855.   Notes on Central America; particularly the
                         states of Honduras and San Salvador. New
                         York.

1858.   The States of Central America. New York.

1859.   Visit to the Guajiquero Indians. (Harper's
                         Magazine, vol. 19, pp. 603–619, New
                         York).

1860.   Collection of Rare and Original Documents
                         and Relations, Concerning the Discovery
                         and Conquest of America (no. 1, New
                         York).

1861.   Monograph of the Authors Who Have Writ-
                         ten on the Languages of Central America
                         or Composed Works in the Native Dia-
                         lects of That Country. New York.

1871–1872.   The Arch in America (Anthropological In-
                         stitute of New York Journal, New York,
                         vol. 1, pp. 78–80, from the Proceedings of
                         the Lyceum of Natural History of New
                         York, series 1, pp. 91–94, New York,
                         1870–1871).

1877.   Peru. Incidents of Travel and Exploration in
                         the Land of the Incas. New York.

Squier, E. G., and Davis, E. H.
     1848.   Ancient Monuments of the Mississippi Val-
                         ley (Smithsonian Institution, Washing-
                         ton).

Starr, F.

1897a.   A Shell Gorget from Mexico (Proceedings, Davenport Academy of Science, vol. 4, 1889–1897, pp. 173–178, Davenport).

1897b.   The Little Pottery Objects of Lake Chapala, Mexico (University of Chicago, Department of Anthropology, Bulletin 2, Chicago).

1897c.   Some Images from Tarascan Territory, Mexico (American Anthropologist, o.s., vol. 10, pp. 45–47, Washington).

1899.   Notched Bones from Mexico (Proceedings, Davenport Academy of Natural Sciences, vol. 7, pp. 101–107, Davenport).

1900.   Recent Mexican Study of the Native Languages of Mexico (University of Chicago, Department of Anthropology, Bulletin 4, Chicago).

1901.   Notes upon the Ethnography of Southern Mexico (Proceedings, Davenport Academy of Natural Sciences, vol. 8, pp. 102–198, Davenport).

1902.   The Physical Characters of the Indians of Southern Mexico (University of Chicago, Decennial Publications, vol. 4, pp. 53–109, Chicago).

1904a.   More Notched Bone Rattles (Proceedings, Davenport Academy of Natural Sciences, vol. 9, pp. 181–184, Davenport).

1904b.   Notes upon the Ethnology of Southern Mexico, Expedition of 1901 (Proceedings, Davenport Academy of Natural Sciences, vol. 9, pp. 63–172, Davenport).

1908.   In Indian Mexico. Chicago.

Staub, Walter
　　1933.　　　　　Zur Uebereinanderschichtung der Völker
　　　　　　　　　und Kulturen an der Ostküste von Mexiko
　　　　　　　　　(Mitteilungen der Geographisch-Ethno-
　　　　　　　　　graphischen Gesellschaft in Zürich, vol.
　　　　　　　　　33, pp. 3–26, Zürich).
Stephens, J. L.
　　1841.　　　　　Incidents of Travel in Central America,
　　　　　　　　　Chiapas and Yucatan (2 vols., New York).

　　1843.　　　　　Incidents of Travel in Yucatan (2 vols.,
　　　　　　　　　New York).

Steward, Julian H., and Setzler, Frank M.
　　1938.　　　　　Function and Configuration in Archaeology
　　　　　　　　　(American Antiquity, vol. 4, pp. 4–10,
　　　　　　　　　Menasha).
Stirling, M. W.
　　1931.　　　　　Mounds of the Vanished Calusa Indians of
　　　　　　　　　Florida (Smithsonian Institution Explora-
　　　　　　　　　tions and Field-work in 1930, pp. 167–172,
　　　　　　　　　Washington).

　　1940.　　　　　An Initial Series from Tres Zapotes, Vera
　　　　　　　　　Cruz, Mexico (National Geographic So-
　　　　　　　　　ciety, Contributed Technical Papers, Mex-
　　　　　　　　　ican Archaeology Series, vol. 1, no. 1,
　　　　　　　　　Washington).
Stoll, Otto
　　1884.　　　　　Zur Ethnographie der Republik Guatemala.
　　　　　　　　　Zürich.

　　1885.　　　　　Supplementary Remarks to the Grammar of
　　　　　　　　　the Cakchiquel Language (Proceedings,
　　　　　　　　　American Philosophical Society, vol. 22,
　　　　　　　　　pp. 255–268, Philadelphia).

　　1886.　　　　　Guatemala: Reisen und Schilderungen aus
　　　　　　　　　den Jahren 1878–1883. Leipzig.
Stone, D. Z.
　　1932.　　　　　Some Spanish Entradas (Tulane University
　　　　　　　　　of Louisiana, Middle American Research
　　　　　　　　　Series, no. 4, pp. 209–296, New Orleans).

Strebel, H.
1885–1889.   Alt Mexiko (2 vols., Hamburg und Leipzig).

1901.   The Sculptures of Santa Lucia Cozumahualpa, Guatemala in the Hamburg Ethnological Museum (Annual Report of the Smithsonian Institution, 1899, pp. 549–561, Washington).

Stromsvik, G.
1938.   Copan (Carnegie Institution of Washington, Year Book no. 37, pp. 11–16, Washington).

Strong, W. D.
1925.   The Uhle Pottery Collections from Ancon (University of California Publications American Archaeology and Ethnology, vol. 21, no. 4, Berkeley).

1934.   Hunting Ancient Ruins in Northeastern Honduras (Smithsonian Institution, in Explorations and Field-Work, 1933, pp. 44–48, Washington).

1935a.   An Introduction to Nebraska Archaeology (Smithsonian Miscellaneous Collections, vol. 93, no. 10, Washington).

1935b.   Archaeological Investigations in the Bay Islands, Spanish Honduras (Smithsonian Miscellaneous Collections, vol. 92, no. 14, Washington).

1936.   Anthropological Theory and Archaeological Fact (Essays in Anthropology in Honor of Alfred Louis Kroeber, pp. 359–370, Berkeley).

Strong, W. D., Kidder, A., and Paul, A. J. D.
1938.   Preliminary Report on the Smithsonian Institution-Harvard University Archaeological Expedition to Northwestern Honduras, 1936 (Smithsonian Miscellaneous Collections, vol. 97, no. 1, Washington).

Studley, Cornelia
  1887.   Notes Upon Human Remains from Caves in
                 Coahuila (Reports, Peabody Museum of
                 American Archaeology and Ethnology,
                 vol. 3, 1880–1886, pp. 233–259; cf. also
                 pp. 10, 21, 32, Cambridge).

Stuebel, A., and Uhle, Max
  1892.   Die Ruinenstaette von Tiahuanaco im Hoch-
                 lands des Alten Peru. Breslau.
Sultan, D. I.
  1932.   An Army Engineer Explores Nicaragua
                 (The National Geographic Magazine, vol.
                 61, pp. 593–627, Washington).
Swanton, J. R.
  1911.   Indian Tribes of the Lower Mississippi and
                 Adjacent Coasts of the Gulf of Mexico
                 (Bureau of American Ethnology, Bulletin
                 43, Washington).

  1915.   Linguistic Position of the Tribes of South-
                 ern Texas and Northeastern Mexico
                 (American Anthropologist, n.s., vol. 17,
                 pp. 17–40, Menasha).

  1924.   Southern Contacts of the Indians North of
                 the Gulf of Mexico (Proceedings, XX In-
                 ternational Congress of Americanists, Rio
                 de Janeiro, 1922, vol. 1, pp. 53–59, Rio de
                 Janeiro).

  1932.   Indian Tribes and Linguistic Stocks in the
                 Eastern Part of the United States about
                 1700 (Conference on Southern Pre-His-
                 tory, National Research Council, Wash-
                 ington).

  1935.   Notes on the Cultural Province of the South-
                 east (American Anthropologist, n.s., vol.
                 37, pp. 373–385, Menasha).

Tannenbaum, Frank
  1934.   Whither Latin America? An Introduction to

its Economic and Social Problems. New York.

Tax, Sol
1937.

The Municipios of the Midwestern Highlands of Guatemala (American Anthropologist, n.s., vol. 39, pp. 423–444, Menasha).

Taylor, Walter W.
1937.

Report of an Archaeological Survey of Coahuila, Mexico (New Mexico Anthropologist, vol. 2, pp. 45–46, University of New Mexico).

Teeple, John E.
1931.

Maya Astronomy (Carnegie Institution of Washington, pub. no. 403, Contributions to American Archaeology, no. 2, pp. 29–115, Washington).

Tellechea, Miguel
1826.

Compendio Gramatical del Idioma Tarahumar. México (Reprinted in Boletín de la Sociedad Mexicana de Geografía y Estadística, vol. 4, pp. 145–166, México, 1854).

Tello, Julio C.
1923.

Wira Kocha (Inca, vol. 1, pp. 93–320, 583–606, Lima).

1929.

Antiguo Perú. Lima.

Ten Kate, H. F. C.
1884.

Materiaux pour Servir à L'Anthropologie de la Presqu'ile Californienne (Bulletin de la Société d'Anthropologie, 3e. série, pp. 551–569, Paris).

Tenayuca
1935.

Tenayuca (Departamento de Monumentos, México).

Termer, Franz
1930.

Zur Ethnologie und Ethnographie des Nördlichen Mittel-Amerika (Ibero-Amerikanisches Archiv, vol. 4, pp. 301–492, Berlin).

1931.   Zur Archäeologie von Guatemala (Baessler-Archiv, vol. 14, Berlin).

Tezozomoc, H.

1878.   Cronica Mexicana (XVI Century) (in: Biblioteca Mexicana, José M. Vigil, ed., Mexico).

Thomas, A. B.

1935.   After Coronado, Spanish Exploration Northeast of New Mexico, 1696–1727. Norman, Oklahoma.

Thomas, Cyrus

1894.   Report on the Mound Explorations of the Bureau of Ethnology (Bureau of American Ethnology, 12th Annual Report, Washington).

Thomas, Cyrus, and Swanton, John R.

1911.   Indian Languages of Mexico and Central America and their Geographical Distribution (Bureau of American Ethnology, Bulletin 44, Washington).

Thompson, E. H.

1886.   Archaeological Research in Yucatan (Proceedings, American Antiquarian Society, n.s., vol. 4, pp. 248–254, Worcester).

1889.   The Ruins of Labna (MS. in the Peabody Museum of American Archaeology and Ethnology, Harvard University, Cambridge).

1897.   The Chultunes of Labna (Memoirs, Peabody Museum of American Archaeology and Ethnology, Harvard University, vol. 1, no. 3, Cambridge).

1898.   Ruins of Xkichmook, Yucatan (Field Columbian Museum, Anthropological Series, vol. 2, no. 3, Chicago).

1904.   Archaeological Researches in Yucatan (Memoirs, Peabody Museum of American

Archaeology and Ethnology, Harvard
University, vol. 3, no. 1, Cambridge).

1911.   The Genesis of the Maya Arch (American
Anthropologist, n.s., vol. 13, pp. 501–516,
Menasha).

Thompson, J. Eric
1927.   A Correlation of the Mayan and European
Calendars (Field Museum of Natural History, Anthropological Series, vol. 17, no. 1,
Chicago).

1927, 1932.   Civilization of the Mayas (Anthropology
Leaflet 25, Field Museum, Chicago).

1929.   Maya Chronology: Glyph G. of the Lunar
Series (American Anthropologist, n.s., vol.
31, pp. 223–231, Menasha).

1930.   Ethnology of the Mayas of Southern and
Central British Honduras (Field Museum
of Natural History, pub. 274, Anthropological Series, vol. 17, no. 2, Chicago).

1931.   Archaeological Investigations in the Southern Cayo District, British Honduras
(Field Museum of Natural History, pub.
301, Anthropological Series, vol. 17, no. 3,
Chicago).

1932.   The Solar Year of the Mayas at Quirigua,
Guatemala (Field Museum of Natural History, Anthropological Series, vol. 17, no.
4, Chicago).

1933.   Mexico before Cortez. New York.

1934.   Sky Bearers, Colors and Directions in Maya
and Mexican Religion (Carnegie Institu-
tion of Washington, pub. no. 436, pp. 209–
242, Washington).

1935.   Maya Chronology: the Correlation Question
                         (Carnegie Institution of Washington, pub.
                         no. 456, Contribution no. 14, Washing-
                         ton).

1936.   Archaeology of South America (Field Mu-
                         seum of Natural History, Anthropology
                         Leaflet 33, Chicago).

1937.   A New Method of Deciphering Yucatecan
                         Dates with Special Reference to Chichen
                         Itza (Carnegie Institution of Washington,
                         pub. no. 483, Contribution no. 22, Wash-
                         ington).

1938a.   Reconnaissance and Excavation in British
                         Honduras (Carnegie Institution of Wash-
                         ington, Year Book no. 37, pp. 16–17,
                         Washington).

1938b.   Sixteenth and Seventeenth Century Reports
                         on the Chol Mayas (American Anthropol-
                         ogist n.s., vol. 40, pp. 584–603, Menasha).

1939.   Excavations at San José, British Honduras
                         (Carnegie Institution of Washington, pub.
                         no. 506, Washington).

Thompson, J. E., Pollock, H. E. D., and Charlot, J.
1932.   A Preliminary Study of the Ruins of Cobá,
                         Quintana Roo, Mexico (Carnegie Institu-
                         tion of Washington, pub. no. 424, Wash-
                         ington).

Thruston, G. P.
1897.   The Antiquities of Tennessee. Cincinnati.

Titterington, P. F.
1938.   The Cahokia Mound Group and Its Village
                         Site Materials. St. Louis.

Torquemada, Juan de
1723.   Los Veinte i Un Libros Rituales i Monarchia
                         Indiana (3 vols., Madrid).

Totten, George Oakley
1926.   Maya Architecture. Washington.

Tozzer, A. M.
1907.   A Comparative Study of the Mayas and the Lacandones (Archaeological Institute of America, New York).

1911a.   A Preliminary Study of the Prehistoric Ruins of Tikal, Guatemala (Memoirs, Peabody Museum of American Archaeology and Ethnology, Harvard University, vol. 5, no. 2, Cambridge).

1911b.   The Value of Ancient Mexican Manuscripts in the Study of the General Development of Writing (Proceedings, American Antiquarian Society for April, 1911, Worcester).
Also in: Smithsonian Annual Report for 1911, pp. 493–506, Washington.

1912.   The Ruins of Northeastern Guatemala (Proceedings, XVII International Congress of Americanists, Mexico, 1910, pp. 400–405, Mexico).

1913.   A Preliminary Study of the Ruins of Nakum, Guatemala (Memoirs, Peabody Museum of American Archaeology and Ethnology, Harvard University, vol. 5, no. 3, Cambridge).

1918.   The Domain of the Aztecs and their Relation to the Prehistoric Cultures of Mexico (Holmes Anniversary Volume, pp. 464–468, Lancaster).

1921a.   Excavation of a Site at Santiago Ahuitzotla, D. F. Mexico (Bureau of American Ethnology, Bulletin 74, Washington).

1921b. A Maya Grammar with Bibliography and Appraisement of the Works Noted (Papers, Peabody Museum of American Archaeology and Ethnology, Harvard University, vol. 9, Cambridge).

1926. Chronological Aspects of American Archaeology (Proceedings, Massachusetts Historical Society, vol. 59, pp. 283–292, Boston).

1927. Time and American Archaeology (Natural History, vol. 27, pp. 210–221, New York).

1930. Maya and Toltec Figures at Chichen Itza (Proceedings, XXIII International Congress of Americanists, New York, 1928, pp. 155–164, New York).

1934 Maya Research (Maya Research, vol. 1, pp. 3–19, New York).

1937a. Prehistory in Middle America (The Hispanic American Historical Review, vol. 17, pp. 151–159, Durham).

1937b. Review of various publications by G. C. Vaillant (American Anthropologist, n.s., vol. 39, pp. 338–340, Menasha).

Tozzer, Alfred M., and Allen, Glover M.
1910. Animal Figures in the Maya Codices (Papers, Peabody Museum of American Archaeology and Ethnology, Harvard University, vol. 4, no. 3, Cambridge).

Trewatha, Glenn T.
1937. An Introduction to Climate and Weather. New York and London.

Tschiffely, A. F.
1929. Buenos Aires to Washington by Horse (The National Geographic Magazine, vol. 55, pp. 135–196, Washington).

1933. Tschiffely's Ride. New York.

Uhle, Max

1903. Pachacamac (Museum of the University of Pennsylvania, Philadelphia).

1920. Los Principios de la Civilización en la Sierra Peruana (Boletín de la Sociedad Ecuatoriana de Estudios Históricos Americanos, vol. 1, no. 1, Quito-Ecuador).

1922a. Orígenes Centroamericanos (Boletín de la Academía Nacional de Historia, vol. 4, pp. 1–6, Quito).

1922b. Influencias Mayas en el Alto Ecuador (Boletín de la Academía Nacional de Historia, vol. 4, pp. 205–240, Quito).

1923. Civilizaciones Mayoides de la Costa Pacífica de Sudamérica (Boletín de la Academía Nacional de Historia, vol. 6, pp. 87–92, Quito).

1924. Cronología y Relaciones de las Antiguas Civilizaciones Panameños (Boletín de la Academía Nacional de Historia, vol. 9, pp. 190–207, Quito).

1925. Der Mittelamerikanische Ursprung der Moundbuilder- und Pueblocivilisationen (Proceedings, XXI International Congress of Americanists, Göteborg, 1924, pp. 674–698, Göteborg).

1930. Desarrollo y Origen de las Civilizaciones Americanas (Proceedings, XXIII International Congress of Americanists, New York, 1928, pp. 31–43, New York).

1931. Las Antiguas Civilizaciones de Manta (Boletín de la Academía Nacional de Historia, vol. 12, pp. 5–71, Quito).

Vaillant, George C.

1927.   The Chronological Significance of Maya Ceramics (MS. Thesis submitted in Partial Fulfillment of the Requirements of the Degree of Ph.D. at Harvard University, Cambridge).

1928.   The Native Art of Middle America (Natural History, vol. 28, pp. 562–576, New York).

1930a.   Excavations at Zacatenco (Anthropological Papers, American Museum of Natural History, vol. 32, part 1, New York).

1930b.   Notes on the Middle Cultures of Middle America (Proceedings, XXIII International Congress of Americanists, New York, 1928, pp. 74–81, New York).

1931a.   A Bearded Mystery (Natural History, vol. 31, pp. 243–252, New York).

1931b.   Excavations at Ticoman (Anthropological Papers, American Museum of Natural History, vol. 32, part 2, New York).

1932a.   A Pre-Columbian Jade (Natural History, vol. 32, pp. 512–520, 557–558, New York).

1932b.   Some Resemblances in the Ceramics of Central and North America (Medallion Papers, Gila Pueblo, no. 12, Globe).

1932c.   *See* Merwin and Vaillant, 1932.

1933.   Hidden History (Natural History, vol. 33, pp. 618–628, New York).

1934.   The Archaeological Setting of the Playa de los Muertos Culture (Maya Research, vol. 1, pp. 87–100, New York).

1935a.	Excavations at El Arbolillo (Anthropological Papers, American Museum of Natural History, vol. 35, part 2, New York).

1935b.	Early Cultures of the Valley of Mexico: Results of the Stratigraphical Project of the American Museum of Natural History in the Valley of Mexico, 1928–1933 (Anthropological Papers, American Museum of Natural History, vol. 35, part 3, New York).

1935c.	Chronology and Stratigraphy in the Maya Area (Maya Research, vol. 2, pp. 119–143, New York).

1935d.	Artists and Craftsmen in Ancient Central America (American Museum of Natural History, Guide Leaflet Series, no. 88, New York).

1937.	History and Stratigraphy in the Valley of Mexico (Scientific Monthly, vol. 44, pp. 307–324, New York).

1938.	A Correlation of Archaeological and Historical Sequences in the Valley of Mexico (American Anthropologist, n.s., vol. 40, pp. 535–573, Menasha).

1939a.	By Their Arts You Shall Know Them (Natural History, vol. 43, pp. 268–277, New York).

1939b.	Indian Arts in North America. New York.

1939c.	A Prehistoric Occurrence of Cotton (American Anthropologist, n.s., vol. 41, p. 170, Menasha).

Vaillant, S. B., and Vaillant, G. C.
1934.	Excavations at Gualupita (Anthropological Papers, American Museum of Natural History, vol. 35, no. 1, New York).

588   BIBLIOGRAPHY

Valcárcel, L.
1932.   El Personaje Mítico de Pukará (Revista del
                       Museo Nacional, vol. 1, pp. 18–30, Lima).
Valentini, P. J. J.
1883.   The Olmecas and the Tultecas (Proceedings,
                       American Antiquarian Society, October
                       21, 1882, Worcester).
Vásquez, Francisco
1714.   Chrónica de la Provincia del Santíssimo
                       Nõbre de Jesus de Guatemala (2 vols.,
                       Guatemala).
Vaughan, T. W.
1918.   Geologic History of Central America and
                       the West Indies during Cenozoic Time
                       (Bulletin, Geological Society of America,
                       vol. 29, pp. 615–630, Washington).
de Velasco, J. B.
1737.   Arte de la Lengua Cahitas (Edited and re-
                       printed by Eustaquio Buelna, México,
                       1890. México).

Verneau, R., and Rivet, P.
1912–1922.   Ethnographie Ancienne de l'Equateur (Mis-
                       sion du Service Geographique de l'Armée
                       pour la mesure d'un arc de meridien equa-
                       torial en América du Sud sous le controle
                       scientifique de l'Academie de Sciences,
                       1899–1900, vol. 6, Paris).
Verrill, A. H.
1927.   Excavations in Coclé Province, Panama (In-
                       dian Notes, Museum of the American In-
                       dian, Heye Foundation, vol. 4, no. 1, New
                       York).
Veytia, Mariano
1836.   Historia Antigua de México (3 vols., Méx-
                       ico).
Villacorta C., J. Antonio
1927.   Arqueología Guatemalteca. Guatemala.

1934.   Estudios sobre Lingüística Guatemalteca
                       (Memorial de Tecpan-Atitlan [Anales de
                       los Cakchiqueles], Colección Villacorta,
                       no. 4, pp. 1–179, Guatemala).

1938a.   Descubrimiento Arqueológico (Nuestro Diario, May 11, 1938, Guatemala).

1938b.   Prehistoria e Historia Antigua de Guatemala. Guatemala.

Villacorta C., J. A., and Rodas, N. Flavio
1927.   Manuscrito de Chichicastenango (Popol Buj). Estudios sobre las Antiguas Tradiciones del Pueblo Quiché (Guatemala).

Villacorta C., J. A., and Villacorta, C. A.
1930.   Arqueología Guatémalteca. Guatemala.

1930–1933.   Codices Mayas. Dresdensis, Peresianus, Tro-Cortesianus. Reproduced and expounded by J. Antonio Villacorta C. and Carlos A. Villacorta. Guatemala.

Villagutierre y Sotomayor, Juan
1701.   Historia de la Conquista de la Provincia de el Itza, etc. (part 1, Madrid).

Viollet-le-Duc, Eugene E.
1863.   See Charnay D., and Viollet-le-Duc.

1876.   The Habitations of Man in All Ages. Translated by B. Bucknall. Boston.

Wafer, Lionel
1699.   A New Voyage and Description of the Isthmus of America. London.

Walckenaer, de Larenaudière, and Jomard
1836.   Rapport sur le Concours Relatif à la Géographie et aux Antiquités de l'Amérique Centrale (Bulletin de la Société de Géographie, 2nd series, vol. 5, pp. 253–291, Paris).

Waldeck, Frédéric de
1838.   Voyage Pittoresque et Archéologique dans la Province d'Yucatan (Amérique Centrale), pendant les Années 1834 et 1836. Paris.

590   BIBLIOGRAPHY

Waldeck, F. de, and Brasseur de Bourbourg, C. E.
1866.   Monuments Anciens du Mexique. Palenqué
                           et Autres Ruines de l'Ancienne Civilisa-
                           tion du Mexique. Paris.
Walde-Waldegg, H. von
1937.   Preliminary Report on the Expedition to San
                           Augustin (Colombia) (Anthropological
                           Series of the Boston College Graduate
                           School, vol. 2, no. 1, Chestnut Hill).
Walker, W. M.
1935.   A Caddo Burial Site at Natchitoches, Louisi-
                           ana (Smithsonian Miscellaneous Collec-
                           tions 94, no. 14, pub. no. 3345, Washing-
                           ton).

1936.   The Troyville Mounds, Catahoula Parish,
                           Louisiana (Bureau of American Ethnol-
                           ogy, Bulletin 113, Washington).
Warden, D. B.
1834.   Recherches sur les Antiquités de l'Amérique
                           du Nord et de l'Amérique du Sud, et sur
                           la Population Primitive de ces Deux Con-
                           tinents (Antiquités Mexicaines, vol. 1,
                           Part 2, div. 2, Paris. See Dupaix, 1834).
Waterman, T. T.
1924.   On Certain Antiquities in Western Guate-
                           mala (Bulletin of the Pan American
                           Union, April, 1924, pp. 1–21, Washing-
                           ton).

1931.   The Architecture of the American Indians
                           (Kroeber, A. L., and Waterman, T. T.,
                           Source Book in Anthropology, revised
                           edition, pp. 512–524, New York).
Wauchope, Robert
1934.   House Mounds of Uaxactun, Guatemala
                           (Carnegie Institution of Washington, pub.
                           no. 436, Contribution no. 7, Washington).

1936.   Zacualpa (Carnegie Institution of Washing-
                           ton, Year Book no. 35, Washington).

1938.   Modern Maya Houses: a Study of Their Ar-
        chaeological Significance (Carnegie Insti-
        tution of Washington, pub. no. 502, Wash-
        ington).

Webb, W. S.
1938.   An Archaeological Survey of the Norris
        Basin in Eastern Tennessee (Bureau of
        American Ethnology, Bulletin 122, Wash-
        ington).

1939.   An Archaeological Survey of the Wheeler
        Basin on the Tennessee River in Northern
        Alabama (Bureau of American Ethnology,
        Bulletin 122, Washington).

Webb, W. S., and Funkhouser, W. D.
1932.   Archaeological Survey of Kentucky (Pub-
        lications, Department of Anthropology
        and Archaeology, University of Ken-
        tucky, vol. 2, Lexington).

Weber, F.
1922.   Zur Archäologie Salvadors (Festschrift Ed-
        uard Seler, pp. 619–644, Stuttgart).

Wedel, W. R.
1936.   An Introduction to Pawnee Archaeology
        (Bureau of American Ethnology, Bulletin
        112, Washington).

Weitlaner, Roberto
1933.   El Dialecto Otomi de Ixtenco, Tlaxcala (An-
        ales del Museo Nacional de Arqueologia,
        4a. Época, vol. 8, pp. 667–692, Mexico).

Weitzel, R. B.
1930.   Maya Chronological Systems (American
        Journal of Archaeology, 2nd series, vol.
        34, pp. 182–189, Concord).

1935a. Maya Moon Glyphs and New Moons (Maya
        Research, vol. 2, pp. 14–23, New York).

1935b. Maya Correlation Problem (Maya Research,
        vol. 2, pp. 278–286, New York).

Weyerstall, A.
1932.   Some Observations on Indian Mounds, Idols
                 and Pottery in the Lower Papaloapam
                 Basin, State of Vera Cruz, Mexico (Mid-
                 dle American Research Series, pub. no. 4,
                 Tulane University, New Orleans).

Whorf, B. L.
1935.   The Comparative Linguistics of Uto-Az-
                 tecan (American Anthropologist, n.s., vol.
                 37, pp. 600–608, Menasha).

1936.   Appendix to J. Alden Mason's "The Classifi-
                 cation of the Sonoran Languages" (Es-
                 says in Anthropology in Honor of Alfred
                 Louis Kroeber, pp. 197–198, Berkeley).

1937a.   The Origin of Aztec *tl* (American Anthro-
                 pologist, n.s., vol. 39, pp. 265–274, Me-
                 nasha).

1937b.   The Relationship of Uto-Aztecan and
                 Tanoan. With G. L. Trager (American
                 Anthropologist, n.s., vol. 39, pp. 609–624,
                 Menasha).

Willard, T. A.
1926.   The City of the Sacred Well. New York.

Willoughby, C. C.
1897.   An Analysis of the Decorations upon Pot-
                 tery from the Mississippi Valley (Journal
                 of American Folk-Lore, vol. 10, pp. 9–20,
                 Boston and New York).

Willson, Robert W.
1924.   Astronomical Notes on the Maya Codices
                 (Papers, Peabody Museum of American
                 Archaeology and Ethnology, Harvard
                 University, vol. 6, no. 3, Cambridge).

Winship. G. P.
1896.   The Coronado Expedition, 1540–1542 (Bu-
                 reau of American Ethnology, 14th Annual
                 Report, part 1, Washington).

Wissler, C.
1914.   Influence of the Horse in the Development

of Plains Culture (American Anthropologist, n.s., vol. 16, pp. 1–25, Lancaster).

1933.   Ethnological Diversity in America and its Significance (Jenness, ed., The American Aborigines, pp. 165–216).

1938.   The American Indian (3rd edition, Oxford University Press, New York).

Woodbury, G.
1937.   Notes on Some Skeletal Remains of Texas (University of Texas Bulletin, Anthropological Papers, vol. 1, pp. 5–16, Austin).

Woodward, Arthur
1936.   A Shell Bracelet Manufactory (American Antiquity, vol. 2, no. 2, pp. 117–125, Menasha).

Ximénez, F.
1931.   Historia de la Provincia de San Vicente de Chiapa y Guatemala de la Orden de Predicadores (2nd edition, 3 vols. [Biblioteca Goathemala], Guatemala).

Yacovleff, E., and Muelle, J. C.
1934.   Un Fardo Funerario de Paracas (Revista del Museo Nacional, vol. 3, pp. 63–153, Lima).

Yde, J.
1938a.   An Archaeological Reconnaissance of Northwestern Honduras (Middle American Research Series no. 9, Tulane University, New Orleans).

1938b.   An Archaeological Reconnaissance of Northwestern Honduras. A Report of the Work of the Tulane University-Danish National Museum Expedition to Central America, 1935 (Acta Archaeologica, vol. 9, Copenhagen).

Young, B. H.
1910.

The Prehistoric Men of Kentucky (Filson Club pub. no. 25, Louisville).

Zavala, Lorenzo de
1834.

Notice sur les Monuments Antiques d'Ush-mal, dans la Province de Yucatan (Antiquités Mexicaines, vol. 1, part 1, Notes et Documents Divers, no. 6, Paris. *See* Dupaix, 1834).

Zies, E. G.
1935.

Volcanes de Centro America en 1932 (Anales de la Sociedad de Geografia e Historia de Guatemala, vol. 11, pp. 277–280, Resumé of a report to the "Geophysical Union," Guatemala, C. A.).

Zurita, A.
1891.

Breve y Sumaria Relación de los Señores de la Nueva España (in García Icazbalceta, Nueva Colección de Documentos para la Historia de México, vol. 3, pp. 71–227, México).

INDEX

acculturation: 135f., 282ff., 342ff., 348, 380, 382, 471f.; *see also* Conquest, Spanish

Africa, diet in: 33

agriculture, crops: 33, 34f., 36, 336, 341, 372, 378, 420, *see also* coca, cotton, maize, manioc; methods: 37ff., 296f., 336, 350; sequence in: 118, 295, 331, 340; *see also* domestication of plants

Aguacate: 387

Ahau Equation: 151

Ahuachapan: 401

Aké: 210, 216

Alta Verapaz: 124, 250; architecture: 258; pottery: 123, 248, 251ff., 269, 271

Alvarado, Pedro de: 180, 250

Amatlan: 403

Amazon basin: 424

Amusgo: 66, 102

Anasazi: 296, 331ff., 480

ancestor cult: 437

Ancona, Elegio: 187

Andrade, Manuel: 70

Andrews, E. Wyllys: 146, 150

animal gods: 163, 433, 434f.

animals, extinct, associated with man: 332, 333, 334, 417, 474f.; *see also* domestication of animals; fauna

Antilles: 12ff., 425

Apache: 60

Arawak: 425, 446, 478; language: 72, 384, 425

arch, true: 220; *see also* vault

archaeology, criticism of: 47, 50f.; in Middle America: 10f., 188ff., 473ff., *see also various sites*

Archaic: 163f., 422f., 424, 430f.; at Kaminaljuyú: 399; and Miraflores: 118ff., 122; and Tarascan: 64; at Tehuacan: 312, 314, 318

architecture: 10, 119, 133f., 162, 179ff., 196, 197ff., 221, 222ff., 308, 387, 451; domestic: 134, 196, 216f., 232ff., 302, 378, 444f., Basket Maker, 337, Missis-

sippi, 351, Southeast, 371; Spanish in Southwest: 345; *see also* dome; epigraphy; mounds; rubble; substructure; temple complex; vault; *and various sites*

Arévalo: *see* Kaminaljuyú

Argentine, vault in: 216, 218, 221

Arica: 424

Arsandaux, H.: 457

art: 134, 163, 198f., 271, 390, 452; alter ego motif: 408, 415, 452f.; evolution of: 402; *see also* sculpture

Asia, diet in: 33; racial type: 7

astronomy: 139, 143, 150ff., 164, 195, 438f., 483; *see also* epigraphy

Asunción Mita: 212, 216

Athabascan: 8, 60, 468

Atitlán: 248

atlatl, 332, 334, 445

Avendaño y Loyola, Andrés de: 181

Awatovi: 345, 346ff.

Ayuc: 72, *see* Mixe

Azcapotzalco: 300

Aztec: 299; archaeology: 137, *see various sites*; language: 69, *see also* Utaztecan; religion: 430ff.

Bagaces: 427

Baking Pot: 247

Balakbal: 146, 205

Baldwin, John D.: 187

ball courts: 134, 195, 446

Bancroft, Hubert Howe: 187, 381

Bandelier, Adolphe F.: 187

Barranca del Aguila: 310

Basket Maker: 36, 332, 335ff.; physical type: 337

basketry: 295, 338

Bastian, A.: 186

Baul, sculpture: 396, 397, 398, 414

Bay Islands: 385, 389, 403, 451; pottery: 390, 455

bead recordings: 164

Belmar, Francisco: 56; on language: 58, 64
Bennet, Wendell C.: 478; on archaeology: 217, 423
Benque Viejo: 127, 128, 133, 228
Berendt, C. H.: 70, 77
Bernasconi, A.: 183, 184
Beyer, Hermann: 142; on epigraphy: 145, 148, 155
Bienvenida, Lorenzo de: 180
Blom, Frans, on architecture: 195, 208, 222, 397
blood type: 6
Bloomfield, Leonard: 468, 469
blowgun: 425, 445
Boa: 112
Boas, Franz, on language: 4, 54, 68, 466 footnote; on race: 9
Bochica: 447
Bolivia, architecture: 217, 218; cultural sequence: 441, 450
Boturini Benaduci, L.: 182
bow: 334, 445
Bowditch, Charles P., influence of: 10, 139; on epigraphy: 141
Bradford, Alexander W.: 187
Brasseur de Bourbourg, C. E.: 186
Brew, J. O.: 341
brick: 206
bridges, Inca: 218
Brinton, Daniel G.: 381; on diffusion: 385; on epigraphy: 139; on language: 56, 61, 63
British Honduras, archaeology: 128, 137, 270, see also various sites
burial, Basket Maker: 337; mound: 254, 260, 351, 371, 390, 392; mummy packs: 449; tomb: 218, 246, 351, 454; tomb, cruciform: 308; urn: 301, 448; see also cremation; embalming
Burkitt, R.: 250
Burnet Cave: 334
Butler, Mary: 250

Cabrera, V. M.: 184
Caddo: 365
Cahal Pichik: 228
Cakchiquel: 234
Calakmul: 132
Calderón, J. A.: 183
calendar: 434; Inca: 438f.; Maya: 122, 123, 135, 136, 143, 147, 164, 165f.,

285f., 302f.; Mexican: 296, 299; Mixtec: 165, 166f., 177; Zapotec: 166; see also chronology; epigraphy; stelæ
California, climate: 19; languages of: 61, 467
Callejón de Huailas: 414, 453
canoes: 428
cantilever: 202f.
Caracol: 208
Cara Sucia: 401
Carib: 72, 77
Caribs, Black: 77, 380
Carrillo, P.: 185
Carrillo y Ancona, C.: 187
Casa del Adivino: 132
Casa Grande: 363
Caso, A.: 318, 488
Caspinchango: 218
Castañeda: 183f., 213
Castillo: 132, 397
Catherwood, Frederick: 185
Catholicism: 285, 286; see also missionaries
Cazcan: 106, 107
cement, lime: 162, 217
Cenote, Chichen Itzá: 272ff., 458
cephalic index: 6f., 8, 136, 274; see also deformation, head
ceramics: see pottery
Cereceda, Andrés de: 381
ceremonial organization: 284, 296, 366; see also calendar
Cerro de las Mesas: 165
Cerro Montoso: 299
chacmool: 401, 402f., 415
Chakantun: 233
Chalchihuites: 69, 380
Chamá: 248, 250, 251ff.; see also Alta Verapaz
Chañabal: 108
Chané: 446
Charnay, Désiré: 186
Chatino: 67, 103f.
Chavero, Alfredo: 187
Chavin: 424, 450; contacts: 425, 454; pottery: 423; vault: 216
Chávin de Huantar: 379
Chenes: 132, 133f.; see also various sites
Chiapanec: 58, 64, 109
Chibcha: 377, 426, 444, 450; language: 59, 74, 75, 76f., 112f., 384, 426, 443
Chicanel pottery phase: 203, 243, 247, 248, 249, 302

Chichen Itzá: 107; contacts: 299, 403; domestic architecture: 232, 233, 234; epigraphy: 142, 165; frescoes: 134; sculpture: 408; vault: 208, 210, 211; *see also* Cenote; Temple of the Warriors

Chichimec, period: 266, 299; language: 64f.

Chihuatal: 250, 256, 261

Chile, climate: 19; language: 425

Chimu: 450; architecture: 425; pottery: 456; religion: 434f., 447

Chinantec: 102; language: 54, 58, 60, 66f., 77, 101, 103

Chinkultic: 149

Chinook: 468

Chipal: 250, 256f., 260ff.

Chiriqui: 379, 454

Chixoy Valley: 250, 261f., 266

Chocho: 77, 101, 103

Choco: 76f.

Chocola: 397

Choctaw: 365

Chol: 288, 290; language: 107f., 109

Cholula: 213, 298, 310

Chontal: 234; language: 61, 65, 71, 108; sculpture: 412f., 416, 453

Chorotega: 164, 404, 424, 451; art: 399, 404ff., 415, 426; contacts: 423, 427; language: 443

chronicles: *see* manuscripts

chronology, Maya-Christian: 142, 143, 145, 151ff., 428, 482f.; Maya-Mixtec: 166ff.; Maya-Peru: 423, 428f., 456; table: 484ff.; *see also* animals, extinct; migrations, into New World; stratigraphy; *and sequences at various sites*

Chuitinamit: 248, 261, 267

Chuj: 108

Chukumuk, architecture: 234; pottery: 248, 254, 267, 269

Chulpa: 218

Cibola: 342

Clavigero, F. S.: 182f.

climate: 27ff.; and agriculture: 37, 121, 422; effect of ocean currents on: 19ff.

clubs, stone: 445

Coahuiltecan: 62, 99, 106; *see also* Hokan-Coahuiltecan

Coba, contacts: 134; pottery: 249; vault: 208, 210, 211

Coban: 248

coca: 393, 425, 444

Coclé: 379; art: 425; metal: 426; pottery: 378; sculpture: 414, 453

codices: 140f., 148, 186, 236, 288, *see also* manuscripts; Dresden: 140, 144, 152, 156, 165; Rickards: 177; Vienna: 166ff., 170, 171; Yolotepec: 177; Zouche: 176

Cogolludo, Diego L.: 181

Colombia, cultural sequence: 450; language: 76; pottery: 455f.; sculpture: 453

colonization, Mexican: 69; Southwest: 343f.

Comalcalco: 206, 208, 212

Comayagua Valley: 386, 393, 403

Comitan: 149, 406

Conant, Kenneth: 196

Conquest, Spanish: 10, 91, 284f., 287, 288f., 388; *see also* Southwest, history

contacts: *see* chronology; migrations; stratigraphy; trade; *and various sites*

Conzemius, Eduard: 75, 110, 112, 383

Copan: 190, 268; architecture: 387; contacts: 269, 270, 399, 412; epigraphy: 142, 157; pottery: 268ff., 302; sculpture: 403, 408ff.; sequence: 132, 133, 137, 410; vault: 210

Copelito: 411 *footnote*, 414

Copilco-Zacatenco: 296, 298f.

copper: 128, 356, 457

Cora: 106

Córdoba: 179

Coronado expedition: 342f.

Cortés, Hernando: 180

Costa Rica: 379; language: 58, 75, 105, 112, 443; pottery: 427, 451, 455

cotton: 298, 341

cremation: 448

Cresson, F. M.: 196

Cuchumatanes: 282ff.

Cuicatec, language: 66, 100, 101f., 103

Cuicuilco-Ticoman: 299

Cuitlatec: 54, 63, 77

culture hero: 433, 447

Cuna: 382

Czekanowski: 461, 462

dairy products: 33

Daly, César: 187

dating: *see* chronology; dendrochronology
dead, disposal of: *see* burial; cremation; embalming
deformation, head: 273ff., 277
dendrochronology: 246, 339, 374
Desaguadero: 427
Diaz, Bernal: 180
Diaz, Juan: 179, 180
diet, balanced: 32ff.; deficiency: 276; of Folsom Man: 333
Dittrich, Arnŏst: 143, 146
Dixon, R. B., on language: 4; on racial type: 6, 7
documents: *see* codices; manuscripts; source material
dome: 216f., 478; *see also* vault
domestication of animals: 33f., 342, 420
domestication of plants: 34ff., 119, 121, 129, 304, 420, 422, 442, 477; *see also* maize
dress: 445, 452
drill, tubular: 347
Dupaix, Guillelmo: 183f., 220

Eastern Woodlands, area of North America, agriculture: 37; community organization: 38f., 296; physical type: 8; *see also* Mississippi; Woodland
Ecker, Lawrence: 66, 67
economics, Cuchumatán district: 282ff.
Ecuador, pottery: 455f.; sculpture: 452; sequence: 424, 450
effigy ware: 358
Ekholm, Gordon F.: 320
El Congo: 401, 402
El Limón: 401
El Palmar: 396
El Paraiso: 224
El Silencio: 414
embalming: 448f.
epigraphy, Maya: 134f., 139ff., 153, 164ff., 192, 423; Mexican: 140, 142, 148
Eskimo: 3 *footnote*, 8, 468
ethnology in Middle America: 126, 135f., 194, 281ff., 444ff., 471ff.
Etowah: 366, 371f.
evolution of culture: 187, 195, 297f.

fauna: 14, 16, 475; *see also* animals, extinct
feather, quetzal: 130
feather work: 332, 338; *see also* serpent, feathered
Fergusson, James: 187
figurines, female: 163, 338, 340
flaying: 448
Folsom Man: 7, 331, 333ff., 420, 474, 476
food-gatherers: 331ff., 424
footprints in mud-flows: 420
Förstemann, Ernst: 139, 140
Fort Ancient: 373
Fowke, Gerard: 218f.
Franciscans: 344, 345
Freeland, L. S.: 73
Friederichsthal, Emmanuel de: 185
Fuentes y Guzmán, F. A. de: 181

Gabb, William M.: 383
Galindo, Juan: 185
games, ball: 446; *see also* ball courts
Gamio, Manuel: 122, 214
Gann, Thomas: 191
García, Agustín: 181
Garibi, Dávila: 68, 106
Gassó, Leonardo: 382
Gates, William: 70
geology, of Middle America: 11ff.; of migration route: 419f., 422
glaciation of New World: 419f.
Gladwin, Harold S.: 120, 466
glyph: *see* epigraphy
gods: *see* pantheon
gold, occurrence: 129, 272, 426, 457, 479
Gómara, Francisco López de: 181, 381
Goodman, J. T., on epigraphy: 139, 140, 145, 151, 160, 161
Gordon, G. B.: 190
government, Maya: 162; Mexican: 296
Grijalva expedition: 179
Guachichil: 63, 68f., 104, 106
Guasave: 300
Guatemala, architecture: 212, 213f., 234; highlands: 117, 250, 298; history: 283, 284f., 287; language: 108, 110; sculpture: 396ff., 406, 415; towns: 39, 234; *see also* Alta Verapaz; Peten; *and various sites*
Guaycura: *see* Waicurian
Guaymí: 382

Guetar: 445, 449; pottery: 390, 455
Guthe, C. E.: 368, 480; on epigraphy: 143, 146, 156
Gypsum Cave: 331, 332f., 334

Habel, S.: 186, 402
hammock: 445
Hartman, C. V.: 379
Hatzcap Ceel: see Mountain Cow
Hawikuh: 342, 345
heads: see deformation; jaguar; trophy
Herrera, Antonio de: 181
Herzog, George: 384
Hewett, Edgar L.: 192
Hissink, Karin: 195
history, Central America: 283, 284f., 287, 472f.; Southwest: 342ff.; see also Conquest, Spanish
Hodge, F. W.: 345
Hohokam: 446, 480; contacts: 296, 340; pottery: 359
Hokaltecan: 58, 59, 60, 61f., 77
Hokan: 59, 61, 384
Hokan-Coahuiltecan: see Hokaltecan
Holmes, W. H.: 191, 379
Holmul, contacts: 304; pottery: 247, 249, 254, 261, 271; sequence: 127, 132, 164, 242, 298, 301; vault: 210
Honduras, language: 74ff., 91, 105, 110, 112; pottery: 248, 249, 269, 387f.; sculpture: 403ff., 406; see also various sites
Hooton, E. A.: 272; on race; 5, 6, 7, 8, 460f.
Hopewell: 351, 372, 373, 481
Hopi: 342, 344, 346; archaeology: 345, 346ff.
horse: 421; extinct: 332, 475
house structure: see architecture, domestic
Howells, W. W.: 3, 460f.
Hrdlička, Ales, method: 274; on race: 7, 461f.
Huasteca: 356; see Huaxtec
Huatusco: 213
Huave: 72, 109
Huaxtec: 234; language: 54, 71, 107
Huichol: 69, 106
Huitzilopochtli: 432
human sacrifice: 130, 172, 272, 398, 432f., 446f., 448

Humboldt, Alexander von: 183, 213
hunting: see food-gatherers

Inca, architecture: 217f.; religion: 436ff.
intoxication: 444
Iñak-Uyu: 217
Iroquois: 39, 477; archaeology: 372
irrigation: see water conduit
Irritila: see Lagunero
Itza: 131, 181; language: 107
Itzamná: 433
Ixcatec: 65, 100f.
Iximché: 124
Izamal: 181

Jacaltec: 108
jade: 128, 130, 260, 266, 310, 346ff.
jaguar god: 163, see also tiger god
jaguar heads: 396, 399f., 402, 415
Jicaque: 383; language: 59, 60, 63, 73, 74f., 113, 426
Jijón y Caamaño, J.: 424, 450
Jiménez Moreno, W., on language: 64, 70, 94, 97, 470
Johnson, F.: 88, 382
Jonuta: 264
Joyce, T. A.: 144, 193

Kabah: 210, 234; pottery: 249
kabal: 266
Kabo: 75, 111
Kaminaljuyú: 119; artifacts: 130; contacts: 122, 123, 249, 304; pottery: 119, 248, 269; sculpture: 399, 410; sequence: 120, 132
Kanhobal: 286
Karankawa: 62
Kekchi: 251
Kidder, Alfred V.: 117, 232, 476; on archaeology: 130, 232, 269; on the calendar: 151, 160; method of: 45, 49f., 197
Kidder, Alfred, II: 441
kiva: 296, 346
Kixpek: 250, 258, 264
Kluckhohn, Clyde: 41
Kreichgauer, Damian: 159f.
Kroeber, A. L.: 460; on language: 50,

Kroeber, A. L. (*continued*)
54, 63, 67, 70f., 104; on South America: 424f., 451, 454
Kukulcan: 447

Labná: 190, 210
Lacandones: 107, 126, 241, 280, 287, 288, 471
La Farge, Oliver: 281, 472f.
La Flora: 398
La Florida: 403, 406, 408, 410
Lagunero: 68, 106
land ownership: 282ff., 388
Landa, Diego de: 180; on calendar: 159; on language: 136
language: 4, 383ff., 463ff.; classification: 52ff., 88ff., 133; table: 60, 78ff.; *see also* map, linguistic
La Paya: 218
La Quemada: 69
Las Casas, Bartolomé de: 181, 381
Las Mercedes: 403
La Venta: 396, 397
law: 284; enacted by Whites: 282, 283f., 286f., 388
Lehmann, Walter, on language: 56, 62, 65, 69, 72, 74, 75, 76, 77, 93, 98, 113, 384, 426
Lenca: 383, 387; language: 59, 60, 63, 73, 74f., 109, 110, 113, 384, 389, 426; pottery: 387f., 393, 394
Lenoir, Alexandre: 184
Léon, N: 56
León: 403
Le Plongeon, Augustus: 186
Leyden plaque: 134
lienzo: *see* codices
Lindenmeier: 333
Linton, Ralph: 32, 43, 47, 477f., 489
literacy: 288, 473
Lizana, Bernardo de: 181
Lizardi Ramos, Cesar: 153
Long, R. C. E.: 142
Longyear, J. M.: 268
Los Naranjos: 387f.
Los Tarros: 397
Lothrop, S. K.: 417; on archaeology: 118, 120, 193, 232, 378, 379, 399, 451, 455; on language: 75, 108, 112; method of: 49, 193, 381; on migrations: 91, 211, 396, 446, 478f.; on

sculpture: 406f.; on trade: 458; on the vault: 216
Lovén, S.: 353
Lower California: 63
Lowie, R. H.: 238
Lubaantun: 214, 242, 302
Ludendorff, Hans, on epigraphy: 143, 145, 151, 153, 154, 156, 157, 158f.
Lundell, A.: 234

Macalaya: 217
MacCurdy, G. G.: 379
Macon: 365
maize, Basket Maker: 337; development of: 118, 119, 120, 443, *see also* domestication of plants; spread of: 121, 336
Maler, Teobert: 139, 189
Maltrata: 165
Mam: 108, 111, 113
Mamom pottery phase: 243, 247, 248, 249, 301, 302
man in New World: *see* migrations, into New World
Managua, Lake: 404, 412
manioc: 121, 425, 442, 444
manuscripts: 186f., 289; Mixtec: 168, 177; Quiché: 288; *see also* codices
map, architectural: 200; linguistic: 56ff., 88ff., 470; Maya area: 204, 212
Marajó: 425
Maribio: 61
Marquina, Ignacio: 196
marriage: 284
Martínez Hernández, Juan: 142, 145, 146, 151, 160, 161
Martyr, Peter: 179, 180
masks: 195, 302, 449
Mason, J. A.: 41, 52; on archaeology: 196; on language: 67, 95, 468, 470
Matagalpa: 75, 112, 443; *see also* Misumalpan
mathematics: *see* numerical system
Matlatzinca: 54, 77, 100
Maucallajta: 217
Maudslay, Alfred P., on archaeology: 10, 189, 192; on art: 134, 408; on epigraphy: 139
Maya, development of: 36, 121f., 162ff., 211, 425, 441; language: 54, 58, 59, 60, 70ff., 74, 444; physical type: 5, 280

Maya area, defined: 211f., 268; map: 204

Maya, Highland: 117ff., 130f., 136, 283ff.; language: 71, 384; *see also various sites*

Maya, Lowland: 126ff.; language: 71; *see also various sites*

Maya, Old Empire: 129, 131ff., 211; contacts: 215; development of: 121, 122f., 127, 128f.; epigraphy: 135; metal: 457

Maya, post-Conquest: 281ff., 290f.

Mazapan: 138

Mazatec, language: 54, 58, 65; neighbors: 101, 103

Means, P. A.: 430

Melanesia, subsistence: 33

Mercado: 211

Merwin, R. E.: 191

metal, occurrence: 129, 130, 265, 422, 450, 456ff., 479f., *see also* copper; gold; techniques: 356, 424, 427, 456f.

method, of dating: 246; review of: 181, 182, 188f., 193f., 197ff.; present day: 41ff., 281f., 484-487

Mexico, geology: 26f.; language: 55; pre-pottery horizon: 331f.; sequence: 298f., *see also* Archaic; *see also* Aztec *and various sites*

Michelson, T.: 468

Michoacano: *see* Tarascan

middens: 245

Middle America, defined: 11; culture stages in: 304f.; *see various topics and sites*

migrations: 91; into New World: 3ff., 16, 118, 163, 280, 417ff., 443; United States-Mexico: 59, 62; Mexico: 69, 100, 319; Mexico-Maya: 124, 300, 396; Maya: 107, 123, 136, 304, 390; Middle America-South America: 76, 377, 378, 423, 424, 426, 427, 434, 440, 443f., 458; South America: 424, 425; *see also* colonization; trade

Miraflores: 119f., 122, 214, 248, 301

Miraflores, Finca: 119

Miskito: 59; *see* Mosquito

missionaries: 287, 289; in Southwest area of United States: 343, 344, 345f.; *see also* Catholicism

Mississippi: 370, 371, 373f.; Middle: 350ff., 480f.

Misumalpan: 59, 75f.

Mitla: 451

Mixco Viejo: 124

Mixe: 54, 59, 102, 103, 109; *see also* Mizocuavean

Mixtec, calendar: 165, 166f., 177; language: 54, 58, 60, 66, 77, 101f., 102; pottery: 137, 264, 310, *see also* Mixteca-Puebla

Mixteca-Puebla: 299ff., 302, 303, 305

Mizocuavean: 60, 72f., 74

Mogollon: 359, 480

Molina Solis, Juan Francisco: 187

Momostecos: 286

Monte Alban, contacts: 123, 318, 427, 458; epigraphy: 165; pottery: 302; sequence: 298, 299, 300, 301; vault: 213, 220

Monte Alto, sculpture: 396, 397, 402, 415

Morgan, Lewis H.: 187

Morley, S. G.: 139, 192, 398, 482

Morris, A. A.: 195

Mosquito: 380f., 383; language: 75, 111, 443, *see also* Misumalpan

Mosquito-Sumo-Matagalpa: *see* Misumalpan

Motagua Valley: 124, 212

Motolinía, de Benavente: 381

Motozintlec: 108

mound-builders: 368

mounds: 350f., 372, 393, 412, 452; classification: 369; sequence: 370f., 373, 486; *see also* burial, mound

Moundville: 366

Mountain Cow: 127, 128, 215; vault: 208, 210

mythology: 433, 447

Naachtun: 224

Nacasola: 406

Naco: 380

Nadillac, Marquis de: 187

Nahuatl: 427; language: 54, 67, 68, 69f., 75, 77, 100, 103, 104f., 384; sculpture: 397f.

Nahuatlato: 427

Nakum: 220, 228, 247

names: 286

Natchez: 365, 373

Nazca: 450; art: 456; religion: 434, 447

Nelson, N. C.: 4

Nevada: *see* Gypsum Cave

Nicaragua, early man in: 420; language: 58, 61, 76, 98, 112; pottery: 427, 451, 455; sculpture: 404ff., 415, 452; *see also various sites*
Nicaragua, Lake: 404, 412
Nicarao: 427, 451
Noguera, Eduardo: 301, 306
Noll-Husum, Herbert: 157, 159
Nordenskiöld, Erland, on South America: 382, 420, 421, 439; on vault: 216
numerical system, Maya: 140, 147, 150, 162; *see also* epigraphy
Nuttall, Zelia: 213, 438

Obero: 397
obsidian, occurrence: 129, 130, 310, 312, 314
Ocuiltec: 65, 77
Old Empire: *see* Maya, Old Empire
Olive: 62
Olmec, art: 397; language: 66, 77
Olson, Ronald D.: 217
Ometepe, Island of: 404
Opico: 401
orange ware: 129, 262, 264, 267, 299, 309, 314
Ordóñez: 183
Orozco y Berra, Manuel, on architecture: 187; on language: 55, 94
Otomanguean: 59, 60, 64f.
Otomi: 54, 58, 99f., 109; *see also* Otomanguean
Oviedo y Valdés, G. F. de: 181, 381
Oxpemul: 224

Pachacamac: 220
Pakawan: *see* Coahuiltecan
Palacio, Diego Gárcia de: 180
Palacios, Enrique Juan: 145, 195
Palenque, Honduras: 133, 391
Palenque, Mexico: 183; pottery: 247; vault: 208, 210; *see also* Temple of the Cross
Palo Verde: 397
Panama: 418, 422; contacts: 426f.; language: 58, 75, 76, 443; sculpture: 414; sequence: 420, 423f.
pantheon: 431ff.; Aztec: 145; Maya: 145, 162f.
Papabuco: 104
Papalguapa: 212

Paracas: 450, 452, 456
Parsons, Talcott: 42
Pasión Valley: 214
Patagonia, early man in: 4, 417, 449
pathology, cranial: 276
Paya: 383, 389f.; language: 59, 60, 73, 74f., 113f., 309, 426, 443; mounds: 392; pottery: 387
Pearl Islands: 378
Pecos: 6, 345
Peet, Stephen D.: 187, 193
Penutian: 58, 59, 73, 74, 384, 426, 467
Pericú: 63
Périgny, Maurice de: 191
Peru: 296; agriculture: 420, 442; architecture: 216ff., 221, 425, 454; metallurgy: 458; physical type: 277; pottery: 379, 423, 426, 455f.; sculpture: 414, 435, 450, 452; sequence: 426, 428f., 441, 450; *see also various horizons and sites*
Peten: 137, 242; archaeology: 122, 123, 127ff., 132; architecture: 134, 236; pottery: 242ff., 264, 270, 302; vault: 203ff., 206, 208, 210, 212; *see also various sites*
peyote: 69
Phillips, P.: 349, 480
physical anthropology: 136, 272ff., 380, 462; *see also* cephalic index; racial type
Piedras Negras: 242; architecture: 132, 133, 215, 245; pottery: 164, 245, 247, 248, 261; *see also* Usumacinta Valley
Pilco-Kayma: 217
Pima: 69
Pimentel, F.: 56
Pipil: 124, 131, 270, 388, 396, 420, 427; language: 69, 105
Plains Indian of North America, and Folsom Man: 335; physical type: 8
plumbate ware: 129, 260, 261f., 265, 299
Pokom: 108
Pollock, H. E. D.: 179, 213, 241
Polynesia, subsistence: 33
Popenoe, Dorothy: 393
Popoloco of Guatemala: 74, 110
Popoloca of Puebla: 65, 72, 100f., 103
Popoloca of Vera Cruz: 109
population: 304; composition of: 197; density of, and food: 32, 34ff., 38; density of, indicated by artifacts: 251; density of, and language: 55;

density of, and security: 164; movements of: *see* migrations
potter's wheel: 266
pottery, recent: 284
pottery, temper: 127, 130, 338
pottery types, Alta Verapaz: 251ff.; Central America: 455f.; Copan: 269ff.; Lake Yojoa: 387f.; Maya: 122, 127, 128, 129, 393; Miraflores: 119, 121; Mississippi: 358f., 362ff.; Monte Alban: 318; Q-complex: 300f.; Tehuacan: 311ff.; Teotihuacan: 122, 269, 308ff., 317, 394; Tzakol: 131; Uaxactun: 243ff.; Ulua: 393f.; use in archaeology: 47, 297; Zapotec: 308f.
pottery, unfired: 338
pre-pottery horizon: 331f., 378
Prescott, William H.: 187
priesthood: 290, 431, 434, 447
pueblo rebellion: 345
pueblos: 421; Rio Grande: 342, 343f.; *see also* Hopi; Zuñi
Punin skull: 8 *footnote*
Pusilhá, pottery: 128, 247, 270; sequence: 242f.; vault: 214
Puuc sites: 133f., 208

Q-complex: 119, 121, 254, 300, 301; in Southeast United States: 362, 363, 364
Quarai: 345
Quelepa: 399
Quen Santo: 123, 214
Quesalteca: 403
Quetzalcoatl: 165, 166f., 171, 433, 447
Quiché: 70ff., 108
Quimbaya: 457
Quintana Roo: *see various sites*
quipu: 439
Quiriguá: 192, 403

race prejudice: 283f., 285
racial type: 5ff., 124, 277, 337, 418, 460ff.; *see also* cephalic index
Radin, Paul: 53, 62, 72, 73
Rama: 111, 112, 443
Ramonal: 132
Ratinlixul: 250
Rau, Charles: 186
Real, Ciudad: 180
Red House, Chichen Itzá: 165
Redfield, Robert: 47

religion: 289, 430ff.; *see also* ancestor cult; Catholicism; ceremonial organization; missionaries; pantheon; priesthood
Richardson, F. B.: 395
Rickards, Constantine George: 191
Ricketson, E. B.: 121, 232
Ricketson, O. G.: 10, 195, 196
Rio, Antonio del: 183, 184
Rio Bec sites: 132, 211
Rivet, Paul, on language: 56, 62, 66, 70, 75, 76, 77, 94; on South America: 424, 457
Roberts, F. H. H.: 331, 480
Robertson, William: 182, 188
Roys, Lawrence: 146, 195, 202, 220
rubber: 446
rubble: 236, 245
Ruppert, K.: 195, 205, 222

Sahagun: 66, 77, 153
Salvador, language: 112, 133; pottery: 248, 249, 266, 270f., *see also* Usulutan; sculpture: 399ff., 415; sequence: 378
San Agustin, Colombia: 398, 450, 452
San Agustín Acasaguastlan: 210, 212, 232
San José: 130, 249, 298; architecture: 134; contacts: 131; pottery: 127, 128, 247, 248; sequence: 127, 133, 242, 243; vault: 210
San Pedro Carcha: 248; *see also* Alta Verapaz
Santa Cruz Michapa: 401
Santa Lucia Cozumalhualpa: 165, 186, 397, 402
Santa Rita: 299
Sapir, Edward, on language: 53, 56, 58, 59, 61, 67, 72, 73, 74, 75, 384, 426, 466
Sapper, Carl: 189f.; on architecture: 200, 232; on the calendar: 286; on language: 70, 73
Satterthwaite, L.: 195, 196, 215
Sauer, Carl, on domestication of plants: 477; on language: 34, 60, 68, 99, 104
Saville, Marshall H.: 190
Sayil: 234, 249
Schellhas, Paul: 139, 140
Scherzer, Karl: 185
Schmidt, P. Wilhelm, on language: 53, 56, 62, 66, 67, 74, 75, 76, 94

Scholes, F. V.: 344
Schuller, Rudolf: 72, 74, 77, 384
Schulz, R. P. C.: 155, 157, 159
sculpture: 271, 300; monumental: 396ff.; *see also* chacmool; *and at various sites*
Seibal: 214
Selden Roll: 168
Seler, Eduard: 190; on the calendar: 165f.; on epigraphy: 139, 140, 201
Seri: 61
serpent, feathered: 360, 408; *see also* Quetzalcoatl
serpent god: 163, 353
sheep, in Southwest United States: 342, 346
shell work: 353, 354, 427
Shepard, Anna: 122, 127
Short, John T.: 187
Sigua: 427
Sinaloa sites: 297, 300
Sioux: 39, 61, 468
Smith, A. L.: 195, 196, 202, 232, 478
Smith, R. E.: 122
social organization: 131; *see also* ceremonial organization; government; marriage; village mobility
Soltec: 104
source material: 136, 148, 179ff., 388, 430, 472; *see also* codices; manuscripts; Sahagun
South America: 417ff.; agriculture: 420; *see also various countries and sites*
Southeast, area of United States: 36, 40, 296; archaeology: 349f., 368ff.; architecture: 218f., 351; agriculture: 350; and Basket Maker: 339; contacts: 349f., 351, 353, 356, 364, 372; and Folsom Man: 335; geology: 12, 13; language: 62
Southwest, area of United States, agriculture: 37, 341; community organization: 40, 477, 489; contacts: 348, 480; culture sequence: 35f.. 123, 331ff., 480; history: 342ff.; physical type: 6, 277; *see also* Basket Maker; Folsom Man; Pueblos
speech scrolls: 164f.
spider: 354
Spinden, H. J.: 162; Archaic theory: 422f., 450; on archaeology: 118f., 207, 213; on art: 134, 143, 192f., 402;

on the calendar: 143, 151, 153ff., 158f., 160, 482, 483; method of: 49, 193
Spiro mound: 366
Squier, E. G.: 185, 220, 381, 401
Starr, F.: 136, 232
stelae: 246, 302; in culture sequence: 127, 128, 203; occurrence: 122, 123, 131, 132, 301, 302, 387, 398, 401, 423
Stephens, John Lloyd: 10, 185, 285
Stoll, Otto: 70, 72
Stone, Doris: 386
stone implements, Folsom: 333f., 476; Gypsum Cave: 332; Mississippi: 351ff.; Old Empire: 128, 129; Southeast United States: 371
stratigraphy, at Alta Verapaz: 250ff.; of architectural sites: 132f., 190, 350; in Central America: 378f.; at Copan: 268ff.; early: 192, 193f., 194; at Holmul: 127, 164, 298; at Monte Alban: 298; Southeast: 365, 369, 370f., 373; at Tehuacan: 311; at Uaxactun: 243ff.; in Valley of Mexico: 120, 137, 295, 298f., 422f., 488
Strong, William Duncan: 51, 377, 455, 463
substructure: 233
Subtiaba: 61, 74, 98, 384, 443
Sulas: 389, 392
Sumo: 383; language: 75, 111, 112, 443; *see also* Misumalpan
sun cult: 438f.
Swanton, J. R., on language: 52, 56, 62, 93, 99; use of documents: 472
sweat houses: 134, 196

Tajin: 165, 213
Talamanca: 382, 418, 427
Tambor: 250, 261
Tancah: 208, 220
Tarascan: 64; language: 54, 58, 60, 64, 114
Tauira: 111
Tayasal: 247
Tazumal: 401, 403
Teeple, John E.: 144, 146, 154, 156, 158
Tehuacan: 306ff.; pottery: 311ff.
Tello, Julio C.: 478
temple complex: 222ff., 296, 298ff., 302, 390f., 477, 489; *see also* kiva
Temple of the Cross: 186

Temple of the Warriors: 132
Tenampua: 393
Tenochtitlan: 179, 432
Teotihuacan: 299; contacts: 121, 122, 131, 138, 249, 270, 300, 304, 308f., 310f., 318f.; epigraphy: 164; pottery: 123, 248, 256, 269, 308, 309f., 394; sequence: 300, 301
Teotitlan del Camino: 311
Tepeaca: 310
Tepecan: 106
Tepehua: 65, 73, 106, 107
Tepeu pottery phase: 243, 247, 248f.
Tequistlatecan: 98; see also Chontal
textiles: see weaving
Tezcatlipoca: 433
theory and fact: 42, 45ff.
Thomas, Cyrus: 52, 56, 93, 139, 140
Thompson, E. H.: 189, 193, 232; on the arch: 207; at Cenote: 272
Thompson, J. Eric: 126, 232; on archaeology: 122, 196; on Chol Mayas: 107, 108, 290; on chronology: 145, 151, 152, 159, 161
Tiahuanaco: 424, 435, 450; epigraphy: 423; sculpture: 435, 452; vault: 216
Tibet, physical type: 8
tiger god: 300f., 302; see also jaguar god
Tikal: 146; architecture: 133, 208, 210, 228
Titicaca, Lake: 217
Tlapanec: 61, 98
Toltec: 69, 122, 164f.; see also Teotihuacan
Toluquilla: 213
Tonina: 149
Tonkawa: 62
Toqueguas: 388
Torquemada, Juan de: 181
Totonac: 234; language: 54, 58, 60, 65, 73, 109f.
Totonicapan: 248
Totten, George O.: 196
Tozzer, A. M.: 10, 41, 460, 473; on art: 195; on chronology: 195; on ethnology: 126; on language: 70; method of: 43, 49, 138, 191f., 197, 232
trade: 426f., 456, 457f., 479; Maya: 129, 130, 249, 267, 393, 427f.; Mexico: 311; Peru: 450
Trager, A.: 57
Travesia: 390ff., 394

tree ring dating: see dendrochronology
Tres Zapotes: 300, 394, 396
Trique: 234; language: 65
trophy heads: 447f.
Tulum: 220
Tunica: 365
Tupi: 384
Tupinamba: 447
turkey: 33
turquoise: 129, 338
Tusapan: 213
Tuxtla statuette: 408, 414, 415, 441
Tzakol pottery phase: 122, 123, 130, 131, 203f., 211, 215, 243, 247, 248, 249, 302
Tzeltal: 286
Tzimin Kax: 254
tzolkin: 140, 156
Tzotzil: 136; language: 108, 109

Uaxactun: 224, 298; arch: 220; architecture: 222ff., 232f.; contacts: 304, 397; epigraphy: 146; frescoes: 134; pottery: 243ff., 254, 261, 264, 302; sequence: 121, 127, 128, 130, 132, 163, 164, 242, 243ff.; vault: 133, 203ff., 208, 210, 215
Ucanal: 228
Uhle, Max: 423, 450, 475, 478
Ulua Valley: 268, 386, 388, 394; pottery: 133, 270, 393f.; sculpture: 403, 406
Ulva: 112, 443
Uolantun: 146
Usulutan ware: 119, 269, 301, 410
Usumacintla Valley: 250; architecture: 134, 234, 245; pottery: 256, 264, 302; vault: 206, 208, 210, 211, 212, 215
Utatlan: 124, 214, 248; fall of: 288
Utaztecan: 58, 59, 60, 67ff., 468
Utcubamba Valley: 216, 217
Uto-Aztecan: see Utaztecan
Uxmal, accounts of: 180, 184; sequence: 132; vault: 208, 210
Uxul: 224

Vaillant, George C.: 295; on Archaic: 423; on archaeology: 118f., 121, 164; on calendar: 160, 266; on dating: 266; method of: 45, 49, 120, 137, 196,

Vaillant, George C. (*continued*) 489; on Mississippi: 362; on War God: 432
Vaillant, S. B.: 306
vault: 122, 127, 131, 133, 163, 202ff., 302f., 451, 478
Venezuela, archaeology: 450
village mobility: 38f., 296f., 304, 336
Villagutierre y Sotomayor, Juan: 181
Viollet-le-Duc, Eugene E.: 187, 193
Viracocha: 435, 439, 447
Votan: 433

Wafer, Lionel: 381
Waicurian: 58, 60, 63
Walckenaer, de Larenaudiére: 184
Waldeck, Frédéric de: 185
Wanki: 111
Warden, D. B.: 184
warfare: 391, 437f.
water conduit: 210, 387
Wauchope, R.: 196, 232
weaving: 284, 295, 422; *see also* cotton
Weitlaner, Robert: 64, 66, 67, 77
Weitzel, R. B.: 146
whistle, figurine: 394
whistling jars: 456
Whorf, B. L., on language: 53, 57, 58, 67, 69, 74, 468
Williams, G. D.: 276
Willson, Robert W.: 143, 151
Winnebago: 39
Wissler, Clark: 3, 4
witchcraft: 286
wood artifacts: 310
Woodland: 370, 371, 372f., 481
woodlands: *see* Eastern Woodlands
writing: 139, 147, 164, 299, 300; *see also* epigraphy; literacy

Xacbal: 210, 212
Xelhá: 208
Xicaque: 389, 443
Xinca: 59, 60, 63, 73, 74f., 109, 110, 384
Xipe: 448
Xochicalco: 165, 213

Yaxchilan: 146, 264
Yaxuna, pottery: 249
Yojoa, Lake: 386, 387, 388; pottery: 249, 387f., 394; *see also* Ulua Valley
Yucatan, architecture: 137, 234, 236f., 302; culture sequence: 134, 298; discovery: 179; geology: 12, 13, 18; pottery: 302; *see also various sites*
Yucatec: 136, 234; language: 107
Yuman: 61, 63, 97

Zacatec: 68, 106
Zacate Grande Island: 403
Zacatenco: 296, 298f.
Zacualpa: 234; architecture: 234; gold: 458; pottery: 248, 264, 456; sculpture: 347
Zaculeu: 214
Zambos: 75
Zapatero, Island of: 404
Zapotec: 300f., 319; architecture: 308; calendar: 166; contacts: 308f., 310f.; language: 54, 58, 60, 64, 66, 67, 101, 102ff.; pottery: 308, 309; sculpture: 398
Zavala, Lorenzo de: 184
Zoque: 72, 108, 109; *see also* Mizocuaven
Zuñi: 342, 344, 345

A CATALOGUE OF
SELECTED DOVER BOOKS
IN ALL FIELDS OF INTEREST

A CATALOGUE OF SELECTED DOVER
BOOKS IN ALL FIELDS OF INTEREST

RACKHAM'S COLOR ILLUSTRATIONS FOR WAGNER'S RING. Rackham's finest mature work—all 64 full-color watercolors in a faithful and lush interpretation of the *Ring*. Full-sized plates on coated stock of the paintings used by opera companies for authentic staging of Wagner. Captions aid in following complete Ring cycle. Introduction. 64 illustrations plus vignettes. 72pp. 8⅝ x 11¼. 23779-6 Pa. $6.00

CONTEMPORARY POLISH POSTERS IN FULL COLOR, edited by Joseph Czestochowski. 46 full-color examples of brilliant school of Polish graphic design, selected from world's first museum (near Warsaw) dedicated to poster art. Posters on circuses, films, plays, concerts all show cosmopolitan influences, free imagination. Introduction. 48pp. 9⅜ x 12¼. 23780-X Pa. $6.00

GRAPHIC WORKS OF EDVARD MUNCH, Edvard Munch. 90 haunting, evocative prints by first major Expressionist artist and one of the greatest graphic artists of his time: *The Scream, Anxiety, Death Chamber, The Kiss, Madonna,* etc. Introduction by Alfred Werner. 90pp. 9 x 12. 23765-6 Pa. $5.00

THE GOLDEN AGE OF THE POSTER, Hayward and Blanche Cirker. 70 extraordinary posters in full colors, from Maitres de l'Affiche, Mucha, Lautrec, Bradley, Cheret, Beardsley, many others. Total of 78pp. 9⅜ x 12¼. 22753-7 Pa. $5.95

THE NOTEBOOKS OF LEONARDO DA VINCI, edited by J. P. Richter. Extracts from manuscripts reveal great genius; on painting, sculpture, anatomy, sciences, geography, etc. Both Italian and English. 186 ms. pages reproduced, plus 500 additional drawings, including studies for *Last Supper,* Sforza monument, etc. 860pp. 7⅞ x 10¾. (Available in U.S. only) 22572-0, 22573-9 Pa., Two-vol. set $15.90

THE CODEX NUTTALL, as first edited by Zelia Nuttall. Only inexpensive edition, in full color, of a pre-Columbian Mexican (Mixtec) book. 88 color plates show kings, gods, heroes, temples, sacrifices. New explanatory, historical introduction by Arthur G. Miller. 96pp. 11⅜ x 8½. (Available in U.S. only) 23168-2 Pa. $7.95

UNE SEMAINE DE BONTÉ, A SURREALISTIC NOVEL IN COLLAGE, Max Ernst. Masterpiece created out of 19th-century periodical illustrations, explores worlds of terror and surprise. Some consider this Ernst's greatest work. 208pp. 8⅛ x 11. 23252-2 Pa. $5.00

DRAWINGS OF WILLIAM BLAKE, William Blake. 92 plates from Book of Job, *Divine Comedy, Paradise Lost,* visionary heads, mythological figures, Laocoon, etc. Selection, introduction, commentary by Sir Geoffrey Keynes. 178pp. 8⅛ x 11. 22303-5 Pa. $4.00

ENGRAVINGS OF HOGARTH, William Hogarth. 101 of Hogarth's greatest works: *Rake's Progress, Harlot's Progress, Illustrations for Hudibras, Before and After, Beer Street and Gin Lane,* many more. Full commentary. 256pp. 11 x 13¾. 22479-1 Pa. $12.95

DAUMIER: 120 GREAT LITHOGRAPHS, Honore Daumier. Wide-ranging collection of lithographs by the greatest caricaturist of the 19th century. Concentrates on eternally popular series on lawyers, on married life, on liberated women, etc. Selection, introduction, and notes on plates by Charles F. Ramus. Total of 158pp. 9⅜ x 12¼. 23512-2 Pa. $5.50

DRAWINGS OF MUCHA, Alphonse Maria Mucha. Work reveals draftsman of highest caliber: studies for famous posters and paintings, renderings for book illustrations and ads, etc. 70 works, 9 in color; including 6 items not drawings. Introduction. List of illustrations. 72pp. 9⅜ x 12¼. (Available in U.S. only) 23672-2 Pa. $4.00

GIOVANNI BATTISTA PIRANESI: DRAWINGS IN THE PIERPONT MORGAN LIBRARY, Giovanni Battista Piranesi. For first time ever all of Morgan Library's collection, world's largest. 167 illustrations of rare Piranesi drawings—archeological, architectural, decorative and visionary. Essay, detailed list of drawings, chronology, captions. Edited by Felice Stampfle. 144pp. 9⅜ x 12¼. 23714-1 Pa. $7.50

NEW YORK ETCHINGS (1905-1949), John Sloan. All of important American artist's N.Y. life etchings. 67 works include some of his best art; also lively historical record—Greenwich Village, tenement scenes. Edited by Sloan's widow. Introduction and captions. 79pp. 8⅜ x 11¼. 23651-X Pa. $4.00

CHINESE PAINTING AND CALLIGRAPHY: A PICTORIAL SURVEY, Wan-go Weng. 69 fine examples from John M. Crawford's matchless private collection: landscapes, birds, flowers, human figures, etc., plus calligraphy. Every basic form included: hanging scrolls, handscrolls, album leaves, fans, etc. 109 illustrations. Introduction. Captions. 192pp. 8⅞ x 11¾. 23707-9 Pa. $7.95

DRAWINGS OF REMBRANDT, edited by Seymour Slive. Updated Lippmann, Hofstede de Groot edition, with definitive scholarly apparatus. All portraits, biblical sketches, landscapes, nudes, Oriental figures, classical studies, together with selection of work by followers. 550 illustrations. Total of 630pp. 9⅛ x 12¼. 21485-0, 21486-9 Pa., Two-vol. set $15.00

THE DISASTERS OF WAR, Francisco Goya. 83 etchings record horrors of Napoleonic wars in Spain and war in general. Reprint of 1st edition, plus 3 additional plates. Introduction by Philip Hofer. 97pp. 9⅜ x 8¼. 21872-4 Pa. $3.75

THE EARLY WORK OF AUBREY BEARDSLEY, Aubrey Beardsley. 157 plates, 2 in color: *Manon Lescaut, Madame Bovary, Morte Darthur, Salome,* other. Introduction by H. Marillier. 182pp. 8⅛ x 11. 21816-3 Pa. $4.50

THE LATER WORK OF AUBREY BEARDSLEY, Aubrey Beardsley. Exotic masterpieces of full maturity: *Venus and Tannhauser, Lysistrata, Rape of the Lock, Volpone,* Savoy material, etc. 174 plates, 2 in color. 186pp. 8⅛ x 11. 21817-1 Pa. $4.50

THOMAS NAST'S CHRISTMAS DRAWINGS, Thomas Nast. Almost all Christmas drawings by creator of image of Santa Claus as we know it, and one of America's foremost illustrators and political cartoonists. 66 illustrations. 3 illustrations in color on covers. 96pp. 8⅜ x 11¼. 23660-9 Pa. $3.50

THE DORÉ ILLUSTRATIONS FOR DANTE'S DIVINE COMEDY, Gustave Doré. All 135 plates from Inferno, Purgatory, Paradise; fantastic tortures, infernal landscapes, celestial wonders. Each plate with appropriate (translated) verses. 141pp. 9 x 12. 23231-X Pa. $4.50

DORÉ'S ILLUSTRATIONS FOR RABELAIS, Gustave Doré. 252 striking illustrations of *Gargantua and Pantagruel* books by foremost 19th-century illustrator. Including 60 plates, 192 delightful smaller illustrations. 153pp. 9 x 12. 23656-0 Pa. $5.00

LONDON: A PILGRIMAGE, Gustave Doré, Blanchard Jerrold. Squalor, riches, misery, beauty of mid-Victorian metropolis; 55 wonderful plates, 125 other illustrations, full social, cultural text by Jerrold. 191pp. of text. 9⅜ x 12¼. 22306-X Pa. $7.00

THE RIME OF THE ANCIENT MARINER, Gustave Doré, S. T. Coleridge. Dore's finest work, 34 plates capture moods, subtleties of poem. Full text. Introduction by Millicent Rose. 77pp. 9¼ x 12. 22305-1 Pa. $3.50

THE DORE BIBLE ILLUSTRATIONS, Gustave Doré. All wonderful, detailed plates: Adam and Eve, Flood, Babylon, Life of Jesus, etc. Brief King James text with each plate. Introduction by Millicent Rose. 241 plates. 241pp. 9 x 12. 23004-X Pa. $6.00

THE COMPLETE ENGRAVINGS, ETCHINGS AND DRYPOINTS OF ALBRECHT DÜRER. "Knight, Death and Devil"; "Melencolia," and more—all Dürer's known works in all three media, including 6 works formerly attributed to him. 120 plates. 235pp. 8⅜ x 11¼. 22851-7 Pa. $6.50

MAXIMILIAN'S TRIUMPHAL ARCH, Albrecht Dürer and others. Incredible monument of woodcut art: 8 foot high elaborate arch—heraldic figures, humans, battle scenes, fantastic elements—that you can assemble yourself. Printed on one side, layout for assembly. 143pp. 11 x 16. 21451-6 Pa. $5.00

THE COMPLETE WOODCUTS OF ALBRECHT DURER, edited by Dr. W. Kurth. 346 in all: "Old Testament," "St. Jerome," "Passion," "Life of Virgin," Apocalypse," many others. Introduction by Campbell Dodgson. 285pp. 8½ x 12¼. 21097-9 Pa. $7.50

DRAWINGS OF ALBRECHT DURER, edited by Heinrich Wölfflin. 81 plates show development from youth to full style. Many favorites; many new. Introduction by Alfred Werner. 96pp. 8⅛ x 11. 22352-3 Pa. $5.00

THE HUMAN FIGURE, Albrecht Dürer. Experiments in various techniques—stereometric, progressive proportional, and others. Also life studies that rank among finest ever done. Complete reprinting of *Dresden Sketchbook*. 170 plates. 355pp. 8⅜ x 11¼. 21042-1 Pa. $7.95

OF THE JUST SHAPING OF LETTERS, Albrecht Dürer. Renaissance artist explains design of Roman majuscules by geometry, also Gothic lower and capitals. Grolier Club edition. 43pp. 7⅞ x 10¾ 21306-4 Pa. $3.00

TEN BOOKS ON ARCHITECTURE, Vitruvius. The most important book ever written on architecture. Early Roman aesthetics, technology, classical orders, site selection, all other aspects. Stands behind everything since. Morgan translation. 331pp. 5⅜ x 8½. 20645-9 Pa. $4.50

THE FOUR BOOKS OF ARCHITECTURE, Andrea Palladio. 16th-century classic responsible for Palladian movement and style. Covers classical architectural remains, Renaissance revivals, classical orders, etc. 1738 Ware English edition. Introduction by A. Placzek. 216 plates. 110pp. of text. 9½ x 12¾. 21308-0 Pa. $10.00

HORIZONS, Norman Bel Geddes. Great industrialist stage designer, "father of streamlining," on application of aesthetics to transportation, amusement, architecture, etc. 1932 prophetic account; function, theory, specific projects. 222 illustrations. 312pp. 7⅞ x 10¾. 23514-9 Pa. $6.95

FRANK LLOYD WRIGHT'S FALLINGWATER, Donald Hoffmann. Full, illustrated story of conception and building of Wright's masterwork at Bear Run, Pa. 100 photographs of site, construction, and details of completed structure. 112pp. 9¼ x 10. 23671-4 Pa. $5.50

THE ELEMENTS OF DRAWING, John Ruskin. Timeless classic by great Viltorian; starts with basic ideas, works through more difficult. Many practical exercises. 48 illustrations. Introduction by Lawrence Campbell. 228pp. 5⅜ x 8½. 22730-8 Pa. $3.75

GIST OF ART, John Sloan. Greatest modern American teacher, Art Students League, offers innumerable hints, instructions, guided comments to help you in painting. Not a formal course. 46 illustrations. Introduction by Helen Sloan. 200pp. 5⅜ x 8½. 23435-5 Pa. $4.00

THE ANATOMY OF THE HORSE, George Stubbs. Often considered the great masterpiece of animal anatomy. Full reproduction of 1766 edition, plus prospectus; original text and modernized text. 36 plates. Introduction by Eleanor Garvey. 121pp. 11 x 14¾. 23402-9 Pa. $6.00

BRIDGMAN'S LIFE DRAWING, George B. Bridgman. More than 500 illustrative drawings and text teach you to abstract the body into its major masses, use light and shade, proportion; as well as specific areas of anatomy, of which Bridgman is master. 192pp. 6½ x 9¼. (Available in U.S. only) 22710-3 Pa. $3.50

ART NOUVEAU DESIGNS IN COLOR, Alphonse Mucha, Maurice Verneuil, Georges Auriol. Full-color reproduction of *Combinaisons ornementales* (c. 1900) by Art Nouveau masters. Floral, animal, geometric, interlacings, swashes—borders, frames, spots—all incredibly beautiful. 60 plates, hundreds of designs. 9⅜ x 8-1/16. 22885-1 Pa. $4.00

FULL-COLOR FLORAL DESIGNS IN THE ART NOUVEAU STYLE, E. A. Seguy. 166 motifs, on 40 plates, from *Les fleurs et leurs applications decoratives* (1902): borders, circular designs, repeats, allovers, "spots." All in authentic Art Nouveau colors. 48pp. 9⅜ x 12¼.
23439-8 Pa. $5.00

A DIDEROT PICTORIAL ENCYCLOPEDIA OF TRADES AND IN-DUSTRY, edited by Charles C. Gillispie. 485 most interesting plates from the great French Encyclopedia of the 18th century show hundreds of working figures, artifacts, process, land and cityscapes; glassmaking, papermaking, metal extraction, construction, weaving, making furniture, clothing, wigs, dozens of other activities. Plates fully explained. 920pp. 9 x 12.
22284-5, 22285-3 Clothbd., Two-vol. set $40.00

HANDBOOK OF EARLY ADVERTISING ART, Clarence P. Hornung. Largest collection of copyright-free early and antique advertising art ever compiled. Over 6,000 illustrations, from Franklin's time to the 1890's for special effects, novelty. Valuable source, almost inexhaustible.
Pictorial Volume. Agriculture, the zodiac, animals, autos, birds, Christmas, fire engines, flowers, trees, musical instruments, ships, games and sports, much more. Arranged by subject matter and use. 237 plates. 288pp. 9 x 12.
20122-8 Clothbd. $14.50

Typographical Volume. Roman and Gothic faces ranging from 10 point to 300 point, "Barnum," German and Old English faces, script, logotypes, scrolls and flourishes, 1115 ornamental initials, 67 complete alphabets, more. 310 plates. 320pp. 9 x 12. 20123-6 Clothbd. $15.00

CALLIGRAPHY (CALLIGRAPHIA LATINA), J. G. Schwandner. High point of 18th-century ornamental calligraphy. Very ornate initials, scrolls, borders, cherubs, birds, lettered examples. 172pp. 9 x 13.
20475-8 Pa. $7.00

ART FORMS IN NATURE, Ernst Haeckel. Multitude of strangely beautiful natural forms: Radiolaria, Foraminifera, jellyfishes, fungi, turtles, bats, etc. All 100 plates of the 19th-century evolutionist's *Kunstformen der Natur* (1904). 100pp. 9⅜ x 12¼.   22987-4 Pa. $5.00

CHILDREN: A PICTORIAL ARCHIVE FROM NINETEENTH-CENTURY SOURCES, edited by Carol Belanger Grafton. 242 rare, copyright-free wood engravings for artists and designers. Widest such selection available. All illustrations in line. 119pp. 8⅜ x 11¼.
     23694-3 Pa. $3.50

WOMEN: A PICTORIAL ARCHIVE FROM NINETEENTH-CENTURY SOURCES, edited by Jim Harter. 391 copyright-free wood engravings for artists and designers selected from rare periodicals. Most extensive such collection available. All illustrations in line. 128pp. 9 x 12.
     23703-6 Pa. $4.50

ARABIC ART IN COLOR, Prisse d'Avennes. From the greatest ornamentalists of all time—50 plates in color, rarely seen outside the Near East, rich in suggestion and stimulus. Includes 4 plates on covers. 46pp. 9⅜ x 12¼.   23658-7 Pa. $6.00

AUTHENTIC ALGERIAN CARPET DESIGNS AND MOTIFS, edited by June Beveridge. Algerian carpets are world famous. Dozens of geometrical motifs are charted on grids, color-coded, for weavers, needleworkers, craftsmen, designers. 53 illustrations plus 4 in color. 48pp. 8¼ x 11. (Available in U.S. only)   23650-1 Pa. $1.75

DICTIONARY OF AMERICAN PORTRAITS, edited by Hayward and Blanche Cirker. 4000 important Americans, earliest times to 1905, mostly in clear line. Politicians, writers, soldiers, scientists, inventors, industrialists, Indians, Blacks, women, outlaws, etc. Identificatory information. 756pp. 9¼ x 12¾.   21823-6 Clothbd. $40.00

HOW THE OTHER HALF LIVES, Jacob A. Riis. Journalistic record of filth, degradation, upward drive in New York immigrant slums, shops, around 1900. New edition includes 100 original Riis photos, monuments of early photography. 233pp. 10 x 7⅞.   22012-5 Pa. $7.00

NEW YORK IN THE THIRTIES, Berenice Abbott. Noted photographer's fascinating study of city shows new buildings that have become famous and old sights that have disappeared forever. Insightful commentary. 97 photographs. 97pp. 11⅜ x 10.   22967-X Pa. $5.00

MEN AT WORK, Lewis W. Hine. Famous photographic studies of construction workers, railroad men, factory workers and coal miners. New supplement of 18 photos on Empire State building construction. New introduction by Jonathan L. Doherty. Total of 69 photos. 63pp. 8 x 10¾.
     23475-4 Pa. $3.00

THE DEPRESSION YEARS AS PHOTOGRAPHED BY ARTHUR ROTH-STEIN, Arthur Rothstein. First collection devoted entirely to the work of outstanding 1930s photographer: famous dust storm photo, ragged children, unemployed, etc. 120 photographs. Captions. 119pp. 9¼ x 10¾.
23590-4 Pa. $5.00

CAMERA WORK: A PICTORIAL GUIDE, Alfred Stieglitz. All 559 illustrations and plates from the most important periodical in the history of art photography, *Camera Work* (1903-17). Presented four to a page, reduced in size but still clear, in strict chronological order, with complete captions. Three indexes. Glossary. Bibliography. 176pp. 8⅜ x 11¼.
23591-2 Pa. $6.95

ALVIN LANGDON COBURN, PHOTOGRAPHER, Alvin L. Coburn. Revealing autobiography by one of greatest photographers of 20th century gives insider's version of Photo-Secession, plus comments on his own work. 77 photographs by Coburn. Edited by Helmut and Alison Gernsheim. 160pp. 8⅛ x 11.
23685-4 Pa. $6.00

NEW YORK IN THE FORTIES, Andreas Feininger. 162 brilliant photographs by the well-known photographer, formerly with *Life* magazine, show commuters, shoppers, Times Square at night, Harlem nightclub, Lower East Side, etc. Introduction and full captions by John von Hartz. 181pp. 9¼ x 10¾.
23585-8 Pa. $6.00

GREAT NEWS PHOTOS AND THE STORIES BEHIND THEM, John Faber. Dramatic volume of 140 great news photos, 1855 through 1976, and revealing stories behind them, with both historical and technical information. Hindenburg disaster, shooting of Oswald, nomination of Jimmy Carter, etc. 160pp. 8¼ x 11.
23667-6 Pa. $5.00

THE ART OF THE CINEMATOGRAPHER, Leonard Maltin. Survey of American cinematography history and anecdotal interviews with 5 masters— Arthur Miller, Hal Mohr, Hal Rosson, Lucien Ballard, and Conrad Hall. Very large selection of behind-the-scenes production photos. 105 photographs. Filmographies. Index. Originally *Behind the Camera*. 144pp. 8¼ x 11.
23686-2 Pa. $5.00

DESIGNS FOR THE THREE-CORNERED HAT (LE TRICORNE), Pablo Picasso. 32 fabulously rare drawings—including 31 color illustrations of costumes and accessories—for 1919 production of famous ballet. Edited by Parmenia Migel, who has written new introduction. 48pp. 9⅜ x 12¼. (Available in U.S. only)
23709-5 Pa. $5.00

NOTES OF A FILM DIRECTOR, Sergei Eisenstein. Greatest Russian filmmaker explains montage, making of *Alexander Nevsky,* aesthetics; comments on self, associates, great rivals (Chaplin), similar material. 78 illustrations. 240pp. 5⅜ x 8½.
22392-2 Pa. $4.50

HOLLYWOOD GLAMOUR PORTRAITS, edited by John Kobal. 145 photos capture the stars from 1926-49, the high point in portrait photography. Gable, Harlow, Bogart, Bacall, Hedy Lamarr, Marlene Dietrich, Robert Montgomery, Marlon Brando, Veronica Lake; 94 stars in all. Full background on photographers, technical aspects, much more. Total of 160pp. 8⅜ x 11¼. 23352-9 Pa. **$6.00**

THE NEW YORK STAGE: FAMOUS PRODUCTIONS IN PHOTO-GRAPHS, edited by Stanley Appelbaum. 148 photographs from Museum of City of New York show 142 plays, 1883-1939. *Peter Pan, The Front Page, Dead End, Our Town,* O'Neill, hundreds of actors and actresses, etc. Full indexes. 154pp. 9½ x 10. 23241-7 Pa. **$6.00**

DIALOGUES CONCERNING TWO NEW SCIENCES, Galileo Galilei. Encompassing 30 years of experiment and thought, these dialogues deal with geometric demonstrations of fracture of solid bodies, cohesion, leverage, speed of light and sound, pendulums, falling bodies, accelerated motion, etc. 300pp. 5⅜ x 8½. 60099-8 Pa. $4.00

THE GREAT OPERA STARS IN HISTORIC PHOTOGRAPHS, edited by James Camner. 343 portraits from the 1850s to the 1940s: Tamburini, Mario, Caliapin, Jeritza, Melchior, Melba, Patti, Pinza, Schipa, Caruso, Farrar, Steber, Gobbi, and many more—270 performers in all. Index. 199pp. 8⅜ x 11¼. 23575-0 Pa. $6.50

J. S. BACH, Albert Schweitzer. Great full-length study of Bach, life, background to music, music, by foremost modern scholar. Ernest Newman translation. 650 musical examples. Total of 928pp. 5⅜ x 8½. (Available in U.S. only) 21631-4, 21632-2 Pa., Two-vol. set $11.00

COMPLETE PIANO SONATAS, Ludwig van Beethoven. All sonatas in the fine Schenker edition, with fingering, analytical material. One of best modern editions. Total of 615pp. 9 x 12. (Available in U.S. only) 23134-8, 23135-6 Pa., Two-vol. set $15.00

KEYBOARD MUSIC, J. S. Bach. Bach-Gesellschaft edition. For harpsichord, piano, other keyboard instruments. English Suites, French Suites, Six Partitas, Goldberg Variations, Two-Part Inventions, Three-Part Sinfonias. 312pp. 8⅛ x 11. (Available in U.S. only) 22360-4 Pa. **$6.95**

FOUR SYMPHONIES IN FULL SCORE, Franz Schubert. Schubert's four most popular symphonies: No. 4 in C Minor ("Tragic"); No. 5 in B-flat Major; No. 8 in B Minor ("Unfinished"); No. 9 in C Major ("Great"). Breitkopf & Hartel edition. Study score. 261pp. 9⅜ x 12¼. 23681-1 Pa. $6.50

THE AUTHENTIC GILBERT & SULLIVAN SONGBOOK, W. S. Gilbert, A. S. Sullivan. Largest selection available; 92 songs, uncut, original keys, in piano rendering approved by Sullivan. Favorites and lesser-known fine numbers. Edited with plot synopses by James Spero. 3 illustrations. 399pp. 9 x 12. 23482-7 Pa. **$9.95**

PRINCIPLES OF ORCHESTRATION, Nikolay Rimsky-Korsakov. Great classical orchestrator provides fundamentals of tonal resonance, progression of parts, voice and orchestra, tutti effects, much else in major document. 330pp. of musical excerpts. 489pp. 6½ x 9¼.   21266-1 Pa. **$7.50**

TRISTAN UND ISOLDE, Richard Wagner. Full orchestral score with complete instrumentation. Do not confuse with piano reduction. Commentary by Felix Mottl, great Wagnerian conductor and scholar. Study score. 655pp. 8⅛ x 11.   22915-7 Pa. $13.95

REQUIEM IN FULL SCORE, Giuseppe Verdi. Immensely popular with choral groups and music lovers. Republication of edition published by C. F. Peters, Leipzig, n. d. German frontmaker in English translation. Glossary. Text in Latin. Study score. 204pp. 9⅜ x 12¼.

23682-X Pa. $6.00

COMPLETE CHAMBER MUSIC FOR STRINGS, Felix Mendelssohn. All of Mendelssohn's chamber music: Octet, 2 Quintets, 6 Quartets, and Four Pieces for String Quartet. (Nothing with piano is included). Complete works edition (1874-7). Study score. 283 pp. 9⅜ x 12¼.

23679-X Pa. **$7.50**

POPULAR SONGS OF NINETEENTH-CENTURY AMERICA, edited by Richard Jackson. 64 most important songs: "Old Oaken Bucket," "Arkansas Traveler," "Yellow Rose of Texas," etc. Authentic original sheet music, full introduction and commentaries. 290pp. 9 x 12.   23270-0 Pa. **$7.95**

COLLECTED PIANO WORKS, Scott Joplin. Edited by Vera Brodsky Lawrence. Practically all of Joplin's piano works—rags, two-steps, marches, waltzes, etc., 51 works in all. Extensive introduction by Rudi Blesh. Total of 345pp. 9 x 12.   23106-2 Pa. **$14.95**

BASIC PRINCIPLES OF CLASSICAL BALLET, Agrippina Vaganova. Great Russian theoretician, teacher explains methods for teaching classical ballet; incorporates best from French, Italian, Russian schools. 118 illustrations. 175pp. 5⅜ x 8½.   22036-2 Pa. $2.50

CHINESE CHARACTERS, L. Wieger. Rich analysis of 2300 characters according to traditional systems into primitives. Historical-semantic analysis to phonetics (Classical Mandarin) and radicals. 820pp. 6⅛ x 9¼.

21321-8 Pa. $10.00

EGYPTIAN LANGUAGE: EASY LESSONS IN EGYPTIAN HIERO-GLYPHICS, E. A. Wallis Budge. Foremost Egyptologist offers Egyptian grammar, explanation of hieroglyphics, many reading texts, dictionary of symbols. 246pp. 5 x 7½. (Available in U.S. only)

21394-3 Clothbd. $7.50

AN ETYMOLOGICAL DICTIONARY OF MODERN ENGLISH, Ernest Weekley. Richest, fullest work, by foremost British lexicographer. Detailed word histories. Inexhaustible. Do not confuse this with *Concise Etymological Dictionary,* which is abridged. Total of 856pp. 6½ x 9¼.

21873-2, 21874-0 Pa., Two-vol. set $12.00

A MAYA GRAMMAR, Alfred M. Tozzer. Practical, useful English-language grammar by the Harvard anthropologist who was one of the three greatest American scholars in the area of Maya culture. Phonetics, grammatical processes, syntax, more. 301pp. 5⅜ x 8½. 23465-7 Pa. $4.00

THE JOURNAL OF HENRY D. THOREAU, edited by Bradford Torrey, F. H. Allen. Complete reprinting of 14 volumes, 1837-61, over two million words; the sourcebooks for *Walden*, etc. Definitive. All original sketches, plus 75 photographs. Introduction by Walter Harding. Total of 1804pp. 8½ x 12¼. 20312-3, 20313-1 Clothbd., Two-vol. set $50.00

CLASSIC GHOST STORIES, Charles Dickens and others. 18 wonderful stories you've wanted to reread: "The Monkey's Paw," "The House and the Brain," "The Upper Berth," "The Signalman," "Dracula's Guest," "The Tapestried Chamber," etc. Dickens, Scott, Mary Shelley, Stoker, etc. 330pp. 5⅜ x 8½. 20735-8 Pa. **$4.50**

SEVEN SCIENCE FICTION NOVELS, H. G. Wells. Full novels. *First Men in the Moon, Island of Dr. Moreau, War of the Worlds, Food of the Gods, Invisible Man, Time Machine, In the Days of the Comet.* A basic science-fiction library. 1015pp. 5⅜ x 8½. (Available in U.S. only) 20264-X Clothbd. $8.95

ARMADALE, Wilkie Collins. Third great mystery novel by the author of *The Woman in White* and *The Moonstone.* Ingeniously plotted narrative shows an exceptional command of character, incident and mood. Original magazine version with 40 illustrations. 597pp. 5⅜ x 8½. 23429-0 Pa. $6.00

MASTERS OF MYSTERY, H. Douglas Thomson. The first book in English (1931) devoted to history and aesthetics of detective story. Poe, Doyle, LeFanu, Dickens, many others, up to 1930. New introduction and notes by E. F. Bleiler. 288pp. 5⅜ x 8½. (Available in U.S. only) 23606-4 Pa. $4.00

FLATLAND, E. A. Abbott. Science-fiction classic explores life of 2-D being in 3-D world. Read also as introduction to thought about hyperspace. Introduction by Banesh Hoffmann. 16 illustrations. 103pp. 5⅜ x 8½. 20001-9 Pa. $2.00

THREE SUPERNATURAL NOVELS OF THE VICTORIAN PERIOD, edited, with an introduction, by E. F. Bleiler. Reprinted complete and unabridged, three great classics of the supernatural: *The Haunted Hotel* by Wilkie Collins, *The Haunted House at Latchford* by Mrs. J. H. Riddell, and *The Lost Stradivarius* by J. Meade Falkner. 325pp. 5⅜ x 8½. 22571-2 Pa. $4.00

AYESHA: THE RETURN OF "SHE," H. Rider Haggard. Virtuoso sequel featuring the great mythic creation, Ayesha, in an adventure that is fully as good as the first book, *She.* Original magazine version, with 47 original illustrations by Maurice Greiffenhagen. 189pp. 6½ x 9¼. 23649-8 Pa. $3.50

UNCLE SILAS, J. Sheridan LeFanu. Victorian Gothic mystery novel, considered by many best of period, even better than Collins or Dickens. Wonderful psychological terror. Introduction by Frederick Shroyer. 436pp. 5⅜ x 8½. 21715-9 Pa. $6.00

JURGEN, James Branch Cabell. The great erotic fantasy of the 1920's that delighted thousands, shocked thousands more. Full final text, Lane edition with 13 plates by Frank Pape. 346pp. 5⅜ x 8½.
23507-6 Pa. $4.50

THE CLAVERINGS, Anthony Trollope. Major novel, chronicling aspects of British Victorian society, personalities. Reprint of Cornhill serialization, 16 plates by M. Edwards; first reprint of full text. Introduction by Norman Donaldson. 412pp. 5⅜ x 8½. 23464-9 Pa. $5.00

KEPT IN THE DARK, Anthony Trollope. Unusual short novel about Victorian morality and abnormal psychology by the great English author. Probably the first American publication. Frontispiece by Sir John Millais. 92pp. 6½ x 9¼. 23609-9 Pa. $2.50

RALPH THE HEIR, Anthony Trollope. Forgotten tale of illegitimacy, inheritance. Master novel of Trollope's later years. Victorian country estates, clubs, Parliament, fox hunting, world of fully realized characters. Reprint of 1871 edition. 12 illustrations by F. A. Faser. 434pp. of text. 5⅜ x 8½. 23642-0 Pa. $5.00

YEKL and THE IMPORTED BRIDEGROOM AND OTHER STORIES OF THE NEW YORK GHETTO, Abraham Cahan. Film *Hester Street* based on *Yekl* (1896). Novel, other stories among first about Jewish immigrants of N.Y.'s East Side. Highly praised by W. D. Howells—Cahan "a new star of realism." New introduction by Bernard G. Richards. 240pp. 5⅜ x 8½. 22427-9 Pa. $3.50

THE HIGH PLACE, James Branch Cabell. Great fantasy writer's enchanting comedy of disenchantment set in 18th-century France. Considered by some critics to be even better than his famous *Jurgen*. 10 illustrations and numerous vignettes by noted fantasy artist Frank C. Pape. 320pp. 5⅜ x 8½. 23670-6 Pa. $4.00

ALICE'S ADVENTURES UNDER GROUND, Lewis Carroll. Facsimile of ms. Carroll gave Alice Liddell in 1864. Different in many ways from final Alice. Handlettered, illustrated by Carroll. Introduction by Martin Gardner. 128pp. 5⅜ x 8½. 21482-6 Pa. $2.00

FAVORITE ANDREW LANG FAIRY TALE BOOKS IN MANY COLORS, Andrew Lang. The four Lang favorites in a boxed set—the complete *Red, Green, Yellow* and *Blue* Fairy Books. 164 stories; 439 illustrations by Lancelot Speed, Henry Ford and G. P. Jacomb Hood. Total of about 1500pp. 5⅜ x 8½. 23407-X Boxed set, Pa. $14.95

HOUSEHOLD STORIES BY THE BROTHERS GRIMM. All the great Grimm stories: "Rumpelstiltskin," "Snow White," "Hansel and Gretel," etc., with 114 illustrations by Walter Crane. 269pp. 5⅜ x 8½.
21080-4 Pa. $3.50

SLEEPING BEAUTY, illustrated by Arthur Rackham. Perhaps the fullest, most delightful version ever, told by C. S. Evans. Rackham's best work. 49 illustrations. 110pp. 7⅞ x 10¾.
22756-1 Pa. $2.50

AMERICAN FAIRY TALES, L. Frank Baum. Young cowboy lassoes Father Time; dummy in Mr. Floman's department store window comes to life; and 10 other fairy tales. 41 illustrations by N. P. Hall, Harry Kennedy, Ike Morgan, and Ralph Gardner. 209pp. 5⅜ x 8½.
23643-9 Pa. $3.00

THE WONDERFUL WIZARD OF OZ, L. Frank Baum. Facsimile in full color of America's finest children's classic. Introduction by Martin Gardner. 143 illustrations by W. W. Denslow. 267pp. 5⅜ x 8½.
20691-2 Pa. $3.50

THE TALE OF PETER RABBIT, Beatrix Potter. The inimitable Peter's terrifying adventure in Mr. McGregor's garden, with all 27 wonderful, full-color Potter illustrations. 55pp. 4¼ x 5½. (Available in U.S. only)
22827-4 Pa. $1.25

THE STORY OF KING ARTHUR AND HIS KNIGHTS, Howard Pyle. Finest children's version of life of King Arthur. 48 illustrations by Pyle. 131pp. 6⅛ x 9¼.
21445-1 Pa. $4.95

CARUSO'S CARICATURES, Enrico Caruso. Great tenor's remarkable caricatures of self, fellow musicians, composers, others. Toscanini, Puccini, Farrar, etc. Impish, cutting, insightful. 473 illustrations. Preface by M. Sisca. 217pp. 8⅜ x 11¼.
23528-9 Pa. $6.95

PERSONAL NARRATIVE OF A PILGRIMAGE TO ALMADINAH AND MECCAH, Richard Burton. Great travel classic by remarkably colorful personality. Burton, disguised as a Moroccan, visited sacred shrines of Islam, narrowly escaping death. Wonderful observations of Islamic life, customs, personalities. 47 illustrations. Total of 959pp. 5⅜ x 8½.
21217-3, 21218-1 Pa., Two-vol. set $12.00

INCIDENTS OF TRAVEL IN YUCATAN, John L. Stephens. Classic (1843) exploration of jungles of Yucatan, looking for evidences of Maya civilization. Travel adventures, Mexican and Indian culture, etc. Total of 669pp. 5⅜ x 8½.
20926-1, 20927-X Pa., Two-vol. set $7.90

AMERICAN LITERARY AUTOGRAPHS FROM WASHINGTON IRVING TO HENRY JAMES, Herbert Cahoon, et al. Letters, poems, manuscripts of Hawthorne, Thoreau, Twain, Alcott, Whitman, 67 other prominent American authors. Reproductions, full transcripts and commentary. Plus checklist of all American Literary Autographs in The Pierpont Morgan Library. Printed on exceptionally high-quality paper. 136 illustrations. 212pp. 9⅛ x 12¼.
23548-3 Pa. $12.50

AN AUTOBIOGRAPHY, Margaret Sanger. Exciting personal account of hard-fought battle for woman's right to birth control, against prejudice, church, law. Foremost feminist document. 504pp. 5⅜ x 8½.

20470-7 Pa. $5.50

MY BONDAGE AND MY FREEDOM, Frederick Douglass. Born as a slave, Douglass became outspoken force in antislavery movement. The best of Douglass's autobiographies. Graphic description of slave life. Introduction by P. Foner. 464pp. 5⅜ x 8½.

22457-0 Pa. $5.50

LIVING MY LIFE, Emma Goldman. Candid, no holds barred account by foremost American anarchist: her own life, anarchist movement, famous contemporaries, ideas and their impact. Struggles and confrontations in America, plus deportation to U.S.S.R. Shocking inside account of persecution of anarchists under Lenin. 13 plates. Total of 944pp. 5⅜ x 8½.

22543-7, 22544-5 Pa., Two-vol. set $12.00

LETTERS AND NOTES ON THE MANNERS, CUSTOMS AND CONDITIONS OF THE NORTH AMERICAN INDIANS, George Catlin. Classic account of life among Plains Indians: ceremonies, hunt, warfare, etc. Dover edition reproduces for first time all original paintings. 312 plates. 572pp. of text. 6⅛ x 9¼.

22118-0, 22119-9 Pa.. Two-vol. set $12.00

THE MAYA AND THEIR NEIGHBORS, edited by Clarence L. Hay, others. Synoptic view of Maya civilization in broadest sense, together with Northern, Southern neighbors. Integrates much background, valuable detail not elsewhere. Prepared by greatest scholars: Kroeber, Morley, Thompson, Spinden, Vaillant, many others. Sometimes called Tozzer Memorial Volume. 60 illustrations, linguistic map. 634pp. 5⅜ x 8½.

23510-6 Pa. $7.50

HANDBOOK OF THE INDIANS OF CALIFORNIA, A. L. Kroeber. Foremost American anthropologist offers complete ethnographic study of each group. Monumental classic. 459 illustrations, maps. 995pp. 5⅜ x 8½.

23368-5 Pa. $13.00

SHAKTI AND SHAKTA, Arthur Avalon. First book to give clear, cohesive analysis of Shakta doctrine, Shakta ritual and Kundalini Shakti (yoga). Important work by one of world's foremost students of Shaktic and Tantric thought. 732pp. 5⅜ x 8½. (Available in U.S. only)

23645-5 Pa. $7.95

AN INTRODUCTION TO THE STUDY OF THE MAYA HIEROGLYPHS, Syvanus Griswold Morley. Classic study by one of the truly great figures in hieroglyph research. Still the best introduction for the student for reading Maya hieroglyphs. New introduction by J. Eric S. Thompson. 117 illustrations. 284pp. 5⅜ x 8½.

23108-9 Pa. $4.00

A STUDY OF MAYA ART, Herbert J. Spinden. Landmark classic interprets Maya symbolism, estimates styles, covers ceramics, architecture, murals, stone carvings as artforms. Still a basic book in area. New introduction by J. Eric Thompson. Over 750 illustrations. 341pp. 8⅜ x 11¼.

21235-1 Pa. $6.95